Dedicated to the Memory of
Sir Henry Campbell-Bannerman
and the
Six Hundred and Twenty-Five
Fellow Former Pupils of
The High School of Glasgow
who gave their lives in
The First and Second World Wars.

REVIEW COPY
Not For Resale

Alexander S. Waugh

SIR HENRY CAMPBELL-BANNERMAN

A Scottish Life and UK Politics, 1836–1908

REVIEW COPY
Not For Resale

AUSTIN MACAULEY PUBLISHERS™
LONDON · CAMBRIDGE · NEW YORK · SHARJAH

Copyright © Alexander S. Waugh (2019)

The right of the estate of Alexander S. Waugh to be identified as author of this work has been asserted by his executors in accordance with section 77 and 78 of the Copyright, Designs and Patents Act 1988.

All rights reserved. No part of this publication may be reproduced, stored in a retrieval system, or transmitted in any form or by any means, electronic, mechanical, photocopying, recording, or otherwise, without the prior permission of the publishers.

Any person who commits any unauthorised act in relation to this publication may be liable to criminal prosecution and civil claims for damages.

A CIP catalogue record for this title is available from the British Library.

ISBN 9781849636667 (Paperback)
ISBN 9781849636674 (Kindle e-book)
ISBN 9781528903929 (ePub e-book)

www.austinmacauley.com

First Published (2019)
Austin Macauley Publishers Ltd.
25 Canada Square
Canary Wharf
London
E14 5LQ

Dr. Alexander (Sandy) Somerville Waugh was born in Dumbreck, Glasgow, in 1934. He attended The High School of Glasgow in 1939-1951 – some 100 years after Sir Henry Campbell-Bannerman – and had degrees in Economics (1955), Divinity (1999) and Scottish Church History (PhD, 2003). He was a Fellow of the Society of Antiquaries of Scotland and a Member of the Glasgow High School Club, the Scottish Church History Society, the Scottish Place-Name Society, the Liberal International (British Group) and the Liberal Democrat History Group, and was also a contributor to the *Journal of Liberal History.*

After National Service, he worked in general publishing, in the iron and steel industry and in newspaper publishing, mainly in personnel and training roles. He joined the old Scottish Liberal Party (SLP) in 1951, serving for some years on its National Executive, convening its Housing Policy and Structure of Government Committees and making a major contribution to the development of SLP policy for an integrated income tax/social security system. He also held a range of offices in the former Glasgow Pollok, West Aberdeenshire and North Angus & Mearns (Kincardineshire) Constituency Liberal Associations and was the unsuccessful Liberal/Alliance candidate for Kincardine and Deeside at the 1983 General Election. In 1954-1955, he was a Vice-President of the old Scottish Union of Students and in 1957-1964, he was Liberal Whip and then Leader in the Glasgow Parliamentary Debating Association. He was latterly a member of the Scottish Liberal Democrats.

As a school pupil and then as a student, he had leadership roles in the Scottish Schoolboys Club (SSC) and the Student Christian Movement (SCM). In later years, as an ordained Elder of The Church of Scotland, he was Session Clerk of Banchory-Ternan West Parish Church for eleven years, a Commissioner at a number of General Assemblies and a member of a number of General Assembly Boards and associated Committees. He was also Convener of the Business Committee of the Presbytery of Kincardine and Deeside, and Convener of Christian Aid Banchory.

Sandy and his wife, Sheila, lived in North-East Scotland after their marriage in 1965 and specifically in Banchory (Banchory-Ternan), Kincardineshire, from 1975. They have two children and four grandchildren, who live in Edinburgh and Newcastle.

Sandy Waugh died at home in Banchory in July 2017.

Foreword

Sir Henry Campbell-Bannerman is a much neglected figure in British political history. The names of Asquith and Lloyd George are more readily associated with the great reforming Liberal governments of the early twentieth century. Yet it can be forcefully argued that neither of them might have come to prominence were it not for the remarkable personality of CB, as he was known, and his success first in re-uniting the Liberals and then leading them to the stunning election victory in 1906. His holding of the office of Prime Minister lasted just over two years until his untimely death, during which much legislation which could have been counted to his credit was vetoed by the House of Lords.

Dr. Waugh spells out a series of justified tributes: He saved the ship of Liberalism from total shipwreck at a time when most of the crew and many of the pilots had lost all hope, all heart and all faith": No premier has ever been more deservedly or more widely popular than he was"; and from Asquith himself: "of all the men with whom I have been associated in public life, I put him as high as any in both moral and intellectual courage". The author also takes us through more of his early life, and he is painstaking in sometimes slightly irrelevant (most concerning their mutual alma mater, Glasgow High School) but nevertheless fascinating detail. For example he tells us that CB as a teenager heard Strauss play in Vienna and that he was distantly related to Fletcher of Saltoun (and correctly reminds us that Fletcher was in favour of the Union and only objected to the abolition of the Scottish Parliament).

He attributes the creation of the Scottish Grand Committee to CB, and in arguments relevant to today reminds us that he advocated a reformed House of Lords as a federal chamber after home-rule all round. CB pointed out: As Scottish Home Rule involves English Home Rule, Scottish Home Rule must wait until the sluggish mind of John Bull [the English] is educated up to that point'. The author also pays due attention to his remarkable 40-year tenure as the Member for Stirling Burghs; all letters from constituents had to be forwarded to him when abroad and every one received a personal reply.

His remarkable post Boer war association with Smuts is well recounted along with perhaps his most famous quote: "When is a war not a war? When it is conducted by methods of barbarism in South Africa". Truly this is an intensively scholarly work which will do much to elevate Campbell-Bannerman's reputation.

Sadly, the author passed away last year whilst the book was still at the proof stage. Sandy was a stalwart of the old Scottish Liberal Party whom I know from the 1960s. His commitment to the Liberal Democrats remained undimmed and we shall miss him greatly.

DAVID STEEL

CONTENTS

Illustrations, Capsules and Tables

Foreword 7
Introduction 12
    Outline Genealogy – 1 – The McOran-Campbells 12
    Outline Genealogy – 2 – The Bannermans and The Hunton Line 13
    Political Timeline 1836-1908 14
The Rt. Hon. Sir Henry Campbell-Bannerman, GCB 15
    PERSONAL PROLOGUE 17
    NOTES 19
1 – Ancestry, Family Business, Birth (1836), Religion and Politics 25
    Afterword – The Family Business and McOran-Campbells in Later Years 46
2 – 1845-1868 – Education, Travels, Career, Marriage (1860) and Politics 48
3 – The Stirling Burghs Constituency and Sir Henry's Election in 1868 69
4 – 1868-1880 – Parliament, Government and Opposition 86
    A – 1868-1874 – Parliament, Government (Junior Office) and Change of Surname 86
    B – 1874-1880 – Opposition 97
5 – 1880-1886 – Government, Opposition and Government 105
    A – 1880-1885 – Government (Junior and Irish Office) and Opposition 105
    B – 1885-1886 – Opposition and Government (Cabinet Office) 116
6 – Meigle, Belmont Castle and Personal Life and Routine 124
    Meigle and Belmont Castle 124
    The Campbell-Bannermans and Belmont Castle 130
    Personal Life and Routine 137
    Afterword – Belmont Castle in Later Years 140
7 – 1886-1894 – Opposition and Government 143
    A – 1886-1892 – Opposition 143
    B – 1892-1894 – Government (Cabinet Office) 152
8 – 1894-1899 – Government and Opposition 159
    A – 1894-1895 – Government (Cabinet Office) and Knighthood 159
    B – 1895-1899 – Opposition 166
9 – 1899-1905 – Liberal Leadership in Opposition 175
    A – 1899-1900 – From Election to Leadership to the 1900 General Election 175
    B – 1900-1905 – From the 1900 General Election to Accession as Prime Minister 182
10 – 1905 – From Challenge to Appointment as Prime Minister 204
11 – The 1906 General Election 218
    A – Liberal Organisation and Strategy, Ancillaries, Allies and the Press 218
    B – The Prime Minister's Campaign 225
    C – The Result 236
    Afterword – The Liberal/Labour MPs and the Labour Party 242
12 – 1905-1908 – 28 Months and Bereavement (1906) as Prime Minister 244
13 – 1905-1908 – Legislative and Executive Action and Frustration 263
    South Africa 263
    The 1906 Trade Disputes and Workmen's Compensation Acts 276
    Social and Other Domestic Policy 277
    The Second Hague Peace Conference of 1907 283
14 – 1907-1908 – Final Illness, Resignation and Death 287

15 – An Appraisal..306
Appendix 1 – Electoral History of Stirling Burghs 1708--1918..........................319
Appendix 2 – Liberal Hegemony in Scotland 1832 to 1918................................326
Appendix 3 – Biographical Notes..332
Appendix 4..344
Appendix 5 – Commemorations...347
Appendix 6 – Glasgow High School Parliamentarians 359
BIBLIOGRAPHY 362

Illustrations

Capsules

Chapter 4

Wording on Stained Glass Window in Port of Menteith Parish Church
Wording on Plaque commemorating Sir Henry at 6 Grosvenor Place, London

Chapter 6

Sale of Belmont Castle – Advertisement in *The Scotsman* of 8 August 1884
Wording on Plaque commemorating Sir Henry inside Meigle Parish Church

Chapter 10

Dream Correspondence – From Sir Henry Campbell-Bannerman to Mr. Winston Churchill

Chapter 14

Wording on the Campbell-Bannerman Gravestone on the Outside Wall of Meigle Parish Church

Appendix 5

Description of Statue of Sir Henry in Stirling (*Stirling Observer*, 4 November 1913)

Wording on Plaque commemorating Sir Henry at 129 Bath Street, Glasgow

Appendix 6

Wording on Plaque commemorating James, Viscount Bryce in Belfast
(Ulster History Circle and Ulster-Scots Agency, 10 May 2013)

Tables

Chapter 1
Table 1   The 1837 General Election in Glasgow
Table 2   The 1841 General Election in Glasgow
Table 3   The Major Scottish Presbyterian Churches and Associated Statistics
Table 4   The Fasque-Stracathro Connection (Ramsay/Gladstone and Cruickshank/Campbell)

Chapter 2
Table 5   The 1865 General Election in Glasgow

Chapter 3
Table 6   Stirling Burghs – 30 April 1868 By-Election
Table 7   Stirling Burghs – 20 November 1868 General Election
Table 8   Stirling Burghs – 1871 Census

Chapter 4
Table 9   The 1868 General Election
Table 10   Scottish Universities – 1868 General Election
Table 11   The 1874 General Election

Chapter 5
Table 12   The 1880 General Election
Table 13   The 1885 General Election
Table 14   The Fifth Liberal Cabinet 1886

Chapter 6
Table 15 –   Owners of Belmont Castle 1800-1884

Chapter 7
Table 16 –   The 1886 General Election
Table 17 –   The 1892 General Election
Table 18 –   The Sixth Liberal Cabinet 1892-1894

Chapter 8
Table 19 –   The Seventh Liberal Cabinet 1894-1895
Table 20 –   The 1895 General Election

Chapter 9
Table 21 –   The 1900 General Election

Chapter 10
Table 22 –   The Eighth Liberal Cabinet 1905-1908

Chapter 11
Table 23 –   The 1906 General Election
Table 24 –   Election Results in Places where Sir Henry spoke in January 1906
Table 25 –   The Fifty Labour Candidatures in 1906

Chapter 14
Table 26 –   Cabinet Changes in April 1908

Appendix 2
Table 27 –   Scotland – General Elections 1832 to 1918

Appendix 4
Table 28 –   Other Members of the 1905-1908 Liberal Administration

Appendix 6
Table 29 –   Glasgow High School Parliamentarians

Introduction

Outline Genealogy – 1 – The McOran-Campbells

John Campbell *(Duinecoir)* of Fernoch, Melfort, Argyll (Died c.1669)
=
Isabella MacLachlan of Craigentreve, Argyll
|
A Young Campbell (Born c.1645)
from Fernoch, Melfort, Argyll to Menteith, Perthshire in 1660x1665
= 1670x1675 =
Nancy Haldane, Daughter of Hugo Haldane of Gleneagles, Perthshire
and Niece of Patrick Haldane of Lanrick Castle by Doune, Perthshire *
(The McOrans of Inchanoch, Port of Menteith, Perthshire) *
|
Donald McOran of Inchanoch
=
Agnes Haldane
|
James McOran of Inchanoch
(Baptised 1 February 1713)
= c.1745 =
Janet MacKerecher
|
James McOran or Campbell of Inchanoch and Glasgow (1752-1831)
=1785=
Helen Forrester of Frew, Stirlingshire (1763-1824)

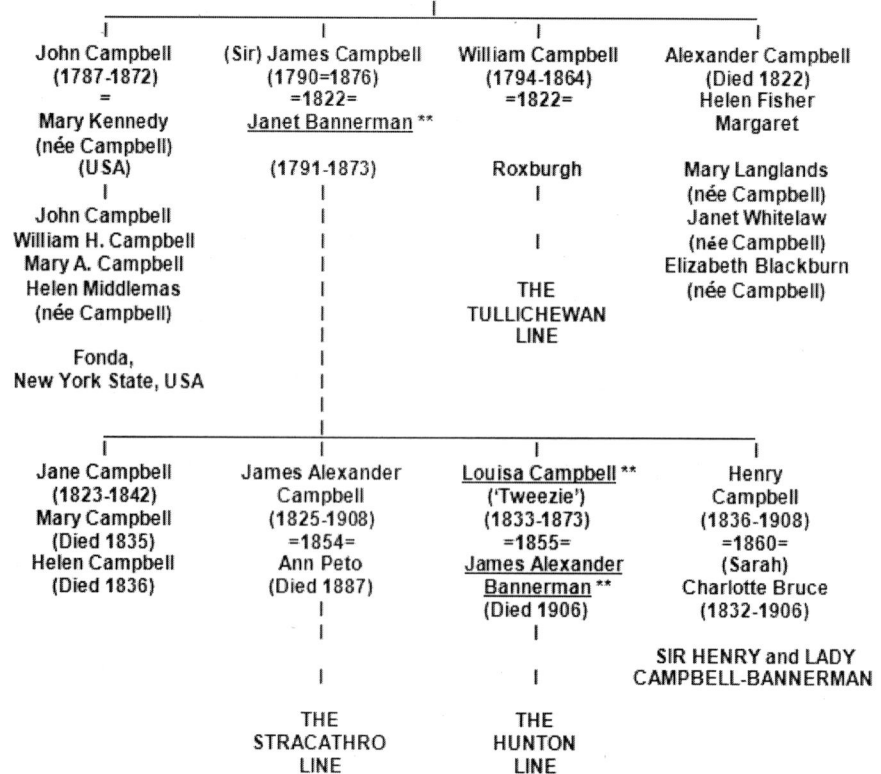

John Campbell (1787-1872) = Mary Kennedy (née Campbell) (USA)	(Sir) James Campbell (1790=1876) =1822= Janet Bannerman ** (1791-1873)	William Campbell (1794-1864) =1822= Roxburgh	Alexander Campbell (Died 1822) Helen Fisher Margaret
John Campbell William H. Campbell Mary A. Campbell Helen Middlemas (née Campbell) Fonda, New York State, USA		THE TULLICHEWAN LINE	Mary Langlands (née Campbell) Janet Whitelaw (née Campbell) Elizabeth Blackburn (née Campbell)
Jane Campbell (1823-1842) Mary Campbell (Died 1835) Helen Campbell (Died 1836)	James Alexander Campbell (1825-1908) =1854= Ann Peto (Died 1887)	Louisa Campbell ** ('Tweezie') (1833-1873) =1855= James Alexander Bannerman ** (Died 1906)	Henry Campbell (1836-1908) =1860= (Sarah) Charlotte Bruce (1832-1906) SIR HENRY and LADY CAMPBELL-BANNERMAN
	THE STRACATHRO LINE	THE HUNTON LINE	

Outline Genealogy – 2 – The Bannermans and The Hunton Line

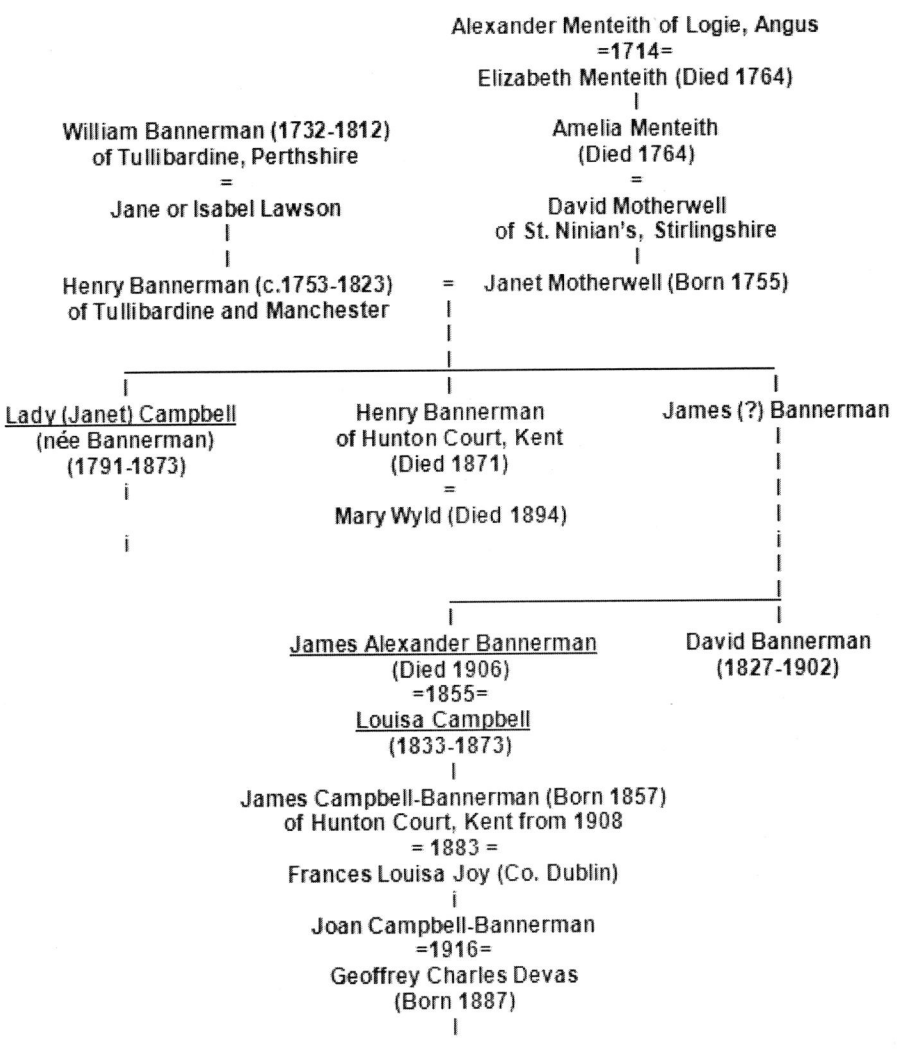

Political Timeline 1836-1908

	Prime Ministers	Government Parties	General Elections
1835-1841	Melbourne	Whig	1837 1841
1841-1846	Peel	Conservative	
1846-1852	Russell	Whig *	1847
1852	Derby	Conservative*	1852
1852-1855	Aberdeen	Peelite/Whig/Radical	
1855-1858	Palmerston	Whig/Peelite/Radical	1857
1658-1859	Derby	Conservative*	1859
1859-1865	Palmerston	Liberal	1865
1865-1866	Russell	Liberal	
1866-1868	Derby	Conservative*	
1868	Disraeli	Conservative*	1868
1868-1874	Gladstone	Liberal	1874
1874-1880	Disraeli	Conservative	1880
1880-1885	Gladstone	Liberal	
1885-1886	Salisbury	Conservative*	1885
1886	Gladstone	Liberal *	1886
1886-1892	Salisbury	Unionist	1892
1892-1894	Gladstone	Liberal *	
1894-1895	Rosebery	Liberal *	
1895-1902	Salisbury	Unionist	1895
1902-1905	Balfour	Unionist	1900
1905-1908	Campbell-Bannerman	Liberal	1906

* Without overall majority in House of Commons

The Rt. Hon. Sir Henry Campbell-Bannerman, GCB

Born, as Henry Campbell, in Kelvinside House, Glasgow on 7 September 1836
Younger Son of James Campbell (1790-1876) & Janet Campbell, née Bannerman (1791-1873)
(James Campbell was Lord Provost of Glasgow in 1840-1843 and was knighted in 1841)
Home Address 1836-1860 – 21 (later 129) Bath Street, Glasgow
The High School of Glasgow, 1845-1850, The University of Glasgow. 1851-1853
Trinity College, Cambridge, 1854-1858 (BA 1858 and MA 1861)
Overseas Travel, Europe, 1848, 1850-1851, 1855, 1860, 1862, 1863, 1864 and from 1872 to 1908
Founder Member (Lieutenant and Captain) First Lanarkshire Rifle Volunteers in 1859
Partner in J. & W. Campbell, 29 (later 137) Ingram Street, Glasgow in 1860-1876
Married (Sarah) Charlotte Bruce (1832-1906) on 13 September 1860
Home Address 1860-1887 – 8 Claremont Gardens, Glasgow
Liberal MP for Stirling Burghs, 20 November 1868 to 22 April 1908
(Stirling, Culross, Dunfermline, Inverkeithing and South Queensferry)
Maiden Speech in the House of Commons on 17 June 1869
London Addresses – 60 Queen's Gate (1868-1872),
117 Eaton Square (1872-1878), 6 Grosvenor Place (1878-1904),
29 Belgrave Square (1904-1906), 10 Downing Street (1906-1908)
Financial Secretary, War Office, 1871-1874 and 1880-1882
Financial and Parliamentary Secretary, Admiralty, 1882-1884,
Chief Secretary for Ireland, 1884-1885, Secretary of State for War, 1886 and 1892-1895
Change of Surname from Campbell to Campbell-Bannerman (CB) in 1872
English Country Address 1872-1908 – Gennings, Hunton Court, Maidstone, Kent
Honorary Doctorate of Laws (LLD), Glasgow, 22 March 1883
Freedom of the Royal Burgh of Stirling, 15 December 1892
Knight Grand Cross of the Order of the Bath (GCB), 1 July 1895
Home Address 1887-1908 – Belmont Castle, Meigle, Perthshire
Liberal Leader and Leader of the Opposition in the House of Commons, 1899-1905
Freedom of the Royal Burgh of Dunfermline, 31 October 1903
South African War 1899-1902
with 'Methods of Barbarism' Speech in London on 14 June 1901
LIBERAL PRIME MINISTER
First Lord of the Treasury and Leader of the House of Commons

5 December 1905 to 3 April 1908
'Enough of this foolery' Speech in answer to Arthur Balfour,
House of Commons, 12 March 1906
Vive la Douma Speech, 14th Inter-Parliamentary Conference, London, 23 July 1906
Death of Lady Campbell-Bannerman on 30 August 1906
at Marienbad, Bohemia, now Marianske Lazne in the Czech Republic
Freedom of the City and Royal Burgh of Glasgow, 25 January 1907
Sworn in as Elder Brother of Trinity House, 8 March 1907
Honorary Doctorate of Laws (LLD), Cambridge, 12 June 1907
Honorary Doctorate of Civil Law (DCL), Oxford, 26 June 1907
Freedom of the Royal Burgh of Montrose, 27 September 1907
Freedom of the Royal Burgh of Peebles, 4 October 1907
Freedom of the City and Royal Burgh of Edinburgh, 20 October 1907
Last Cabinet Meeting and Last Attendance and Speech,
House of Commons on 12 February 1908
Resignation as Prime Minister on 3 April 1908
Death in 10 Downing Street on 22 April 1908

PERSONAL PROLOGUE

My particular interest in Sir Henry Campbell-Bannerman started in June 1948 when that month's *Glasgow High School Magazine* took the form of a Campbell-Bannerman Centenary Edition with the centenary being one hundred years since Sir Henry (then known as Henry Campbell and about the time of his 12th birthday) was Dux of the Junior Division of the Third Form. (In Scotland, the word DUX [*Dux Litterarum*] is used to refer to the top pupil in a school, form, class or subject in terms of academic achievement) In 1948 I was myself then (aged 13) in the Third Form of the School.

Specially invited contributors to the June 1948 *Magazine* included Jan Christiaan Smuts (then Prime Minister of the Union of South Africa), Viscount Samuel (a former Cabinet Minister and Liberal Leader), Viscount Simon (a former Cabinet Minister and Liberal National Leader), Dr. Andrew Browning (Professor of History, Glasgow University), Dr. William A. Cunningham (Librarian, Glasgow University), Professor Henry Contamine (University of Caen), Gilbert Murray (formerly Professor of Greek in Glasgow and Oxford Universities), George Macaulay Trevelyan (Master of Trinity College, Cambridge) and Lady Ponsonby of Shulbrede, whose late husband had been Principal Private Secretary for most of Sir Henry's Premiership.

The *Magazine* article which most impressed me was perhaps that by Field Marshall Smuts, who wrote in his covering letter, 'It is of course possible that the little article may attract wider attention and other papers may wish to quote from it or to reproduce it. It is my wish that no objection be raised to this. Let it all be in honour of Campbell-Bannerman and his remembrance in these confused days'. The Field Marshall's article concluded with the words, 'Don't forget Campbell-Bannerman'.

Coincidentally, Sir Henry's motto, as a Campbell, as granted and recorded by Lord Lyon King of Arms in Edinburgh in 1872, was *Ne obliviscaris* [Do not forget]. The motto, which was also the motto of his father, Sir James Campbell of Stracathro [Grant and Record of 1859], is also the motto of the Scottish Dukes of Argyll, Chiefs of Clan Campbell. Such duplication would probably not be allowed nowadays. The motto was also used by Lady Frances Balfour as the title of her *Ne Obliviscaris, Dinna Forget* [1929-1930]. Lady Frances was a daughter of the 8th [Scottish] and 1st (UK) Duke of Argyll and a sister-in-law of both the Campbell-Bannermans' friend Princess Louise [a daughter of Queen Victoria] and Arthur Balfour, Conservative Prime Minister in 1902-1905.

As a Campbell, Sir Henry's coat of arms had a boar's head crest. As a Bannerman, his crest was 'a demi-man in armour proper', with the motto *Patriæ fidelis* [Faithful to fatherland].

Some years later, I was equally impressed by statements made by John Wilson in Herbert Van Thal (Editor), *The Prime Ministers,* Volume Two (1975), p.194 that Sir Henry 'was one of the nicest and most sensible men ever to be leader of a political party or prime minister' and by Colin Clifford in his *The Asquiths* (2002), p.134 that Sir Henry 'was probably the most decent man ever to hold the office of Prime Minister'.

On the other hand, I am very much aware of what John Wilson wrote in his *CB – A Life of Sir Henry Campbell-Bannerman* (1973), p.15, that Sir Henry 'today is almost forgotten. Most people have never heard of him, and those who have tend to class him as a dim and secondary figure'. Accordingly, my determination to help in making him much better known and much better appreciated.

It should also be appreciated that this publication has its origins in my *A Scottish Liberal Perspective 1836-2008 – A Centenary Commemoration for Sir Henry Campbell-Bannerman 1836-1908* which was published privately in December 2008 with a reprint in January 2009, Indeed, as I then stated, it was my hope that appropriate parts of the *Perspective* would be of assistance to a qualified Scottish historian in producing a long overdue biography of Sir Henry which is not too anglocentric, too localised or too error-strewn. I now have the temerity to present myself as that biographer.

As for evidence of anglocentricity, I need only refer to the statement by John Wilson (1973), p.15 that Sir Henry was "an unusual person to emerge as the leader of a great political party in **England**"! (England ≠ The United Kingdom)

Sir Henry's constituency of Stirling Burghs included not only the Royal Burgh of Stirling (with some 43 % of the population) but also the Royal Burghs of Dunfermline (45 %), Inverkeithing (5 %), South Queensferry (5 %) and Culross (2 %). Accordingly, it should be appreciated that the early *The Model Member – Sir Henry Campbell-Bannerman* (1914), by John Beveridge Mackie of the *Dunfermline Journal,* was somewhat localised in that it was written very much from a Dunfermline perspective,

I also aim to correct some errors in previous biographies. For example, John A. Spender's statement, in his *Life of the Rt. Hon. Sir Henry Campbell-Bannerman, GCB* (1923), Volume 1, p.22, that Sir Henry and Lady Campbell-Bannerman married within a few months of their first meeting (rather six years later), was repeated by two later biographers – John Wilson, as above, in 1973, p.38, and Roy Hattersley in his *Campbell-Bannerman* (2006), p.10 – and by A.J.A. Morris in the entry (2004) for Sir Henry in the *Oxford Dictionary of National Biography (ODNB).* (The error arose in that Spender dated the marriage of Sir Henry's brother, James Alexander Campbell, at which the future Lady Campbell-Bannerman was bridesmaid, to 1860 rather than to the correct date of 1854.)

More positively. I believe that an individual's way of life is conditioned by a number of inter-related factors such as family identity, education, religious affiliation and other formative experiences, including, for Sir Henry, much overseas travel and the history and interests of the five Royal Burghs he represented in the House of Commons. Accordingly, particularly in the early chapters, I have gone much further than previous biographers in referring to Sir Henry's ancestry, his school (and its history and traditions of public service), the many places with which he and/or his family were connected, the family business, the political activities of his father and brother, what he himself wrote (mainly before he became an MP) and did in a non-political context, the family's other interests, achievements and relationships and Scottish Church matters. I have also been able to refer to commemorative events held in 2008, 2009 and 2010 and other events as recently as May 2013.

Further, it is not so much that there have been new discoveries about Sir Henry but that there is little or no evidence that earlier biographers referred to the interesting political history of Stirling Burghs before the mid-19th century or, other than John B. Mackie for Dunfermline, to such sources as the archival material now held by Stirling Council Archives and the Dunfermline Carnegie Library or to such held by The High School of Glasgow (a selection of which was published in a *Scrapbook* in 1995) or to the items held by the Stirling Smith Art Gallery and Museum or to appropriate entries in the invaluable *Statistical Accounts of Scotland*.

Moreover, since the last major biography of Sir Henry (by John Wilson in 1973), much material has become readily accessible online, including, for example, the *Glasgow Digital Library, Hansard 1803-2005, UK Parliament* and the *Oxford Dictionary of National Biography (ODNB)*. Also, by way of family history, reminiscences and the like, I have been able to have research exchanges with a number of Sir Henry's present-day relatives and to refer to a dissertation about him written by another such relative in 2009.

The availability of digital or other modern reprints of some, relatively inaccessible, books, some originally published over a hundred years ago (and not available on inter-library loan) – as indicated in the Bibliography – has also been very helpful.

NOTES

With the Campbell-Bannerman Papers originally deposited in what was the Library Department of the British Museum but, since 1973, located in the British Library, references to such are indicated as (CB/BL). References to Parliamentary business (speeches, votes, etc.) are taken from *Hansard* for the appropriate date. Extracts from Election Addresses for 1886 (February) and from 1892 to 1900 and the full text of such for 1906 are taken from originals held in the Dunfermline Carnegie Library. Refer to the Bibliography for sources for General Political Data (Election Results and Biographical Notes). Otherwise, full citations for all books mentioned in this introductory context and/or specifically quoted hereinafter are included in the Bibliography.

The McOran Campbells and Bannermans
Henry Campbell to Henry Campbell-Bannerman to Sir Henry-Campbell-Bannerman

The future Sir Henry Campbell-Bannerman's paternal ancestors had adopted the surname McOran in the mid-17th century while living in Perthshire but resumed the surname Campbell on moving to Glasgow in 1804 – hence references to the McOran Campbells as a sept (branch) of Clan Campbell. Thus he was known as Henry Campbell from his birth in 1836 until 1872 when he adopted, by royal licence, the surname Campbell-Bannerman as a condition of an 1871 legacy – the life rent of the Hunton Court estate in Kent – from a maternal uncle, Henry Bannerman. He was thereafter commonly and affectionately known as CB. He was invested as a Knight Grand Cross of the Order of the Bath (GCB) by Queen Victoria at Windsor on 1 July 1895. Accordingly, hereinafter, references to Henry (Campbell), to CB and to Sir Henry (Campbell-Bannerman).

Electoral Law and Practice

There were four major electoral enactments or groups of such during Sir Henry's lifetime, The 1867 Reform Act for England and Wales and the 1868 Reform Acts for Scotland and Ireland, (effective from the 1868 General Election) extended the franchise to adult male householders in the burgh/borough constituencies and redistributed constituencies. As will be considered, the extension of the burgh/borough franchise in 1868 was of particular significance at the start of Sir Henry's electoral career in the constituency of Stirling Burghs. The 1872 Ballot Act introduced secret voting. The 1883 Corrupt and Illegal Practices Act placed a maximum limit on election expenses incurred by candidates. The 1884 Reform Act and the 1885 Redistribution Act (effective from the 1885 General Election) extending the franchise to adult male householders in the county constituencies and redistributing constituencies.

Further, until 1918, General Elections were held over a period of some weeks, with polling in Orkney and Shetland and the University constituencies often being completed a week or so after polling in the other constituencies had been completed, Thus, for example, The 1906 General Election – 12 to 29 January (to 8 February), in Chapter 11 Table 23, indicates that the English boroughs started to poll on 12 January with such in all the boroughs, burghs and counties (except Orkney & Shetland) being completed by 29 January but with such in the Universities and Orkney & Shetland not being completed until 8 February. (Polling started in the Scottish burghs, including Edinburgh and Glasgow, on 18 January with such in the counties starting on 19 January) Accordingly, General Election campaigns continued after the early results were declared. For example, Sir Henry's final campaign speech in 1906 not being until 22 January at Larbert in Stirlingshire. (Refer also to J. Blair and David Chapel, *A Handbook of Parliamentary Elections in Scotland* [1909])

Ministerial By-Elections

Ministerial By-Elections were caused by a provision in the 1707 Succession to the Crown Act – as modified in 1919 and totally repealed in 1928 – that MPs appointed to certain senior ministerial and other public offices were required to seek re-election at a by-election, unless, as in December 1905, a General Election was called immediately following the appointment(s). Such MPs were more often than not re-elected unopposed as at all four such 19th century by-elections in Stirling Burghs – Archibald Primrose (Courtesy Title – Lord Dalmeny), father of the 5th (Scottish) Earl of Rosebery (Liberal Prime Minister in 1894-1895), when appointed Civil Lord of the Admiralty in 1835 and Henry Campbell-Bannerman following his appointments as Chief Secretary for Ireland in 1884 and as Secretary of State for War in 1886 and 1892.

Others were not so fortunate. William Gladstone did not contest a ministerial by-election in Newark on 29 January 1846 when he was appointed Secretary of State for War and the Colonies and was out of Parliament until elected for Oxford University at the July/August 1847 General Election. Winston Churchill was defeated at a ministerial by-election in Manchester North-West on 24 April 1908 when he was appointed President of the Board of Trade, but was elected, fifteen days later, at a by-election in Dundee on 9 May.

Peerages

Unless otherwise stated all peerages mentioned hereinafter are Peerages of Great Britain (1707-1801) or of the United Kingdom (from 1801)

Until legislation from 1963 onwards, Peers of Scotland and Ireland who also held English or, from 1707 or 1801, British or UK peerages were entitled to sit in the House of Lords by reason of such other peerages rather than as Scottish or Irish Representative Peers. George Hamilton-Gordon, 4th (Scottish) Earl of Aberdeen, when Peelite Prime Minister in 1852-1855, sat in the Lords as 1st (UK) Viscount Gordon. Archibald Primrose, 5th (Scottish) Earl of Rosebery, Liberal Prime Minister in 1894-1895, sat in the Lords for most of his parliamentary career as 2nd (UK) Lord Rosebery. Victor Alexander Bruce, 9th (Scottish) Earl of Elgin and 13th (Scottish) Earl of Kincardine, Liberal Colonial Secretary in 1905-1908, sat in the Lords as 2nd (UK) Lord Elgin. However, John Stuart, 3rd [Scottish] Earl of Bute, while briefly Tory Prime Minister in 1762-1763, sat in the Lords as a Scottish Representative Peer.

No Scottish Peerages, as such, were created after 1707. Scottish Representative Peers were elected for a Parliament with the last such elections being in 1959. However, Irish Peerages continued to be created until 1898. Irish Representative Peers were elected for life with the last such peer being elected in 1919 and the last such peer dying in 1961.

Nevertheless, unlike all other Peers who, until recently, were not eligible, other Peers of Ireland were eligible for election as MPs. Thus Henry Temple, 3rd (Irish) Viscount Palmerston (Prime Minister as a Whig in 1855-1858 and as a Liberal in

1859-1865) not being an Irish Representative Peer or having any British or UK Peerages, was able to serve in the House of Commons between 1807 and 1865.

Sons and some grandsons of Peers, including Lord Dalmeny as above mentioned, who were elected to the House of Commons usually used a courtesy title. John Russell (Prime Minister as a Whig in 1846-1852 and as a Liberal in 1865-1866), third son of the 6th (English) Duke of Bedford, was known as Lord John Russell until he was created Earl Russell in 1861. Spencer Crompton Cavendish (a Cabinet Minister as a Liberal in 1866, 1868-1874 and 1880-1885 and as a Liberal Unionist in 1895-1903) was known as Lord Cavendish until his father succeeded as 7th (English) Duke of Devonshire in 1858 and then as the Marquis of Hartington until he succeeded as 8th Duke in 1891. Alexander Murray (a Liberal MP in 1900-1912 and Chief Whip in 1910-1912) was known as the Master of Elibank, a traditional title for an heir to a Scottish Peerage, until he was created Lord Murray of Elibank in 1912. He predeceased his father and a younger brother succeeded to the family peerages.

Purchasing Power of the £ Sterling 1836 to 1908

The purchasing power of the £ Sterling during Sir Henry's lifetime was in the range of from 80 to 100 times current money values.

Acknowledgements

I would like to acknowledge the work of all those at Austin Macauley who have been involved in the production of this book, especially Annette Longman, Chief Editor and Vinh Tran, my Production Coordinator.

I am also particularly grateful to Lord Steel of Aikwood not only for writing the Foreword but also for other helpful comments.

My thanks also to The High School of Glasgow for giving me access to School publications dating from 1906, some including material dating back to the 16th century, and for confirming that extracts and illustrations from such may be reproduced provided due acknowledgement is given. Particular thanks to Colin D.R. Mair, Rector from 2004 to 2014, for continuing courtesies in this connection and otherwise. Many thanks also to Karen McDonald, the School's Development Director, Marjory Grimmond, School Librarian, Katie Keenan, the School's former Development Director, and Dr. Robin Easton, Rector in 1983-2004, for their good offices in this connection.

Thus and otherwise, citations/credits for all illustrations have been given in the list of such immediately after the Contents Page. Efforts have also been made to obtain permission for the use of other copyright material, with apologies for any omissions in this respect.

I am also grateful to those others with whom I have had relevant research exchanges over the years and/or have supplied illustrations and/or have commented helpfully on early drafts of various parts of this publication. Such include the late R. Ian Elder, the late T.R.L. (Ronnie) Fraser, Hugh Campbell Adamson, Dr. Malcolm Baines, Duncan Brack (Editor, *Journal of Liberal History*), Hugh Brown (CrossReach, The Church of Scotland), Councillor Robert Brown, Professor Stewart J. Brown, Professor Ewen Cameron, Lord Campbell of Pittenweem, Robert Adair Campbell, Gordon Casely, Richard Crossick, Martin Cook (AOC Archaeology), Professor Russell Deacon, Gillian Devas, James C. Devas, Andrew Driver (Perth and Kinross Heritage Trust), David Eaton (Meigle and District History Society), Sir Angus and Lady Farquharson, Berkley Farr, Barry Gardiner, MP, James Gray, MP, Jane Hamilton (Mary's Meals), Andrea Hertz, Patrick Jackson, Dr. Elspeth King (Director, Stirling Smith Art Gallery and Museum), John Lawrie, Nigel Lindsay, Graham Lippiatt, Brian Lockhart, Tom Lynch, Iain Macnair (Glasgow Cathedral), Alastair McOran-Campbell, Professor Roger Mason, Michael Meadowcroft, John Miller (Stirling Bowling Club), Galen Milne, Linna Monteath and Sheena Maitland-Makgill-Crichton (Session Clerk and Treasurer, Port of Menteith Parish Church), Dr. Willis Pickard, Dr. Jack Priestley, Willie Rennie, MSP, Elizabeth Roads, (Snawdoun Herald and Lyon Clerk), The Rev. John Russell (Clerk, Presbytery of Dunkeld and Meigle), Councillor Lewis Simpson, Dr. Tony Trower (Westminster Abbey), Dr. Adam Watson, W. Stewart Wilson, and Councillor Willie Wilson (now also Deputy Provost of Perth and Kinross).

Ronnie Fraser had Sir Henry Campbell-Bannerman as his special subject when he won a round of Mastermind some years ago. Hugh Campbell Adamson is a descendant of Sir Henry's brother (James Alexander Campbell), James C, Devas of Sir Henry's sister (Louisa Bannerman, née Campbell) and Robert Adair Campbell and Alastair McOran-Campbell of Sir Henry's uncle (William Campbell). Hugh's daughter, Rosie was the author of a Durham University Dissertation (2009) on CB – *The Thwarted Prime Minister.* Mrs. Gillian Devas is James Devas' step-mother. Brian Lockhart is the author of *The Town School – A History of The High School of Glasgow* (2010). John Russell and I shared a desk in Sixth Year English in 1950-1951, before which both our names appeared on three other pages of the above-mentioned *Glasgow High School Magazine* of June 1948. Nigel Lindsay, a former Liberal Councillor in Aberdeen and a leading light in the Scottish commemorative events for Sir Henry in 2008, has been exceedingly supportive at all stages. As Nigel wrote in January 2008, 'It has always seemed to me that Liberals of our age are the (not always worthy) legatees of a powerful tradition. Encouraging an understanding of that may help people better to link policy thinking to underlying principle'.

There are biographical notes for Nigel and for Councillor Robert Brown in *The Little Yellow Book – Reclaiming the Liberal Democrats for the People* (2012) which they edited.

Many thanks also to archivists, librarians, office-bearers and other correspondents of the organisations and institutions mentioned above and of Aberdeen Central Library, Aberdeen University Libraries, Banchory Library, Christ's College Library (Aberdeen), Dundee City Archives, Dunfermline Bowling Club, Dunfermline Carnegie Library, Faculty of Advocates (Edinburgh), Glasgow University Archives, *Life and Work* (The Magazine of The Church of Scotland), Mitchell Library (Glasgow) for *The (Glasgow) Herald* Archives, National Archives of Scotland (Edinburgh), National Galleries of Scotland (Edinburgh), National Liberal Club (London), National Library of Scotland (Edinburgh), Oxford University Archives, Perth and Kinross Council Archives, Presbytery of Stirling, Reform Club (London), St. Deniol's Residential Library (Hawarden, Flintshire) as founded by William Gladstone in 1889, *The Scotsman* (Edinburgh), Scottish Outdoor Education Centres, Stirling Council Archives, Stirling Bowling Club, The Stirling Highland Hotel and Trinity House (London).

Last but not least, my thanks to my wife, Sheila and to our son, Angus and our daughter, Dr. Sheila and their families for their love, tolerance and support. Sheila, my wife has not only provided a translation of *Sir Henry Campbell-Bannerman dans L'Histoire de France* by Professor Henry Contamine of the University of Caen (*Glasgow High School Magazine,* June 1948), helped with Sir Henry's Italian and commented helpfully on many of my drafts but also continues to be and increasingly a very present help in all things.

Note:
Matters of fact have been updated where appropriate since Dr Waugh completed the manuscript of this book in 2013.

1 – Ancestry, Family Business, Birth (1836), Religion and Politics

As indicated in the Outline Genealogy of the McOran-Campbells in the Introduction, in the 17th century Sir Henry Campbell-Bannerman's paternal ancestors occupied the farm of Fernoch in Melfort (south of Oban) in Argyll. Sir Henry's great-great-great-great-grandfather, John Campbell (Died c.1669) had the nickname of *Duinecoir,* from the Gaelic *duine* ('man') and *coir* ('just/right') but taken to mean 'honest man'. In 1660x1665,[1] John Campbell's son (Born c.1645) accidentally killed a young McColl. Although apparently forgiven by the deceased's family, he thought it best to leave the district. Thus he arrived in the Menteith district of Perthshire and, under the assumed surname of McOran (taken to mean 'son of the honest man') entered into the service of William Graham, 8th (Scottish) Earl of Menteith. On The McOran's marriage, in 1670x1675,[1] to Nancy Haldane, a daughter of Hugo Haldane of Gleneagles and a niece of Patrick Haldane of Lanrick Castle, he was settled by the Earl on the farm of Inchanoch in the Parish of Port of Menteith. The farm, apparently between the lands of Rednock and Gartmore, was held by the family rent free until 1799 and then by a one year lease in 1799-1800, with the lease being renewed for nine years in 1800.

The Earl, who was also 2nd (Scottish) Earl of Airth, and had succeeded his grandfather in 1661, died, without issue, in 1694. However, fourteen years earlier, by reason of indebtedness, he had disposed of most of the already much reduced lands of the Menteith Earldom. One portion went to James Graham, 3rd (Scottish) Marquis of Montrose, the head of the senior branch of the Graham family. Another portion, including Inchanoch, went to the Earl's nephew, the then Graham of Gartmore. Thus, from 1680, the McOrans held Inchanoch of the Grahams of Gartmore. Gartmore is in the Civil Parish of Port of Menteith which is now within the jurisdiction of Stirling Council, The Parish is now also part of the Loch Lomond and Trossachs National Park.

The 7th Earl had been deprived of his Menteith Earldom by Charles I in 1632 for allegedly claiming that his ancestor, David Stewart, rather than David's older half-brother, John Stewart (who reigned as Robert III) should have succeeded their father, Robert II as King of Scots in 1390. The Earl was given a new Earldom (Airth) instead, but was subsequently allowed to resume the Menteith title.

The McOran-Campbells continued to be mindful of their Argyllshire origins, being responsible in later years for reclaiming two farms – Easter and Western Lorne – from the Moss in the Melfort area.[2] (Also, as will be considered in Chapter 8, by reason of another family connection, a village in what is now Zimbabwe was named

---

[1] 1660x1665 and 1670x1675 indicate a time span of earliest and latest possible dates when an exact date is unknown,

[2] Margret Olympia Campbell (1882, 2012 Reprint), p.8

Melfort). Further, a Dugald McCorran is recorded at Fernoch, Melfort in 1689.[3] So, the often quoted local saying, 'there was never a Campbell in Menteith or a McOran out of it', has to be interpreted as meaning that the McOran-Campbells never used the surname Campbell in Menteith.

Donald McOran, the son of the original McOran and Nancy Haldane of Inchanoch, also married a Haldane (Agnes, probably a cousin). Their son, James was a great-grandfather of Sir Henry Campbell-Bannerman. In the Port of Menteith Parish Register for 1 February 1713 – which records James' baptism – the spellings are 'Haldan' and 'Inchie-noch', with also 'McCorran' recorded, as above, as an alternative (and perhaps the more authentic) spelling of 'McOran' The Gaelic word *oran* is usually translated as 'song'. Accordingly, it is appropriate to note that James McOran-Campbell, a descendant of the McOrans of Inchanoch, has become a leading concert and operatic singer in recent years.

Lanrick Castle (demolished illegally in 2002) was four miles north-west of Doune in Perthshire. It was held by the Earls of Menteith until 1460 when it was sold to a branch of the Haldanes of Gleneagles. The Haldanes of Lanrick Castle having been forfeited for their part in the Jacobite Rising of 1745-1746, the Castle was acquired in 1776 by General John Murray who was really a MacGregor.

The penal statutes against the MacGregors having been finally repealed in 1774, the General was publicly acknowledged as Chief of Clan Gregor and created a Baronet in 1795. The 2nd Baronet resumed the surname MacGregor by royal license in 1822. After reconstruction in the 1790s Lanrick Castle was known as Clan Gregor Castle until sold out of the family in 1831. The new owner was William Jardine, co-founder of the Hong Kong trading company Jardine Matheson, who was Whig MP for Ashburton, Kent in 1841-1842.[4] His heir was his nephew, Sir Robert Jardine, Bt. who was a Liberal MP in 1865-1874 [Ashburton and Dumfries Burghs] and MP for Dumfries-shire as a Liberal in 1880-1886 and as a Liberal Unionist MP in 1886-1892

Coincidentally, two Haldanes of Gleneagles were among Sir Henry's 18th century predecessors as MPs for Stirling Burghs. (Refer to Chapter 3 and Appendix 1) Further, the descent of Sir Henry from the Haldanes of Gleneagles also means that he was very distantly related to Richard Burdon Haldane (Viscount Haldane 1911), who served in his 1905-1908 Cabinet as Secretary of State for War. As from the same descent, Sir Henry was also very distantly related to such maternally Haldanes as Andrew Fletcher of Saltoun (c.1653-1716), and Admiral Adam Duncan (1731-1804), Viscount Duncan of Camperdown.[5]

---

[3] Online *Clan Campbell Society of North America – Septs of Clan Campbell*

[4] Online *Clan Gregor History – Lanrick* and William Jardine, *ODNB* (Richard J. Grace)

[5] Online *ODNB* Andrew Fletcher (John Robertson) and Admiral Duncan (P.K. Crimmin)

Andrew Fletcher served in the old Scottish Parliament in 1681-1682 and again, after a period of political outlawry and exile, in 1702-1707. During the debates in 1706-1707, he favoured a federal, rather than an incorporating, union of Scotland with England (and Wales). Admiral Duncan was the victor of the sea battle of Camperdown in 1797. His son was created Earl of Camperdown and his son, known by his courtesy title of Viscount Duncan, was a Whig MP for Southampton in 1837-1841, for Bath in 1841-1852 and for Forfarshire (Angus) from 1854 until he succeeded to the family peerages in 1859. One of his residences was on inherited land at Gleneagles in Perthshire, reflecting his connection with the Haldanes. He was in favour of secret ballots and the ending of all religious discrimination. Robert Haldane-Duncan, 3rd Earl of Camperdown served in Gladstone's First Administration as a Government Whip in the House of Lords in 1868-1870 and as Civil Lord of the Admiralty in 1870-1874. The Earl was responsible for persuading Richard Burdon Haldane, his distant relative and near neighbour in Perthshire, to enter active Liberal politics in 1878. [6] The Camperdown estate on the outskirts of Dundee has been converted into a large public park, a golf course and a nature reserve.

Port of Menteith (Gaelic *Port Loch Innis Mo Cholmaig*) – on the north-east shore of what is usually known nowadays as the 'Lake' of Menteith (Gaelic *Loch Innis Mo Cholmaig*) – is the base for the ferry (Gaelic *port*) for the Island of Inchmaholme (Gaelic *Innis Mo Cholmaig*, meaning 'My Colmac's Island'.) In past times Port of Menteith itself, although giving its name to the Parish, was never more than a small hamlet – with church, manse, inn, school, schoolhouse and a few cottages – although given the status of a Burgh of Barony, in favour of the then Earl of Menteith, by King James III in 1466.

Scottish Burghs of Barony, as distinct from Royal Burghs, were granted in favour of tenants-in-chief who held their lands directly from the Crown. This gave the landowner various trading rights (to hold weekly markets and/or to trade overseas). The remaining Burghs of Barony were, as such, abolished in 1893 by the 1892 Burgh Police (Scotland) Act.

In records and maps of 1646, 1654 and 1742 and in the *(First) Statistical Account* – with the entry for the Parish written by the then Parish Minister in 1791-1793 – the 'Lake' was known as a 'Loch', as also by Sir Walter Scott. Both 'Loch' and 'Lake' were used by Dr. Patrick Graham in his *Sketches of Perthshire* (c.1812). In the mid-19th century *New Statistical Account* – with the entry for the Parish written by the then Parish Minister – the reference was to the 'Lake of Inchmaholme', a very 'English' translation of the Gaelic. Queen Victoria, who visited the area in 1869, referred, in her *Highland Journal* to 'the Loch of Menteith (the only loch in Scotland

---

[6] Matthew (1973), p.4

which is ever called lake)'.[7] Further, according to Andrew F. Hutchison, writing in 1899, during the 19th century, many locals referred to the 'Loch o' Port'.[8] The Loch/Lake, with its surface less than 100 feet above sea level, lies within a natural basin surrounded by hills. Hence, in early maps, the Loch/Lake is shown as within the Laicht of Menteith, with Laicht (otherwise 'laich' and 'laigh') meaning 'lowland'. So, rather than refer to the 'Lake of Menteith', it would be more appropriate to refer to the <u>Loch of the Laicht (Lowland) of Menteith.</u> Nearly all the other 'Lakes' in Scotland are man-made except Manxman's Lake which is a sea bay near Kirkcudbright.[9]

Inchmaholme Island's Augustinian Priory, dating from c.1238, was visited by King Robert I (The Bruce) and King Robert II. It also provided refuge for three weeks in 1547 for Mary, Queen of Scots (then aged four) during a period of English incursions. By the time of the Reformation the Priory had 'lay' Abbots, known as Commendators. (A Commendator held his office *in commendam* [in trust] rather than *in titilum* [by entitlement] as did Abbots and Priors who were monks and lived in their monasteries.) Indeed, one such Commendator, David Erskine of Cardross (whose family became Patrons of the Parish of Port of Menteith) represented the Priory at the Reformation Parliament in Edinburgh in August 1560. By 1606, the Priory was no more than a secular possession of the Scottish Earls of Mar (Erskines) and later of the Scottish Marquises and Dukes of Montrose (Grahams), with the 6th Duke passing the Priory into the care of the State in 1926. The Priory's remains are now in the care of Historic Scotland, with the ferry now running only from April to October.

Coincidentally, the Rev. Linda Stewart, who was, in 2001-2008, Parish Minister of Meigle (where Sir Henry and Lady Campbell-Bannerman are buried) was Parish Minister of Port of Menteith (as linked with Aberfoyle in 1983) in 2008-2012. (The Parish Churches of Aberfoyle and Port of Menteith are about 4 miles apart.)

Another coincidence is that Lord Campbell of Pittenweem, Leader of the Liberal Democrat Party in 2006-2007, and Lady Campbell owned a little farmhouse near Port of Menteith for about twenty years from the 1970s.[10] Further, the Glasgow

---

[7] Duff (1983), p.145

[8] Hutchison (1899, Reprint 2010), p.67-68

[9] The artificial 'Lakes' in Scotland include the Lake of the Hirsel (Berwickshire) in the grounds of the home of the Scottish Earls of Home (Douglas-Homes), Lake Louise (Sutherland) in the grounds of Skibo Castle, Pressmennan Lake in East Lothian, Raith Lake in Kirkcaldy, Cally Lake near Gatehouse of Fleet and Lake Superior in Wigtownshire. It is also noted that, on recent and current OS maps, the lochs at Fyvie Castle in Aberdeenshire, at Hatton Castle in Angus (Forfarshire) and at least one at Haddo House, also in Aberdeenshire, are marked as 'Lakes' I am indebted to Dr. Adam Watson for drawing such markings to my attention.

[10] Campbell (2008), p.91

birthplaces of Sir Henry (in 1836) and of Sir Menzies (in 1941), were only about half-a-mile apart, as the crow flies, or a half-hour walk, Moreover, both were born into Clan Campbell, educated at school and at university in Glasgow (and at universities furth of Scotland), married the daughters of Major-Generals, had an interest in the Speakership of the House of Commons and were thereafter elected party leaders in their sixties.

In 1785 Sir Henry's paternal grandfather, James McOran (1752-1831), great-grandson of the first McOran of Inchanoch, married Helen Forrester (Born 1763). The Forresters had tenanted the farm of Frew (near Kippen) in Stirlingshire for over 300 years. Kippen was also in Menteith but, unlike the seven other Menteith parishes which were in Perthshire, Kippen Parish was divided between Perthshire and Stirlingshire. Unlike her husband, and most other people in Menteith at that time, Mrs. McOran did not have the Gaelic. Therefore, their four sons and four daughters did not learn Gaelic. Thus, the future Prime Minister was only one complete generation away from having Gaelic.

Apparently, both before and after his marriage in 1785, James McOran had exchanged visits with Captain Neil (or Niel) Campbell, a Melfort landowner. Indeed, the Captain had promised the young James a commission if he would enter the army. When the McOrans' first son was both in 1787, the Captain expressed a wish that the child should be called Neil (or Niel). However, the parents preferred John as the child's name. The Captain took the choice amiss and never visited Inchanoch again.[11]. So, the family's future lay elsewhere, in particular as from 1803 when the then 'Graham' of Gartmore (who used the surname Bontine) transferred the superiority of Inchanoch to the adjacent proprietor, Graham Shepherd of Rednock.

Robert Graham (1735-1797) of Gartmore had assumed the surname Bontine in 1770 by reason of an inheritance of land but, after the death of his father (Nicol Graham), and as Radical MP for Stirlingshire in 1794-1796, he was again known as Robert Graham. Then, in 1796, he added Cunninghame to his surname by reason of another inheritance of land. He was a close friend of Charles James Fox and Rector of Glasgow University in 1785-1787 (in between Edmund Burke and Adam Smith.) His son, who inherited in 1797, was always known as Bontine but his colourful Harrow-educated grandson (1852-1936) resumed the surname Cunninghame-Graham in 1883 to become, as Robert Bontine Cunninghame-Graham of Gartmore, Liberal/Labour MP for North West Lanarkshire in 1886-1892. Thereafter, he was a founder member of the Independent Labour Party (ILP) in 1893, the unsuccessful Liberal Candidate for West Stirlingshire in 1918, first Chairman of the National Party of Scotland (in 1928), which, in 1934, merged with the Scottish Party (formed in 1932) to form the Scottish National Party (SNP), of which he was first President.[12]

---

[11] Margret Olympia Campbell (1882, 2012 Reprint), p.8

[12] In 1887 Cunninghame-Graham and John Burns, who would be a Liberal Cabinet Minister in 1905-1914, were charged in connection with disturbances in Trafalgar Square. Burns defended

Then, in 1804, the McOrans relinquished the lease of the family farm to Mr. Shepherd in return for a payment of £525 and moved to Glasgow where they resumed the surname of Campbell. They had in mind to move on to North America but – except for the eldest son, John – this notion was soon abandoned. The parents opened a grocer's shop at 304 Gallowgate (east of Glasgow Cross). After moving to the Saltmarket (south of Glasgow Cross), they, gave up the business in 1807, and eventually retired to Parkhead, then in open country to the east of Glasgow.

The family also continued to be mindful of their Menteith connection. Sir Henry's father, Sir James Campbell had known before his death in 1876 that a new Parish Church was to be built in Port of Menteith – to replace the Church, built in 1771, in which the family had worshipped – and had promised to make some provision for the new building as the means of fulfilling his promise to his parents to commemorate their association with the Parish. Thus, after Sir James' death, the funding by his sons – James Alexander Campbell and Henry – of the Stained Glass Window for the new Church building, as opened on 3 October 1878.[13] (Refer also to Chapter 4)

John Campbell (1787-1872), who had already worked for a year as a grocer's apprentice in Glasgow went to the USA where he married a Mary Kennedy He subsequently returned to Glasgow for a few years and worked in his brothers' business. He then went back to the USA and eventually settled in Fonda (formerly Caughnawaga) in the Mohawk Valley, Montgomery County, New York State.

In 1863, during the US Civil War, he and his wife were involved in raising funds in Fonda to pay for two flags as then presented to the 115th New York Infantry Regiment. In 1885 John Campbell's family were still living in Fonda.[14]

The Regiment, with headquarters in Fonda, was mustered on 26 August 1862 with men from Fonda serving in four of its ten companies. It was mustered-out at Raleigh, North Carolina on 17 June 1865. Caughnawaga was renamed Fonda after a late 18th century settler, Douw Fonda, an ancestor of Henry Fonda the actor. One wonders if any members of John Campbell's family in Glasgow were aware that the former Confederate President, Jefferson Davis, after his release from imprisonment, visited Glasgow in 1869. He stayed with his friend, James Smith – a merchant who had supported the Confederates financially – at his residence of Benvue in Dowanhill.

---

    himself and Cunninghame-Graham was defended by H.H. Asquith. Both were sentenced to six weeks imprisonment. This was the first case that brought Asquith to public notice.

[13] *Stirling Journal (and Advertiser)* 4 October 1878

[14] Online *New York Military Museum – Civil War Newspaper Clippings.*

James Smith's younger brother, Robert had been killed while serving as a Colonel in the Mississippi Rifles.[15]

James Campbell (1790-1876), Sir Henry's father, served an apprenticeship until 1810 with Messrs. McLachlan and McKeand (Warehousemen) whose business was in the High Street (between Glasgow Cross and the Cathedral.) Mr. McLachlan had known the family at Port of Menteith and would be a good friend in Glasgow.

James was then, for two years, in partnership with Matthew Paterson as clothiers at 163 Trongate (west of Glasgow Cross). The business failed by reason of a previous partner withdrawing his capital. With Mr. Paterson not wishing to continue in business, James, with the help of friends, offered the creditors a settlement of ten shillings in the pound. The offer was declined, with the creditors preferring to liquidate the business. Although in time legally discharged of liabilities, the two partners undertook to reimburse the creditors for the amount by which James' offer had fallen short of the full amount of their claims. With Matthew Paterson having died, James eventually settled this obligation, with interest, in 1828. In the meantime, James was in business on his own as James Campbell Tertius & Co. for four to five years, as a clothier at 41 Brunswick Place (north of the Trongate).

In this and other similar Scottish contexts 'gate' refers to a 'way/road/path/street'. The famous Saracen's Head Inn, visited by Boswell, Johnson and Burns, was built on a site in the Gallowgate in 1754. It became the Glasgow terminus for the London mail coach in 1788 but was converted into houses and shops in 1792 and demolished in 1903. The Trongate was named for the 'tron' (public weigh-bridge) erected in 1491.

In 1817 James Campbell disposed of his business in Brunswick Place and entered into partnership with his youngest brother, William (1794-1864) as J & W Campbell (Wholesale and Retail Drapers) in an old tenement at 5 Saltmarket. His former employers – Messrs. McLachlan and McKeand – advanced the capital (£ 100) for the new business and were also partners until later in 1817 (Mr. McKeand) and until 1822 (Mr. McLachlan). William had previously been employed by John Craig, a merchant in the High Street. The third brother, Alexander was also a partner from 1820 until his death in 1822. During this time the business was known as J, A. & W. Campbell.

The brothers owed much of their success to introducing a system of fixed prices, narrow margins and quick returns for their goods rather than the then common practices of haggling, broad margins and slow turnover of stock. It is said that they departed from haggling after hearing a sermon by Thomas Chalmers, later Moderator of the first General Assembly of the Free Church of Scotland at the time of the Disruption of the Church of Scotland in 1843. Thomas Chalmers, who denounced

---

[15] Urquhart (2000), p.28

haggling as dishonest especially to the poor,[16] was a Church of Scotland Minister in Glasgow in 1815-1823 – Tron Parish in 1815-1819 and St. John's Parish in 1819-1823.

James and William Campbell both married in 1822. William Campbell married Margaret Roxburgh, with their eldest son, James, later becoming senior partner in the family business. James Campbell married Janet Bannerman (1791-1873) in Manchester Cathedral. Janet was the sister of Henry Bannerman (Died 1871), formerly of Manchester and later of Hunton Court in Kent, who was married to Mary Wyld. (According to the Online *Sue Young Histories,* the Wylds were related by marriage to the Gladstones.) Janet's father was Henry Bannerman (c.1753-1823) a prosperous Manchester merchant. He had been sent (with his family, including Janet and her siblings) by his father, William Bannerman (1732-1812) from the family farm and distillery at Tullibardine in Strathearn, Perthshire to Manchester to engage in the cotton trade. Tullibardine is just over a mile north-west of Auchterarder, off the road to Crieff, with the family also having a farm near Crieff and business premises in Auchterarder.

The Bannermans' Tullibardine is now little more than a hamlet, with three adjacent farms. Its Castle (belonging to the Murray Dukes of Atholl) was destroyed after the 1745-1746 Jacobite Rising, with Marquis of Tullibardine being one of the Dukes' lesser titles. However, the well-preserved Medieval Chapel, at West Mains of Tullibardine, survives in the care of Historic Scotland. The Bannerman's former distillery at Tullibardine should not be confused with the present-day Tullibardine Distillery [opened in 1949] which is four miles to the south-west at Blackford is adjacent to the bottling plants of Highland Spring Water and its local subsidiary, Gleneagles Water. The nearby Gleneagles Hotel and golf complex [opened in 1924) is in the Parish of Blackford.

In his old age William Bannerman followed his son to Manchester and took charge of the finances of Henry Bannerman and Sons, although returning to Tullibardine to die in 1812. William Bannerman just made it to Manchester – by road to Glasgow and then by sea with, after the sailing ship had spent fourteen days beating about in a stormy Irish Sea, twenty miles in a rowing boat to Liverpool.[17]

Janet Motherwell (Born 1755), mother of Janet Campbell (née Bannerman), came from St. Ninian's, Stirlingshire, being of the same family as, and probably an aunt of, William Motherwell (1797-1835), the Glasgow poet. William Motherwell, author of the ballad *Jeanie Morrison,* used to meet other *literati,* including William Millar, author of *Wee Willie Winkie,* in a snuggery at the back of a bookshop at the foot of

---

[16] O'Connor (1908), p.12

[17] *Stirling Journal (and Advertiser),* 1 May 1908

Glassford Street [18] William Motherwell was also Editor of the Tory-supporting *Glasgow Courier* from 1830 until his death.[19]

For several years James Campbell went regularly as a buyer to English and Irish markets, in particular to Lancashire, Yorkshire, Nottinghamshire, London and Dublin. It may be that he met Janet Bannerman on one or more of his visits to Lancashire and/or through her Glasgow or Perthshire connections. James and Janet Campbell's first married home was in the centre house of the New Building in George Square. The Square was laid out in 1781 and completed in 1804. The New Building was later incorporated into the North British Railway Hotel (now the Millennium Hotel), beside Queen Street Station (opened in 1842). James' and Janet's first child, Jane (1823-1842) and their first son, James Alexander were born in George Square on 20 April 1825. (He died at Stracathro on 9 May 1908).

A new suburban house was built for James Campbell at 21 (later 129) Bath Street in 1828. At that time, the houses further west in that part of the town, except in Blythswood Square (as developed from 1832) were suburban villas. The three-storeyed house, with attics and basement, had stables and coach-houses behind in Bath Lane. The site, which had been bought from James Auchie, a Glasgow merchant, was described as 'the fourth steading east from Campbell Street on the south side of Bath Street'. After Sir James Campbell's death, the house was sold by his trustees (including Henry) to the recently created School Board of Glasgow for £ 7,200 in 1878.

The surveyor then stated that 'the public rooms are spacious, well furnished and the whole house is superior in style… I do not know of a more suitable lot for offices'.[20] In 1872, James Alexander had been elected to the first Glasgow School Board, becoming its Deputy Chairman and Convener of its Property and High School Committees and serving until 1876.

James and Janet Campbell's three other daughters were born in Bath Street – Louisa (1833-1873), Mary who died in infancy in 1835 and Helen who died in childhood in 1836. All the daughters predeceased their parents with the exception of Louisa who died in the same year as her mother. Louisa was also the only married daughter, her husband being James Alexander Bannerman, a cousin. A bronze plaque commemorating Sir Henry's association with the building was unveiled by David, Lord Steel of Aikwood in December 2008. At that date the building was The ABode Glasgow Hotel, as renamed The Arthouse Glasgow in 2014. (Refer also to Appendix 5)

---

[18] Oakley (1946), p.57

[19] Cowan (1946), pp.39 and 141

[20] *Glasgow High School Magazine,* June 1948, p.113

In 1832 the Campbell business moved to new premises at 34 Candleriggs (north of the Trongate), with manufacturing departments on the upper floors. A large export trade was now also being developed with valuable connections in North America, the West Indies, the Cape of Good Hope and eventually in Australia and New Zealand.

The Glasgow Herald of 17 September 1830

[Kelvinside House is] beautifully situated on the banks of the Kelvin. [It is] in good condition, and fit to accommodate a genteel family, with an abundance of Offices and a productive Garden. The beauty of this situation is not surpassed in this part of the country; it is now very retired, and as the west end of Glasgow is extending rapidly in that direction, it will soon be in contact with the principal streets at the west end of the town, and in consequence become much more valuable,

However, the then owner of Kelvinside House, Mrs. Elizabeth Cuthill, failed to sell the House in 1830. Accordingly, it was rented-out throughout the 1830s, being rented by James Campbell for several summers from 1835 until acquiring a new rented summer residence on part of the site now occupied by Jordanhill College of Education, with the Jordanhill district not becoming part of Glasgow until 1912.

The Glasgow Herald of 9 September 1836
At Kelvinside, on the 7th Sept., Mrs. James Campbell, of a son

Thus the future Sir Henry Campbell-Bannerman was born, as Henry Campbell, on 7 September 1836 at Kelvinside House, being the youngest child and second son of James and Janet Campbell, who were then aged about 46 and 45, respectively.

Kelvinside House, originally known as Bankead, was built in 1749-1750 for Thomas Dunmore, one of Glasgow's 'Tobacco Lords' and demolished in about 1890. It stood on a hill (since occupied by Clouston Street [formerly Montgomerie Street], Derby Crescent and Kelvin Drive) overlooking the future site of Glasgow Botanic Gardens (opened in 1842) on the other side of the River Kelvin. The House was approached from Garscube Road by a carriage drive corresponding to the present-day Kelvinside Avenue. Until, at least, some 40 years after the demolition of Kelvinside House, it was possible to see, from the west end of Clouston Street, four carved pillars, which were what was then left of the House and its gateways. [21] Nevertheless, in 1836, the House was in open country in an area which was not annexed by Glasgow until 1891.

---

[21] Barr (1928), p.219. The Rev. James Barr, while Labour MP for Motherwell in 1924-1931, lived at 75 Clouston Street.

In 1836, with a Scottish population of about 2.5 million, Glasgow had a population of c.250,000. Thirteen townships around Glasgow became Burghs during the 19th century – from Gorbals in 1808 to Pollokshields East in 1880. However, all were eventually annexed by Glasgow – from Anderston, Calton and Gorbals in 1846 to Govan, Pollokshaws and Partick in 1912. Twenty-nine originally suburban districts were also annexed by Glasgow between 1846 (Bridgeton]) and 1975 (Carmlye). The Royal Burgh of Rutherglen became part of Glasgow for local government purposes in 1975 but was restored to (South) Lanarkshire in 1986.[22]

However, summers apart, Henry was brought up in Glasgow in Bath Street which remained his home base until he married in 1860. A family portrait of Henry, aged two, was reproduced in the *Glasgow High School Magazine* of June 1948.

Glasgow's Botanic Gardens had their origin in the Physic Garden created in 1706 next to the University's Old College in the High Street, with the Royal Botanic Institute of Glasgow opening new Gardens near Charing Cross in about 1815. After that site was sold, the Gardens move to the present-day site in Kelvinside in 1842. Until taken over by Glasgow Corporation in 1891, the Gardens were usually only open to Institute members. However, on Saturdays the public were allowed in for a shilling each with occasionally the payment being reduced to one penny. But there was eventually free admission during the Fair Fortnight in July, thanks to a payment of £ 500 by Henry's Uncle, William Campbell.

Kibble Palace, a soaring iron and glass structure, with at one time a seating capacity of 6000, erected within the Gardens in 1871-1873, was recently re-erected after a three-year renovation. It was the location of the delayed installation of Gladstone as Rector of Glasgow University in 1879, which, incidentally, was attended by Bonar Law, a future Conservative Prime Minister, then aged 21 years.

In January 1837 James Campbell was one of the delegation which travelled to Deyton Manor in Staffordshire to invite Sir Robert Peel to attend a banquet in his honour on the occasion of his installation as Rector of Glasgow University, Apparently, they did not allow the wheels of their carriage to be washed during the journey so that the mud would bear witness to their haste and eagerness. The banquet was held in a temporary wooden pavilion in the very large back garden of a villa, the very first house to be built (1778) in Buchanan Street. It. was attended by some 3,430 people with William Gladstone, then a Tory MP for Newark, being one of the speakers.

The villa was demolished within four years to allow for the erection of the Prince of Wales building with an enclosed commercial courtyard at the back. The courtyard was eventually roofed over in 1987 and the Princes Square shopping centre created.

---

[22] At the same time (1836), Edinburgh had a population of about 175,000, including the Parishes of Canongate, St. Cuthbert, Duddingston and North and South Leith., Aberdeen of about 65,000, including the Parish of St. Machar, and Dundee of about 50,000.

In the summer of the same year (1837) James Campbell stood unsuccessfully as a Tory for the then two-member Glasgow constituency.

Table 1 - The 1837 General Election in Glasgow - Electorate 8,676		
Lord William Bentinck	Whig	2,767
John Dennistoun	Radical	2,743
James Campbell	Tory	2,416
Robert Menteith	Tory	2,090

The 1837 General Election was caused by the death of William IV on 20 June, the succession of Queen Victoria and the then custom that a change of monarch necessitated a General Election. The overall result – and the election of 385 Whig and Radical and 273 Tory MPs – was such that Lord Melbourne's Whig Government, formed in 1835, continued in office.

James Campbell, having been first elected to the Town Council in 1831, was Lord Provost of Glasgow in 1840-1843. As such he was knighted in 1841 being included in the special honours list to mark the birth of Prince Albert Edward (the future King Edward) on 9 November 1841.[23] The railway from Glasgow to Edinburgh was not opened until 1842 and to London, via Carlisle, until 1848. So when James Campbell went to London to receive his knighthood in late 1841, the journey involved sea travel between Glasgow and Liverpool and train journeys between Liverpool and London.

Twenty-one years earlier (in 1820) one of his business journeys from Dublin to London involved seven hours by sea to Holyhead and then thirty-seven hours in a mail coach. The goods he had bought in Dublin were expected to take three weeks to reach Glasgow.

When the Glasgow to/from London direct mail coach service was introduced in 1788 the journey time was 63 hours. The record time from London to Glasgow was 35 hours and 50 minutes taken by a reporter during the debates on the Reform Bills in 1832. The normal time was eventually 44 hours, with 45 changes of horses (using a total of 180 horses) and a one-way fare of £ 40.

During his term as Lord Provost, Sir James was twice censured. Firstly, in connection with a large fire which broke out at Barrowfield (Barrowland) just east of the Gallowgate but then in the separate Burgh of Calton. An application made for assistance to the Glasgow Fire Brigade was refused with the reason given being that the Brigade had no right to do duty beyond Glasgow's boundaries. Application was then made to Sir James at his home and not only did he order the Brigade out on his

---

[23] Roy Hattersley (2006), p.11 stated that James Campbell was a (hereditary) 'knight baronet' whereas, in fact, he was a (non-hereditary) knight bachelor.

own responsibility but he also went to the fire with the Brigade. As a result he was severely censured by the Police Commissioners with one Commissioner declaring that, if the offence was repeated, the Lord Provost should be taken into custody.

Secondly, when he helped the Conservative Government of Sir Robert Peel to prepare a new Glasgow Police Bill, to extend the City boundaries, with which his own Council disagreed. The legislation led to the annexation of the Burghs of Gorbals, Calton and Anderston by Glasgow in 1846.

While Lord Provost, Sir James was also much concerned with solving Glasgow's water supply problem. Thus, having taken over the Glasgow Water Company, the Town Council's decision in 1854 to tap Loch Katrine, with the work completed and the system inaugurated by Queen Victoria in 1859.

Although dominated by businessmen in the 19th century, Glasgow Town Council was strangely reluctant to entrust the welfare of the people to the mechanics of capitalism. In addition to the municipal water supply, legislative powers were acquired in 1866 to clear slums and build municipal housing, the city's gas companies were taken over in 1869, municipal electricity was generated from 1892, the tramway system (opened on a horse-drawn basis in 1872) was taken over in 1894, the subway/underground was opened in 1896 and a municipal telephone network operated from 1901.

Given Sir Henry's expressed support for such municipal improvement when he received the Freedom of Glasgow in 1907, having also (in 1904) anticipated the nationalisation of the railways, one wonders what he would have thought of the extent to which such public sector utilities have since passed to the private sector by reason of social conservative intervention or inaction.

While Lord Provost, James Campbell again stood unsuccessfully as a Tory for the two-member Glasgow constituency in the summer of 1841.

Table 2 - The 1841 General Election in Glasgow - Electorate c.8,241		
James Oswald	Radical	2,776
John Dennistoun	Radical	2,728
James Campbell	Tory	2,416
George Mills	Chartist	353

The 1841 General Election was caused by Lord Melbourne's Whig Government losing a vote of confidence in the House of Commons on 4 June. The overall result – and the election of 367 Tory, 271 Whig and Radical and 20 Irish Repeal (Home Rule) MPs – was such that Sir Robert Peel formed a Tory Government in August. This was the last majority Tory-Conservative Government until 1874.

In later years Henry was much influenced by a former Chartist in Glasgow and another former Chartist in Dunfermline would be one of his earliest active supporters in his future constituency of Stirling Burghs.

The Chartist reform movement consisted of a number of un-coordinated local groups, taking its name from the People's Charter issued by one group in 1838. It called for universal adult male suffrage, constituencies of equal size, no property qualifications for candidates, secret ballots, annual general elections and payment for MPs. All such were eventually achieved by-and-large, except annual elections, but after Chartism, as such, had ceased to be. There were never more than nine Chartist candidates at the General Elections of 1841, 1847, 1852, 1857 and 1859 and none thereafter. The only Chartist MP was Feargus O'Connor who was elected for the two-member constituency of Nottingham in 1847 and served until he retired in 1852. [24]

Also in 1841 the Campbell family business opened a new retail department in the Prince of Wales Building (now the frontage for the Princes Square shopping centre) in Buchanan Street and William Campbell purchased Tullichewan Castle Estate in Dunbartonshire. The Estate was sold out of the family by 1930, the Castle was demolished in 1954 and the area is now occupied by a dual carriageway (A82), the Vale of Leven Hospital, housing developments and a caravan site.

William Campbell, although a member of Glasgow Town Council in 1845-1852, was not much involved in municipal affairs, being best known, apart from business, for his philanthropy, In addition to his benevolence anent access to the Botanic Gardens, he was, for example, a co-founder of the Glasgow Night Asylum for the Homeless and took an active interest in the Royal Infirmary, the City Improvement Scheme and the Indigent Gentlewoman's Fund. He was also much involved in church extension fund-raising for the Church of Scotland before the Disruption in 1843 and in fund-raising for the Free Church thereafter. In such ventures, before and after 1843, he was closely associated with Sir William Collins (1817-1895) – the founder of the Collins printing and publishing dynasty and Lord Provost of Glasgow in 1877-1880.

---

[24] A wee Chartist hymnbook of 1845, recently discovered by a Manchester University researcher in a library in Todmorden (West Yorkshire), includes a hymn written by Dr. William Villiers Sankey of Edinburgh. A contemporary Scottish Chartist was the Rev. Patrick Brewster (1788-1859), a Church of Scotland Parish Minister in Paisley. In 1842 he was referred to the Commission of (the General) Assembly for political preaching in Paisley Abbey. However, luckily for him, the occurrence of the Disruption in 1843 and the fact that he remained in the Church of Scotland caused his case to be dealt with very gently. Thus, he was formally acquitted of all charges. (Refer to the article, headed 'Songs of History', by Jackie Macadam in *Life and Work – The Magazine of The Church of Scotland* [April 2013]).

```
Table 3 - The Major Scottish Presbyterian Churches and Associated Statistics
Church of Scotland
|
|_____ Original Secession 1733 _____ Original Secession Churches to 1847
|
|_____ Second Secession 1752 _____ Relief Church to 1847
|
|_____ The Disruption 1843 ___ Free Church to 1900
|
|              Church Union 1847                 United Presbyterian Church to 1900
|
|              Church Union 1900       United Free Church to 1929
|                                      |
|              Church Reunion 1929     |
|                                      |
The Church of Scotland from 1929 ---------------- ←
```

Percentages of all Scottish Worshippers as from the 1851 Census

Church of Scotland 32 %, Free Church 32%, United Presbyterian Church 19 %, Other Presbyterians 2 %, Episcopalians/Anglicans 3 %, Other Protestants 6 %, Roman Catholics 5 %, Others 1 %

Scottish Communicant Estimates 1900 [xxv]

Church of Scotland 662,000, United Free Church 493,000, Episcopalians/Anglicans 48,000, Baptists 17,000, Methodists 8,000, Roman Catholics 413,000

Scotland's Census 2001

Church of Scotland 42.40 %, Roman Catholic 15.88 %, Other Christians 6.01 %, Other Religions 1.87 %, No Religion 27.55 %, No Reply 5.49 %

The Disruption of the Church of Scotland and the formation of the original Free Church of Scotland took place on 18 May 1843. William Campbell joined the newly-formed Free Church (having been again much influenced by the aforementioned Thomas Chalmers, Moderator of that Church's first General Assembly) and became a Whig (from 1859 a Liberal). Sir James and his family stayed in the Church of Scotland though remaining on excellent terms with William and his family.

Immediately after the Disruption, Sir James, as Lord Provost, took an active part in nominating ministers for the seven (out of ten) Burgh Churches in Glasgow which had been vacated by seceders. The Town Council was then the patron of all such Burgh Churches.

Sir Robert Peel's Tory Government of 1841-1846 was politically responsible for the Disruption. A final attempt to avert the Disruption, a motion moved by a Whig MP, Fox Maule, was defeated in the House of Commons on 8 March 1843 by 211 votes to 76, although supported by 25 of the 37 Scottish MPs present and voting. Those voting in the majority included such future Peelites (Tory Free Traders) and Liberals as Sir James Graham and William Gladstone.

However, a minority of Whigs including Lord John Russell, a future Whig and Liberal Prime Minister, voted with the Tories. On the other hand, Archibald Primrose, Lord Dalmeny (Courtesy Title) – then Whig MP for Sir Henry's future constituency of Stirling Burghs and father of the future Liberal Prime Minister, the 5th (Scottish) Earl of Rosebery – voted in favour of Fox Maule's motion.[25]

There had been two earlier unsuccessful legislative attempts to respond to the Church of Scotland's grievances anent Patronage and the interference of the secular courts (including the House of Lords) in the internal affairs of the Church. Those responsible for drafting the unsuccessful Bills were the future Peelite Leader, George Gordon, 4th (Scottish) Earl of Aberdeen (Prime Minister, 1852-1855) and George Campbell, 8th (Scottish) Duke of Argyll, a future Peelite and Liberal Cabinet Minister,

Roy Hattersley (2006), p.10 implied that, by joining the Free Church, William Campbell became something other than a Presbyterian whereas, in fact, the Free Church was just as much Presbyterian as the Church of Scotland. A similar mistake was made, in the same 2006 series of short biographies, by Andrew Taylor in his *Bonar Law* (p.110) in stating that Bonar Law was "the first Presbyterian to hold the office" of UK Prime Minister.

Sir Henry Campbell-Bannerman was a faithful member of the (Presbyterian) Church of Scotland all his life. The Earls of Aberdeen and Rosebery and Arthur Balfour, at least when they were at home in Scotland, attended their local (Presbyterian) Church of Scotland Parish Church. Indeed, one Sunday morning in June 1922, Balfour took Lloyd George, then Prime Minister, to Whittinghame Parish Church in East Lothian. 'The praise [was then] led by the little Welshman in a loud and high pitched tenor which reached above the voices of the congregation'.[26]

Further, William Gladstone's father had contributed to the cost of building the first Scots (Presbyterian) Kirk in Liverpool, as opened in 1793. However, some twenty or so years later he decided to join the Church of England by reason of the then limitations on the educational and political ambitions of non-Anglicans in England (and Wales). Until then the entire Gladstone family, including William, were Presbyterian worshippers.

In later years, the Gladstone family also worshipped in the nearby Fettercairn Parish Church when in residence at Fasque in Kincardineshire until an Episcopalian Chapel was opened at Fasque in 1847. William Gladstone is also known to have attended Presbyterian worship in Edinburgh during his first Midlothian campaign although he

---

[25] *Hansard*, 8 March 1843

[26] Farquharson-Lang (1987), pp.87-88. The late William Marshall Farquharson-Lang, an active Liberal, was the son of the Very Rev. Marshall Laing, Parish Minister of Whittinghame from 1918. Marshall Lang, Moderator of the 1935 General Assembly, was a younger brother of Cosmo Lang, Archbishop of Canterbury in 1928-1942. The brothers' father, John Lang, who attended the High School of Glasgow for one year, was Moderator of the 1893 General Assembly and Principal of Aberdeen University in 1900-1909.

is not known ever to have attended Crathie Parish Church while visiting Queen Victoria at the nearby Balmoral.

Some Gladstone biographers have suggested that (Sir) John Gladstone became an Anglican because, by the early 19th century, many of the Presbyterian congregations in England had become, or were becoming, Unitarian. (Refer to the 1850 Titles of Religious Congregations Act.) But this was not the case with the Scots Kirks in England, such as in Liverpool, which remained staunchly Presbyterian and Trinitarian. John Gladstone was also originally a Whig and only became an active Tory by about 1812 when he supported George Canning's candidature in Liverpool to the extent of being his Election Agent.

The height of William Gladstone's Anglicanism was reached in 1838 when he published *The State in its Relations with the Church.* In this he suggested that, as all Presbyterians had rejected episcopacy and the apostolic succession, the Church of Scotland had no claim to independent spiritual jurisdiction. (What Gladstone thought of Queen Victoria taking Communion in Crathie Parish Church from 1873 onwards is not recorded.)

Henry's mother's family, the Bannermans (apart from the William Motherwell connection) were always Whigs/Liberals. Indeed it was said, 'Mr. Henry's no a Campbell – he's just a Bannerman'.[27] Uncle William's influence may also have encouraged his nephew to depart from the Conservatism of his father and elder brother. However, Henry was probably well on the way to becoming a Liberal by the time he left Cambridge University in 1858.

Other factors bringing about Henry's entry into active Liberal politics were (1) his reading of the writings of Herbert Spencer (1820-1903), a fervent advocate of the rights of the individual against the state, (2) the influence of Daniel Lawson, an employee in the Campbell's family business and a Radical and former Chartist, and (3), after 1860, a long correspondence with his brother-in-law, Colonel Herbert Bruce.

Colonel Bruce, having served in the East India Company's armies and distinguished himself during the Indian Mutiny, was then Chief of Police in Oudh in India. Early in their correspondence, Henry sent him a copy of John Stuart Mill's *On Liberty* as published in 1859. Apparently, however, there was disagreement during the US Civil War, with the Colonel attempting to refute Henry's sympathies for the North and his belief that the Yankees would win.

Nevertheless, in August 1865, the Colonel repeated earlier advice that 'the sooner you get into Parliament the better. I am quite sure you ought to be in Parliament – indeed you ought to have been there two years ago…'". (CB/BL)

---

[27] As quoted in Spender (1923), Volume 1, p.5.

In 1844, J G. Kohl, a German visitor to Glasgow, wrote "I visited the greatest warehouse of manufactured goods in the town, that of the brothers Campbell, who employ no fewer than two hundred clerks in their establishment. The largest warehouses in Paris do not boast of employing more than a hundred clerks.... The receipts of this house amounted, in the year 1834 to £ 433,021 sterling, an amount probably unequalled by any other retail dealers in the world'.[28] Also in 1844, the Campbell business was visited by the Crown Prince of Denmark, the future Frederick VII.[29]

It was his share of the firm's profits and the income from associated investments (managed by his father and brother) which would enable Sir Henry to devote himself to politics from his early thirties, given that MPs were not paid a salary until 1911. Nevertheless, his commitments were such that, when Prime Minister, with heavy expenses, he had to borrow £ 2,700 from his Conservative brother, James Alexander. (CB/BL)

In May 1845 Sir James Campbell, by way of recognition of his initiatives and associated difficulties as Lord Provost, was 'presented, by upwards of 200 subscribers, with a handsome and costly piece of gold plate [as] the expression of a grateful sense entertained in the community of his liberal spirit and charitable disposition [and] of his faithful, unremitting and firm discharge of the duties of Chief Magistrate'.

In making the presentation, Sheriff Alison referred to both the initiatives for which Sir James had been censured when Lord Provost 'Citizens will not easily forget the vigorous efforts you made to procure for the suburbs of this great city that protection from fire of which they so lamentably stood in need. It must [also] be to you a source of the greatest satisfaction to see that, whatever differences of opinion formerly existed, the measures about to receive the sanction of the Legislature, with the general concurrence of all parties in the community.[30] (This anticipated the annexation of the Burghs of Gorbals, Calton and Anderston by Glasgow in 1846).

Also in 1845, William Campbell was one of a group of Glasgow businessmen, associated with the new Free Church of Scotland, who formed a private company to found a new school which, as Glasgow Academy, was opened in Elmbank Street in 1847. Thirty years later, following the passing of the 1872 Education (Scotland) Act, the Academy's directors initially took the view that there was no future for privately-run schools. Accordingly, the Academy's buildings were sold to the Glasgow School Board for £ 32,000 in 1877, with the High School (which the future Sir Henry

---

[28] *Glasgow High School Magazine* (June 1948), p.115.

[29] Oakley (1946), p.123

[30] Online *Glasgow Digital Library – Memoirs and Portraits of 100 Glasgow Men* – 19

Campbell-Bannerman had attended in 1845-1850) moving from John Street and taking possession of what became known as the 'Centre Block', the gymnasium and janitor's house in June 1878. (Four other 'blocks' and two janitors' houses [replacing the original janitor's house] were eventually built on the site) A new Glasgow Academy at Kelvinbridge was opened four months later.

In mid-1846, given an alliance of Peelites (Tory Free Traders) also known as Liberal Conservatives, Whigs and Radicals, the Corn Laws were repealed. This was followed almost immediately by the defeat of Sir Robert Peel's Tory Government in the House of Commons, his resignation on 29 June and the accession of a minority Whig Government headed by Lord John Russell.

By the summer of 1847, Lord John, wishing to obtain a clear mandate, and also take advantage of the division of the Tories [now also known as Conservatives] into Protectionists and Peelites, called a General Election for July/August. With no Conservatives nominated in Glasgow, the overall result – and the election of 325 Conservatives (including about 100 Peelites), 293 Whigs and Radicals, 36 Irish Repeaters, 1 Chartist and 2 Other MPs – was such that Lord John Russell's minority Whig Government continued in office.

Also In 1847 Sir James Campbell bought the 4,000 acre Stracathro Estate (including Stracathro House) in Forfarshire (Angus) from the Cruickshank family. The Estate had been bought by Patrick Cruickshank (who had made his fortune in Jamaica) in 1775. In due course, his brother, James Cruickshank inherited the property and employed the Aberdeen-based architect, Archibald Simpson to build the Palladian-style House in 1824-1827.[31] Stracathro – apart from earlier legendary associations – is said to be where John Balliol was deposed as King of Scots by Edward I of England in July 1296.

Stracathro is 7 miles south of Fasque (in Kincardineshire) as purchased in 1829 by John Gladstone (1st Baronet from 1846), William Gladstone's father. Fasque House had been built, at the cost of near bankruptcy, by Sir Alexander Ramsay, 1st Baronet of Balmain in 1809. There was a family connection between Stracathro and Fasque. Jane Cruickshank of Stracathro was a sister-in-law of Sir Alexander Ramsay, 2nd Baronet of Balmain who inherited Fasque in 1810 and sold it to John Gladstone nineteen years later.

On Sir James Campbell's death in 1876, Stracathro was inherited by his elder son, James Alexander and, on his death in 1908, by his grandson, Hugh Campbell. On Hugh Campbell's death in 1934, Stracathro was inherited by his cousins, the Adamsons of (the nearby) Careston, also descended from James Alexander Campbell.

Stracathro House was acquired by the Government in 1938, with a major regional hospital (originally a war emergency hospital) being built within the grounds in

---

[31] Archibald Simpson (1790-1847) also designed such Aberdeen buildings as the headquarters of the North of Scotland Bank (1840) and the Triple Kirks (1843)

1940. The House was used as a staff residence until it was sold by Tayside Health Board in 2003 for refurbishment as a private residence. However, Millden of Stracathro – with, by reason of acquisitions, more than the original 4,000 acres – remains in family ownership in the person of Hugh A. Campbell Adamson, James Alexander Campbell's great-great grandson.

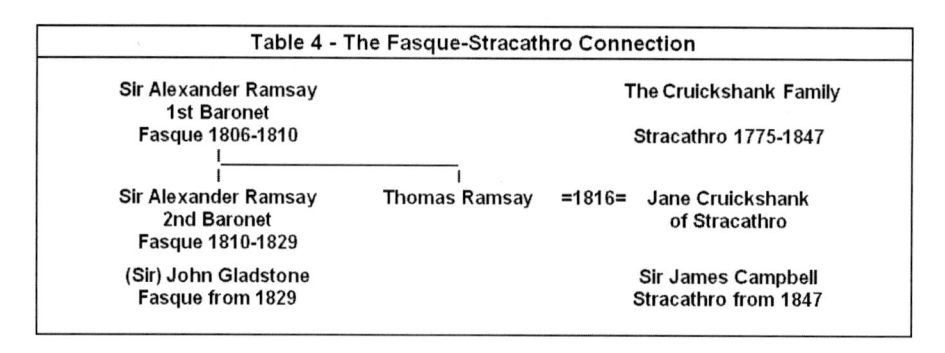

Table 4 - The Fasque-Stracathro Connection		
Sir Alexander Ramsay 1st Baronet Fasque 1806-1810		The Cruickshank Family Stracathro 1775-1847
Sir Alexander Ramsay 2nd Baronet Fasque 1810-1829	Thomas Ramsay =1816=	Jane Cruickshank of Stracathro
(Sir) John Gladstone Fasque from 1829		Sir James Campbell Stracathro from 1847

Apparently, at one time, the Campbells also had premises in John Street as in March 1848, a year of revolution in Europe, a crowd, which was about to attack their silk mill in John Street, was driven off by the militia to Glasgow Green.[32]

In 1856 the Campbells sold their premises in both Candleriggs and Buchanan Street, moving to 29 (later 137) Ingram Street – 'a yellow sandstone, gabled, turreted confection of a warehouse' – as built in 1854-1856. Thereafter the business concentrated exclusively on the wholesale trade. When the new building in Ingram Street was at the planning stage, Sir James anticipated an extension of the then Municipal Buildings into Ingram Street. Accordingly, he "was so anxious that his handsome new building should not be obscured that he arranged for the front of his building to be slightly angled to the south so that anyone walking along the street would have an unrestricted view of it",[33]

Ingram Street was originally laid out in 1781 along the line of Black Cow Loan (a grassy cattle-track) which led from the east to the grazing grounds in Cowcaddens. Black Cow Loan was the location of the Star Inn, the meeting place for the Reform Association under the leadership of Thomas Muir (1765-1799), an advocate, who, with some of his associates, was sentenced to 14 years transportation to Botany Bay for sedition in 1794. By the end of the 18th century, the Star Inn was the Glasgow terminus for the Glasgow-Edinburgh coach, *The Royal Telegraph.*

When in Glasgow, the Campbells (and the Campbell-Bannermans) worshipped in St. George's Parish Church (St. George's Tron Parish Church from 1940), dating from 1808, in St. George's Place (now Nelson Mandela Place) off Buchanan Street.[34]

---

[32] Oakley (1946), p.143

[33] Carol Foreman (2007), pp.100-101.

[34] St. George's Place – then the location of the South African Consulate – was renamed for Nelson Mandela in 1986. He had been awarded the Freedom of the City in 1981 but was unable to

Charles Hutcheson (1792-1860), a member of the St. George's Congregation and a friend of the Campbell family, named his hymn tune, *Stracathro* after the Campbells' house and estate in Angus. (*Church Hymnary,* Fourth Edition [2005], 548, 637. Refer also to Appendix 5)

The Minister of St. George's in 1843-1870 was the Rev. Dr. James Craik (1801-1870), Moderator of the General Assembly in 1863. He was the father of Sir Henry Craik (1846-1927) who had attended The High School of Glasgow in 1857-1860 and was Permanent Secretary of the Scottish Education Department in 1885-1904 and a Conservative MP for Scottish Universities in 1906-1927.

Sir Henry Craik well remembered Sir James Campbell's pew in his father's Church and the unfailing presence of each member of the Campbell family. The young Henry Campbell was a frequent visitor to the Manse, with Dr. Craik taking a special interest in plans for his education. The younger Craik's early impressions of the future Prime Minister's family in Glasgow were quoted by John Spender (1923), Volume 1, pp.8-9.

The figures of Sir James and Lady Campbell stand out in my memory…. Henry took after his mother in personal appearance. Sir James was a man of somewhat rough exterior and with character of marked force… In politics Sir James was a Tory of the old school…

But whatever he thought of his son Henry's politics, he was nonetheless proud of his abilities and the promise of his Parliamentary career. His elder son, James Alexander, followed more nearly the political predilections of his father, although in somewhat modified form… The two brothers, although cordial in their friendship, were formed in strongly contrasting moulds. Their widely different views of politics and their fundamental disagreement on almost all public questions did. However, keep them asunder in many ways… They loved and respected one another; but each disliked the opinions of the other.

After the retirement and deaths of Sir James and William Campbell, and given also the political priorities of Sir James' sons – James Alexander and Henry – the senior partnership in the family business passed to William Campbell's sons and grandsons.

---

come to Glasgow to receive the award until 1993. The Glasgow Liberal Club was also formerly situated in what was then St. George's Place, at the northern corner with Buchanan Street.

Afterword – The Family Business and McOran-Campbells in Later Years [35]

> *The Glasgow Herald*, 3 December 1912
>
> During Sunday night's blaze in Ingram Street there were two incidents which attracted the attention of the [assembled] crowd... Several firemen were stationed on the roof of the warehouse of Messrs J & W Campbell, directing a stream of water on the flames, when one of them was seen to place a pipe in his mouth and light it with a match. He was so closely silhouetted against the glare of the fire that his action was clearly visible to the spectators. Just when the fire was at its height a bird was seen to rise apparently out of the flames, and circle once or twice... before disappearing...

However, 137 Ingram Street survived, then, in 1922, with at least ten Campbells having been partners or directors in the business, J. & W. Campbell merged with Stewart and Macdonald (located between Buchanan, Argyll and Mitchell Streets). The new company, Campbells, Stewart & Macdonald was based in the Campbells' premises in Ingram Street, with Sir Andrew Pettigrew as head of the new company. As from the Online *Commercial Overprint Society of Great Britain*, it is noted that the Society has overprinted stamps for receipts for J & W Campbell and Stewart & Macdonald (One Penny, as used before 1922) and for Campbells, Stewart & Macdonald (Two Pence, as used after 1922).

In 1938 the company acquired the stock and goodwill of Mann Byars (of Glassford and Virginia Streets) when that business, founded in 1847, was closed. By 1946 a Campbell, Sir James Clark Campbell of Lochwinnoch had become the last head of the company, with shares being no longer traded by the 1950s, and like so many other buildings in Glasgow's 'Merchant City', 137 Ingram Street has since been converted into residential flats.

Stewart & Macdonald had been originally founded in 1826 as a drapery warehouse in which Hugh Fraser (1815-1873) – founder of the House of Fraser from 1849 – had served an apprenticeship. In 1913, Stewart and Macdonald's retail business in Buchanan Street became a separate company as Macdonalds Limited which in 1951 was bought by the House of Fraser.

Thus at least eleven Campbells were Partners and/or Directors of J. & W. Campbell, J. A. & W. Campbell and Campbells, Stewart & Macdonald – Sir James Campbell, William Campbell and Alexander Campbell (Brothers), James Alexander Campbell and Sir Henry Campbell-Bannerman (Sons of Sir James Campbell), James Campbell and William Campbell (Sons of William Campbell), Matthew Pearce Campbell,

---

[35] I am indebted to Alastair McOran-Campbell and Robert Adair Campbell for much of the family information in this Afterword.

James Adair Campbell and William Alexander Campbell (Grandsons of William Campbell) and Sir James Clark Campbell (Son of Matthew Pearce Campbell).

James Ronald McOran Campbell, a great-grandson of William Campbell, was killed in action in South Africa in 1899. William Campbell Adamson, a great-grandson of Sir James Campbell, was killed in action while serving with the Royal Flying Corps in 1916. Adair Melfort Gerald Campbell and Frederick Godfrey Burr, great-grandsons of William Campbell, were both killed during the Naval Battle of Jutland in 1916.

Adair Melfort Gerald Campbell, a Midshipman on the armoured cruiser, HMS *Defence* (based at Cromarty) was on leave at the family home at Tullichewan, Dunbartonshire when the recall telegram arrived. His father, James Adair Campbell hired a locomotive as the only way for his son to get to the ship before she sailed. During the battle the ship was struck by German salvoes which detonated the magazines, causing *Defence* to blow up. There were no survivors from a crew of about 900. The Midshipman's nephew, James Melfort Paul Gordon Campbell, was more fortunate while serving in the Royal Navy during the Second World War. His ship was torpedoed in mid-Atlantic, with the torpedo striking just below his cabin where he would have been if he had not been on watch on the bridge.

The service and connections of four other members of the family are noteworthy. Vice Admiral George William McOran Campbell, another great-grandson of William Campbell, led, as a Commander, a Destroyer Flotilla, from its Scapa Flow base, at the Battle of Jutland in 1916. Lieutenant-Colonel Sir John Graham, yet another great-grandson of William Campbell, was awarded a VC for gallantry in Mesopotamia (Iraq), also during the First World War. Sir John was the son-in-law of Sir Alexander Sprot (Conservative) who defeated Aquith in the enlarged constituency of East Fife at the 1918 General Election. Hannah Ranken Campbell, a grand-daughter of William Campbell, was the second wife of Sir William Smith, founder of the Boys Brigade in 1883. Isobel Mary Campbell, CBE, a great-great-grand-daughter of William Campbell, was Deputy Director of the Women's Auxiliary Air Force (WAAF) in South-East Asia during the Second World War.

2 – 1845-1868 – Education, Travels, Career, Marriage (1860) and Politics

The School, which the future Sir Henry Campbell-Bannerman attended in 1845-1850, originated in the 12th century as the 'Sang Schule' (Choir School) of Glasgow Cathedral. By the 15th century it had become the Grammar School. (For a comprehensive history of the School, from the 12th century, refer to Brian R.W. Lockhart's *The Town School – A History of The High School of Glasgow* [2010])

Although the School no longer has marked pews in the Cathedral as it used to have, the connection otherwise continues in modern times, with an Annual Service of Commemoration and Thanksgiving therein. The School was also one of the three Glasgow schools which mainly funded the Millenium Stained Glass Window, on the north wall of the nave, as unveiled by Princess Anne on 3 June 1999. Then, in session 2007-2008, the Cathedral's newly inducted Minister, The Rev. Dr. Laurence Whitley accepted the position of School Chaplain

Notable pupils during the 15th century included, from c.1438, William Elphinstone (1431-1514) who was briefly Chancellor of Scotland in 1488 and, as Bishop of Aberdeen, founder of Scotland's third University, King's College, Aberdeen in 1495. Accordingly, Sir Henry was not the first native of Glasgow (or Former Pupil of its High School) to become a First Minister of the Crown as stated by Professor Andrew Browning in the *Glasgow High School Magazine* of June 1948. Nor was Elphinstone the only Former Pupil to be involved in the foundation of a university, The legacies of James McGill (1744-1813), who attended the School in 1749-1756, facilitated the foundation of McGill College (in Montreal) which achieved university status in 1821. Thomas Campbell, as follows, was involved with Henry Brougham (Lord Brougham 1830) in the foundation of London University in 1826.

However, within ten years of the foundation of Glasgow University in 1451, the School was displaced from the Cathedral precincts. It was then endowed with a tenement, in what became known as Grammar School Wynd, on the west side of the High Street and across from the University (what became to be known as the Old College). The endowment, dated 20 January 1461, in favour of the Rector and Master of the School and his successors in office, designated the Provost, Bailies and Councillors of the Burgh as the School's patrons and governors. The original school building was extended in 1577-1578 and rebuilt in 1600-1601. When the new building was opened, there was mounted above the doorway a stone inscribed with Glasgow's Arms and the words *Schola Grammaticor, A Senatu Civibusque Glasguanis Bonar. Literar, Patronis Condita,* (The Grammar School, built by the Town Council and Citizens of Glasgow, Patrons of Sound Learning). The lintel was to move with the School as it moved thereafter to different parts of Glasgow,

Notable pupils at the School during the 16th century included John Spottiswoode (1510-1585) who after contributing to the *Scots Confession* of 1560 and the (First) *Book of Discipline* of 1560-1561, was appointed Superintendent (Synod Moderator) of Lothian. As such, he officiated at the Coronation of the infant King James VI in Stirling in July 1567, with John Knox preaching. Notable pupils during the 17th century included the 4th (Scottish) Duke of Hamilton (1658-1712) and the 1st (Scottish) Marquis of Annandale (1664-1721). The Duke and the Marquis served in both the old Scottish Parliament and, as Scottish Representative Peers, in the UK House of Lords. The Marquis (then 2nd [Scottish] Earl of Annandale and Hartfell) was President/Presiding Officer of the Scottish Parliament in 1695. He was Lord High Commissioner to the General Assembly of the Church of Scotland in 1701, 1705 and 1711.[36] The Duke, after being created Duke of Brandon in the peerage of Great Britain in 1711, was killed in a duel in 1712.

Further substantial building work in Grammar School Wynd was undertaken in 1656 and 1735 but by 1786 the School had so outgrown its premises that the decision was taken to build a new School in George Street as completed and opened in 1788. However, by 1807, and again more decisively in 1820, it was agreed that yet another new and more commodious new School was required and this was completed and opened in John Street in 1821.

Notable pupils of the School during the 18th century included Lieutenant-General Sir John Moore (1761-1809) who left School in 1772 and was killed in victory at Corunna in 1809, the poet, Thomas Campbell (1777-1844), who left School in 1791 and was the author of *Lord Ullin's Daughter, Ye Mariners of England'*, etc. and Field Marshall Sir Colin Campbell (1792-1863), who attended School (as Colin McLiver) from his birthplace and home in John Street in 1797-1803, also fought at Corunna and was a victorious army commander during the Crimean War and the Indian Mutiny, being created Lord Clyde of Clydesdale in 1856.

During the Crimean War, the Queen's cousin, the then Duke of Cambridge was commander of a Division (Guards and Highland Brigade) when at the Alma (1854) it came under heavy grapeshot fire. He asked Sir Colin Campbell what was to be done. He was advised to put himself (on horseback) at the head (front) of the Division and lead it right up to the Battery.[37] The Duke, when later the London-based Army Commander-in-Chief, would have encounters with another Glasgow

---

[36] More recently, Sir Hector MacLennan (1905-1978), who attended the High School in 1918-1924, was Lord High Commissioner to the Generals Assembly in 1975 and 1976, He was the father of the Liberal Democrat Life Peer, Robert, Lord MacLennan. Sir Norman Macfarlane, KT, Lord Macfarlane of Bearsden (Born 1926), who attended the School in 1941-1945, was Lord High Commissioner in 1992, 1993 and 1997. He is currently Hon. President of the School Club (Former Pupils). Over the years a number of Former Pupils have also been Moderator of the General Assembly including, most recently, the Very Rev. Dr. David Lacy in 2005 and the Very Rev. Dr. David W. Lunan in 2008.

[37] Wilson (1973), p.51

Grammar/High School Former Pupil, Henry Campbell-Bannerman during his four periods of ministerial service at the War Office between 1871 and 1895.

The first statute to be erected in George Square was that for Sir John Moore in 1819. Such for two other Former Pupils followed in 1868 (Lord Clyde) and in 1877. (Thomas Campbell) Sir John was MP for Linlithgow Burghs (also including Lanark, Peebles and Selkirk) in 1784-1790.

As mentioned in Chapter 1, in 1878 the School moved to Elmbank Street, its fourth location, where, on 30 June 1976, it was closed as a public sector school.[38] However, it was immediately (on 1 July 1976) re-constituted as an independent co-educational school, with, since 1977, its main location being at Old Anniesland on part of the 27 acre site owned by the School Club (Former Pupils) since 1922-1924. The lintel of 1601, the School's War Memorial (with the names of 478 Former Pupils from the First World War and 147 from the Second World War), plaques commemorating the School's two Prime Ministers (Sir Henry and Bonar Law) were brought, together with other items pertaining to the School's heritage, from Elmbank Street to Old Anniesland in 1976-1977. Associated with the School Club in the re-constitution of 1976 were the former Drewsteignton School (1922-1976) in Bearsden and the Old Girls' Club of the former Glasgow High School for Girls (1894-1973).

The names of the four Senior School Houses have remained unchanged since session 1926-1927 when the name of Campbell House – originally named in 1917 for the aforementioned Thomas Campbell – was changed to Law House for Andrew Bonar Law the School's other Prime Minister, The other Houses, as from 1917, are also named for aforementioned Former Pupils – Bannerman for Sir Henry Campbell-Bannerman, Clyde for Lord Clyde and Moore for Sir John Moore.

However, In 1834, reflecting the view that many pupils, destined for careers in science and commerce, should study the Classics as part of a broad-based education rather than as a vocational necessity, the name of the School had been changed from 'Grammar' to 'High'. It was probably for this reason that many members of Glasgow's commercial community, such as (Sir) James Campbell, sent their sons to the High School.

Thus it was in the High School in John Street that the future Prime Minister, then known as Henry Campbell, was enrolled in 1845. He joined the Classics Department, specifically the Junior Division of Dr. Patrick McKindlay's First Form. He took first place in the Junior Division of his Form in 1845-1846, 1846-1847 and 1847-1848. Also, in 1848, he won the Tennent (Wellpark) Medal for the best Latin

---

[38] The High School was forced out of the public sector in 1976 by an earlier decision of the Labour-controlled Glasgow City Council (endorsed by Gordon Campbell, Tory Secretary of State for Scotland, 1970-1974). Such Tory-supported Socialist dogmatism was no doubt supported by Dr. Vincent Cable, Labour Candidate for Glasgow Hillhead in 1970, a Glasgow Labour Councillor in 1971-1974, a Liberal Democrat MP since 1997 and a Liberal Democrat Cabinet Minister from 2010 to 2015, and Liberal Democrat Leader since June 2017.

scholar of the Third Year, being placed fifth overall in Greek and first in a 'Writing' (Commercial Subjects) class.[39]

The Prize Lists for Henry's Fourth Year were not divided into Junior and Senior Divisions and in 1849 he was placed third in Latin, fourth in Greek and ninth in 'Writing'. Dr. McKindlay, one of the School's two Classics Masters in 1844-1866, who taught Henry Latin and Greek, was himself a Former Pupil. Alan McNab was the School's 'Writing' (Commercial subjects) Master in 1841-1868 and presumably, taught Book-Keeping to Henry.

Assuming that Henry took the maximum number of subjects, he would also have been taught Mathematics (with Geography) by Dr. James Bryce (the father of James, Viscount Bryce),[40] English (and some History) by the Rev. Alexander D'Orsey, French (and some German) by Felician Wolski and perhaps some Art and Drawing by James Hutchinson. There was no Rector at this time with all the senior masters reporting directly to the Convener of the Town Council's High School Committee.

Only Dr. McKindlay, Dr. Fletcher Low (the other Classics Master) and D'Orsey and Wolski were paid annual salaries (£ 50) by the Town Council. (With the High School being then the Town Council's only school, such salaries accounted for, at least, half the Council's annual education budget) The four salaried masters were also paid fees directly by their pupils' parents, with all the other masters being entirely dependent on such fees. Quarterly fees per subject, depending on teaching hours, ranged from 5 shillings to 21 shillings.

By way of comparison, in an official report in 1868, average total annual fees per pupil were stated as £12 7s 3d for Edinburgh Academy (Private), £10 3s 0d for Edinburgh Royal High School (Council), £8 13s 9d for Glasgow Academy (Private), £5 11s 10d for the High School of Glasgow (Council) and £4 3s 9d for Aberdeen Grammar School (Council).[41]

Dr. Low was Vice-President of the Educational Institute of Scotland (founded in 1847) when it was granted a Royal Charter in 1851. In the Charter, Queen Victoria referred to the High School of Glasgow as the Royal High School of Glasgow.

The day after the former Henry Campbell received the Freedom of the City and Royal Burgh of Glasgow in 1907, an interesting letter from a former class-mate was published in *The Glasgow Herald*.

22 Renfield Street, Glasgow – 25 January 1907

---

[39] The Prize List for the Third Form of 1847-1848 was published in *The Glasgow Herald* of 29 September 1848.

[40] In 1892, some forty-two years after Sir Henry's time at the High School, the author H.G. Wells was turned down for a mathematics post because of his unusual approach to teaching. (*The Scotsman,* 20 September 2010)

[41] Lockhart (2010), p.101.

Sir – I account it an honour that for five years I was a class-fellow of the Prime Minister and was privileged to study Latin and Greek in his company. It was a fairly large class, and it may be interesting to know that the boy, Henry Campbell occupied the same distinguished position in it that the statesman, Sir Henry Campbell-Bannerman has since done in public life.

When the class came to its natural termination in the early fifties, the boys blossomed into young manhood and began a series of commemorative dinners which went on from year to year with unfailing regularity for nearly half a century. The first of these dinners was presided over by the Prime Minister, which sufficiently testifies to the estimation in which he was held by his class-fellows at that early stage; and it says much for his goodness of heart that as recently as the years 1897 and 1898 he was able to find time in the midst of multifarious engagements to give an evening to his class-mates for the interchange of reminiscences of Auld Lang Syne.

Throughout this long term of years his class-fellows never ceased to watch the career of Sir Henry Campbell-Bannerman with sympathetic interest, and – whatever their political opinions might happen to be – they rejoiced in his success and were proud of it. The surviving members of the class are, alas, few in number, but I think I may venture to say on their behalf that none can be more heartily congratulate the Premier on his well-won honours than his old schoolmates who, looking back to the days of their common boyhood now regard the Prime Minister with a curious mixture of respect and affection as their superior in the classroom and their equal in the playground.

I am, etc. MacLean Brodie

In the Third Form Prize List for 1847-1848, MacLean Brodie [then living in Carlton Place] is named as fifth in Latin (Senior Division). Sir Henry's own papers record his attendance at two of the class dinners – 'October 8th, 1897, attended Class Dinner at Brodie's' and 'November 18th, 1898, High School Class Dinner at Pearce's'.

Henry was preceded at the High School by his older brother, James Alexander Campbell. He was followed at the High School by three other future Cabinet Ministers – James, Viscount Bryce (1838-1922), Andrew Bonar Law (1858-1823) and Sir William Sutherland (1880-1949) – and by one other member of his 1905-1908 Administration, Thomas (Tom) Ryburn Buchanan (1846-1911).

The Glasgow High School Magazine of June, 1948 (p, 120) recorded Bonar Law saying, when Prime Minister in 1922, 'My mind goes back to my career as a pupil at the High School of Glasgow. Among the teachers was the father of Lord Bryce. I remember on one occasion his saying to me, *you have every kind of sense except common-sense'*

However, returning to the mid-19th century, Sir James and Lady Campbell valued knowledge of the world as highly as book learning. So they and their children were then very much used to overseas travel. They were with their first daughter, Jane when she died in Zurich in 1842, James Alexander was with them in Dresden in 1844 and Henry was with them in Paris in 1848.

Thus it was that, having left school three weeks before the September 1850 examinations, Henry (just before his 14th birthday) undertook a nine-ten months tour of Europe. He was with his brother, James Alexander (aged 25) and their cousin, David Bannerman (aged 23). David's elder brother, James Alexander Bannerman was then based in Paris. He would marry the Campbell's sister Louisa five years later.

They travelled some 5,500 miles, by water, rail and road, visiting seventeen countries and their capitals, seeing the rulers of Prussia, Austria and all the Italian states. They sailed on Lake Trasimene where Hannibal and his Carthaginians and their allies defeated the Romans in 217 BC, climbed Vesuvius, visited Pompeii and Herculaneum and, on their homeward journey, the field of Waterloo.

They went as far south as Sicily, though not as far east as Constantinople (Istanbul) as originally planned. They spent three winter months in Rome where Henry was tutored in the Classics, French and Italian, in which the others participated to some extent. For the three months in Rome, they rented a flat in the Via della Fontanella for the equivalent of £ 11 monthly. Purchases sent home included macaroni, wine, cheese, bonnets, earthenware, marble and bronze replicas and books. However, James Alexander was mainly looking for markets for the family business, regularly reporting by letter to his parents on business interviews (and also doing pencil sketches of many of the places visited). Henry was expected to write regular letters to the family on all other matters. Thus ninety-seven copious letters – more than two a week – to his sister, Louisa ('Weezie') who copied them into jotters. They were eventually edited by John Sinclair (Lord Pentland, 1909), Sir Henry's literary executor and published, after Lord Pentland's death, by T. Fisher Unwin, London in 1925.[42]

As from Lord Pentland's introductory comments, such letters – of which a selection of extracts follows – indicate – 'what a store of physical, political and artistic knowledge [was] taken in through the eyes and ears of a boy of fourteen who seems for his years already particularly intelligent and well-informed and full of good-natured humour. [Given also his later European ventures], as a public man, Sir Henry was exceptionally equipped for his understanding of the Continent and its languages. This experience must have been one cause of the breadth of his views and of his capacity for friendly intercourse with the subjects and statesmen of other countries.

---

[42] A selection of extracts from the letters were also published in the *Glasgow High School Magazine* of June 1948.

As Prime Minister these qualities enabled him to serve Britain in the best way by helping to carry out the ideal of mutual confidence between nations'.

> Paris (31 August 1850) – We are fairly at Paris at last, comfortably settled in Meurice's [Hotel in the Rue de Rivoli]. [After] a bath and some luncheon, we sallied forth – James to business and the rest of us to see the town. We (the sightseers) hired a fiacre [hackney cab] to take us to the Madeleine, to the Arc d'Etoile at the end of the Champs Elysées, along the Boulevards to the Hôtel de Ville and Notre Dame, and then to the Parthenon. On arriving here [Meurice's] we found James waiting and dined at the table d'hôte. After dinner we went to Franconi's and were very much pleased.
>
> Geneva (7 September) – [Yesterday] we entered Switzerland and arrived at the Hôtel des Bergues at about 10 p.m. We were at first refused admittance, the house being too full, but were at last accommodated, a bed being put in a sitting room. This morning we have been all over the town. It is a very beautiful town.
>
> Milan (22 October) – Saw Leonardo da Vinci's celebrated fresco of the Last Supper. It is from it that all the representations of the Last Supper are taken. It is very old, the room it is in has been a cavalry stable, a door has been made in it, and to complete its desolation, it was been daubed over entirely. But it is still splendid even in its ruins.
>
> Milan (26 October) – How is 'Copperfield' getting on?

David Copperfield was first published in twenty monthly parts from 1 May 1849.

> Alessandria (7 November) – At Villa Nouva [now part of Livigno in the Italian Alps] last night, James had a sizeable saucer to wash in (!) and when he gave it to the cameriere [chamberlain] to throw out the dirty water, he coolly threw it out on the floor of the next room. There is no such thing as a chambermaid here – it is all one man – he is boots, waiter, landlord and chambermaid.
>
> Sienna (20 November) – On Monday morning [at Leghorn/Livorno] we went out to Messrs. Henderson's, and were shown round their warehouse. So many Scots and even Glasgow goods, and above all the old fusty warehouse smell, that puts me in mind of Candleriggs Street[43]

---

[43] The Henderson brothers, from Fife, started business in Glasgow in 1825 and had trading interests in north-west Italy, including this warehouse in Leghorn/Livorno. However, they eventually gave up trading in soft goods and marble and concentrated on their shipping interests including the management of the Burmese Irrawaddy Flotilla Company. All its river steamers and ferries were scuttled when the Japanese invaded in 1942.

> Florence (25 November) – [Yesterday afternoon] we went to a Scots service in the Swiss Church [where] the Rev. [William] Hanna, who resides here for his health, officiates regularly.[44] In the evening James went to Mr. Hanna's and David and I called on [the Rev.] Dr. [William] Black, who gave us another *Constitutional* which like its predecessor is a great source of amusement in the long evenings. This morning we went out as we regularly do to a café for breakfast. We go because it is the custom and with an eye to the money for in the hotel we pay 20 pence each for coffee, eggs and bread, whereas in the café we pay 8 pence each for the same thing and see the company beside.

The *Glasgow Constitutional* was a Conservative weekly which was published from 1835 to 1860. About the time he became Lord Provost in 1840, James Campbell, Henry's father, had a leading interest in the *Constitutional*.[45]

> Rome (13 December) – Yesterday morning we went to St. Peter's. Thence we went to the Vatican, adjoining St. Peter's. Here we saw some men of the Pope's Swiss Guard, who wear the oddest dress I have ever seen – stripped clothes (black and yellow), pantaloons, and carry a pike or halberd which looks as it were made of tin.

The dark blue, red and yellow uniforms of the Papal Swiss Guard were designed by Michelangelo Bounarotti [1475-1564] Henry was to become somewhat of an expert on Michelangelo and, on one occasion, applied that expertise in a lecture to the Dunfermline Literary Society.

> Rome (18 December) – Yesterday we began lessons. M. Agu de Vaux comes at 9 every morning and David and I have an hour's French. On Monday, Wednesday and Friday at 10, James gets an hour's French from him, and from two till three Italian from Signor Rossi. Every day but Saturday I go out at 3.30 to Mr. Robert T. Austin and get an hour and a half's Classics.

> Rome (Christmas Day, 1850) – We got up at 6.30 and went to see High Pontifical Mass performed by the Pope. We went in dress coats, etc. and so got a splendid position, quite near the Pope. It is needless for me to go through all the ceremony we saw, but they were uncommonly fine, but without the smallest particle of devotion.

---

[44] The Rev. William Hanna (1808-1882) had left the Church of Scotland for the Free Church at the Disruption in 1843. He was a son-in-law of Thomas Chalmers, Moderator of the Free Church's first General Assembly. The Rev. Dr. William Black (1801-1851) was Minister of Barony Parish Church in Glasgow from 1829 until his death in Florence in 1851.

[45] Cowan [1946], p.143

> Rome (3 January 1851) – Today I began to learn Italian from Signor Rossi, three days a week. He comes from 2 till 4 and divides that time between James and me.

> Rome (3 March) – We learned today that Lord John Russell [UK Prime Minister] has resigned. Who is talked of as his successor? We heard Lord Aberdeen, Sir James Graham and Lord Claredon.

Such speculation was somewhat premature. Lord John had resigned in February but as the Conservatives were unable to form a Ministry, Lord John resumed office. Thus, as will be considered hereinafter, Lord John and his first [Whig] Cabinet, although tottering, survived until February 1852, followed by a minority Conservative Administration and then, in December 1852, by Lord Aberdeen's Peelite/Whig/Radical Coalition.

> Naples (31 March) – On Thursday we made the excursion to Baia, the Dunoon of the Ancient Romans.

Baia, a coastal town, 10 miles west of Naples, had hot sulphur springs and was a favourite resort of the Emperors and other wealthy Romans It was where Tiberius and Hadrian died.

> Vienna (15 May) – To a place called the Beer Garden, where we heard the great musician J. Strauss [Johann Strauss the Younger] play all evening. The music was very fine and we enjoyed it vastly.

Next evening, they heard Strauss play in the Volksgarten 'but the music was not so good as last night, the evening was cold, and there were not many people, so we did not stay long'.

> Berlin (29 May) – We have today made the excursion to Potsdam, the Prussian Versailles. Leaving by railway at 11, we were there in three quarters of an hour…. On leaving the New Place [now a barracks], we met a carriage, with two men behind and two ladies inside. We took off our hats and received a most gracious bow and soon after learned it was the Queen [of Prussia] and her maid…. We had in the train [back to Berlin] with us the Prince of Prussia (brother of the King and heir of the throne) with his son…. Their valet was in the carriage with us, with the young Prince's helmet – so some day when we hear of him as king, we may say we once travelled in company with his hat.

The Prince of Prussia succeeded as Wilhelm I of Prussia in 1861 and was proclaimed German Emperor in 1871. His son, the young Prince, who married the UK's Princess Royal in 1858, was, as Frederick III of Prussia, briefly German Emperor in 1888. Their son was the Kaiser, whom Sir Henry would encounter personally when UK Prime Minister in 1907.

Berlin (31 May) – This morning we were up by 6.30. We [had] got tickets for the roof of the Opera House [and from there] we saw the King of Prussia [Frederick William IV] unveil the new statue of Frederick the Great.

Amsterdam (6 June) – While in Frankfurt we saw the Ariadne of Danneckrr. It is very much admired as a work of art, I have no doubt, but why should Ariadne, daughter of Minos, King of Crete, a stately fair dame of two or three thousand years ago be represented by a mincing young French miss of the 19th century.

London (18 June 1851) – We have been at the Exhibition [in the Crystal Palace] two whole days and it quite surpasses our expectation in size, completeness, beauty and the quantity of articles exhibited. The police returns yesterday are not given in but it is supposed there were about 70,000 (£ 3,191 is what they got) – the day before there were 63,000.

On returning to Glasgow, Henry, aged fifteen, entered the University, then centred in the Old College in the High Street, in the autumn of 1851. Another future Prime Minister, William Lamb (2nd Viscount Melbourne 1828) had attended the University in 1799-1801. Three other future Prime Ministers also attended a Scottish University (Edinburgh), Palmerston in 1800-1803, Lord John Russell in 1809-1812, and Gordon Brown (MA 1972, PhD 1982).

Henry's name appears in the prize lists for 1851-1852 and 1852-1853, winning the Cowan Gold Medal for Greek in 1853. This was a significant achievement with other Cowan Gold Medalists including three other distinguished High School Former Pupils – Francis, Lord Sandford (first Permanent Under-Secretary at the Scottish Office from 1885), James, Viscount Bryce and Sir Henry Craik (first Secretary of the Scottish Education Department from 1885). As from Professor George E. Ramsay, 'These [Cowan] Medals are amongstthe most coveted and Important distinctions which the University has to give and many of their winners have not only been the ablest classical scholars of their time but have added to the fame of their Alma Mater in every sphere of public and private life'.[46]

As an indication of the immediate academic competition which he faced, Henry's undergraduate contemporaries at Glasgow University included David Binning Monro (Homeric scholar and future Provost of Oriel), J.W. Hales (future Professor of English at King's College, London),[47] James Pettigrew (future Professor of Medicine at St. Andrews), and (Sir) Thomas Millwright (future Premier of Queensland).

---

[46] As quoted in Mackie (1914), p.13
[47] Professor Hales (1836-1914) was a contemporary, but apparently not a classmate, of Henry at the High School.

Henry left Glasgow University without graduating, although later (March 1883) receiving an Honorary Doctorate of Laws (LLD) from it in recognition of his being an MP and then Financial and Parliamentary Secretary to the Admiralty. Given that there is no record of his attendance (class or prize lists) at Glasgow University in session 1853-1854, this may indicate another (otherwise unrecorded) long overseas trip and/or employment in the family business.

Given his recorded interest in politics as from early 1851 [aged 14], Henry would have taken an interest in the 1852 General Election. This followed the defeat of Lord John Russell's Whig Administration in the House of Commons on 20 February 1852 and the accession of a minority Conservative Government headed by the Earl of Derby. Then, in the hope of securing a clear mandate, the Earl called a General Election for July. With two Whigs being elected in Glasgow, the overall result – with the election of 336 Conservatives [including about 45 Peelites] and 324 Whigs and Radicals – was such that an alliance of Whigs, Radicals and Peelites defeated the Conservative Government in a Budget vote in December. A Coalition Government, of Whigs, Radicals and Peelites was then formed, headed by the Earl of Aberdeen, who had succeeded as the Peelite Leader on the death of Sir Robert Peel in 1850.

On 25 April 1854, James Alexander Campbell, Henry's elder brother, married Ann Peto (Died 1906) – a second cousin of H.H. Asquith's first wife, Helen Melland (Died 1891) [48] – with her (Ann's) former school friend, (Sarah) Charlotte Bruce as bridesmaid and, presumably, Henry as best man. This is when Henry (then seventeen) and his future wife, Charlotte (then about twenty-one) first met and not, as already mentioned, a few months before they married in 1860. (James Alexander Campbell and Ann Campbell had four children – Nora Jane [Mrs. Adamson], Hilda Sophia [Mrs. Hunter], Elsie Louisa and James Morton Peto, born on 29 January 1863 and known as Morton, as was his maternal grandfather)

Ann Peto's father was Sir (Samuel) Morton Peto (1809-1889) who was created a Baronet in 1855 for unpaid services as a public works and railway contractor during the Crimean War. He was Whig/Liberal MP for Norwich in 1847-1854, for Finsbury in 1859-1865 and for Bristol in 1865-1868. Later generations of Petos provided Conservative MPs for various constituencies between 1910 and 1950.

Henry entered Trinity College, Cambridge (aged eighteen) in 1854 graduating as a BA in 1958 with a Third in Classics, being also ranked as twentieth Senior Optima in the Mathematics Tripos. In Mathematics he was bracketed with another future Chief Secretary for Ireland, the ill-fated Lord Fredrick Cavendish but there is no reason to believe they were acquainted as undergraduates. Henry returned to Cambridge in 1861 to graduate as an MA and again in 1907 to receive an Honorary Doctorate of Laws (LLD). Apparently, as from incoming correspondence when he was Prime Minister, most of Henry's friends at Cambridge were men who went on to become parish clergy in the Church of England.

---

[48] Packer (2006) p.117

Given Henry's previous prize-winning record in Classics, his Third at Cambridge was somewhat uncharacteristic. Indeed, Christopher Harvie (1976, p.12) refers to him as 'an undistinguished and unenthusiastic graduate of Trinity'.

However, as attested by Asquith – speaking after he had unveiled the statue of Sir Henry in Stirling on 1 November 1913 – he (Henry) had no difficulty in, at least, holding his own among all the apparently better qualified Classical scholars, including Gladstone and Asquith himself, in the 1892-1894 Liberal Cabinet. (Refer to Appendix 5)

In 1855 Henry's sister, Louisa married their cousin, James Alexander Bannerman. Also that summer Henry undertook a short summer tour of France and Switzerland. Extracts (a selection of which, with comments, follows) from relevant entries in Henry's manuscript diaries were first published as 'Journey to Switzerland – 1855' in the *Glasgow High School Magazine* of June 1948,

> Paris, 27 June 1855 – Scarcely had we entered [the Exhibition] when we heard heavy tramping behind us and found that we were being followed by the Emperor [Napoleon III]. He is short, neatly made, with a French cut, pale faced, with a pleasant air – almost bonhomie – about him.
>
> 28 June – Hence to the Invalides. Made an attempt to see Napoleon's tomb, but failed for want of a passport. Shopped in the afternoon. Dined at Frascati's (2.5 francs). Started *for Strasbourg at 8 o'clock.*

The Invalides (*Hôtel National* [formerly *Royal*] *des Invalides*) was built in 1671-1676 for Louis XIV for wounded, homeless French soldiers. Napoleon's body was brought to the Invalides from St. Helena in 1840. Passports for international travel were not generally required until the First World War, However, Henry and co, did have passports some five years earlier, to which visas were attached, when they arrived at Calais in late August 1850.

> 29 June – At Strasbourg about 7.15. After breakfast in a café, to the Cathedral' A polite, kindly and gentlemanly American, having procured a ticket to ascend to the summit (474 feet above the pavement, 112 feet higher than St. Paul's) which was available for two, offered to share it. I embraced his offer, tho' with some misgivings. Here [at the top] we stood about 10 minutes, and enjoyed the finest view I ever saw. The Vosges Mountains on the west and the Black Forest on the east bounded the magnificent valley of the Rhine.
>
> Left about 12 for Kehl [across the Rhine from Strasbourg]. From Kehl by railway (3rd Class) to Freiburg. Reached Bâle [Basle/Basel] at about 7.15. Our rooms looked down on the broad, full rushing stream of the Rhine.

> 30 June – Left Bâle at 9.30 and had railway to Liesthal. After that by diligence [coach], very slowly to Waldenburg. Our road lay thro' richly wooded country, very like Dunkeld and thereabout. Then over the Ober Hauenstein (3,000 feet) and down to Ballsthal. Between Ballsthal and Soleure we saw great crowds and preparations as if for a fete. This is occasioned by the Tir Fédéral which was to commence next day at Soleure. This is an assemblage of all the Swiss nation for the purpose of rifle shooting. At Soleure the whole place was in confusion and the hotel teeming with noisy Swiss.
>
> 1 July – At 10 o'clock a procession formed and marched to the place d'armes. Here canon were fired off and some speeches delivered, evidently with intent to arouse patriotic feelings. The [rifle] firing was to continue until the late evening. At about 3.39 p.m. started for the Weissenstein.

The purpose of the Tir Fédéral is to promote marksmanship among the Swiss whose Army was and is made up, almost completely, of part-time militia. Nowadays the event is held on a competitive basis once every three years, with over 60,000 taking part over three weeks. Henry's encounter with the event in mid-1855 was probably a unique experience for a future rifle volunteer officer in Scotland and a future UK Secretary of State for War.

> 2 July – Started for Berne (en voiture [carriage]) at 7 and got there at 10. Got visas and money. Left for Thun at 6 and got there at 10. To the Pension Baumgarten at Thun.

There was a General Election while Henry was at Cambridge. In the circumstances of the Crimean War, Lord Aberdeen's Coalition had been defeated in the House of Commons on 29 December 1855. There followed a further Whig, Radical and Peelite Coalition headed by Lord Palmerston, although three of the Peelites resigned from the new Cabinet within a fortnight. Just over two years later, Palmerston's Government was defeated in the House of Commons in a vote of censure on 3 March 1857. Palmerston immediately called a General Election for March/April. With no Conservatives being nominated and two Whigs being elected in Glasgow, the overall result – with the election of 239 Conservative, 25 Peelite, 377 Whig and Radical and 13 Other (Irish) MPs – was such that Palmerston's Coalition continued in office until it was defeated in the House of Commons in April 1858. This resulted in Palmerston's resignation and the accession of another minority Conservative Administration again headed by the Earl of Derby.

Lord Derby's Government survived for over a year until it was defeated in the House of Commons on 31 March 1859 and a General Election called for April/May. Although not yet known to be active politically, Henry (now back in Glasgow and aged 22) would have been very much aware of this General Election – when two fellow Glasgow High School Former Pupils (a Whig and a Radical) were returned unopposed in Glasgow – and its aftermath.

The overall result – with the election of 273 Conservative, 25 Peelite and 356 Whig and Radical MPs – was such that 274 Whig, Radical and Peelite MPs, at a meeting in London on 6 June, decided to unite on an assured basis, to defeat Lord Derby's continuing Conservative Government in a no confidence vote and thereafter form a broad ministry committed to a programme of reform. Thus, the inauguration or accouchement of the Liberal Party which would be a major party of government for fifty-six years – that is, until the Asquithian Coalition of 1915-1916 gave way to the Tory-dominated Lloyd George Coalition.

The meeting took place in Willis' Rooms in King Street, Westminster. On the initiative of the Liberal Democrat History Group, and in conjunction with Westminster City Council, a green commemorative plaque was unveiled by Nick Clegg, then Liberal Democrat Leader and Deputy Prime Minister, on the outside of Almack House [a modern office building which now occupies the site] on 14 January 2013.[49]

The long debate on the no confidence motion in the House of Commons, as from 7 June 1859, concluded with a division on the night of 10/11 June in which the Conservative government was defeated by 323 votes to 310. Lord Derby immediately resigned and, after some manoeuvring, Lord Palmerston formed his second [and first Liberal] Administration as from 13 June. (William Gladstone, who had voted with the Conservatives in the division, was nevertheless soon persuaded to go and see Lord Palmerston and accept office as Chancellor of the Exchequer)

In the previous year (1858), after graduating from Cambridge, Henry joined the family business in Ingram Street in Glasgow. Then late in the following year (1859) he and his brother were founder members of the First Lanarkshire Rifle Volunteers. Henry was Lieutenant and then, in succession to his brother, Captain of M Company, known as 'Campbell's Corps' because all its members worked for J.& W. Campbell and had indoor drills in the warehouse. The formation of such units had been authorised, in the interests of Home Defence, by Jonathan Peel – a Protectionist son of Sir Robert Peel – as Conservative Secretary of State for War, in a letter to Lords Lieutenant in Scotland, England and Wales on 12 May 1859, just a month before he (Peel) left office with the minority Conservative Administration.

Next year, on 7 August (1860), Henry commanded his Company at the Royal Review by Queen Victoria in Edinburgh. Next day, *The Scotsman* described how 'peal after peal of cheering broke out from Arthur's Seat, all one mighty mass of human beings, as more than twenty thousand men, the best men of every class and district, presented themselves before their Queen, a self-formed and self-armed army'. Those watching Queen Victoria drive out that day from Holyrood included the parents of John Sinclair (Sir Henry's Secretary for Scotland in 1905-1907) who had the one month old John with them [50]

---

[49] *Journal of Liberal History* (Spring 2013), p.4

[50] Lady Pentland (1928), p.5

When, more than thirty years later, when himself Secretary of State for War, Henry continued to attend annual reunions of his old unit, recalling 'frequent occasions when he was made to tramp about a plot of ground in Burnbank [now part of Hamilton in Lanarkshire] which was miscalled a field, and which was covered with something which they fondly imagined to be grass, but did not always present the appearance of that natural product'.[51]

Some forty-nine years later another member of the family, Matthew Pearce Campbell (a grandson of Henry's Uncle William) held the rank of Major in the First Lanarkshire Battalion His (Matthew's) brother-in-law, Lieutenant-Colonel Sir William Smith, founder of the Boys Brigade in Glasgow in 1883, was at one time the Battalion Commander.

In 1881, during Henry's second term as Financial Secretary at the War Office, his experience as a Volunteer officer contributed, no doubt, to the decision to attach all the Rifle Volunteer units to regular regiments. Thus, Battalions 1, 2, 3, 4 and 7 of the Lanarkshire Rifle Volunteers were attached to the Cameronians (Scottish Rifles) and Battalions 5, 6, 8 and 9 to the Highland Light Infantry (HLI).[52]
When formed in 1902, the Glasgow High School's Cadet Corps – Officers Training Corps [OTC] – was attached to the First Lanarkshire Battalion and thus to the Cameronians. From 1904-1905 to 1911-1912 the School colours were green, blue and white as from the Cameronian tartan, with such colours still used in one of the Former Pupil ties. OTCs were given official recognition in terms of the 1907 Territorial and Reserve Forces Act, passed when Sir Henry was Prime Minister. The High School's OTC received War Office recognition in December 1909.

In 1860 Henry and his brother were admitted as partners in the family business. Henry did not have the same commitment to the business as the other male members of the family. He was soon seeking to quit business for Liberal politics, perhaps even then looking for a constituency some distance from Glasgow to avoid the appearance of directly challenging his Conservative father and brother.

Also in 1860 when Lord Brougham (then aged 82) was in Glasgow as President of the Social Science Congress he was the house guest of Sir James Campbell and probably then met Henry. At that time Brougham was Chancellor of Edinburgh University, having previously been Rector of Glasgow University.

---

[51] As quoted in Spender (1923), Volume 1, p.21

[52] The Third Lanark Football Club (1872-1967), a founder member of the Scottish Football Association (SFA) on 13 March 1873, had its origins in the Third Lanarkshire Rifle Volunteers. (What is now the Scottish Rugby Union was formed as the Scottish Football Union three days earlier than the SFA). St. Bernard's Football Club (1878-1943), also an early member of the SFA, was originally, in 1874-1878, the football club of the Third Edinburgh Rifle Volunteers.

One wonders if the conversation in Bath Street on that occasion included discussion of Brougham's experiences as a Whig MP between 1810 and 1830 and as a rather erratic Whig Lord Chancellor in 1830-1834 during the passage of the 1832 Reform Acts. Was there also discussion of his inconsistent part in the events leading to the Disruption of the Church of Scotland in 1843? In 1834 he had supported the General Assembly's Veto Act (allowing congregations to veto patrons' nominations of parish ministers). In 1839 he had joined in a House of Lords judgement that patrons' rights were absolute and no objections by parishioners were relevant.

The Glasgow Herald, 17 September 1860

> At All Souls' Church, Langham Place, London, on the 13th instant, by the Rev. George March, rector of Sutton Benger, Wilts, Henry Campbell, Esq., second son of Sir James Campbell of Stracathro, to Sarah Charlotte, only daughter of the late Major-General Sir Charles Bruce, KCB'.

Thus the highlight of Henry's life that year – and indeed of his whole life – his marriage to Sarah Charlotte Bruce – known as Charlotte (and called Charley by Henry) – in All Souls Church, Langham Place, London on 13 September (1860).[53]. She was the daughter of the late Major-General Sir Charles Bruce, sometime Military Governor of Portsmouth, and Lady Charlotte Bruce, daughter of James Forbes of Hutton-hall, Essex and Kingairloch, Arygll. Sir Charles, who had fought in the Napoleonic Wars, died in 1854, the year of his daughter's birth. Thereafter mother and daughter lived in the Isle of Wight, apart from when Charlotte was away in France receiving part of her education

As already mentioned, Henry had first met Charlotte in 1854 and their engagement followed occasions earlier in 1860 when they both staying with Henry's brother and sister-in-law in Glasgow. No doubt, Charlotte's friendship since schooldays with Ann Campbell (née Peto) much helped her acceptance by the Campbell family. John Wilson (1973) suggested (p.38) that 'from her photographs she appears to have been a fairly plain girl with a severe expression', but this must have been with reference to photographs taken later in life. In a photograph, taken about the time of her marriage and published in Spender (1923), Volume 1, she looks far from plain and her expression far from severe. Also, at this time, Henry wore a monocle and had not yet grown a moustache.

Charlotte influenced her husband to a considerable extent and was an instinctively shrewd judge of character, with also a keen sense of humour. She guarded his interests, resenting the least supposed slight to his reputation, with her hopes for his advancement compensating for his lack of ambition. However, the marriage was

---

[53] All Souls Church is best known nowadays in Scotland for its annual PROM PRAISE Orchestral and Choral presentations in the major concert halls in Glasgow, Edinburgh, Perth, Inverness and Aberdeen.

childless and in later life she was much overweight, being a diabetic and in poor health. (Insulin was not isolated until 1921 and regulatory medications, such as the biguanides including Metformin, were not available until very much later.) Indeed, in July 1901, Dr. Maclagan of Alyth – then the Campbell-Bannermans' GP in Scotland – told Sir Henry that, given the long continuance of sugar in the blood, she ought not to be in London during the winter and spring and that she ought to spend winters in a warmer climate. (CB/BL) This would have meant the end of Sir Henry's political career and this Charlotte herself would not have wanted – so they carried on. About a year later, in the early summer of 1902, she had a paralytic stroke from which she only slowly recovered, and was thereafter virtually an invalid, having to be wheeled about the grounds of Belmont Castle (their Scottish home from 1887) in a bath chair.

Nevertheless, in her time, Charlotte was a very active political hostess. Indeed, on 22 February 1894, when the Gladstones, Asquith and his fiancée, Margot Tennant were dining with the Campbell-Bannermans in London, Margot lost her temper when, after the ladies moved to the drawing room, she found herself being lectured by Mrs. Gladstone and Charlotte on the duties of a politician's wife. When Gladstone joined the ladies, she told him that she had been adjured to give up dancing, riding and acting, and he told her that he knew no-one better fitted to be a politician's wife then herself.[54] Perhaps significantly, Henry was not one of the past, present and future Prime Ministers – Gladstone, Rosebery, Balfour and Asquith himself – signing the register at the Asquith-Tennant wedding on 10 May (1894).[55] Other London guests of the Campbell-Bannermans about this time were Princess Alexandra (the future Queen Consort) and Mark Twain.[56]

Henry's and Charlotte's month long honeymoon in 1860 followed some of the Italian itinerary of his tour ten years earlier – the Italian lakes, Milan, Venice, Genoa, Pisa and Rome. Thereafter, their first married home – their only home for the next eight years and their only Scottish home until 1887 – was at 8 Claremont Gardens, Glasgow as presumably bought for them by Sir James Campbell. It must have been a new or fairly new house as the first house in Claremont Gardens – west of Charing Cross, on the site of the Botanic Gardens of c.1815-1842 – was built in 1857.[57] (Although situated in Glasgow's 'respectable and fashionable' Victorian West End, Claremont Gardens was also within Glasgow's 'Square Mile of Murder', with four notorious cases from that involving Madeleine Smith in 1857 to that involving Oscar Slater in 1909.[58] (House [1984])

---

[54] Margot Asquith (1962), p.198

[55] Clifford (2002), p.11

[56] *Glasgow High School Magazine,* June 1948, p.112

[57] Amanda Foreman (2007), p.49.

[58] Anent Oscar Slater, refer to Chapter 13

Henry and Charlotte were overseas again in 1862 (Avignon, Arles, Nimes, Toulouse and Biarritz). (As Prime Minister and after Charlotte's death, he revisited Biarritz. His memories of happier days must then have been particularly poignant) They were abroad again in 1863 (Normandy, Brittany and the Loire), followed, in 1864, by an autumn holiday in Spain, apparently with Henry's cousin, James Campbell and his wife, Jessie (née Black).[59] Extracts (of which a selection follows) from entries in Henry's manuscript diaries were first published as 'In Spain – 1864' in the *Glasgow High School Magazine* of June 1948,

> 28 September 1864 – We there [Bordeaux?] joined the train – the same one we came by yesterday – and went off, passing through a pretty broken country by Biarritz and S. Jean de Luz to Hendaye which is the French border town, or rather station. Between that and Irun we entered Spain. At Irun we changed carriages. The Spanish gauge is wider than the French – that is from political motives, to prevent a French invasion – and they suffer from it. A good deal of delay and at last started. [Then via Passages, S. Sebastian, Beasain, Olazagulia and Vittoria] We supped decently at Miranda and reached Burgos at about 10.40 instead of 10.7. Found an omnibus there and drove to the [Hotel] Fonda del Norte. The people were all in bed but we got them up and were shown into a decent set of rooms.

> 29 September – Up about 8. Breakfasted fairly, and went off to the Cathedral [Burgos]. We had had a comfortable night, but were disturbed by various noises – cocks crowing, people knocking on doors, and the watchman shouting the time and state of the weather every quarter of an hour.

> 1 October – At 6.30 left for Madrid. At Villalba a long delay to put an extra carriage on – which ultimately we left behind – the men had neglected to hook it on. We went on about a quarter of mile and then stopped and went back. Great delay and bungling to get the mistake remedied. Crowds of country people everywhere going into Madrid. At last reached Madrid, about one and a half hours after time, arriving at our hotel at a quarter to 10. A good dinner and so to bed.

> 6 October – Were told there was a bull fight at 4 o'clock and [James] and I resolved to go. Took tickets at 24 reals each, and started, with a flask of cognac in my pocket. [25 Centimos = 1 Real, 4 Reals = 1 Peseta and 5 Pesetas = 1 Duro] When we reached the Plaza, two horses were already lying dead in the arena. The bull, a large brown one, was pretty tired and the second part of the performance was going on. We saw this bull killed and the next one, a large dull black one. The worst part of the whole affair is the butchery of the horses. They are blinded, otherwise they could not face the bull. The picador rides and his

---

[59] 1864 was also the year of the death of William Campbell, Henry/s uncle and James' father,

cleverness is shown in keeping his seat while the poor horse was being gored by the bull. This is very disgusting. The third bull we saw was a small black one, very plucky and lively, he immediately disposed of two horses. We then left, having seen enough of it. On the whole, disgust and indignation...

7 October – Reached Sta. Cruz sooner than expected – about 5.30. Here the railway stops and we took our places in the diligence for Cordova. Several diligences started, some for Grenada. Three went to Cordova. Bailen about 12.30 p.m. There half an hour for a poor dinner. At last we found ourselves jolting through the streets of Cordova. At 10.30 p.m. in an omnibus to Fonda Suiza [Hotel], where we were shown a gorgeous suite of rooms. Had some supper, and thankfully to bed.

15 October – At 6.30 to the house of the Capitan of the Gypsies. The house was clean and tidy. We were in a square room with tiles on the floor. There were dancing girls and the Capitan who played. The four girls (in print dresses, with handkerchiefs over their shoulders and flowers in their hair), who danced, were short in stature and not very good looking. The male performer (dancer) was a tall fellow in Spanish costume. The Capitan played the guitar, with seven strings, wonderfully. We had some solos from him, [and] some songs from [one of] the girls. The dancing was accompanied by the guitar; the tambourine managed by the dancing man; and the castanets in the hands of the girls. At the close of each dance the girls came for money and had to be given a peseta or half a peseta. They were not impudent. Left after about an hour it, giving the Capitan 5 Duros for the performance. He is a blacksmith by trade. Took places on the Vittoria diligence on the Monday.

In the following year (1865), with Parliament nearing the end of its statutory life span, then of seven years, a General Election was called for July. The overall result – with the election of 369 Liberal and 289 Conservative MPs – was such that Lord Palmerston's Liberal Government continued in office.

Henry had an opportunity to be a Liberal candidate for the then two-member constituency of Glasgow at that year's General Election but delayed his response and missed the chance. However, for the family reasons already suggested, it is probable that the procrastination was deliberate.

With no Conservative candidate being nominated in Glasgow (as also at the 1857 and 1859 General Elections) the three 1865 candidates were all (sorts of) Liberals. One of the incumbent Liberal MPs (Walter Buchanan), having retired, the other incumbent Liberal MP (Robert Dalglish) was re-elected, and with a new Liberal candidate (William Graham) topping the poll and continuing as a Glasgow MP until he retired in 1874.

Table 5 - The 1865 General Election in Glasgow - Electorate 16,819		
William Graham	Liberal	8,272
Robert Dalglish	Liberal	8,713
John Ramsay	Liberal Conservative	5,820

By not being a candidate in Glasgow in 1865 Henry did not then have as an opponent John Ramsay (1814-1892), then Glasgow's Lord Dean of Guild, a Whiggish Liberal (from 1886 a Liberal Unionist) who defeated Henry at the Stirling Burghs by-election in April 1868 and was defeated by Henry in that constituency at the General Election seven months later.

Nor did he have as an opponent another Glasgow High School Former Pupil (Robert Dalglish) until he (Henry) was unsuccessfully challenged by (Sir) John Pender (Liberal Unionist) at the 1886 General Election.

Within three months of the General Election, Lord Palmerston died [on 18 October 1865] and was succeeded, as Prime Minister and Liberal Leader, by Lord John Russell, now in the House of Lords as Earl Russell, with William Gladstone becoming Liberal Leader in the House of Commons. However, seven months later (on 19 June 1866) the Government was defeated in the House of Commons, resigned the following week and was replaced by yet another minority Conservative Government, again headed by the Earl of Derby, with Benjamin Disraeli as Leader in the Commons.

Then, in the following year (1867) Henry entered active Liberal politics by addressing his first public meeting in his future constituency of Stirling Burghs. The meeting in Dunfermline Music Hall was chaired by a local shoemaker, Thomas Morrison (an old Chartist and uncle of Andrew Carnegie). In introducing the speaker, Mr. Morrison asserted that he (Henry Campbell, the Glasgow Radical) would one day be Prime Minister, with the Whiggish Liberals present laughing and jeering at such a monstrous idea. Thomas Shaw (Lord Shaw 1909, Lord Craigmyle 1929), Sir Henry's Lord Advocate in 1905-1908 – who was then working in a solicitors' office in Dunfermline between school and university – was at the meeting and joined in the derision. This fact much amused Sir Henry in later years.[60]

Henry's appearance in Dunfermline in 1867 was probably in response to the notion that there would soon be a by-election in Stirling Burghs. Laurence Oliphant, who had been elected unopposed as a Liberal at the 1865 General Election, was thought to be about to depart to join a spiritualist community in the USA, led by Thomas Lake Harris. As from an entry (8 May 1867) in John Bright's diary, 'Mr. Oliphant called. Long conversation on his change of views and life, and on Mr. Harris, Very curious and interesting'.[61]

---

[60] Shaw (1921), p.27

[61] As quoted in Wilson (1973), p.42

Oliphant did indeed depart for the USA in early 1868. He wrote from there on 10 February to say that he would be unable to resume his duties in the House of Commons for some time to come. The reaction to this in Stirling Burghs was such that Oliphant took the hint and resigned as an MP by way of appointment to the Chiltern Hundreds in early April. By then John Ramsay and Henry Campbell were already in place as the by-election candidates.

3 – The Stirling Burghs Constituency and Sir Henry's Election in 1868

The single-member UK Constituency of Stirling Burghs, which Sir Henry Campbell-Bannerman represented in the House of Commons from late 1868 until his death in April 1908, was defined in the 1707 Act of the outgoing Scottish Parliament anent the Election of Scottish Representative Peers and Members of the House of Commons as comprising the Royal and Parliamentary Burghs of Stirling in Stirlingshire, Dunfermline and Inverkeithing in Fife, Culross, originally an exclave of Perthshire in Fife but transferred to Fife in 1889, and (South) Queensferry in Linlithgowshire (West Lothian).[62] After the first General Election for the UK Parliament in 1708, the Stirling Burghs Constituency was unaffected by redistribution until the constituency, as such, was abolished in 1918. (Refer to Appendix 1 for a summary of the constituency's electoral history from 1708)

Stirling (Gaelic *Struiglea*, original meaning uncertain but 'enclosure by the meandering river/stream' has been suggested). It was probably the *Urbs Iddeu* or *Urbs Guidi*, as at 656, referred to by Bede and in other contemporary annals. It was originally the location in the Manau (district) of Gododdin of one of the three major hill-forts – the others being at Edinburgh *(Din Eidyn)* and at Traprain Law *(Dinpender)* in East Lothian – of the Kingdom of Gododdin. Until Anglo-Saxon conquests culminating in the capture of Stirling in 641, Gododdin stretched from the Forth to the Tweed. During the process of the unification of Scotland, all parts of the former Kingdom of Gododdin were liberated between 685 (Battle of Nechtanesmere) and 1018 (Battle of Carham).[63]

---

[62] It is noted that Roy Hattersley (2006), p.11 referred to Culross as 'Culdross' and to South Queensferry as 'the fishing village of Cowesferry'.

[63] The Kingdom of Gododdin (from Forth to Tweed) was based on the northern territory of the tribe known to the Romans as the Votadini. The southern tribal territory (Tweed to Tyne) became, firstly, the Celtic Kingdom of Brynaich, with its coastal fortress at *Din Guari* (→ Bebbanburge → Bamburgh), and then, after c.570, Bernicia, the northern kingdom of the Anglo-Saxon Northumbrians.

It is said that, sometime before 442, Cunedda, a chieftain from Manau of Gododdin, moved with his extended family and war-band to North Wales to help combat Irish incursions, thus founding the First Dynasty of Gwynedd. Traditionally, other members of his family – Ceredig (hence Ceredigion/Cardigan) and Meirion (hence Meirionydd/Merioneth) – gave their names to other parts of Wales. The name Manau survives in such place-names as Clackmannan and Slamannan.

Helen (or Ellen) – possibly a natural daughter of Llywelyn the Great (c.1172-1240), a later Prince of Gwynedd – married the future 6th (Scottish) Earl of Mar. Their daughter, Isabella was the first wife of Robert I (The Bruce), King of Scots. Their daughter, Marjorie married Walter, 6th High Steward of Scotland and thus founded the Royal Stewart Dynasty.

Since 1565 there have been two Scottish Earldoms of Mar – the senior Earldom, dating from c.1115, currently held by Margaret, Countess of Mar (31st in line) and the junior Earldom,

As by then a community of merchants and craftsmen, Stirling was created a Royal Burgh by David I, King of Scots in 1124x1127. Its medieval Castle was one of the major royal strongholds in Scotland, with its strategic importance leading to the nearby Battles of Stirling Bridge (1297) and Bannockburn (1314) during the Wars of Independence. Henry Campbell-Bannerman's good offices, as the local MP in the early 1890s, ensured that the Abbey Craig part of the 1297 battleground was preserved for the nation, with the Abbey Craig being the site of the dominating statue of Sir William Wallace as erected in 1869.[64]

The nearby Cambuskenneth Abbey, dating from about 1140, was the location of a number of early meetings of the Scottish Parliament, including that of 1324, at which for the first time the Royal Burghs were represented. James III, King of Scots, who was killed in the aftermath of the nearby Battle of Sauchieburn in 1488, was buried in the Abbey.

Two Kings of Scots died in Stirling Castle – Alexander I in 1124 and William I (The Lyon) in 1214. However, the present-day Castle buildings date from only the 15/16th centuries including the Great Hall built for James III and occasionally used for meetings of the Scottish Parliament, the Palace built for James V, and the Chapel Royal built for James VI.

The future King James VI (and I) was baptised as Charles James in the Castle on 17 December 1566 and his Scottish Coronation took place in the Burgh's medieval (and present-day) Parish Church of the Holy Rude on 29 July 1567.

In the mid-19th century Stirling was a centre for the manufacture of tartans, shawls, carpets, yarns and cotton goods, leather, malt, soap and rope, with also a considerable river trade.

The position of hereditary Governor of Stirling Castle was restored to the Scottish Earls of Mar and Kellie in 1923. Currently the position is held by James Erskine, 15th Earl of Mar and 17th Earl of Kellie who sits in the House of Lords as a Liberal Democrat Life Peer [Lord Erskine of Alloa Tower]. One of his ancestors, James Erskine (aka Lord Grange) was MP for Stirling Burghs in 1741-1747.

The University of Stirling was founded in 1967. Stirling was granted city status on the occasion of the Queen's Golden Jubilee in 2002.

It is of interest to note that Stirling Burgh Council was controlled in 1772-1775 by three Councillors who had signed a secret agreement to run the Burgh's affairs to their own political and financial advantage. When this so-called Black Bond became public knowledge in 1775, the Burgh was placed under the supervision of a UK

---

dating from 1565, currently held by James Erskine, as above, 15th Earl of Mar and 17th Earl of Kellie.

[64] *Stirling Observer,* 21 December 1892

Government Commission and lost its status as a Parliamentary Burgh. Accordingly, the Burgh was unable to take part in the 1780 General Election. However, in 1781 the government of the Burgh was returned to a Burgh Council, with also the restoration of its Parliamentary Status.[65]

Dunfermline (Gaelic *Dun Phàrlain,* original meaning uncertain but 'fortified hill by a winding stream' has been suggested). It is about 24 miles east of Stirling, and was created a Royal Burgh by David I, King of Scots in 1124x1127. The marriage of Malcolm III (Canmore), King of Scots and the Anglo-Saxon Princess Margaret (canonised in 1250 as Saint Margaret of Scotland) took place in 1069 in a chapel on the site of the Priory, dating from 1070 and of the Abbey, dating from 1128. Their daughter, Edith-Matilda, was born in the Priory's Guest House in c.1080 as were, in the same Guest House, two later Kings of Scots, David II in 1324 and James I in 1394. Edith-Matilda was the wife of Henry I of England and thus ancestress of all subsequent Kings and Queens Regnant of England, except Stephen who married Matilda, a grand-daughter of Malcolm III and Queen/Saint Margaret.

At least seven Kings of Scots were buried in Dunfermline Priory/Abbey – Duncan II in 1094, Edgar in 1107, Alexander I in 1124, David I in 1153, Malcolm IV in 1165, Alexander III in 1286, and Robert I (The Bruce) in 1329.

Malcolm III (Canmore), who was killed near Alnwick, Northumberland in 1093, was originally buried in Tynemouth Priory. His remains were removed to Dunfermline Abbey in 1115 and thereafter, together with most of the remains of his wife, Queen/Saint Margaret, to the Escorial, 28 miles from Madrid.[66]

In 1330, The Bruce's casketed heart was carried in battle against the Moorish Kingdom of Grenada in Spain by Sir James of Douglas. After the battle, the casket was recovered from The Douglas' dead body, brought back to Scotland and buried at Melrose. During excavations in 1818, prior to the erection of a new Dunfermline Abbey Parish Church beside the old Abbey site, The Bruce's body (identified from the evidence for the removal of the heart and the composition of the shroud) was discovered. It was placed in a new coffin and re-interred below the pulpit of the new Church. Other royal burial places in Scotland were Iona, Dunkeld, Arbroath, Melrose, Holyrood, Scone, Paisley and Perth.

---

[65] The opportunities for such municipal corruption in Scotland were greatly reduced by the Scottish Burgh Reform Act of 1833 in that elected town councils replaced self-perpetuating councils, thus also increasing popular representation among the Elder Commissioners appointed by the Royal Burghs to the General Assembly of the Church of Scotland. This helped to ensure that the popular party had a majority in General Assemblies from 1834. However, that majority was lost, by reason of decisions of the Court of Session in 1841, 1842 and early 1843 excluding the one-fifth of Ministers who were Chapel (Church Extension) Ministers from Presbyteries and General Assemblies. This was followed, in May 1843, by the Disruption of the Church of Scotland and the formation of the original Free Church, which 162 (70 %) of the Chapel Ministers joined,

[66] Alison Weir (2008). p.186

The Abbey's Guest House was converted into a Royal Palace about the time of the Coronation of Anne of Denmark and Norway as Queen Consort of Scotland in 1590. Princess Elizabeth (maternal grandmother of George I) was born therein in 1596 as also Charles I in 1600. Andrew Carnegie, industrialist and philanthropist, was born in a weaver's cottage (now a museum) in Dunfermline in 1835. Henry Beveridge – the father of Sir William Beveridge (Lord Beveridge 1946) – was born in Dunfermline in 1837. This connection explains why Sir William was invited to become the Prospective Liberal Candidate for Dunfermline Burghs before he was elected as Liberal MP for Berwick-upon-Tweed in 1944.

In the mid-19th century Dunfermline's staple industry was the manufacture of fine linen goods, especially table linen, mostly produced on hand-looms although six steam-powered spinning mills were operating by 1831. There were also four breweries, four tobacco factories and an iron foundry. The Dunfermline Building Society was founded in 1869, the year after the future Sir Henry Campbell-Bannerman became the Burgh's MP. Before its merger with Nationwide in 2009, the Dunfermline Society was the largest in Scotland.

In 1911 the Burgh secured parliamentary approval to extend its boundaries five miles southwards to the Firth of Forth and thus include the 'new town' of Rosyth as built on land acquired by the Admiralty in 1903. Sir Henry Campbell-Bannerman had speculated about this when he received the Freedom of Dunfermline in 1903. [67]

Broomhall, the main residence of the Scottish Earls of Elgin, etc. (Bruces) is nearby Dunfermline, with the 9th Earl serving in 1905-1908 in Sir Henry's Cabinet as Colonial Secretary. Two Bruces of Broomhall represented the nearby Royal Burgh of Culross in the old Scottish Parliament in the 17th century.

It is of interest to note that in 1819 a House of Commons Select Committee reported that the Dunfermline Burgh Council was dominated by the Beveridge family who filled vacancies in the Council with their own nominees and got rid of any Councillors who opposed the family's wishes, with also the Provost being related to the Beveridges. As already mentioned, in later years the family included Henry Beveridge – the father of Sir William Beveridge (Lord Beveridge 1946) – who was born in Dunfermline in 1837. John Beveridge Mackie (1848-1919), one of Sir Henry Campbell-Bannerman's early biographers (in 1914) was also related to the family. [68]

Inverkeithing (Gaelic *Inbhir Céitein,* meaning [Place] at the mouth of the Keithing Burn [wooded stream]). It is about 4 miles south-east from the centre of Dunfermline and was created a royal burgh by Malcolm IV, King of Scots in 1153x1162. It was the location of a Franciscan Friary, dating from c.1260, with its Guest House having been restored for use as a museum. It was also the location of the original *Curia*

---

[67] During the Second World War, my late sister, Jane (Jean), then serving in the Women's Auxiliary Air Force (WAAF), was stationed for some time at the RAF's northern HQ at Pitreavie, also in Dunfermline.

[68] Refer to Endnote 4

Quattuor Burgorum – The Court of the Four Burghs (Edinburgh, Stirling. Roxburgh and Berwick-upon-Tweed) – the precursor of the Convention of Royal Burghs which had its first official meeting in Edinburgh in 1552.[69]

In the mid-19th century it had a distillery and a brewery. For long also a coal exporting centre, it became a shipbuilding centre in the 19th century but, since the First World War, it has been a major ship-breaking centre with many famous ships – from HMS Dreadnought in 1921 onwards – meeting their end here.

Culross (pronounced 'Coo-ros', Gaelic *Cuileann Ros*, probably meaning 'holly point'). It is about 6 miles west of Dunfermline and was created a royal burgh by James VI in 1592. It is said to have been the 6th century birth-place of Kentigern (aka Mungo), later the patron saint of Glasgow, who also evangelised in Cumbria and Wales.[70] It was the location of a Cistercian Abbey, dating from about.1217. It was for long famed for its coalmines and saltpans.[71] Many of its 16th to 18th century buildings have been restored by the National Trust for Scotland.

The Primroses – the family of the later Earls of Rosebery – were originally burgesses in Culross, with also properties in Inverkeithing. One of them, Gilbert – from whom my wife is descended – became principal physician and surgeon to King James VI (and I). A younger brother, James Primrose, became Clerk to the Scottish Privy Council in 1599. James' son, Archibald (1616-1679) held the same office from 1641 until, as an active supporter of James Graham, 1st (Scottish) Marquis of Montrose, he was captured at Philiphaugh in 1645, after which he only narrowly escaped execution for treason. On the restoration of Charles II, he was appointed Lord Clerk Register (Clerk to the Scottish Parliament) in 1660 and was the author of the Acts of the Scottish Parliament in 1661 which annulled all the Acts of the Covenanting Parliament of 1640-1649.[72] His fourth son and namesake, was given three Scottish peerages in 1703 – Earl of Rosebery (from the name of a place in Dumfries-shire), Viscount of Inverkeithing and Lord Dalmeny.

The Scottish Earls of Dundonald (Cochranes) were major local landowners in Culross, with the family providing MPs for Stirling Burghs in 1791-1797 and 1800-1806. Sir Alexander Cochrane, MP for Stirling Burghs in 1800-1806, was, as a Vice-

---

[69] In 1357, by reason of the English occupation of Roxburgh and Berwick-upon-Tweed, such royal burghs were replaced by Lanark and Linlithgow in The Court of the Four Burghs

[70] Kentigern (aka Mungo) is commemorated in the arms of the City of Glasgow, of the University of Glasgow and of The High School of Glasgow. The School's modern Arms Memorial, with the Motto *Sursum Semper,* were granted by Lord Lyon King of Arms in 1919.

[71] Ben Johnson, the poet and playwright, visited the coalmines and saltpans of Culross during his walking tour of Scotland in 1618. While in Culross on a Sunday, 'he endured a long sermon, in both the morning and afternoon'. (Dr. Anna Groundwater, 'Ben Johnson in Scotland'. *History Scotland,* May/June, 2013).

[72] After the abdication by flight of James VII (and II) the Acts of 1661 were effectively repealed by the Revolutionary Parliament in 1689-1690.

Admiral, responsible for the bombardment, with rockets and bombs, of Baltimore in 1814 which prompted the poem which became *The Star Spangled Banner,* the US National Anthem – "And the rockets' red glare, the bombs bursting in the air, Gave proof through the night that our flag was still there".

South Queensferry (Gaelic *Taobh a Deas Chas Chaolais,* meaning '([Place] at the Southern Side of [the] Steep Strait [the Firth of Forth]'). It is about nine miles north-west of the centre of Edinburgh and eight miles across the Forth from the centre of Dunfermline.

Apart from the nave, which was lost in the nineteenth century, its Carmelite Friary, dating from c.1440, was restored for Episcopalian/Anglican worship in 1889. Originally a dependency of Dunfermline Abbey, the town was created a royal burgh by Charles I in 1636. (Originally in West Lothian, it has been part of the City of Edinburgh since 1975.)

'Queensferry' refers to the above-mentioned Queen Margaret who is said to have established the ferry (to/from North Queensferry) for travellers on their way from Edinburgh and the Lothians to Dunfermline and St. Andrews and vice-versa.

In early years the ferry crossing was alternatively from Dalmeny (two miles east of South Queensferry) to/from Inverkeithing. Indeed, that was the route taken by Alexander III, King of Scots one dark wet night in 1286 on his way from Edinburgh to join his second wife (to whom he had been married for less than five months) in Fife. His horse then lost its footing on an embankment near Kinghorn (10 miles east of Inverkeithing) with the King being found dead next morning with a broken neck. Dynastic instability, English intervention and the Wars of Independence followed.

The still functioning 17th century Hawes Inn in South Queensferry features in Scott's *The Antiquary* and in Stevenson's *Kidnapped*. The ferry continued to be a vital link until the opening of the Forth Rail Bridge in 1890 and was only discontinued when the Forth Road Bridge was opened in 1964. The main residence of the Scottish Earls of Hopetoun (UK Marquises of Linlithgow from 1903) is two miles to the west and that of the Scottish Earls of Rosebery at Dalmeny, two miles to the east.[73] The Dundas Estate, two miles to the south, is the location of an annual open-air passion play.

It is of interest to note that two Haldanes of Gleneagles – and, therefore, very distant relatives of Sir Henry – were MPs for Stirling Burghs in the 18th century – George Haldane in 1747-1758 and his uncle, Robert Haldane in 1758-1761. Further, two members of the family of the Primrose Earls of Rosebery were Whig MPs for Stirling Burghs with the first such, in 1819-1820, being Francis Ward Primrose, a younger son of the 3rd Earl and the second, in 1832-1847, being Archibald Primrose (known

---

[73] The Scottish Earls of Hopetoun/UK Marquises of Linlithgow are descended from Sir Thomas Hope who was Lord Advocate during the reign of Charles I. The 1st Marquis was briefly Tory Secretary for Scotland in 1905.

by his courtesy title of Lord Dalmeny). His premature death, aged 41, in 1851 resulted in his only son, another Archibald Primrose (Liberal Prime Minister in 1894-1895) succeeding directly as 5th Earl on the death of his grandfather, the 4th Earl in 1868. The 4th Earl had been given a UK peerage as Lord Rosebery in 1828 and thus his grandson entered the Lords as 2nd (UK) Lord Rosebery.[74]

Lord Dalmeny successfully contested four General Elections (1832, 1835, 1837 and 1841) and a Ministerial By-Election (later in 1835) in Stirling Burghs. While a Ministerialist as Civil Lord of the Admiralty in 1835-1841 he was subjected to the same sort of heckling by Radicals which would afflict Sir Henry's opponents in later years. On one occasion Lord Dalmeny winced under the scathing invective of the aforementioned (Chapter 2) Thomas Morrison whereas another Radical, Thomas Inglis simply asked questions and received answers, leaving the rest of the audience to judge matters for themselves.

'Did not your Lordship support the vote for £ 70,000 to build and repair stables for the horses of Her Majesty?'
'Yes, I did.'
'Did not your Lordship vote against a certain application which was made to Parliament for £ 30,000 for educational purposes?'
'Yes, I did.' [75] Both Thomas Morrison and Thomas Inglis eventually became Town Councillors and Bailies in Dunfermline.

At the 1841 General Election, by reason of his opposition to political change and his position on ecclesiastical matters. Lord Dalmeny faced serious opposition from a Radical, supported by the Presbyterian Dissenters who would unite in 1847 to form the United Presbyterian Church. Then, at the 1847 Dissolution, Lord Dalmeny stood down on the arrival of a new Radical candidate, James Benjamin Smith who in, due course, defeated the replacement Whig candidate.

J.B. Smith, a Manchester merchant and first Chairman of the Anti-Corn Law League in 1840, had been the unsuccessful Radical candidate in Dundee at the 1841 General Election. However, he stood down in Stirling Burghs at the 1852 Dissolution by reason of local hostility to his religious opinions as a Unitarian.

The new Radical candidate, Sir James Anderson, who had been knighted as Lord Provost of Glasgow in 1849, then defeated the new Whig candidate at the 1852 General Election, being returned unopposed in 1857, as also were, as Liberals, Sir James Caird in 1859 and Laurence Oliphant in 1865.

No Tory/Conservative was nominated for the constituency after 1832 until 1880 with, until then, either the unopposed election or re-election of a Whig, Radical or

---

[74] The Fourth Earl, before succeeding in 1814, had been Whig MP for Helston (Cornwall) in 1805-1806 and for Cashel (in Ireland) in 1806-1807. The Fifth Earl, the former Prime Minister, was granted three UK peerages in 1911 – Earl of Midlothian, Viscount Mentmore and Lord Epsom.

[75] Mackie (1914), pp.12-13

(after 1859) a Liberal or contests between Whigs and/or Radicals or, as at the by-election on 30 April 1868 and the General Election later that year, between two Liberals. The 1868 by-election – caused by the resignation of Laurence Oliphant – was, as anticipated in Chapter 2, contested by John Ramsay (1814-1892), a Whiggish Liberal and by a Radical Liberal, then known as Henry Campbell.

It should also be appreciated that, when Benjamin Disraeli had succeeded in February 1868 as Prime Minister of a Conservative Administration, without a majority in the House of Commons, it was understood that he would soon seek to secure a clear mandate from the electorate. However, it was also understood that he would wait until later in the year until new electoral registers were available on the basis of the provisions of the 1867 Reform Act for England and Wales and the 1868 Reform Acts for Scotland and Ireland, providing for the extension of the franchise and redistribution.

Accordingly, the Stirling Burghs by-election was contested with John Ramsay hoping to have somewhat of a walkover and thus perhaps secure an unopposed return at the forthcoming General Election while Henry Campbell's campaign was addressed not only to the current electorate but also to those who would be enfranchised later in the year when the 1867 and 1868 Acts (as converted by Liberal amendments into burgh/borough householder suffrage measures) would be implemented. Electioneering started locally in March, with by the 26th the *Stirling Observer* committed to supporting John Ramsay and by the 28th the *Dunfermline Press* committed to supporting Henry Campbell and, after referring to Ramsay's inconsistencies on such matters as the introduction of secret ballots and the disestablishment of the Church of England in Ireland, concluding –

> On personal as well as public grounds we cherish the hope that Mr. Campbell may be elected the representative of these burghs. The family to which he belongs have been long noted for their good deeds... These qualities do not in themselves entitle any man to Parliamentary honours, but, added as they are, to sound political views and considerable commercial experience, they greatly enhance our estimate of the man.

Nomination day was Tuesday, 28 April, 1868, with the proceedings taking place in Stirling and Sheriff Sconce presiding.[76] John Ramsay was accompanied by nearly seventy supporters from Stirling and Dunfermline and Henry by over ninety supporters from Stirling, Dunfermline, Inverkeithing and South Queensferry. John Ramsay was proposed by Provost Rankin of Stirling and seconded by Provost Whitelaw of Dunfermline. Henry was proposed by ex-Bailie Andrew Drummond of Stirling and seconded by ex-Provost Robertson of Dunfermline. Both candidates then made speeches, followed by a show of hands for the two candidates, which showed a majority in favour of Mr. Campbell. A poll was then demanded on behalf

---

[76] This account of the proceedings in Stirling and Dunfermline in April and May 1868 is based on the *Dunfermline Press* report of 2 May 1868.

of Mr. Ramsay and the Sheriff adjourned proceedings until polling day – with open voting – on Thursday, 30 April.

John Ramsay, who made much of a Stirling connection, drew most of his support from that Burgh being also, given his active support in Glasgow for the union of the Free and United Presbyterian Churches, warmly recommended to the clergy of such denominations in the five Burghs.

The hope for such Church Union in the 1860s was rather premature. Although there had been draft Articles of Agreement in 1864, further discussions on union were terminated in 1873 because of disagreement on the establishment question. Accordingly, the Free Church (majority) did not unite with the United Presbyterian Church, as the United Free Church, until 1900. (Refer to Table 3 in Chapter 1)

Henry drew most of his support from Dunfermline and from the electors and non-electors in the constituency who not only supported his progressive policies but objected to a candidate of the Old Whigs and the dissenting clergy being foisted upon them.

John Ramsay's Stirling connections were rather overplayed in that his mother came from the nearby Craigforth, Henry could have countered that his maternal grandmother came from the equally nearby St. Ninian's. Further, Ramsay's main business interest was in a distillery in Islay and, indeed, throughout his political career, his home address was given as Kildalton, Port Ellen, Islay.

Henry's electoral appeal in April 1886 was based on household suffrage for the counties as well as the burghs/boroughs, secret ballots, national and compulsory education, religious equality and disestablishment, self-government for the counties, local democratic control of licensing, land reform and a strong dose of anti-jingoism. All of this was a wee bit too much for the Whiggish majority in the electorate in April, although Henry's meetings were a great success, particularly with the, as yet, 'non-electors' who gave him great support.

Table 6 - Stirling Burghs - 30 April 1868 By-Election - Electorate c.1,257 (Turnout c.82.2 %)

	Stirling	Dunfermline	Culross	Inverkeithing	Queensferry	TOTAL
Ramsay	312	184	9	34	26	565 (53.4 %)
Campbell	204	251	11	17	11	494 (46.6 %)

After the result was declared at Stirling Corn Exchange, where and when only John Ramsay made a speech, Henry then came to Dunfermline where a large gathering of his supporters wanted him to speak to them from an open window in the Town House but access was denied. Accordingly, he and others had to speak from a window of the Burgh's Reading Room. Thereafter, the Radical majority in the Council passed a resolution which Provost Whitelaw and two Bailies, as supporters of John Ramsay, regarded as a vote of censure and, accordingly, resigned. Ex-Provost Robertson, Henry's seconder on 28 April, was then re-elected as Provost.

The *Stirling Observer,* published late on polling day, suggested that the result was 'conclusive enough to deter Mr. Campbell from standing again', hoped that 'some awful nonsense about Mr. Campbell's gifts and qualities as a politician will not be revived again' and referred to articles in the *Dunfermline Press,* in support of Henry, as 'simply disgraceful, brimful of lies and misrepresentations'. The *Stirling Journal (and Advertiser),* published the following day (Friday), suggested that Stirling Burghs had 'hitherto been content to be represented by men of no name and no renown' but now had, in Mr. Ramsay, a representative who 'will prove a great ornament to the House of Commons'. The *Stirling Journal* was clearly unaware of the many men of renown who had represented the constituency in the previous 160 years.

However, Henry and his core of active local supporters were in no way discouraged by the result and within two days he was committed to stand again. Thereafter he devoted himself to improving his local organisation with, for example, a local Agent, Alexander Macbeth of Dunfermline (supported by local committees) instead of Gordon Smith, a Glasgow solicitor who had been his Agent in April. Prospects in Stirling were enhanced as from a dinner there on 26 May, with ex-Bailie Drummond presiding and eighty other supporters in attendance. Thus when, as expected, Disraeli called the General Election for November/December (1868), Henry and his active supporters were well prepared.

In the meantime, Mr. Ramsay had not been particularly active and indeed it was said that, during his brief service in the Commons, he had made only one short speech, 'I'll thank you to shut that window'. (Apparently, nearly 100 years later, exactly the same was said about Commander Donaldson, David Steel's Conservative predecessor as MP for Roxburgh, Selkirk and Peebles. 'So I think it may have been in regular use as an antagonistic joke'. [Lord Steel of Aikwood, e-mail of 12 June 2013]).

On the other hand, Ramsay's supporters accused Henry of being a Tory in disguise, a more insidious way of countering his opinions with a more progressive electorate than a frontal attack.[77] Further, on 18 August one of Ramsay's supporters – signing himself 'Theodore' – published an altered version of *The Campbells are Coming* – as written by Robert Burns in 1790 – with, for example, the chorus starting 'The Campbells are coming to woe, to woe' instead of 'The Campbells are coming, Oho, Oho'.[78]

---

[77] Spender (1923), Volume 1, p.28

[78] As from a copy in the Dunfermline Carnegie Library

Nomination day for the General Election was Tuesday, 18 November, with the proceedings again taking place in Stirling and Sheriff Sconce again presiding.[79] John Ramsay was accompanied by twenty-nine supporters from Stirling and Dunfermline and Henry by thirty-four supporters from Stirling, Dunfermline and Inverkeithing.

John Ramsay was proposed by Provost Rankin of Stirling and seconded by ex-Provost Whitelaw of Dunfermline. Henry was proposed by ex-Bailie Andrew Drummond of Stirling and seconded by Provost Robertson of Dunfermline. Both candidates then made speeches with that by Henry including the following statement –

> Now some of my kind friends in the crowd say I'm a Tory. Well, my father is a Tory and I am proud of him, and my brother is a Tory and I am not ashamed of him. My father is, as you well know, because you have been told it, chairman to the Tory candidate for Glasgow, and my brother is chairman of the [Tory] Lord Advocate's Committee of Glasgow University. Therefore, they say I am a Tory.
>
> I would like to see the man who would come to my face and tell me that. All I can say is this, that if I am a Tory in disguise, I would be unfit for my position, but in the proof of the fact that I am not a Jesuit [Judas?], as my opponents suppose, I may add that this morning I took the trouble of going to Glasgow and recording my votes for the Liberal candidates.[80]

A show of hands was then taken for the two candidates, which the Sheriff declared was in favour of Mr. Campbell. A poll was then demanded on behalf of Mr. Ramsay and the Sheriff then adjourned proceedings until polling day – again with open voting – on Thursday, 20 November.

More positively, during his campaign, to his policies of six months earlier, Henry added his specific support for the Liberal intention to disestablish the Church of England in Ireland and expressed his support for Mr. Gladstone on that and other issues. Gladstone had become Leader in the Commons when Viscount Palmerston died in October 1865 and *de facto* overall Liberal Leader from December 1867 when the 1st Earl Russell (formerly Lord John Russell) resigned the overall leadership in that month.

> [Thus his eve-of-poll speech concluded] Now, gentlemen, some time ago you had an election here, and at that election I failed to get a majority of the suffrages. Against that decision as representing the opinions of the peoples of the Burghs this candidature of mine is, of

---

[79] This account of the proceedings in Stirling and Dunfermline in November 1868 is based on the report in the *Stirling Journal (and Advertiser)* of 20 November 1868.

[80] The 1868 result in Glasgow, a three-member constituency in 1868-1885, was 18,287, 18,062 and 17,803 (Liberals elected) and 10,820 (Conservative)

course, an open protest. I know that I possess the sympathy and the goodwill of the working-classes of the Burghs. I say I know it. Not that I hope for it – I say I have it. And there has been nothing that has occurred during the last six months which has belied that conviction. Wherever I have gone I have been received with the greatest kindness and hearty goodwill, and in every part of the constituency the general public have crowned me with honours I have done nothing to deserve. All that I want from you is to afford me the opportunity of deserving this honour. Entrust your Parliamentary interests to me. I promise to devote myself to your service and to show by my conduct that I reciprocate the great sympathy, kindness, and confidence which you have placed in me.[81]

Henry's tactics in appealing at both elections to the new electors of November 1868 were vindicated in that, with also an increase in the turnout, he now secured the support of over 60 % of such electors. Indeed, *The Stirling Journal* admitted that 'Mr. Campbell was right in appealing from the old constituency [electorate] to the new one' (20 November 1868).

Table 7 - Stirling Burghs - Thursday, 20 November 1868 General Election - Electorate 4,372 (Turnout 88.8 %)						
	Stirling	Dunfermline	Culross	Inverkeithing	Queensferry	TOTAL
Campbell	759	1,224	26	105	87	2,201 (56.7 %)
Ramsay	752	687	85	143	65	1,682 (43.3 %)

The result was known unofficially in Stirling shortly after the close of poll at 4.00 p.m. and Henry then spoke from a window in the Golden Lion Hotel –

> Ladies and Gentlemen – for I perceive there are some of the fair sex present (Loud cheers). Men and women of Stirling, I do not know really what to say to thank you for the honour, the great honour, you have conferred upon me (Renewed and prolonged cheering).
>
> It is certainly a great honour to be called a Member of Parliament; but it is a greater honour to represent a constituency such as this; and furthermore it is a still greater honour to have the majority of the suffrages in both the principal burghs – Stirling and Dunfermline. (Loud cheers). I thank you, gentlemen from the bottom of my heart for the hearty reception you have given me, and the honour you have crowned me with (Loud cheer) and, above all, for the great victory you working men have delivered in the present contest.[82]

---

[81] Mackie (1914), 23-24

[82] *The Glasgow Herald,* 21 November 1868

Henry arrived in Dunfermline mid-evening and, this time, was allowed to speak from a window in the Town House. However, as very few of the very large crowd could hear what was being said, he was carried shoulder-high to his hotel, suffering en route with a torn coat and a battered hat. He was then able to speak to a considerable number of his supporters in the hotel (Mr. Milne's)

Immediately after the official declaration in Stirling next morning, Henry made his first speech as officially a member of Parliament, concluding –

> I can make no return for what you have done except one, and that is to endeavour to do my duty to the best of my ability. You may depend upon this, that I shall act up to all the principles I have professed and that nothing will deter me from that which I think right, and that which the constituency desire. I do not wish to say any more, but from the bottom of my heart I am grateful for the great honour you have conferred upon me.[83]

The *Dunfermline Press* (21 November 1868) stated that 'in electing Mr. Campbell, the Burghs have done honour to themselves, as well as to him. There are many questions which Mr. Campbell has already pledged himself to support, and not the least important of these are education and vote by ballot. His earnest promotion of these will confirm the sympathy which already exists between him and the working classes. [In conclusion] A Member who has obtained so large a share of the suffrage of his constituency, is not likely to be disturbed in a seat which has been so honourably and so triumphantly won'.

However, The *Stirling Observer* (26 November 1868) was not too happy with the result, expressing surprise that the electors should have 'without any tangible cause or complaint, ousted an old, staunch and experienced Liberal and placed in his stead the scion of a Tory family, but said-to-be a converted Radical'.

Thus the start of Henry's nearly forty years of representation of the constituency. He had given an assurance that, if elected, he would make such business arrangements as were necessary to enable him to be a full-time MP. Indeed, his father and brother, far from resenting his break from their Tory politics, did everything possible to ensure that he had every opportunity to succeed in his chosen career.

So much so that when Henry returned briefly to Glasgow, before Parliament assembled on 10 December, Sir James and James Alexander Campbell attended a complimentary dinner for Henry held in the Western Club, with representatives of Glasgow's ecclesiastical, municipal, business, educational and legal communities, including both Liberals and Tories.

---

[83] *Stirling Observer,* 26 November 1868

On that occasion, the chairman for the evening was Lord Provost Sir William Lumsden – another Glasgow High School Former Pupil and Chairman of the Clydesdale Bank – who also proposed a toast to the health of the new MP's father. The conclusion of Sir James' speech in reply is worthy of note.

> There are those in this company, and others scattered over the nations of the earth, I may say, who are rejoicing in the fete of this evening, and I am sure that so far as they have succeeded, and many have succeeded well in the world, I rejoice and glory in their success. With regard to any interest I have taken in the municipal affairs of Glasgow, or in the interests and prosperity of Glasgow, I have no hesitation in saying that Glasgow owes me nothing. I owe it a great deal. I think that the business with which I am connected has been carried on the very shoulders of the friendship and confidence of the citizens of Glasgow,[84]

For Henry an early constituency priority was to reconcile the rival Liberal factions in the Burghs and thus to ensure that, in the future, he would not be challenged by other Liberal candidates. Most of Ramsay's supporters, including ex-Provost Whitelaw, were soon 'converted' and some remained among Henry's most faithful supporters to the end of his or their lives.

The legal firm in Dunfermline, which had provided Ramsay with his Agent at both elections in 1868, thereafter represented Henry in the person of (Sir) John Ross who continued as Henry's Dunfermline Agent until 1886 when he was succeeded by David Gorrie. Sir John went on to be Chairman and Treasurer of the Carnegie Trusts. Some thirty years later it was said that what Henry accomplished by way of party unity in his own constituency justified the hope that he would achieve, as he did, overall party unity when he became Leader and Prime Minister.

John Ramsay was thereafter Liberal MP for Falkirk Burghs [also including Airdrie, Hamilton, Lanark and Linlithgow] from February 1874 to June 1886, with a short break later in 1874 when he was disqualified by reason of being a Government contractor, being returned unopposed at the subsequent by-election. He received the Freedom of Linlithgow in November 1876 for his services as an MP in securing compensation for the Burgh for its losses under the Roads and Bridges Act. Prior to the 1885 General Election he had to contend with the challenge of two other would-be Liberal candidates. Hamilton Liberal Association did not want Ramsay and nominated J. Roskill who withdrew after arbitration by the Scottish Liberal Association but his name remained on the ballot papers and he polled 14 votes. Another Liberal, J.G. Weir would not accept arbitration and polled 814 votes as an Independent Liberal, with Ramsay polling 3,104 against the Conservative's 2,204.

Ramsay became a Liberal Unionist in 1886 but did not contest that year's General Election when Falkirk Burghs was won by another Liberal Unionist with a majority

---

[84] Online *Glasgow Digital Library – Memoirs and Portraits of 100 Glasgow Men – 19*

of 19 over his Liberal opponent. Apparently, in 1887, John Ramsay was spotted by Henry in Stirling, having just given £ 1.000 to the Town Council for education in the Burgh. However, whatever the accuracy of Henry's surmise as to his motives, Mr. Ramsay died, aged 78, just before the next (1892) General Election when Henry was opposed by another Liberal Unionist.

A continuing constituency priority for Henry – in addition to exemplary attention to correspondence, printed communications, supplying his town councils with copies of Bills and Blue Books, responding to specific requests and invitations and the like – was to set up a system of regular stewardship exchanges (which he called colloquys) with his constituents (supporters and opponents), centred on, in each of the five Burghs, an annual public meeting followed by an informal house meeting with the leading citizens of the Burgh, with also walk-abouts and house calls. The annual Stewardship Meetings were held on a non-party basis – for example, the Dunfermline meeting in 1894 was chaired by Provost Walker, a Unionist'.

Henry was equally at home in his fireside chats in Culross, in his exchanges with South Queensferry fishermen, with shipbuilding workers in Inverkeithing as at large meetings in Stirling and Dunfermline. From time-to-time he was also able to share his artistic and literary interests with his constituents. As already mentioned (Chapter 2), on one occasion he lectured on Michelangelo at a meeting of the Dunfermline Literary Society.

> The sketch he presented of [Michelangelo] this marvellous genius, bore the impress of enthusiasm for a character representing his 'own ideal knight'. He reviewed his hero's achievements as scholar, painter, sculptor, engineer and philosopher; and, remarking it was rare to find in one man such a combination of gifts, he said Italy might well claim him as the noblest heritage of her children, while men of all nationalities might strive to imitate his example.
>
> He pictured him not as 'The Happy Warrior' but as 'the perfect gentleman', as a man and a citizen, pure, temperate and unblemished; proud and independent where duty called for the assertion of his position; generous, open and earnest; humble and lovely in his devotion to duty; true to his country; true and tender to his friends. Are not these the characteristics of a perfect gentleman? [85]

Apart from anything else, this approach and diligence, supported by his personal kindliness, sincerity, geniality and wit, not only saved him from the electoral vicissitudes which afflicted so many other prominent politicians but also ensured that he had a solid base on which his reputation throughout Scotland and at Westminster would be based.

---

[85] Mackie (1914), pp.46-47

Such past, present and future Prime Ministers as Russell, Palmerston, Gladstone, Balfour, Asquith, Law, MacDonald, Churchill, Macmillan and Douglas-Home all suffered defeat, some more than once, in their constituencies after their first election as MPs, as also such (other) Liberal Leaders as Samuel, Sinclair and Thorpe. Further, Russell represented no fewer than seven different constituencies, Palmerston six, Gladstone five and Churchill four during their political careers.

Otherwise, his constituency organisation was centred on the Liberal Associations in Stirling, Dunfermline (including Culross and Inverkeithing) and South Queensferry, with Election Committees based in Stirling and Dunfermline. With Alexander, Macbeth, (Sir) John Ross and then David Gorrie as his Agents in Dunfermline, Robert Taylor was his Agent in Stirling from 1886 onwards.

His Election Committee Chairmen included, over the years, Andrew Drummond, Andrew Young and (Sir) James B. Smith in Stirling and Provost Robertson and his son, (Sir) William Robertson in Dunfermline. Sir William was later Vice-Chairman of the Carnegie Trusts, Lord Lieutenant of Fife and Chairman of the Scottish Liberal Federation.

Strangely enough, not until after Sir Henry's death was a unified Stirling Burghs Liberal Association set up 'to be representative of all the [five] burghs' which would be enabled 'to give expression to its views and to take concerted action with regard to a candidate in a more businesslike way than had been the case in the past'. (19 November 1908), [86] This was presumably an indication of some local disquiet as to the way in which in which Sir Henry's successor as Liberal Candidate [and MP] had been 'selected' in April 1908.

(Sir) Henry was also scrupulous in avoiding any accusations of corrupt practices. Indeed, only three significant gifts to his constituents are recorded. In 1875 he donated a trophy – the Campbell-Bannerman Challenge Cup – for annual competition between the Bowling Clubs of Stirling and Dunfermline. (The competition continues to this day, with the Cup currently [2018] held by Dunfermline Bowling Club). In 1890 he contributed to the cost of an extension to Stirling High School (then in Spittal Street) which enabled the building of an observatory tower and dome which gave the pupils a head start in the study of astronomy. (The Building is now occupied by The Stirling Highland Hotel which continues to feature a working Observatory). In 1897 when opening the triennial Stirling Fine Art Association Exhibition in the Smith Institute (now the Stirling Smith Art Gallery and Museum) he bought a sea-scape painting by the Scottish artist, T. Campbell Noble and presented it to the Institute.

He was re-elected for Stirling Burghs on eleven occasions. He was returned unopposed at three General Elections (1874, 1885 and 1906) and at three Ministerial By-Elections (1880, 1884 and 1886). He was virtually unopposed at another General

---

[86] As quoted in Hutchison (1986), p.231

Election (1880) when his Conservative opponent withdrew after nomination. He defeated Liberal Unionists at three General Elections (1886, 1892 and 1900) and another Conservative at the 1895 General Election.

During his thirty-nine years and five months as a Member of Parliament, Sir Henry was a Government back-bencher for approx. three years, a Junior Minister for approx. seven years, an opposition front-bench spokesman for approx twenty-three years (including just under six years as Liberal Leader in the Commons) and for approx. six years as a Cabinet Minister (including two years and four months as Prime Minister).

It is of interest to compare the Stirling Burghs electorate of 4,372 in November 1868 with the local statistics from the Census three years later.

Table 8 - Stirling Burghs - 1871 Census					
	Population			Houses	Families
	Males	Females	Total		
Culross	201	266	467	108	138
Dunfermline	6,783	8,200	14,983	1,638	3,486
Inverkeithing	856	889	1,745	300	480
South Queensferry	735	786	1,521	139	335
Stirling	6,670	7,609	14,279	1,481	3,261
	15,245	17,750	32,995	3,666	7,701

Thus, there must have been over 1,000 electors in November 1868 who qualified other than on the basis of adult male householder suffrage and also a large number of sub-tenants who were not qualified as electors.

4 – 1868-1880 – Parliament, Government and Opposition

A – 1868-1874 – Parliament, Government (Junior Office) and Change of Surname

Table 9 - The 1868 General Election - 17 to 30 November (to 7 December)												
Candidates (Unopposed), Percentages and MPs Elected												
	England				Wales				Scotland			
Liberals	412	(46)	59.7	244	29	(10)	62.1	23	70	(23)	82.5	51
Conservatives	334	(54)	40.2	211	20	(4)	37.9	10	20	(3)	17.5	7
Others	1	(0)	0.1									
	747	(100)		455	49	(14)		33	90	(26)		58
	Ireland				Universities				UNITED KINGDOM			
Liberals	85	(41)	57.9	66	4	(1)	44.6	3	600	(121)	61.5	387
Conservatives	53	(26)	41.9	37	9	(4)	55.4	6	436	(91)	38.4	271
Others	2	(0)	0.2						3	(0)	0.1	
	140	(67)		103	13	(5)		9	1039	(212)		658

Net Gains/Losses in MPs Elected compared to the 1865 General Election

	England	Wales	Scotland	Ireland	Universities	UK
Liberals	minus 7	plus 5	plus 9	plus 8	plus 3	plus 18
Conservatives	minus 2	minus 4	minus 4	minus 8		minus 18

Stirling Burghs - Electorate 4,372

Henry Campbell	Liberal	2,201
John Ramsay	Liberal	1,682

Lancashire South Western (Two Members) Electorate 21,261			Greenwich (Two Members) Electorate 15,581		
R.A. Cross	Conservative	7,729	D. Solomons	Liberal	6.684
C. Turner	Conservative	7.676	W.E. Gladstone	Liberal	6,386
W.E, Gladstone	Liberal	7,415	Sir H.W. Parker	Conservative	4,704
H.R. Grenfell	Liberal	6.939	Viscount Mahon	Conservative	4,372

Accordingly, Disraeli and his minority Conservative Government resigned before the new House of Commons met on 10 December and Gladstone (aged 59) formed his first administration. Gladstone, having been the only Liberal MP for the three-member constituency of South Lancashire in 1865-1868, was defeated in the new two-member constituency of South-West Lancashire. However, he was elected as the second-placed Liberal in the two-member constituency of Greenwich which he continued to represent until 1880.

Oxford and Cambridge Universities and Trinity College, Dublin each continued to elect two MPs. Three new single-member University constituencies were created – London, Edinburgh & St. Andrews and Glasgow & Aberdeen. Each of such elected a Liberal MP, with Robert Lowe (London), who was about to become Chancellor of the Exchequer, being unopposed. Otherwise, the number of English MPs was reduced by nine, with one extra MP for Wales (in Merthyr Tydfil) and five for Scotland (in Dundee, Glasgow, Aberdeenshire, Ayrshire and Lanarkshire).

The 1868 General Election also marked the appearance of the first Liberal/Labour candidate on the electoral scene in the two-member constituency of Tower Hamlets in London. From 1869 onwards, such candidates were sponsored by the Labour Representation League formed by trade union leaders to promote the registration of working men as voters irrespective of their political opinions and also to secure the election of working men as MPs.

With the exception of Tower Hamlets in 1868 and 1880 and Southwark in 1870 and 1874, all Liberal/Labour candidates stood without (other) Liberal opposition and all the Liberal/Labour MPs elected from 1874 onwards took the Liberal Whip. Indeed, in 1875, it was formally stated that the League was allied to the Liberal Party.[87]

This being the last General Election with open voting, it is possible, as from the poll books, to analyse the voting in the two new Scottish University constituencies.

	Table 10 - Scottish Universities - 1868 General Election -					
	Edinburgh & St. Andrews	Glasgow & Aberdeen	TOTAL	Church of Scotland Ministers	Other Presbyterian Ministers	Others
Liberal	2,322	2,067	4,389	67	1,081	3,241
Conservative	2,067	2,020	4,087	1,221	34	2,832

The Other Presbyterian Ministers were mainly of the Free and United Presbyterian Churches. (Refer also to Table 3 in Chapter 1) The Others (otherwise mainly members of other professions) included 82 Episcopalian clergy of whom 78 voted Conservative and 4 Liberal. Such alignments were significant, given the correlation between denominational affiliation and party political allegiance in Scotland for most of the 19th century. (Refer also to Appendix 2)

Organisationally, given Disraeli's intention to improve Conservative organisation particularly in the urban constituencies, the National Union of Conservative Associations had been formed in 1867. However, this was too recently to have much impact in 1868. On the other hand, the Liberal Registration Association, as formed in 1860, was beginning to develop into the Liberal Central Association as it was renamed in 1874. This was eventually under the control of the Chief Whip in the Commons, with responsibility for assisting constituency associations in such matters as candidatures and, to a very limited extent, financially. There would be other significant Liberal organisational developments during the next (1874-1880) Parliament.

Also, in December 1868 Henry and Charlotte moved into 60 Queen's Gate which was to be their London home until 1872. All their London homes were leased – usually from the Grosvenor Estates – and not purchased outright. Henry soon joined five London Clubs – Athenaeum, Devonshire, Brooks, Oxford & Cambridge (which

---

[87] Boothroyd (2001), p.142

he used mainly for lunching) and the Reform. In due course, he also joined or was associated with the Scottish Liberal Club (founded in Edinburgh in 1879), the National Liberal Club in London (of which he was a founding member in 1882), the Glasgow Liberal Club (founded in 1887) and the Dunfermline and Stirling Liberal Clubs. He was eventually President of both the Scottish and Dunfermline Clubs, being also, at one time, a member of the Glasgow Club's Committee. In London, the Reform Club and the National Liberal Club were mainly used by Henry, particularly in later years, for party political purposes.[88] Before the creation of central political organisations with premises in London, the Conservative Carlton Club (founded in 1832) and the Liberal Reform Club (founded in 1836) provided offices for their parties, complete with printing presses and facilities for franking mail.[89]

The National Liberal Club had its origins in the Radical Club, of which Henry is listed as a member in 1871. The other thirty or so members, men and women, listed in that year included John Stuart Mill, Millicent Garret Fawcett (for whom refer also to Chapter 9) and such (other) future Liberal Cabinet Ministers as Sir Charles Dilke, John Morley and (Sir) George Otto Trevelyan. During the Parliamentary session, the members of the Club, as founded in 1870, met for dinner on Sunday evenings in an inn in London or along the Thames, with dinner followed by the reading of a paper on a current political topic or opportunity for action which was then debated by the members present.[90]

In the new Liberal Government's early years Irish affairs dominated, with Henry supporting all legislative initiatives. The Church of England in Ireland was disestablished in 1869. The 1871 Irish Land Act sought to respond to the grievances of Irish tenant farmers by providing compensation for unfair eviction and for improvements to farms undertaken by tenants. However, the Land Act was considered too moderate by majority opinion in Ireland as it did not provide for fair rents and fixity of tenure.

The 1873 Irish Universities Bill was defeated by three votes in the Commons due to forty-three (mainly Irish) Liberal MPs voting with the Conservatives as the Bill did not provide for a state-funded Roman Catholic university.[91] (Gladstone attempted to

---

[88] The Reform Club has in its Coffee Room a portrait of Sir Henry by J.H.F. Bacon. The National Liberal Club has a portrait of Sir Henry by B. Morgan (after J.C. Forbes).

[89] Coincidentally, Henry's brother's father-in-law, [Sir] Morton Peto was one of the contractors for building the Reform Club in 1836 and the Oxford & Cambridge Club in 1836-1838. He was also one of the contractors for building the superstructure of the new Houses of Parliament as begun in 1840.

[90] Harvie (1976), pp.187 and 262

[91] The successful Liberal Irish Universities Bill which was enacted in 1908, but after Sir Henry's death, created the federal National University of Ireland and gave Queen's College, Belfast separate university status. Roman Catholics were also given enhanced access to university education in Ireland. In 1918, the National University and Queen's University, Belfast were given the stuns of single-member constituencies, with Trinity College, Dublin continuing to elect two MPs.

resign after this defeat but, as Disraeli would not take office, the resignation was withdrawn.)

This loss of support led to most Irish Liberal MPs elected in 1868 contesting the 1874 General Election as candidates of the new Irish Home Rule Party or being defeated by such candidates. This had disastrous consequences for the Victorian Liberal Party in Ireland, reaching a nadir at the 1886 General Election, when there was only one Liberal candidate in Ireland.

Henry's maiden speech on 17 June 1869 was in seconding a procedural amendment, moved by Dr. Lyon Playfair (Liberal MP for Edinburgh & St. Andrews Universities, 1868-1885), to delay for three months further consideration of the Government's Endowed Hospitals (Scotland) Bill. The Bill, which had the backing of the Edinburgh Merchant Company, concerned endowed schools in Scotland – such as George Heriot's in Edinburgh – which were known as Hospitals. The purpose of the amendment was to give the Government time to consider criticisms of the Bill before it returned to the House of Commons.

> [Mr. Campbell said] what appeared to him to be the great objection to the Bill was the fact that it was suited only to those institutions which were anxious to reform themselves.... If the Bill passed into law, there would be spasmodic efforts enough, but no uniform system of administering the funds. The whole circumstances of the case were such as to render obvious the necessity for immediate inquiry.... the insertion of clauses in this measure, such as had been suggested... might make it more effectual in developing those great forces that were latent in Scotland for informing the ignorance, and, to a certain extent, relieving the necessities of the people.

After a short debate, in which five other MPs took part, Dr. Playfair's amendment was, by leave, withdrawn. Accordingly, consideration of the Bill resumed on the following Monday, with the royal assent being granted on 26 July.

Given Henry's close connection with Meigle, Perthshire as from late 1884, it is of interest to note that Dr. Playfair's grandfather, the Rev. Dr. James Playfair, was Parish Minister of Meigle in 1775-1800. (Refer also to Chapter 6) Further, the son of Sir Edward Colebrooke, who also took part in the debate, would as a Lord-in-Waiting, (as appointed by Henry, as Prime Minister, in February 1906) represent King Edward at Lady Campbell-Bannerman's funeral in Meigle in September 1906. (Refer also to Chapter 12)

Twelve days later (29 June), Henry spoke in an early debate on the successful Bill, as enacted in 1871, which abolished most of the remaining religious tests for the English Universities. His speech including such comments as that 'not only do these Universities [Oxford and Cambridge] with a maximum of endowments educate a minimum of the young men of the nation, but to those young men they afford a minimum of education at a maximum of expense'. He also questioned the value of what he described as cursory religious education at Oxford and Cambridge for undergraduates generally. He concluded, 'We wish to see the Universities thrown altogether open to the nation, and thus, while the nation derives the full benefits of the high traditional position of these great institutions, my hope is that the freer and fuller life of the nation will in turn react on the Universities and render them better qualified to fill their high position'. Significantly, this was all in the hearing of Gladstone who was devoted to Oxford University and had been one of its MPs in 1847-1865. Further, *Hansard* reported Henry's speech in the first person, an unusual compliment in the mid-19th century.

A month later (27 July) Henry did not proceed with a motion, of which he had given notice, regretting that the Scottish Parochial Schools Bill, while providing for compulsory rating for educational purposes, did not include 'the power of enforcing the attendance of children at school'. Nevertheless, he took the opportunity to deride Conservative opposition to compulsory education, citing the examples of other European countries and also stating that there was no fear of compulsory education in Scotland.

In 1870 Henry voted in favour of Jacob Bright's unsuccessful Bill for women's suffrage – a cause to which he (Henry) adhered consistently throughout his parliamentary career. (Jacob Bright, a younger brother of John Bright, was then one of Manchester's two Liberal MPs.)

In the following year (27 February 1871) Henry spoke in favour of the (Scotland) Act 1872Scottish Education Bill. This, when enacted in 1872, brought parochial schools and many other schools within a new state system with also the creation of directly-elected local school boards. In particular, with regard to that part of the Bill which allowed compulsory powers, he thought (as he had said in 1869) that 'Scotland [was] perfectly ripe for universal compulsion'. Indeed, he thought the Bill 'was the most statesmanlike measure for education which had been presented to Parliament for many years'.

In the same month (February 1871) he spoke in favour of the unsuccessful Deceased Wife's Sister's Marriage Bill – to allow widowers to marry their deceased wife's sister – and assured the House that majority Scottish opinion was not unfavourable. No doubt, Henry's early and continuing support for such legislation helped see through a successful Bill when he was Prime Minister in 1907.[92]

In Henry's early years as an MP, his reputation as a coming man was greatly helped by the extent of the coverage of his speeches by *The Scotsman* and *The Glasgow Herald,* both then Liberal newspapers. Stirling was a dividing point between their base circulation areas (and thus a circulation battleground). Both were also anxious to secure an increase in their sales in the Fife Burghs. Thus Henry enjoyed much

---

[92] Although in Scotland a man was not allowed to marry his deceased wife's sister as from the 1567 Scottish Marriage Act, such a marriage, although prohibited in the Anglican Book of Common Prayer, was not absolutely void in the rest of the UK and the colonies until the 1835 Marriage Act. Thus, for example, the artist Holman Hunt had to go to Switzerland to marry Edith Waugh in 1875 after the death of his first wife, Fanny Waugh, her sister in 1866.

more attention in the Edinburgh and Glasgow based press than most Scottish members, other than those representing such cities.[93]

Also in early 1871 the House of Commons voted on an allowance for Princess Louise (1848-1939), fourth daughter of Queen Victoria on her marriage to John Campbell (1845-1914), son and heir of the 8th (Scottish) Duke of Argyll, then a Liberal Cabinet Minister.[94]

After the vote Henry was at a dinner when John Stuart Mill (previously Liberal MP for Westminster in 1865-1868) said that the Duke was rich enough to provide for a royal daughter-in-law without help from the taxpayer. Henry then said that, as a Scotsman and a Campbell, he thought that Scotland was entitled to what she could out of England, and that he was only sorry that the vote for the allowance had not been larger. As Henry said later, 'Mill looked daggers at me and seemed to be wondering who was this flippant Philistine who has found his way into the Holy of Holies'. (CB/BL – Memo. by Henry Higgs)

In later years Henry (in London and at Balmoral and overseas) and Charlotte (in London and overseas) met and made friends with Princess Louise (Duchess of Argyll from 1900). They often dined with her at Kensington Palace and she sent personal wreaths for Charlotte's and Sir Henry's funerals at Meigle on 5 September 1906 and 28 April 1908.

It may have been such friendship with Princess Louise and thus Henry's good offices which led to her appointment as the President of Glasgow's Queen Margaret College (for the higher education of Women). One of the College's founders in 1883 was Mrs. Jessie Campbell, the wife of his cousin, James Campbell of Tullichewan. Indeed, the Princess and Mrs. Campbell were present when Queen Victoria paid a brief visit to the College on the occasion of her final visit to Glasgow in August 1888 for the opening of the new City Chambers in George Square and the International Exhibition in Kelvingrove Park.[95] (Refer to Chapter 8 for the Liberal opinions of Princess Louise and her good offices in connection with Henry's relations with her mother, Queen Victoria).

Henry's maternal uncle, Henry Bannerman died on 13 September (1871), leaving Henry a life interest in his estate at Hunton near Maidstone in Kent provided that,

---

[93] Mackie (1914), pp.33-34

[94] John Campbell was then known by his courtesy title of Marquis of Lorne. The marriage (which was childless) took place at Windsor on 21 May 1871. The Marquis was Liberal MP for Argyll in 1868-1878, Governor-General of Canada (appointed, on Queen's Victoria's 'recommendation' by Disraeli) in 1878-1883 and Liberal Unionist MP for Manchester South from 1895 until he succeeded as 9th (Scottish) Duke and 2nd (UK) Duke of Argyll on 24 April 1900. After the Canadian years the couple lived mostly apart.

[95] Urquhart (2000), pp.80-81

within 18 months, he adopted the surname Bannerman instead of, or in addition to, Campbell. Henry reluctantly complied in 1872, by changing his surname to Campbell-Bannerman by royal licence. Charlotte was even more reluctant and, for some time thereafter, continued to use the signature 'Charlotte Campbell'.

Thus the Campbell-Bannermans were enabled to take over the property which included a number of valuable farms, 150 acres of garden and parkland and lakes covering over two acres.[96] However, most of the rental income went on providing new cottages for the tenants and on estate management, with not much left for the Campbell-Bannermans. The bailiff is said to have left £ 10,000 for each of his ten children – in total £ 100,000 compared to the net total of £38,000 which Sir Henry left on his death.[97]

After Sir Henry's death in 1908, the outright ownership of the Hunton estate passed to James Campbell-Bannerman (son of Sir Henry's sister, Louisa and their cousin, James Alexander Bannerman), with their daughter, Joan marrying Geoffrey Charles Devas in 1916. With the exception of a Lodge (Grove Lodge in Grove Lane) the residue of the estate was recently sold out of the family.

The main house, Hunton Court was occupied (until 1894) by Henry's uncle's widow. So the Campbell-Bannermans took over, as their only country home until 1887, another house on the estate, called Gennings. However, they normally only lived in the house at weekends when they were otherwise based in London. Writing in 1938, Mr. J. Bartholomew, a former choirboy in Hunton, recalled the presence in the local church of 'Henry Campbell-Bannerman and some members of one of Gladstone's Cabinets'.[98]

Henry, who became a JP (Justice of the Peace) for Kent,[99] was also for some years President of the Kent Liberal Association. When at Gennings he identified himself with the Liberals of Maidstone. Maidstone's Liberal MP in 1870-1880 was Sir John Lubbock, afterwards MP for London University as a Liberal in 1880-1886 and as a Liberal Unionist from 1886 until he was created 1st Lord Avebury in 1900. (Eric Lubbock, Liberal MP for Orpington in 1962-1970, succeeded as 4th Lord Avebury in 1971)

---

[96] The lands of Hunton have an interesting history. Originally (11th century) *Huntindune* – 'huntsman's [or huntsmen's] homestead [or enclosure]' – at one time the Lords of the Manor were the monks of Christ Church Priory, Canterbury. In the 16th century Hunton was given, by Henry VIII, to Sir Thomas Wyatt, High Sheriff of Kent, whose son and namesake was executed for treason during the reign of Mary Tudor. The lands were then forfeited to the Crown until granted, by Elizabeth Tudor, to Sir John Baker (of Sissinghurst) who was followed by a succession of landowners until the acquisition by Henry Bannerman. The main house, Hunton Court was built in the late 18th century (on the same site as earlier houses including the immediately preceding Court-Lodge, with alterations and additions in about 1850

[97] Wilson (1973), p.122

[98] Morey (2000), pp.10-11.

[99] (Sir) Henry was also a JP for Lanarkshire.

(There is a Plaque in the vicinity of St. Mary's Church in Hunton commemorating Sir Henry as a local landlord in 1872-1908. His maternal uncle, Henry Bannerman is buried in the Churchyard.)

However, within three years of his first election as an MP, Henry was, in November 1871, appointed Financial Secretary at the War Office. This was a new appointment – which was part of a scheme to reform War Office administration and stop bickering between departments – involved responsibility for the Estimates, ongoing War Office finances and the Army Pay Department. This followed the appointment of John Vivian, a former Captain in the Royal Hussars, a Whig MP in 1841-1847 and 1857-1859 and a Liberal MP from 1865, as Permanent Under-Secretary at the War Office three months earlier.

Henry was initially somewhat concerned that, by joining the Government, his loss of independence would not be appreciated by his constituents. However, he was soon made aware that his selection for office strengthened rather than weakened his reputation in the constituency, bringing honour to it as well as to its MP. There was even talk locally that he was now well on the way to being Chancellor of the Exchequer and then Prime Minister. On the other hand, Henry gave an assurance that if ever what was required of him in office conflicted with the interests of his constituents or the principles which he professed, he would not hesitate to resign from office.[100]

Henry joined the War Office at a time of extensive Army reforms known as the 'Cardwell Reforms', all of which he supported, initially as a back-bencher and then as a Junior Minister. Edward Cardwell (1813-1886), a former Peelite, had been Secretary of State for War, since the formation of the Cabinet in December 1868, (Cardwell had significant Scottish connections in that he had married, in 1838, Annie Parker, a lady from Fairlie in Ayrshire and, in 1852, had unsuccessfully contested the Ayrshire county constituency.) There were two Under Secretaries, both in the House of Lords, at the War Office in 1868-1874. Firstly, in 1868-1872, Thomas George Baring, 2nd Lord Northbrook, under whom Henry would serve at the Admiralty in 1882-1884.[101] Secondly, in 1872-1874, Charles Petty-Fitzmaurice, 5th Marquis of Lansdowne (a Liberal Unionist from 1886) who, as Unionist Leader in the Lords, would mention this early association with Henry when paying tribute to him after his death in 1908.

The earliest of the Cardwell reforms was the abolition of flogging in peace-time in 1868 (with flogging in war-time not abolished until 1880). In 1869 troops were withdrawn from self-governing colonies which were encouraged to raise their own local forces. In 1870 bounty money for recruits was abolished. The basis of enlistment was also changed so that a soldier could serve for six years as a regular followed by six years in the reserves during which he was paid for attending a short

---

[100] Mackie (1914), p.37
[101] Thomas George Baring, 2nd Lord Northbrook should not be confused with his cousin, Evelyn Baring, 1st Earl of Cromer as did John Wilson (1973), p.438. After being Viceroy of India for four years from 1872, Lord Northbrook was created 1st Earl Northbrook in 1876.

annual period of training. In 1871 the UK was divided into districts within which all line infantry regiments had a depot and a recruitment area. All infantry regiments were also to have two battalions, one serving overseas and one stationed at home for training.

Henry's arrival at the War Office coincided with the abolition of the sale of Army commissions on 1 November 1871. (The sale of commissions applied only up to the rank of Colonel in infantry and cavalry regiments and, therefore, not to the Royal Engineers or the Royal Artillery [or to the Royal Navy]. For example, the cost of promotion from Captain to Major was £ 3,500 in the Guards, £ 1,750 in the Household Cavalry, £ 1,400 in other infantry regiments and £ 1,350 in other cavalry regiments.)

All such reforms were opposed by the ultra-conservative Army officers, led by the Commander-in-Chief, Prince George, Duke of Cambridge, the Queen's cousin. He was not to be deposed until his retirement was arranged by Sir Henry himself as Secretary of State for War in 1895. Indeed, many of the reforms, such as the sale of commissions, had to be implemented by Order in Council such was the extent of the obstruction tactics pursued by Conservative opposition in the Lords.

Nevertheless, the extremities of Military Law continued to be inflicted until, after modifications in 1925 and 1928, Parliament in 1930, removed cowardice and desertion from the Army's list of capital sanctions, effectively limited its use of capital punishment to the same offences as carried that sanction for civilians. The barbarity of what was known as Field Punishment No.1 had earlier (in 1923) been abolished by the Army Council. This followed an inquiry prompted by an amendment to the annual Army Bill moved by Major Evan Hayward (Liberal MP for Seaham. County Durham) in 1918-1922. (Refer to Clive Emsley on 'Why Crucify Tommy' in *History Today* [November 2012])

In 1872 the Campbell-Bannermans moved from Queen's Gate to 117 Eaton Square which was to be their London home until 1878. Also, from 1872 (the year in which it got a railway connection) visits to the spa town of Marienbad in Bohemia in the Austro-Hungarian Empire (now Marianske Lazne in the Czech Republic) became a yearly fixture until Charlotte died there in August 1906. Henry spoke fluent French (as did Charlotte) and German and passable Italian and they already had the habit of annual visits to France and various other countries in mainland Europe.

Bohemia is named for its earliest recorded inhabitants, the Celtic *Boii* who, by the 2nd century, had been completely displaced or absorbed by Germanic tribes from the north. Western Slavonic (Czech) settlement followed in the 6th century, The German population, including other settlers from the 13th century, was eventually mainly confined to the border regions (including Marienbad), later known as the Sudetenland, with, until the Second World War, more than 90 % of its population being ethnic Germans.[102]

---

[102] In 1918-1919, with the break-up of the Austro-Hungarian Empire, the Sudetenland, with the rest of Bohemia (and Moravia and Slovakia), became part of the newly created

At Marienbad, Henry and Charlotte always stayed in the rather old-fashioned Klinger, the largest hotel in the town, with 200 bedrooms, including some suites with bathrooms, a resident orchestra and its own carriages, although eventually it had three lifts, a telephone and vacuum cleaning! [103]

At Marienbad, whatever the benefits of its mineral waters, Charlotte undoubtedly benefited from being there. They both greatly appreciated the attentions and advice of the spa's most famous physician, Dr. Alfred Ott and, after 1897, his son, Dr. Ernst. Both such model society doctors became personal friends, with the elder Ott staying with them when in London.

Over the years other seasonal visitors to Marienbad included Czar Nicholas II, the German Grand Admiral Tirpitz, the French General Gallifret (who was involved in the Dreyfus case), Goethe, Chopin, Edison, Wagner, Earl Spencer, Lloyd George, Lord Rosebery (after his wife's death in 1890), Richard Haldane, Sir Rufus Isaacs (later Marquis of Reading), Admiral Lord Fisher and, as already mentioned, Princess Louise.

King Edward also visited Marienbad twice before his accession and annually from 1903. He stayed in the Hotel Weimar, with its proprietor being, in due course, granted the right to advertise as 'By Appointment, Hotel Proprietor to HM King Edward VII'. [18]

However, Sir Henry, as he was then, was not fully admitted to the royal circle at Marienbad until the autumn of 1905, just two to three months before he became Prime Minister. This followed a brief conversation about travel arrangements in September 1899, a one hour interview at the King's request in Marienbad in 1904 and socialising privately in London earlier in 1905.

Thus the Marienbad connection enabled Henry to develop a wide range of contacts in circumstances when normal protocol and ceremony were waived and holiday conditions prevailed. As Admiral Lord Fisher – who once managed to go there and

---

Czechoslovakia. Then, following the 15-29 September 1938 Berchtesgaden and Munich Agreements between the UK, France, Fascist Italy and Nazi Germany – with no Czechoslovak representation – the Sudetenland was ceded to Germany, with military occupation by 10 October. After the Second World War, the Sudetenland was restored to what was then Czechoslovakia. Of the German population, about 500,000 were expelled with more than 100,000 others later leaving voluntary.

There are now only about 40,000 ethnic Germans in the entire Czech Republic. Thus whereas most of the basic population of Marienbad was ethnic German in the Campbell-Bannerman's time, it is now, with re-settlement since the Second World War, almost entirely Czech.

One wonders what Sir Henry would have thought of the part played by Walter Runciman (Viscount Runciman 1937), one of his Junior Ministers in 1905-1908, in the diplomacy leading up to the 1938 Sudetenland settlement.

[103] *Bradshaw's* (1913), p.926

back, staying for three weeks for £ 25 – wrote, 'At Marienbad, I met some very celebrated men, and the place was so small I became great friends with them... You can't help knowing each other quite well. I almost think I knew Campbell-Bannerman the best. He was very delightful to talk to'.[104]

Given his determination that a letter from a constituent would not remain unanswered for long, before going abroad Henry always left instructions that any communication bearing the post mark of any of the five Burghs should be forwarded to him. Further, all letters from constituents, almost without exception, received a personal reply.

In addition to Irish, Army and Educational reforms, the 1868-1874 Liberal Government was responsible for the abolition of compulsory Church of England rates in England and Wales in 1868. Competitive examinations for entry into the civil service were introduced in 1870 and 1873. The 1871 Trade Union Act gave trade unions legal status (and to some extent protected their funds). The 1873 Judicature Act established the English High Court and Court of Appeal,

The 1871 Criminal Law Amendment Act, which sought to protect trade unions from prosecution for conspiracy when undertaking peaceful picketing was frustrated by court decisions from 1872 onwards. The 1871 Ballot Bill to introduce secret voting at elections was rejected by the House of Lords but, when re-introduced in 1872, was enacted. The Act was, in part, in response to the eviction, by Tory landowners, of 269 Liberal-voting tenant farmers in Wales at the 1868 General Election.[105]

Having also taken over the additional office of Chancellor of the Exchequer in August 1873, Gladstone faced opposition within the Cabinet to his Budget proposals. Accordingly he called a General Election for January/February, 1874, with Henry Campbell-Bannerman being returned unopposed in Stirling Burghs. The Liberals had lost 33 by-elections since the 1868 General Election including Glasgow & Aberdeen Universities in November 1869 and the other Liberal seat in Gladstone's two-member constituency of Greenwich in August 1873.

---

[104] As quoted in Wilson (1973), p.139

[105] Morgan (1991), pp.25-26

B – 1874-1880 – Opposition

Table 11 - The 1874 General Election - 31 January to 17 February 1874

Candidates (Unopposed), Percentages and MPs Elected

	England				Wales				Scotland			
Liberals	335	(26)	53.8	171	32	(7)	60.9	19	61	(16)	68.4	40
Conservatives	387	(100)	46.2	280	23	(5)	39.1	14	36	(6)	31.6	18
Others	1	(0)										
	743	(126)		451	55	(12)		33	97	(22)		58

	Ireland				Universities				UNITED KINGDOM			
Liberals	39	(1)	18.4	10	2	(2)		2	489	(52)	52.7	242
Conservatives	54	(7)	40.8	31	7	(7)		7	507	(125)	43.9	350
Irish Home Rulers	80	(10)	38.6	60					80	(10)	3.3	60
Others	3	(0)	1.2						3	(0)	0.1	
	176	(18)		101	9	(9)			1080	(187)		652

Net Gains/Losses in MPs Elected compared to the 1868 General Election

	England	Wales	Scotland	Ireland	Universities	UK
Liberals	minus 73	minus 4	minus 11	minus 56	minus 1	minus 145
Conservatives	plus 69	plus 4	plus 11	minus 6	plus 1	plus 79
Irish Home Rulers				plus 60		plus 60

Stirling Burghs - Electorate 4,779

Greenwich (2 Members) - Electorate 17,599

Henry Campbell-Bannerman	Liberal	Unopposed

T.W. Boord	Conservative	6,193
W.E. Gladstone	Liberal	5,968
J.E. Liardet	Conservative	5,561
J.B. Langley	Liberal	5,255

Gladstone and his Government resigned later in February – that is, before the new Parliament assembled on 5 March 1874 – and Disraeli (1st Earl of Beaconsfield from 1876) formed the first majority Conservative Government since 1841-1846,

This was the first General Election since the 1872 Ballot Act and the introduction of secret voting. As already mentioned, most of the Irish Liberal MPs elected in 1868 had joined Isaac Butt's Irish Home Rule Party as formed in 1873 or were defeated by Home Rule candidates. Since the 1868 General Election there had been a reduction of four English and two Irish MPs The two-member English Borough Constituencies of Beverley and Bridgwater and the single-member Irish Borough Constituencies of Cashel and Sligo had lost their status as Parliamentary Boroughs in 1870.

The Liberals elected included the first two Liberal/Labour MPs. (The Rt. Hon.) Thomas Burt, a native of Northumberland, sometime Secretary of the Northumberland Miners Association, was elected for Morpeth which he continued to represent as a Lib/Lab MP until he retired in 1918. He was Parliamentary Secretary to the Board of Trade in 1892-1895 and 'Father' of the House of Commons in 1910-1918. In 1908 he represented the Liberal back-benchers as a pall-bearer at the Westminster Abbey Service on the day before CB's funeral in Meigle,

Perthshire. He refused to join the Labour Party after the Miners Federation decided to affiliate later in 1908. Alexander Macdonald from Holytown in Lanarkshire, sometime Secretary of the Miners Association for Scotland and President of the Miners National Association, was elected in the two-member constituency of Stafford which he continued to represent until his death in October 1881.

Gladstone resigned the Liberal leadership in February 1875 with Spencer Cavendish MP (known by his courtesy title of Marquis of Hartington as heir of the 7th [English] Duke of Devonshire) elected to the Liberal leadership in the House of Commons and Lord Granville continuing as Leader in the House of Lords. The two gentlemen were cousins.

Throughout the 1874-1880 Parliament, CB was Liberal (Opposition) spokesman on the War Office in the House of Commons as Edward Cardwell had been created a Viscount at the Dissolution. CB had a brief to ensure that none of the Army reforms of the 1868-1874 Parliament were challenged and, in this connection, was in regular contact with the Viscount, who was, for six years from 1872, a London neighbour in Eaton Square.

Early in the new Parliament (21 May 1874) CB had to make a short and effective speech to defend the action of the War Office when, with himself as Financial Secretary, the Commander-in-Chief in Ireland had been required to repay £ 750 of his pay by reason of absence from duty. As a result of his intervention, a motion critical of the previous War Office administration was withdrawn.

The Conservative Secretary of State for War gave relatively few openings for the Cardwellian watchmen. However, there was one occasion when it was proposed to legalise the sale of regimental exchanges by officers, when CB had to intervene (22 February 1875) to challenge this proposed resumption of trafficking in appointments.

Otherwise, in 1874-1880, CB was primarily concerned with Scottish matters. He joined other Scottish MPs in complaining that many Bills in which they took a particular interest were pushed into the early hours of the morning or shunted aside. Such complaints eventually resulted in the revival of the office of Secretary for Scotland and the institution of the Scottish Office in 1885. This was after the unfortunate experiment of having an Under-Secretary for Scottish Affairs (the Earl of Rosebery) at the Home Office from August 1881 to June 1883. (The inability of Rosebery and Sir William Harcourt [then Home Secretary] to work together in 1881-1883 was perhaps the origin of their personal estrangement in later years when Rosebery was Prime Minister [and Liberal Leader] and Harcourt was Liberal Leader in the Commons.).

However, on 13 July 1874, CB spoke in opposition to the Church Patronage (Scotland) Bill which, when enacted, conclusively abolished patronage in the Church of Scotland as re-imposed unconstitutionally by the Westminster Parliament in 1712. He stated that what was proposed was intended to bolster up the Church of Scotland at the expense of the other Scottish Presbyterian Churches and also checkmate the movement for the union of the Free and United Presbyterian (UP) Churches. He also pointed out that the Disruption of the Church of Scotland in 1843 and the formation of the (original) Free Church of Scotland had been caused not only by the matter of patronage but also by the matter of spiritual independence.

However, he was clearly unaware, or chose to ignore, that in 1873 the then Liberal Lord Advocate had been instructed to draft a Bill much as the Conservative Bill initially introduced in the House of Lords in May (1874) – that is, after the Liberals had lost office at the January/February General Election. Further, far from being intended to frustrate Presbyterian union (and reunion) it was a necessary first step towards optimum Presbyterian reunion in Scotland. However, CB was correct in the matter of spiritual independence. Indeed, during the Bill's passage, an attempt was made to assert the spiritual independence of the Church of Scotland but this was set aside as providing a precedent for the Church of England. (Refer to Table 3 in Chapter 1)

CB's mother having died on 3 October 1873, his father, Sir James Campbell died on 10 September 1876, leaving the house in Bath Street, Glasgow and the Stracathro estate to James Alexander Campbell and a property in Glasgow, £25,000 and the silver in the house in Bath Street to CB. Thus, CB acquired some free capital and a marketable asset which would be used some eight-ten years later to purchase, reconstruct and refurbish Belmont Castle in Perthshire. Also in 1876 both CB and his brother retired as partners in the family business in order to concentrate on public affairs and domestic responsibilities. Thereafter, the family's active interest in the business was maintained by Uncle William Campbell's Tullichewan line.

As mentioned in Chapter 1, Sir Henry's father, Sir James Campbell had known before his death that a new Parish Church was to be built in Port of Menteith and thought that some contribution to such would be an ideal means of fulfilling his promise to his parents to make provision for commemorating their association with the Parish. Thus, after Sir James' death, the funding by his sons – James Alexander Campbell and Henry – of the Trefoil Stained Glass Window (depicting Faith, Hope and Charity) designed by Stephen Adam, commemorating the brothers' paternal grandfather and grandmother, in the east gable wall of Port of Menteith Parish Church. Accordingly, at the opening of the new building on 3 October 1878, there were references to that promise and to 'the love of the country of their ancestors which [had] induced the sons of Sir James to offer so beautiful a window (applause) in memory of their ancestor who was born in the parish'.[106]

> **In Memory of**
> **James McOran: or**
> **Campbell: born at Inchanoch**
> **in this parish: 1752 died at Glasgow 1831**
> **and of Helen Forrester his: wife died: at Glasgow: 1824**

---

[106] *Stirling Journal (and Advertiser)*, 4 October 1878.

Stephen Adam (1848-1910) was born in Edinburgh, where he was a school classmate of Robert Louis Stevenson. He moved to Glasgow in 1870 and, by 1877, was established as the foremost stained glass artist in the west of Scotland. His Glasgow studio was in Bath Street, near to the house built for Sir James Campbell in 1828.

Meanwhile, on 14 March 1877, CB had spoken on a private member's Scottish Temperance Bill. He suggested that the only point on which Scottish opinion was agreed was that licensing should be dealt with and judged locally. Otherwise, all the facts could only be ascertained by way of a Royal Commission or some other sort of Enquiry. Needless to say Disraeli's Government did not take the matter further and local opinion had to wait.

CB's brother, James Alexander Campbell was a member of no fewer than four Royal Commissions – Scottish Universities 1876, Endowed Institutions [Scotland] 1878, Educational Endowments [Scotland] 1882 and Universities [Scotland] 1889

In the following year (1877), on the initiative of Joseph Chamberlain the National Liberal Federation (for England and Wales) was launched in Birmingham on 31 May, with Gladstone as the principal speaker (Chamberlain would be a Liberal Cabinet Minister in 1880-1885 and again briefly in 1886 before becoming a Liberal Unionist). The Federation had much the same objectives as the Conservatives' National Union. However, there was the added intention of countering the Whiggish elements in the Liberal Party leadership. Significantly the Marquis of Hartington had refused to attend the Birmingham meeting.

Hartington had spent Christmas Day 1862 making eggnog for Confederate cavalry officers in General Robert E. Lee's army. [107] Hartington's family eventually acquired the pocket book of Robert E. Lee in which permission was scribbled for the young Hartington to visit the Confederate troops.

In 1878 the Campbell-Bannermans moved from Eaton Square to 6 Grosvenor Place which was to be their London home until 1904. This house, which was taken at a yearly rent of £185, looked across to the gardens of Buckingham Palace. Until Charlotte became virtually an invalid, her dinners and parties in Grosvenor Place – often as many as four or five a month for up to twenty people during the London season – were regarded as events of importance. There is a Blue Plaque at 6 Grosvenor Place commemorating Sir Henry's association with the building.[108]

---

[107] Amanda Foreman (2011), p.xxiii

[108] Such blue plaques have been erected in London since 1867 to mark buildings where well-known persons lived or worked. The responsibility of English Heritage since 1986, with more than 800 in London, responsibility for the scheme has passed to the English Heritage Trust. (*Current Archaeology,* March 2013). The English Heritage blue plaques should not be confused with the green plaques which are the responsibility of Westminster City Council.

> Sir HENRY CAMPBELL-BANNERMAN, 1836-1908, Prime Minister lived here.

Meanwhile, Gladstone was emerging from semi-retirement although he had already publicly pursued a critical line on such matters as the purchase of shares in the Suez Canal in 1875 and the Royal Titles Act of 1876 which created Queen Victoria as Empress of India. From September 1876 he also denounced, in print and speech, Turkish atrocities in Bulgaria.

CB also criticised the manner in which Disraeli had acquired the Canal shares and expressed his sympathy for the oppressed Christian subjects of the Ottoman (Turkish) Empire, On the Royal Titles Act, he said that 'We could not add to the lustre and dignity of our [Monarchy], the most ancient and august in Europe, by tricking it out in a brand new title'. He also expressed keen concern lest, in the future, our Heir Apparent should come to bear the title Prince Imperial.

Also, as from the autumn of 1876 the 5th (Scottish) Earl of Rosebery – with a special interest in foreign affairs and in alignment with Gladstone – was becoming more active on Liberal platforms in Scotland and from the Liberal benches in the House of Lords Then, in autumn of 1878, he defeated the Conservative candidate for the Rectorship of Aberdeen University by three votes.

Rosebery, in addition to being Rector of Aberdeen University in 1878-1881, was also later Rector of Edinburgh, Glasgow and St. Andrews Universities and Chancellor of Glasgow University. Rectors of Scottish Universities have also included such other Liberal Leaders as Palmerston, Lord John Russell, Gladstone, Asquith, Lloyd George, Sir Archibald Sinclair, Jo Grimond and David Steel. Sir Henry Campbell-Bannerman would probably have been elected as Rector of Glasgow University in 1908 but for his death before the election.

Recently two Liberal Democrats have been Rectors of Scottish Universities – the late Charles Kennedy (Glasgow 2008-2014), the late Maitland Mackie III (Aberdeen 2012-2014), with Lord Campbell of Pittenweem having been Chancellor of St. Andrews University since 2006.

Strangely enough, apparently by reason of personal friendship with Disraeli, eleven years earlier (1867) Rosebery had been invited to become the Conservative candidate for Darlington. But he was never to stand for the House of Commons. His grandfather died on 4 March 1868 and he then succeeded to the family peerages, taking his seat in the House of Lords in May 1868, just after his 21st birthday,[109]

---

[109] Rhodes James (1963), pp.46-47, 49

Meanwhile, William Patrick Adam (1823-1881), Liberal MP for Clackmannan and Kinross since 1859 and Liberal Chief Whip since 1874, in addition to his London-based commitments, was taking a particular interest in Liberal organisation in Scotland. Thus in 1876-1877 he had set up two regional Liberal organisations in Scotland – The East & North and the West & South of Scotland Liberal Associations. This was with a particular concern for the seats, including Midlothian (Edinburghshire), which the Liberals had lost in 1874. The Edinburgh-based Secretary of the East & North Association, John James Reid was effectively the Liberal agent for all of Scotland and the Chief Whip supplied him with funds to the extent that, even after the 1880 General Election, he had over £ 1,500 in-hand.[110]

Given Gladstone's renewed political activity and his intention to depart from his marginal Greenwich constituency, Adam had, in 1876, attempted unsuccessfully to persuade him to stand for a Scottish constituency. However, given Gladstone's election as rector of Glasgow University in 1877, the attempt was renewed in the autumn of 1878, now specifically with Midlothian in mind. (Gladstone had been rector of Edinburgh University in 1859-1865 and although elected in Glasgow in 1877 would not be installed until late 1879, that is, during his first Midlothian Campaign.) After extensive exchanges, the matter was settled and the Midlothian Liberal Association, meeting on 7 January 1879 – with Roosebery having travelled from Paris to attend – in effect adopted Gladstone as its prospective parliamentary candidate.[111]

Midlothian was held for the Conservatives – without opposition, since a by-election in 1853 – by the Earl of Dalkeith (Courtesy Title), eldest son and heir of the 5th (Scottish) Duke of Buccleuch.[112] He first faced opposition at the 1868 General Election when he lost to a Liberal. However, at the 1874 General Election, he won back the constituency by 1,194 votes to 1,058 for a new Liberal candidate. After being defeated by Gladstone at the 1880 General Election, he succeeded as 6th Duke in 1884.

It should be appreciated that, in Gladstone's time, the county constituency of Midlothian (Edinburghshire) included many areas which later became part of the City and Royal Burgh of Edinburgh. Such included Corstorphine which was not

---

[110] Hutchinson (1886), pp.145-146

[111] To the extent that William Adam was responsible for providing Gladstone with constituency security for the next fifteeen years and, organisationally, for Liberal electoral success generally in 1880, he was somewhat ill-rewarded when the new Liberal administration was formed in late April 1880. He returned to the then non-Cabinet post of First Commissioner of Works which he had occupied for six months in 1873-1874. He was appointed Governor of Madras in December 1880 and died in office five months later (May 1881). The following year (1882) his son, Charles was created a Baronet and his widow was given the status of a Baronet's wife.

[112] The Dukes of Buccleuch are descended from the ill-fated James Scott, Duke of Monmouth and Buccleuch, an illegitimate son of Charles II.

anexed by Edinburgh until 1920. Thus my mother (who was born in Corstorphine in 1894) had Gladstone as her MP for the first year of her life.[113] However, when my mother's father, Alexander Somerville, (after whom I am named) died in 1933, he was a member of the West Edinburgh Liberal Association.

Following his adoption in January 1879, Gladstone's first Midlothian Campaign took place later that year from 24 November to 8 December. Most of the innovations were on the initiative of Rosebery (Gladstone's host at Dalmeny), as from his attendance at a Democrat Convention in New York. CB was fully in sympathy with the campaign and when the Gladstones stopped in Dunfermline on an excursion to Perthshire he was one of the many demonstrative Liberals on the station platform. He was shouldering a bulky parcel of Dunfermline linen which when presented to Mrs. Gladstone resulted in increased applause.[114]

Then, three months later, on 8 March 1880, Beaconsfield's Government faced the possibility of defeat in the House of Commons. This was in connection with a bill to unify the private water companies in London into a municipal undertaking with compensation for the private shareholders entailing large capital gains. Accordingly, a General Election was called for late March/April.

In anticipation of serious opposition from the first Tory/Conservative candidate to contest Stirling Burghs since 1832, CB duly issued his election address –

> The great kindness which you have invariably shown me in the past, and for which I shall always feel grateful, induces me to hope that you will not be unwilling again to entrust your interests to me. During the past six years little progress has been made in the great work of legislative reform, while the attention of the country has been mainly absorbed by the foreign policy of the Government.
>
> I have repeatedly given my vote against that policy, not so much on account of any individual force of judgement which it may have displayed as in condemnation of its whole tone and tendency which I have deemed to be lowering to the national dignity and injurious to our higher interests.
>
> I trust that the new Parliament will witness again the predominance of Liberal ideas, alike in domestic legislation, in current administration, and in the conduct of foreign affairs, believing as I do by this means alone can our liberties be preserved, our prosperity be fostered and the integrity of the Empire be maintained.[115]

---

[113] My father also had Gladstone as his MP for a year or so after his family returned to Midlothian after his birth, in what is now part of Glasgow, in 1893. Further, both my parents, my two sisters and my brother – as then resident in Paisley – had H.H. Asquith as their MP for a few months in 1924.

[114] Mackie (1914), pp. 51-52
[115] Mackie (1914), p.52.

In the meantime Sir James Gibson Maitland, a wealthy Midlothian landowner with Dunfermline family connections had been nominated by the Conservatives. However, his lack of political knowledge and his inability to cope with questions were such that after only one election meeting (in Dunfermline) he returned home a wiser man. Thus he became convinced that his effort to oust CB was not only a hopeless task but a stupendous folly. Accordingly, he withdrew from the contest. However, with polling arrangements having already been made and Sir James' name remaining on the ballot papers, polling had to take place.

Many of CB's supporters thought that this personal withdrawal was a Tory ploy to encourage Liberal voters not to vote as their support would be unnecessary while their opponents might make a sudden rally before polling. So, under this apprehension and in order to give proof of their devotion to CB and to the Liberalism he represented, electioneering efforts on his behalf continued, resulting in an impressive display of Liberal strength in Stirling Burghs, with CB being re-elected by 2,906 votes to 132, with a 63 % turnout.

5 – 1880-1886 – Government, Opposition and Government

A – 1880-1885 – Government (Junior and Irish Office) and Opposition

Table 12 - The 1880 General Election - 30 March to 14 April (to 27 April)

Candidates (Unopposed), Percentages and MPs Elected

	England				Wales				Scotland			
Liberals	372	(19)	56.2	254	32	(9)	58.8	29	60	(12)	70.1	52
Conservatives	390	(47)	43.7	197	22	(1)	41.2	4	43	(0)	29.9	6
Others	2	(0)	0.1									
	764	(36)		451	54	(10)		33	103	(12)		58

	Ireland				Universities				UNITED KINGDOM			
Liberals	32	(1)	22.7	15	3	(0)	50.8	2	499	(41)	55.4	352
Conservatives	57	(4)	39.8	23	9	(6)	49.2	7	521	(58)	42.0	237
Irish Home Rulers	81	(10)	37.5	63					81	(10)	2.6	63
Others									2	(0)		
	170	(15)		101	12	(6)		9	1104	(109)		652

Net Gains/Losses in MPs Elected compared to the 1874 General Election

	England	Wales	Scotland	Ireland	Universities	UK
Liberals	plus 83	plus 10	plus 12	plus 5		plus 110
Conservatives	minus 83	minus 10	minus 12	minus 8		minus 113
Irish Home Rulers				plus 3		plus 3

Stirling Burghs - Electorate 4,807

	Henry Campbell-Bannerman	Liberal	2,906
	Sir J.R.G. Maitland	Conservative	132

Leeds (Three Members) - Electorate c.49,000 *

W.E. Gladstone	Liberal	24,622
J. Barran	Liberal	23,647
W.L. Jackson	Conservative	13,331
W. St.J. Wheelhouse	Conservative	11,965

Midlothian - Electorate 3,260

W.E. Gladstone	Liberal	1,579
Earl of Dalkeith	Conservative	1,368

* At the 1868, 1874 and 1880 General Elections, in such three-member constituencies, individual electors could vote for only two candidates.

Lord Beaconsfield (Benjamin Disraeli) and his Conservative Government resigned before the final results were declared. After some manoeuvring, Gladstone resumed the Liberal Leadership and formed his second Liberal administration from 23 April.

The Liberals had made five net gains at by-elections during the 1874-1880 Parliament, and this was the first General Election at which the National Union of Conservative Associations, the National Liberal Federation and the two regional Liberal Associations in Scotland had significant impacts. Three of the Liberals elected were Liberal/Labour MPs.

Given his dual mandate, William Gladstone opted to represent Midlothian and his son, Herbert was returned unopposed at the subsequent by-election in Leeds on 10 May. This Gladstonian connection with Leeds would be of significance at the time of the Liberal split over Irish Home Rule in 1886. James Kitson (1835-1911), then President of the Leeds Liberal Association, ran William Gladstone's campaign for him in Leeds in 1880 and was thereafter President of the National Liberal Federation in 1883-1890. Thus it was under his leadership that the Federation remained resolutely Gladstonian in 1886. (Kitson was created a Baronet in 1886 and a peer, as Lord Airedale, in 1907, having been Liberal MP for Colne Valley from 1892.)

Charles Parnell had assumed the leadership of the Irish Home Rule Party in 1877 which during the course of the 1880-1885 Parliament became known as Irish Nationalist.

CB's elder brother, James Alexander Campbell was first elected as Conservative MP for the Universities of Glasgow & Aberdeen with 2,531 votes to 2,139 for Alexander Asher. (Asher was subsequently Liberal MP for Elgin Burghs in 1881-1905 and Solicitor-General for Scotland in 1881-1885, February-July 1886 and 1892-1894.)

James Alexander had been one of the two prospective Conservative candidates for the then three-member constituency of Glasgow. However, he was ousted by the Orange Order's nominee, Sir James Bain, who came bottom of the poll, with three Liberals being elected. The Glasgow Orange Lodges then had a representative on the City's Conservative Executive, an arrangement which only ended at the time of the Irish Free State Treaty in late 1921.

James Alexander (aged 55 when first elected) continued to represent Glasgow & Aberdeen Universities until retiring (aged 80) prior to the January 1906 General Election. He was unopposed at the 1885, 1886, 1892, 1895 and 1900 General Elections, having become a Privy Councillor in 1897. Thus the two brothers, CB and James Alexander, sat on opposite sides of the House of Commons for twenty-five years.

Other examples of brothers representing different parties in the Commons at the same time were William Gladstone (Liberal) and John Neilson Gladstone (Conservative) in 1859-1863, (Sir) William Harcourt (Liberal) and Edward Harcourt (Conservative) in 1878-1886, John Bright (Liberal Unionist) and Jacob Bright (Liberal) in 1886.-1889), John A. Bright (Liberal Unionist) and William Bright (Liberal) in 1889-1895 and George Mackie (Liberal) and John Mackie (Labour) in 1964-1966. Stanley Baldwin (Conservative) sat on the opposite side from his son, Oliver Baldwin (Labour) in 1929-1931. At the 1929 General Election in Flintshire, F.L. Jones was the successful Liberal candidate while his brother, C.O. Jones was the third-placed Labour candidate.

CB was again Financial Secretary at the War Office from April 1880 to May 1882, with the new Secretary of State, Hugh Childers, also sitting in the Commons. This was again a period of significant reforms in the Army, all of which CB supported. Flogging was completely abolished. The minimum age for recruitment was raised to nineteen years and to twenty years for service in India. The period of enlistment was revised to seven years as a regular and five years in the reserves. The numbering of infantry regiments was replaced by names and, as already mentioned anent the Lanarkshire Rifle Volunteers, by grouping volunteer battalions with regular regiments. Also, in this period, CB was Chairman of a Committee overseeing the reorganisation of coastal defences.

Lord Beaconsfield (Benjamin Disraeli) died in April 1881 and was replaced as Conservative Leader by Robert Cecil, 3rd Marquis of Salisbury with Sir Stafford Northcote as Conservative Leader in the Commons.

Also in 1881 the two regional Liberal organisations in Scotland merged to form the Scottish Liberal Association, while maintaining regional offices in Edinburgh and Glasgow. The new Association corresponded more to the London-based Liberal Central Association than to the then Birmingham-based National Liberal Federation.

Then in May 1882, CB was transferred from the War Office to the Admiralty, serving until October 1884 as Parliamentary and Financial Secretary and Government spokesman for the Admiralty in the House of Commons as the First Lord of the Admiralty, Thomas Baring, 1st Earl Northbrook was in the Lords. (CB succeeded George Otto Trevelyan at the Admiralty and would, in due course, succeed him as Chief Secretary for Ireland). Thus, for the first time CB was answerable in the Commons for a Government department.

On one occasion, in early May 1883, as also a founder member (1882) of the National Liberal Club in London, he had to answer a complaint from a Scottish Conservative MP that the Club had hoisted a White Ensign. CB replied that 'the penalties provided by the Merchant Shipping Act only applied to the improper use of flags afloat, and there is no restriction as to the flags which anyone can hoist on shore'.

However, much more significantly, on the two occasions when he presented the Naval Estimates in the Commons he had to face criticism not for Admiralty extravagance but for its allegedly dangerous economies. However, being in full command of facts and figures, he was able to defend effectively – although, as it turned out, somewhat provisionally on his part – the Government's refusal to enter into a new era of naval shipbuilding, pointing out the difficulty of designing any sort of ship which might not be out-of-date before it was launched.

Nevertheless, in early October 1884, when the First Lord was away in Egypt, and impressed by a press-centred campaign insisting on the Navy being strengthened and aware of the political hazards of not responding, he took it upon himself to approach Childers (now Chancellor of the Exchequer) to suggest, deliberately by way of understatement, an increase of £ 500,000 in the Naval Estimates,

He also pointed that the facilities in the UK for making armour plate, torpedoes and guns were far inferior to those in France. This approach resulted in the Cabinet, without waiting for the First Lord's return, approving a Supplementary Estimate, not of £ 500,000, but of £ 3 million, out of which two battleships and thirteen cruisers were built,

He also took a considerable interest in conditions of employment in the Naval Dockyards being accompanied on visits to such by Charlotte who took a particular interest in the conditions of women workers. As previously mentioned (Chapter 2) while serving in the Admiralty, CB received an Honorary Doctorate of Laws (LLD) from Glasgow University on 22 March 1883.

Further, in February 1884 the Liberal Cabinet had in mind to nominate CB for the vacant Speakership of the House of Commons. However, the nomination was first offered as a compliment to Arthur Peel, MP (a son of Sir Robert Peel) who unexpectedly accepted and held the post until April 1895 when CB virtually 'applied' unsuccessfully for the vacancy.

In August 1884 there was a large open-air demonstration in Dunfermline in support of CB's commitment to extend householder suffrage from the burghs/boroughs to the counties. It was also in support of CB's attitude to the House of Lords in that 'it has been for some time merely part of the machinery of the Tory Party' and that we should 'not rest until this source of delay and disappointments in reforms and of obstruction of legislation is finally settled'.[116]

CB was then Chief Secretary for Ireland from 24 October 1884 to 30 June 1885. He was sworn in as a member of the UK Privy Council on 29 November 1884 and thereafter (1885) as a member of the Privy Council of Ireland, However, he remained outwith the Cabinet. No Liberal Chief Secretary for Ireland was given Cabinet membership from after 1880-1882 (William Foster) until John Morley in 1886.

Strangely enough, when George Otto Trevelyan had demitted office as Chief Secretary for Ireland in October 1884, he was appointed Chancellor of the Duchy of Lancaster with Cabinet membership. Further, if CB had not accepted the Chief Secretaryship in October 1884, it would have been offered to Sir Henry James (the Attorney-General) with Cabinet membership. Gladstone was not very consistent in such matters.

The Chief Secretary was junior to the Lord Lieutenant (Viceroy) who was then John Spencer, 5th Earl Spencer.[117] As Chief Secretary, CB succeeded Lord Frederick Cavendish, MP (a younger brother of the Marquis of Hartington) who had been assassinated in Dublin on 6 May 1882 four days after his appointment and George Otto Trevelyan, MP (a future Liberal Secretary for Scotland), Chief Secretary in 1882-1884. After an initial refusal, CB accepted the Chief Secretaryship only on the urgings of Charlotte as it was rightly said to be the most dangerous and disagreeable

---

[116] Mackie (1914), pp.60-61

[117] Prince William, Duke of Cambridge and Earl of Strathearn is not descended, through his mother, Lady Diana Spencer from the 5th Earl but from that Earl's younger half-brother who succeeded as 6th Earl in 1910

post in the public service. Indeed, on leaving the Admiralty, his Secretary 'thoughtfully presented him with a pocket revolver'.[118]

The appointment necessitated a Ministerial By-Election in Stirling Burghs, at which he was returned unopposed on 31 October (1884).

> It is my duty to inform you that I have accepted the office of Chief Secretary to the Lord Lieutenant of Ireland, and I trust you will approve of the decision I have taken. I am well aware of the arduous duties attached to this honourable office, and it is with sincere diffidence that I have undertaken to discharge them. My steadfast aim and earnest desire will be to render such service as I can in promoting the welfare of the Irish people, in the administration of whose affairs I am called to take part. My seat being vacant, I beg to ask you to confer on me the favour of again returning me as your representative. The friendly confidence which you have extended to me during so many years, with a kindness for which I cannot be sufficiently grateful, leads me to hope that you may be disposed to leave your Parliamentary interests in my hands.
>
> My political opinions are so well known to you that I need not recapitulate them; but I may say that my attachment to and belief in Liberal principles have become stronger and stronger as my political experience has increased. With regard to the great question of the day, I hope that the unmistakeable indication that has been given during the last three months of the overwhelming feeling of the country may induce those who have hitherto resisted the immediate extension of the suffrage in the counties to abandon their opposition.
>
> If, however, they persist in delaying this great measure of justice, it will become necessary to take such steps as shall not only enforce the passing of the Franchise Bill but prevent the recurrence of similar obstructions to useful and progressive legislation. If you are pleased to favour me with a renewal of your confidence I need not say that I shall do my utmost to deserve it.[119]

CB had first been to Ireland (Dublin) as Chief Secretary for a few days in late October. But he had to return to London for Parliamentary business from the beginning of November, with a first appearance in the Commons as Chief Secretary on 3 November.

In the Commons CB had, at first, to face the baiting of the Irish Nationalist MPs with which his predecessors, William Forster and George Otto Trevelyan, had been unable to cope. (Frederick Cavendish never appeared in the Commons as Chief

---

[118] Wilson (1973), p.66

[119] Mackie (1914), p.63

Secretary.) Indeed, in the first Irish debate at which CB appeared as Chief Secretary, one Irish Nationalist MP, T.P. O'Connor, expressed the prevailing feeling of his party by saying that 'the Government reminded him of a beleaguered capital. First they tried stone fortifications, then they tried guns; finally they resorted at the last extremity to a sandbag.' But with CB "there was no human being so impervious to attack… thunders of denunciation from his [Irish Nationalist] opponents opposite. There was nothing to be done with an opponent like this. He laughed at vituperation; he was jaunty under a cyclone of attack".[120]

Thus CB gained the respect and trust of the Irish Nationalist MPs which was to stand him in good stead for the rest of his life. Indeed, O'Connor (his first biographer), came to regret what he had said, and he and CB became personal friends to the extent that, when confined to bed in 10 Downing Street not long before his death, CB asked his then Principal Private Secretary to ask O'Connor to recommend some books.

One of the early exchanges, involving CB and an Irish Nationalist MP – Thomas Sexton, a future Lord Mayor of Dublin – was with reference as to why the Commissioners of National Education in Ireland had not deemed it advisable to include the teaching of Irish history in their schools.

CB replied that the Question 'opens up an old standing subject of concern and difficulty which the Commissioners have had to encounter. Having to deal with schools designed for the united education of children of different religious denominations, they felt constrained to regard it as impracticable to include the teaching of history [all history whatsoever] in the curriculum of the schools'.

Before Christmas (1884) CB spoke at meetings in his constituency and then, with Charlotte, returned to Dublin early in the New Year and, having had a drainage problem sorted, stayed in the Chief Secretary's Lodge until mid-February. (The water supply had been only three yards from the cesspool.) Then, after a visit to Belfast on 16 February, they returned, via Larne, Stranraer and Glasgow, to Parliamentary duties in London.

However, the most critical weeks in Ireland during CB's seven-eight months as Chief Secretary were at the time of the visit of Prince Albert Edward (the future King Edward) and Princess Alexandra to Ireland in April 1885. Henry and Charlotte were again based in the Chief Secretary's Lodge. There had been threats from extremists, backed by the *United Irishman* in New York publishing a letter offering $ 10,000 for the body of the Prince, dead or alive. Dublin City Council had voted against the visit by a majority of 41 to 17. It was also necessary to keep the temperature down between Nationalists and Orangemen during the visit. In which connection, CB thought that, if all else failed, it would be better to close the whiskey shops than to send in troops.

---

[120] O'Connor (1908), pp.23-24

Nevertheless, the crowded schedule was completed without too much trouble and CB was able to report that the positive aspect of the visit was unmistakable with the feeling in the House of Commons being of "admiration and gratitude for a great public service".[121]

At about this time, Earl Spencer had suggested, without success, not only that one of Queen Victoria's sons should be appointed as a non-political Viceroy but also that there should be a permanent royal residence in Ireland.

When in Ireland, CB shared, with Earl Spencer, a military escort commanded by Captain John (Jack) Sinclair of the 5th Royal Irish Lancers. After leaving the army, Sinclair was to become a close friend and political colleague of CB, a Liberal MP and Whip, Secretary for Scotland, 1st Lord Pentland and Governor of Madras.

CB was in an even more than usually difficult tactical political position in the Commons as Chief Secretary. The more radical Liberal MPs were opposed to coercion in Ireland. The Cabinet, to which CB did not have adequate access, was divided on whether or not to renew the coercive legislation when it was due to expire. Further, although the Conservatives were not really opposed to coercion in Ireland there was always the possibility, as did come to pass, that they might come to some sort of understanding with the Irish Nationalists resulting in the defeat of the Government in the Commons and/or at the General Election which had to take place by the spring of 1887.

CB's only legislative initiative as Chief Secretary was a Bill introduced on 24 March to improve elementary education in Ireland, given that such education had been earlier made compulsory in England, Wales and Scotland and that Irish teachers were underpaid. During the course of his speech, in considering the financing of the extra costs, he pointed out that in the rest of the UK, 41 % of elementary educational costs were financed from the UK Exchequer, with the balance coming about equally from local rates and fees paid by parents, as against 80 %, 10 % and 10 % in Ireland. Accordingly, the Bill provided that – for example, as concerning teachers' pay – the local rates contribution be increased to half that of the Exchequer contribution.

From the Irish point of view the flaw was that so much of the extra cost was to be financed from local rates in Ireland and not from the UK Exchequer. Although the Bill received an unopposed Second Reading, it made no further progress and CB eventually advised Earl Spencer that the matter would be better left until Irish County Councils were established.

In the meantime the Liberal Cabinet continued to be divided on Irish questions, not only on coercion but also on land and local government reform and on the suggestion by Joseph Chamberlain (President of the Board of Trade) that a Central Board be set up with administrative functions for the whole of Ireland. Thus, from late February

---

[121] Weintrub (2000), pp.289-290

onwards, CB was involved in soundings among Liberal MPs and in exchanges with Lord Spencer on such matters.

However, by now, firstly Lord Spencer and then CB were privately coming to the conclusion that, as concerning the Government of Ireland, there was no half-way house. There had to be continuing rule by the UK Parliament and Government, with the necessary powers (including coercion) to maintain such rule or an Irish Parliament with full domestic responsibility.

In particular, they anticipated nothing but confusion and conflict if an elected Irish Central Board was set up with administrative functions while executive authority remained vested in those answerable to the UK Cabinet. However, the 'big question' – continuing coercion or Home Rule – was about to be considered no longer relatively privately in Liberal and Conservative circles but in a public context.

The Liberal Government had taken office in April 1880 with a substantial overall majority in the Commons. Thus, although the Liberals had suffered a net loss of 17 MPs at by-elections, the Government, on the face of it, retained its overall majority. However, on 8 June 1885, during the Budget debates, a critical Conservative amendment was carried by 264 votes to 252.

There were seventy-six Liberals absent (with no more than a dozen or so being paired), with thirty-six Irish Nationalists and six Liberals voting with the Conservatives. The Conservative-Irish Nationalist alliance followed exchanges involving Lord Randolph Churchill (who would serve as a Conservative Cabinet Minister in 1885-1886 and in 1886) and Charles Parnell, the Irish Nationalist Leader and the completely fallacious understanding that an incoming Conservative Government would avoid coercive policies in Ireland.

The Liberal Government eventually resigned and on 24 June the Marquis of Salisbury formed a minority Conservative administration. This was on the understanding that, given the 1884 Representative of the People Act (which extended the franchise to householders in the counties) and the 1885 Redistribution Act, the Conservatives would be allowed to remain in office until the new electoral registers were ready in the autumn when Parliament would be dissolved followed by a General Election.

During exchanges prior to the passage of the 1885 Redistribution Act (which gave Scotland 12 additional MPs) it was suggested that the Royal Burgh of Dunfermline be removed from Stirling Burghs and, with Kirkcaldy, form a new Burgh constituency. This was welcomed in Stirling but not in Dunfermline. Happily the suggestion was withdrawn and CB was able to retain his connection with all five Burghs without giving offence by making a premature choice.

The understanding of June 1885 allowed the Liberal Bill, which CB supported, reviving the office of Secretary for Scotland (Secretary of State from 1926) to proceed to a successful Second Reading in the House of Lords on 9 July. (The office of Secretary for Scotland had continued on and off after the Parliamentary Union of

1707 but was discontinued after the Jacobite Rising of 1745-1746 with, thereafter, Scottish business at Westminster being the responsibility of the Lord Advocate and the Home Office until late August 1885.) At that stage, the Bill was amended to transfer responsibility for Scottish education from the Privy Council to what would become the Scottish Office. The Bill reached the House of Commons on 21 July, was passed within two weeks and received the Royal Assent on 14 August.

Thus the first in the new line of Scottish Secretaries, as from 17 August 1885, was not a Liberal but a Conservative, Charles Henry Gordon-Lennox, Duke of Richmond, Lennox and Gordon, a descendant of Charles II and Louise de Keroualle. He had then been President of the Board of Trade for just under two months, having previously been President of the Board of Trade in 1867-1868 and Lord President of the Council in 1874-1880. His initial appointments included Sir Francis Sandford as Permanent Under-Secretary at the Scottish Office and Sir Henry Craik as Secretary of the Scotch (sic) Education Department. Both Sir Francis and Sir Henry were, like CB, Former Pupils of the High School of Glasgow.

At this time it was Gladstone's hope that a Conservative Government – with its assured majority in the House of Lords and with Liberal and Irish Nationalist support – would introduce a settlement of the Irish constitutional question on Home Rule lines – much as cross-party action had earlier ensured Roman Catholic Emancipation and the Repeal of the Corn Laws.

Indeed, such a solution had been implied by Lord Carnarvon (Conservative Lord Lieutenant for Ireland from late June 1885) in a secret discussion with Charles Parnell. Accordingly, given also Lord Randolph Churchill's fallacious assurances, Charles Parnell urged his supporters with votes in British constituencies to vote for Conservative candidates at the General Election in Nov-Dec 1885. This may have ensured the election of as many of thirty extra Conservative MPs at the expense of the Liberals.

Given the 30 votes by which the Irish Home Rule Bill was defeated at the Second Reading stage on 8 June 1886, if there had then been something like 30 fewer Conservative MPs and, at least, 17 more pro-Home Rule Liberal MPs, the Bill would have secured a Second Reading. Thus the next challenge to the Liberal Government would not have been defeat in the Commons and a General Election but the Conservative (and Liberal Unionist) majority in the House of Lords.

It should be appreciated that, as from his October 1885 election address, CB had not yet answered the 'big question' and was only publicly committed to a large extension of local government in Ireland.

> The dissolution of Parliament being about to discharge me from the honourable function of your representative, I beg, with great respect and with the warmest sense of your past kindness and consideration, to offer myself for election to serve in the same capacity in the new House of Commons. I venture to hope that my public conduct during 17 years has been such as to merit your general approval. But I do not found my

> claim to your favour upon the fact of the long association so much as on the substantial community of opinion on all public questions which I believe to subsist between us.
>
> I am not aware that I have departed in any particular from the profession of political faith which I made on the occasion of my first election. I then declared myself in favour of household suffrage in the counties; of the [secret] ballot; of a national and compulsory system of education; of complete religious equality involving disestablishment; of representative county government; of [land reform]; of a simplified form of land transfer; and of investing localities with direct control of licences for the sale of intoxicating liquor.
>
> During the years which have since elapsed, a period made up of two-thirds of reforming energy under Liberal Government, and one-third of legislative soupiness under Tory Government many of these reforms have been achieved; while others which then seemed equally needed remain unaccomplished.
>
> This delay in the work of legislation is mainly due to two causes – obstruction in the House of Commons and opposition, direct or indirect, in the House of Lords, which fails, as at present constituted, to sympathise with the general feeling of the country. I would, therefore, add to the unfulfilled elements of my former programme a drastic alteration in the rule of the Lower Chamber, and the complete reconstitution of the Upper.

[Commitments to landed property being held subject to the general interests of the community and to the abolition of fees for primary and secondary public sector education]

> My recent connection with the Government of Ireland has only served to increase my appreciation of the difficulties to be met by those who administer the affairs of that country. I am desirous of seeing at the earliest possible moment a large extension of local self-government in Ireland... I am strongly opposed to a meddlesome foreign policy, and I earnestly hope that our interference in Egypt... will soon be brought to an end... [122]

However, less than thirteen weeks later (26 December), after two days of discussion with Earl Spencer, he wrote to Earl Northbrook saying "There is no alternative to the grant of a Parliament" to Ireland.[123]

---

[122] Mackie (1914), pp.69-70

[123] As quoted in Spender (1923), Volume 1, p.93

In the meantime, the local Conservatives appreciated that they had no chance of organising any opposition to CB which would have the slightest hope of success. Further, although some Conservatives elsewhere urged the nomination of a Tory candidate, if only for the purpose of restricting CB electioneering to Stirling Burghs, this notion received little support from the local Tories. Accordingly, CB was returned unopposed for the third, but not for the last, time.

B – 1885-1886 – Opposition and Government (Cabinet Office)

Table 13 - The 1885 General Election - 24 November to 9 December (to 18 December)

Candidates (Unopposed), Percentages and MPs Elected

	England				Wales				Scotland			
Liberals	452	(4)	51.3	238	34	(4)	58.3	29	70	(5)	53.3	51
Conservatives	440	(1)	47.5	213	29	(0)	38.9	4	55	(0)	34.3	8
Irish Nationalists	2	(0)	0.1	1								
Others	26	(0)	1.1	4	2	(0)	2.8	1	32	(0)	12.4	11
	920	(5)		456	65	(4)		34	157	(5)		70

	Ireland				Universities				UNITED KINGDOM			
Liberals	14	(0)	6.8		2	(1)	46.3	1	572	(14)	47.4	319
Conservatives	70	(2)	24.8	16	8	(7)	53.7	8	602	(10)	43.5	249
Irish Nationalists	92	(19)	67.8	85					94	(19)	6.9	86
Others	10	(0)	0.6						70	(0)	2.2	16
	186	(21)		101	10	(8)		9	1338	(43)		670

Net Gains/Losses in MPs Elected compared to the 1880 General Election

	England	Wales	Scotland	Ireland	Universities	UK
Liberals	minus 16		minus 1	minus 15	minus 1	minus 33
Conservatives	plus 16		plus 2	minus 7	plus 1	plus 12
Irish Nationalists	plus 1			plus 22		plus 23
Others	plus 4	plus 1	plus 11			plus 16

Stirling Burghs - Electorate c.5,178 **Midlothian - Electorate 12,924**

Henry Campbell-Bannerman	Liberal	Unopposed	W.E. Gladstone	Liberal	7,879
			C. Dalrymple	Conservative	3,248

There was an increase of 18 in the number of Constituencies (England 5, Wales 1 and Scotland 12) with the increased electorate, votes and majority in Midlothian reflecting the enfranchisement of householders in the counties.

Eleven of the Liberals elected were Liberal/Labour MPs. In the Irish territorial constituencies, all 16 Conservatives and 8 of the Nationalists were elected in what became Northern Ireland after 1922.

The Irish Nationalist elected in England was T.P. O'Connor in Liverpool Scotland, a constituency he continued to represent until his death in 1929 as a Privy Councillor and 'Father' of the House of Commons. He had been MP for Galway from 1880 and was also elected for Galway in 1885 but opted to represent Liverpool Scotland. (Refer to Biographical Notes in the Bibliography)

The Others elected were 4 Independent Liberals in England, an Independent Liberal/Labour MP in Wales and 11 Independent Liberals in Scotland including four Crofter MPs associated with the Highland League and George Goschen (a former Liberal Cabinet Minister) who was elected in Edinburgh East with Liberal opposition and Conservative support.

Before the final results had been declared, the deeply divided Conservative Cabinet, meeting on 14 December, decided to reject Lord Carnarvon's plea for a Conservative-led Irish Home Rule Bill and he resigned from the Cabinet two days later. However, presumably aware of divisions in the Cabinet but not of the Cabinet's decision, the next day (15 December) Gladstone had a meeting with Arthur Balfour (then President of the Local Government Board), Lord Salisbury's nephew, during which the possibility of a Conservative-led Irish Home Rule Bill was discussed.

Nevertheless, the very next day (16 December) the Liberal Leader's son, Herbert Gladstone – at what was supposed to be a confidential meeting with a representative of the National Press Agency – said that his father was now personally committed to an Irish Home Rule Bill. Although, following press reports on 17 December, there was an ambiguous denial of this intention, any remaining faint hope that the Conservatives would introduce their own Home Rule Bill was now effectively extinguished.

One the other hand, just after the new Parliament assembled on 12 January (1886), Albert Grey (Liberal MP for Tyneside), at a meeting of Liberal MPs, anticipated the forthcoming schism by urging like-minded (and more senior) colleagues to declare themselves against Irish Home Rule.[124]

The Conservative position was confirmed in the Queen's Speech on 21 January followed by the announcement of a new Conservative Irish Coercion Bill on 25 January and the transfer of Irish Nationalist support from the Conservatives to the Liberals. Thus, later (on 25 January) when Jesse Collings (an associate of Joseph Chamberlain) moved an agrarian amendment to the Address in reply to the Queens' Speech, the thoughts of MPs were not on agricultural matters but on Ireland.

Nevertheless, in the division the Conservatives were defeated by 331 votes to 252. However, seventeen Liberals and one Independent Liberal, including two former Liberal Cabinet Ministers (George Goschen and the Marquis of Hartington) and Sir Henry James (a former Liberal Attorney-General) voted with the Conservatives. Some seventy other Liberal MPs – including two other former Liberal Cabinet Ministers (John Bright and C.P Villiers) – were absent or abstained.

The Conservative Government then resigned on 29 January and Gladstone was invited to form his third administration. He had considerable difficulty in constructing a ministry. This followed those invited to serve being advised that the new Cabinet would examine the possibility of setting up a legislative body in Dublin. This was too much for the Marquis of Hartington and Sir Henry James who, together

---

[124] Albert Grey (elder son of General Charles Grey, Private Secretary to Queen Victoria) failed to be re-elected as the Liberal Unionist Candidate for Tyneside at the July 1886 General Election, being defeated by the Liberal Candidate.

with the Duke of Argyll, the Earl of Derby. Earl Northbrook and the Marquis of Lansdowne, refused to serve.[125]

There were also difficulties with Joseph Chamberlain and George Otto Trevelyan but, with reservations, they agreed to serve as President of the Local Government Board and Secretary for Scotland, respectively. Jesse Collings also accepted office as Parliamentary Secretary to the Local Government Board and a Privy Counsellor.

Table 14 - Fifth Liberal Cabinet - February to July 1886	
Prime Minister	**William Ewart Gladstone,** (Third Cabinet as PM) MP for Midlothian
Lord Chancellor	Sir Farrer Herschell, 1st Lord Herschell
President of the Council	John Spencer, 5th Earl Spencer
Chancellor of the Exchequer	Sir William Harcourt, MP for Derby
Home Secretary	Hugh Childers, MP for Edinburgh South
Foreign Secretary	Archibald Primrose, 5th (Scottish) Earl of Rosebery & 2nd (UK) Lord Rosebery
Secretary for War	**Henry Campbell-Bannerman**, MP for Stirling Burghs
Colonial Secretary	George Leveson-Gower, 2nd Earl Granville, (Leader in the House of Lords)
First Lord of the Admiralty	George Robinson, 1st Marquis of Ripon
President of the Board of Trade	Anthony Mundella, MP for Sheffield
Secretary for India	John Wodehouse, 1st Earl of Kimberley
Chief Secretary for Ireland	John Morley, MP for Newcastle-upon-Tyne
President of the Local Government Board	
02/1886 -04/1886	Joseph Chamberlain, MP for Birmingham West
04/1886 -	James Stansfeld, MP for Halifax
Scottish Secretary	
02/1886 -04/1886	George Otto Trevelyan, MP for Hawick Burghs

Thus CB, having had junior office in both of Mr Gladstone's previous administrations now achieved Cabinet membership for the first time at the age of forty-nine and after seventeen years in the Commons. He was not Mr. Gladstone's first choice for the War Office as he had preferred Hugh Childers. Queen Victoria had taken strong exception to such a re-appointment and, with the support of Prince Albert Edward and the Duke of Cambridge (Commander-in-Chief), urged that CB was the most suitable man for the position.

Thus, the Queen's Private Secretary, reported to her on 8 February (1886), "Mr. Gladstone said that he wished to please Your Majesty to the best of his power, and

---

[125] The 15th (English) Earl of Derby, son of the former Conservative Leader and Prime Minister, was a senior Conservative Cabinet Minister in 1858-1859, 1866-1868 and 1874-1878. He joined the Liberals in 1880, serving as Liberal Colonial Secretary in 1882-1885 and joining the Liberal Unionists in 1886. Perhaps significantly, the family of the Marquis of Hartington owned a castle and land in Ireland and the Marquis of Lansdowne, who also held Scottish and Irish peerages, owned 121,000 acres in Ireland.

therefore at a great sacrifice would give up Mr. Childers and would select the gentleman named by Your Majesty, Mr. Campbell-Bannerman, for the War Office'.[126] However, the Prime Minister's family interests were secured by the appointment of his fourth son, Herbert Gladstone as CB's Financial Secretary.

(Accordingly, Hugh Childers became Home Secretary, having been defeated in Pontefract at the 1885 General Election but elected at a by-election in Edinburgh South on 29 January 1886)

And, once again – having received the congratulations of Stirling and Dunfermline Town Councils, the local Liberal Associations and Andrew Carnegie – CB had to submit to a Ministerial By-Election, being returned unopposed for Stirling Burghs on 10 February (1886).

Given that he had 'so recently received the honour of re-election' at the hands of the Stirling Burghs electorate', CB thought it unnecessary that he should make any further statement of his well-known political opinions. However, in his short election address, he necessarily referred to his appointment to the Cabinet, adding "From my previous experience in the War Department, I know how onerous are the duties which with much diffidence I have undertaken, and I can only promise to spare no effort to serve the country faithfully in the administration of its Army'. He also anticipated that, in encountering difficulties almost unexampled, Mr. Gladstone would 'receive the generous support of patriotic men throughout the country'.

CB's five month's tenure at the War Office was, of course, almost entirely overshadowed by the Irish Question. His first priority was to prepare the Army Estimates, as from the drafts left by his predecessors and involving an increase of £2.5 million. He presented the Estimates to the House of Commons on 16 March when, with the assistance of an intervention by Gladstone, he successfully resisted an attempt to add to the vote for the Volunteers. He was also involved in supporting an unopposed Bill to repeal the Contagious Diseases Acts (in the interests of the health of the Army and the moral conditions of the garrison towns) as achieved in April. With the approval of the Queen, the Duke of Cambridge (Commander-in-Chief) and the Admiralty, a new Naval and Military decoration, the Distinguished Service Order (DSO) was instituted in early July.

It is of interest to note that, in discussions leading to the institution of the DSO, an alternative considered was to add a new, fourth or fifth class to the Order of the Bath, given that, within nine years, CB was himself admitted to the first class as a GCB.[127] The election of four Crofter (Highland Land League) MPs at the 1885 General Election prompted the new Liberal Government to consider implementing the recommendations of the Royal Commission of Inquiry into the Condition of Crofters and Cottars (The Napier Commission) which had been appointed by the previous

---

[126] Spender (1923), Volume 1, p.99

[127] Risk (1972), pp.83-84

Liberal Government in 1883 and which reported in 1884. Accordingly, the passage of the 1886 Crofters Holdings Act which gave crofters the right to a fair rent, the right not to be evicted if they paid their rent and, on giving up their tenure, the right to compensation for any improvements they had made and eventually the formation of the Scottish Land Court in 1912. Such backing for the Crofting community was thereafter of much significance for Liberal support in the Highlands and Islands.

Meanwhile, on 13 March, Gladstone outlined his Irish proposals to the new Cabinet and only with difficulty persuaded Chamberlain and Trevelyan to withhold their resignations. However, thirteen days later (26 March), when the Prime Minister submitted his more detailed proposals, both Chamberlain and Trevelyan resigned, effectively from 6 April. Collings also then resigned from junior office and thereafter was unseated as an MP on petition.

James Stansfeld, MP for Halifax succeeded as President of the Local Government Board and the 13th (Scottish) Earl of Dalhousie – who sat in the House of Lords as 2nd (UK) Lord Ramsay – succeeded as Secretary for Scotland but without Cabinet membership.

After Gladstone introduced his Irish Home Rule Bill in the Commons on 8 April, a cross-party meeting – indicative of a new political alignment – was held on 14 April. The chairman was the 7th Earl Cowper who was also, as a result of the reversal of a Jacobite attainer, 4th (Scottish) Lord Dingwall.[128] The leading speakers were the Marquis of Hartington and George Goschen (1831-1907) for the Liberal and Independent Liberal dissidents and the Marquis of Salisbury and W.H. Smith (a former Chief Secretary for Ireland) for the Conservatives. As already mentioned, Goshen, a Liberal Cabinet Minister in 1866 and 1868-1874, had been elected as Independent Liberal MP for Edinburgh East at the 1885 General Election with official Liberal opposition and Conservative support. Earl Cowper and William Forster, respectively Liberal Lord Lieutenant and Liberal Chief Secretary for Ireland in 1880-1882, had resigned in May 1882 in opposition to the Government's so-called 'Kilmainan Treaty' with Parnell [the Irish Nationalist Leader], an attempt at compromise with the Irish Nationalists.

Chamberlain, Trevelyan and their 'Radical' associates did not attend the 14 April meeting, However, after the general committee of the National Liberal Federation, meeting in London on 5 May, overwhelmingly passed a motion of confidence in Gladstone, Chamberlain resigned from the Federation, which he had been mainly responsible for founding in 1877.[129]

Francis Schnadhorst, formerly Secretary of the highly successful, Chamberlain-dominated Birmingham Liberal Association, remained as Secretary of the National Liberal Federation which moved its headquarters from Birmingham to London in

---

[128] Currently (2018), the 8th (Scottish) Lord Dingwall who is also 12th (English) Lord Lucas of Crudwell sits in the Lords as an elected hereditary Conservative Peer.

[129] *Daily News,* 6 May 1886 and Cawood (2012), p.12

1887, with Schnadhorst having also become Secretary of the London-based (and resolutely Gladstonian) Liberal Central Association in 1886. (A final Liberal Unionist attempt to persuade the Federation to depart from its unconditional support for Gladstone's Irish policy was made at its Annual Conference on 3 November [1886] but this was easily seen off by the Gladstonians under the leadership of the Federation's President, Sir James Kitson of Leeds.)

During April (1886) Chamberlain had written to Schnadhorst saying 'The Liberal Party is going forward to certain disaster unless some steps are taken immediately to reunite us by mutual concession'.[130]

The Scottish Liberal Association and the National Liberal Federation of Scotland (formed in 1885 and corresponding to the National Liberal Federation in England and Wales) were initially divided on the Irish question. But later in 1886 the two bodies amalgamated, as an enlarged Scottish Liberal Association, with Gladstonians in control. Thereafter, the Association's annual autumn conferences became occasions for policy discussion and the adoption of programmes of radical reform. (The Scottish Liberal Association later became the Scottish Liberal Federation and, from 1946, the Scottish Liberal Party). At the time of his death in 1908, CB was President of the Scottish Liberal Association in succession to Rosebery. Also in 1886 the North and South Wales Liberal Federations were formed, with both being resolutely Gladstonian.

CB spoke at length, on 13 May, during the long debate on the Second Reading of the Government of Ireland Bill. He spoke immediately after Sir Henry James (Liberal Attorney-General in 1873-1874 and 1880-1885) who, speaking in opposition to the Bill, concluded by saying that he had to reject the inducement to follow the path of his former Leader (Gladstone) because that path would lead to nothing 'except confusion and darkness' and, accordingly, would follow the path which would 'maintain untouched the Empire of our Queen'.

In reply, CB started by noting that many of the opponents of the Bill – in particular, those who objected to any large extension of Home Rule in Ireland and those who had alternative schemes of their own – had spoken, not so much in terms of irreconcilable hostility to the Bill but with reference to certain points in the Bill, in particular the proposed virtually complete exclusion of Irish members from the House of Commons. He went on to consider the 'ticklish' religious question, stating that he knew of no instance 'comparable to that which is conjured in Ireland where we are excepted to believe that alone in the whole of Europe the two great branches of the Christian Church will be unable to deal on equal terms with the administration of their common affairs'.[131]

---

[130] From a collection of 'Liberal Letters' found in an old filling cabinet and auctioned in Elgin on 15 May 2013 for £ 600, Refer to reports in *The Herald* (Glasgow) and *The Press and Journal* (Aberdeen) of 7 May 2013 and to my letters, correcting errors in such reports, in *The Herald* of 8 May and *The Press and Journal* of 11 May.

[131] On the Irish religious question, it is of interest to note what was said by Dr. Gordon Lucy, speaking in Belfast on 10 May 2013 in the premises of the Ulster Scots Agency after the

Returning to the question of the retention or non-retention of Irish members in the House of Commons, CB indicated that, respecting the principle of no taxation without representation, the Government would be prepared to amend the Bill to provide that, before any tax applying to Ireland is created, increased, reduced or repealed, 'the Irish members will be summoned and restored to their full position in this House'. He concluded –

> I am a firm believer in the sobering effect of direct responsibility, and I am an equally firm believer in the healing effect of joint co-operation in public life between men of all creeds and classes. I advocate the adoption of the policy contained in this Bill, not only because I believe it will facilitate good government in Ireland, but because I believe it will be in the end the surest and shortest way of promoting concord within her shores, and restoring friendship and good feeling between the three [sic] parts of the United Kingdom.

Nine days later, on 22 May, when Hartington and his associates adopted a constitution as Liberal Unionists, Chamberlain and his associates continued to stand somewhat apart. Then on 27 May Gladstone called a meeting of some 280 Liberal MPs – those not yet known to be associated with Hartington or Chamberlain. He asked for support for the principle of Irish Home Rule, adding that the Bill could be amended in committee and indicating specifically that he was prepared to amend the Bill to allow a number of Irish MPs to remain at Westminster – thus going further than CB had done two weeks earlier. However, on the following day (28 May), a meeting of Liberal Unionists convened by Hartington was advised that the Conservative Chief Whip had said that his party would not oppose, at an ensuing General Election, any Liberal MP who opposed the Home Rule Bill. Despite such an assurance three such MPs did have Conservative opposition at the General Election.

Then, Chamberlain, at a meeting with fifty-four of his associates on 31 May, suggested that they all abstain on the Bill's Second Reading. But a letter was then read from John Bright advising his intention to vote with the Conservatives. Thereafter Chamberlain, Trevelyan and over forty of their associates took a belated and decisive decision to join the Liberal Unionists and vote with the Conservatives.

Thus the result of the division in the early hours of 8 June (1886) when 93 Liberal (now Liberal Unionist) MPs voted with the Conservatives against the Second Reading of Gladstone's first Irish Home Rule Bill resulting in its defeat by 343 votes to 313. Accordingly, a General Election was called for July (1886) with the

---

unveiling of a plaque, commemorating James, Viscount Bryce who born an Ulster Scot. Dr. Lucy concluded by saying that 'if Bryce had been more successful in persuading Gladstone of the reality of the Ulster question in 1886 or 1892/1893 the history of the island in the 20th century might make more pleasant reading... Bryce's failure to educate the Liberal political elite in these matters might be regarded as a matter of serious regret'.

Liberals and Irish Nationalists on one side of the divide and the Conservatives and Liberal Unionists on the other.

With, as in many other constituencies, the Liberals divided, the Conservatives aroused and with an injection of Liberal Unionism, CB faced his first serious opposition in Stirling Burghs since first being elected in 1868. His Liberal Unionist opponent was (Sir) John Pender, a Liberal MP in 1862-1866 and 1872-1885 (and later a Liberal Unionist MP in 1892-1895) and, like CB, a Former Pupil of the High School of Glasgow.[132]

CB took nothing for granted, speaking frequently in all five Burghs. He asked wavering Liberals to concentrate on the principle of Irish Home Rule and not to be concerned with details, with all concerns and objections as to such details to receive attention when the next Home Rule Bill was drafted and debated. He also very much relied on his personal relationships within the Constituency, particularly with key individuals. His Agent in Dunfermline, John Ross, had to be persuaded not to resign. His Chairman in Stirling, James B. Smith, who had indicated his opposition to Irish Home Rule on 20 April, got down on the same side as CB on 15 May. Accordingly, CB was re-elected by 2,440 votes to 1,471 on a 74.8 % turnout.

Before nominations for the July General Election, an attempt, supported by Gladstone, was made to persuade CB to transfer his candidature to Edinburgh East in order to challenge George Goschen. The idea was also to provide the Liberal Party with another rallying point in south-east Scotland in addition to Gladstone's Midlothian. Fortunately, nothing came of this as if CB had left Stirling Burghs it would probably have been lost to the Liberal Unionists. Further, Gladstone was not confined to Midlothian, being returned unopposed. In any case, Goschen, as a Liberal Unionist, was defeated by 3,694 votes to 2,253 by another Liberal, Professor Robert Wallace.[133]

---

[132] There were three other General Elections with Glasgow Grammar/High School Former Pupils in direct opposition. In 1835 the incumbent Whig MP, James Ewing was defeated by Colin Dunlop (Radical) in the then two-member constituency of Glasgow. In 1905 the incumbent Conservative MP, Charles Scott Dickinson was defeated by James Cleland (Liberal) in Glasgow Bridgeton. In 1922 the incumbent Coalition/National Liberal MP, Sir William Sutherland defeated Harry Watt (Liberal) in Argyll.

[133] The Professor was a native of Culross and formerly a Church of Scotland Minister and Editor of *The Scotsman*. He remained MP for Edinburgh East until his death in 1899.

6 – Meigle, Belmont Castle and Personal Life and Routine

Meigle and Belmont Castle

In 1887 the Campbell.-Bannermans moved into their new country home, Belmont Castle (less than half-a-mile westwards from the centre of Meigle) in Perthshire which was to be their Scottish home for the rest of their lives. As will be considered, Sir Henry was not the first UK MP, Privy Councillor or Cabinet Minister to be the owner of Belmont Castle.

Meigle is on the A94 between Coupar-Angus (5 miles to the west) and Forfar (12 miles to the east). As from the 1881 Census, local populations then were 966 (Ecclesiastical Parish which included part of Coupar-Angus Civil Parish) and 696 (Civil Parish). Meigle and Belmont are 28 miles south-west of the Stracathro estate owned by Henry's father, Sir James Campbell and his descendants in whole or part since 1847.

Meigle – *Meggill* (1183), *Migdele* (c.1200), *Mygghil* & *Myglle* (1378), *Megle* & *Meggill* (1561), *Meggle* (1566) – as from the Gaelic *Migeil,* or more likely the Pictish *mig+dol,* meaning 'marshy meadow'.[134] This reflects the village's situation between originally marshy ground to the south and the River Isla to the north. Further, Meigle lies in the plain of Strathmore, an area long associated with rich arable farmland. As from the development of larger urban communities, Meigle came to be where the roads from Perth to Forfar and from Dundee to Alyth intersect. The village was created a Burgh of Barony in 1608 but thereafter failed to develop into more than a village. (Refer to the earlier reference to Burghs of Barony in Chapter 1)

Meigle is also said to be the oldest village in Scotland, given (1) the evidence in the vicinity of the Parish Church for souterrains (semi-subterranean chambers used for storage) dating from as early as c.100 BC, (2) the settlement associated with the 1st to 3rd century Roman encampment at nearby Cardean, (3) the Pictish cemetery, probably dating from the 3rd to 8th centuries,[135] and (4) the village's outstanding collection of sculptured Pictish Stones, nearly all originating locally, dating from the 8th century onwards. Indeed, Meigle was, briefly in the early 9th century, a Pictish capital.

---

[134] The place-name Migvie in Aberdeenshire also includes the Pictish *mig* (marsh), with Migvie also having Pictish 'evidence in stone', in that there is a 9th century Pictish cross-slab in the Kirkyard.

[135] 'A Pict-and-Mix Selection – Meigle, Perthshire' in *Current Archaeology* (December 2012) and 'A Pictish Cemetery in Perthshire', 2013 (Online AOC Archaeology Group). The site is between Coupar-Angus and Meigle and, therefore, somewhat westwards of Belmont Castle.

There are many legends associated with Meigle. For example, there is, near the front entrance to the Parish Church, *Vendora's Mound* which is supposed to contain the remains of King Arthur's Queen Guinevere! Further, Meigle is associated with the legends connecting some of the 'relics' of Andrew the Apostle with the place in Fife that came to be known as St. Andrews from c.1158.[136] According to a St. Andrews foundation text written in the 12th century,[137] in about 840 a Pictish Scribe called *Thana,* based in Meigle, wrote or rewrote one of the stories about how St. Regulus (aka Rule) was shipwrecked at Crail, near 'St. Andrews'. He was carrying some 'relics' of St. Andrew from Patras in Greece to an unknown destination. He then met *Onuist* (son of *Urguist),* King of Picts, 729-761 who gave him some land so that he (and his 'relics') could settle at the place which became known as St. Andrews.

Thana is said to have been instructed to write or rewrite the story by *Uurad,* King of Picts, 839-842. *Uurad* – whose Gaelic name was *Ferat,* and who was related to the Kings of Dál Riata – was one of the last Kings of Picts before the conclusive dynastic union of Picts and Scots under Kenneth Mac Alpin in the mid-9th century.[138]

It is said that the first church in Meigle was built – on the site of the present-day Parish Church – early in the 7th century, as the focus of a Christian community committed to a range of spiritual and other creative activities. However, the 'evidence in stone' for a 7th century church is inconclusive and it may be that it was constructed basically of wattle – wooden stakes or rods, interlaced with twigs. (Such a construction is the origin of the place-names BANCHORY and BANGOR, with one such being the Banchory on the River Isla near Meigle.). A succession of churches have been built on the site until the church, as built or rebuilt in 1791-1799, was rebuilt (providing 600 sittings) in 1869-1870 after a fire in 1869.

1791-1799 was also the time of the production of the [First] *Statistical Account of Scotland,* with the entry for Meigle being written by the Rev. Dr. James Playfair (1739-1819) Parish Minister in 1777-1800. (His grandson, Dr. Lyon Playfair, MP is mentioned in Chapter 4 in connection with Sir Henry Campbell-Bannerman's maiden speech in the House of Commons on 17 June 1869.) The entry for Meigle in the *New Statistical Account of Scotland* (1834-1845) was written by the Rev. James Mitchell [1769-1855], Parish Minister in 1808-1855. *The Statistical Accounts* were historical and contemporary accounts of all parishes in Scotland. The (First) *Statistical Account,* for 936 parishes, was published by Sir John Sinclair (1754-1835), 1st Baronet of Ulbster in Caithness founder of the Sinclair political dynasty,

---

[136] St. Andrews in Fife was originally known as Kilrimont (or Chilrimunt or Kilrimund) with the change of name coinciding with the decision to start work on the Cathedral to be dedicated to St. Andrew, although the Cathedral was not completed and consecrated until 1318. The medieval Scottish Church did not have metropolitans (Archbishops) until 1472 (St, Andrews) and 1492 (Glasgow), but the primacy of St. Andrews was confirmed in a Papal Bull of 1225, giving the Scottish bishops the right to hold provincial councils with the Bishop of St. Andrews usually acting as conservator (convener).

[137] Online *ODNB – Kings of the Picts*

[138] Smyth (1991), Tables XII and XIV

now in its seventh UK generation. However, two earlier Sinclairs of Ulbster represented Caithness in the old Parliament of Scotland in the 17th century,

During Dr. James Playfair's time at Meigle, the village gained some notoriety when, in September 1797, the Depute Lord Lieutenant of Perthshire had to call out the local Company of the Perthshire Yeomanry and Volunteers to defend his house in Coupar-Angus against what he described as a 'Mob from Meigle', who were protesting against the Militia Acts. Such Acts provided for a form of conscription by ballot and it was suspected that the conscripts were going to be shipped off to the West Indies where disease took toll of so many UK soldiers. The tumult in Coupar-Angus was easily suppressed and nine of the rioters from Meigle were escorted to Dundee for trial.[139]

After the Disruption of the Church of Scotland in 1843, there was also a Free Church (United Free from 1900), built in 1853, in Meigle. After the reunion with the Church of Scotland in 1929, the local United Free Church gradually fell into disrepair and is now used as a store. The Episcopal (Anglican) Church of St. Margaret of Scotland was built in Meigle in 1852, but was served from Alyth from 1854, closed in 1952 and was demolished thereafter. (Within The Church of Scotland, the adjacent Ecclesiastical Parishes of Ardler [centred on a mission church built in 1883] and Kettins were united with Meigle in 1981).

Belmont Castle, bought by the Campbell-Bannermans in late 1884, was originally built as a three-storey tower house (with a garret within a parapet) in the late 15th century and was then known as Kirkhill,[140] being a residence of the late medieval Bishops of Dunkeld. In 1183 the patronage and major teinds (tithes) of Meigle Parish had been granted by Simon de Meggill, the then local landowner to the Canons of St. Andrews Augustinian Cathedral Priory (as founded in the 1140s) and later, by 1249, to the Bishop and Canons of Dunkeld Cathedral. Indeed, in the late 18th century it was recorded that "the greater part of the stipend of Dunkeld [was] paid out of this parish" [of Meigle].[141] (With Dunkeld and Meigle being among the first fifty or so Church of Scotland Presbyteries created by 1593, the medieval and later connection has since been restored in that they are now united in the present-day Presbytery of Dunkeld and Meigle.)

In 1404 the Meggill family, in the person of William Meggill, resigned their lands to Sir David Lindsay (c.1360-1407), 1st (Scottish) Earl of Crawford from 1398. In 1474, David Lindsay (1440-1495), 5th Earl from 1453, endowed a perpetual chaplaincy in the Parish Church of Meigle for the soul of King James III and that of his Queen (Margaret). The Earl was created Duke of Montrose by King James III on 18 May 1488 but the title and other offices were forfeited after the Battle of Sauchieburn and the murder of the King on 11 June 1488. However, the title was

---

[139] Tennant (1970), pp.67-68

[140] Kirkhill was otherwise known as Kirkhill of Meigle or Kirklands

[141] (First) *Statistical Account of Scotland, Meigle.*

restored, but only for life, by the new King (James IV) on 18 September 1489.[142] Thus in 1495 the Dukedom reverted to the Crown until it was conferred on James Graham, 4th (Scottish) Marquis of Montrose in April 1707, that is just before the Anglo-Scottish Parliamentary Union in the following month. Further, given a Lindsay-Lyon blood feud, it was probably in the circumstances of the 1488 forfeiture, that the Lyons of Glamis then acquired, at least, some lands in the Parish of Meigle. (The Lyons of Glamis are descended from a daughter of Robert II, the first Stewart King of Scots)

Certainly, by the immediate post-Reformation period, the Kirkhill estate (originally over 8,690 acres and reaching a height of 759 ft. above sea-level) was a possession of the Lyons (Bowes-Lyon from 1776) of Glamis. Indeed, it is recorded that in 1589 Sir Thomas Lyon's house at Kirkhiill was attacked and burned by rebels led by Sir Patrick Gordon (acting for George Gordon, 6th [Scottish] Earl of Huntly) with Sir Thomas himself being captured and not released until later in the year.[143] Sir Thomas (c.1546-1608) was the younger brother of John Lyon (c.1544-1578), 8th (Scottish) Lord Glamis and guardian during the minority of his son (Sir Thomas's nephew), Patrick Lyon (1575-1615), 9th Lord Glamis and, from 1606, 1st (Scottish) Earl of Kinghorne, (The designation was changed to Strathmore and Kinghorne in 1677.)

However, no later than 1686 the Kirkhill estate was sold to Sir George Mackenzie (1636-1691) of Rosehaugh in the Black Isle (Ross and Cromarty). Sir George was known as 'Bluidy Mackenzie' because, as Lord Advocate, he was responsible for prosecuting ("persecuting to death") prominent Covenanters during the reigns of Charles II and James VII and II. On the other hand, he founded the Advocates Library (the National Library of Scotland from 1925) in 1682 although it was not formally opened until 15 March 1689.

After the abdication by flight of James VII and II in 1688, Sir George opposed the declaration of the Scottish Convention of Estates on 4 April 1689 that the throne was vacant. Being also an associate of the Jacobite John Graham of Claverhouse, 1st (Scottish) Viscount of Dundee (aka 'Bluidy Clavers' or 'Bonnie Dundee'), Sir George found a pressing need to leave Scotland later in the month for England where he died in 1691. After Sir George's death, ownership of Kirkhill passed to a son (George Mackenzie), then to a daughter (Lady Elizabeth Mackenzie) and then to a grandson, James Stuart, 2nd (Scottish) Earl of Bute, the son of Sir George's daughter, Agnes and the 1st Earl. (The Stewarts or Stuarts of Bute are descended, in the male line, from Sir John Stewart, Hereditary Sheriff of Bute from 1385, an illegitimate son of Robert II).[144]

---

[142] Online *ODNB – The Lindsay Family*

[143] Online *ODNB – Sir Thomas Lyon*

[144] The Stewarts of Bute changed the spelling of their surname to Stuart during the 16th century as from the spelling used by Mary, Queen of Scots while in France in 1548-1561. However, her son (James VI and I) always referred to himself as a Stewart.

On the 2nd Earl's death in 1723, ownership of Kirkhill passed to his second son, James Stuart (1719-1800), a younger brother of John Stuart, 3rd (Scottish) Earl of Bute who was briefly Tory Prime Minister in 1762-1763. As an adult, James Stuart took the additional surname of Mackenzie and was successively Tory MP for Argyll (1742-1747), Bute (1747-1754), Ayr Burghs (1754-1761) and Ross-shire (1761-1780).

In 1758 Stuart-Mackenzie was appointed Envoy-Extraordinary to the King of Sardinia. Five years later he was recalled to assist in the management of Scottish affairs on behalf of his elder brother, the Prime Minister, being also appointed to the UK Privy Council and made Lord Privy Seal for Scotland with considerable powers of patronage.

However, the intimacy of his brother with the King (George III) brought unpopularity to the whole family and when George Grenville (Prime Minister 1763-1765) removed the Earl as an adviser to the King in 1765, Stuart-Mackenzie was also forced out of office. Nevertheless, when William Pitt the Elder, 1st Earl of Chatham, formed a ministry (as UK Lord Privy Seal) in 1766, Stuart-Mackenzie was reinstated as Lord Privy Seal for Scotland for life at an annual salary of £ 3,000 but without any real powers or responsibilities. (From 1766, the only responsibility of the Lord Privy Seal of Scotland was as nominally the Keeper of the Privy Seal of Scotland but with duties undertaken by a Deputy Keeper. The Lord Privy Seal's annual salary was restricted to a maximum of £ 1,200 in 1817, with the office remaining unfilled since 1922.).[145]

Having in 1752, as the feudal superior, taken possession of Kirkhill from Sir William Nairne of Dunsinnan, Stuart-Mackenzie had the old tower house rebuilt in 1765-1769 at a cost of £ 10,000, with the name being changed to Belmont Castle. As much as possible of the old Kirkhill tower house was incorporated in the new building including the fortified clock tower (complete with shot hole) which survives to this day. On Stuart-Mackenzie's death in 1800, Belmont was inherited by his nephew, Lieutenant-Colonel James Archibald Stuart-Wortley, MP, a younger son of the 3rd Earl, with the ownership remaining with him and his descendants for the next seventy-two to eighty-five years. (The additional surname of Wortley had been added in 1795 after inheriting his mother's family estates in Yorkshire and Cornwall in 1794. The additional surname of Mackenzie was again added to the family's main line surname name in 1803 but later removed.)

---

[145] The last holder of the office of Keeper of the Privy Seal of Scotland from 1907 to 1922 was Sir Gavin Campbell, KG (1851-1922), 1st Marquis of Breadalbane from 1885. He held junior office in the Liberal Administrations of Gladstone in 1873-1874, 1880-1885 and 1892-1894 and of Rosebery in 1894-1895.

Table 15 – Owners of Belmont Castle – 1800-1884
Lieutenant-Colonel James Archibald Stuart-Wortley (1747-1818) Tory MP for Bossiney (Cornwall) 1797-1802 Owner of Belmont Castle from 1800 I James Archibald Stuart-Wortley-Mackenzie (1776-1845) Tory MP for Bossiney (Cornwall) 1802-1818 Tory MP for Yorkshire 1818-1826 1st Lord Wharncliffe 1826 UK Lord Privy Seal 1834-1835 (Sir Robert Peel's First Cabinet) UK Lord President of the Council 1841-1845 (Sir Robert Peel's Second Cabinet) Owner of Belmont Castle from 1818 I John Stuart-Wortley-Mackenzie (1801-1855) Tory MP for Bossiney (Cornwall) 1823-1830 Tory MP for Perth Burghs 1830-1831 Tory MP for West Riding of Yorkshire 1831-1845 2nd Lord Wharncliffe 1845 Owner of Belmont Castle from 1845 I Edward Montagu Stuart-Wortley-Mackenzie (1827-1899) 3rd Lord Wharncliffe 1855 1st Earl of Wharncliffe 1876 Owner of Belmont Castle from 1855 to 1884

The 1st Lord Wharncliffe at first opposed the 1832 Reform Bills but eventually took an important part in helping the Bills through the House of Lords. As then Lord President of the Council, he was due to be present (with the Archbishop of Canterbury and others) at the birth of Prince Albert Edward (the future King Edward) in 1841, but he (and the Archbishop) were late and missed the birth. Charles Beily Stuart-Worley (1851-1926), a grandson of the 1st Lord, was Conservative MP for Sheffield (1880-1885) and for Sheffield Hallam (1885-1916). He was Under-Secretary at the Home Office in 1885 and again in 1886-1892. He was created Lord Stuart of Wortley in 1917 with the peerage becoming extinct on his death. (Nick Clegg, Liberal Democrat Leader from 2007 and Deputy Prime Minister and Lord President of the Council from 2010 to 2015 , was MP for Sheffield Hallam from 2005 to 2017) Lord Stuart's father, James Archibald Stuart-Wortley (1805-1881), was MP for Halifax (1835-1837) and for Bute (1842-1859). A Conservative until 1846, he was thereafter, as a supporter of Free Trade, a Peelite. He served in Lord Palmerston's Whig-Peelite-Radical Administration as Solicitor-General for England and Wales in 1857-1858. Edward Montagu Stuart-Wortley-Mackenzie, as 3rd Lord Wharncliffe, was a supporter of the Confederate States during the US Civil War

(1861-1865) to the extent of being President of the Manchester Southern Independence Association.[146]

In 1872 the Belmont estate was broken up and sold off in lots by the 3rd Lord Wharncliffe However, the Castle, with 400 acres, failed to sell, with the ownership being retained by Edward Montagu Stuart-Wortley-Mackenzie (1st Earl of Wharncliffe from 1876) until the sale to the Campbell-Bannermans.

The Campbell-Bannermans and Belmont Castle

The sale and purchase is said to have been at a bargain price as, during the residential tenancy of a Mr. Low and not long before 7 July 1884, much of the Castle was destroyed by fire. This was its condition when it and its policies were advertised in *The Scotsman* on 8 August 1884.

BELMONT CASTLE, STRATHMORE, AND POLICIES

To be SOLD by Public Roup, within Dowell's Auction Rooms, Edinburgh, on a day in September to be afterwards named, unless previously disposed of by Private Bargain – Private Offers are invited –

BELMONT CASTLE (unfortunately to a great extent destroyed by a recent fire) and the POLICIES' The Remains of the Castle are easily capable of restoration, as the outer walls stand and are nearly uninjured, or their site is admirably suited for a modern Mansion. The Policies, consisting of Lawn, Grass Parks, and Arable Land, within Ring Fence, extend to about 400 acres, and embrace a quantity of valuable Wood. The Grass Parks always command Good Rents, and the Arable Land is well Let. The Ornamental Timber in the Park is unequalled in Scotland for size and beauty. Access by Rail to all parts is most convenient. Alyth Junction, a principal Station of the Caledonian Railway, is within Ten Minutes' Drive.
(William Kerr, Solicitor) 26 Castle Street, Dundee

Accordingly, the Castle was almost entirely reconstructed for the Campbell-Bannermans, with their original country house (Gennings) in Kent not being much used after 1887 when they took up residence at Belmont. Presumably, their Glasgow house was sold about this time if not earlier. During 1885 the Castle was reconstructed on a larger scale with beautiful fireplaces, cornices, etc. The stair hall (originally a covered-in courtyard), adjacent to the main lounge (or living hall), is particularly impressive, with its grand staircase and a dome (cupola) of strained glass, with the round face of a heraldic sun beaming cheerfully down. A large annexe was built on, providing spacious guest rooms and staff quarters. Two new lodges

---

[146] Amanda Foreman (2010-2011), p.xxxv

were also constructed and the others brought up-to-date.[147] In 1886 the stables were built, using the same quarry stone that had been used for the Castle.

The grounds were planned to look their best in winter when the Campbell-Bannermans were in residence. There were great sweeps of lawns, a flower garden in the shape of a coat of arms, and a two acre walled kitchen garden. It is said that Sir Henry used to sit thinking in the shade of 'Old Maggie', a large copper beech tree at the front of the Castle. When in London, flowers, fruit and vegetables were sent regularly in season from Belmont, with a white gardenia being posted daily to Charlotte.

When at Belmont, and not too busy with public affairs, Sir Henry often took a walk into the village, usually calling at the bank and post office (which was never so busy before or after Sir Henry's time). He was a liberal contributor to local purposes, giving freely in cases of distress and with annual donations to both the local Parish (Church of Scotland) and Free (United Free from 1900) Churches, the Horticultural Society, School Soup Kitchen, Public Library, Strathmore Ploughing Society and the like.

The Campbell-Bannermans also presented annually medals to the Meigle School duxes, boy and girl. David Eaton, a present-day Meigle resident, has seen (and has a drawing of) one such silver medal, made by Hamilton & Inches, Edinburgh, as engraved 'Meigle School – Boy Dux – William Leslie – 1900' and 'Presented by Lady Campbell-Bannerman'. After her death in 1906 and Sir Henry's in 1908, the presentations were continued by Mrs. Alice Campbell – Sir Henry's niece by marriage – the new lady of Belmont Castle. After she left the district (by early 1913), the presentations were continued by Sir George Kinloch, 3rd Baronet of Kinloch – then the major local landowner in and around Meigle – until the Kinloch estate was sold off in lots in 1922-1923.[148]

The Meigle Cricket Club had the use of a field within the Belmont grounds where, with Sir Henry's consent, a pavilion was erected in 1907.[149] In 1901, the Strathmore Curling Club also received some ground, at a nominal rent, from Sir Henry on which a curling pond was created, His farming tenants, including William Tasker who would be one of those helping to carry the coffin on the day of Sir Henry's funeral in April 1908, found him to be a good and sympathetic landlord. All the local tradesmen and shopkeepers also benefited greatly from the Campbell-Bannermans' patronage which thus brought much prosperity to the village. Nor was the welfare of

---

[147] There is, beside the Castle's south lodge, a very large upright boulder – a 'menhir' – some 11 feet high, tapering roughly to a point and featuring ring- and cup-marks. It is known as 'Macbeth's Stone', but it pre-dates that King of Scots (1040-1057) by over two thousand years, being probably upended and carved before 1,000 BC. (Gifford [2007], p.195).

[148] *Stirling Observer* (29 April 1908), Meigle SWRI, *Our Meigle Book,* (1932, p.8), David Eaton of Temple Hall, Meigle, 2013 and Perth and Kinross Council Archives.

[149] The Meigle Cricket Club is now based in the village's Victoria Park which is fronted by the War Memorial, with sixteen names from 1914-1918 and eight from 1939-1945.

estate and domestic staff neglected. For example, two sisters, the Misses Alderson, who had worked for Charlotte, were given a furnished house on the estate on their retirement and, after one of them died, the other, being lonely, was provided with comfortable accommodation in the Castle.[150] (For Sir Henry's welcome by the people of Meigle at the time of his accession as Prime Minister in December 1905 and during the 1906 General Election campaign, refer to Chapters 10 and 11.)

In early 1948, Duncan Macfarlane who in his youth had been employed for four years by the Campbell-Bannermans, was interviewed for the *Glasgow High School Magazine*. He recalled times at Belmont Castle and in Europe (including Marienbad) and London, and meeting such Campbell-Bannerman guests as Princess Alexandra (later Queen Consort), Lord Rosebery and Samuel L. Clemens (Mark Twain). Mr. Macfarlane then wrote a paragraph about the Campbell-Bannermans for the *Magazine* of June 1948.

> My own memory of them will never fail. They were a devoted husband and wife and a golden example to their fellow-creatures – kind and considerate to all their employees and always with a helping hand to the poor and needy. Their service to the country, to my way of thinking, was never fully appreciated. We need his help very badly today.

When at Belmont the Campbell-Bannermans had daily (evening) prayers domestically. They also worshipped regularly on Sundays in Meigle Parish Church. Their pew was in the east gallery overlooking the later memorial plaque for Sir Henry and near the windows which have overlook their graves since 1906-1908.

To the memory of
The Right Hon. Sir Henry Campbell-Bannerman of Belmont Castle
Prime Minister from 1905 to 1908
Born 7 September 1836 – Died 27 April 1908

When in office Sir Henry took his paperwork up to Belmont. Particularly after the opening of the Forth Rail Bridge in 1890, he would tell his friends, colleagues and officials that, if they left London at noon, the train would take them directly to Alyth Junction Station by the evening, with then a carriage journey of ten minutes to Belmont. Alyth Junction was one of the many junctions on the Strathmore line from Perth and the south to Aberdeen which was closed in 1967, as was Alyth Junction Station, although the line from Perth (via Stanley Junction) to Forfar remained open until 1982. Alyth Junction, with its station known as Meigle from its opening in 1862 until 1876, was where the line from Dundee to Alyth crossed the main line. The Alyth Junction station was unusual in that it had three through platforms – two for the main line and one for the Alyth line, with connections between the three lines immediately east of the station.

---

[150] *Stirling Observer*, 29 April 1908

Apart from London-based and more local guests, John Morley was a frequent visitor, at the time of and after his election as MP for Montrose Burghs in 1896, on his way to/from the nearby five burghs in that constituency. Sir William Harcourt (then MP for a Welsh constituency and Liberal Leader in the Commons) was also a guest when he received the Freedom of the nearby City and Royal Burgh of Dundee in November 1897.

An alcove off the main lounge at Belmont was and is still known as 'Gladstone's Walk' or the 'Cabinet Room'. Presumably named not for William Gladstone (Prime Minister) – as is local legend – but for his fourth and youngest son, Herbert Gladstone who was Sir Henry's Chief Whip in the House of Commons in 1899-1905 and thereafter his Home Secretary. It has also been suggested that an emergency Cabinet meeting was once held at Belmont Castle when Sir Henry was Prime Minister.[151] However, although there were a number of occasions when a number of Cabinet Ministers were together at Belmont – for example, at the time of Lady Campbell-Bannerman's funeral in 1906 – there is no record of a formal Cabinet meeting ever being held there.

The local (East Perthshire) Liberal MP when the Campbell-Bannermans arrived at Belmont was Robert Menzies with whom they were friendly until he died in 1889. Thereafter, they remained friends of his family. Another near neighbour and friend was Blanche, Lady Airlie (1830-1921) whom they often visited at Airlie Castle. (Indeed, Lady Airlie was the first person visited locally by Sir Henry after Lady Campbell-Bannerman's burial in Meigle in September 1906). She was the widow of the 10th (Scottish) Earl of Airlie (who died in 1861) and a daughter of the 2nd Lord Stanley of Alderley who was a Liberal Cabinet Minister (Postmaster-General) in 1860-1866 and established the Post Office Savings Bank in 1861.[152]

Her daughter, Clementina married the 1st Lord Redesdale, with the 6th Lord currently sitting in the House of Lords as a Liberal Democrat Life Peer (Lord Mitford) although he continues to be known as Lord Redesdale. Blanche was also the grandmother of Clementine Hozier (the wife of Winston Churchill) and of the Mitford sisters (one of whom married Sir Oswald Mosley). Her great-grandson (Sir) Angus Ogilvy married Princess Alexandra in 1963.

---

[151] The Rev. Lewis Cameron, then Director of The Church of Scotland's Social Services, writing about Belmont Castle in 1971.

[152] Blanche, Lady Airlie was also an aunt of Bertrand Russell and of Venetia Stanley (1887-1948) who was a particular friend and correspondent of H.H. Asquith in 1910-1915 while he was Prime Minister. In mid-1915 she married Edwin Montagu, a Liberal and then a Coalition Liberal MP in 1906-1922 who served in both Asquith's and Lloyd George's Cabinets.

However, the major landowners in and around Meigle in the Campbell-Bannermans' time were the Kinlochs.[153] Dr. David Kinloch (1559-1617) of Dundee, *Medicinae Doctor Regius* to King James VI, purchased the estates of Aberbothrie and Balmyle which he re-named Kinloch, being in the Ecclesiastical Parish of Meigle but in the Civil Parish of Coupar Angus. Dr. David's grandson, another David Kinloch (who died in about 1700) was created Baronet of Kinloch in the Baronetage of Nova Scotia in 1685.

The third Baronet, Sir James (Died 1766), took part in the 1745-1746 Jacobite Rising, being captured, condemned to death, with forfeiture of his baronetcy and his lands. However, the sentence was commuted to permanent exile from Scotland, with the restoration of his lands but not the baronetcy. His son, William Kinloch then sold the lands to his cousin, John Kinloch, a sugar planter in Jamaica, and when he died there in 1770 the Kinloch estate was inherited by his brother, George Oliphant Kinloch.

His son, George Kinloch (Born 1775), known as the Radical Laird, was such an extreme advocate of political reform that he was declared an outlaw in Edinburgh in 1819 and had to spend some years in exile in France. However, he was able to return to Scotland in time to be elected Radical MP for Dundee at the 1832 General Election, serving briefly until his death in early 1833,

The Radical Laird's son, George Kinloch (1800-1881) was created Baronet of Kinloch in the Baronetage of the United Kingdom in 1873, having in 1871 also become proprietor of the village of Meigle by purchase (£ 75,000) from the late Queen Mother's grandfather, Claude Bowes-Lyon, 13th (Scottish) Earl of Strathmore and Kinghorne. With a new Primary School having been built in 1876-1877, in 1877, Sir George Kinloch (First UK Baronet) housed the local collection of Pictish Stones in the Meigle Museum (The Old School House, dating from 1844), as now with its contents in the care of Historic Scotland.

Most of the Stones were taken from the Kirkyard and others from the Church after it was burned down in 1869. Unfortunately, some were lost at this time including the only Pictish Stone to show a wheeled vehicle or chariot. Others were found when an old malt kiln was being demolished to build what would have been a wash house, but is now the kitchen and workshop of Temple Hall house across the road from the Church. These Stones are included in the title deeds of Temple Hall with the instruction that 'should the Museum ever close the owner has to make room to put them back on Temple Hall property'.[154]

Thanks to the initiative of the Perth and Kinross Heritage Trust, the Meigle Churchyard is no longer in the extremely dilapidated condition of a few years ago. Disabled access has also been provided between the Churchyard and the Museum.

---

[153] Refer to Charles Tennant's *The Radical Laird – George Kinloch of Kinloch, 1775-1833* (1970)

[154] David Eaton of Temple Hall, Meigle, 2012

It is to be hoped that the good work will continue and also that the Campbell-Bannerman grave will eventually come to have the setting intended at the time of Lady Campbell-Bannerman's burial in 1906. (Refer to Chapter 12) It is unfortunate that Parish Churchyards in Scotland were effectively secularised by legislation in 1925.

Sir George's son, Sir John Kinloch (1849-1910), Second Baronet from 1881, was, from 1887, a particular friend of Sir Henry, and would be another of those helping to carry the coffin on the day of Sir Henry's funeral in April 1908. Sir John was also the local Liberal MP (East Perthshire) in 1889-1903, being succeeded by Tom Buchanan, another Glasgow High School Former Pupil, who served until he retired in December 1910. He would be Financial Secretary at the War Office in Sir Henry's 1905-1908 Administration and then Under-Secretary at the India Office in 1908-1909. (Refer also to the Biographical Notes in Appendix 3)

The extent of the Campbell-Bannerman's hospitality at Belmont can be illustrated by reference to an occasion in early December 1897 when a number of overnight guests were entertained. The guests included Dr. Robert Farquharson (Liberal MP for Aberdeenshire West, 1880-1906), and Sir Charles Cameron, Bt (Liberal MP for Glasgow [as a three-member constituency], 1874-1885, for Glasgow College, 1885-1895 and for Glasgow Bridgeton, 1897-1900).

Dr. Farquharson was, by request, kilted as was a young Scots Greys officer, Alexander Dingwall Fordyce, whose father had been a Liberal MP (Aberdeenshire in 1866-1868 and Aberdeenshire East in 1868-1875). A fiddler had been engaged and there were some vigorous reels involving also the younger ladies who were present. This was probably the only time that the spacious halls at Belmont was used for such revelry. Sir Henry could not be induced to take the floor with Charlotte also a sympathetic spectator.

To mark the occasion, Sir Charles wrote a song (dated 9 December, 1897) including the following verses

> *In the north-east end of Perthshire, near the ancient town of Meigle,*
> *The broad-based Belmont Castle lies – of truth a seat vice-regal;*
> *But my muse sings not its stone and lime, but its owner, as you'll see,*
> *A Right Honourable, hospitable, jolly GCB.*

> *And well I wot with helpmate he's exceptionally blest,*
> *For of hostesses Her Ladyship stands forth among the best –*
> *In "half a mo" her guest's at ease – she's poured him out his tea,*
> *This kindly, worthy helpmeet of this jovial GCB.*

> *Then the guests are well assorted – and you know that's half the fight,*
> *If you'd have a pleasant party, and want everything to go right;*
> *He selected youth and beauty, wit and wisdom – you and me,*
> *Doth this tactful, genial hospitable, jovial GCB.*

And now to end my little song, and likewise to conclude,
(For to keep the breakfast waiting any longer would be rude)
Let's give our host three hearty cheers – his lady three times three –
The Right Honourable, hospitable, jovial GCB. [155]

---

[155] Farquharson (1911), p.286

Personal Life and Routine

After the Campbell-Bannermans settled into Belmont Castle as their Scottish home there was somewhat of a change in their annual routine and way of life – that is, apart from the interventions of official, constituency and other public duties and autumn sittings of the House of Commons. (During his thirty-nine autumns as an MP, the House of Commons only met in October and/or November in eight years.)

After spending Christmas and seeing-in the New Year at Belmont, he would go down to London for the opening of the Parliamentary session. During the Easter recess, he would often go over to Paris for a few days. Occasionally, if he found London too oppressive, he would go down to Dover to stay for a day or so at the Lord Warden Hotel, spending most of the time sitting at the end of the pier, reading and enjoying the sea air. Sometimes, he would go across to Calais just for lunch at the Gare Maritime.

While in London, until Charlotte became virtually an invalid, in addition to hosting dinners and parties and attending such given by other people, the Campbell-Bannermans were regular theatre-goers. For example, in June 1881, they saw the Gilbert and Sullivan comic opera *Patience,* within two months of its first performance, on both the 14th and 25th. Also, on the 17th, they saw Sarah Bernhardt in *Frou Frou.*[156] However, when a Cabinet Minister-in-Attendance on Queen Victoria at Osborne and Balmoral, Henry did not much appreciate the amateur dramatics which he had to attend.

After the closure of the Parliamentary session in the summer and, in some years, a round of public meetings and constituency visits, Henry took Charlotte to Marienbad, often for as much as five or six weeks. Then there often would be a week in Austria or Italy or Switzerland followed by a few days in Paris and, in late October, at least a week in London. For the rest of the year he and Charlotte would be based at Belmont.

For example, after he returned to office as again Secretary of State for War in August 1892, Parliament adjourned on the 18th (and did not meet again until 31 January 1893). Also on 18 August he went to Osborne to receive his seals of office from the Queen and thereafter spent two days at the War Office and departed for Marienbad with Charlotte on the 21st. (He was re-elected unopposed, *in absentia,* at a ministerial by-election on 25 August.) He stayed at Marienbad until 27 September, returning to London for a Cabinet meeting on the 29th. On 31 September he went off to Zurich to meet Charlotte, on her way back from Marienbad and together they spent a week in Paris before he returned to London for another Cabinet meeting. The rest of October was spent in Scotland, including a week at Balmoral as Minister-in-Attendance. He was then back in London, at the War Office, for nearly the whole of November, being based at Belmont for all of December.

---

[156] Wilson (1973), p.125

In London, Sir Henry's transport was either his own brougham, drawn by the same favourite horse for fourteen years, or a hansom cab which he thought was 'eighteen pence worth of danger' – the fare when he was going to the Commons. At Belmont, his transport was one of his own coaches, driven by a coachman or by Sir Henry himself. The death of a coachman, surnamed Hadenman, in 1892 was a terrible blow. 'There was never a better coachman, kinder to his horses and more faithful to his duties'.[157] On one occasion, in later years, when he was driving a friend round at Belmont, he was asked why he didn't keep a motor car. When he pulled up he went to the horses' heads and stroked them, while they nuzzled up to him. Then he said, 'That's why I don't keep a motor'.[158]

In addition to his attachment to his horses, he had a great affection for a grey African parrot, brought in the year he became an MP, which outlived him. He also had a large collection of French bulldogs. One such, the much spoilt *Zuli,* from Bordeaux, was so much of a terror – planting his teeth in the butler's calves at meals – that Arthur Ponsonby (his Principal Private Secretary in 1906-1907) used to hand round the tea things at Belmont, carrying the fire-guard over his legs by way of defence.[159]

He never smoked and, perhaps reflecting that, at school, he had been only the equal of his fellow-pupils in the playground, rather than their superior as in the class-room, as an adult he did not take part in any sports or games except billiards. At one time he did try to play golf but, on discovering that he had no aptitude for the game, did not persevere. In a speech at a Montrose Golf Club Bazaar in September 1907, he recalled how he 'often came over from the banks of the North [Esk] water to Montrose and thought he played golf. He raised a good deal of their best turf and smashed a good many of his best clubs, and he called that playing golf'.[160] On his way to Montrose he would have passed Northwaterbridge, the birth-place of James Mill (the father of John Stuart Mill) in 1773.

He once referred to the dismal mysteries of bridge and thought that chess was a disease not a game and felt pity for those staring at a board for long minutes with every symptom of acute mental distress. For some years he did shoot at Belmont but then gave that up, He was too fond of living things to be happy killing them. He liked to see rabbits on the lawn at Belmont and, to the despair of the gardeners, refused to let them be shot or trapped,

Otherwise, the gardeners had a free hand although they were not allowed to touch any of the trees without his specific consent, Sir Henry's great favourite was a tall fir tree. He would take off his hat to it when he passed and speak to it in French, *Comment ça va, chérie?* He also had a great collection of walking sticks and is said, when selecting one for an airing, to have muttered words of consolation to the ones left behind. Indeed, he always took a little, old walking stick abroad with him. 'I

---

[157] Spender (1923), Volume 2, p.49

[158] Mackie (1914), p.139

[159] *Glasgow High School Magazine,* June 1948, p.87

[160] Spender (1923), Volume 2, p.364.

never use this one, but, poor little chap, he would have minded if I had left him behind'.[161]

He and Charlotte had a liking for all things French. Some of the original eighteenth century furniture at Belmont came from châteaux in provincial France. Other pieces were copies of furniture in the Louvre and there was also a collection of Sèvres china. Other continental interests were represented by some good nineteenth century pictures by Dutch artists and a large Meissen clock made to order.

He had somewhat of an addiction to French novels and memoirs and French food. Indeed, he did read and re-read the novels of Balzac, Flaubert, Anatole France, Zola and De Maupassant in French – often before English translations were available. However, he also read all sorts of literature, in English and Italian as well as in French.

Nor was his interest in continental catering confined to France, He was very knowledgeable about the specialities of restaurants all over Europe and about the best places to go to buy certain kinds of provisions. On one occasion he advised Princess Louise to patronise a particular shop in Vienna which he believed stocked the best coffee beans in Europe.

Nevertheless, his Scottishness came out in that he was devoted to the poems of Robert Burns and once described his ideal meal as from a menu of broth, herring or salmon, haggis, mutton, apple tart and strawberries, ending with buttered gingerbread, (Refer also to Appendix 5) However, as from his attachment to the Auld Alliance, he believed that claret, not whisky, should be the national drink of Scotland.

He was very precise in managing his own affairs. Throughout his life, except when overseas, he entered every item of personal expenditure in little pocket-books – bills, subscriptions, railway and other fares, hair-dressing charges, gratuities, etc., etc.

However, when abroad, he just recorded the total cost of travel to/from and of the stay at a particular place – for example, £ 120 for two weeks in Paris in 1888. Although he employed a bailiff in Kent and a factor at Belmont, when able to do so, he personally paid his employees' wages and settled staff expenses. For many years, he made up the final annual accounts for the Hunton estate in Kent in his own handwriting. He also recorded – in both UK and Austrian measures – his own and Charlotte's weights at Marienbad on a particular day every year.

Another note-book contained nothing but the addresses of shops in Paris where he liked to go about buying presents for family and friends. He would poke about in odd little shops he knew of and was greeted and welcomed by the proprietors who knew him of old.

---

[161] *Glasgow High School Magazine,* June 1948, p.89

Afterword – Belmont Castle in Later Years

On Sir Henry's death in April 1908, the ownership of Belmont passed to his trustees – John Sinclair, Matthew Pearce Campbell and William Alexander Campbell, with Hugh Campbell replacing William Alexander Campbell in 1914 – for the benefit of Mrs. Alice Campbell (the wife of his nephew, James Morton Campbell) who had been acting as his hostess in London and at Belmont since the death of Lady Campbell-Bannerman in August 1906 – with reversion to her son Hugh. Matthew Pearce Campbell and William Alexander Campbell were sons of cousins of Sir Henry, with both being Directors of the family business in Glasgow.

Hugh Campbell was the owner of the family's estate of Stracathro in Angus, having inherited it from his grandfather, James Alexander Campbell, Sir Henry's elder brother, in 1908. Then, later in 1914, the trustees sold Belmont to Sir James Key Caird, Bt (1837-1916), a wealthy Dundee jute manufacturer and philanthropist.[162] (Sir James was presumably the '– Caird, Esq. [Dundee]' listed by Asquith for a Liberal peerage in 1911 if the Parliament Bill had not been passed by the House of Lords in August.)

However, Sir James had apparently taken up residence at Belmont by early 1913 – that is, after Mrs. Alice Campbell left the district, presumably to live with her son at Stracathro. Indeed, Sir James was created Baronet of Belmont Castle on 8 February 1913.

Thereafter, until he died at Belmont on 9 March 1916, Sir James was somewhat of a recluse. He left Belmont to his only close surviving relative, his elder half-sister, Mrs. Emma Grace Marryat who allowed the Castle to be used as a convalescent home for disabled servicemen. She then presented it, in memory of her brother and her late husband (formerly a Colonel in the Manchester Regiment) to Dundee Corporation in April 1918 to be used for as long as possible for such convalescents and then to be used at the Corporation's discretion. In 1918 the Dundee City Architect valued the entire estate at £ 55,000 with an annual rental value of £ 1,292. (Dundee City Council Archives)

Then in 1930, while Dundee City Council continued and continues to retain responsibility for the management of the rest of the estate, including the gardens, the Castle was leased to The Church of Scotland as a retirement home (and originally also a convalescent home for men), being formally opened as such by the Duchess of York (the future Queen Elizabeth, the Queen Mother) on 19 September 1931, The Duchess and a gathering of approx. 700 people were welcomed by the Lord Provost

---

[162] Sir James Caird's best known benefaction was a gift of up to £ 100,000 in 1914 for building new Council Chambers and a new City Hall (the Caird Hall) in Dundee, The foundation stone of the Hall was laid by King George V and Queen Mary later in 1914, with the formal opening by Prince Edward (the future King Edward) on 26 October 1923. Roy Jenkins in his *Churchill* (2001, p.131) referred to Churchill speaking in the Caird Hall in 1908. As that Hall was not completed until 1923, Churchill would have spoken in 1908 in the Kinnaird Hall, which became a cinema after 1919, was closed in the 1960s and then demolished.

of Dundee and the Rev. John Mansie of Dundee (formerly of the United Free Church) and the Rev. Dr. David Watson, Joint Conveners of the General Assembly's Social Work Committee. (Dr. Watson [1859-1943] was Parish Minister of St. Clement's, Glasgow in 1888-1938 and, in 1901, the founder of the Scottish Christian Social Union, the aim of which was to stimulate positive criticism of the social effects of industrial capitalism.)

For some years Dundee Corporation retained the north wing as a holiday home for men and also as accommodation for evacuees (thirty deaf and dumb children and their teachers) from Dundee during the Second World War, but the Corporation's reservation of the wing was discontinued in 1949. Then in 1981 the Queen Mother returned to Belmont for the Home's Golden Jubilee, planting a crab apple tree opposite the front door. (One wonders if the Queen Mother was aware in 1931 or 1981 that her Bowes-Lyon ancestors were the one-time owners of both Kirkhill (as later rebuilt as Belmont Castle) and the village of Meigle.) In May 1996 Princess Anne visited Belmont while Lord High Commissioner to the General Assembly using the same chair as used by her grandmother in 1931 and 1981.

For over 80 years Belmont was the longest serving Home for Senior Citizens run by The Church of Scotland, specifically, by what is now its Social Care Council, now known as CrossReach. (Coincidentally, one of CrossReach's 2011 Christmas Cards included a Belmont recipe for gingerbread with which, as already mentioned, Sir Henry liked to end his meals.)

However, in 2013, the Church announced that it was to give up the lease of Belmont Castle. The 16 residents, their families and 21 staff were told of the decision on 22 April (2013). Apparently, despite an extensive marketing campaign to increase the number of residents, it had simply become unviable, with 16 residents representing an occupancy level of less than 60 %. Thus, after more than eighty years of care, the closure of The Church of Scotland's longest serving home for older people.

The Church had previously thought, many years ago, about giving up Belmont Castle and establishing a Home in Dundee. Some suggested that putting out money into a building that did not belong to the Church was bad policy. A visit was made to the Town Clerk of Dundee to ascertain if there was any likelihood of the Town Council making any other use of Belmont Castle. His answer was an emphatic negative. He said that if The Church of Scotland were to give up the Castle, the Town Council would put it to no other use and would take the roof off. Accordingly, the Church then gave up the idea of terminating its lease of Belmont.[163] Fortunately, as from legislation of 1947, the Castle is now a Grade A Listed Building of architectural or historic, national or international importance, thus ranking with some 3,800 other such listed buildings in Scotland.

---

[163] The Rev. Lewis Cameron, then Director of The Church of Scotland's Social Services, writing about Belmont Castle in 1971.

A Service of Thanksgiving to mark the caring work at Belmont Castle since 1931 was held in Newtyle Parish Church (in Angus but just over two miles from Meigle) on 4 July (2013).

Nevertheless, whatever the future for the Castle, 100 of the Estate's 400 acres will continue to be occupied by the Belmont Centre, the most northerly of the Scottish Outdoor Education Centres, providing a wide range of on-site activities for groups of up to 240 in size, with overnight accommodation for up to 148 pupils and accompanying staff.

7 – 1886-1894 – Opposition and Government

A – 1886-1892 – Opposition

Table 16 - The 1886 General Election - 1 to 17 (to 27) July											
Candidates (Unopposed), Percentages and MPs Elected											
	England				Wales				Scotland			
Liberals	347	(23)	47.2	123	32	(10)	53.9	26	68	(7)	53.6	43
Conservatives				278				6				10
Liberal Unionists				54				2				17
	432	(105)	52.6	332	24	(2)	46.1	8	63	(2)	46.4	27
Irish Nationalist	1	(0)	0.1	1								
Others	3	(0)	0.1									
	783	(128)		456	56	(12)		34	131	(9)		70
	Ireland				Universities				UNITED KINGDOM			
Liberals	1	(0)	1.0		1	(0)	13.8		449	(40)	45.0	192
Conservatives				14				8				316
Liberal Unionists				3				1				77
	35	(3)	50.4	17	9	(6)	84.7	9	563	(118)	51.4	393
Irish Nationalists	97	(66)	48.6	84	2	(0)	1.5		100	(66)	3.5	85
Others									3	(0)	0.1	
	133	(69)		101	12	(6)		9	1115	(224)		670

Net Gains/Losses in MPs Elected compared to the 1885 General Election

	England	Wales	Scotland	Ireland	Universities	UK
Liberals	minus 115	minus 3	minus 8		minus 1	minus 127
Conservatives	plus 65	plus 2	plus 2	minus 2		plus 67
Liberal Unionists	plus 54	plus 2	plus 17	plus 3	plus 1	plus 77
	plus 119	plus 4	plus 19	plus 1	plus 1	plus 144
Irish Nationalists				minus 1		minus 1
Others	minus 4	minus 1	minus 11			minus 16

Stirling Burghs - Electorate 5,226				East Fife - Electorate 9,233		
Henry Campbell-Bannerman	Liberal	2,440		H.H. Asquith	Liberal	2,863
John Pender	Liberal Unionist	1,471		J.B. Kinnear	Liberal Unionist	2,489
Midlothian - Electorate c.12,965				Leith Burghs - Electorate 11,779		
W.E. Gladstone	Liberal	Unopposed		W.E. Gladstone	Liberal	Unopposed

With their former Liberal MP, J.B. Kinnear having become a Liberal Unionist and having been repudiated by the East Fife Liberal Association, Asquith's candidature was secured only two weeks before polling day. The East Fife constituency did not then include St. Andrews and six other Burghs which were within the separate constituency of St. Andrews Burghs until 1918.

Asquith was already one of the first Secretaries of The Eighty Club, as formed to celebrate the Liberal victory at the 1880 General Election and to promote political education and organisation within the Liberal Party. Within a year of his election as an MP, in May 1887, Asquith had to write a letter to *The Times* defending the Club's action in causing the resignation of its Liberal Unionist members including Joseph Chamberlain, John Bright, Hartington and Goschen. (Spender and Asquith [1932], Volume 1, p. 56).[164]

Ten of the Liberals elected were Liberal/Labour MPs. In the Irish territorial constituencies, all seventeen Unionists and seven of the Nationalists were elected in what became Northern Ireland after 1922. However, overall the early results were such that Gladstone, who opted to represent Midlothian,[165] resigned on 20 July and Lord Salisbury formed a Conservative administration with initially Liberal Unionist support rather than participation.

There was a very significant increase in the number of unopposed returns to 224 as against 43 at the 1885 General Election, mainly due to a reduction in the number of Liberal candidates from 572 to 449.

Of the 93 dissident Liberal MPs (Liberal Unionists) of 8 June, 16 retired, 13 were defeated by Liberals, 2 were defeated by Conservatives, 25 were returned unopposed (including 1 as a Liberal and one who re-joined the Liberals immediately afterwards), 1 was re-elected with Conservative opposition and 36 were re-elected with Liberal opposition. 16 of the Liberal Unionists elected had not been Liberal MPs in 1885-1886 although two had been elected as Independent Liberals at the 1885 General Election.

One of the Scottish constituencies for which the former Liberal MP was re-elected as a Liberal Unionist was Ayr Burghs (also including Campbeltown, Inverary, Irvine and Oban). The unsuccessful Liberal candidate, making his first electoral appearance, was John Sinclair, CB's friend and, *inter alia,* his future Cabinet colleague as Secretary for Scotland in 1905-1908.[166] However, in two other Scottish constituencies, two former Cabinet Ministers standing as Liberal Unionists were defeated by Liberals – George Goschen (as already mentioned) and Sir George Otto Trevelyan who was defeated in Hawick Burghs (also including Galashiels and

---

[164] At its peak The Eighty Club had 600 members, with its Presidents including Campbell-Bannerman and Lloyd George. On 12 December, 1952 Harry Willcock – the leading figure in the 1951 case which led to the abolition of Identity Cards – died suddenly when taking part in an Eighty Club debate. The Club closed in 1978 with the name being later adopted by the Association of Liberal Democrat Lawyers for a series of annual Lectures.

[165] The resulting by-election in Leith Burghs (also including Musselburgh and Portobello) on 20 August resulted in the contested election of R.C. Munro-Ferguson (Liberal), later a Liberal Imperialist, who ended his political career as Viscount Novar and Conservative Secretary for Scotland in 1922-1924.

[166] Two years later (in 1888), John Sinclair was asked by the Liberal Whips to contest a by-election in Mid-Lanarkshire caused by the resignation of the incumbent Liberal MP. However, he declined, being unwilling to oppose the Independent Labour Candidate, Keir Hardie who had failed to secure the Liberal nomination. The contest was won by another Liberal candidate, with Hardie in third place with 617 votes (8.4 %).

Selkirk) by 2,523 votes to 2,493,[167] Of the 16 Independent Liberals elected in 1885, in addition to George Goschen, two had died, two had retired, eight were re-elected as Liberals, two were re-elected as Liberal Unionists and one was defeated as a Liberal.

It should also be noted that a significant number of other Liberal Unionist MPs and candidates subsequently returned to the Liberal Party – for example, in Scotland, from Sir George Otto Trevelyan in 1887 to Cameron Corbett (Glasgow Tradeston) in 1910, and two of Glasgow's three other Liberal Unionist MPs. (Cameron Corbett, 1st Lord Rowallan 1911, was the father-in-law of Jo Grimond's very much older sister.)

Such returns to the Liberal Party occurred on 'conversion' to Irish Home Rule (particularly after a failed attempt at Liberal reunion in early 1887), in opposition to Conservative quasi-permanent coercive policies in Ireland (from later in 1887), in opposition to Imperial Preference/Tariff Reform (Protectionism) after Joseph Chamberlain announced his support for such in May 1903 and in support of Irish Land Reform in February 1904. By 1910 the number of Liberal Unionist MPs had fallen to 36 and thus their merger with the Conservatives in 1912 was perhaps inevitable.

However, as from mid-1886, the Liberal cause in Scotland was not helped by *The Scotsman* and *The Glasgow Herald* – formerly Liberal newspapers – changing their allegiance to the Unionists. This resulted in the demise of the Tory *Scottish News* in 1888, which had been founded by a merger of *The Edinburgh Courant* and *The Glasgow News* earlier in 1886, with one of the financial backers of *The Glasgow News* when founded in 1873, being CB's brother, James Alexander Campbell.

The change in *The Scotsman's* allegiance prompted CB to write to Gladstone later in 1886 saying that 'there is no limit to *The Scotsman's* malignant distortion of the facts'.[168] (At the time of the 1906 General Election, *The Glasgow Herald* changed its allegiance again to become a Free Trade Unionist newspaper and a supporter of Scottish land reform)

CB had joined in the Commons in opposing the Conservatives' 1887 coercive policies (The Irish Crimes Bill) which included the loss of the right to trial by jury for those accused of offences against law and order.

---

[167] George Otto Trevelyan had succeeded his father as Second Baronet on 19 June 1886. Sir George was a nephew of Thomas Babington Macaulay (Lord Macaulay 1857) who was Rector of Glasgow University in 1848-1851 and a Whig MP for Edinburgh in 1840-1847 and 1852-1856. George Macaulay Trevelyan, then Master of CB's old College, Trinity, Cambridge – who, as already mentioned, wrote about CB in the *Glasgow High School Magazine* of June 1948 – was a younger son of Sir George's. Sir Charles Trevelyan, Third Baronet from 1928, was a Liberal MP in 1899-1918 and a Labour MP in 1922-1931. He served as a Liberal Junior Minister in 1908-1914 and as a Labour Cabinet Minister in 1924 and in 1929-1931.

[168] As quoted in Wilson (1973), p.157

Also in July (1887) he took part in the Second Reading debate on the Conservatives' Irish Land Bill saying that, after six months, 'a tumult of evictions would burst upon the country' and that the Conservatives were fulfilling the Scriptural maxim, 'from him that hath not shall be taken that which he seemeth to have'.

After the 1886 General Election the Liberal Unionists, despite their alignment with the Conservatives and thus providing Lord Salisbury with an overall majority in the Commons, continued to sit on the same side of the House as the Liberals. However, following Lord Randolph Churchill's resignation, George Goschen had joined Lord Salisbury's second administration as Chancellor of the Exchequer in December 1886. Nevertheless, he did not return to the Commons as a Liberal Unionist MP until a By-Election in London St. George's Hanover Square in 9 February 1887. He sat as a Conservative after the 1892 General Election.

Also in early 1887 five former Liberal Cabinet Ministers had a series of meetings – known as the Round Table Conference – with a view to Liberal re-unification, with Sir William Harcourt, John Morley and Lord Herschell representing the Gladstonians and Joseph Chamberlain and Sir George Otto Trevelyan representing the 'Radical' Liberal Unionists. Although the exchanges were inconclusive, as also was Gladstone's meeting with Chamberlain in April, Sir George was 'converted' to Irish Home Rule and re-joined the Liberal Party. He then contested Glasgow Bridgeton at a by-election – caused by the resignation of the Liberal MP who had been re-elected in 1886 with a 797 majority – on 2 August (1887) and was elected with 4,654 votes against 3,253 for his Liberal Unionist opponent.

Thus CB's optimism when he wrote on 29 July, 'Things are going first rate all over... If G.O.T. [Sir George Otto Trevelyan] gets a thumping majority and we win the Cheshire seat (which we ought to do) it will take out of them [Conservatives and Liberal Unionists] the little wind they have left'.[169] Cheshire (Northwich) had been lost by John Brunner (Liberal) by 458 votes to a Liberal Unionist whose death caused the By-Election on 13 August which was indeed won by Brunner with a majority of 1,129.

Later in 1887 suggestions started to be made that CB, as now, second only to Gladstone, the most distinguished of the Scottish Liberal MPs, move from Stirling Burghs to contest another Scottish constituency with being suggested specifically, Glasgow Central, Forfarshire (Angus) and West Perthshire – all Conservative or Liberal Unionist gains in 1886 – and Dunbartonshire which had only Conservative MPs since 1841.

Indeed, the West Perthshire Liberals sent CB a lengthy petition stating that only a leader of his calibre could attain a Liberal victory in their constituency, which was answered by a counter-petition from Stirling Burghs.

---

[169] As quoted in Spender (1923), Volume 1, p.112

> We, the undersigned electors, being a few of your many most loyal supporters, ardent admirers and warmest friends in the constituency, having heard with much concern and regret that you have been invited to contest West Perthshire at the next election, and that you have requested time to consider the invitation, humbly desire to approach you with an expression of our most grateful recognition and high appreciation of the splendid service and great honour you have rendered to and conferred upon us during the twenty years you have most faithfully represented us in Parliament; and also to express our most sincere and earnest wishes that you may long continue our Representative in Parliament. [170]

Such sentiments agreed with CB's own inclinations, although the matter was not settled for eighteen months, to remain with Stirling Burghs which he was to do for the rest of his life. West Perthshire was not again won by a Liberal until 1906 although John Sinclair, CB's friend and close colleague, after being MP for Dunbartonshire in 1892-1895, won Forfarshire at a by-election in January 1897.

Glasgow Central, as created in 1885, was only held by Liberals in 1885-1886 and 1906-1909. Otherwise, it remained Conservative until it was gained by Labour in 1950. The trouble was the business vote which, for example, at the 1945 General Election – the last with plural voting – comprised 9.5 % (3,387) of the total electorate and thus accounted for the Conservatives majority of 1,516 over Labour.

Plural voting – basically, the business vote and votes in the University Constituencies – was not abolished until the Labour Government's 1948 Representation of the People Act. However, there were earlier Liberal attempts to abolish plural voting, not only in the 1905-1908 Liberal Government's Bill as frustrated by the House of Lords but also in an earlier attempt to abolish the University Constituencies as such. A motion proposed by Edmund Robertson (Liberal MP for Dundee, 1885-1908) and seconded by Dr. Robert Farquharson (Liberal MP for Aberdeenshire West, 1880-1906) was carried at an evening sitting in the House of Commons but the initiative made no further progress.[171]

Generally, during the 1886-1892 Parliament, CB was very much the handy man of the Opposition front bench, being spokesman on the War Office, having enough experience of the Admiralty to take part in naval debates, and, as a former Chief Secretary, having a special standing in Irish debates. Further, as apart from

---

[170] Spender (1923), Volume 1, p.115

[171] Edmund Robertson was created Lord Lochee on 22 May 1908 and his earlier resignation as an MP created the vacancy which enabled Winston Churchill having lost the Ministerial By-Election (on his appointment as President of the Board of Trade) for Manchester North West on 23 April 1908, to be elected for Dundee at a By-Election on 9 May. Refer to Anne Newman on 'Dundee's Grand Old Man – Biography of Edmund Robertson MP' in *Journal of Liberal History* (Spring 2005)

From 1886 onwards and until 1918, the University Constituencies elected only Conservative or Liberal Unionist MPs

Gladstone being the most distinguished of the Scottish Liberal MPs, he was the natural guardian of Scottish interests. Thus he gained a reputation as an all-rounder, with the certainty of being reported at length when he spoke In the Commons or in the country. Also, while in London, he dined out frequently and entertained freely, with his political invitations being usually as suggested by the Liberal Whips.

In the spring of 1889 CB had his first serious illness which prevented him from taking a full part in the deliberations of the Hartington Commission on naval and military administration. The recommendations in the Commission's First Report (July 1889), which dealt mainly with the Admiralty, are no more than interesting curiosities, However, some of the recommendations in the Second Report (February 1890), dealing with the War Office, would be the basis of changes made later, including some when CB was again Secretary of State for War in 1892-1895.

At a very late hour on 9 April (1889) the House of Commons had a major debate on Scottish Home Rule within a Federal UK. The motion was moved by Dr. Gavin Clark (Liberal MP for Caithness) [172] and seconded by William Hunter (Liberal MP for Aberdeen North), with an amendment being moved by Professor Robert Wallace (Liberal MP for Edinburgh East) and seconded by Edmund Robertson (Liberal MP for Dundee).

> [The Motion] That, in the opinion of this House, it is desirable that arrangements be made for giving to the people of Scotland, by their representatives in a National Parliament, the management and control of Scottish affairs.
>
> [The Amendment to add the words] at such time and of such a character as may be desired by the Scottish people.

During the debate the front bench speakers were Gladstone and Arthur Balfour (then Chief Secretary for Ireland). Gladstone concluded, 'I do not think this question is ripe for our decision, and until it is ripe for our decision, I should forfeit any title I have to the favourable attention and kindness of the House and the confidence of my constituency were I to support the proposal which is now brought before the House'.

---

[172] Dr. Clark, had originally been elected as the Independent Liberal/Crofter MP for Caithness in 1885, defeating the official Liberal candidate, Clarence Sinclair (father of Sir Archibald Sinclair, Liberal Leader in 1935-1945). Dr. Clark was first President of the Scottish Home Rule Association as founded in May 1886 and virtually a Liberal/Labour MP from 1888. As the Transvaal's former Consul-General in the UK, he was not re-adopted by the Caithness Liberals in 1900 due to his pro-Boer activities and, as an Independent Liberal candidate, was in third place at that year's General Election when Caithness was won by Robert Harmsworth (Liberal) with a majority of 28 over the Conservative candidate. Dr. Clark ended his political career as the unsuccessful Labour candidate for Glasgow Cathcart at the 1918 General Election. (Clarence Sinclair died in 1895 and thus Sir Archibald succeeded his grandfather directly as 4th Baronet of Ulbster in 1912.)

Balfour concluded, 'We [in Scotland] have gained the inestimable privilege of feeling ourselves citizens of one great community, and of taking our full share in the management of this great Empire. I will not be a party, and those on this side of the House will never be parties, to anything which can, even in the smallest degree, tend to diminish the great heritage which has been handed down to us'.

The debate ended with a division on an attempt to proceed to votes on the motion and the amendment which was defeated by 200 votes to 79. Then, 'It being after One of the clock [1.00 a.m.], Mr. Deputy Speaker adjourned the House without question put'. Thus there was no vote on Mr. Clark's motion or on Professor Wallace's amendment,

However, CB then wrote to his friend, Donald Crawford (Liberal MP for North-East Lanarkshire) who had spoken in the debate, In the letter, CB while confirming his support for Scottish Home Rule, also took the opportunity to express his opposition to asymmetrical devolution (and thus anticipate the 'West Lothian Question').

> It should be pointed out that Scottish Home Rule involves English Home Rule; and that not one in a thousand Englishmen has ever grasped the idea of having a local [English] Parliament, as apart from the common Imperial Parliament, so that Scottish Home Rule must wait until the sluggish mind of John Bull is educated up to that point. (CB/BL)

Donald Crawford had cited Sir Charles Dilke in a divorce action in 1886. Dilke, also a Liberal MP, had served as a Liberal Cabinet Minister in 1882-1885. Although discharged from the otherwise successful divorce action, his political career never recovered. Nine years later, in the 'Cordite Vote', as discussed in Chapter 8, he was one of the few Liberal MPs to vote with the Conservatives and Liberal Unionists against CB. For that reason alone, and given that Charlotte never forgave him, as a former Liberal Cabinet Minister, for his action that day, he had no reason to be upset when he was not given a place in CB's Cabinet in December 1905. In any case, Dilke had not been given office by Gladstone in 1886 or 1892-1894 or by Rosebery in 1894-1895.

Between 1890 and 1914 Scottish Home Rule was on the 'agenda' – Motions and Bills – of the House of Commons on no fewer than 13 occasions, being accepted in principle on eight occasions. However, none of the Bills reached the Committee stage.

In mid-1889 Gladstone asked CB to lead for the Liberal Opposition in the Commons on the Local Government (Scotland) Bill, 'a task which he enlivened with abundant local knowledge and characteristic flashes of humour'.[173] This legislation was very much in line with the self-government for the counties which he had been advocating for over 23 years. When enacted the legislation replaced the outdated Commissioners

---

[173] Spender (1923), Volume 1, pp.120-121

of Supply with new county councils directly elected (as were small burgh councils) on a triennial basis. However, 15 years later he wrote to James Bryce that 'County Councils in Scotland are nearly all Tory. The areas are so large that the body of the people and their possible representatives are excluded because they could not attend. Payment of travelling expenses would help a little. At present it is all lairds and farmer toadies'.[174]

On 24 December 1889 Charles Parnell, the Irish Nationalist Leader was cited by William O'Shea in a divorce case. A decree of divorce was granted on 17 November 1890 with Parnell offering no defence (although he could have offered the defence of the husband's collusion). Accordingly, it was generally believed that the uncontested evidence showed him to have been treacherous and deceitful. A meeting of the Liberal leadership (Gladstone, Rosebery, Sir William Harcourt and CB) with Parnell planned for later that month was cancelled and CB summed-up his attitude in a letter to Harcourt, dated 20 November, 'the feeling among our own people in Scotland is very strong against Parnell remaining as the recognised leader of his Party – my belief is that the Scots will not tolerate Parnell in his position of quasi-partnership with the Liberal leaders'.[175]

Harcourt then wrote to Gladstone on 22 November, quoting CB and adding 'if Parnell is allowed to remain as leader of the Irish Party all further co-operation between them and the English Liberals must end'.[176] Nevertheless, as yet unaware of the depth of Scottish and English Liberal feeling, the Irish Nationalist MPs re-elected Parnell as their leader on 25 November. However, following direct intervention by Gladstone, a further meeting, requisitioned for 1 December resulted in a split into anti- and pro-Parnell factions with, after Parnell's death in 1891, the Parnellite Nationalists being led by John Redmond, MP until the he became Leader of the reunited party in 1900, a position he held until his death in 1918.

O'Shea had been a Liberal MP for County Clare in 1880-1885 and then a Nationalist MP for Galway Town for five months from a by-election in February 1886. His candidature for the by-election had been forced through by Parnell. Although Mrs. O'Shea [Kitty] – who had been acting as an intermediary between Gladstone and Parnell – had been Parnell's mistress for some years and had been living with him since mid-1886, O'Shea had not taken action earlier – hence the notion of collusion. After the O'Shea divorce, Parnell married Kitty in June 1891, four months before his death in October.

During the 1886-1892 Parliament there were 19 Liberal by-election gains including, on 10 April 1890, the start of David Lloyd George's 54 years as MP for Caernarfon Boroughs (also including Bangor, Conway, Criccieth, Nevin and Pwllheli) when he won (by 1,963 votes to 1,945) a by-election caused by the death of the Conservative MP who had defeated the incumbent Liberal MP at the 1886 General Election.

---

[174] As quoted in Wilson (1973), p.157

[175] As quoted in Spender (1923), Volume 1, pp.121-122

[176] As quoted in Wilson (1973), p.105

In mid-1892, after the failure to enact an Irish Local Government Bill and as the House of Commons was within a year of its then statutory life span of seven years, Lord Salisbury called a General Election for July 1892, with CB, in anticipation of Liberal Unionist opposition, issuing his election address, as from Belmont Castle, Meigle on 21 June, with polling day being on 8 July.

> In view of the impending dissolution of Parliament, I beg most respectfully to offer myself again as a candidate for the honour of representing you… on the question of the government of Ireland, which is still the main question before the country, I support the policy of Home Rule, which I am convinced will conduce to the good government of that country, the contentment of the Irish People and the strength of the Empire, while at the same time greatly increasing the efficiency of the [Westminster] Parliament by relieving it of its duties regarding exclusively Irish business.
>
> During the last six years I have done my best… in opposing the old alternative policy of repression which the Tory Government has pursued. In the adaptation of our Parliamentary system [to Irish Home Rule] there will necessarily be difficulties and inconveniences which will be encountered, but these are as nothing in comparison with the benefits which can reasonably be expected to follow from it to Ireland herself and to her relations with the Empire, in the creation and maintenance of which her children have borne so large a part.

Apparently, this was the first election at which, in addition to the election address, the local Liberals issued polling cards to individual electors, The Dunfermline Carnegie Library has one such for 1892 and another for 1895.

B – 1892-1894 – Government (Cabinet Office)

Table 17 - The 1892 General Election - 4 to 17 (to 26) July 1892

Candidates (Unopposed), Percentages and MPs Elected

	England				Wales			Scotland			
Liberals	426	(9)	48.0	190	34	(4)	62.5	31	70	(0)	53.9	50
Conservatives				233				3				9
Liberal Unionists				28								11
	441	(22)	51.1	261	29	(0)	37.2	3	68	(0)	44.4	20
Irish Nationalist	1	(0)	0.1	1								
Others	18	(1)	0.8	4					11	(0)	1.7	
	886	(32)		456	63	(4)		34	149	(0)		70

	Ireland				Universities				UNITED KINGDOM			
Liberals	2	(0)	1.1						532	(13)	45.1	271
Conservatives				17				8				270
Liberal Unionists				4				1				44
	59	(11)	20.6	21	9	(7)	80.9	9	606	(40)	47.0	314
Irish Nationalists	133	(9)	78.1	80					134	(9)	7.0	81
Others	1	(0)	0.2		1	(0)	19.1		31	(1)	0.9	4
	195	(20)		101	10	(7)		9	1303	(63)		670

Gains/Losses in MPs Elected compared to the 1886 General Election

	England	Wales	Scotland	Ireland	Universities	UK
Liberals	plus 67	plus 5	plus 7			plus 79
Conservatives	minus 45	minus 3	minus 1	plus 3		minus 46
Liberal Unionists	minus 26	minus 2	minus 6	plus 1		minus 33
	minus 71	minus 5	minus 7	plus 4		minus 79
Irish Nationalists				minus 4		minus 4
Others	plus 4					plus 4

Stirling Burghs - Electorate 5,590				East Fife - Electorate 9,133			
Henry Campbell-Bannerman	Liberal	2,791		H.H. Asquith		Liberal	3,743
Walter T. Hughes	Liberal Unionist	1,695		Sir John Gilmour	xiv	Conservative	3,447

Midlothian - Electorate 13,234				Caernarvon Boroughs - Electorate 4,732			
W.E. Gladstone	Liberal	5,845		D. Lloyd George		Liberal	2,154
A.G. Wauchope	Conservative	5,155		Sir J.H. Puleston		Conservative	1,958

This was the first General Election for the UK Parliament at which, on a population basis and compared to England, Scotland was not to be under-represented in the House of Commons, with, on the same basis, Wales and Ireland being under-represented until about 1861.

Of the 81 Irish Nationalists elected nine were of the faction that had supported Charles Parnell at the time of the Party split in 1890-1891. In the Irish territorial constituencies, nineteen of the Unionists and five of the Nationalists elected were in what became Northern Ireland after 1922. In the South of Ireland, the Unionists gained a seat from the Nationalists in Dublin and another in County. Dublin.

The 4 Others elected in England were three Independent Labour MPs – John Burns (subsequently a Liberal-Labour MP and Liberal Cabinet Minister), Keir Hardie (founder Chairman of the Independent Labour Party in 1893) and John H. Wilson (who ended his parliamentary career as a Liberal and then a Coalition Liberal MP in 1918-1922) – and one Independent Liberal MP, Sir Edward Watkin (Hythe). Ten of the Liberals elected were again Liberal/Labour MPs.

Lord Salisbury and his Conservative administration remained in office until defeated (350-310) in the Commons on 11 August (1892) on a no confidence motion (moved by Asquith) during the debate on the Queen's Speech.[177] Lord Salisbury then resigned and Gladstone (now 83) formed a minority government, his fourth and last administration.

CB was now senior enough to be consulted about the appointment of the Secretary for Scotland. Gladstone had thought of appointing James Bryce. However, the others consulted, including CB, opted for Trevelyan, who had been briefly Scottish Secretary in 1886 before his temporary dalliance with the Liberal Unionists, and he was appointed. (Trevelyan's successor as Liberal Scottish Secretary, for just under four months in 1886, Sir John William Maule Ramsay, 13th [Scottish] Earl of Dalhousie had died, aged 40, in November 1887.)

Table 18 - Sixth Liberal Cabinet - August 1892 to March 1894	
Prime Minister	**William Ewart Gladstone,** (Fourth Cabinet as PM) MP for Midlothian
Lord Chancellor	Sir Farrer Herschell, 1st Lord Herschell
Lord President and Secretary for India	John Wodehouse, 1st Earl of Kimberley (Leader in the House of Lords)
Chancellor of the Exchequer	Sir William Harcourt, MP for Derby
Home Secretary	Herbert Henry Asquith, MP for East Fife
Foreign Secretary	Archibald Primrose, 5th (Scottish) Earl of Rosebery & 2nd (UK) Lord Rosebery
Secretary for War	**Henry Campbell-Bannerman, MP** for Stirling Burghs
Colonial Secretary	George Robinson, 1st Marquis of Ripon
First Lord of the Admiralty	John Spencer, 5th Earl Spencer
President of the Board of Trade	Anthony Mundella, MP for Sheffield Brightside
Chief Secretary for Ireland	John Morley, MP for Newcastle-upon-Tyne
President, Local Government Board	Henry Fowler, MP for Wolverhampton East
Scottish Secretary	Sir George Trevelyan, Bt, MP for Glasgow Bridgeton
Chancellor, Duchy of Lancaster	James Bryce, MP for Aberdeen South
Postmaster-General	Arnold Morley, MP for Nottingham East
First Commissioner of Works	George Shaw-Lefevre, MP for Bradford Central
Vice-President of the Council (with responsibility for Education)	Arthur Acland, MP for Rotherham

---

[177] *Hansard,* 11 August 1892

All the MPs were re-elected at Ministerial By-Elections later in August with only Sir William Harcourt and John Morley not being returned unopposed, with CB being again Secretary of State for War as from 18 August 1892. On resuming his 1886 office as Secretary of State for War, CB appointed his friend, John Sinclair as his Parliamentary Private Secretary. Sinclair had entered the Commons as from the (1892) General Election when he gained Dunbartonshire from the incumbent Conservative MP,

CB was also Minister-in-Attendance at Balmoral in the autumns of 1892, 1893 and 1894 and, on other occasions, at Osborne and Nice. As wives were not then invited to be with their husbands, almost all the letters of CB to Charlotte which have survived are letters from Balmoral which describe Court life in the Highlands in particular detail, such as his attendance at Crathie Parish Church on Sundays and his allocation of five new wax candles each night.

CB received the Freedom of the Royal Burgh of Stirling and was admitted as an Honorary Member of the Guildry Incorporation of Stirling on Thursday, 15 December 1892,[178]

He arrived from Belmont during the morning and shortly before 12 noon received, in the Barnton Street office of his Stirling Agent, Robert Taylor, a deputation and congratulatory address from the local branch of the Educational Institute of Scotland, noting that he had done everything in his power to secure national recognition and facilities for secondary and elementary education in Scotland, with reference also to the position on higher education he had taken up during the last session of Parliament. CB replied that it was with very great pleasure that he had the opportunity of meeting with the deputation. He had always taken a great interest in educational matters, and that he had been able to receive from the best sources all the information he could receive on the subject – the teachers themselves.

The Freedom ceremony was held in a crowded Public Hall as from 2.00 p.m., with Provost Kinross and Thomas Galbraith, Town Clerk presiding and with the others joining them and CB on the platform including James Alexander Campbell, MP (CB's brother), James Campbell (his cousin), the Provosts of Dunfermline and Inverkeithing (with apologies from the Provosts of South Queensferry and Culross) and the Town Clerks of Dunfermline, South Queensferry, Inverkeithing and Culross. After speeches by the Provost and Town Clerk and the presentation of the Burgess Ticket, in a specially engraved silver casket, CB replied at length, concluding –

> I shall always see in your kindly recognition of my feeble services, imperfect as I know them to be, fresh proof that honest public work will never fail to be met by all our countrymen with due encouragement and reward,

---

[178] This account of events in Stirling on 15 December 1892 is based on reports in the *Stirling Journal (and Advertiser)* of 16 and 23 December 1892 and in the *Stirling Observer* of 21 December 1892.

CB and a number of the guests then accompanied the Provost and the other members of the Town Council to the Lesser Public Hall for a reception, where after honouring the toast to the Queen, the Provost proposed the health of CB as the Burgh's newest Burgess, it being noted during the day that earlier recipients of the Freedom of Stirling had included James VII and II (as Duke of York), John Churchill, 1st Duke of Marlborough and the Elder and Younger William Pitts, with the Younger Pitt being the last honorary Burgess before CB came upon the scene. CB then replied to the Provost's toast by proposing the health of the Provost and Town Council.

Most of the company then proceeded to the Guild Hall where, with Samuel Miller, Dean of Guild presiding, CB was admitted as an honorary member of the Guildry Incorporation of Stirling, with CB speaking in acceptance and again in reply to the Dean's toast to the health of the Guildry's newest member. Then unexpectedly Provost Kinross rose to propose a toast to the health and happiness of Mrs. Campbell-Bannerman who had recently patronised a bazaar on behalf of one of the Stirling churches.

CB then replied on her behalf, saying, among other things, 'when my wife hears that her health has been drunk in these circumstances, I have no doubt she will be highly gratified, and it will add to her regret at not been present, because then she might have replied herself' (Laughter and Cheers). The proceedings then closed, with CB proposing a toast to the Dean's health, to which he briefly replied.

In the evening, the Guildry entertained CB and all the other guests at a dinner in the Golden Lion Hotel. Hopefully, CB did not have to make another speech as surely six were enough for one day. Given the attitude of the Stirling newspapers to CB, as Henry Campbell, twenty-four years earlier and that of the *Stirling Journal (and Advertiser)* when he became Prime Minister in December 1905, it is of interest to quote from an editorial in that newspaper of 23 December 1892 –

> The presentation of the freedom of the Burgh of Stirling to the Right Hon. Henry Campbell-Bannerman cannot be allowed to pass without comment. It is the most graceful compliment the town could offer him, and it was not one undeserved. Quarter of a century is a long time to represent a place in Parliament, and it is some satisfaction, even to those of our way of thinking politically, that the Stirling District of Burghs has been represented all these years by a member who is not a nonentity but one of the cleverest of his party.
>
> Mr. Campbell-Bannerman's ability none can doubt, and Unionists are the first to admit, he has held high office, holds high office now, and it is possible he may even rise higher in the service of the State.

However, away from the more local scene, almost immediately, on resuming office, Gladstone formed a Cabinet Committee, to which CB was eventually added, to draft a second Irish Home Rule Bill which was introduced in 1893, with the only major difference from the 1886 Bill being the retention of Irish MPs in the Commons but only able to vote on Irish and 'imperial' matters. With CB having taken a leading part in the debates, the Bill received a Second Reading by 43 votes on 21 July (1893) and a Third Reading by 34 votes on 1 September.

However, on 8 September, the Lords declined to give the Bill a Second Reading by a massive 419 votes to 41. Gladstone wanted a dissolution and an appeal to the electorate but received no support in the Cabinet for such a course of action.

During his second, and much longer term, as Secretary of State for War, CB – while remaining on good terms with Queen Victoria – had a number of difficult exchanges with her and other members of the Royal Family. The Queen had her own way as to the future of the Cameron Highlanders despite CB pointing out that the Regiment was mainly recruiting in the East End of London but she had to depart from her objections to any of her Guards serving overseas.

Although CB also remained on good terms with the Duke of Cambridge (still Commander-in-Chief), he was constantly at odds with the Duke's reactionary views such as his belief in promotion by seniority or special favour rather than by merit. Significantly, CB's last success in the War Office was to arrange the retirement of the Duke in June 1895.

There was also a disagreement with the Queen when she appointed the Kaiser as Honorary Colonel of the 1st Royal Dragoons, given that she had not consulted any Cabinet Minister. The Kaiser had wanted to be appointed Honorary Colonel of a Highland Regiment but this was not on because he had banned the wearing of the kilt at his Court Balls.

CB was also responsible for introducing an eight-hour day for workers in the ordnance factory at Woolwich. This followed a Dinner at the Campbell-Bannerman's in London on 22 March 1893, also attended by John Sinclair, when Sir John Mather (then Liberal MP for the Gorton Division of Lancashire), gave details of a successful eight-hour day experiment introduced in his Salford Iron Works as from August 1892.[179] The Woolwich experiment was a complete success, being extended to the Army Clothing Department, with other Ministries following the War Office initiative.

As for War Office reorganisation, CB was responsible for the creation of a Cabinet Defence Committee, the origin of the later Committee of Imperial Defence and with the term of office of future Commanders-in-Chief to be restricted to five years. (The Duke of Cambridge, was then 75 years of age in 1895 and had held the post since 1856)

Early in 1894, CB was, with others, consulted about the appointment of a new Viceroy of India. CB and the others opted for the Earl of Elgin and he was appointed. CB did not know that both Gladstone and 'The Palace' had independently thought

---

[179] Lady Pentland (1928), p.39

of appointing CB himself, but that Gladstone had then decided that CB could not be spared from the Cabinet.

Given an understanding that CB would assist Sir William Harcourt with his burdens as Chancellor of the Exchequer, Harcourt wrote to him on 7 January (1894) saying that 'I am in need of your strong sense and judgement [in London] to help me in controlling the extravagance and looseness of other Departments'. CB replied that he had been speaking at public meetings in Scotland and that he had had the Adjutant-General up at Belmont for a few days to go through the Army Estimates.

> I have been sweating in the stoke-hole to keep the steam up, while certain other people have been lolling in the smoking-room or enjoying the breezes on the quarter deck. Mine have been meetings without the plum pudding unless that word can be applied figuratively to the varied but stodgy oratory of the War Minister.[180]

Shortly afterwards, CB was involved in a Cabinet crisis over the Naval Estimates which lasted for two months, culminating in Gladstone's resignation, aged 85, as Prime Minister and Liberal Leader. CB, although opposing Gladstone's demand for cuts, had attempted, without success, to reconcile the difference between Harcourt (Chancellor of the Exchequer) and Earl Spencer (First Lord of the Admiralty), but Gladstone went, and the Navy got its ships.

Throughout the 1892-1895 Parliament, CB also persisted in his support for disestablishment all-round. With the Scottish Liberal Association already committed to the disestablishment of the Church of Scotland, at its last annual conference before the 1892 General Election, the National Liberal Federation approved what was known as the 'Newcastle Programme' which while giving primacy to Irish Home Rule also included disestablishment in Scotland and Wales, land value taxation, the reform of the House of Lords and other radical policies. In October 1891, the Scottish Liberal Association had adopted an even more radical programme including also women's suffrage, payment of MPs, triennial parliaments and the abolition of the House of Lords.

There were two Welsh Disestablishment Bills during the 1892-1895 Parliament, in 1894 and 1895, with both lapsing by reason of the instability of the minority Liberal governments and then the resignation of that Government following the 'Cordite Vote' in June 1895. (Refer to Chapter 8)

The next Welsh Disestablishment Bill, in 1909, lapsed by reason of the necessity to give priority to the resolution of the conflict with the House of Lords anent the 1909 Budget. The conclusive Disestablishment Bill, introduced in 1912 by another minority Liberal Government, was rejected by the House of Lords but, following the procedures of the 1911 Parliament Act, received the Royal Assent as the Welsh Church Act on 18 September 1914. However, on the same date, the Royal Assent

---

[180] Wilson (1973), p.152

was given to a Suspensory Act which effectively postponed Disestablishment until after the War. Thus, after an Amending Act in 1919, with 30 March 1920 as the effective date for Disestablishment, the end of a campaign for religious freedom and equity, noting that the final settlement also involved extensive disendowment of the Welsh Anglican Church with the secularisation of approx, 60% of its assets.

As for Scottish Disestablishment, this was always supported by the United Presbyterian Church of 1847-1900 and, after 1874, by a majority in the Free Church of 1843-1900 but not by a minority as represented by the small, present-day Free Church or by the Scottish Episcopal and Roman Catholic Churches.

With Disestablishment as a major issue at General Elections in Scotland between 1874 and 1892, a number of Bills were tabled but none came anywhere near to enactment. Then, in 1894, Queen Victoria is said to have made pro-active use of the Royal prerogative in refusing to sanction the Queen's Speech if it included, as the minority Liberal Government had in mind, a commitment to Scottish Disestablishment, so effectively killing the Government's plans.[181] The Queen was devoted to the Church of Scotland – as a consequence of her long periods of residence at Balmoral – and, much to the consternation of her Anglican advisors, had come to take Communion in the local (Crathie) Parish Church as from 1873.[182]

Further, Sir George Otto Trevelyan as Liberal Secretary for Scotland in 1892-1895, in drafting the Queen's annual message to the General Assembly, once omitted the usual reference to the Queen's Accession Oath for the Security of the Church of Scotland. The then Lord High Commissioner, the 1st Marquis of Breadalbane [183] and others took prompt action and the missing words were put back in their place and the Secretary for Scotland in his. [184]

---

[181] Bradley (2002), p.124.

[182] Refer to Owen Chadwick, 'The Sacrament at Crathie, 1873', in Stewart J. Brown and George Newlands (Editors), *Scottish Christianity in the Modern World* (2000)

[183] The Marquis, a Junior Liberal Minister in 1873-1874, 1880-1885 and 1892-1895, was Lord High Commissioner in 1893, 1894 and 1895. A number of Liberals/Liberal Democrats have subsequently been Lord High Commissioner including Edward Tennant, 1st Lord Glenconner (Asquith's brother-in-law) in 1911, 1912, 1913 and 1914 and most recently David, Lord Steel of Aikwood in 2003 and 2004 – that is, after serving as the first Presiding Officer of the new Scottish Parliament.

[184] Lady Frances Balfour (1924), pp.65-66

8 – 1894-1899 – Government and Opposition

A – 1894-1895 – Government (Cabinet Office) and Knighthood

When Gladstone went to Windsor to resign on 2 March he intended, if asked, to advise the Queen to appoint Earl Spencer as his successor as Prime Minister. But no such advice was requested, with Rosebery already knowing that he was the Queen's choice. So Rosebery became Prime Minister (and Liberal Leader) with Sir William Harcourt (Chancellor of the Exchequer), who had hoped (and many expected) to be Gladstone's successor, becoming Liberal Leader in the Commons.

During the reconstruction of the Cabinet, as there had not been a Liberal Foreign Secretary in the Commons since 1861 (Lord John Russell), there were objections to yet another peer succeeding Rosebery as Foreign Secretary. However, Rosebery appointed the Earl of Kimberley (previously Lord President and Secretary for India), with the indications being that, if an MP had been appointed, it would have been Henry Campbell-Bannerman.[185]

Table 19 - Seventh Liberal Cabinet - March 1894 to June 1895	
Prime Minister and Lord President	**Archibald Primrose,** 5th (Scottish) Earl of Rosebery & 2nd (UK) Lord Rosebery
Leader in the House of Commons and Chancellor of the Exchequer	Sir William Harcourt. MP for Derby
Lord Chancellor	Sir Farrer Herschell, 1st Lord Herschell
Lord Privy Seal and Chancellor, Duchy of Lancaster	Edward Marjoribanks, 2nd Lord Tweedmouth
Secretary for India	Henry Fowler, MP for Wolverhampton East
Home Secretary	Herbert Henry Asquith, MP for East Fife
Foreign Secretary	John Wodehouse, 1st Earl of Kimberley
Secretary for War	**Henry Campbell-Bannerman, MP** for Stirling Burghs
Colonial Secretary	George Robinson, 1st Marquis of Ripon
First Lord of the Admiralty	John Spencer, 5th Earl Spencer
President of the Board of Trade	James Bryce, MP for Aberdeen South
Chief Secretary for Ireland	John Morley, MP for Newcastle-upon-Tyne
Scottish Secretary	Sir George Trevelyan, Bt, MP for Glasgow Bridgeton
Postmaster-General	Arnold Morley, MP for Nottingham East
President, Local Govt. Board Vice-President of the Council (with responsibility for Education)	George Shaw-Lefevre, MP for Bradford Central Arthur Acland, MP for Rotherham

---

[185] Rhodes James (1963/1965), p.321

The 1894-1895 Cabinet was not a happy band of brothers. Indeed it is said that CB was the only member on speaking terms with all the others. Rosebery, whose first speech as Prime Minister was an attempt to distance himself from Gladstone on Irish Home Rule, is said to have had only two successes in the sixteen months when he was Prime Minister, when his horses won the Derby in 1894 and 1895.

In the meantime, In February 1894, CB had written to his cousin, James Campbell that the Lords 'have raised a wind which will not go down until their wings are clipped in one way or other'. (CB/BL) Then, as from his annual stewardship meeting in Dunfermline later in 1894 –

> The present relationship of the two houses to each other is indefensible... It has been ever so since these happy and halcyon days in which the same class which now dominates the House of Lords dominated the House of Commons. It has been a growing evil, increasing with the growing intellect of the electorate, and increasing also with the more perfectly representative character of the House of Commons. And now that the year is not long enough for the work demanded of the House of Commons, that we should submit that House to the chance of obstruction by a hostile Upper Chamber is, to put it plainly, intolerable.[186]

Further, Rosebery, speaking at Bradford in October 1894, said that the issue of the House of Lords was an intolerable situation, with CB, in the same month, saying at Stirling that the House of Lords had ceased to be a Senate and had become a body of violent and reckless partisans. CB had, of course, for long called for action to reduce the powers of the House of Lords. As early as August 1884 he had written in support of a demonstration in Dunfermline declaring that 'It is absurd that the Second Chamber should be worked... as a mere part of the machinery of the Tory Party'.[187]

Queen Victoria was not amused by what Rosebery had said (in October 1894) about the House of Lords and when CB was Minister-in-Attendance at Balmoral in the following month, he had, at her request, a talk with her, on 7 November, about the House of Lords. In her old age the Queen was becoming increasing conservative and inflexible but CB's talk with her managed to lower the temperature. Before his talk with the Queen, CB had talks with Sir Arthur Bigge (Lord Stamfordham 1911), then the Queen's Assistant Private Secretary,[188] with also CB's friend, Princess Louise – described by CB as the divine influence at Balmoral – and Princess Beatrice being involved off-stage. CB, in a letter to Charlotte, reported that 'Princess Beatrice is open minded but had said that the Queen had been terribly hurt by Rosebery's speech and that Princess Louise favours Home Rule all-round and condemns the action of

---

[186] Mackie (1914), p.85

[187] As quoted in Wilson (1973), p.549

[188] Bigge was thereafter Principal Private Secretary to Queen Victoria in 1895-1901 and also served as such to George V in 1910-1931.

the Lords, etc. Really, it is quite marvellous and I think her influence will have best effect'. (CB/BL)

Before CB saw the Queen, Bigge summarised, with the Princesses' assistance, what CB had said to him in a memorandum for the Queen – 'Mr. Campbell-Bannerman and the House of Lords' – with the main points being –

> The present state of things has become indefensible. The extension of the Franchise has given a democratic basis to Parliament which does not admit of a House in its spirit antagonistic to the democratic tendency of things… The huge (intemperate) majorities in the House of Lords against recent measures are not representative of the opinion of the country, He has seen for the past ten years that the two Houses could not continue without things coming to a deadlock. He alludes to the view held by many that there should be Parliaments (single chamber) for England, Scotland, Ireland and even Wales – and one Chamber like the Reichstag – for imperial purposes – but of course this would have to be a representative chamber,[189]

Ten days after the Balmoral exchanges, Bigge wrote to Prince Albert Edward (the future King Edward) reporting that CB had also said that half the Cabinet are in favour of a single Chamber. (But CB was never, in the context of a unitary UK, in favour of the abolition of the House of Lords. In 1899, he wrote in the *Annual Register* that he wanted the Lords' veto abolished, but he wished to leave them some of their ancient constitutional powers.)

In March 1895, with Arthur Peel, MP (1st Viscount Peel from 8 May) having decided to retire as Speaker of the House of Commons, CB indicated that he was willing to be nominated for the vacancy, with the Tories also advising that if he was nominated they would make no difficulties.

However, Rosebery as Prime Minister and Sir William Harcourt as Leader in the House of Commons – for once in agreement – while believing that CB would make an excellent Speaker, opposed the move as they were reluctant to lose such an effective and popular member from the Cabinet and also wished to avoid an awkward reshuffle. Further, on 23 March, Queen Victoria minuted that "even if [Lord Rosebery] had not been so strong about Mr. C. Bannerman, She [would] never [have] allowed Mr. C. Bannerman to leave the Cabinet".[190] Thus, William Gully, a rather obscure MP was nominated by the Liberals and defeated Sir Matthew White Ridley, the Tory nominee by 11 votes.

CB was somewhat disappointed and Gladstone (still an MP) made it known that he thought that CB had been ill-used by his colleagues. Significantly, many of the Stirling Burghs constituents were not too pleased at the possibility of their MP

---

[189] As quoted in Wilson (1973), p.551

[190] As quoted in Wilson (1973), p.257

becoming Speaker. Some thought it would mean their virtual disenfranchisement and others thought it would put an end to their hopes for much higher office for their MP. It was later suggested by Admiral Fisher that CB's political opponents were cursing that CB had not been got out of their way as Speaker. (CB/BL)

The 'Cordite Vote' on 21 June (1895) was a snap vote, contrived by the Opposition Whips, on a Conservative motion – moved by St. John Brodrick – to reduce the salary of CB as Secretary of State for War by reason of an alleged shortage of cordite and small arms ammunition. (Brodrick, then Conservative MP for Guilford, would himself be Secretary of State for War in 1900-1903. He was defeated in Guilford by a Liberal at the 1906 General Election.) The motion was carried by 132 votes to 125 in a House of Commons with a total membership of 670, with the House being in Committee to consider the Army Estimates.

Three Cabinet Ministers were absent without being paired as also, being preoccupied with the Welsh Disestablishment Bill, all but four of the Welsh Liberal MPs. Even Tom Ellis, the Government Chief Whip did not arrive on the scene until just before the Speaker put the question. A few Liberal MPs also voted against CB including, as already mentioned, Sir Charles Dilke. One of the Conservatives who voted against CB, George Whiteley, subsequently joined the Liberal Party and was appointed Chief Government and Liberal Whip by CB in December 1905. Leonard Courtney, one of the Liberal Unionists who then voted against CB and later re-joined the Liberal Party, received a peerage, on CB's recommendation in 1906.

Dr. Robert Farquharson, MP, who had served for nine years as an Assistant Surgeon with the Coldstream Guards and 'was sitting just behind CB when the result was announced', later wrote –

> He [CB] shut up his portfolio with a snap, and hurried out of the House, and although we surrounded him and begged him not to resign, nothing would move him from his resolution. His word had been called in question. I have always bitterly lamented that I had not the pluck to get up and talk [during the debate] for I could have done so to some effect.
>
> I could have told the House that cordite was dangerously unstable apt to resolve itself into its pristine elements and explode spontaneously; that it would be a criminal act of folly to store it up in any quantity; for it could be rapidly produced in several factories, that it was really in the experimental stage, and that its use rapidly deteriorated guns by eating out their interiors.
>
> I could thus have consumed the half-hour or so that elapsed before the dinner hour, when the Whips could have scoured the town and brought back the wanderers, and more especially the three Cabinet Ministers who were away unpaired [but] perhaps his [CB's] decision to resign [and thus bring about the resignation of our minority Government] was a wise one, for our majority [which depended on Irish Nationalist

> votes] never rose above thirty and often fell below three, and we were in a state of almost depressing thraldom [191]

It is also of interest to note that, six years later at a critical point in the Boer War, the War Office had only just over three million rounds of small arms ammunition in-hand in the UK, far less than the one hundred million rounds for which CB had been censured in 1895. As CB himself had written at the time (on 24 June 1895) –

> It was a blackguard business. We have too much ammunition rather than too little; but Kynoch & Co. of which Joe's [Joseph Chamberlain's] brother & son are directors would like a larger order, and the Chilworth Company in Brodrick's constituency was unsuccessful in getting any orders from us because their prices were prohibitive. (CB/BL)

Nevertheless, CB immediately resigned followed by the Government, with such resignations effective from 29 June. Queen Victoria was not amused! Indeed, before the Government resigned, she sent a telegram to Lord Rosebery stating that if CB confirmed his resignation, she would not accept it. She also wrote "that the Government should be defeated by an attack on the most popular of its members is too extraordinary".[192] As it was, she had to hurry back from Balmoral – where she had been attending the dedication of the new Crathie Parish Church on 19 June – to Windsor to receive Lord Rosebery's and the Government's resignation.[193]

The Times commented on 22 June, "With Mr. Campbell-Bannerman personally much sympathy will be felt… [He] had just effected a grand coup [dislodging the Duke of Cambridge – Queen Victoria's cousin and an obstacle to army reforms – as Commander-in-Chief] when a motion to reduce his salary was carried by a majority of seven votes"

The Manchester Guardian commented on 24 June that there was "the greatest sympathy with Mr. Campbell-Bannerman [who was] certainly the most popular War Minister of this generation" and had shown a real desire to improve the position of the officer and the soldier and had done much to speed up the rearming of the forces.

Queen Victoria's attention to duty in returning from Balmoral to Windsor at this time contrasts with the absence of King Edward in Biarritz in April 1908 when the King had to communicate by telegram before the dying Sir Henry could resign as Prime Minister and when Asquith had to go off to Biarritz to receive the King's commission as the new Prime Minister.

---

[191] Farquharson (1911), pp.223-224.

[192] As quoted in Wilson (1973), p.206

[193] Court Circular (Balmoral Castle), 19 June 1895, as included in *Transactions of the Aberdeen Ecclesiological Society for 1895* (Aberdeen, 1897).

One of Rosebery's last acts as Prime Minister was to recommend CB for a knighthood – a GCB for CB – and thus he was invested as a Knight Grand Cross of the Order of the Bath (GCB) by Queen Victoria at Windsor on 1 July. As CB himself wrote that day, 'the award is specially meant as a mark of her [and Rosebery's] appreciation of my conduct of negotiations about the poor old Duke of Cambridge. She had repeatedly told me that no one but myself could have managed it! That is a bit strong, but she is very effusive about it'. (CB/BL)

Rosebery, a Knight of the Garter [KG] from 1892, had been invested with the Order of The Thistle [KT] three days earlier. In addition to Royal and Overseas Knights and Ladies, the Order of the Garter [instituted in 1348] is restricted to 24 members and the Order of the Thistle [revived in 1687] to 16 members. Knights and Dames Grand Cross of the Order of the Bath [instituted in 1729] rank, as such, immediately after Knights and Ladies of the Garter and Thistle.

Just before the 'Cordite Vote', CB had announced arrangements for the retirement of the Duke of Cambridge as Command-in-Chief, but he had not indicated in the Commons who would succeed the Duke. However, knowing that the Liberal Cabinet had decided on General Sir Redvers Buller (then the Adjutant-General), Lord Salisbury, the incoming Prime Minister, in order to avoid such a last minute appointment by the outgoing Liberal Government, asked CB to surrender his seals of office directly to him (Salisbury). CB replied that his seals would only be surrendered to the Queen from whom they came.

In this CB was supported by the Queen who thought Salisbury's behaviour scandalous, and by Rosebery and Harcourt who confirmed that Salisbury's behaviour was unprecedented. Salisbury had to apologise and, with the matter having become public knowledge, when CB and his colleagues went to Windsor to give up their seals, CB was given a great reception at Paddington Station. Further, Salisbury did CB an injustice as he was the last man to take advantage of a technicality – that, until he surrendered the seals he could still act as Secretary of State for War – as to commit his Conservative successor as Secretary of State for War.[194]

In due course the Conservatives appointed Field Marshall Sir Garnet Wolseley (a former Adjutant-General) as Commander-in-Chief after he had been offered the choice between that post and that of UK Ambassador in Berlin. Although a progressive in matters of Army reform, Wolseley was otherwise a committed Conservative to the extent that, about this time, he put himself up unsuccessfully for membership of the Carlton Club.

On demitting office as Secretary of State for War, CB sent John Sinclair, who had been his Parliamentary Private Secretary, a tie-pin to remind him of their War Office days. 'I need not add how pleasant it has been for me to have had your help for these three years, for which I am sincerely obliged to you, and I hope our friendly relations

---

[194] Wilson (1973), p.211

will not diminish but rather increase in intimacy now that we have more timer to do as we like'[195]

Also, at about this time (Summer 1895), CB was sounded out about a peerage, with reversion to his nephew, James Morton Campbell – the only son of his elder brother, James Alexander Campbell – but CB had no wish to leave the House of Commons. Further, as Morton Campbell was considered to be the 'black sheep' of the family, the alternative of a baronetcy was also rejected. Perhaps, this was also why James Alexander Campbell refused the offer of a baronetcy but instead accepted membership of the Privy Council on the occasion of Queen Victoria's Jubilee in 1897.

In the meantime Lord Salisbury, as now Prime Minister, called a General Election for July/August. Sir Henry faced Conservative opposition, as such, for the first time since the nominal challenge in 1880. Accordingly, as from 6 Grosvenor Place, London, he issued his election address on 3 July. After referring to the successes of the late Liberal Government, he stated that other measures equally beneficial had failed to become law for three main causes –

> Firstly, the resistance of the House of Lords; and this obstacle can only be overcome by taking from the irresponsible Chamber the power of overruling the judgement of the representatives of the people

> Secondly, the facilities of delay afforded by the traditional methods of procedure in the House of Commons, which are now out of date, and to which stringent reform should be applied.

> Thirdly, the excessive burden of work now imposed upon Parliament, from which relief can be found only in a large system of devolution…

Having gone on to refer to his support for 'free Church[es] in a free State', for popular control of the licensed sale of alcohol and measures to improve the conditions of life, to prevent overpressure of work and to secure healthy dwellings and workshops, he concluded –

> All of these opinions are closely consistent with, and developed from the principles which I have during my whole public life professed among you, and as these principles have for so long secured for me your confidence, I trust that you will be willing to renew to me the honour I have so long – however unworthily – enjoyed.

---

[195] Lady Pentland (1928), pp.56-57

B – 1895-1899 – Opposition

Table 20 - The 1895 General Election - 13 to 29 July (to 7 August)

Candidates (Unopposed), Percentages and MPs Elected

	England				Wales				Scotland			
Liberals	342	(8)	46.7	112	34	(2)	56.8	25	66	(1)	51.7	39
Conservatives				292				8				17
Liberal Unionists				51				1				14
	442	(10€)	51.9	343	31	(0)	42.2	9	68	(4)	47.4	31
Independent Labour Party	21	(0)	1.1	-					7	(0)	0.8	-
Irish Nationalist	1	(0)	0.1	1								
Others	9	(0)	0.2	-	2	(0)	1.0	-	1	(0)	0.1	-
	315	(114)	q	456	67	(2)		34	142	(5))		70

	Ireland				Universities				UNITED KINGDOM			
Liberals	5	(0)	7.1	1					447	(11)	45.7	177
Conservatives				15				8				340
Liberal Unionists				4				1				71
	38	(13)	26.0	19	9	(9)		9	558	(132)	49.1	411
Independent Labour Party									28	(0)	1.0	
Irish Nationalists	104	(46)	66.9	81					105	(46)	4.0	82
Others									12	(0)	0.2	
	147	(59)		101	9	(9)		9	1180	(189)		670

Net Gains/Losses in MPs Elected compared to the 1892 General Election

	England	Wales	Scotland	Ireland	Universities	UK
Liberals	minus 78	minus 6	minus 12	plus 1		minus 95
Conservatives	plus 59	plus 5	plus 10	minus 2		plus 72
Liberal Unionists	plus 23	plus 1	plus 2			plus 26
	plus 82	plus 6	plus 12	minus 2		plus 98
Irish Nationalists				plus 1		plus 1
Others	minus 4					minus 4

Stirling Burghs - Electorate 6,007

Sir Henry Campbell-Bannerman	Liberal	2,793
S.C. Macaskie	Conservative	1,656

East Fife - Electorate 9,432

Caernarvon Burghs - Electorate 4,881

H.H. Asquith	Liberal	4,332	D. Lloyd George	Liberal	2,265
J. Gilmour (Senior)	Conservative	3,616	H.J.E. Nanney	Conservative	2,071

This was the first General Election which Gladstone had not contested since 1832, Four members of the former Liberal Cabinet were defeated – Harcourt in Derby, John Morley in Newcastle upon Tyne, Arnold Morley in Nottingham East and Shaw-Lefevre in Bradford Central. That was the end of Arnold Morley's parliamentary career, with Shaw-Lefevre not returning to Parliament until created 1st Lord Eversley in June 1906. However, having been defeated in Derby on 14 July, as county nominations and polling had not yet taken place, the Liberal candidate for West Monmouthshire withdrew and Harcourt was duly elected for that constituency. John Morley had to wait eight months for a by-election opportunity in order to return to the House of Commons.

John Sinclair was also defeated in Dunbartonshire by a majority of 33. As recorded by Lady Pentland (1928, p.42) a few days later, Sir Henry wrote to him saying,' I did not write or wire you the other day when we were all weeping over you in Glasgow, for I am not convinced that messages of condolence do not increase the bitterness. I know that everyone laments your defeat and those who know you the best will do the most. You did all that mortal could do, but you fall a victim to the general *bouleversement.* All our fellows will miss you sorely in the H of C, the two ex-law officers were loud about it… My wife is most pressing that I should convey her kindest regards and sympathy'. Four months later, Sinclair departed for Canada to become Secretary to Lord Aberdeen, who had been appointed Governor-General in 1893.

Of the 82 Irish Nationalists elected twelve were of the faction that had supported Charles Parnell at the time of the Party split in 1890-1891. In the Irish territorial constituencies, seventeen Unionists, a Liberal and six of the Nationalists were elected in what became Northern Ireland after 1922. The Rt. Hon. Charles Hemphill, Solicitor-General for Ireland in 1892-1895, elected in North Tyrone, was the first Irish Liberal MP to be elected since the 1880 General Election. The constituency remained in Liberal hands – with majorities of 91, 55, 9, 7, 102, 132 and 10 – until 1918.

Including Russellite land reformers, five other Northern Irish constituencies had Liberal MPs after 1895 – Down East 1902-1906, Fermanagh North 1903-1906, Tyrone South 1904-1910, Antrim North 1906-1910 and Londonderry City 1913-1918.

Eleven of the Liberals elected were Liberal/Labour MPs. Keir Hardie, founder chairman of the Independent Labour Party (ILP) in 1893 was defeated by a Conservative in West Ham South which he had won as an Independent Labour candidate in 1892.

The decisive result of the election was such that Lord Salisbury now had a substantial majority in the Commons which was further secured by the inclusion of further Liberal Unionists, in addition to George Goschen (now a Conservative), in his Cabinet. Thus all the Liberal Unionist MPs now sat alongside the Conservatives on the Government benches, with the two parties hereinafter being referred to collectively as Unionists. Joseph Chamberlain became Colonial Secretary, the former Marquis of Hartington, now the 8th Duke of Devonshire, became President of the Council, the 5th Marquis of Lansdowne became Secretary of State for War and Sir Henry James, now Lord James of Hereford, became Chancellor of the Duchy of Lancaster.

Although Rosebery retained the nominal overall Liberal Leadership after the General Election defeat, the two Liberal Opposition front benches, in the Lords and Commons, tended to operate independently. Indeed, even before the new Parliament met, any co-operation between Rosebery and Harcourt, as Leader in the Commons, had been ruled-out. Rosebery in replying, on 12 August, to an approach by Earl

Spencer on Harcourt's behalf, wrote that his political connection with that gentleman had 'terminated with the late Government. In no shape or form can it be renewed'.[196]

John Morley, after his defeat at Newcastle, was ready to return to the literary career which he had partly abandoned for politics. Thus he had to be coaxed back into active politics, mainly by Harcourt who persuaded him to stand at a by-election in Montrose Burghs (also including Arbroath, Brechin, Forfar and Inverbervie) caused by the resignation of its Liberal MP in early November 1895.

Perhaps significantly, when Morley was created a Viscount in 1908, he was succeeded as Liberal MP for Montrose Burghs by Sir William Harcourt's second son, Robert Harcourt.

Morley, in a letter (26 November) to Sir Henry, expressed doubts as whether he would 'suit the Scotch' [sic] as, in particular, he was not yet prepared for 'Home Rule All Round, like you advanced men'.[197] (In this connection, Sir Henry's good offices were necessary not only as he was now the senior Scottish Liberal MP but also because all five Burghs in Montrose Burghs were only a few miles from his home base at Belmont, to which thereafter Morley would be a frequent visitor. However, these reservations were overcome. Morley was duly elected on 22 February 1896 and on his return to the House of Commons on 26 February was escorted to the Table by Sir Henry.

Some two months' later – on 21 April 1896 – Sir Henry attended a gathering in the Glasgow Liberal Club to celebrate the golden wedding anniversary of his cousin, James Campbell of Tullichewan and his wife, Jessie. Alastair McOran Campbell, a great-great grandson of James and Jessie, has a leather-bound volume of the Address then presented to the couple. It contains the actual signatures, in alphabetical order, of 430 members of the Club including the Trustees, Vice-Presidents and Committee members, with Sir Henry's signature as a member of the Committee.[198]

In the meantime the situation in Southern Africa was taking a turn for the worse which would bring about the Second Boer War of 1899-1902. Ever since the UK had taken control of the Cape from the Dutch East India Company in 1795, the earlier, mainly Dutch settlers had objected to such control, to further settlement from the UK, particularly in the eastern region (Natal) which was annexed by the UK in 1843, to the granting of rights to coloured peoples and a failure to support them against native resistance.

Accordingly, from the 1830s onwards, the Boers (from the Dutch-Afrikaans word for farmer) had undertaken treks northwards leading to the creation of the South

---

[196] As quoted in Jackson (2004), p.272

[197] As quoted in Jackson (2012), p.285

[198] Alistair McOran-Campbell, 23 May 2013. As mentioned in Chapter 1, the Glasgow Liberal Club was in St. George's Place (Nelson Mandela Place since 1986) at its northern corner with Buchanan Street.

African Republic (Transvaal) and the Orange Free State, with such states being recognised by the UK Government in 1852 and 1854, respectively. The inability of the Boers to control such peoples as the Zulus within and along their borders led to the annexation of the Transvaal by the UK Conservative Government in 1877.

Such rule was short-lived, with the First Boer War of 1880-1881 concluding with a Boer victory at the Battle of Majuba in 1881, after which the Transvaal secured what the Boers regarded as independence and the UK as limited self-government. However, the then UK Liberal Government restored the Transvaal to full independence in 1884.

Thereafter, the situation was again aggravated by the flood of UK immigrants (and capital) into the borderlands of the Orange Free State to develop the diamond resources, as originally discovered in 1867, and into the Transvaal to develop its gold resources, as discovered in 1886. The UK Government's demands, that the new immigrants (Uitlanders or Outlanders) should have the same political rights as the Boers, were resisted by the Boers in order to retain control of their own countries. Then, in December 1895, Dr. Leander Jameson of the British South Africa Company and 600 armed men – mainly Company policemen from Rhodesia and Bechuanaland – staged a raid into the Transvaal in order to link up with an anticipated rising by the Outlanders. The rising did not materialise, Jameson was captured and thereafter tried and imprisoned in England, with the fiasco increasing the tensions which led to the outbreak of war within four years.

Although Dr. Jameson was sentenced to fifteen months imprisonment in mid-1896, he was released six months later, on account of illness, and subsequently pardoned. On the evening of the committal proceedings in the Police Court, he dined at the Asquiths' with Rosebery. Thereafter, he served as Prime Minister of Cape Colony in 1904-1908.

Sir Henry served on the resulting House of Commons Select Committee which reported in July 1897, censuring Cecil Rhodes (who had resigned as Prime Minister of Cape Colony) and others but, perhaps by reason of the suppression of vital documentation, clearing the Colonial Secretary, Joseph Chamberlain.

Strangely enough, James Adair Campbell (1860-1932) – a son of Sir Henry's cousin, James Campbell – was a colleague of Cecil Rhodes during the formation of the British South Africa Company in 1889, to the extent of being given lands in Southern Rhodesia, now Zimbabwe. There is a village called Melfort – reflecting the McOran-Campbell's origins in Argyll – in Zimbabwe and a plaque commemorating James Adair Campbell and Rhodes jointly in Harare's Anglican Cathedral.[199]

Many Liberal backbenchers were severely critical of the role of Harcourt, the senior Liberal on the Committee, who had taken the line that he had to accept

---

[199] Alistair McOran-Campbell, 29 May 2013

Chamberlain's word not only as a personal friend for some thirty years and a former Cabinet colleague but also as a fellow Privy Councillor.

Although he had condemned the Jameson Raid as 'a sordid and a squalid picture of stock-jobbing imperialism',[200] such criticism was probably the start of a general disillusionment with Harcourt's Liberal Leadership in the Commons which would lead to his resignation of such within two and a half years.

Sir Henry escaped such criticism as it was appreciated that he had gone along with Harcourt out of loyalty. Sir Henry's position with the Liberal back-benchers was also helped by Chamberlain saying, when the Committee's report was debated in the Commons, that he much preferred Harcourt's [so-called] frontal attack to Sir Henry's insinuations.

Significantly, Sir Henry said later that the Jameson Raid would never have happened under a Liberal Government and that it would have been better if the Unionist Government's interests in Southern Africa had been handled by Lord Salisbury (who was both Prime Minister and Foreign Secretary in 1895-1902) rather than by Joseph Chamberlain, with his aggressive policies as Colonial Secretary.

Meanwhile, the Earl of Rosebery had resigned as Liberal Leader on 8 October 1896, by reason of the difficulty of leading the Party in opposition from the House of Lords and his estrangement from Harcourt, the Leader in the Commons. John Wodehouse, 1st Earl of Kimberley succeeded as Leader in the Lords with Harcourt continuing as Leader in the Commons. Sir Henry had been briefly Harcourt's Deputy in the Commons but John Morley wanted the job back and got it.

Two months later (Decembers 1896), John Sinclair was snow-bound in the Governor-General's train in the Canadian Rockie Mountains when a message arrived asking him to return to Scotland to contest a by-election in Forfarshire (Angus) caused by the resignation of its Liberal MP. After an initial refusal and further telegrams from the Liberal Whips and from Sir Henry saying that he must come unless absolutely debarred, Sinclair departed for Scotland on 26 December. He duly won the by-election on 30 January (1897), becoming Sir Henry's Chief Political Assistant and also, in 1900, Scottish Liberal Whip, As Sir Henry wrote later, if it had not been for Sinclair's unceasing efforts and work on his behalf, he would not have become Leader of the Party.[201]

By 1897 Sir Henry was clearly becoming somewhat less enthusiastic about Scottish Disestablishment. Indeed, in writing to Sir William Harcourt on 4 October (1897), he referred to the notion that the Auld Kirk (the Church of Scotland) should be left alone.

---

[200] As quoted in Jackson (2004), p.277

[201] Lady Pentland (1928), p.57

> As to Disestablishment... There are very few of our public men who care much about it just now, and fewer still in private. 'Let the Auld Kirk alane, she's da'ing nae hairm' is the prevailing feeling.[202]

In December 1898, when he rendered his annual accounts of his stewardship to his constituents, he directed most of his speeches to the recently enacted Irish Local Government Act, a reform he had favoured since his time as Chief Secretary. He welcomed the Act as putting 'the new wine of democracy into an entirely new elective system of administration' and expressed satisfaction at the degree of unanimity with which the Act had been passed. Nevertheless, he added that the Act had not changed his attitude to Irish Home Rule, his advocacy of which was based on the demands of the Irish electorate.[203]

Then, later in December (1898), Sir Henry (now aged 62) was at Belmont on the 14th when Sir William Harcourt (now aged 71) resigned as Liberal Leader in the House of Commons. This followed repeated attempts to discuss his leadership in such organisations as the National Liberal Federation and, as already mentioned, a general disillusionment with his leadership among the Liberal MPs, all of which Harcourt interpreted as disloyalty. A more personal reason was probably that his elder son, Lewis (Loulou), who had been acting as his private secretary since 1881 and on whom he greatly depended, was about to get married.

However, on 17 December, the *Manchester Guardian* suggested that the real reason for Harcourt's decision was the fundamental divergence of view within the party between Palmerstonians (imperialists) and Cobdenites (anti-imperialists)

Apart from Harcourt, there remained only six other members of the 1894-1895 Liberal Cabinet in the Commons – Sir Henry, John Morley, Asquith, James Bryce, Henry Fowler and Arthur Acland. Acland was about to resign as an MP and it was assumed, perhaps wrongly, that Morley had ruled himself out of the succession. In any case, he was heavily committed in writing the 'official' biography of Gladstone (as published in 1905) and would soon indicate his support for Sir Henry's election as Leader.[204]

Bryce (on 16 December) and Fowler (on 22 December) wrote directly to Sir Henry supporting his accession, followed, after some uncertainty, by Asquith (on 31 December). Bryce wrote, 'You are the person who will best unite the party and be followed by our men in the H. of C. with the most general satisfaction'. (CB/BL) Fowler wrote, 'I am satisfied that you will be the choice both of your colleagues – all of us, and of the party' (CB/BL) Asquith wrote, 'I hear that you [were] thinking of taking counsel with your doctor... but I hope you will not [have forgotten] to tell him that you have the assurance that (the burdens and responsibilities of the post)

---

[202] Spender (1923), Volume 1, p.188.

[203] As quoted in Mackie (1924), p.90

[204] Wilson (1973), p. 286

will be lightened as far as possible by the co-operation and loyalty of others'. (CB/BL)

However, before Asquith wrote to Sir Henry, his (Asquith's) wife was so determined that her husband should succeed Harcourt that, using Richard Haldane (Liberal MP for Haddingtonshire / East Lothian) as an intermediary, Lord Rosebery and Arthur Balfour (a Conservative Cabinet Minister!) were asked to approach her wealthy Liberal father, Sir Charles Tennant to ask him to make up his son-in-law's loss of earnings (over £ 5,000 annually) as a barrister which he would have to give up if he succeeded Harcourt. Apparently, Sir Charles, who was already giving the Asquiths an annual allowance of £ 5,000 and had just remarried at the age of seventy-five, replied that Sir Henry, a fellow Glaswegian, was entitled to the Leadership and he would do nothing to prevent him getting the post.[205]

In the meantime, Lord Tweedmouth had visited Sir Henry at Belmont to take soundings and thereafter (on 22 December 1898) reported that 'his inclination would be to accept the responsibilities of leadership provided than he is allowed to do so by his doctor'.[206] (Edward Marjoribanks, 2nd Lord Tweedmouth from 4 March 1894, had been previously, as an MP, the Liberal Government's Chief Whip in the House of Commons from August 1892).

Sir Henry did indeed consult his local doctor (Dr. Thomas Maclagan of Alyth) who wrote on 26 December, 'There is no *a priori* reason why you should not take the post and none for my asking you to give up the idea'. (CB/BL)

Soundings, by Thomas Ellis, the Liberal Chief Whip and others, were also being taken among the Liberals MPs generally. Thus, for example, Andrew Provand (MP for Glasgow Blackfriars in 1886-1900) wrote on 2 February that Sir Henry 'is undoubtedly the most popular front bencher on our side'.(CB/BL) By then Sir Henry probably realised that his election was inevitable, as he anticipated in a letter (3 February) to John Ellis (Liberal MP for Rushcliffe in 1885-1910), 'there is no room for shirking [and] I am enough son of my country [Scotland], and have enough of

---

[205] Wilson (1973), p. 288 and Koss (1976), p.44.
Sir Charles Tennant, Bt, (1825-1906|) of St. Rollox, Glasgow and The Glen, Peebles-shire was Liberal MP for Glasgow (as a three-member constituency) in 1879-1880 and for the counties of Selkirk and Peebles in 1880-1886. His eldest son, Sir Edward Tennant (1859-1920) was Liberal MP for Salisbury in 1906-1910, being created 1st Lord Glenconner in 1911. His widow married Viscount Grey (Liberal Foreign Secretary in 1905-1916) as his (Grey's) second wife in 1922. Sir Charles' youngest son, Harold Tennant (1865-1935) was Liberal MP for Berwickshire in 1894-1918 and served in his brother-in-law's (Asquith's) Administrations as a Junior Minister in 1911-1916 and as Secretary for Scotland in July-December 1916. Kathleen, Sir Charles' daughter from his late second marriage, was the second wife of Walter Elliot, a Conservative Cabinet Minister in 1932-1940. After Walter Elliot's death, she was the unsuccessful Conservative candidate at a by election in 1958 in his former constituency of Glasgow Kelvingrove. She was, thereafter, created a Conservative Life Peeress.

[206] Wilson (1973), p. 286

the *Shorter Catechism* still sticking about my inside, to do my best with a thing if it comes straight to me'.[207]

Sir Henry had received a letter, dated 1 January, from Tweedmouth suggesting a dinner at which 'you could find yourself the unanimous choice of those present". (CB/BL) However, having receive a letter from James Bryce confirming that he was the choice of the immense majority of Liberal MPs (CB/BL), Sir Henry wrote to Asquith, on 17 January, suggesting a meeting of all Liberal MPs in the Reform Club,[208] thus following the precedent set when Lord Hartington was elected Liberal and Opposition Leader in the Commons in 1875, This was duly agreed, with circulars being sent to all the Liberal MPs on Saturday, 28 January calling the meeting for Monday, 6 February.

On Saturday, 4 February – two day before the meeting – Harcourt left London for a visit, of considerable duration, to the South of France. It was reported that this was by reason of his desire that the leadership question should be settled without reference to himself.[209]

Also that day the *Dunfermline Journal* reported that 'the occupants of the Opposition front bench agree with what they believe to be the prevailing opinion of the rank and file of the party that the claims of Sir Henry are unquestionable', adding that the dinner party to be given by Sir Henry at his London residence that (Saturday) evening for many of his colleagues would be a private and unofficial function.

On the morning of the meeting, *The Glasgow Herald* (also) reported, as from its London Correspondent on the Sunday evening, that the bulk of the Liberal MPs have arrived in town, and at such political centres as the Reform and National Liberal Clubs were seen yesterday and today in great force. There seems to be wonderful unanimity in approving the choice of Sir Henry Campbell-Bannerman as Leader of the Opposition in the House of Commons'.

Thus on Monday, 6 February, 1899, Sir Henry was unanimously elected as Liberal Leader and Leader of the Opposition in the House of Commons. The meeting was chaired by the oldest Liberal MP, Sir Wilfrid Lawson, Bt, (Cockermouth, Cumberland), with the election being proposed by Sir Joseph Pease, Bt (Saffron Walden, Essex) and seconded by Sir Francis Channing, Bt (Northamptonshire East). Also speaking in support were Henry Labouchere (Northampton) for the English Liberal MPs, Abel Thomas, QC (East Carmarthenshire) for the Welsh Liberal MPs and Dr. Robert Farquharson (West Aberdeenshire) for the Scottish Liberal MPs.

---

[207] As quoted in the *Glasgow High School Magazine* of June 1948, p.86

[208] Wilson (1973), p.292

[209] *The Glasgow Herald,* 6 February 1899

Extracts from Speech of Acceptance [210]

It is quite impossible for me to express, by any words I could find to use, the sense I entertain of the honour you have just conferred upon me [but] I will yield to none of the distinguished men who have gone before me in my devotion to the Liberal Party and in my faithful adherence to Liberal principles.... I believe there are no differences at this moment in the Liberal Party greater than those natural and wholesome differences which must always exist in a body of men habituated to think and act for themselves instead of thinking and acting to order. We are members of the party of progress and action and movement not the party of mere resistance and delay...

It is with the utmost confidence that I call upon you, my loyal comrades in the House of Commons, to give me support... And not to me personally but to me as representing the cause of the Liberal Party and its principles... [Thus] there must be deference paid to the Leader's ideas of tactical necessity, without which it would be impossible for him to maintain his position... My whole heart goes out to you; my warmest thanks are due to you for the signal and distinguished honour you have paid me; and my best and freest services shall be cordially rendered to you.

Sir Henry's accession to leadership was also very much welcomed in Stirling Burghs which he had now represented for thirty years. There were appreciative comments on the qualities he was now displaying in his new office which were taking his critics by surprise. There was also much local speculation as to what next, with much depending on how he would succeed in the Commons in a formidable task, given that he must now imbue each of his followers with his own spirit of loyalty to a party which only a few years previously had been a party of government and which, with judicious nurture, might be so again.[211]

John Spender (1923), Volume 1, p.222 reported a fellow Scot then sending a warning to Sir Henry, 'Don't play the bagpipes too loud; it's rather trying for the Saxon when both the Leader of the House [Arthur Balfour] and the Leader of the Opposition are Scots'.

---

[210] *The Times*, 7 February 1899

[211] *Stirling Journal (and Advertiser),* 10 February 1899

9 – 1899-1905 – Liberal Leadership in Opposition

A – 1899-1900 – From Election to Leadership to the 1900 General Election

Sir Henry's first speech in the Commons as Leader of the Opposition on 7 February (1899) was a marked success, exceeding expectations, with colleagues, such as Morley and Spencer, writing to express appreciation. Even Arthur Balfour, as Leader of the House, in reporting to the Queen, wrote that 'it was a good beginning to a term of leadership'.

> Sir H. Campbell-Bannerman [spoke] extremely well; perhaps more aggressively than is usual on such occasions, but this was perhaps not unnatural. He apparently aimed at proving that no more vacillating Foreign Secretary than Lord Salisbury ever existed, His criticisms [were] at times grossly unfair. But they were well delivered and full of humorous touches and eloquent passages.[212]

However, seventeen days later, on 24 February, there was an indication of future divisions in the Liberal front-bench on imperialist (expansionist) issues. In a poorly attended House, Sir Edward Grey's views on the Sudan were opposed by John Morley in a motion supported by Sir Henry and thirty-eight other Liberal MPs, with Grey and twelve others voting with the Unionist Government. Three of Grey's supporters did not take part in the division. Asquith and Henry Fowler were deliberately and Haldane unintentionally absent.

Then in Hull on 8 March Sir Henry addressed the National Liberal Federation for the first time in his new capacity. His speech outlined Liberal policy on Ireland, Egypt and the Sudan, imperial and foreign affairs generally including armament levels, public finance including the taxation of ground (land/site) values, education and the House of Lords. However, in speaking about social questions, he included a major section on Old Age Pensions, discussing whether such a benefit 'should be given to all or only to a certain number' and the question of the source from which the money for this purpose is to be obtained –'contributions or general taxation'.[213]

Such questions would be answered, at least for the foreseeable future, when in December 1906 Sir Henry's own Cabinet approved a limited non-contributory means-tested pension scheme for the elderly poor, to be funded from general taxation, which would be the basis of legislation, after Sir Henry's death in 1908 with implementation from 1 January 1909.

---

[212] Wilson (1973), p.302

[213] *The Times*, 9 March 1899

In view of later developments, it is of interest to note what Rosebery wrote about Sir Henry, also in March 1899, to Munro-Ferguson, MP, the Scottish Liberal Whip – 'Remember he is thoroughly straight, a gentleman, a friend of yours, a Scot, and do not be hasty to despair of him'.[214]

Sir Henry's first major administrative decision as Liberal Leader in the Commons was to appoint a new Chief Whip when Tom Ellis died on 6 April, with Herbert Gladstone being appointed, He had been Sir Henry's Financial Secretary at the War Office in 1886 and had also held junior office in 1892-1895. As Chief Whip, he was loyal, hardworking, assiduous and effective, with his appointment proving vital for future party management – in particular in the run-up to the 1906 General Election.

However, within two months of Sir Henry's accession to leadership, the situation in South Africa became critical, with the Outlander (UK Nationals) grievances in the Transvaal being the basis of a petition to Queen Victoria on 24 March, supported by a cable (which was not published in London until 14 June) from Sir Arthur Milner, the UK High Commissioner based in the Cape, and the failure of a conference involving Milner and the two Boer Presidents (Paul Kruger and Martinis Steyn) at Bloemfontein from 31 May to 5 June. Significantly, during the discussions, Milner played down attempts at compromise by the Transvaal State Attorney, Jan Christiaan Smuts.

Given differing Liberal alignments during the War, it should be appreciated that Asquith and Milner had been close friends since their student days at Balliol College, Oxford. Further, Margot (Tennant), Asquith's second wife, was also a close friend of Milner's to the extent that, before her marriage, he is said to have fallen head-over-heels in love with her.[215]

Smuts was of Cape Dutch ancestry. After attending Christ's College, Cambridge and being admitted to the English Bar (Middle Temple), he practised for about two years in Cape Colony before moving to the Transvaal where he was appointed State Attorney in 1898.

As the situation in South Africa deteriorated, Sir Henry spoke at a meeting in Ilford on 17 June with a carefully balanced statement challenging the necessity and even the probability of war, supporting the Outlanders' grievances, but also saying that there should be no desire to humiliate the people of the Transvaal or deprive them of their independence,[216] Three days later (20 June) Chamberlain, having requested a meeting, asked Sir Henry to support the sending of 10,000 UK troops to the Cape on the basis that it was all a bluff, that the Boers would not fight and that there was no expectation of the UK troops would be actively engaged.

---

[214] Rhodes James (1963 and 1995), p.420

[215] Clifford (2003), pp.4 and 39-41

[216] *The Times*, 19 June 1899

Sir Henry replied that such a policy was rash and dangerous and counter to his hope for an entirely peaceful solution in that it might inflame rather than pacify the Boers and thus demonstrations of this kind, if not successful, meant war. Therefore, the Unionist Cabinet could not expect the Liberal Opposition to share any responsibility for their actions. (Sir Henry later referred to this meeting during a debate in the House of Commons on 5 February 1904).[217]

However, by September (1899), a majority in the Unionist Cabinet thought that war was inevitable. Indeed, an ultimatum to the Boers, demanding full equality for the Outlanders in the Transvaal, was sent by Joseph Chamberlain as Colonial Secretary. However, this was pre-empted by an ultimatum from the two Boer Republics on 9 October that, unless UK troops were withdrawn from their borders within 48 hours, war would be declared. With that ultimatum being rejected, war was declared immediately, followed by attacks on Natal and Cape Colony before reinforcements from the UK could arrive.

Three days before the Boer ultimatum, Sir Henry, speaking at Maidstone (6 October) had taken the opportunity to review the situation, concluding with 'an appeal to those who bear the tremendous and overwhelming responsibility of government in this crisis, whether it be in London or in Cape Town or in Pretoria, to save if possible the states of South Africa and the Empire and indeed the whole civilised world from so dire a calamity incurred upon grounds so wholly insufficient'.[218]

After the war started Sir Henry developed what has been described as 'a finely constructed and consistent policy'.[219] This reflected his long political experience and the likely reactions of his fellow-citizens over the longer term, given that, when the war ended and jingoism had died down, the public would start to question how an imperial power had been dragged into a war with two very small states. The Unionist Government's aggressive policy had provoked the Boers into going to war. However, the rapid and effective prosecution of the war was necessary because of the Boer ultimatum and the invasion of Natal and Cape Colony.

Further, after early defeats and our army having performed so badly against a small number of part-time farmer-soldiers, and with the war continuing far longer than anyone had expected, the Unionist Government, not the soldiers in the field, had to be criticised for not making adequate preparation. One example of the Unionists' inadequate war planning was that the team sent out to run the railways, in an area the size of Central Europe, consisted of one officer, one batman, one groom and one horse. Sir Henry also totally opposed the Unionists' insistence on unconditional

---

[217] *The Times,* 6 February 1904

[218] *The Times,* 7 October 1899

[219] Bill Inglis, 'Sir Henry Campbell-Bannerman and the Boer War' (*History Scotland,* July/August 2008). Refer also to Professor Stewart J. Brown on 'Echoes of Midlothian – Scottish Liberalism and the South African War', 1899-1902 (*The Scottish Historical Review,* October 1992)

surrender by the Boers, favoured a negotiated settlement and while eventually agreeing that the two Boer states would have to be annexed, believed that they should thereafter be given, as rapidly as possible, self-government within the Empire.

While the Liberal Party generally agreed with Sir Henry, the Liberal MPs were divided into three distinctive and apparently irreconcilable groups with only a third or so being consistently loyal to their Leader, given also that, at least initially, the unprecedented degree of jingoism among the British public, any criticism of the country's war effort was likely to make the Liberal Party very unpopular. Nevertheless, the Party was able to hold its own, except in Scotland, at the 1900 General Election and, within six years, Sir Henry would be able to create a balanced, united and electorally successful Administration.

Otherwise, the two wartime groups, standing apart from their Leader's position, were the so-called pro-Boers led by Harcourt, who were totally opposed to the War and wanted the UK to withdraw and leave the Boer republics to themselves and the Liberal Imperialists, including Asquith, Sir Edward Grey, Richard Haldane and Henry Fowler (with also the adherence of Rosebery), who were enthusiastic supporters of the War and uncritical of its conduct and the Unionist Government's objectives.

The war continued to go badly until the arrival of Field Marshall Lord Roberts as the new Commander-in-Chief, with Lieutenant-General Lord Kitchener as his Chief-of-Staff, in late December 1899, with the last major disaster being the defeat of the Highland Brigade, advancing to the relief of the besieged Kimberley, on 19 December, with its commander, Major-General Andrew G. Wauchope being killed. On that very day (19 December), in what was known as 'Black Week', Sir Henry, speaking in Aberdeen, said that 'The Liberal Party accepts no responsibility for this War and has never acquiesced in the policy and proceedings that led to it'. He also referred to 'the appalling catalogue of lives lost and sufferings endured' with our hearts going out to the 'relatives at home who are worn out by anxiety or else overwhelmed by grief and desolation'.[220] Indeed, his own family had suffered bereavement in South Africa only eight days earlier when Lieutenant James Ronald McOran Campbell – a grandson of his cousin, James Campbell – had been killed in action.

Major-General Wauchope had been the unsuccessful Conservative candidate at the 1892 General Election in Midlothian (in opposition to William Gladstone) and at a by-election in June 1899 in Edinburgh South.

Five weeks after the Aberdeen meeting, on 26 January 1900, Rosebery resigned as President of the Scottish Liberal Association, with Sir Henry being elected as President on 27 February. Rosebery had previously resigned in late 1898 but

---

[220] *The Times,* 20 December 1899

withdrew his resignation on receiving certain assurances from the Association's Executive.

However, with the changes in command and massive reinforcements, real progress was made in the second phase of the War. Bloemfontein, the Orange Free State capital was captured on 13 March 1900 and Pretoria, the Transvaal capital on 5 June, with the relief of all the besieged garrisons between 15 February (Kimberley) and 18 May (Mafeking) with also other local surrenders, The strength of the Empire's forces in the field reached about 450,000 during this second phase – nearly 350,000 from the UK (the largest ever overseas expeditionary force until the First World War) with the others being from Cape Colony, Natal, Rhodesia, Canada, Australia, New Zealand and India. The Boer strength peaked at about 88,000 – some 25,000 from the Transvaal, some 15,000 from the Orange Free State, with the others being Cape Dutch and foreign volunteers.

Nevertheless, Liberal disarray continued to the extent of a three-way split in the House of Commons on 25 July. A pro-Boer amendment moved by Sir Wilfred Lawson was supported by 30 other Liberal MPs including Sir Robert Reid (the future Liberal Lord Chancellor) and Lloyd George, with 40 Liberal MPs, including Sir Edward Grey and Haldane voting against the amendment and with the Unionists. During the debate Sir Henry said that he could not vote for the amendment because of the extreme views of the mover and equally he could not vote against it as that would imply support for the Government's policies, Thus 35 Liberal MPs followed him in walking-out. Such three-way splits in Liberal voting in the Commons would be a common feature during the War.

In the meantime, in April (1900) a number of Liberal Imperialists had formed the Imperial Liberal Council, with by May (1900) 220 members, but then including only three Liberal MPs. Initially, the front-bench Liberal Imperialists, specifically Asquith and Grey, refused to co-operate.

Then, in September (1900) – during what appeared to be a lull in the War before final victory – Lord Salisbury considered that, with favourable economic and military circumstances and Liberal divisions, it would be to the Unionists advantage to have an election, Accordingly, a General Election (The Khaki Election) was called for October.

Sir Henry again faced a Liberal Unionist opponent in Stirling Burghs, Colonel Oliver T. Duke who had been placed as candidate by the Unionist Whips. The Colonel had been Deputy Secretary and then Secretary of the Liberal Unionist Party from 1886 but had resigned in order to become a parliamentary candidate, He was the unsuccessful Liberal Unionist candidate for Luton at a by-election in 1892 and at the 1895 General Election.[221]

---

[221] Colonel Duke later became a prominent Unionist opponent of Tariff Reform/Imperial Preference)

In 1900 the Colonel asked the electors of Stirling Burghs to send him to Parliament to support the Unionist administration 'so that the blood of our soldiers may not have been in vain or sacrifices may not be rendered fruitless and the loyal affection of our Colonies may not be irretrievably alienated'.[222] Further, as from a document, dated 2 October (1900), in the Dunfermline Carnegie Library, Colonel Duke had apparently accused Sir Henry of not only agreeing with, but having authorised supportive letters sent by two Liberal MPs – Henry Labouchere, Northampton and Dr. Gavin Clark, Caithness – to the Boer authorities. The letters had been discovered when Bloemfontein, the Orange Free State capital was captured by UK troops six-seven months earlier.

Dr. Clark had been de-selected by the Caithness Liberals and only achieved third place as an independent at the October General Election. As already mentioned, he subsequently joined the Labour Party.

But Sir Henry did not quail. In his leadership capacity he issued an election address, in the form of a manifesto, reiterating the opinions he had already expressed about the war. He blamed the Government for lack of prudence and judgement in the exchanges preceding the outbreak of hostilities. He protested against the assumption that only the Unionists had a monopoly of patriotism. He did not identify territorial extent with strength or the beating down of other peoples. Thus, as also in his speeches, he showed the same resolution as he had displayed when he had been assailed because of his support for Irish Home Rule fourteen years earlier.

Then after referring, *inter alia,* to 'satisfying the aspirations of the Irish people… by some scheme of devolution' [home rule all-round], to 'the great question of religious equality', to an electoral system allowing 'an unfair plurality of votes', to 'the necessity of readjusting the powers of the two Chambers so as prevent the ascertained will of the people being set at nought', and to the necessity for a 'more peremptory method than now exists of conciliating opposing interests' [employers and workers], he concluded –

> Gentlemen, the question before you and before the electorate of these kingdoms is not the narrow question which concerns the war or the South African policy, it is the question – with what object, and in what spirit, the affairs of our country, legislative and administrative, at home and abroad, are to be conducted… The views I have set before you are those of a Liberal… We seek the good of the people through the people and by trusting the people. We wish to destroy privilege or monopoly, whether of class or sect or person, when it is hurtful to the people, and whether in internal constitution or external policy we hold that it is not power, nor glory, nor wealth, that exalted a nation, but righteousness, justice and freedom. It is for you to say whether you are with us or against us.[223]

---

[222] As quoted in Mackie (1914), p.93

[223] As from an original in the Dunfermline Carnegie Library

The campaign was unusually bitter overall with, however, the Liberal Party trying to pull itself together and bury its differences, The manifesto of the National Liberal Federation followed Sir Henry in attacking the Unionists for their mismanagement of negotiations before the war and, thereafter, for their mismanagement of the war effort. The Federation also stated that after the annexation of territories there 'remains the delicate and difficult task of reconciling a humbled but brave people and reconstructing free institutions for men who before have owed no direct allegiance save to themselves'.[224]

On the other side, Chamberlain's theme was that every seat lost by the Government was a seat gained by or sold to the Boers. Winston Churchill, who would enter the Commons for the first time as one of the two successful Conservative candidates for Oldham (and join the Liberal Party four years later) had a poster stating, 'Be it known that every vote given to the Radicals means two pats on the back for Kruger and two smacks on the face for our country'. However, except in Scotland, the Liberals did much better than expected, with in total the election of 183 MPs compared to 177 in 1895.

---

[224] The full text is given in F.W.S, Craig's *British General Election Manifestos* (1975), pp,.4-6

B – 1900-1905 – From the 1900 General Election to Accession as Prime Minister

Table 21 - General Election - 1 (to 15) to 24 October 1900

Candidates (Unopposed), Percentages and MPs Elected

	England				Wales				Scotland			
Liberals	302	(12)	45.6	121	33	(10)	58.5	27	66	(0)	50.2	34
Conservatives				286				6				20
Liberal Unionists				46								16
	441	(139)	52.4	332	21	(1)	37.6	6	70	(3)	49.0	36
Labour	13	(0)	1.4	1	2	(0)	3.9	1				
Irish Nationalist	1	(0)	0.1	1								
Others	6	(0)	0.5	1					3	(0)	0.8	
	763	(151)		456	56	(11)		34	139	(3)		70
	Ireland				Universities				UNITED KINGDOM			
Liberals	1	(0)	2.0	1					402	(22)	45.0	183
Conservatives				15				7				334
Liberal Unionists				4				2				68
	28	(11)	32.2	19	9	(9)		9	569	(163)	50.3	402
Labour									15	(0)	1.3	2
Irish Nationalists	100	(58)	57.4	81					101	(58)	2.6	82
Others	6	(0)	8.4						15	(0)	0.8	1
	135	(69)		101	9	(9)		9	1102	(243)		670

Net Gains/Losses in MPs Elected compared to the 1895 General Election

	England	Wales	Scotland	Ireland	Universities	UK
Liberals	plus 9	plus 2	minus 5			plus 6
Conservatives	minus 6	minus 2	plus 3		minus 1	minus 6
Liberal Unionists	minus 5	minus 1	plus 2		plus 1	minus 3
	minus 11	minus 3	plus 5			minus 9
Labour	plus 1	plus 1				plus 2
Irish Nationalists						
Others	plus 1					plus 1

Stirling Burghs - Electorate 6,442

| Sir Henry Campbell-Bannerman | Liberal | 2,715 |
| Colonel O.T. Duke | Liberal Unionist | 2,085 |

East Fife - Electorate 9,505

Caernarvon Burghs - Electorate 5,202

| H.H. Asquith | Liberal | 4,141 | D. Lloyd George | Liberal | 2,265 |
| A.H.B. Constable | Conservative | 2,720 | H. Platt | Conservative | 2,116 |

The two Irish Nationalist factions had now united under the leadership of John Redmond, the former Parnellite leader. In the Irish territorial constituencies, eighteen Unionists, a Liberal and five of the Nationalists were elected in what became Northern Ireland in 1922.

Eight of the Liberals elected were Liberal/Labour MPs. The Labour candidates were nominees of the Labour Representation Committee as formed in February 1900. The Labour MPs elected were Richard Bell (who subsequently took the Liberal Whip as a Liberal/Labour MP) in the two-member constituency of Derby which was contested by only one Liberal candidate and Keir Hardie in the two-member constituency of Merthyr Tydvil where the defeated Liberal MP was too much in favour of the Boer War for the mining community. The Other MP elected was an Independent Liberal in the West Riding of Yorkshire who had Liberal but not Conservative opposition.

This was the first General Election in Scotland since the 1832 Reform Acts at which the majority of MPs elected in Scotland were not Whigs, Radicals or Liberals with, for example, only Conservatives and Liberal Unionists being elected in Glasgow. Indeed, Sir Henry said, 'Glasgow is damnable'.[225] He also wrote, 'Scotland has been horrible, for one thing the [Roman] Catholics have voted against us for the first time'.[226] Much of the temporary increase in pro-Unionist jingoism in Scotland was in reaction to the defeat of the Highland Brigade in South Africa less than a year earlier and the bread and butter influence of the popularity of warlike expenditure in Clydeside. The temporary loss of RC support was by reason of Unionist support for the establishment of a Roman Catholic University in Ireland. (Refer also to Appendix 2)

But Sir Henry was inimitable, 'Now that we have dried our clothes, and washed the salt out of our eyes, we mariners, survivors of the storm, can communicate with each other in peace'.[227]

However, the political imbalance (38 Unionists, including the two University MPs, to 34 Liberals) was soon rectified with four net Liberal gains at by-elections in Scotland between May 1903 and March 1905 and two of the Liberal Unionists defecting to the Liberal Party in support of Free Trade. Thus, at the Dissolution in January 1906, there were in Scotland 40 Liberal MPs and only 32 Unionist MPs. (At the 1906 General Election, no Conservatives would be elected in Glasgow and the two Liberal Unionists who were then elected subsequently re-joined the Liberal Party also in support of Free Trade).

Towards the end of the 1900 election campaign, Munro-Ferguson (Liberal MP for Leith Burghs), a Liberal Imperialist, resigned as Scottish Whip. (As already mentioned, Munro-Ferguson ended his political career as Viscount Novar and Conservative Secretary for Scotland in 1922-1924) Sir Henry was delighted to replace him with the faithful Jack Sinclair, now MP for Forfarshire (Angus).

Then, in a speech in Dundee on 15 November (1900), Sir Henry reviewed the outcome of the previous month's General Election, describing the Unionists' tactics as 'scandalous' and calling for greater cohesion in the Liberal ranks and loyalty to his leadership in the Commons. He also referred to a recent Liberal Imperialist

---

[225] *Glasgow High School Magazine* of June 1948, p.85
[226] As quoted in Wilson (1973), p.335. Less significantly, probably as many Irish Roman Catholics electors in Scotland had not voted Liberal in 1885.
[227] As quoted by Lady Frances Balfour (1929-1930), Volume 2, p.336

Council meeting at which the chairman (Lord Brassey) had said that 'there were disloyal men within the Liberal Party who wished success to the enemies of our country'.[228]

> Who are these men? Who is disloyal? Surely it has not come to this – that they have taken a leaf out of the book of the Colonial Secretary [Chamberlain] and that everyone who does not approve of his goings on is to be condemned as a disloyal person?

> If a man holds the strong opinion that his country is taking a wrong step, disloyalty on his part lies in holding his tongue'... A few members of the Liberal Party have thought fit to form themselves into a separate society [and] to claim for themselves exclusive possession and exclusive rights in that party'.

> 'I have publicly condemned this action of the Liberal Unionist Council – I mean the Liberal Imperialist Council – there is not much difference perhaps in the general effect upon the Liberal Party [as] fatal to our efficiency in Parliament'.[229]

The front-bench Liberal Imperialists were now moving closer to the Imperial Liberal Council. Indeed, Grey wrote to Sir Henry to complain about his Dundee speech and, by October (1901) he (Grey) would succeed Lord Brassey as President of what had become the Liberal Imperialist League, with which Rosebery and Haldane (who was helping with organisation) were already associated, with Asquith and Fowler becoming honorary members in late November.[230]

Queen Victoria died on 22 January (1901) with, as Sir Henry said, 'a pause in which 'the House of Commons forgets all differences of party and political strife'. Accordingly, when the Commons met on 25 January to pay tribute to the late Queen and to welcome the new King, he seconded Arthur Balfour's resolution, which was agreed, *nomine contradicente,* that 'A Humble address be presented to His Majesty' expressing sympathy and sorrow on the death of the late Queen and assuring him of loyalty and 'the earnest conviction that His reign will be distinguished under the blessing of Providence...'

However, as Balfour had not mentioned Alexandra, now Queen Consort in his speech, Sir Henry, in concluding his speech, took care to do so. 'It is an additional

---

[228] Thomas Brassey (1836-1918) a peer since 1886 – first President of the Imperial Liberal Council from later in November 1900 – had been a Liberal MP briefly in 1865 and again in 1868-1886. He held been Civil Lord of the Admiralty when (Sir) Henry was Parliamentary and Financial Secretary and had succeeded to that post in 1884. He was thereafter Governor of Victoria (Australia) in 1895-1900. He was created an Earl in 1911. Two years' later, in presenting his apologies for absence from the unveiling of Sir Henry's statue in Stirling on 1 November 1913, he described himself as a friend of the late Prime Minister.

[229] *The Times,* 16 November 1900

[230] Matthew (1973), pp.77-78.

satisfaction to us to know that His Majesty will have by his side his august Consort, who has reigned in the hearts of the British people ever since she first set foot on our soil'.

Sir Henry was ill ('run down') in London in late March (1901) to the extent that his London doctor forbade him to go to Dunfermline for a meeting and speech on the 27th and he had to ask Thomas Shaw, a native of Dunfermline, to deputise. [231]

Meanwhile, the Liberal Imperialists had failed in an attempt to take control of the National Liberal Federation in February 1901. Further, the Council of the Scottish Liberal Association on 3 October 1901 would give 'strenuous and unreserved support' to Sir Henry's leadership.[232] The Liberal Imperialists had little influence or impact in Wales. Thus, in these difficult times, Sir Henry was greatly sustained by support in the constituencies. Also, public meetings, at which he was always given a great reception by rank and file Liberals, played a large part in keeping up his morale.

The South African War had continued into its third phase, with Lord Kitchener having succeeded Lord Roberts as Commander-in-Chief on 29 November (1900). The Boers now adopted guerrilla tactics, attacking trains and supply convoys and isolated UK and allied units. Smuts had remained in Pretoria when President Kruger and other colleagues fled in May but escaped, taking with him the republic's remaining gold reserves, before the city was captured in early June. He (Smuts) then became a commando leader in western Transvaal and Cape Colony until early 1902.

The British response to the Boers' new tactics was to burn down the Boer farms (homes and barns), shoot the sheep and cattle and hack down the orchard trees, so as to deprive the commandos of their bases and supplies. Further, about 107,000 Boer civilians – mainly women and children – were confined in concentration camps. The camps were very badly run, tents and rations were in short supply, sanitary arrangements were unhygienic and water supplies inadequate. Nearly 26,000 internees, of whom about 22,000 were children, including the Smuts' firstborn child, died of exposure, dysentery, pneumonia and other afflictions. Kitchener made matters worse by blaming the mortality of the children on the criminal neglect of their mothers.

When Lloyd George raised the appalling state of things in the camps, during a debate, in Committee, on the Army Estimates in the Commons on 24 May (1901), in reply, St. John Broderick, the Unionist Secretary of State for War, said that no doubt there are hardships but 'war can be war', thus using a phrase to which Sir Henry would refer dramatically some three weeks later. As a gesture, Lloyd George had moved a motion to reduce the Vote for Engineering Services in the Field in South Africa – New Works, etc., but this was defeated by 123 votes to 46.

---

[231] Shaw (1921), p.147

[232] As quoted in Matthew (1973), p.77

In the meantime, Emily Hobhouse (sister of the Liberals theorist and writer, L.T. Hobhouse), defying the injunction by the authorities in Cape Town that nobody who was not employed in the War was welcome in South Africa, had gone out in December 1900 as Secretary of the South African Women and Children Distress Fund. She bullied the authorities into letting her travel round the concentration camps. Horrified at what she had seen, on her return to London, she went straight to Sir Henry to brief him on 12 June (1901).

The very next day, he asked Arthur Balfour, the Unionist Leader in the Commons, 'whether an early opportunity will be given to the House on obtaining full information on the condition of affairs in South Africa', Balfour replied that the Government was not encouraging peace negotiations and that, otherwise, the Government had no information which 'the public are not already acquainted with'. As Sir Henry later commented, it was difficult to believe that the Government was so callous and indifferent as to be content with the small amount of information generally available.

However, the next evening (14 June), he spoke at a dinner in the Holburn Restaurant in London given for him and Sir William Harcourt by the (Radical) National Reform Union. After opening courtesies, he reviewed the political situation coolly and calmly, but then in the middle of his speech he switched in a raised voice to a savage assault on the Government's policy in South Africa.

> What was that policy? That now we had got the men we had been fighting against down, we should punish them as severely as possible, devastate their country, burn their homes, break up their very instruments of agriculture, and destroy the machinery by which food was produced.
>
> It was that we should sweep the women and children into camps in which they are destitute of all the decencies and comforts, and many of the necessities, of life, and in some of which the death rate rose as high as 430 in 1,000... It was the thing that was being done at that moment in the name and with the authority of this most humane and Christian nation... **When is a war not a war? When it is conducted by methods of barbarism in South Africa.**[233]

As from the next day most of the press launched ferocious attacks on Sir Henry for his lack of patriotism, for becoming rabid, for being a wilfully blind partisan, for being pro-Boer, for insults that are as false as they are vexatious, for being on the side of our enemies, and such like. Rudyard Kipling denounced the 'Mildly nefarious, Wildly barbarous, Beggar that kept the cordite down'. Even such close colleagues as Lords Spencer and Crewe questioned his judgement. Predictably, the Unionists and the Liberal Imperialists were having a field day at Sir Henry's expense

---

[233] *The Times,* 15 June 1901

Haldane even defended the clearances and the concentration camps in the content of a series of mutual public denunciations within the Liberal Party.

Sir Henry now knew that the Liberal Party was in crisis. He appreciated that both Rosebery and Harcourt had departed from leadership because they had failed to face up to intolerable criticism and opposition within the Party. Accordingly, he called a meeting of all the Liberal MPs at the Reform Club in London on 9 July.

He concluded his opening remarks by saying, 'I make this appeal to you against courses which I see, every day that I live, to be fatal to the efficiency of the Party. You know me, you know my faults, you know my good points, if I have any. You know my views on all public subjects. You know my course of conduct which has been perfectly consistent throughout. It is for you to say whether I enjoy that confidence which my position requires'.[234] The line taken by the Liberal Imperialists in their speeches during the meeting was that the expression of honestly entertained convictions should not result in imputations of party disloyalty. However, the meeting ended with a unanimous vote of confidence in Sir Henry's leadership.

However, ten days later, on 19 July, at an afternoon meeting of the London City Liberal Club, which had Liberal Unionist members, Rosebery stated that a party could not contain 'irreconcilable divisions of opinions on a group of questions of the first importance', and that the Reform Club meeting had been 'organised hypocrisy'. He also called for Liberal Unionists to re-join a Liberal Party 'with a clean slate' [meaning Irish Home Rule] and 'disembarrassed from some entangling alliances' [meaning the Irish Nationalists].[235].

There is no doubt that what Sir Henry said on 14 June was essentially an expression of righteous indignation. On the other hand, although he had to suffer severe criticism for the rest of 1901, the Government was forced onto the defensive, as hostilities dragged on, the public became increasingly critical of the conduct of the war. So much so that the Government appointed a Royal Commission, chaired by the 9th (Scottish) Earl of Elgin, who would be Liberal Colonial Secretary in 1905-1908.

The Commission's 1903 Report, which was highly critical of the conduct of the war, was not debated in the Commons until February 1904, with Sir Henry's speech being challenged by Chamberlain as to what had happened at their meeting on 20 June 1899.[236]

With the concentration camps having been already transferred to civilian (Colonial Office) control the Government also appointed an all-woman Commission, chaired

---

[234] *The Times,* 10 July 1901

[235] *The Times,* 20 July 1901

[236] *The Times,* 6 February 1904

by Millicent Fawcett, a suffragette leader but also a Liberal Unionist,[237] The Commission toured the camps in November-December 1901 and confirmed the truth of everything that Emily Hobhouse has said. As a result of the immediate implementation of the Fawcett recommendations, mortality rates in the camps fell to the level of the rates in most UK cities.

The civilian in charge was briefly John Buchan, then Milner's Secretary. He was later a Conservative MP in 1927-1935 and, as 1st Lord Tweedsmuir, Governor General of Canada in 1935-1940.

Meanwhile in Scotland Liberal divisions were accentuated by the circumstances and outcome of a by-election in Lanarkshire North Eastern on 26 September (1901). For an apparently 'safe' Liberal seat, the local Liberal Association had adopted a Liberal Imperialist, Cecil Harmsworth. Accordingly, Sir Henry refused to endorse Harmsworth and instead made it clear that he preferred Robert Smillie, President of the Scottish Miners' Federation and the nominee of the Scottish Workers Representation Committee. A number of Scottish Liberal MPs, led by John Sinclair, the Scottish Whip, went to Lanarkshire to campaign for Smillie, Thus the election of a Liberal Unionist with 42.6 % of the vote against 36.7 % for Harmsworth and 21.7 % for Smillie.[238]

The Liberal Imperialists complained to the Scottish Liberal Association about the conduct of Sinclair and co. but, with Sir Henry's (and Sinclair's) supporters now in control of the Association, no action was taken.

Thereafter, the Liberal Imperialist cause in Scotland suffered as from support for Sir Henry at the autumn conference of the Scottish Liberal Association in Stirling on 25 October and an anti-war meeting in an overflowing Music Hall in Edinburgh on 30 October, at which Lloyd George spoke.[239]

Meanwhile, Rosebery had been asked, in August, by the Liberal Imperialist League, to speak at a meeting of the Chesterfield Liberal Association. After an initial qualified refusal, he agreed to speak at Chesterfield on 15 December (1901). With a special train arranged to bring MPs and reporters from London, Rosebery – flanked by Asquith, Grey and Fowler – again advocated a 'clean slate' policy approach and the need for Liberal association with 'the new sentiment of Empire which occupies

---

[237] As mentioned in Chapter 4, thirty years earlier, Millicent Fawcett was one of Sir Henry's fellow members in the Radical Club.

[238] Cecil Harmsworth was subsequently Liberal MP for Droitwich, Worcestershire in 1906-1910 and for Luton in 1911-1922, being re-elected as a Coalition Liberal in 1918. Robert Smillie was subsequently Labour MP for Morpeth in 1923-1929.

[239] There had been earlier anti-war meetings in Scotland, at which Lloyd George had also spoken, in Glasgow, Edinburgh and Dundee in March 1900 but no further such large-scale meetings were held in Scotland until October 1901.

the nation' He also condemned Sir Henry's use of the words 'methods of barbarism' six months earlier.[240]

Sir Henry was outraged by Rosebery's Chesterfield speech, particularly the 'clean slate' (which he had already denounced as both a philosophical concept and a practical possibility), and wrote to Herbert Gladstone on 18 December saying that it 'was an affront to Liberalism and pure claptrap'.[241] However, having been urged by his friends to make peace, a week later (23 December), he had a meeting with Rosebery, with his request for co-operation and consultation being rebuffed. Then, some two months later (14 February 1902) in a speech in Liverpool, Rosebery, in a bold challenge to Sir Henry, developed the 'clean slate' doctrine, with particular reference to Ireland.[242]

Five days later (19 February), Sir Henry spoke at a meeting of the National Liberal Federation in Leicester. He referred to the ordinary and reputable meaning of imperialism – 'that we should knit together in close friendship all the peoples and states within [our Empire's] borders'. But he also went on to say that 'when a man chooses to be always boasting about it, and whenever he hears the very name of Empire uttered, throws up his hat and shouts, he does nothing to exalt the object of his adoration – he only vulgarises it and makes himself ridiculous'.

On South Africa, he deprecated the Unionist Government's apparent renewed insistence on unconditional surrender by the Boers. (This was with reference to peace negotiations during a truce a year earlier, involving Kitchener and the Boer General Louis Botha. However, the rather meagre terms offered by Kitchener were rejected by the Boers and fighting resumed, until the Boers asked for further negotiations in April 1902). On Ireland, he suggested that a future Home Rule Bill 'may fall within a wider scheme of devolution'. Then having said that '<u>I do not know down to this moment of my speaking to you whether Lord Rosebery speaks to us from the interior of our political tabernacle or from some vantage ground outside</u>', he concluded with an appeal for Liberal unity, saying that with such 'we may be perfectly confident we shall win a triumphant victory for our cause which we know to be the cause of freedom and justice and good government'.[243]

Rosebery immediately replied to Sir Henry in a letter published in *The Times* of 21 February (1902). In the letter, Rosebery announced his '<u>definite separation</u> from Sir Henry and declared himself '<u>outside [Sir Henry's] tabernacle, but not, I think in solitude</u>'.

Three days later (on 24 February) at a meeting in Rosebery's London home, the Liberal Imperialists set up the Liberal League with Rosebery as President and

---

[240] Matthew (1973), pp.79-80

[241] As quoted in Wilson (1973), p.371

[242] Spender (1923), Volume 2, pp.26-27

[243] *The Times,* 20 February 1902

Asquith, Grey and Fowler (and later also Haldane) as Vice-Presidents. The League's purpose was to promote Liberal Imperialism (the development of the Empire) and a 'clean slate' policy approach. (The Liberal Imperialist League was dissolved two weeks later with most of its members joining the new Liberal League)

As Sir William Harcourt commented, 'All the traditions, the pledges, and the faiths of the Liberal Party are to be wiped out... The whole language is an insult to the whole history of the Liberal Party and a betrayal of its growth in the future'.[244]

In view of later developments, it should be appreciated that Rosebery, as from Liverpool on 14 February, was now opposed to Irish Home Rule not in any form but until such time as 'some scheme of Imperial Federation should allow a local and subordinate Irish legislature as part of that scheme'.

Sir Henry, as from Leicester on 19 February, had suggested that a future Irish Home Rule Bill 'may fall within a wider scheme of devolution'.

It is unfortunate that the common ground of 'Home Rule All-Round' was not pursued instead of the step-by-step approach to Irish Home Rule which Rosebery's Vice-Presidents in the Liberal League would support, with which Sir Henry would concur in November 1905 and which would be attempted in the ill-fated Irish Council Bill which his Government introduced in 1907.

However, later in 1902, with also the general public beginning to re-assess the causes of the war, increasingly blaming the Government for involving the UK in an unnecessary war, the Government now meaningfully adopted the policy which Sir Henry had been advocating for over two years – peace by negotiation with relatively generous terms for the Boers. Thus, with also further implementations by a united Liberal Cabinet when he became Prime Minister, the complete vindication of Sir Henry's longer-term South African policies.

The War ended with the Treaty signed at Pretoria on 31 May 1902, following negotiations at Vereeniging (also in the Transvaal) with Kitchener and Milner leading for the UK and Botha and Smuts leading for the Boers and Cape Dutch. The Treaty required the Boers to disarm (except for weapons required for the protection of their properties), to recognise King Edward as their sovereign, guaranteed them immunity from all civil and criminal proceedings (except for actions contrary to the usages of war), secured them in their liberty and property, conceded the use of Dutch-Afrikaans in schools and law courts, promised that civilian administration would soon be restored in the two new crown colonies and that £3 million and interest-free loans would be provided to facilitate the restoration of farms.

Further, the banishment clauses in a proclamation of September 1901 were dropped, with the only punishment for rank and file Cape Dutch rebels being

---

[244] As quoted in Rhodes James (1963), p.433

disenfranchisement and, in the case of officers and public sector officials, there would be no death sentences. The Treaty also provided that there would be no extension of the franchise to the natives in the Transvaal or Orange River Colonies until the grant of responsible self-government.

It is also significant that during the negotiations Milner was being so obdurate that all hope of a settlement appeared to be lost. However, Kitchener retrieved the situation by taking Smuts outside and suggesting to him that a Liberal Government would probably be in power in the UK within a few years when all of South Africa would be granted a sell-governing constitution.

Milner was created a Viscount later in 1902, opposed the Liberal South Africa settlement after 1905, and thereafter served in the Tory-dominated War Cabinet of Lloyd George [a former pro-Boer] as successively War and Colonial Secretary.

Nevertheless, Kitchener maintained one tradition of imperial conquest. When he returned to the UK in July 1902 he brought with him the Boer statues looted from their capitals. At the then Liberal Government's insistence they were returned to South Africa in 1909.

Sir Henry joined in the general congratulations in the House of Commons on 2 June when he looked forward to an era of peace and concord in South Africa. A week later both he and Asquith spoke at a dinner in London, an apparently a welcome sign of peace within the Liberal Party, although there was a long way to go before real party unity was achieved.

There were two major changes in party leadership during 1902. The Earl of Kimberley died in April and was succeeded by Earl Spencer as Liberal Leader in the House of Lords, with Rosebery taking no part in the replacement process. Lord Salisbury retired in July and was succeeded by his nephew, Arthur Balfour, as Prime Minister and Unionist Leader.

There was also a significant change in the Campbell-Bannerman's Marienbad routine in 1902. Charlotte had had a paralytic stroke from which she was only slowly recovering. So, as soon as his duties in the Commons wound up at the end of July, Sir Henry took her to Marienbad, leaving her there in the care of Dr. Ernst Ott. He then returned to London on his own to attend the delayed Church of England Coronation of King Edward on 9 August, leaving again for Marienbad on the following day.

However, it was believed that Charlotte's particular pain at this time was not helped by the altitude of Marienbad. So Dr. Ott suggested a move to the spa town of Baden-Baden which is at a much lower altitude than Marienbad and which, over the years, was frequented by the likes of Queen Victoria, Napoleon III, Wilhelm I, Berlioz, Brahms and Dostoyevsky. At Baden-Baden, Charlotte got somewhat better, thanks to the ministrations of a Swedish masseuse, recommended by a Baden-Baden doctor. Miss Thorbjörn, the masseuse became a special friend and companion and remained with Sir Henry and Charlotte for the next four years, also remaining with Sir Henry for some time after Charlotte's death in 1906.[245]

Meanwhile, in Scotland, the Free and United Presbyterian Churches had united to form the United Free (UF) Church on 31 October 1900, Thus were brought together all but a few of the heirs of the seceders who had left the Church of Scotland in 1733, 1752 and 1843 in opposition to Patronage and other erastian impositions contrary to the constitutional settlement of 1706-1707.

However, twenty-seven (3%) ministers of the Free Church – known as the 'Wee Frees' – opted out of the 1900 union and claimed all the assets of the pre-1900 Free Church. Their legal actions were initially dismissed in the Outer House of the Court of Session with, on appeal by the Wee Frees, that judgement being unanimously upheld in the Inner House (Second Division) of the Court of Session on 4 July 1902.

The Wee Frees then appealed to the House of Lords, with the appeal being upheld (by a majority of five to two) by the Law Lords on 1 August 1904. It is clear, from what one of the Lords' majority, Lord Albertson (Lord Chief Justice of England) later wrote, that he, if not others in the majority, was totally confused as to the facts of the case.[246]

Soon afterwards, at a public meeting in Edinburgh, Sir Henry, having consulted Thomas Shaw, who would be his Lord Advocate in 1905-1908, suggested the appointment of a Commission to extricate the United Free Church from the confusion and further litigation caused by the unworkable House of Lords decision. Thomas Shaw was a member of the United Presbyterian Church until 1900 and thereafter of the United Free Church. (Refer to Table 3 in Chapter 1)

Another of the speakers at the Edinburgh meeting was the Rev. Principal Robert Rainy of New College, Edinburgh who had attended the High School of Glasgow ten years before Sir Henry. The Principal was Moderator of the Free Church General Assembly in 1887 and of the United Free Church General Assembly in 1900 and 1905. His son, Dr. Adam Rainy was Liberal MP for Kilmarnock Burghs (also including Dumbarton, Port Glasgow, Renfrew and Rutherglen) in 1906-1911 being succeeded by William G.C. Gladstone (grandson of the former Prime Minister and the last Gladstone to serve in the Commons) who served until his death in action in 1915. The next Liberal MP for the constituency was Alexander Shaw, son and heir of Thomas Shaw.

---

[245] It is stated in the Online *Sue Young Histories* that Sir Henry, as a cousin of the homeopathic practitioner, Dr. George Wyld, was a patient of Allan Broman, with the implication that Broman was also a homeopathic practitioner. However, although Sir Henry, through Mary Wyld (the wife of his uncle, Henry Bannerman), was related to Dr. Wyld, the connection with Allan Broman, who was basically a Swedish masseur who occasionally lectured at the London Homeopathic Hospital, may simply have been that he was a one-time colleague of, or used the same methods as Miss Thorbjörn,

[246] Shaw (1921), pp.171-192

Then, later in 1904, with cross-party support, the Government appointed a Royal Commission, with, as Chairman, the above-mentioned Earl of Elgin, his third Royal Commission in four years. (In December 1905 he would probably have become Foreign Secretary, rather than Colonial Secretary, if Sir Edward Grey had not accepted office,) The Commission's Report (April 1905) was the basis of the Churches (Scotland) Act of August 1905 which ensured a fair and equitable distribution of the disputed assets.

As requested by the Church of Scotland, the 1905 Act (Clause V) also repealed a provision in the old Scottish Parliament's 1693 Ministers Act. This eventually enabled the 1910 General Assembly to determine its own formula of subscription to its confessional standards by Ministers (and Elders).

Further, the very fact that the United Free Church had to accept state intervention to secure its assets, together with Church and State in Scotland becoming increasingly preoccupied with prospects for further Scottish Presbyterian union – as achieved in large measure in 1929 – meant that the Scottish disestablishment campaign was becoming increasingly irrelevant,

Although he generally supported the 1905 Act, Sir Henry objected (18 July) to Clause V on the strange (and erastian) grounds that an ecclesiastical assembly should not enjoy the right of determining the faith of an established church. He should have read the provisions for the security of the Church of Scotland in the constitutional settlement of 1706-1707 from which is clear that the basis of establishment in Scotland was and is entirely different from that in England. Indeed, as was pointed out in 1905, Clause V set an important precedent for the release of all churches from state control in matters of faith and doctrine.

Further, in his opposition to Clause V, Sir Henry was, somewhat contradicting what he had said six years earlier (1899) when he had drawn attention to the extent to which the Church of Scotland, unlike the Church of England, was becoming less and less dependent on state-enforced sources of income.

> [The Church of Scotland] does not include among its members the main part of the most exalted and the most wealthy of the community; it is a Church comprising the great mass of the trading, farming and labouring people of Scotland – at least it has a share of all these classes. It came home to the Church of Scotland a few years ago that a large number of its ministers were not in receipt of sufficient incomes to maintain their position. So what did it do?
>
> It instituted a fund and it collected subscriptions, so that a minimum income [stipend] might be established which every one of the ministers was to receive, and that has been done by the free will effort and self-sacrifice of the people of the Church. Here is an instance of an

established Church which can take the right way in dealing with difficulties of this sort.[247]

However, if enacted in his lifetime, Sir Henry would surely have welcomed the legislation of 1921 and 1925 which together redefined the relationship between Church and State in Scotland. Alternatively, it may be suggested that, in particular, the 1921 Act merely re-asserted what had been thought to be entrenched in the constitutional settlement of 1706-1707.[248] The only vestige of support for the disestablishment of The Church of Scotland remains in the present-day United Free Church, representing the minority which opted out of the reunion of 1929, by reason of objection to any relationship between Church and State giving The Church of Scotland 'a privileged position' and the presence of 'a state official' (the Lord High Commissioner) at its General Assemblies.[249]

In this connection, it is worth quoting from the Report (Appendix 1) of the Church, Community and State Group in the 1966 Report on *Anglican-Presbyterian Conversations.*

> The fundamental essence of 'establishment' consists simply in recognition by the State of some religious body as the 'State Church', that is, as the body to which the State looks to act for it in matters of religion, and which it expects to consecrate great moments of national life by liturgical or official ministrations.

Meanwhile, on 18 June 1902, the Corn Duty (intended to raise £ 2.5 million annually), proposed by Sir Michael Hicks Beach, the Unionist Chancellor of the Exchequer, was passed in the House of Commons. Sir Michel called it a registration duty on imported corn and flour – equivalent to a third of a penny on a loaf – necessary to broaden the base of taxation and thought it would be paid (absorbed) by the exporter or importer and not passed on to the consumer. The bakers thought otherwise and instantly added a halfpenny to the price of a loaf.

It had been known for some time that Canada would seek to have the new duty exempted from, or reduced on its exports. Accordingly, on 13 May, Sir Henry asked in the Commons, 'Are our free ports to be shut up by preferential duties? This would

---

[247] Lady Frances Balfour (1924), pp.39-40

[248] The 1921 Church of Scotland Act (and the associated Articles Declaratory) and the 1925 Church of Scotland (Property and Endowments) Act. Unfortunately, the phased financial provisions of the 1925 Act were not linked to inflation. Otherwise, The Church of Scotland, as reformed in 1560, would not have suffered, in final local settlements, the loss of much of 96 % of the real value of its ancient Spiritualities (Teinds [Tithes], etc.) Thus, in many cases, the descendants or successors of the lords and lairds who benefited greatly from the alienation of the Church's ancient Temporalities (Lands) in the 16th century (before and after the Reformation) also benefited greatly from the 20th century settlements.

[249] A.W. Wishart, *Why a United Free Church Continues* (1953), p.1.

be a tremendous departure from the traditional [Free Trade] policy of the country, and we are not going to have it smuggled into existence in the form of this innocuous, little, imperceptible, intangible duty on corn'.

However, despite being assured that the new tax had nothing to do with preferential treatment for Canada, three days later, Joseph Chamberlain, speaking in Birmingham, left no doubt that the new tax could and should lead to preferential relations with our colonies. However, this particular controversy was broken off when the Corn Duty was repealed a year later.[250]

Also in 1902, the Unionist Government had adhered to the Brussels Sugar Convention with the associated legislation, in mid-1903, described by Winston Churchill as a working model of the Tariff Reform (anti-Free Trade) policies which Joseph Chamberlain (as Colonial Secretary) had advocated earlier in the year. The Convention, which involved nine other countries, was an attempt to stabilise world sugar prices. It was opposed by Liberals as not only threatening UK sovereignty but also fostering the interests of West Indian sugar producers and UK refiners against the interests of UK bakers, confectioners and consumers. Accordingly, the Convention was denounced by Sir Henry in a speech to the Cobden Club on 28 November (1902).

> It means that we abandon our fiscal independence, together with our free-trade ways; that we subside into the tenth part of a Vehmgericht [criminal tribunal] which is to direct us what sugar is to be countervailed [subjected to retaliatory tariffs] and this being the established order of things, the British Chancellor of the Exchequer in his robes obeys the orders he receives from this foreign convention in which the Britisher is only one in ten, and the House of Commons humbly submits to the whole transaction. [Shame] Sir, of all the insane schemes offered to a free country as a boon this is surely the maddest. [Cheers].[251]

However, it was not the fate of specific commodities which caused the Unionist Parties to receive a shattering blow and the Liberal Party to receive a massive unifying uplift. It was a speech in Birmingham on 15 May 1903 by Joseph Chamberlain in which he urged that Free Trade be abandoned in favour of Tariff Reform – Protectionism and Imperial Preference, that is with lower rates of duty on imports from within the Empire.

In four major speeches during the next eighteen months, Sir Henry attacked Tariff Reform and defended Free Trade – at Perth on 6 June, at Bolton on 15 October, at Alexandra Palace, London on 5 June 1904 and in Limehouse, London on 20 December. In all four speeches, his arguments were centred on much the same declaration

---

[250] Spender (1923), Volume 2, pp.66-67 and 95

[251] *The Times,* 29 November 1902

[Free Trade] is good for us, good for this free country, good for every man whatever his calling or station in the country may be. We are satisfied that it is right because it gives the freest play to individual energy and initiative and character and the largest liberty to both producer and consumer. We say that trade is injured when it is not allowed to follow its natural course, and when it is either hampered or diverted by artificial obstacles.

We are not willing to substitute for a system, which safeguards the interests of the whole community, a system based on favouritism and involving the transformation of healthy trades giving strength to the community into parasitic industries sapping its vitality, Besides we have the experience of fifty years [of Free Trade] during which our prosperity has become the envy of the world,[252]

When the Unionist Cabinet discussed Chamberlin's proposals on 13 August 1903, Arthur Balfour as Prime Minister offered the alternative policy of introducing only retaliatory tariffs to counter unfair competition from overseas exporters.

However, a conclusive Cabinet decision was delayed for a month. In the interval, Charles T. Ritchie (now Chancellor of the Exchequer) and Alexander Henry Bruce, 6th (Scottish) Lord Balfour of Burleigh (Scottish Secretary) [253] were trying to persuade the Duke of Devonshire, formerly Marquis of Hartington (Lord President) to assume the Unionist leadership and form a Free Trade coalition with the Liberal Imperialists.

Thus when the Cabinet met on 14 September it split three ways, with the majority supporting the Prime Minister's retaliatory policy. Ritchie and Lord George Hamilton (Secretary for India) resigned from the Cabinet on 17 September, followed by Lord Balfour on 20 September, when Arthur Elliott also resigned as Financial Secretary to the Treasury. Then, after a delay, the Duke of Devonshire also resigned from the Cabinet. A number of Free Trade Unionist MPs (including Winston Churchill) defected directly to the Liberal Party before the 1906 General Election. As Sir Henry had written later in 1903, 'Young Winston and all that lot are furious. We are in for a great time'.[254]

Chamberlain also resigned from the Cabinet in order to conduct his protectionist campaign in the constituencies. This succeeded to the extent that, by mid-1904, he secured the support of the Liberal Unionist Council for Tariff Reform followed by

---

[252] *The Times,* 16 October 1903

[253] The 5th Lord Balfour of Burleigh had been attained (forfeited) as an active Jacobite in 1716 but, in 1869, the title was restored to the young Alexander Henry Bruce who thus became 6th Lord.

[254] As quoted in the *Glasgow High School Magazine* of June 1948, p.115

that of the National Union of Conservative Associations on 14 November 1905, thus confirming that the three-way Unionist split had spread to the constituencies.

Sir Henry received the freedom of the Royal Burgh of Dunfermline in St. Margaret's Hall on the afternoon of 31 October 1903 'in recognition of the eminent services he has rendered to the Burgh of Dunfermline for the last thirty-five years, during which he has represented the Burgh in Parliament, and of the high and honourable position he holds as a statesman in Great Britain and Ireland'.[255] Provost Scobie, who presided at the ceremony, said, 'What more than anything else endeared Sir Henry to his constituents was his prompt attention to their interests no matter how small, and with the ease and freedom with which at all times he could be approached. Between him and the poorest citizen there was no barrier of pride'.[256]

Then, given that earlier in 1903 the Admiralty had acquired the adjacent lands of Rosyth beside the Firth of Forth, with the intention of building a naval base and dockyard and a 'new town' to house dockyard workers, and that this was the talk of the town, Sir Henry posed a few questions in his acceptance speech.

> Would Dunfermline extend her borders, embrace the new town, impart to it her own good influence, and absorb it? Or would the new community stretch its arms up to the grey town on the hill and wrap itself round her… Would Dunfermline dominate the new colony, or would she be altered in tone and character by it? Who could tell?[257]

As mentioned in Chapter 3, Dunfermline received parliamentary approval in 1911 to extend its boundaries to the Firth of Forth and thus include Rosyth in the Burgh.

The afternoon ceremony was followed by a dinner (described as a cake and wine banquet) in the evening in the Lecture Theatre with those attending including Andrew Carnegie (another Freeman of Dunfermline). The speakers, in addition to Sir Henry, included three other future members of his 1905-1908 Administration – Sir Robert Reid, MP (Lord Chancellor as Lord Loreburn from 1905), Thomas Shaw, MP (a native of Dunfermline and Lord Advocate from 1905) and the Earl of Elgin (Colonial Secretary from 1905) and also, as was his father, a Freeman of Dunfermline. Earlier Freemen had included Sir Walter Scott and the Hungarian patriot Louis Kossuth.

Two days later, on the afternoon of 2 November, the Dunfermline Liberal Club was opened, with Sir Henry 'in the chair as President (an' wha daur say nay?) and you [Thomas Shaw] making the oration. Admirable!'.[258]

---

[255] *Dunfermline Press,* 31 October 1903

[256] As quoted in Mackie (1914), p.101

[257] Mackie (1914), pp.104-105

[258] As quoted in Shaw (1921), p. 24€

Five years earlier (in 1897), in response to an appeal by Thomas Shaw on the needs of Scottish education, Carnegie had made available £ 1 million to assist, among other things, with the payment of university fees. Sir Henry had agreed to be a Trustee, although both he and Thomas Shaw were upset when Carnegie later modified the scheme to the extent that assistance with fees was to be based on parental means-testing.[259] (One wonders what Sir Henry's attitude to Carnegie would have been if he had known about his unscrupulous employment practices in the USA.)

Meanwhile, in addition to somewhat of a switch in public opinion generally in the aftermath of the South African War (particularly after the publication of the Fawcett and Elgin Reports) and the Free Trade versus Protection issue, three contentious Acts of Parliament in 1902, 1904 and 1905 and executive action in South Africa combined to provoke hostility to the Unionists, reconcile the Liberal Imperialists with the Party leadership and enhance Liberal election prospects, as confirmed by by-election results.

At by-elections during the 1900-1906 Parliament, the Unionists had a net loss of 25 seats, Liberals a net gain of 16, Labour 3 gains and Others 6 gains. Thus, at the end of that Parliament, there were four Labour MPs – Keir Hardie, as elected in 1900, and three other MPs who had gained their seats at by-elections in 1902 and 1903. D.J. Shackleton had been elected unopposed in Clitheroe on 1 August 1902 following the elevation to the peerage of the former Liberal MP. W. Crooks had been elected, with only Conservative opposition, in Woolwich on 11 March 1903. Arthur Henderson had been elected, with Conservative and Liberal opposition, in Barnard Castle on 24 July 1903. None of these three Labour MPs would have Liberal opposition in 1906. As already noted, the other Labour MP elected in 1900 had subsequently taken the Liberal whip as a Liberal-Labour MP.

For Sir Henry personally there was, in early 1903, a significant by-election in East Perthshire, in which he was an elector, caused by the resignation of its Liberal MP, Sir John Kinloch, Sir Henry's friend and neighbour. The Liberal candidate for the by-election was Tom Buchanan, a fellow Glasgow High School Former Pupil, who had lost East Aberdeenshire at the 1900 General Election. Writing to James Bryce, another Glasgow High School Former Pupil, on 26 January Sir Henry hoped 'we shall easily get Tom Buchanan in for E. Perthshire and he will be a most useful reinforcement. But there may be a drop in the majority'. However, Tom Buchanan was elected unopposed on 26 February.

The 1902 Education Act for England and Wales abolished school boards and transferred their responsibilities to county and borough councils' The Act was subject to criticism in that it required ratepayers to aid Anglican and RC schools and thus subsidise schools promoting doctrines and/or ecclesiastical arrangements with which nonconformists disagreed.

---

[259] Wilson (1973), p.156

So much so that the Welsh local authorities refused, in response to encouragement by Lloyd George, to administer the Act and the Government had to introduce direct control from Whitehall. Sir Henry described the Bill, in a letter to James Bryce on 23 September, as 'an attempt to relieve Church funds while retaining Church supremacy... the supremacy of Church interests is incompatible with popular control...'.[260]

The 1904 Licensing Act, for England and Wales – drafted in the offices of the Licence Trade Defence League – was regarded by temperance interests – including nonconformists and trade unionists – as being too lenient to the brewers. Sir Henry was not of the extreme school of temperance reformers but he took the view that it was outrageous for the Government to make such proposals, forced through under guillotine closure and without any electoral mandate whatsoever. Accordingly he took an active part in resisting the measure both in and out of the Commons.

The 1905 Aliens Act introduced modern immigration controls and registration. The Act confirmed the right of asylum for religious and political refugees but was otherwise intended to prevent criminals and paupers entering the country. However, the legislation was really a reaction to the arrival of large numbers of Jewish refugees, mainly from Russia and Russian Poland, and as many as 150,000 since 1890, with an initial concentration in the East End of London.

Anti-Semitic elements wanted to stop all Jewish immigration while others, such as the racist British Brothers' League and many trade unionists, wanted numerical restrictions on all immigration. Liberals were, of course, totally opposed to numerical restrictions and were troubled by the complications of registration and associated documentation and by the definition of a pauper. Many religious and political refugees are necessarily paupers. However, the Parliamentary Liberal Party did not vote against the Bill's Second Reading (although many Liberal MPs spoke against it in debate) but unsuccessfully fought practically every line of it in Committee. Sir Henry then led a substantial minority in voting against the Bill's Third Reading by reason of its being illiberal and unfair and discriminating unjustly between rich and poor.

> The hardest working man, the most laborious and intelligent man, the man most likely to make a good citizen if he settles here... has no chance to come into this country unless he has money in his pocket. But the worthless man, the scamp, the lazy man... can come in if he has money in his pocket.

An elderly Jewish gentleman living in Glasgow Gorbals in the late 1950s was a Liberal because, when his parents had arrived in the UK fifty years earlier, they had been helped with their registration documentation by Liberal Councillors.

---

[260] As quoted in Wilson (1973), p.392

Also In 1905 the Unionist Government drafted a Constituency Redistribution Bill which did not proceed to enactment. But as a potentially significant reduction in the number of Irish MPs was envisaged, this tended to fortify the *de facto* Liberal – Irish Nationalist alliance at Westminster, which had been upset by Liberal opposition to the 1902 Education Act.

On a population basis, there was then justification for a reduction in the number of Irish MPs. The number of Irish MPs had remained at about the 1801 level despite subsequent increases in the populations of England, Wales and Scotland and an overall decrease in the Irish population. However, the Irish argued that the number of Irish MPs could not be reduced below the number agreed in their Act of Union with Great Britain.

The executive action in South Africa, which the Unionist Government justified on economic grounds but which the Liberals depicted as being only to the advantage of international financiers, was the importation of 46,000 Chinese labourers to work in the Rand gold mines, They were forced to live in compounds, to work very long hours for low pay, forbidden to leave the compounds and mines during their terms of service and were subject to corporal punishment.

> [As Sir Henry said], To import aliens from outwith the Empire and to make them bondsmen under degrading conditions for the mere purpose of benefiting, not the whole community into which they are introduced, but a wealthy industry and speculators in that industry, can anyone conceive a more flagrant denial on all points of the principles of freedom and equity, by adherence to which we have gained our place in the world. [261]

Sir Henry was greatly sustained in the difficult 1899-1905 period by support in the constituencies and by a loyal core of Liberal MPs and Peers, including, until his death in the autumn of 1904, Sir William Harcourt, his predecessor as Liberal Leader in the Commons. As Sir William said himself at a meeting in the National Liberal Club on 27 June 1904 –

> [I have] done what I could to sustain our leader, Sir Henry Campbell-Bannerman, who has shown consistency and courage in perhaps the most difficult days that any man in his position has ever to pass through… I believe that he and you all are going to reap your reward for your constancy to the principles which you profess.[262]

In response, next day Sir Henry wrote to thank Sir William for his 'loyalty and much needed assistance and suggestion and advice for which I am indebted to you through

---

[261] As quoted in Mackie (1914), p.108

[262] *The Times,* 28 June 1904.

these years, and without which I could not have stood out for a month. Be sure that I feel it deeply'.[263]

Sir William Harcourt died some three months later (on 1 October) when Sir Henry was in Marienbad. However, on returning to the UK, he took the first opportunity, in a speech at Norwich in late October, to pay tribute to 'this greatest of Parliament men'. In the same speech, he supported the Government's initial outrage at the recent sinking of a British fishing boat in the North Sea by the Russian Baltic Fleet on its way to destruction by the Japanese Navy.[264]

1904 was also the year of the *Entente Cordiale* with France which was warmly welcomed by Sir Henry when the Anglo-French Convention Bill was introduced the Commons on 1 June. He took the opportunity to say that King Edward, the French President, the Ambassadors and Foreign Ministers on both sides 'all deserve our thanks for the part they have taken. I share the hope... that this arrangement with France may be a model for other arrangements with other countries'. Lord Rosebery almost alone had doubts about this linking of UK and French policy, a view perhaps coloured by his own experience of French diplomacy when Foreign Secretary.

One would, however, tend to agree with Francis W, Hirst (1947, p.252) that Sir Henry did not anticipate the *Entente Cordiale* developing into 'an instrument of war with Germany and that he would have wished 'to follow up the *Entente* with France with a similar *Entente* with Germany'.

Certainly, in his speech in the Albert Hall in launching the General Election campaign on 21 December 1905, while reaffirming his adhesion to the *Entente Cordiale* with France, he added that, in the case of Germany, he saw no cause for estrangement in any of the interests of either people and welcomed 'the unofficial demonstrations of friendship which have lately been passing between the two countries'.[265]

The *Entente Cordiale* replaced the Auld Alliance of Scotland with France in that all particular French rights in Scotland were dissolved. However, the French Government declared that, in terms of an Edict (Dieppe, 1 March 1607), pre-1560 Franco-Scottish treaties remained valid in French law to the extent that every Scot alive at the time of the *Entente* – such as Sir Henry – would continue to possess the full rights and privileges of Franco-Scottish nationality.[266]

Although Sir Henry's power struggle with the Liberal Imperialists, and in particular with Rosebery, would not be finally resolved, very much in his favour, until late 1905, two reasons may be suggested for that outcome. Firstly, Sir Henry was an

---

[263] As quoted in Wilson (1973), p.402

[264] *The Times,* 22 October 1904

[265] *The Times,* 22 December 1905

[266] Dr. Siobhan Talbott, 'The Auld Alliance' in *History Scotland* (January/February 2013)

astute politician who well understood the importance of developing and maintaining a power base among the party activists in the constituencies, Secondly, the Liberal Imperialist leaders had no understanding of what was necessary to secure real political power in the party. Sir Henry's success with the party activists was by reason of a real identity with them and their aspirations and a willingness to work with them to achieve party unity. As was written in the *British Congregationalist* (p.411) on 30 April 1908, shortly after his death, he 'spoke and acted as if he were always one of rank and file of Liberalism, well content to do spade work himself and not simply satisfied to leave the spade work to others'.

In contrast, the Liberal Imperialists alienated most of the local activists by appearing to promote schism rather than unity and apostasy rather than loyalty to traditional Liberalism. They also alienated the Chief Whip and local Liberal leaders by appearing to be trying to create an alternative party organisation.[267]

For, example, on 25 October 1902, Rosebery spoke at a meeting in the Empire Theatre in Edinburgh under the auspices of the Edinburgh and East of Scotland Branch of the Liberal League, having declined invitations from the Scottish Liberal Association and the United Edinburgh Liberal Council to speak at meetings in the same venue that autumn.

As Thomas Shaw wrote a month earlier (on 25 September), 'that he [Rosebery] should reject the whole and chose a section is indeed strange, and, had it not happened, would have been declared incredible. It is especially regrettable at a time when the country is justly hostile to the present Government and is earnestly looking for that unity and cohesion in the Opposition which alone can secure an effective change in the direction of public affairs'.[268]

On the domestic front, the Campbell-Bannerman's London home, from later in 1904, was at 29 Belgrave Square, into which they had moved from 6 Grosvenor Place. Grosvenor Place had become too noisy, with the last straw for Charlotte being when a hansom cab fell into the basement area of No. 6. The lease of the Belgrave Square house cost £ 4,816, with an annual rent of £ 170. Thus Belgrave Square was to be Sir Henry's London base as Prime Minister until moving into 10 Downing Street in early 1906. He thought that No. 10 was a rotten old barrack of a house and Charlotte thought it a place of doom.

Sir Henry was assisted in the search for a new house by John Sinclair, as detailed in a letter to his fiancée on 14 June (1904). He married Lady Marjorie Hamilton-Gordon, daughter of the Earl and Countess of Aberdeen, a month later (on 12 July).

> I walked down... to lunch with CB. They are house-hunting. After luncheon, he and I chartered a handsome, and took a non-stop

---

[267] Refer to George L. Bernstein on 'Sir Henry Campbell-Bannerman and the Liberal Imperialists' in the *Journal of British Studies* (*Chicago Journals,* 1983), pp, 105-124.

[268] Shaw (1921), p.230

comparative survey of his various possible houses – south side of the Peak – north side – Park Lane, Portland Place, Grosvenor Square, Belgrave Square, and round and round about. We guided the driver by umbrella-semaphore, and at first he thought we were clean off our heads. I want him to go to Berkeley Square: but at present Belgrave Square is first favourite.[269]

---

[269] Lady Pentland (1928), p.77

10 – 1905 – From Challenge to Appointment as Prime Minister

As already suggested, the ending of the South African War in mid-1902 and Joseph Chamberlain's tariff reform/imperial preference (protectionist) initiatives from May 1903 onwards removed much of the antagonism between the Liberal Imperialists and the mainstream of the Party. Further, by September 1905, even the leading Liberal Imperialist MPs had come to accept that Sir Henry would be the next Liberal Prime Minister. Most people thought that he had established his position not only as Liberal Leader in the Commons but as *de facto* Leader in the country and, therefore should and would be the head of the next government.

Indeed, at about this time, when there was some discussion in Joseph Chamberlain's presence as to who should be the next Liberal Prime Minister, Chamberlain said, 'There can be no question about that. Campbell-Bannerman has kept the Liberal Party together as no other man could have done and he is their only possible leader'. And then he went on to pay a glowing tribute to the dogged way in which Sir Henry had stuck to the ship in spite of the presence of a half-mutinous crew, and in face of unpopularity in the country.[270]

Lord Rosebery was out of contention by reason of his increasing isolation from the mainstream Party. He was no longer even sitting on the Liberal front-bench in the House of Lords and would soon move over to the cross-benches. Earl Spencer was out of contention by reason of his health. He had a cerebral attack on 13 October 1905, with the Marquis of Ripon [aged 78] succeeding as Liberal Leader in the House of Lords. In any case, as became known later, Sir Henry and Spencer had come to a private arrangement in early 1904, by which Spencer would give up his claim by seniority to be Prime Minister as the Prime Minister had to be in the Commons.[271]

Indeed, John Morley, while staying with Sir Henry at Belmont in January (1905), had made some suggestions as to the composition of a Liberal Cabinet – including Morley himself for India, James Bryce for Ireland, with also the inclusion of the Liberal/Labour MP, John Burns. Later that month (on 27 January), Sir Edward Hamilton (Joint Permanent Under-Secretary, Treasury, 1902-1907) wrote that 'John Morley had been in Scotland where he said they were heart high for C. Bannerman. He [Sir Henry] had no wish that he should be Prime Minister, but he was like a man in an express train. He could not alight'.[272]

However, as early as October 1903, Sir Edward Grey had given an indication of difficulties to come in telling Asquith that he must lead the next Liberal Government

---

[270] Mackie (1914), pp.138-139

[271] Wilson (1973), p.403

[272] Wilson (1973), p.424

in the Commons and that he (Grey) would not take office in any government with Sir Henry as both Prime Minister and Leader in the Commons.[273] Accordingly, in early September (1905), Asquith, Grey and Haldane had a meeting at Grey's Scottish fishing lodge at Relugas on the River Findhorn in north-east Scotland. There they agreed that they would refuse to serve under Sir Henry as Prime Minister unless he agreed to go to the House of Lords. Given that condition, Asquith would serve as Chancellor of the Exchequer and Leader in the Commons, Grey as Foreign (or Colonial) Secretary and Haldane as Lord Chancellor. This was to ensure that, with a figurehead Prime Minister, Asquith would have a free hand in leading the Government and Party from the Commons.

While all this was going on, Sir Henry was at Marienbad as also was the King. As Sir Henry wrote to John Sinclair on 26 August, the King had sent for him 'to have a talk, when he expressed his satisfaction of having a frank conversation on things abroad and at home, as I must soon be in office and very high office. Most significant and very discretely done. Of course this is secretissimo'.[274] Thereafter, they had lunch or dinner together nearly every day for some two weeks. As already mentioned, although, after his accession, the King and Sir Henry had both been at Marienbad in 1903 and 1904, they did not really socialise there together until 1905. This followed their first private social encounter in London at a dinner, in the home of the Earl Carrington, on 28 June 1905. They sat together after dinner and got on splendidly, with the King not leaving until 1.00 a.m. (CB/BL)

Meanwhile, Haldane – who was thought by Sir Henry to be a clumsy intriguer – was chosen to bring the King into the plot. Thus a letter from Haldane to the King's Principal Private Secretary on 12 September and thereafter an invitation to talk to the King at Balmoral in early October.

However, by then Sir Henry knew what was going on as his friend (and fellow Glasgow High School Former Pupil) Tom Buchanan had been staying with the Haldanes, with Asquith also present, at the end of September. Thus he was able to write to Sir Henry on 1 October advising that 'They would like to shove you into the Lords, but that, I told them, would be fatal to your position and influence'. (CB/BL)

Then Rosebery, speaking at Stourbridge on 25 October (1905), demanded an official statement of Liberal policy on Irish Home Rule. In fact, Sir Henry had said in a House of Commons debate as early as 16 February 1899 – ten days after his election to leadership in the Commons – that Irish Home Rule would probably not be the first subject Liberals would deal with on their return to power. Further, as indicated in Chapter 9, Rosebery's Vice-Presidents in the Liberal League now favoured a step-by-step approach to Irish Home Rule, with which Sir Henry would concur, both privately and publicly between 13 and 23 November.

---

[273] Robbins (1971), p.109

[274] As quoted by Lady Pentland (1928), pp.77-78

In the meantime the Campbell-Bannermans had left Marienbad on 28 September for three weeks at Merano (in the South Tyrol),[275] followed by ten days in Vienna and a week in Paris. In Paris there was a letter, dated 3 November, from John Morley saying, 'There are some floating icebergs in the political ocean, but your Sun will melt them'. (CB/BL) Accordingly, when Sir Henry returned to London on 12 November he was able to act swiftly and effectively to start to break up the Relugas conspiracy.

When Asquith saw him next day the idea was to persuade him to agree to go to the Lords as Prime Minister but Sir Henry seized and retained the initiative. He told Asquith that 'nothing but the point of a bayonet would induce [him] to go to the Lords'.[276] So, the meeting had quite a different outcome, with Asquith agreeing unconditionally to become Chancellor of the Exchequer. Thus the Relugas conspiracy had started to be broken up at the first encounter with the prospective victim. Asquith later suggested that what had been agreed at Relugas had assumed that a Liberal Government would take office after and not before a General Election. However, this cannot be sustained as, from a letter written to Herbert Gladstone, Liberal Chief Whip, on 25 November, he appreciated that there was a possibility of the Party taking office before a General Election.

While in London, Sir Henry also took the opportunity to consult Asquith and Grey as to how he should reply not only to Rosebery's recent challenge (Stourbridge, 25 October) on Irish Home Rule but also to John Morley's demand, also in October, that the Party should put such at the forefront of its legislative programme. Having secured Asquith's and Grey's agreement that he should reply in terms of a gradualist (step-by-step) approach, he then invited Redmond and O'Connor, for the Irish Nationalist leadership, to breakfast at Belgrave Square on 14 November. Redmond later recorded what Sir Henry had then said –

> He said he was stronger than ever for [Irish] Home Rule. It was only a question of how far they could go in the next Parliament. His own impression was that it would not be possible to pass a full Home Rule Bill but he hoped it would be possible to pass some serious measure which would be consistent with and would lead up to the other.... He would speak his mind plainly on the question to his constituents on the following Thursday week.[277]

Three years later, O'Connor – after writing that 'There were constant knockings at the door; telegrams seemed to be coming in every second; and cards were piling themselves up in the hall. It seemed as if one had entered not a private dwelling house, but a great public department' – recorded –

---

[275] Merano was then an Austrian possession. It was annexed by Italy after the First World War. Currently, rather more than half the population still speak German.

[276] Waterhouse (2013), p.117

[277] Wilson (1973), p.111

This exchange of views was brief, for there was complete agreement as to both policy and tactics. There was no need for discussing any such possibility as the abandonment of [Irish] Home Rule by Campbell-Bannerman… One point only could be suggested for discussion [what he had agree with Asquith and Grey], and a few words showed that even that required little if any discussion. [278]

Having accomplished his main purposes Sir Henry went home to Belmont with Tom Buchanan and his wife coming to stay. Thus it was from Belmont, that Sir Henry went to Stirling to make his Irish Home Rule by stages speech on 23 November.

My opinion has been long known to you. The only way of healing the evils of Ireland, of giving consent and prosperity to her people, and of making her a strength instead of a weakness to the Empire, is that the Irish people should have the management of their own domestic affairs. [But] if I were asked for advice by an ardent Irish Nationalist, I would say, 'Your desire is, as mine is, to see the effective management of Irish affairs in the hands of a representative Irish Parliament. If I were you I would take it in any way I can get it, and if an instalment of representative control was offered to you, or any administrative improvements, I would advise you thankfully to accept it provided it is consistent with and led up to the larger policy. [279]

Two days later (25 November), Rosebery, misunderstanding and not knowing until later that what Sir Henry had said at Stirling, had been agreed with Asquith and Grey, declared, in a speech at Bodmin, that the flag of Irish Home Rule had again been hoisted, adding that 'emphatically and explicitly and once and for all that I cannot serve under that banner'.[280]

It was anticipated that Sir Henry would reply to the Bodmin speech a few days afterwards at a meeting in Partick, by Glasgow. However, in his speech Sir Henry did not say a word about Rosebery. As many at the meeting had gone away disappointed, he was asked why he had not mentioned Rosebery 'He smiled and said he had consulted Lady Campbell-Bannerman. She had told him to pay no attention to [Rosebery's] speech, and he had taken her advice',[281]

More positively, Sir Henry soon realised, that the Bodmin speech had cleared the air, that he no longer had to face the difficulty of having to find a place for Rosebery in a Liberal Cabinet and that those most embarrassed by what had been said at

---

[278] O'Connor (1908), pp.73-74

[279] *The Times,* 24 November 1905

[280] As quoted in Wilson (1973), p.406

[281] William Webster, then Joint Secretary of the Scottish Liberal Association, writing, in retirement, in the *Glasgow High School Magazine* of June 1948, p.94

Bodmin would be Rosebery's colleagues in the Liberal League, specifically Asquith and Grey. (CB/BL) Rosebery was indeed now virtually isolated.

Meanwhile, Rosebery had returned to London and learned that Asquith and Grey were appalled by what he said at Bodmin, Thus, on 30 November, Herbert Gladstone wrote to Sir Henry saying that Rosebery was in a savage and despairing mood, denouncing Asquith and Grey in unmeasured terms, accusing them of having abandoned him, and saying he had done with public life, having no party and no friends. (CB/BL)

However, Arthur Balfour took this new public difference between Rosebery and Sir Henry as indicating a renewed and major split in the Liberal Party to the extent that Sir Henry would not be able to form a Government or, if so, only a very weak Government. Accordingly, he (Balfour) and his Unionist Government resigned on 4 December. Not for the last time he had underestimated Sir Henry who was a very much better strategist and tactician than Balfour (or Rosebery or Asquith or Grey or Haldane).

Rosebery also failed because he was so enigmatic that people became exasperated with him. He also lacked common sense and Sir Henry was a success precisely because he had common sense in abundance. Asquith's strategic and tactical deficiencies allowed him to be manoeuvred out of office by Lloyd George in 1916 and were again evident in 1924 when he failed, as Leader of a reunited Liberal Party, to engage with the possibility of a minority Liberal Government assuming office.

Further, if Sir Henry had formed an administration after winning a General Election, its composition would almost certainly have been rather different from that formed in December 1905. As he wrote to Lord Rendel in 1907, if his (Sir Henry's) government had been formed after the election, the constituency associations and new House of Commons would not have stood for the inclusion of the Liberal Leaguers.[282] This does not, of course, imply the exclusion of Asquith, given that Sir Henry did not know for certain that he would become Prime Minister before a General Election when he offered Asquith the position of Chancellor of the Exchequer three weeks before becoming Prime Minister.

There followed many exchanges by letter and telegram over the next two-three weeks, concluding with a summons to London. This was in anticipation of the resignation of Arthur Balfour as Prime Minister and his Unionist Government when the King returned to London from Sandringham on Monday, 4 December. So Sir Henry left for London on the Sunday, accompanied by John Sinclair but not by Charlotte, arriving in the early hours of Monday morning.

When the King arrived, from Sandringham, at St. Pancras Station at about 2.30 p.m., he did not go directly to the Palace but instead went to a Fat Stock Show at Islington. So Balfour was waiting for him when he did arrive at the Palace. The audience of

---

[282] Stuart Rendel was Liberal MP for Montgomeryshire in 1880-1894

about 15 minutes or so started at 4.00 p.m., with Balfour's resignation being made known generally shortly thereafter. Accordingly, at 4.45 p.m., Francis Knollys, the King's Principal Private Secretary wrote to Sir Henry asking him to attend at Buckingham Palace on the Tuesday at 10.45 a.m. Thus the Court Circular (Buckingham Palace) of 5 December –

> **His Majesty summoned the Right Hon. Sir Henry Campbell-Bannerman, MP to an audience this morning, and invited him to form an Administration. The Right Hon. Sir Henry Campbell-Bannerman accepted His Majesty's Commission, and kissed hands on his appointment as Prime Minister and First Lord of the Treasury.**

The Royal Warrant recognising the position and precedence of a Prime Minister was prepared on 2 December, announced on 4 December and also gazetted 5 December. Thus Sir Henry was the first person to have the official title of Prime Minister. Until then 'Prime Minister' was an unofficial title with the UK's Head of Government usually having only the official title of First Lord of the Treasury although the elder William Pitt, 1st Earl of Chatham headed a ministry as Lord Privy Seal in 1766-1768. Further, Arthur Balfour was First Lord of the Treasury not only when Prime Minister in 1902-1905 but also in 1891-1892 and 1895-1902 when his uncle, Lord Salisbury was Prime Minister.

During the audience, the King – perhaps as a result of Haldane's approaches – had suggested that Sir Henry take a peerage for the sake of his health. Also, the previous evening, at 10.00 p.m., Sir Edward Grey had told him that unless he took a peerage he (Grey) would not accept office in the new Government. Sir Henry's reply was a point-blank refusal. Indeed, he had already told Grey, in November, that the House of Lords was 'a place for which [he had] neither liking, training nor ambition'.[283]

After arriving in London with Sir Henry on 4 December, John Sinclair stayed with him at 29 Belgrave Square for a fortnight, acting as confidential secretary and messenger during the formation of the Government and warding off clusters of reporters.[284] An offer from Lewis (Loulou) Harcourt to help with arrangements for making up the Government was also accepted, with Sir Henry and John Sinclair also being much helped by Tom Buchanan.

Before he went to the Palace on the Tuesday morning. Sir Henry had seen Asquith and again later in the day. However, although backing up Grey, Asquith did not withdraw or qualify his earlier (13 November) unconditional acceptance of office as Chancellor of the Exchequer.

During the early part of this week, Asquith was staying at Hatfield in Hertfordshire and commuting to/from London daily. His host at Hatfield was Arthur Balfour's

---

[283] Waterhouse (2013), p.117

[284] Lady Pentland (1928), p.78-79

cousin, the 4th Marquis of Salisbury, President of the Board of Trade in the outgoing Unionist Cabinet – who had succeeded his father (the former Prime Minister) as Marquis in 1903.

The Prime Minister's state of mind at this time was recorded in the *Glasgow High School Magazine* of June 1948 (p.18). Herbert Samuel wrote that, when he was being offered and accepting the position of Under-Secretary at the Home Office, 'He [Sir Henry] was for the time being, no longer the genial, easy personality, fluent in talk, whom we knew well and liked so much. Without going into detail, he told me that a grave difficulty had arisen – serious enough perhaps to cause the failure of his efforts. He still hoped, however, that the obstacle might be overcome'.

It should be appreciated that there was never any prospect of Haldane becoming Lord Chancellor at this time. That position was earmarked by Sir Henry for Sir Robert Reid, who had been called to the English Bar (Inner Temple) in 1871, Liberal Solicitor-General for England and Wales and then Attorney-General in 1894-1895. Moreover, Sir Henry wanted Sir Robert, a Radical, in the Cabinet to help balance the Liberal Leaguers.

Haldane, although an MP since 1885, had never held Government office. He was not even Sir Henry's first choice as Secretary of State for War. That post had been offered to two other men with Haldane being considered as Attorney-General or Home Secretary before Haldane was specifically offered the War Office by Sir Henry on the Thursday.

Haldane did become Lord Chancellor under Asquith in 1912-1915 and ended his political career as Labour Lord Chancellor in 1924 and Labour Leader in the House of Lords in 1924-1928 – a strange fate for a Liberal Imperialist!

Further, Sir Edward Grey was not Sir Henry's first choice as Foreign Secretary. Indeed, although he had been a Junior Minister at the Foreign Office in 1892-1895, his reputation was not then as it would become. At one point in his university career, he had been sent down from Balliol College, Oxford, for idleness, although allowed to return to graduate with a Third in Law, spoke no foreign languages and, before 1906, is only known to have been abroad on three occasions – two days in Paris, a three month holiday in India in 1887 and to the West Indies in 1897 as a member of a Royal Commission on the sugar industry.

So much so that, immediately after seeing the King on the Tuesday, Sir Henry had sent a telegram offering the Foreign Office to Evelyn Baring, Lord Cromer, who had been UK Commissioner in Egypt since 1876 and had been virtually running that country since 1883. However, Cromer cabled back on the Wednesday refusing the offer, ostensibly by reason of insufficient health and strength, thus leaving the office open for Grey.

Otherwise, consultations and meetings at Belgrave Square and elsewhere and press speculation continued. By the Wednesday evening, as from an early dinner with Sir Henry and John Sinclair, Tom Buchanan feared that the Prime Minister was about to yield and go to the Lords. However, later that evening Charlotte arrived in London from Belmont and a joint decision was taken that Sir Henry should not move to the Lords. Charlotte was not going to have her beloved Henry forced onto the shelf. From then on the Prime Minister was a happier and more determined man.

Thus, the next morning he told Asquith that he was not going to the Lords and asked him to go and tell Grey he may have the Foreign Office and Haldane the War Office. Thus it was Grey and Haldane who now started to wobble and then yield by early on the Friday morning.

Thomas Shaw, who had been so disturbed by a report in *The Times* that Friday morning – which, by stating that Grey had declined office unless Sir Henry went to the Lords, was virtually out--of-date by the time it was published – had immediately written to Tom Buchanan asking him to tell the Prime Minister to stand firm.[285] However, when he went to Belgrave Square that afternoon, Sir Henry's state of mind was very different from that noted by Herbert Samuel earlier in the week. Shaw opened the meeting by asking, 'How is her Ladyship?' Sir Henry's reply and what he said thereafter are now summarised.

> Never was better; she likes the stir – no monotony here. That poor door-bell. Don't believe *The Times*. Do you know it was the comically of it that I could hardly get over. They were to serve <u>under</u> me but not <u>with</u> me! Well, this thing began on Monday; and I let it go on for three days; and then I said to each and all of them, 'It is I who have the King's Command: I am on horseback, I will not go to the Lords, I will not have any condition of the kind imposed upon me. You must take your own course on that footing. So, they all came in – no conditions – there they are'.[286]

Sir Henry then went on to say that, although the Irish Nationalist leadership had wanted Shaw to be Chief Secretary for Ireland, that post was to go to James Bryce, 'a difficult man to place', with Shaw becoming Lord Advocate. John Sinclair then entered the room to say that Lord Ripon and Henry Fowler had arrived and Shaw then departed.

The new Cabinet was completed by Sunday, 10 December, when Sir Henry presented his list to the King at 6.30 p.m., announced next morning and sworn-in on that afternoon, Monday, 11 December. (Refer to Appendix 3 for Biographical Notes). It was a day of thick black fog in London and some of the new office-holders got lost on their way to/from the Palace and/or their departmental offices.

---

[285] The Press Association had put out a statement at 12 noon saying that the report in *The Times* was unauthorised and incorrect.

[286] Shaw (1921), pp. 262-263

However, that same evening the entire Cabinet dined together as the guests of the Prime Minister in Belgrave Square. It was a cheerful occasion – all amity and harmony, with differences forgotten.

The Cabinet – the largest Liberal Cabinet ever to that date – had nineteen members, included seven Scots, two who were half-Scots and five others with Scottish connections by education, marriage and/or constituency represented. Six had been at Eton or Harrow and ten at Oxford or Cambridge Universities (including the Prime Minister and three others at Trinity College, Cambridge) and seven were lawyers.

The ages of the Cabinet were in the range from 42 (Lloyd George) to 78 (Lord Ripon) who was serving in his seventh Liberal Cabinet and was also to serve from April to October 1908 in the next Liberal Cabinet. He did not serve in the fourth Liberal Cabinet as he was then Viceroy of India. He had been born in 10 Downing Street when his father, then known as Viscount Goderich, was very briefly Prime Minister in 1827-1828.[287]

Only seven members of the new Cabinet had previously been Cabinet Ministers. One (the Earl of Crewe) had been Lord Lieutenant of Ireland, another (the Earl of Elgin) had been Viceroy of India, five had previously held junior office and five – Lloyd George, Haldane, John Sinclair, John Burns and Augustine Birrell – were newcomers to Government office.

On the Monday (11 December), the King wrote to his sister, the Campbell-Bannerman's friend, Princess Louise (now Duchess of Argyll) saying 'The new Government promises to be a strong one and I find Sir H. Campbell-Bannerman charming to do business with'.[288] Even Rosebery gave the new Government – as including his son-in-law, the Earl of Crewe as Lord President – a generous welcome, congratulating Sir Henry on the position he had achieved as entirely his due and applauding the presence of four Liberal Leaguers – Asquith, Grey, Haldane and Fowler – in the Cabinet. However, although the League was not formally wound-up until 1910, the four would soon forget that it had ever existed. Further, as will be noted, as concerning his attitude to the Prime Minister, Rosebery would again change his tune within two months.

A letter from Marienbad (via Vienna) and a later comment by John Morley on the events of that week in December 1905 and letters written later to Sir Henry by two of the Relugas conspirators are also worthy of note.

Dr. Ernst Ott, the Campbell-Bannerman's physician and friend in Marienbad wrote on 9 December (1905), offering heartiest congratulations on Sir Henry's accession as Prime Minister but advised that, at the age of sixty-nine and for the sake of his

---

[287] Goderich, when Vice-President of the Board of Trade in 1812-1818, was the Minister responsible for the passage of the protectionist 1815 Corn Importation Act (The Corn Laws.)

[288] As quoted in Wilson (1973), p.460

precious health, it would be best to go to the House of Lords.[289] However, the letter arrived too late for consideration and, as John Wilson has suggested, 'Perhaps on this occasion the Gods were kind'!

John Morley wrote on 5 September 1907, '[Charlotte] was indeed a valiant lady and her valour saved us and the party from the very brink of disaster, the famous night when she came from Belmont to Belgrave Square. We were very near the brink of disaster'.[290]

Sir Edward Grey was gracious enough to write to Sir Henry on 31 December 1907 that 'your presence in the House of Commons has been not only desirable but essential to manage this party and keep it together...' [291]

On 6 April 1908, Haldane wrote, 'None of your Cabinet has more real cause to be grateful to you. In a task of great magnitude and difficulty you trusted and helped through... Without your strong hand and guidance and complete sympathy my effort for you would have been a hopeless one... Yours has been a great and notable administration and there is no member of your Cabinet who has realised more what he has learned and gain from you than myself'. (CB/BL)

On 7 April 1908, Grey again wrote to Sir Henry saying, 'I have long recognised that the difficulties I made when the Government was formed were short-sighted and ill-advised. I hope you realise how widespread and sincere is the regard and goodwill which is felt for you I wish the time had come when I could retire as honourably and with as good fame as you are doing'. (CB/BL)

An exchange during Sir Henry's last visit to Marienbad in August 1906 is also worthy of note.

An old lady of his acquaintance was particularly effusive in her compliments but added that she had no idea that he was likely to become Prime Minister as her friends had told her that he was simply a warming-pan for Lord Rosebery, to which Sir Henry replied that 'Scotsmen never make good warming-pans'.[292]

---

[289] As quoted in Spender (1923), Volume 2, pp.119-120

[290] As quoted in Wilson (1973), pp.449-450

[291] As quoted in Spender (1923), Volume 2, pp.198-199

[292] *Stirling Observer,* 29 April 1908

Table 22 - Eighth Liberal Cabinet - December 1905 to April 1908

From 5 December 1905

Prime Minister, First Lord of The Treasury and Leader of the House of Commons	**Sir Henry Campbell-Bannerman**, MP for Stirling Burghs

From 10 December 1905

Chancellor of the Exchequer	Herbert Henry Asquith, MP for East Fife
Lord Chancellor	Sir Robert Threshie Reid, KC, 1st Lord Loreburn
President of the Council	Robert Offley Ashley Crewe-Milnes, 1st Earl of Crewe
Lord Privy Seal	George Robinson, 1st Marquis of Ripon, (Leader in the House of Lords)
Home Secretary	Herbert John Gladstone, MP for Leeds West
Foreign Secretary	Sir Edward Grey, Bt, MP for Berwick-upon-Tweed
Colonial Secretary	Victor Alexander Bruce, 9th (Scottish) Earl of Elgin, 13th (Scottish) Earl of Kincardine and 2nd (UK) Lord Elgin
Secretary for War	Richard Burton Haldane, MP for East Lothian
Secretary for India	John Morley, MP for Montrose Burghs,
First Lord of the Admiralty	Edward Marjoribanks, 2nd Lord Tweedmouth
President, Board of Agriculture	Charles Robert Wynn-Carrington, 1st Earl of Carrington
President, Board of Education (to 23 January 1907)	Augustine Birrell, MP for Bristol North from January 1908
Chief Secretary for Ireland (to 23 January 1907)	James Bryce, MP for Aberdeen South
Chancellor, Duchy of Lancaster	Henry Fowler, MP for Wolverhampton East
President, Local Government Board	John Burns, MP for Battersea
Postmaster-General	Sydney Charles Buxton, MP for Poplar, Tower Hamlets
Secretary for Scotland	John Sinclair, MP for Forfarshire
President of the Board of Trade	David Lloyd George, MP for Caernarvon Burghs

From 23 January 1907

Chief Secretary for Ireland	Augustine Birrell, MP (as above)
President, Board of Education	Reginald McKenna, MP for North Monmouthshire

From 27 March 1907

First Commissioner for Works *	Lewis Harcourt, MP for Rossendale

* Held Office, without Cabinet Membership, from 10 December 1905

Sir Henry's accession as Prime Minister was generally enthusiastically welcomed in Scotland and particularly in Stirling Burghs. For example, congratulatory telegrams were sent by the Town Councils of Stirling and Dunfermline and by the Scottish Liberal Association and the Scottish Liberal Club, both of which mentioned that Sir Henry was their President. Sir Henry had been due to speak in Dunfermline on the Thursday (7 December) but this was necessarily postponed until 29 December.

However, the *Stirling Journal (and Advertiser) of* 8 December was far from gracious, not only referring to 'all that the Unionist Party has done for us during the past ten years' but also suggesting that 'Sir Henry will find his position impossible, and the country will have the joy of calling back to power the Unionist Party'.

The first *Glasgow High School Magazine* to be published (April 1906) after Sir Henry's accession referred to him as 'at the head of the Old Boys who sit on the Ministerial benches'. The *Magazine's* frontispiece was 'a very successful reproduction of a photograph presented to the School Gallery by Sir Henry himself'. (Unfortunately, there were two errors in the caption printed below the photograph. Sir Henry was not a Baronet and he was at the School in 1845-1850, not 1847-1852.)

The School *Prospectus* for the following session 1906-1907 included the Rector's Report for 1905-1906 to the Glasgow School Board. The Rector noted that one of the School's Old Boys in Parliament 'occupies the high position of His Majesty's Prime Minister – perhaps the only instance in which this honour has fallen to an *alumnus* of a Scottish Burgh School. This high and unusual distinction was marked by you [the School Board] granting a special holiday to the School to mark the occasion'.

The new Cabinet had its first meeting on 14 December when committees were set up to consider education and unemployment. The decision to dissolve Parliament was announced on 16 December, with thus a General Election being called for January/February 1906. At the Cabinet's second meeting on 20 December it was decided to stop any further importation of indentured Chinese labour into the Transvaal. A committee on South African matters generally was also set up, with Lord Loreburn, as chairman, and the Earl of Elgin (Colonial Secretary), Lord Ripon, Asquith and Bryce being the other members.

At the third Cabinet meeting on 21 December it was decided to set up a Royal Commission on Canals. Sir Henry had in 1904 written to Herbert Gladstone suggesting the development of a State canal network with also a reference to taking over the Railways eventually, although he thought that any such proposal would scare those who depended on railway dividends.[293]

Significantly, at one of such early Cabinet meetings, the Prime Minister asked all his colleagues for details of their directorships and, in most cases, asked that they be relinquished in order to avoid conflicts of interest. This request and action also extended to the Junior Ministers. What T.P. O'Connor (1908, pp.100-101) wrote about this is worth quoting.

> There were some exceptions, and two of these were Mr. Hudson Kearley [Parliamentary Secretary, Board of Trade] and Mr. [Thomas] Lough [Parliamentary Secretary, Education], both chairmen of prosperous provision and grocery companies, in which tea was the main article of consumption. When Campbell-Bannerman was pressed as to exceptions, he replied that, of course, a Minister could not be

---

[293] Wilson (1973), pp. 469-470

expected to give up a family directorship or a directorship in a philanthropic institution. 'Is the sale of tea a philanthropic business?' asked the persistent Unionist questioner. 'That,' replied Campbell-Bannerman promptly, 'depends on the tea'.

The 7th (Scottish) Earl of Aberdeen & 4th (UK) Viscount Gordon was appointed Lord Lieutenant of Ireland on 11 December with most of the Junior Ministers appointed on 12, 14 and 18 December. (Refer to Appendix 4)

Winston Churchill, having been elected as a Conservative in Oldham in 1900, was about to be elected as a Liberal in Manchester South-West. He had been offered the office of Financial Secretary to the Treasury (at an annual salary of £ 2,000) in December 1905 but, knowing that the Colonial Secretary would be in the Lords, had instead asked to be Colonial Under-Secretary (at an annual salary of £1,500) so that he would represent the Colonial Office in the Commons.

Churchill's progression of offices was as a Liberal – Under-Secretary, Colonial Office, 1905-1908; President of the Board of Trade; 1908-1910, Home Secretary, 1910-1911; First Lord of the Admiralty, 1911-1915; Chancellor of the Duchy of Lancaster, 1915 – as a Liberal and, from 1918, a Coalition Liberal – Minister for Munitions, 1917-1919; Secretary for War and Air, 1919-1921; Colonial Secretary, 1921-1922 – and as a Conservative – Chancellor of the Exchequer, 1924-1929; First Lord of the Admiralty, 1939-1940; Prime Minister and Minister of Defence, 1940-1945 and 1951-1952 and Prime Minister, 1952-1955.

He contested ten elections as a Conservative, five as a Liberal, one as a Coalition Liberal, one as a National Liberal and two as a Constitutionalist/Anti-Socialist.

The following, as from *Punch* of 13 December 1905, was reproduced in the *Glasgow High School Magazine* of June 1948 as 'Dream Correspondence or letters which never reached them – From Sir Henry Campbell-Bannerman to Mr. Winston Churchill'

Dear Mr. Churchill,

I trust you will see your way to join my Administration as Secretary of State for War. It is imperatively necessary that we should keep a tight hand on Kitchener, and you are the only man to do it. Otherwise I should have preferred to offer you the Chancellorship of the Exchequer or the Foreign Office Perhaps, however, you could manage to take all three?

Obediently Yours,

Henry Campbell-Bannerman

11 – The 1906 General Election

A – Liberal Organisation and Strategy, Ancillaries, Allies and the Press

Liberal Organisation and Strategy

As Chief Liberal Whip and head of the Liberal Central Association, Herbert Gladstone was mainly responsible for overall election preparations in England. Fortunately, he had a very good working relationship with Sir Henry, having been his Financial Secretary at the War Office in 1886 and having been appointed as Chief Whip by him in 1899. After the 1900 General Election at which over a hundred seats in England were not contested by Liberals, Herbert Gladstone appointed an advisory committee with representatives of the Liberal Central Association (LCA), the National Liberal Federation (NLF) and local constituency associations.

Co-operation between the LCA and the NLF was already assured in that R.A. Hudson, the honorary secretary of the LCA was also organising secretary of the NLF. The organising secretary of the LCA, from 1902, was Arthur Ponsonby who would become Principal Private Secretary to Sir Henry, as Prime Minister, in January 1906. The President of both the NLF and the Liberal Publication Department, also from 1902, was Augustine Birrell, MP for West Fife in 1889-1900, who would join Sir Henry's Cabinet in December 1905 and be elected as MP for Bristol South in January 1906.

Herbert Gladstone also appointed a separate committee for the sixty-one constituencies in Greater London as, despite a thriving Progressive (Liberal and Labour) presence on London County Council, the Liberal record had been abysmal at the 1895 and 1900 General Elections.

However, instead of accepting the national committee's recommendation that the Party should re-organise on a broad front, he decided to avoid an unnecessary and costly duplication of federations and officials. Instead, he adopted a selective approach, concentrating the limited financial resources available to him on London, the English Home Counties and, otherwise, on constituencies where men of ability, who could not make much of a financial contribution to their own candidatures, were willing to come forward as Liberal candidates.

On the basis of the London committee's recommendations, a new London Liberal Federation (LLF) was created, with J.R. Segar, its organising secretary, brought over from the moribund London Liberal and Radical Union. The honorary secretary off the LLF was Hubert Carr-Comm. who, after being elected as an MP in January 1906, would serve as Sir Henry's Assistant Parliamentary Private Secretary. The new Federation's sixty-one constituencies were then divided by Herbert Gladstone and Segar into three groups to determine priorities in financial assistance, including the appointment of eventually seven or eight professional organising secretaries/agents.

Twenty-eight were thought likely to be won, of which twenty-five were won. Ten were classified as 'might be won', of which all were won. Twenty-three were thought unlikely to be won, of which seven were won.

Thus Herbert Gladstone changed the balance of power between the Party's central and local organisations. Financial help from central funds was refused except to constituency associations with already <u>approved</u> and adopted prospective candidates, with the expectation of pound-for-pound local contributions. Many local associations objected to the extent of central intervention but, where an allocation of central funds was wanted, they had to accept the measure of central control involved.

It should also be appreciated that, despite fears to the contrary, the Liberal League operated locally, for electoral purposes, within the Party structure. All forty-one League-supported candidates also received the support of their local associations and nearly half of them received financial help from the LCA.[294]

However, and certainly in the longer term, of much greater significance than any of Herbert Gladstone's other initiatives as Chief Whip, was the non-aggression pact which he and Jesse Herbert (of the LCA) negotiated, with Sir Henry's knowledge and approval, with Ramsay MacDonald (as Secretary of the Labour Representation Committee [LRC]) in early 1903. The pact was intended to avoid Labour having Liberal opposition in a significant number of single-member constituencies, with Liberal and Labour candidates running in tandem in a significant number of two-member constituencies. On the other hand, MacDonald undertook to do his best to ensure that there was no Labour opposition to Liberal candidates in other constituencies.

Herbert Gladstone believed that many working men who had been voting Tory would now vote for a Labour but not for a Liberal candidate. Jesse Herbert believed that the LRC election fund of about £ 100,000 provided the possibility of fighting on a common front to some extent at Labour's expense. However, Herbert Gladstone was as much concerned at maximising the anti-Unionist vote in areas where the Liberals had been traditionally weak. On the other hand, MacDonald knew that the LRC could not make much headway against combined Liberal and Unionist opposition,

For the next two-three years, Herbert Gladstone and MacDonald did their best to make the agreement hold. Indeed, MacDonald had to intervene personally to prevent Herbert Gladstone having a Labour opponent in Leeds West. Thus, at the 1906 General Election Labour candidates would not have Liberal opposition in twenty single-member English constituencies, with Liberal and Labour candidates running in tandem in ten two-member English constituencies, However, in sixteen single-member constituencies – twelve in England, one in Wales and three in Scotland – and in three two-member constituencies – one in England, one in Wales and one in Scotland – Liberal and Labour candidates would be in opposition. Specifically, in

---

[294] Russell (1973), p.43

the two-member constituency of Merthyr Tydvil the new Liberal candidate refused to withdraw thus denying the incumbent Liberal and Labour MPs – David Thomas and Keir Hardie – unopposed returns. Thus, in practice, the Herbert Gladstone-MacDonald pact did not extend to Wales, nor to Scotland.

Perhaps significantly, three of the leading Labour MPs elected or re-elected in 1906 had only turned to Labour after being rejected as Liberal candidates by local Liberal Associations. As already mentioned (Chapter 7), Keir Hardie was rejected in Mid-Lanarkshire in 1888. Ramsay MacDonald was rejected in Southampton in 1894 and Arthur Henderson in Newcastle-upon-Tyne in 1895. Further, Philip Snowden had been an active Liberal before joining the Independent Labour Party on its formation in 1893. After being a Labour and then a National Labour Cabinet Minister, he would, as a Viscount in 1935, advise electors to vote Liberal.

With the Welsh Liberals having contested all but one Welsh seat in 1900 and having then elected more MPs than in 1895, the need for organisational improvement was not as great as in England or Scotland, However, at least seven constituency associations had to be reorganised and one (Merioneth) re-constituted, Further, progress had been made in creating a unified (rather than a regional) organisational structure for Welsh Liberalism with, on Lloyd George's initiative, the formation of the Welsh National Liberal Council in 1898. The Council 'was quite well organised and structured. It played a central role in campaigning and policy determination across Wales and was well supported. It didn't match the aspirations of the more radical Welsh Liberal Nationalists but what would have?' [295]

A Welsh Liberal MP, Tom Ellis, had been Liberal Chief Whip in 1894-1899. After his death, both Sir Henry and Herbert Gladstone offered to appoint a separate Welsh Whip in the person of Herbert Lewis (then MP for Flint Boroughs) but the offer was declined although he did accept office (as then MP for Flintshire) as a Junior Government Whip when Sir Henry's Administration was formed in December 1905.

Further, Welsh Liberal General Election prospects were greatly enhanced by the appointment of Lloyd George to the Liberal Cabinet in December 1905. Indeed, he opened the Welsh Liberal election campaign in Caernarfon on the same evening (21 December) as the Prime Minister opened his campaign in London.

Moreover, if organisational adequacy can be judged by election results, one can only point to the success of the Welsh Liberals at the 1906 General Election in eliminating Unionist representation in Wales and securing all but two of the Welsh seats.

John Sinclair, the Scottish Liberal Whip since 1900, had, of course, an even closer working relationship with Sir Henry than had Herbert Gladstone. Sinclair believed that Liberal leaders and followers, candidates and constituency associations all needed to be brought together as a party in a way ultimately free from personal

---

[295] Professor Russell Deacon, e-mail of 28 January 2013

differences and difficulties. To this end he started annual gatherings of Scottish Liberal MPs and candidates which he continued to hold when Secretary for Scotland, As Scottish Whip he was constantly adjusting, persuading and restraining at Westminster, elsewhere in London, visiting the Liberal regional headquarters in Edinburgh and Glasgow and local associations all over Scotland,

A General Election committee was also formed to represent and co-ordinate the activities of the Scottish Liberal Association (SLA) – of which Sir Henry was President – the Liberal League and ancillary organisations such as the Young Scots. Financial help for constituencies was on much the same basis as in England, with the SLA able to report, in 1904, that a special organiser had been appointed in virtually every constituency. Thus, with also much success in voter registration and the organisation of motor cars – making their first significant appearance on the political scene – for candidates and supporting speakers during the campaign and for electors on polling day, the *Daily Chronicle* had good reason to report on 6 December 1905 that Liberal organisation in Scotland had never been so good.

Both Herbert Gladstone and John Sinclair were also active in looking out for good, new Liberal candidates and getting such adopted for the most appropriate constituencies, Thus Herbert Gladstone succeeded in placing a number of promising young men in 'safe' or winnable constituencies, including such future Cabinet Ministers as Herbert Samuel who retained Cleveland, Yorkshire for the Liberals at a by-election in November 1902 and Christopher Addison in Shoreditch, Hoxston and Charles Masterman in West Ham North which were Liberal gains at the 1906 General Election.[296]

In Scotland, by December 1905, the University Constituency of Edinburgh & St. Andrews was the only constituency for which a Liberal candidate had not yet been adopted.[297] Accordingly, knowing that Arthur Conan Doyle had been a Liberal Unionist candidate in 1900 (as he would be again in 1906), and that such other *literati* as Hilaire Belloc and A.E.W. Mason would be Liberal candidates in England,[298] Sinclair hoped to persuade his friend, James M. Barrie [299] – a native of

---

[296] Charles Masterman, who had been unsuccessful at a by-election in Dulwich in 1903, was unseated on petition in West Ham North in June 1911. Having been elected for S.W. Bethnal Green at a by-election in July 1911, he lost a Ministerial By-Election therein on being appointed to the Cabinet in February 1914. After unsuccessfully contesting another by-election in May 1913, he resigned from the Cabinet in February 1915. Later, in 1923-1924, he was briefly MP for Manchester Rusholme,

[297] In 1906, Edinburgh and St. Andrews was held by a Conservative with only an Independent Free Trade candidate in opposition. Aberdeen and Glasgow Universities was held by a Conservative with Liberal and Independent Free Trade candidates in opposition.

[298] Conan Doyle was defeated by Liberals in Edinburgh Central in 1900 and in Hawick Burghs (also including Galashiels and Selkirk) in 1906. In 1906, Belloc was elected for Salford South (a Liberal gain) and Mason for Coventry (also a Liberal gain).

[299] Barrie, who became a Baronet in 1913 and a member of the Order of Merit in 1922, was elected as Rector of St. Andrews University in 1919 and Chancellor of Edinburgh University in 1930.

Kirriemuir in his (Sinclair's) Forfarshire Constituency – to stand. However, he was unsuccessful,

> The Universities would have been an ideal seat if I had been able to stand at all but I am convinced it is wiser that I should not. Public life would be too much out of my line. Politics is a great and a fine calling but it is not for me, Thank you very heartily, I am with you heart and spirit in the Liberal cause.
>
> Yours sincerely,
> J.M. BARRIE [300]

Ancillaries

Also, in both England and Scotland, the Liberal Party's ancillaries were at the peaks of activity and efficiency by the time of the 1906 General Election, bringing over 100,000 voluntary workers into action. In England the main ancillaries were the Women's Liberal Federation (WLF), formed in June 1886 at the height of the Irish Home Rule crisis, and with eventually 732 branches and the Young Liberals (formed in Birmingham as the British League of Young Liberals in 1903, with a separate League being formed in London) with 300 branches by 1905.[301] In Scotland the main ancillaries were the Scottish Women's Liberal Federation and the Young Scots. In September 1905, the Countess of Aberdeen, President of the WLF, wrote to Sir Henry assuring him that he had 'no more devoted and loyal supporters [who would] give a good account of themselves during [an] election.[302]

The Countess was also President of the Scottish Women's Liberal Federation, being succeeded in that position by her daughter. Lady Marjorie Sinclair, John Sinclair's wife. Edward Marjoribanks, 2nd Lord Tweedmouth from 1894 and brother of the Countess, had been, as an MP, Liberal and Government Chief Whip in 1892-1894.

The Young Scots Society was formed – three years earlier than the National League of Young Liberals – following a letter in the *Edinburgh Evening News* on 28 October 1900 in response to the Liberal losses in Scotland earlier that month.[303] Having eventually 10,000 members in fifty mainly urban branches, it was committed to the political education of its members (complemented by campaigning) and a range of policies such as home-rule-all-round (federalism), land value taxation, licensing law reform, the effective solution of housing problems, women's suffrage and old age

---

When he died in 1937, he left the bulk of his estate, excluding the copyright of *Peter Pan*, to his Secretary, Cynthia Asquith, a daughter-in-law of the former Prime Minister.

[300] Marjorie Sinclair, Lady Pentland (1928), p.78

[301] The two English Young Liberal Leagues amalgamated in 1908.

[302] As quoted in Russell (1973), p.42

[303] The Young Scots first major venture was a massive anti-war rally in October 1901 in the Waverley Market in Edinburgh which attracted an estimated 10,000.

pensions. Campaigning zeal was effectively displayed between 1903 and 1910 but with also, particularly at the 1906 General Election (when they were commended for their work by Sir Henry) an emphasis on social questions, with many Young Scots office-bearers becoming MPs.[304]

Allies

As from 1899 the Presbyterians, Methodists, Congregationalists and Baptists in England and Wales – accounting for about 10 % of the English electorate and well over 50 % in Wales – had been organised in the National Free Church Council which in 1905 affirmed that the pressures of political circumstances and social concerns drove it towards political action. It established a department for electoral work and circulated millions of leaflets attacking Unionist policies, specifically education and licensing. Its 1906 election manifesto made the Liberal cause its own by proclaiming that Campbell-Bannerman's government 'represented the people as no other has before'.[305] There was also much local co-operation with Liberal (and Labour) candidates.[306]

The Liverpool-based Irish Defence League attempted to ensure that Irish Nationalist supporters in Great Britain were brought over to the Liberals (and Labour) by endorsing 165 Liberal (and 21 Labour) candidates in appropriate constituencies. Further, in reaction to the Unionists' 1906 Aliens Act, as due to come into force on 1 January 1906, Jewish electors were told by the Federation of Synagogues that the return of the Unionists to power would be 'the death blow for Jewish freedom in this country',[307]

In 1903, with Chamberlain having formed the Tariff Reform League, the Free Trade Union was also formed to give Free Trade Unionists, who were unwilling to go straight over to the Liberals, the opportunity to play their part in defence of Free Trade. This 'non-party' organisation, with Liberals as directors and treasurer, did not have the financial resources of the Tariff Reform League. However, financial parity was unnecessary for effectiveness, given a country-wide network of local Free Trade associations which also emerged.

The Press

In a letter to Herbert Gladstone in June 1905, when a new Liberal daily newspaper, *The Tribune* was being planned, Sir Henry wrote, 'the great thing we suffer from is

---

[304] Refer to the late R. Ian Elder on 'The Young Scots Society', *Journal of Liberal History* (Autumn 2002). The 1914-1918 War had adverse effects on the Society, which never thereafter recovered its momentum and by about 1922 had virtually ceased to be

[305] *The Times*, 4 January 1906

[306] Russell (1973), pp, 182-183

[307] As quoted in Russell (1973), p.104

that we have no organ in the press',[308] meaning that three of the London-based daily newspapers with the largest circulations – *The Daily Mail* (c.750,000), *The Daily Express* (c.300,000) and *The Daily Telegraph* (c.285,000) – were all Unionist. Further, speaking in Culross, seven months later, on 12 January (1906), Sir Henry deplored the fact that 'the newspaper press has largely got into the hands of combinations of capitalists and that they [the readers] could not have their former confidence in individual newspapers giving personally disinterested advice'.[309]

However, the two leading London-based Liberal newspapers, *The Daily News* and *The Daily Chronicle,* by reducing their cover price from a penny to a halfpenny in 1904, both increased their circulations to c.200,000 by 1906. The erstwhile Independent *Daily Mirror,* with a circulation of c.350,000, eventually came out strongly against the Unionists and the Unionist newspapers' attempts to cover up divisions on fiscal policy merely confirmed that the Unionists were hopelessly divided. Elsewhere in England the balance between Liberal and Unionist newspapers was much more even than in London, with a number of newspapers, such as the *Liverpool Daily Post,* which had turned Unionist in 1886 in opposition to Irish Home Rule, coming back to support the Liberals in defence of Free Trade.

In Scotland, John Sinclair, while MP for Dunbartonshire in 1892-1895, had attempted unsuccessfully to start a Liberal newspaper to challenge *The Scotsman* (Edinburgh) and *The Glasgow Herald,* both of which had also turned Unionist in 1886.[310] In January 1897, when Sinclair returned from Canada to contest successfully the Forfarshire by-election, *The Scotsman* hoped that 'Captain Sinclair would be able to return to the pleasant land he was so unwilling to leave in order to enjoy its winter pastimes'.[311]

However, as already mentioned (Chapter 7), by 1905, *The Glasgow Herald* had again changed its allegiance becoming a Free Trade Unionist newspaper and a supporter of land reform. Further, by 1905, the *Aberdeen Free Press,* also a Unionist newspaper since 1886, had returned to its original Liberal allegiance.[312]

Three media-owning families provided five (successful) Liberal candidates in England, Wales and Scotland. Cecil Harmsworth (Droitwich) and Robert Harmsworth (MP for Caithness since 1900) were connected with the Amalgamated Press, Sir George Newnes (MP for Swansea Town since 1900) and Frank Newnes (Bassetlaw, Nottinghamshire) controlled the *Westminster Gazette* and *Country Life* and George W. Agnew (West Salford) was the proprietor of *Punch.*

---

[308] As quoted in Russell (1973), p.139

[309] *The Times,* 13 February 1906

[310] Lady Pentland (1928), p.40-41

[311] As quoted by Lady Pentland (1928), p.49

[312] In 1922, *The Aberdeen Free Press* merged with *The Aberdeen Journal* to become *The Press and Journal*

B – The Prime Minister's Campaign

On the evening of his third Cabinet meeting (21 December 1905) Sir Henry spoke, at a Liberal Rally in the Albert Hall, to launch his General Election campaign. The packed and enthusiastic gathering, of about 9,000 people, rose to acclaim the new Prime Minister and, as he rose to receive the ovation, tears ran down his cheeks. He then lambasted the Balfour Government as having departed in a moonlight flitting, run away in a murky December and died of tactics. In the election it would be the Unionists not the Liberals who were on trial.

As an example of the mess left for the Liberals to clear up, he referred to the quarrel between Curzon (Viceroy) and Kitchener (Army Commander) in India. He could imagine nothing less like a sense of our imperial responsibility than such a controversy, rashly raised and tactlessly handled and referred to the Liberal principle of the subordination of the military to the civil authority.

He then outlined the past week's Cabinet decisions. Turning to Foreign affairs, he reaffirmed his support for the *Entente Cordiale* with France, adding that, in the case of Germany, he saw no cause for estrangement in the interests of either people. On Home Affairs, he referred to the necessity for legislative action on education, licensing and land reform.

Describing militarism, extravagance and protectionism as weeds that grew in the same field, he urged the central importance of Free Trade to all aspects of government – to foreign policy, to the economy and social reform. He warned that, if once the door was opened to protectionism, there would be little hope for the great objects of reform on which Liberals were set.

> [In conclusion] I would ask you not to be over-confident. Against you is a strong coalition of interests and powers. Against you is a great party – divided on the details of fiscal strategy, but united in its determination to undermine and overthrow the citadel of Free Trade. Let us be worthy of our fathers who went before us and won for us this great privilege of freedom, and let us beware lest, through any fault of ours, so great and vital a national interest is imperilled.[313]

The Rally was one of the first major events to be interrupted by Suffragettes. Otherwise, despite the dreadful acoustics, the occasion was an unqualified success, with a number of colleagues writing next day to the Prime Minister and to Charlotte (who had not been present) to express their appreciation of his speech.

On 23 December Sir Henry left London for Belmont. On arrival he was greeted by a large gathering of Meigle residents. Including many local schoolchildren to whom he said –

---

[313] *The Times,* 22 December 1905

Nothing has pleased me more than to see so many young people, boys and girls, taking part in this little demonstration. They will, I have no doubt, remember all their days that they were here when a Primer Minister took up his residence at Meigle. It will show them that there is no office under the Crown that is not open to an honest man if he has sufficient ability to hold it, and if he also devotes himself to the labours necessary to maintain it.[314]

Given Lady Campbell-Bannerman's death some eight months later, it was the last Christmas they were to spend together. Then, after Christmas, he started his election tour in his own constituency in Dunfermline on Tuesday, 29 December when he spoke at a public meeting in St. Margaret's Hall and at a dinner in the Royal Hotel, He also met privately a Trades Council delegation to discuss the unemployment problem.

In answer to a question, at the St. Margaret's Hall meeting, on Irish Home Rule, he said that 'any legislative body I have ever voted for was to be subordinate to the Imperial Parliament'. He also compared Balfour's transports of alarm on the Irish issue to the false fits of professional beggars. He reiterated that fiscal policy was the outstanding issue and appealed for a verdict against Balfour's obscurities and against Chamberlain's more intelligible but none the less objectionable policy of 'limited and obstructed trade, false imperial instinct and wealth in its most objectionable form'.[315]

From Dunfermline, he returned to London for a fourth Cabinet meeting, then back to Belmont before another trip to London for the Dissolution Council. His election address, although as from 10 Downing Street and dated 6 January 1906, was printed in Dunfermline by the publishers of the *Dunfermline Press* and not published locally until the 8th. The long address took the form of a Manifesto and indeed is included as such in full in F.W.S. Craig's *British General Election Manifestos 1900-1974* (1975), pp.10-13.

---

[314] *Stirling Observer,* 29 April 1908

[315] Russell (1973), p.104

However, as from an original in the Dunfermline Carnegie Library –

TO THE ELECTORS
OF THE
Stirling District of Burghs

GENTLEMEN,

The dissolution of Parliament imposes upon you the duty of returning a representative to the new House of Commons, and I respectfully place my services at your disposal. I do so with confidence, bearing in mind the eight successive Parliaments through which our relations have been unbroken, and having a vivid sense of the kind indulgence which during that long time you have uniformly extended to me.

I make this appeal, however, not merely as your Member in the past Parliaments, but as the head of the Administration recently appointed by His Majesty the King, and I am confident that in undertaking these duties I had your approval.

After ten years of Unionist rule, the country now has an opportunity of saying whether it desires a further period of government at the same hands, and whether the Administration which has been called on to fill the gap created by Mr. Balfour's unexpected resignation shall be confirmed in office; In coming to a decision the electors will, I imagine, be largely guided by the consideration, in the first place, of the record of the late government, and secondly, of the policy which the leaders of the Unionist party are now submitting to them for their judgment.

With regard to their record, it will hardly be disputed that they have had advantages such as few Governments in recent times have enjoyed. For ten years they have been supported by an immense majority in the House of Commons; and throughout this period the House of Lords, by its docility, has done its part to facilitate their task. But, as if these advantages were not enough, they have further, by an unprecedented use of restrictive powers, curtailed the freedom of discussion in the House of Commons, and impaired its authority, reducing the Legislature, so far as was in their power, to a machine for registering the decrees of the Executive.

Of the opportunities so secured, we have to ask ourselves what use they have made, what have they accomplished for the benefit of the country and the Empire? What claim can they establish on the strength of their performances to the confidence of the electors which they are about to solicit?

The period over which we are looking back presents itself to me, I confess, as a well-nigh unbroken expanse of mismanagement, of legislation conducted for the benefit of privileged classes and powerful interests, of wars and adventures abroad hastily embarked upon and recklessly pursued. The legacy which they have bequeathed to their successors – and I say it in no partisan spirit, but with a full sense of responsibility – is in the main a legacy of embarrassment, an accumulation of public mischief and confusion absolutely appalling in its extent and ramifications.

The last General Election was fought on the single issue of the situation created by the war in South Africa. The Government of the day asked for, and obtained, a mandate for concluding the war, and for settling our newly acquired territories. So far as that settlement has proceeded, I ask whether it has been conducted in such a manner as to justify the confidence reposed in them. It seems enough to remind you that the late Prime Minister now declares to us that as a result of the policy which involved such sacrifices on the part of the people of this country, South Africa has been reduced to a condition in which loss of prosperity, nay, even ruin, can only be avoided by the use of servile labour imported in unlimited quantities from China.

Ten years ago the incoming Conservative Government found the national finances in good order. The public debt was being steadily reduced. The burden of taxation was moderate. The coffers of the Exchequer were made to overflow year after year by the operation of the Estate Duty Act, which had been carried in the teeth of their violent opposition. What do we find today? Expenditure and indebtedness have been piled up. The Income Tax stands at a shilling. War taxes are continued in peacetime. The national credit is impaired, and a heavy depreciation has taken place in securities of every description. You have only to look around to see the result. Industry is burdened. Enterprise is restricted. Workmen are thrown out of employment, and the poorer classes are straitened still further in their circumstances. Again I ask whether by their conduct of affairs in this province of administration alone they do not stand condemned as unfit to administer the business of a great commercial State. I confess I am astonished when I find the very men who have so conducted their stewardship appealing for a new lease of power in order that they may assume a still closer control of our industries and exercise a free hand in the imposition of yet further taxes.

One word more on this question of expenditure. If the amount of money expended be a criterion of effective administration, then the defence of the country and the Empire should be secure indeed. But let me remind you that our predecessors, when they left office after four years spent in a series of costly and confused experiments upon the Army and the Volunteers, were still engaged in groping after the true principles of Army reform, still speculating and debating as to the objects for which an Army was required at all, These proceedings have had a demoralising and disheartening effect upon our Regular and Volunteer forces, and the country has just cause for indignation at the levity with which they have been conducted.

If we look back on the field of domestic legislation, the retrospect is no less gloomy. Whether we have regard to their treatment of the supreme national interest of education, or to the licensing question, or to the rating system, we find them approaching and dealing with these matters animated more by a desire to propitiate their powerful friends in the country than to settle problems of national consequence with regard to the needs, the sentiments and the convictions of all concerned.

Of their failure to deal in a serious spirit with the social questions of which so much was heard at the General Election of 1895, I say nothing. The constructive social programme served its purpose at the polls. Little has been heard of its promises during the ten years that have supervened, and today its promoters seem to have forgotten that such a programme ever existed.

So much for the record the authors of which appear before you to-day burning with indignation at the iniquities of a Government which has been in office for just a month, and evidently well satisfied with their own handiwork. Assuredly the terms on which they propose that you should recall them to power betray neither signs of repentance nor promise of amendment. The policy which they offer for your acceptance appears to me, indeed, to embody the most mischievous characteristics of their past.

The thing which they describe as fiscal reform, what is it, after all, but another and a larger item in that series of reforms in which the Unionist party have proved themselves adepts – reforms introduced for the benefit of minorities, classes, interests. This policy – and I shall take the liberty of describing it as Protection – which they will consummate if you allow them, I hold to be fraught with incalculable mischief to the nation and the Empire, and I will endeavour briefly to state the grounds of my conviction.

We are Free Traders because we believe that under Free Trade our people and our industries stand to derive greater benefits than under any other system known to mankind up to the present time; and in this belief we are confirmed by the teaching of our own experience, the safest guide that I know of for a nation to follow. Similarly our fathers abandoned Protection because they found it to be a bad system under which to live and labour.

But we are told that conditions have changed since then, and that inasmuch as certain great industrial States are thriving and expanding under Protection, we should hasten to resume our cast-off garments, with such alterations in their style as modern tariff fashions may dictate. I cannot follow the argument. Nothing in the experience afforded by these countries leads me to suppose that the factors in the case have altered, or that what was profoundly injurious half a century ago has become vital to our prosperity to-day. Nothing in their experience leads me to suppose that by limiting our imports we shall increase our exports, or that by raising prices, no matter by what kind of tariff expedients, we shall assist in equalising the conditions of international competition, or in enlarging the area of employment. Still less so am I persuaded by the experience of these countries that the taxation of food conduces to the welfare of the people. Heartily as I should welcome the adhesion of other States to Free Trade, I am not prepared to sacrifice conditions which I believe to be indispensable to our social welfare and our industrial greatness and expansion, because individual industries here and there are hampered and obstructed by foreign tariffs.

I hold that Protection is not only bad economy, but that it is an agency at once immoral and oppressive, based as it is and must be on the exploitation of the community in the interest of favoured trades and financial groups. I hold it to be a corrupting system, because honesty and purity of administration must be driven to the wall if once the principle of taxes for revenue be departed from in favour of the other principle, which I conceive to be of the essence of Protection – that, namely, of taxes for private beneficiaries. I hold that a method which, even if it be not deliberately contrived to secure the public endowment of such beneficiaries, including trusts and monopolies, must inevitably operate in that direction, is a most grave menace to freedom and to progress, and an outrage on the democratic principle

Last, but not least in order of importance, I hold that any attempt to rivet together the component parts of the Empire with bonds so forged or to involve them with us in a fiscal war against the world is not and cannot come to good. An Empire "united" on a basis of food taxes would be an Empire with a disruptive force at its centre, and that is a prospect with the realization of which, both in the interests of the colonies and the mother country, I can have nothing to do.

Let me only add, in case I am told that it is unfair to identify the late Prime Minister, the chief of the party of Tariff Reform, with the extreme proposals of his leading colleague, that I understand Mr. Balfour to be agreed in principle with Mr. Chamberlain, and also that the Unionist party is committed to the programme of tariffs and preferences put forward by Mr. Chamberlain. This being so, I conceive that the minor fiscal policy indicated by Mr. Balfour occupies, at any rate of the majority of our opponents, little more than a nominal place in the contest in which we shall shortly be engaged. It is the larger policy, therefore, with which we are confronted, and which we are called upon to fight. Our concern in any case is with the results that must flow from the adoption of either of these policies, and not with the question of whether Mr. Balfour conceives himself to be a Free Trader or a Protectionist, or both, or neither.

I am well aware that our opponents claim to be in a position to establish some kind of indeterminate fiscal limbo, in which the advantages of Free Trade and Protection are to be combined with the disadvantages of neither – a fiscal paradise, perhaps, I ought to call it, where tariffs will bless the producer and consumer in equal measure, where workmen will find employment by the exclusion of foreign commodities, and the taxpayer will be relieved by the golden stream of tribute with which the foreigner will still, I know not how, continue to provide him. These fairy stories will be dismissed by serious men, and so I hope will be the illusory assurances that the protection imposed will be of such a moderate description that nobody will be any the worse for it. The man who sets a stone rolling down a steep place may intend that it shall fall slowly and stop before it reaches the foot of the slope. But the stone follows its own course. In the same way the forces that will determine the course and momentum of the tariff movement, once it has started on its way, are beyond the control of the tariff propagandists; and we shall do well to remember that every country which started on the Protectionist path set out in a gradual and tentative way, and with the declared intention of executing a strictly moderate tariff policy.

Neither in their past record nor in their present policy is there anything to entitle the late Government to a vote of confidence from the country.

One word in conclusion. Our own policy is well known to you, and I need not here repeat the terms of the public declaration which it fell to me to make shortly after assuming office. Should we be confirmed in office it will be our duty, whilst holding fast to the time-honoured principles of Liberalism – the principles of peace, economy, self-government and civil and religious liberty – and whilst resisting with all our strength the attack upon Free Trade, to repair, as far as it lies in our power, the mischief wrought in recent years, and, by a course of strenuous legislation and administration, to secure those social and economic reforms which have been too long delayed.

As to the spirit in which foreign affairs will be conducted, it is satisfactory to be able to say that, by renouncing those undesirable characteristics which we formerly detected in their foreign policy, the Unionist party have made it possible for us to pursue a substantial continuity of policy without departing from the unprovocative and friendly methods which, under Liberal Governments in the past, have determined the relations of Great Britain with her neighbours.

Assuring you at all times of my devotion to your interests,

I have the honour to be.

GENTLEMEN,

Your obedient, faithful servant,
H. CAMPBELL-BANNERMAN

10 Downing Street, 6th January 1906

Printed and Published by A. Romanes & Son, *Press* Office, Dunfermline

---

Sir Henry's election tour continued after 8 January – with meetings in Liverpool (evening of 9 January) and next day Chester (noon). Wrexham (afternoon) and Shrewsbury (evening). At all such meetings, with reference to bad housing, rural depopulation and old age, he emphasised that the election was about the whole 'tone, spirit and temper' of public policy.[316]

Detailed electioneering planning at this time may be illustrated by Sir Henry's note to William Robertson (Dunfermline) on 11 January –

---

[316] Russell (1973), p.117

> I expect to arrive tomorrow at 3.37, and shall have to leave for Culross, I suppose at 4.15 or thereabouts, and will gladly have a cup of tea if Mrs. Robertson will kindly allow me. No. 2 will be at the Dundonald Arms [Culross]. No. 3 possibly at Q'ferry [South Queensferry]. No. 4 at Perth before midnight. Thus is the combatant sustained. I had a great time at Liverpool and Chester. Wrexham. among the Welsh, was a prolonged rapture. Shrewsbury – a small opposition (from Birmingham, led by a man named Pentland, Joe's [Chamberlain's] leader of roughs) but an enormous gathering, most enthusiastic.[317]

Further, as from the first declarations of results next day (12 January) the Meigle Post Office was kept open late in the evening and on Sundays, to handle telegrams in order to keep the Prime Minister, when at Belmont, up-to-date with constituency results.[318]

Thus he was back in Dunfermline on 12 January, going on to Culross, South Queensferry, Edinburgh, Stirling, Perth, Crieff (West Perthshire) and Inverness, travelling to/from the Highland Capital on the same train as Arthur Balfour, as newly defeated in Manchester East on 13 January. To the good people of Inverness it was as if it had been decreed that their city would be the arena for the supreme effort in the contest. It was not easy for the Prime Minister, behind pipers and police, to get through the crowds from the station to his evening meeting. Afterwards, the crowds gathered outside his hotel demanding another word from CB. As Sir Henry wrote to Arthur Ponsonby on 20 January –

> I have been so busy and so bucketted about that all private correspondence has been made to stand over. What a cataract and it will probably run quite as high to the end. We have done splendidly in Scotland. It was a needless humiliation to send AJB [Arthur Balfour] up to Inverness to counteract my meeting. We travelled there and back on the same train (though at different ends – we never met) with exultant crowds at the station, my meeting was greatly bigger than his and his man was kicked out. (CB/BL)

On Monday, 15 January, Sir Henry was in Glasgow. By that date 54 results (including Ipswich, Manchester, Salford and Bradford) had already been declared, with 96 further results (including Liverpool, Leeds and Sheffield) declared that day. Polling in most of London (on 16 January), Birmingham (on 17 January), Glasgow and Edinburgh (on 18 January) was later in the week, with a cumulative total of 479 declarations, including the first county results by Saturday, 20 January.

In Glasgow the Prime Minister was greeted as a conquering hero and spoke to a capacity audience of 4,500 in the Grand Hall of the St. Andrew's Halls complex at

---

[317] Wilson (1973), p.473

[318] Sue Cole (2000), p.28

7.30 p.m. and to an overflow meeting in the nearby Berkeley Hall at 8.40 p.m. with an audience of 1,400.

> What a moment it is in which we have met! What a week it is that we are living in! We Liberals have passed through bleak and dreary days, when we seemed to be enshrouded and enwrapped in a cloud of depression, but we have never allowed it to become a cloud of despair. [Now] can the oldest man among you remember anything like it? Not one seat lost by the Government, not a single seat even in danger.

> Everywhere the same tale is told. Manchester and Salford, at the beginning of last week had but one sole representative of Liberalism. Manchester was the home of [Arthur Balfour] the leader of the party of the late Government [yet] by the end of the day Manchester and Salford were wholly Liberal.

Then, with polling in Glasgow to follow in three days' time and with Glasgow until then having had no Liberal MPs since 1900, he concluded –

> Let Glasgow rise and shake off the lethargy and indifference that had beset her so long. Let her show that the men who created one of the great and model cities of the earth were also ready to take a leading part in elevating the physical, intellectual and moral standard of the nation to which they belonged.[319]

The Rev. James Barr – then a United Free Church Minister in Dennistoun, Glasgow, who would be a Labour MP in 1924-1931 and 1935-1945 – had the closing word, at this great meeting in St. Andrew's Hall. Mr. Barr remembered, in particular, Sir Henry's 'reply to Mr. Balfour's declaration that his Licensing Act was based on the eternal principles of justice.

> Justice it would have been to protect the poor and weak and helpless from the temptations which were spread in their sight by a powerful and wealthy vested interest. Justice it would have been to save localities from being injured by the planting among them, against their will, of public houses.[320]

The Prime Minister's Glasgow programme concluded with a late-night Supper in the Glasgow Liberal Club. After the Supper, he settled down in his chair and read out a selection of election results, delighting those present with not merely the bare statistics but also with humorous comments on the people involved.

---

[319] *The Times,* 16 January 1906

[320] Barr (1948), p.230

On returning to Meigle and Belmont next day (Tuesday, 16 January), Sir Henry was again greeted as a conquering hero. When his carriage reached Belmont's entrance gates, the horses were removed from the carriage and the members of the Meigle football team then pulled the carriage by a rope to the front door of the Castle. The rope was then cut up into pieces with the pieces divided amongst the men and kept as mementoes of the great occasion.[321]

Perhaps the good people of Meigle had heard from John Sinclair that when he had been elected for Dunbartonshire in 1892, some of his supporters unyoked the horses from his carriage and pulled it to Clydebank Hall. There were also fireworks along the coast at Helensburgh and a bonfire at Kirkintilloch.[322]

Meanwhile, the prospective Unionist candidate for Stirling Burghs, Charles Kenneth Murchison had withdrawn by reason of influenza and the local Unionists accepted this as an excuse for not contesting the election.[323] Accordingly, later on 16th January, Sir Henry issued a letter of thanks to his constituents for re-electing him without opposition.

> I beg to thank you most sincerely and cordially for the honour you have done me in again returning me as your representative in Parliament and I trust that I shall not show myself unworthy of this renewed mark of confidence. I am deeply indebted to my political friends among you for the strenuous efforts they made in anticipation of a contest which, for the most regrettable cause, did not take place, and I am at the same time sensible of the considerate and even friendly spirit manifested by those of you who are opposed to me in political opinion. I beg to assure you all of my desire to be of service to you to the utmost extent of my power.[324]

He then remained at Belmont with Charlotte and John Sinclair, Secretary for Scotland who was staying with them for the last few days of the contest in his adjacent constituency of Forfarshire (Angus).

After the Forfarshire declaration on Monday, 22 January, with the Liberal majority having increased from 248 in 1900 to 3,150 in 1906, when Sinclair got back to Belmont, Sir Henry came to the door, both hands held out in congratulations, Charlotte was beaming with pleasure as telegrams kept coming in with news of one amazing victory after another.[325]

---

[321] Sue Cole (2000), p.28

[322] Lady Pentland (1928), p.35

[323] Charles Kenneth Murchison was subsequently Conservative MP for East Hull in 1918-1922 and for Huntingdonshire in 1922-1923 and 1924-1929. He was knighted in 1927.

[324] Mackie (1914), p.99

[325] Lady Pentland (1928), p.80

The Prime Minister's final election meeting was in Larbert, Stirlingshire later on 22 January, during which week further results declared assured that the Liberals would have an overall majority in the new House of Commons. (In Stirlingshire, Conservative held since 1895, a Conservative majority of 302 in 1900 was converted into a Liberal majority of 3,669 in 1906).

From Larbert, where he said that the results encompassed a tremendous disproportion of power, he again returned to Belmont before going to London with Charlotte. He saw the King at Windsor on 26 January, with the new Parliament assembling on 13 February, before which Sir Henry and Charlotte had taken full possession of 10 Downing Street.

C – The Result

Table 23 - General Election - 13 (to 29) January to 8 February 1906

Candidates (Unopposed), Percentages and MPs Elected

	England				Wales				Scotland			
Liberals	421	(14)	49.0	306	34	(12)	60.2	32	70	(1)	56.4	58
Conservatives				105								5
Liberal Unionists				17								5
	435	(3)	44.3	122	20	(0)	33.8	-	69	(0)	38.2	10
Labour	43	(0)	5.3	26	2	(0)	3.5	1	4	(0)	2.3	2
Irish Nationalist	1	(0)	0.1	1								
Others	28	(0)	1.3	1	1	(0)	2.5	1	8	(0)	3.1	-
	828	(17)		456	57	(12)		34	151	(1)		70

	Ireland				Universities				UNITED KINGDOM			
Liberals	9	(0)	19.7	3	2	(0)	19.4	-	536	(27)	49.5	399
Conservatives				14				7				131
Liberal Unionists				1				2				25
	23	(6)	47.0	15	9	(4)	60.6	9	556	(13)	43.4	156
Labour	1	(0)	3.4	-					50	(0)	4.8	29
Irish Nationalists	85	(73)	23.9	81					86	(73)	0.7	82
Others	5	(1)	6.0	2	3	(0)	20.0	-	45	(1)	1.7	4
	123	(80)		101	14	(4)		9	1273	(114)		670

Net Gains/Losses in MPs Elected compared to the 1895 General Election

	England	Wales	Scotland	Ireland	Universities	UK
Liberals	plus 185	plus 5	plus 24	plus 2		plus 216
Conservatives	minus 181	minus 6	minus 15	minus 1		minus 203
Liberal Unionists	minus 29		minus 11	minus 3		minus 43
	minus 210	minus 6	minus 26	minus 4		minus 246
Labour	plus 25		plus 2			plus 27
Others		plus 1		plus 2		plus 3

Stirling Burghs - Electorate c.7,274

Sir Henry Campbell-Bannerman   Liberal   Unopposed

East Fife - Electorate 9,998   **Caernarvon Burghs - Electorate 5,668**

H.H. Asquith	Liberal	4,723	D. Lloyd George	Liberal	3,221
John Gilmour (Junior)	Conservative	3,279	R.A. Naylor	Conservative	1,997

Thus, in 1906, the Liberals had overall their best result – in terms of MPs elected – since the Whigs and Radicals at the 1832 General Election (MPs Elected – Whigs and Radicals 441, Tories 175, Irish Repeal 42). Further, apart from Palmerston in 1865, Sir Henry was the only serving Liberal Prime Minister to lead his party to a decisive victory at a General Election. Nearly all the seats lost at the 1886 and/or 1895 General Elections were recovered as also most of the seats lost in Scotland at the 1900 General Election. Moreover, a number of constituencies, particularly in England, thought to be 'safe seats' were lost by the Unionists. The Unionists only held on in any strength in some parts of England – in parts of London (The City, The Strand, Westminster, Marylebone and a few wealthy suburbs), in Birmingham, Liverpool and the Black Country in the West Midlands – in Northern Ireland and the Universities. As the Prime Minister has said in Glasgow on 15 January –

Is there not something in the earnestness, in the fury, with which voters were going to the polls which suggests a deeper significance [than attachment to Free Trade]? Is it the mind only of the people that is moved? Is it not also the heart and the conscience?... The springs of action which the late government avowed seemed to take no account of the better side of our national life.[326]

Of course the electoral system greatly exaggerated the extent of the Liberal victory. Excluding Ireland (with 80 unopposed returns) the Liberal share of the popular vote was 49.6 % with 69.6 % of the MPs elevated. However, the 49.6 % does not take account of the twenty-seven Liberals returned unopposed (including the Prime Minister) and the twenty English single-member constituencies where Labour candidates did not have Liberal opposition.

Twenty-three of the Liberals elected in 1906 were Liberal/Labour MPs with thirteen sponsored by the Mineworkers Federation of Great Britain, with the minority being sponsored by other trade unions.

In the Irish territorial constituencies, all fifteen Unionists, all three Liberals and six of the Nationalists were elected in what became Northern Ireland after 1922. The Irish Liberal candidates and MPs included Russellite Land Reformers led by T.W. Russell.[327]

The Others elected were an Independent Labour candidate in County Durham who joined the Labour Party when the new Parliament assembled, an Independent Liberal/Labour candidate in Gower who eventually joined the Labour Party, an Independent Conservative in Belfast South and an Independent Nationalist in Cork City.

Only three MPs from the former Unionist Cabinet escaped defeat in their constituencies. Such Unionists defeated included, as already mentioned, Balfour (Conservative Leader and former Prime Minister) in Manchester East and also Bonar Law (a future Conservative Leader and Prime Minister) in Glasgow Blackfriars on 18 January. Both were subsequently elected in other constituencies at by-elections.

---

[326] *The Times*, 16 January 1906

[327] The Rt. Hon. Sir Thomas Wallace Russell, Bt (1843-1920), born and educated in Cupar, Fife, was the unsuccessful Liberal candidate for Preston in 1885. He was MP for South Tyrone as a Liberal Unionist in 1886-1904 and then as a Liberal until he was defeated in January 1910. He was thereafter Liberal MP for North Tyrone from a by-election in October 1911 until he retired in 1918. While a Liberal Unionist he was Parliamentary Secretary to the Local Government Board in 1895-1900. As a Liberal he was Vice-President of the Irish Board of Agriculture in 1907-1918. In 1906 the Russellites were not supporters of Irish Home Rule as they subsequently became.

In Scotland, the ten Unionists elected were in Ayr Burghs and St. Andrews Burghs (reversals of by-election losses to Liberals in 1903 and 1904), in Lanarkshire Govan and Lanarkshire North-Western (Liberal losses by reason of the intervention of Labour and Scottish Workers Representation Committee [SWRC] candidates), and in Glasgow Camlachie, Glasgow Tradeston, Edinburgh West, Wick Burghs, Ayrshire Northern and Wigtownshire (where incumbent Unionist MPs were re-elected).

Sir Henry was particularly upset by the loss of St. Andrews Burghs which he thought was 'provoking'. However, given what happened twelve years later, it was Asquith who should have been more concerned. When St. Andrews Burghs (also including the two Anstruthers, Crail, Cupar, Kilrenny and Pittenweem) was merged with Asquith's East Fife (from 1886) for the 1918 General Election, he was defeated in the new enlarged constituency of East Fife.[328]

However, Sir Henry would have been very pleased by the results in the fifteen places where he had spoken in January – accounting for twenty-eight constituencies, including all 9 in Liverpool, all 7 in Glasgow and all 4 in Edinburgh.

---

[328] The enlarged East Fife constituency was won by a Liberal in 1922. He was defeated in 1924 but was re-elected in 1929 and joined the Liberal Nationals in 1931. As North-East Fife the constituency was won by (Sir) Menzies Campbell (Liberal) in 1987 and he continued to serve until 2015, becoming thereafter Lord Campbell of Pittenweem.

In 1982 when Roy Jenkins arrived in St. Andrews (Jo Grimond's birthplace) for a Scottish Liberal Party Conference on the day after he won Glasgow Hillhead for the SDP/Alliance, he said that he was pleased to be in Asquith's old constituency. But, of course, Asquith never represented the Royal Burgh of St. Andrews in Parliament.

Table 24 - Results in Places where Sir Henry spoke in January 1906

Stirling, Dunfermline, Inverkeithing, Culross, South Queensferry	STIRLING BURGHS	Liberal (Sir Henry) re-elected unopposed
CHESTER		Liberal Gain
Crieff	PERTHSHIRE WEST	Liberal Gain
Edinburgh	CENTRAL	Liberal Hold (Majority 569 → 2,076)
	EAST	Liberal Hold (Majority 1,291 → 4,171)
	SOUTH	Liberal Gain
	WEST	Liberal Unionist Hold
Glasgow	BLACKFRIARS	Labour Gain
	BRIDGETON	Liberal Gain
	CAMLACHIE	Liberal Unionist Hold
	CENTRAL	Liberal Gain
	COLLEGE	Liberal Gain
	ST. ROLLOX	Liberal Gain
	TRADESTON	Liberal Unionist Hold
Inverness	INVERNESS BURGHS	Liberal Gain
Larbert	STIRLINGSHIRE	Liberal Gain
Liverpool	ABERCROMBY	Liberal Gain
	EAST TOXTETH	Conservative Hold (Unopposed)
	EVERTON	Conservative Hold
	EXCHANGE	Liberal Gain
	KIRKDALE	Conservative Hold (No Liberal Candidate)
	SCOTLAND	Irish Nationalist Hold (No Liberal Candidate)
	WALTON	Conservative Hold
	WEST DERBY	Conservative Hold
	WEST TOXTETH	Conservative Hold (No Liberal Candidate)
PERTH		Liberal Hold (Majority 344 → 1,008)
SHREWSBURY		Conservative Hold
Wrexham	DENBIGH BOROUGHS	Liberal/Labour Gain

The 1906 results in his native Glasgow – having described the 1900 results as 'damnable' – would also have been particularly pleasing to Sir Henry, with four Liberals gains. The two Liberal Unionists re-elected in Glasgow (and the Conservative re-elected unopposed in Liverpool East Toxteth) subsequently re-joined or joined the Liberal Party. George Barnes (Labour), who defeated Bonar Law in Glasgow Blackfriars, would later serve with him in Lloyd George's Cabinets in 1917-1921. Having been expelled from the Labour Party before the 1918 General Election. Barnes was then elected, with Labour opposition, for Glasgow Gorbals while Bonar Law was elected for Glasgow Central.

Table 25 - The Fifty Labour Candidatures in 1906

		MPs Elected		
		Liberal	Labour	Unionist
10 Two-Member Constituencies with Labour and Liberal Candidates running in Tandem				
Blackburn	Labour Gain from Unionist		1	1
Bolton	Labour Gain from Unionist	1	1	
Halifax	Labour Gain from Unionist	1	1	
Leicester	Labour Gain from Unionist	1	1	
Newcastle-upon-Tyne	Liberal and Labour Gains from Unionists	1	1	
Norwich	Labour Gain from Unionist	1	1	
Preston	Liberal and Labour Gains from Unionists	1	1	
Stockport	Labour Gain from Unionist	1	1	
Sunderland	Liberal and Labour Gains from Unionists	1	1	
York	Liberal Gain from Unionist	1		1
21 Single-Member Constituencies with no Liberal Candidates				
London - Woolwich	Labour Hold from 1903 By-Election Gain		1	
Barrow-in-Furness	Labour Gain from Unionist		1	
Birmingham Bordesley	No Change			1
Birmingham East	No Change			1
Chatham	Labour Gain from Unionist		1	
Darlington	No Change			1
Leeds East	Labour Gain from Unionist		1	
Liverpool Kirkdale	No Change			1
Liverpool West Toxteth	No Change			1
Manchester North-East	Labour Gain from Unionist		1	
Manchester South-West	Labour Gain from Unionist		1	
St. Helens	Labour Gain from Unionist		1	
West Ham South	Labour Gain from Unionist		1	
Wolverhampton West	Labour Gain from Unionist		1	
Durham - Barnard Castle	Labour Hold from 1903 By-Election Gain		1	
Lancs - Clitheroe	Labour Hold from 1902 By-Election Gain		1	
Lancs - Gorton	Labour Gain from Unionist		1	
Lancs - Ince	Labour Gain from Unionist		1	
Lancs - Newton	Labour Gain from Unionist		1	
Lancs - Westhoughton	Labour Gain from Unionist		1	
Belfast North	No Change			1
3 Two-Member Constituencies with Labour and Liberal Candidates in Opposition				
Portsmouth	Two Liberal Gains from Unionists	2		
Merthyr Tydvil	No Change	1	1	
Dundee	Labour Gain from Liberal	1	1	
16 Two-Member Constituencies with Labour and Liberal Candidates in Opposition				
London - Deptford	Labour Gain from Unionist		1	
Bradford West	Labour Gain from Unionist		1	
Croydon	No Change			1
Dewsbury	No Change	1		
Gravesend	No Change			1
Grimsby	No Change			1
Huddersfield	No Change	1		
Leeds South	No Change	1		
Stockton-ion-Tees	No Change			1
Wakefield	No Change			1
Durham - Jarrow	No Change	1		
Lancs - Eccles	Liberal Gain from Unionist	1		
Monmouth Boroughs	Liberal Gain from Unionist	1		
Glasgow Blackfriars	Labour Gain from Unionist		1	
Glasgow Camlachie	No Change			1
Lanarkshire - Govan	Unionist Gain from Liberal			1

Thus, excluding the only Labour candidate in Ireland (who did not have Liberal opposition), in the twenty single-member constituencies, in which Labour candidates did not have Liberal opposition, fifteen Labour and five Unionist candidates were elected. In the ten two-member constituencies, in which Liberal and Labour candidates ran in tandem, nine Liberal, nine Labour and two Unionist candidates were elected.

In the sixteen single-member constituencies in which Labour and Liberal candidates were in opposition, seven Unionists, six Liberal and three Labour candidates were elected. In the three two-member constituencies in which Labour and Liberal candidates were in opposition, four Liberal and two Labour candidates were elected. The average swing away from the Unionists was 16.8 % in Unionist v Labour contests but only 9.4 % in Unionists v Liberal contests. In Unionist v Liberal v Labour contests, the average swing was 32.0 % to Labour –15.3 % from Unionist and 16.7 % from Liberal.[329]

As from J.W.S. Craig (1969), pp.597, 622 and 625, it is of interest to analyse the voting in 1906 in the two-member constituencies of Blackburn, Merthyr Tydvil and Dundee.

BLACKBURN had elected two Conservatives in 1900 with only one candidate (Labour) in opposition. In 1906 one Conservative MP (originally elected in 1886) and one Labour MP (Philip Snowden, the unsuccessful candidate in 1900) were elected, with a new Conservative and a new Liberal candidate being unsuccessful. In 1906, of the 10,282 who voted Labour, 76.6 % also voted Liberal, 14.6 % voted for only the Labour candidate, 8.0 % also voted for the successful Conservative candidate and 0.8 % also voted for the other (new) Conservative candidate. Of the 8,892 who voted Liberal, 88.5 % also voted Labour, 7.0 % also voted for the successful Conservative candidate, 3.5 % voted for only the Liberal candidate and 1.0 % also voted for the other (new) Conservative candidate. Accordingly, given also the relative popularity of the re-elected Conservative MP, the tandem arrangement worked to advantage of Labour rather than Liberal.

MERTHYR TYDVIL had elected one Liberal MP and one Labour MP (Keir Hardie) in 1900, with the other (Liberal) candidate being unsuccessful. In 1906 both the incumbent MPs were re-elected, with the second (new) Liberal candidate being unsuccessful. In 1906, of the 10,187 who voted Labour, 74.0 % also voted for the successful Liberal candidate, 22.7 % voted for only the Labour candidate and 4.3 % also voted for the other Liberal candidate.[330] Accordingly, given also the relative popularity of the re-elected Liberal MP, the pattern of Labour voting ensured the success of both the incumbent Liberal MP (who topped the poll) and the incumbent Labour MP.

---

[329] Russell (1973), Appendix J

[330] As at the Labour Agent's request, the Returning Officer did not issue an official analysis, these percentages are based on what was published in the *Merthyr Express*.

DUNDEE had elected two Liberal MPs in 1900, with Conservative and Liberal Unionist candidates in opposition. In 1906 one Liberal MP (originally elected in 1885) and one Labour candidate (Alexander Wilkie) were elected,[331] with a new Liberal candidate and Conservative and Liberal Unionist candidates being unsuccessful. In 1906, of the 6,833 who voted Labour, 46.6 % also voted for the successful Liberal candidate, 37.4 % voted for only the Labour candidate, 11.3 % also voted for the Liberal Unionist candidate, 2.9 % also voted for the Conservative candidate and 1.8 % also voted for the other Liberal candidate. Accordingly, given also the relative popularity of the re-elected Liberal MP, the pattern of Labour voting ensured the success of both the incumbent Liberal MP (who topped the poll) and the Labour candidate.

The twenty-nine Labour MPs and the Independent Labour MP in County Durham formed the Parliamentary Labour Party when the new Parliament assembled on 13 February. Thus the arrival in significant numbers in Parliament of a second social conservative class-based party which would become a party of government within eighteen years. Accordingly, the Herbert Gladstone-MacDonald pact helped the Labour Party in both the short- and long-terms. It helped the Liberal Party only marginally and only – and, as it turned out, unnecessarily – in the short-term.

Afterword – The Liberal/Labour MPs and the Labour Party

The Mineworkers Federation of Great Britain – having voted not to affiliate to the Labour Party later in 1906 – voted to affiliate (by a majority of approx. 12 %) in 1908 and did affiliate in 1909.[332] In the meantime the TUC had instructed its affiliated unions to require their sponsored MPs to stand as Labour candidates at the next General Election and, if then elected, to take the Labour whip. Thus by the January 1910 General Election, 11 Liberal/Labour MPs, representing mining interests, had formally severed their connection with the Liberal Party. This almost exactly accounts for the increase in the number of Labour MPs elected at that General Election.

However, two other such miner MPs refused to adhere to the Labour Party and continued to sit as Liberals for the remainder of their parliamentary careers – The Rt. Hon. Charles Fenwick (MP for Wansbeck, Northumberland, 1885-1918) and, as already mentioned, the Rt. Hon. Thomas Burt (MP for Morpeth, Northumberland, 1874-1918). Charles Fenwick was Parliamentary Secretary of the TUC in 1890-1894. Thomas Burt was Parliamentary Secretary at the Board of Trade in 1892-1895. He represented the then Liberal back-benchers in carrying Sir Henry Campbell-

---

[331] Alexander Wilkie would be re-elected in tandem with Winston Churchill at both the 1910 General Elections. Thereafter, until the two-member constituency was divided in 1950, there were various successful *de facto* tandem arrangements in Dundee – Prohibitionist and Labour in 1922, 1923, 1924 and 1929 and Liberal and Unionist in 1931 and 1935

[332] In South Wales there was a majority for affiliation in 1906.

Bannerman's coffin at the Memorial Service in Westminster Abbey on 27 April 1908. He was 'Father' of the House of Commons when he retired in 1918.

The last Liberal/Labour MPs to be elected were at by-elections in August 1913 and February 1917. However, Barnet Kenyon, elected for Chesterfield in 1913, sat as a Liberal from 1914 until he retired in 1929. Arthur Richardson, elected for Rotherham in 1917, was defeated as a Liberal in another constituency in 1918. Thus the Liberal/Labour category of MPs ceased to be as from the 1918 General Election.

Strange to relate, at the time of Sir Henry's death in April 1908, it was reported (*Dunfermline Press*, 25 April 1908) that there would be a miners' meeting in Dunfermline on 1 June to discuss the question of affiliation to the Labour Party – that is, after the ballot papers had been issued. The speakers at the meeting were to be Keir Hardie, MP and William Adamson. Adamson, like Hardie originally a Liberal, had been elected to Dunfermline Town Council on a Labour ticket in 1905. He was thereafter Labour MP for West Fife (including Culross) from December 1910 until 1931 and Labour Secretary for Scotland in 1924 and 1929-1931.

12 – 1905-1908 – 28 Months and Bereavement (1906) as Prime Minister

As Prime Minister, Sir Henry's Principal Private Secretary (until January 1908) was Arthur Ponsonby who looked after relations with the Palace and other Ministers. The Assistant Private Secretaries were Vaughan Nash who did the political work, research and helped with speeches and who succeeded as Principal Private Secretary in January 1908, Henry Higgs who worked on patronage and ecclesiastical matters, and Hubert Montgomery who served briefly from January to April 1908. However, such a small 10 Downing Street staff meant that the Prime Minister had to deal personally with some other tasks, including apparently deciphering.

In his boyhood, Ponsonby was a Royal Page and as such he first met Sir Henry when he was Minister-in-Attendance at Osborne in 1886.[333] Although the unsuccessful Liberal candidate for Taunton in January 1906, Ponsonby was with Sir Henry during the early part of the Prime Minister's own campaign – for example, at Dunfermline in late December – and thereafter they kept in touch until Ponsonbly was able to resume his duties in London later in January. After his death, 'Some Recollections of Sir Henry from the Private Diaries of Arthur Ponsonby' edited by Lady Ponsonby, were published in the *Glasgow High School Magazine* of June 1948.

(For fuller Biographical Notes for Ponsonby and for such for Nash, Higgs and Montgomery, refer to Appendix 3. For Sir Henry's Government's legislative and executive initiatives in 1905-1908, refer to Chapter 13, and for his final illness from November 1907 and his resignation and death in April 1908, refer to Chapter 14)

With the new Parliament assembling on 13 February 1906, the previous evening Sir Henry gave a dinner in the Palace of Westminster for his principal colleagues, followed by a reception hosted by Charlotte in a crowded 10 Downing Street. For a start she remained standing, shaking hands with her guests, but fatigue came over her and she had to sit, with lowered head, with Sir Henry, standing beside her, doing the honours. It was her first and last Downing Street reception. She hardly ever left 10 Downing Street thereafter, except for a trip to Dover in May which left her with an attack of influenza. Thus she gradually became very much worse, with Sir Henry having to double as nurse and Prime Minister, although Charlotte continued to be helped by the ministrations of her Swedish masseuse, Miss Thorbjörn. As Sir Henry said, after Charlotte's death, 'How strange to have a whole night in bed; it has not happened to me for six months'.[334]

In an attempt at reconciliation with Rosebery, Sir Henry asked Harry Primrose (1882-1974),[335] Rosebery's son and heir as the newly elected Liberal MP for

---

[333] Hirst (1947), p.292

[334] As quoted in the *Glasgow High School Magazine,* June 1958, p.104

[335] Harry Primrose (1882-1972), who had become Captain of Surrey County Cricket Club in 1905, did not contest the January 1910 General Election. After his father had a severe stroke in 1919,

Midlothian, to second the Reply to the Royal Address (King's Speech) at the Opening of the new Parliament. However, on his father's instructions, the invitation was refused. In the following year (1907), the former Liberal Prime Minister moved to the cross-benches in the House of Lords.

There were six major speeches on the opening day (19 February) of the debate on the King's Speech. Willoughby Dickinson, the newly elected Liberal MP for North St. Pancras, moved the Reply, which was seconded by Francis Dyke Acland, the newly elected Liberal MP for Richmond, Yorkshire and the son and heir of Arthur Acland, a Liberal Cabinet Minister in 1892-1895.[336] With Arthur Balfour, Leader of Opposition, having been defeated in Manchester at the General Election, Joseph Chamberlain replied for the Unionists, with Sir Henry speaking next as Prime Minister. The two other party leaders followed with John Redmond speaking for the Irish Nationalists and Keir Hardie for the Labour Party.

On 7 March (1906) the Prime Minister took part in a debate on a Private Member's Motion advocating the payment of salaries to MPs, following similar (unsuccessful) motions in 1893, 1895 and 1905. Sir Henry had voted for the 1905 motion when in opposition. Now, while stating that he was 'cordially in agreement with the principle of the motion... at this moment, when we are tackling this great question of expenditure and retrenchment, it would be most inopportune of me to make any promise of action on this subject'.[337]

However, the new House of Commons in 1906 was a very different place from its predecessor. This was perhaps most fully appreciated after Arthur Balfour returned to the Commons and resumed the Unionist Opposition leadership as from a by-election for the City of London on 27 February (1906). On 12 and 13 March there was a debate on a Motion moved by Sir James Kitson, Liberal MP for Colne Valley

---

he entered the House of Lords as 2nd (UK) Earl of Midlothian (a title conferred on his father in 1911). After succeeding to the family's other peerages on his father's death in 1929, he became a Liberal National in 1931 and was Secretary of State for Scotland in Churchill's basically Conservative 'Caretaker' Cabinet from May to August, 1945. (Of the nine 'Tory' Scottish Secretaries between 1922 and 1962, six were former Liberals) Gwilym Lloyd George, the son of another Prime Minister, also served as effectively a Liberal National in Churchill's 'Caretaker' Administration in 1945. Further, when Churchill returned to power in 1951, he offered the position of Lord Chancellor to Cyril Asquith, the former Prime Minister's fourth son. Ostensibly for health reasons, the offer was declined (Clifford [2007], p.447)

[336] Willoughby Dickinson (1859-1945), a member of the Privy Council from 1914, served as a Liberal MP from 1906 until defeated at the General Election in 1918, in which year also he was knighted as a KBE. He joined the Labour Party in 1930, in which year also he was created 1st Lord Dickinson. He followed Ramsay MacDonald into the National Labour Party in 1931. Francis Dyke Acland (1874-1939), a member of the Privy Council from 1915, succeeded his father as 14th Baronet in 1926. He was a Liberal MP for different constituencies from 1906 to January 1910, from December 1910 to 1922, from 1923 to 1924 and from 1932 until his death in 1939. He held junior ministerial office in 1908-1916.

[337] At that time, the only direct benefits received by MPs were the privileges of free telephone calls, within the UK from Westminster, and of posting parliamentary papers without charge. Salaries for MPs, at £ 400 p.a., started in 1911.

– 'That this House, recognising that in the recent General Election the people of the United Kingdom have demonstrated their unqualified fidelity to the principles of Free Trade, deems it right to record its determination to resist any proposal, whether by way of taxation on foreign corn or of the creation of a tariff on foreign goods to create in this country a system of protection'.

Early in the debate, Balfour, making his first appearance in the new House of Commons, intervened to ask a series of questions. The intervention was so ineffective that the cheers on his side gradually grew fainter. His suggestion that the Liberals were raising unnecessary controversies was greeted with a roar of ironical laughter. When he sat down, no Minister rose to reply and only after he had asked more questions and, supported by Chamberlain, demand immediate replies, did Sir Henry rise and deliver.

> The Rt. Hon. Gentleman is like the old Bourbons in the oft-quoted phrase he has learnt nothing. He has come back to this new House of Commons with the same airs and graces, the same subtle dialectics, the same light and frivolous way with a great question, and he little knows the temper of the new House of Commons if he thinks these methods will prevail here. He has put some questions to me on this resolution. He has split it up and tortured it, and pulled it to pieces, and he thinks he has put some posers to us...
>
> Then he says we are to stop the proceedings in this debate, and his amendments are not to be moved until we have answered these terrible questions... I have no direct answers to give to them. They are utterly futile, nonsensical and misleading. They are invented by the Rt. Hon. Gentleman for the purpose of occupying time in this debate. I say enough of this foolery. It may have served very well in the last Parliament, but is altogether out of place in this Parliament. The tone and temper of this Parliament will not permit it. Move your amendments and let us get to business.

The Liberals greeted every sentence with a roar of applause, with the final cheer said to be the greatest ever heard in the House of Commons. Thus, in a four minute speech, the man that Asquith, Grey and Haldane had sought to remove to the House of Lords established a commanding position in the House of Commons which he was to hold until his death.

(There were three intermediate divisions during the debate, each of which were lost by the Unionists. The debate concluded on the second day, with the Free Trade motion being agreed by 474 votes to 98)

Sir Henry's ascendancy in the Commons was also established in the Cabinet. As John Morley later wrote, '[Sir Henry] was cool, acute, straight, candid, attentive to affairs, considerate. He always knew his mind and we were all aware he knew it'. It is also said that, under Sir Henry's leadership, even Lloyd George behaved himself, more or less.[338] (One wonders if Sir Henry, unlike Asquith, would have accepted Lloyd George's resignation in the context of the Marconi Scandal of 1912-1913).[339]

On 19 May 1906 Sir Henry received a deputation of some three hundred suffragettes who urged him to include in the Government's legislative programme a measure for female enfranchisement. In general they were told that, although he thought that the activities of the more militant agitators were counter-productive, in his opinion "they had made out before the country a conclusive and irrefutable case" and "should go on pestering". His reply was fully reported in *The Times* of 21 May.

> [He could] not give [for the Government] anything in the way of a pledge as to time or method in achieving this object, as there were other people who did not share the same convictions and sentiments. They could not shut their eyes to the fact that there was no party in the State, and no Government that had ever been formed, was united entirely on this question. He might have disappointed them – to some extent he disappointed himself... But he could assure them sincerely from the bottom of his heart of his profound sympathy with the object they had in mind.

Accordingly, when a Private Member's Women's Enfranchisement Bill was presented in the Commons on 8 March 1907, Sir Henry said that he would vote for it as he had for similar (unsuccessful) Bills as far back as 1870. On this (1907) occasion he said that "the exclusion of women from the franchise is neither expedient, justifiable nor politically right", but the Bill's opponents succeeded in having it talked-out. Thus a letter from King Edward to his son, the future King George V, on 12 March stating 'Thank heaven these dreadful women have not yet been enfranchised. It would have been more dignified if the PM had not spoken on the Bill – or backed it up'. A letter to Sir Henry followed on 29 March when the King wrote 'The conduct of these so-called suffragettes has been so outrageous and done that cause such harm (for which I have no sympathy) that I cannot understand why the Prime Minister could speak in their favour'.[340]

The following month (April), when travelling by train to Cannes, Sir Henry had another encounter with suffragettes. Annie Kenney and Mary Gawthorpe were travelling to a suffragette meeting on the French-Italian border and had gone to the restaurant car for tea when Sir Henry came in and sat at the same table. They introduced themselves and had a long talk.[341] Apparently, thereafter he would refer to this conversation whenever Annie Kenney's name came up. (Both Annie Kenney and Mary Gawthorpe were imprisoned on several occasions for their more militant suffragette activities.)

---

[338] Wilson (1973), p.501

[339] Refer to A.N. Wilson (2006), pp.119-120.

[340] As quoted in Wilson (1973), pp,500-501

[341] Pankhurst (1911), p.222

There were other such (less peaceful) encounters at a meeting in Bristol in November 1907 and again at the time of a Cabinet meeting in January 1908 when two ladies got into 10 Downing Street. Even in death he was not spared such attentions. When Asquith and his daughter, Violet were driving, in an open-topped car to Stirling in 1913 for the unveiling of Sir Henry's statue, they were held up near Bannockburn (of all places) by a band of furious women and assaulted with pepper and a dog whip. (Refer to Appendix 5)

On 23 July 1906 the 14th Inter-Parliamentary Conference – at which Russia was represented for the first time – assembled in London with Sir Henry welcoming the 522 delegates and speaking in French. Just before he left Downing Street to go to the opening the news came through that the Tsar had dissolved the First Russian Duma after only ten weeks of its existence.

So Sir Henry in his speech, inserted, without consulting the Foreign Office, a few sentences to the official draft, concluding with the words, *La Douma est morte – Vive la Douma.* The improvised peroration was received with great enthusiasm. Inevitably, the Czar, as represented by his Ambassador in London, was not amused. Grey (as Foreign Secretary), when the Ambassador complained, blandly told him that, as the Czar intended to summon a new Duma, *'La Douma est morte – Vive la Douma'* was merely the equivalent of *'Le Roi est mort – vive Le Roi'*.[342]

> How glad we are to welcome today the representatives of the youngest of Parliaments – the Russian Duma… I make no comment on the news which has reached us this morning… We have not a sufficient acquaintance with the facts to be in a position to justify or criticise. But this at least we can say, we with our confidence and our hopes in the Parliamentary system – New institutions often have a disturbed, if not a stormy youth. The Duma will revive in one form or other. We can say with all sincerity, **'The Duma is dead – Long live the Duma'**.[343]

The Socialist [Social Democrat – Bolsheviks and Mensheviks – and Socialist Revolutionary] parties had refused to participate in the elections for the First Duma which, accordingly, was dominated by the liberal Constitutional Democrat Party [The Kadets] who were committed to parliamentary government, an amnesty for political prisoners and partial expropriation of the larger estates. The Second Duma was equally unacceptable to the Tsar and it was dissolved in June 1907 when the basis of representation was changed to ensure that future Dumas would be dominated by the property-owning elite.

On 8 August (1906) – shortly after the House of Commons adjourned for the recess on 4 August – Sir Henry, the now terminally ill Charlotte, Miss Thorbjörn (Masseuse) and Arthur Ponsonby (Principal Private Secretary) left for Marienbad

---

[342] As quoted in Wilson (1973), pp,536-537

[343] *The Times,* 24 July 1906 (Translation)

(where Charlotte always felt better) and, travelling by easy stages, arrived on 13 August. The King and his entourage arrived three days later. Dr. Ernst Otto was constantly in attendance on Charlotte and the Campbell-Bannermans' London doctor, Robert Burnett came out but there was nothing they could do and, having not been able to take food for three days, Charlotte died at about 5.00 p.m. on Thursday, 30 August. On hearing the news, the King immediately wrote to Sir Henry that same evening.

> The sad news has just reached me that Lady Campbell-Bannerman has passed away, and although I hardly like intruding on your great grief, still I am anxious to express my warmest sympathy at the great loss you have sustained. I know how great your mutual devotion was, and what a blank the departed one will leave in your home. Still I feel sure that you can now only wish that your beloved wife may be at peace and rest, and free from all suffering and pain, All the British community here, I know, share feelings for you on this truly sad occasion, which I entertain.[344]

A bilingual Memorial Service was then held in Marienbad Protestant Chapel on the afternoon of Saturday, 1 September. The King attended (as Duke of Lancaster) and placed a wreath at the foot of the coffin and, on leaving, shook hands with Sir Henry, speaking a few words of comfort in a low voice.[345] Before leaving for home. Sir Henry sent a letter to Dr. Diet, Burgomaster of Marienbad, expressing his gratitude for the town's expressions of regret and condolence, adding 'my wife loved Marienbad and its people', concluding that he shared her regard. Queen Alexandra, then in Norway, also telegraphed from Christiania (Oslo) a gracious message of sorrow and sympathy.[346]

The coffin was then brought via Frankfurt, Ostend, Dover and London, to Belmont for her burial beside Meigle Parish Church on the afternoon of Wednesday, 5 September. (The like of the funeral had not been seen in Meigle until Sir Henry's own funeral within less than two years). Before the committal, there was a short Service in Belmont Castle led by the Rev. Hugh Climie (Parish Minister of Meigle), the Rev. Peter Maltman of Meigle United Free Church and the Rev. A.S. Aglen of Alyth Episcopal Church. (Mr. Aglen, who also served the Episcopal Church in Meigle, and his wife had been frequent visitors to the Campbell-Bannermans at Belmont Castle.)

---

[344] Spender (1923), Volume 2, p.205

[345] In order to avoid (unsuccessfully) publicity and the attention of the crowds, when at Marienbad, the King adopted the style of Duke of Lancaster. However, for the local parade on the birthday of the Austro-Hungarian Emperor, he dropped the incognito and took the salute as King, wearing the uniform of an Austrian Field Marshall. On one occasion, Sir Henry said to him, 'It would not be agreeable to you, Sir, if they did not take any notice [of you] at all'. (As quoted in Wilson [1973], p.144).

[346] *Dunfermline Press,* 8 September 1906

The grave, beside the Parish Church, had been prepared under the personal supervision of Miss Thorbjörn. The pallbearers at the graveside were Sir Henry, his brother, James Alexander Campbell, a nephew, three cousins and the Provosts of Stirling and Dunfermline. After the committal all the many wreaths (including one from Princess Louise), which had been brought from Belmont, London and Marienbad were placed on the grave, with the intention that it would eventually be lined with planted laurel bays, heliotropes and roses.[14]

Others supporting Sir Henry at Belmont and Meigle at this time included Lord Colebrooke representing the King, Asquith (Chancellor of the Exchequer), Lord Loreburn (Lord Chancellor), John Morley (Secretary of State for India), Herbert Gladstone (Home Secretary), Lord Tweedmouth (First Lord of the Admiralty), Lord Elgin (Colonial Secretary), John Sinclair (Secretary for Scotland) and his wife, Lady Marjorie Sinclair, Lord Portsmouth (Under-Secretary, War Office), the Archbishop of Canterbury (Randall Davidson), Arthur Ponsonby and Thomas Shaw (Lord Advocate).

Sir Edward Colebrooke, Bt [1861-1939] had been created Lord Colebrooke on 21 February 1906, as a Lord-in-Waiting [Liberal Government Whip in the House of Lords]. As mentioned in Chapter 4, his father had spoken in the same debate as that in which Sir Henry had made his maiden speech in the House of Commons in 1869.

James Alexander Campbell, Asquith, Morley, Lord Portsmouth and Ponsonby stayed at Belmont overnight and Thomas Shaw stayed for some days at Sir Henry's request. 'When after the [funeral] I shook hands with him to go, he looked blankly at me, and sat down in a chair, saying 'Thomas, you are not to leave me tonight. So I remained'[347]

At noon on the day of the funeral there was also a Memorial Service in St. Margaret's Church, Westminster, which was led by the Rector and the Chaplain of the House of Commons, Those in attendance included five Cabinet Ministers (Lords Ripon and Carrington, Lloyd George, John Burns and Sydney Buxton), a number of Junior Ministers, other official representatives (including such for the USA, France, Austria-Hungary, Germany, Russia, Denmark. Greece and China) and many other members of both Houses of Parliament.

Charlotte's death was felt in her husband's constituency with a sense of personal loss and the local tributes of respect and affection were instinct with the tenderest sympathy. As from The *Stirling Journal (and Advertiser)* of 31 August, 'Now that the parting has come among those who will offer their sympathy to the Prime Minister none will be more sincere than the constituents he has represented so long. On such occasions politics are forgotten, and today Unionists and Liberals alike sorrow with their old Member in his sore bereavement'. As from the *Dunfermline Press* of 1 September, 'The community, without distinction of political party, will

---

[347] Shaw (1921), p.67

deplore the misfortune that has overtaken Sir Henry Campbell-Bannerman. The sympathy that is bring expressed for the bereaved statesman is of a world-wide character. Her ladyship's death is nothing short of an irreparable loss for the Prime Minister and, knowing this, the nation shares his sorrow'. As from the *Dunfermline Journal* of the same date, 'After a prolonged illness, borne with beautiful and inspiring fortitude, Lady Campbell-Bannerman has passed to her rest.... She performed with scrupulous fidelity and unfailing grace the highest of wifely duties. For nothing lovelier can be found in woman than to study household good and good works in her husband to promote'.

On the Sunday after the funeral Sir Henry attended Morning Worship in Meigle Parish Church where and when appropriate reference was made to the death of his wife. After the Service, he shook hands and talked to several friends at the church door and then paid a visit to Charlotte's grave where a large number of people had already gathered. They moved away respectfully when they saw the bare-headed Prime Minister approaching, but after looking at the wreaths he turned round and said, 'they're going', referring to the fading flowers. It was with difficulty that he overcame his emotion and as he left the grave many of the eye-witnesses were in tears.[348]

Sir Henry was not, of course, the first or last serving or future Prime Minister to become a widower. Lord John Russell's first wife died in 1838, Lord Rosebery's wife in 1890, Asquith's first wife in 1891, Lord Salisbury's wife in 1899 and Bonar Law's wife in 1909.

After Charlotte's death, the Prime Minister's hostess at Belmont and in 10 Downing Street was Mrs. Alice Morton Campbell (an Australian), the wife of his nephew, James Morton (Peto) Campbell, with Arthur Ponsonby also coming to live in 10 Downing Street.

For some time plans were in hand for an event or events to celebrate Sir Henry's 70th birthday on 7 September (1906) as a fitting recognition of the character and services of the Prime Minister. However, such plans were abandoned, given that he could not be in a mood on that date to take part in any celebration of his successes and achievements.

Some extracts from what a *Westminster Gazette Extra* had to say about Sir Henry in its 'The House of Commons in 1906', are of interest. Such comments were written and published after Sir Henry's 70th birthday. The author was apparently unaware of, or deliberately ignored, what had been going on in the previous nine months and, therefore, of the commanding position which Sir Henry had established in the House of Commons and in the Cabinet.

---

[348] *Stirling Observer,* 12/09/2006

The new Prime Minister is a man whose best friends and most devoted admirers would never dream of describing as 'brilliant'. In spite of the unquestionable fact that he has enriched the language with one or two phrases – 'methods of barbarism' and 'the larger policy' – which will certainly live a great deal longer than the Government, of which their author is the head. But as the old saying puts it, 'It's dogged as does it', and no man can fairly deny that quality of doggedness to CB. That is all the more creditable to him inasmuch as he has arrived at a time of life when most men feel inclined to take things more easily than is possible for the Leader of the Liberal, or any other, Party.

But mediocrity – persistent and consistent – will succeed where more brilliant qualities fail, and nobody today denies that CB has won his way to the front largely through his remarkable capacity for taking any amount of punishment with stolid indifference and for coming up for the next round as if nothing had happened.

By contrast, it is of interest to note the concluding paragraph in an entry in *The Harmsworth Encyclopaedia,* published in late 1906 which otherwise summarised Sir Henry's political career and the achievements and hopes of his administration in its first year in office.

> Sir Henry Campbell-Bannerman has a keen sense of wit and humour, and it is told how on some occasions he has kept the House of Commons in laughter for half an hour, and on others has turned many a dangerous attack by some clever raillery of his opponents. His most successful passages do not perhaps lend themselves readily to quotation, and are rarely epigrammatic, but can best be described as a continual diffusion of pleasantries without a touch of bitterness in them, and a sustained drollery with not a little reserve about it – a humour typically Scottish.

With the appointment of James Bryce (Chief Secretary for Ireland) as Ambassador to the USA, the Cabinet was reconstituted in January 1907. (On the King's suggestion, the position of Ambassador to the USA had first been offered to Rosebery but he had declined the offer, ostensibly for the reason that he no longer had a wife to act as his hostess in an embassy). Augustine Birrell (formerly President of the Board of Education) became Chief Secretary for Ireland and Reginald McKenna (Financial Secretary at the Treasury) joined the Cabinet as Birrell's replacement. Louis Harcourt (First Commissioner for Works from December 1905 but not in the Cabinet) joined the Cabinet in March 1907 with the Cabinet thus increasing to twenty members.

There had been some talk at this time about Churchill's promotion to the Cabinet but Sir Henry thought that although Winston had 'done his job brilliantly where he is, and is full of go and ebullient ambition... he is only a Liberal of yesterday [since 1904], his tomorrow being a little doubtful'.[349]

The Cabinet changes in January also resulted in a number of changes in the junior ranks of the Government. Walter Runciman (MP for Dewsbury) replaced Reginald McKenna at the Treasury and Dr. Thomas McNamara (MP for Camberwell North) replaced Runciman at the Local Government Board. John Ellis (Under-Secretary at the India Office) had resigned and he was replaced by Charles Hobson (MP for East Bristol). John Morley, Secretary for India, had wanted Tom Buchanan from the War Office but this had to wait until after Sir Henry's death in 1908. There were also a number of other changes in the junior ranks of the Government between February 1907 and January 1908. (Refer to Appendix 4)

Not for the first time, proposals for a Channel Tunnel were circulated that January with the King's opposition being advised to his Prime Minister. Sir Henry replied that although he had never thought much of the military objections he doubted the alleged commercial advantages. In due course, the Cabinet agreed and he made a statement in the Commons on 21 March saying that the Government was against the Tunnel and suggesting it would be better to consider alternatives such as the further development of ferry services. Indeed, regular Dover-Calais ferry services were approved six months later,

However, Sir Henry spent most of January (1907) at Belmont, with overnight house guests including the Sinclairs, the Buchanans, John Burns, George Whiteley (Government Chief Whip) and a lunch and dinner visit by Asquith on the 12th. On 24 January he went to Glasgow to receive the Freedom of the City and Royal Burgh next day in the St. Andrew's Halls "in recognition of the distinguished services rendered by him as a Statesman and Minister of the Crown", with the following being extracts from his Speech of Acceptance –

> I occupy, it is true, the most conspicuous and, it may be, the most powerful office under the Crown, but I am profoundly conscious that I owe this exalted position not to any merits or qualifications of mine, but, in the first place, to the grace of the Sovereign; and in the second place to the uniform confidence towards me of the House of Commons, in which I have passed the greater part of my life – and last, but not least – do not let me forget it – to the fidelity and favour of my political friends throughout the country...

> The concentration of human beings in towns is contrary to nature, and this abominable existence is bound to issue in suffering, deterioration, and gradual destruction to the mass of the population... countless thousands of our fellow-men, and a still larger number of children are starved of air and space and sunshine... This view of city life, which is

---

[349] Sheldon (2013), pp.148-149

gradually coming home to the heart and the understanding and the conscience of our people, is so terrible that it cannot be put away.

What is all our wealth and learning and the fine flower of our civilisation and our Constitution and our political theories – what are all these but dust and ashes, if men and women, on whose labour the whole social fabric is maintained, are doomed to live and die in darkness and misery in the recesses of our great cities?

We may undertake expeditions of behalf of oppressed tribes and races, we may conduct foreign missions, we may sympathise with the cause of unfortunate nationalities; but it is our own people, surely, who have first claim upon us... the air must be purified, the sunshine must be allowed to stream in, the water and the food must be kept pure and unadulterated, the streets light and clean... the measure of your success in bringing these things to pass will be the measure of the arresting of the terrible powers of race degeneration which is going on in sunless streets.[350]

It is noted that Sir Henry had already spoken forcibly on the subject of infantile mortality to a deputation received by him and John Burns on 23 November 1906. The Rev. James Barr, who had been a platform speaker at Sir Henry's St. Andrew's Hall meeting a year earlier, was again on the platform on this occasion. He remembered, in particular, Sir Henry, in 1907, referring to Glasgow as 'a city set upon a hill, inspiring and encouraging others in the career of municipal improvement'.[351]

At the lunch that followed the St. Andrews Hall ceremony, the Prime Minister also spoke, delighting those present with reminiscences of his early days in Glasgow. Thus and otherwise, two days later (27 January) Vaughan Nash was able to write to Arthur Ponsonby, 'Glasgow was a tremendous success and it has freshened the PM up and brought him back to his best Downing Street form... The stay at the Lord Provost's was a great success – nice, simple, warm-hearted people who did it to perfection'.[352]

The St. Andrew's Halls complex was opened by a private company in 1877 and taken over by the Town Council in 1890. St. Henry had previously spoken in the Grand Hall during the 1906 General Election campaign. In 1962 the entire complex was almost totally destroyed by fire. One of the surviving facades was subsequently incorporated in an extension of the adjacent Mitchell Library, providing multi-purpose accommodation and facilities. (The last Liberal Leader to speak in the old Grand Hall was Clement Davies in the early 1950s when I recall his saying that the

---

[350] *The Glasgow Herald*, 25 January 1907

[351] Barr (1928), p.320

[352] As quoted in Wilson (1973), pp,587-588

cause of Home Rule for Wales could be advanced by following the example of the Scottish Covenant Association.)

On 8 March (1907) Sir Henry was sworn in as an Elder Brother of Trinity House, thus becoming a member of the board (then with some 31 members) with maritime and associated responsibilities in England, Wales and the Channel Islands. (The Northern Lighthouse Board has similar responsibilities in Scotland and the Isle of Man, with a joint Board for all of Ireland).

During the 2008 Campbell-Bannerman Centenary Commemorations in Scotland (refer to Appendix 5), there was speculation as to how Sir Henry, if he had lived longer, would have interacted with Bonar Law (another Glasgow High School Former Pupil) who became Conservative Leader in 1911. Law had returned to the Commons as from a by-election for Dulwich on 15 May (1906). However, not much was heard from him in the House until March (1907). Then 'a new and harsh voice was heard from the Conservative benches in the House. In a combative speech, Bonar Law warned the Government that they would not be allowed to forget Chinese Labour and accused them of gerrymandering the Transvaal Constitution to bribe the Boers. Sir Henry indignantly repudiated such charges'.[353]

On 15 April (1907) Sir Henry opened the Imperial Conference in London – The UK, Australia, Canada, New Zealand, Cape Colony, Natal, the Transvaal and Newfoundland – with the attendance including Dr. Leander Jameson (of the Jameson Raid of 1895) as Prime Minister of Cape Colony and Louis Botha as Prime Minister of the Transvaal. (The Orange River Colony was granted self-government two months later [in June 1907]. Newfoundland ceased to be self-governing in 1934 and confederated with Canada in 1949.) During a dinner in the Holburn Restaurant, Botha was told by Sir Henry that this was the place where he had made the 'methods of barbarism' speech six years earlier. Before he left London, Botha had breakfast with Sir Henry in 10 Downing Street. (Two years later [1909] when Botha was next in London, he gave a dinner for Asquith's Cabinet at which, after the toast to the King, Botha rose again and said simply 'To the memory of Sir Henry Campbell-Bannerman').

Sir Henry had made it clear, when opening the Conference, that the UK Government could and would not go behind the declared opinion of the electorate and the Commons on Free Trade v Tariff Reform/Imperial Preference. However, the opportunity was too good for the Unionists to miss, with a series of dinners and public meetings, at which the Colonial Premiers were assured of unflagging efforts to break down the obstinacy of the Cobdenite UK Government. The matter was debated for several days by the Conference at the end of the month. The UK representatives maintaining their Government's position, Botha and Sir Wilfred Laurier (Canada) arguing that each country should decide its own fiscal policy and the other Premiers arguing that the UK should adopt Imperial Preference. Balfour then joined the debate and, at a demonstration in the Albert Hall on 3 May, stated

---

[353] Wilson (1973), pp,593-594

that the UK should adopt Imperial Preference because of the clear proof that that was what the Colonies wanted.

At Easter, Sir Henry spent a few days in Cannes as the guest of Lord Rendel (Liberal MP for Montgomeryshire in 1880-1892) from where he visited his stricken friend, Earl Spencer. Also, about this time, his dinner engagements in London included one at which Bertrand Russell was present and another at Marlborough House, hosted by Prince George, the future King George V. (Bertrand Russell was about to be defeated as an Independent Liberal at a by-election in Wimbledon on 14 May.)

On 12 April he was back in the Commons after the Easter recess and personally saw through the adoption of new procedural rules. The number of Standing Committees was increased to four, including one for Scottish business. The Committee Chairmen were given powers to enable many measures to be passed which would have had little or no chance under the previous system.

On 9 May Sir Henry spoke for an hour at a banquet in Manchester – speaking mainly about the Imperial Conference, the Transvaal, Free Trade v Imperial Preference and the House of Lords – being described in the *Manchester Guardian* as 'alert vivacious and robust'. In his references to Imperial Preference (and the Imperial Conference), the Unionists were berated for seizing on the Conference as an opportunity for a party demonstration and for trying unsuccessfully to sow dissention between the present UK Government and the Colonies. He concluded, 'all we want to do is to claim for ourselves the same freedom which these self-governing Colonies and communities enjoy, and which nothing on earth will tempt them to forgo'.[354]

On the death of the Rt. Hon. George H. Finch (Conservative MP for Rutland from 1867) on 22 May 1907, Sir Henry became the 'Father of the House of Commons' the only serving UK Prime Minister to do so to date. (Lloyd George, Winston Churchill, Edward Heath and James Callaghan became 'Fathers of the House' after they had been Prime Minister).

About this time Sir Henry was given a private dinner at the Reform Club by some Liberal Peers and MPs, at which Asquith made an impromptu speech testifying to the absolute unanimity of the Cabinet and their unqualified trust in, and personal affection for their leader.[355]

Sir Henry received an Honorary Doctorate of Laws (LLD) at Cambridge on 12 June. With the Duke of Devonshire (the former Marquis of Hartington) presiding as Chancellor of the University, the other honorary graduands that day were two other members of the Liberal Cabinet, the Earl of Elgin and Haldane and two Unionists, Alfred Milner and George Curzon, 1st (Irish) Lord Curzon of Kedleston. That evening, Sir Henry made a witty after-dinner speech in Trinity College and the

---

[354] As quoted in Spender (1923), Volume 2, pp.335-336

[355] Wilson (1973), p,586

following morning had breakfast and went for a drive with the Master, Dr. Montagu Butler.[356]

The three Liberal graduands must have been somewhat embarrassed as when the company assembled in the Senate House, before the graduations, most fuss was made of Milner whose maiden speech in House of Lords on 26 February (1906) had been a bitter attack on the Liberal Government's South African policy. Sir Henry and George Curzon may also have been embarrassed by their presence together on 12 June. Earlier in 1906 the Prime Minister had followed Balfour in refusing to recommend Curzon, Viceroy of India in 1899-1905, for a UK Earldom.

Curzon never forgave Sir Henry and his decision to challenge him for the Rectorship of Glasgow University in 1908 may have been taken out of pure spite He was again to be frustrated as Sir Henry died before the election.[357] Curzon was eventually created a UK Earl in 1911 and succeeded his father as 5th (UK) Lord Scarsdale in 1916.

Sir Henry received an Honorary Doctorate of Civil Law (DCL) at Oxford on 26 June, along with Prince Arthur of Connaught, Sir Edward Grey, Kipling, Rodin, Mark Twain and General Booth of the Salvation Army. (As already mentioned, Mark Twain had been a guest of the Campbell-Bannermans in London in 1894) Sir Henry and Kipling may also have been embarrassed by their presence together on 26 June, given Kipling's response to the 'methods of barbarism' speech in 1901.

In early August, Sir Henry was in touch with the Palace, with also discussion in Cabinet, as to whether or not to accept the offer of the Transvaal Government to present the Culluinan Diamond to the King. Objections were centred on the opposition of the English-speaking South African Progressive Party and the fact that a large UK loan to the Transvaal was being negotiated. Accordingly, on 21 August, Sir Henry wrote to the Palace saying that only the King's well-known tact and right and prudent instincts could find a way out and thus the offer was accepted.[358]

He had no wish to return to Marienbad after Charlotte's death, so – after the Commons adjourned on 28 August – he went up to Belmont where he stayed until the start of his autumn round of engagements (Many of Sir Henry's activities from the summer of 1907 onwards are necessarily also considered in Chapter 14.) Visitors to Belmont at this time included John Morley and Lord Crewe. A letter arrived from Sir Edward Grey on 31 August confirming the conclusion of the Anglo-Russian Convention on spheres of influence in Persia (Iran), removing motives for Russian intrigues in Afghanistan and elsewhere on the Indian frontier. Then, on 2 September, he wrote from Belmont to his Chief Whip, George Whiteley –

---

[356] Spender (1923), Volume 2, p.343

[357] Wilson (1973), pp,586

[358] Wilson (1973), pp,601-602

You know what everybody has been saying for the last week? That the splendid success of our session is due to the driving force and courage of the Chief Whip. And so say I. I assure you it is universally felt, and you have your reward now for all your labour and sacrifices. I need not tell you how warmly I feel about it; and I am doubly glad for Mrs. Whitley's sake, who has borne the brunt of it even more than yourself.[359]

Sir James Guthrie came to Belmont to paint his portrait. In the portrait, which was presented by the Scottish Liberal Association to the National Galleries of Scotland in 1912, Sir Henry is dressed, sword and all, as a Knight Grand Cross of the Order of the Bath.[360]

A black and white photograph (by Annan of Glasgow) of the portrait was published, as a frontispiece in the *Glasgow High School Magazine* of June 1948. Sir James Guthrie, RSA [1858-1930], a pupil at the High School of Glasgow in 1869-1874 – that is, nineteen years after Sir Henry – was President of the Royal Scottish Academy in 1902-1919.

The Stirling Smith Art Gallery and Museum has a portrait sketch of Sir Henry, also by Sir James Guthrie, as presented by J.J. Monroe in 1944. It was presumably painted by Sir James as a by-product of his full-length portrait of Sir Henry as above. The head and shoulders sketch shows Sir Henry wearing the collar of a Knight Grand Cross of the Order of the Bath, as in the full-length portrait.

Sir Henry received the Freedom of the Royal Burgh of Montrose on 27 September on which day he also opened a golf club bazaar and made three speeches. He took the opportunity to praise small burghs, such as Montrose, contrasting their 'sweet clean air' with the conditions in the great cities. After Montrose he went to Balmoral to see the King, returning to Belmont, but not for long, on 2 October. After receiving the Freedom of the Royal Burgh of Peebles on 4 October, he was in Edinburgh on 7 October to give a major speech to a crowded and excited meeting on the relationship between the House of Commons and the House of Lords, citing, in particular, the mutilation of Scottish legislation in the Upper Chamber. Judging by the interruptions, there was much support for the notion that what was really necessary was not to reform the relationship but to abolish the House of Lords.[361]

He was back in Edinburgh on 30 October to receive the Freedom of the City and Royal Burgh. This was probably the last occasion on which Rosebery and Sir Henry met, and nothing pleased the Prime Minister more than when the former Liberal

---

[359] Spender (1923), Volume 2, p.367

[360] There is also a watercolour drawing of Sir Henry by Sir Francis C. Gould (1844-1925) in the National Portrait Gallery in London

[361] Spender (1923), Volume 2, p.368

Prime Minister joined in the tributes to his fellow Scot. Rosebery was not on the platform but was called forward at the end of the proceedings. He then said that in their occasional [!] differences of opinion they had always retained their personal feelings of friendship for each other.[362] Rosebery must have been on his best behaviour!

In his speech of acceptance, given that the year (1907) was the 200th anniversary of the parliamentary union of Scotland with England and Wales, Sir Henry referred to such as a 'mighty combination', with its 'profound effect for good upon the world', going on to say –

> We are living in days when heart-searchings, sometimes carried to morbid lengths, are rather fashionable. In the South we hear of a Celtic invasion and in the North the cry is raised that Scotland is being anglicised. In every sort of union there must be some give and take; but, so far as I can see, Scotland is Scotland still, and the Scot, so far from being de-scotticised, still loves his country, has in him the old, stubborn, ever-turbulent spirit and is still devoted to things of the mind.
>
> He has met with success – he is often gibed at and mocked on that account – but success has not effaced his ancient characteristics or vulgarised or debased the type. If his speech is nearer to English than it once was, he can still read Robert Burns and on occasion recite him intelligibly.
>
> Here in Edinburgh, where one would expect, if anywhere, to detect signs of national decay or backsliding, you will find a centre of learning and cultivation, a home of the arts, great lawyers, doctors, teachers, and a spacious and dignified common life, not unworthy of the high traditions and associations of this ancient capital. We owe much to the wisdom and foresight of the bygone custodians of the city, and we thank them for their planning of this new town. And this heritage which the custodians of what is known among us as "the common good" have handed down, you, the municipality, will guard with jealousy as nothing less than a national trust.
>
> Depend upon it, that in maintaining and adorning and equipping this, our national capital, you are helping to promote the development of our own literature, our own art and our own industries, and our national life, and you are doing what can be done to check and neutralise the natural, but in many ways mischievous, tendency to absorption and eclipse by the greater imperial metropolis on the Thames.[363]

---

[362] O'Connor (1908), p.147

[363] *The Scotsman,* 31 October 1907.

Also in October, having taken over responsibility for remembering the birthdays of Charlotte's god-children, he sent a letter and presents (a photograph of Charlotte and a small brooch she had worn as a child) to one of them, Margaret (Peggy) Sinclair – the daughter of the Secretary for Scotland, and Lady Marjorie Sinclair – for her second birthday on 12 October to be read by her in later years, 'The sight of you, and even the thought of you, cheered her, and brightened for her the last months of her life, which were months of pain, feebleness and distress… Good-bye then, Baby Sunshine; and so will you best please your good father and mother and do your duty to the good God who implanted that spirit in you'.[364]

Later in October, he was in Dunfermline during his last visits to his constituency – making a speech, attending a lunch and a reception, meeting a local Trades Council delegation and making a round of personal visits. He was particularly pleased to meet the senior citizens making use of Pittencrieff House which had been gifted to the local community by Andrew Carnegie. The Pittencrieff purchase must have been especially pleasing as the previous proprietor had banned the Morrison family from the grounds by reason of the chartist and radical opinions of Andrew Carnegie's uncle, Thomas Morrison who was, of course, one of Sir Henry's earliest supporters in Dunfermline.

> Scour and polish as you like the outside of the cup and platter, what avails it to the strength of the Empire if you and your people at home are weakened and demoralised by the efforts to which I have referred [colonial wars and foreign adventures]. These are the motives and these are the objects at least of the Bills of ours which they have managed somehow or other to prevent becoming Acts of Parliament – the English Education Bill, our Land Values (Scotland) Bill, our Scottish Small Holders' Bill, yes, and our one man one vote Bill, which have all been summarily rejected or destroyed.[365]

The meeting in a packed St. Margaret's Hall on the evening of the 22nd was chaired by Alexander Macbeth, formerly the Liberal Agent in Dunfermline and now Provost. The meeting concluded with the enthusiastic adoption of a vote of thanks and confidence. This was moved by John Weir, Secretary of the local Miners' Association, who directed special attention to the unity and ability of the Cabinet and made grateful acknowledgement of the appointment for the first time of a 'working man' (John Burns) as a Cabinet Minister.

At the reception hosted by the Robertsons he enjoyed meeting many old friends, including veterans of early election contests, but also the sons and daughters of parents whose memory he cherished. Unfortunately, despite Provost Macbeth

---

[364] Spender (1923), Volume 2, p.365-366

[365] Mackie (1914). p.125

having commented on his healthy appearance and vigour, Sir Henry was heard to say, at the reception, 'I really do not feel very well'.[366]

By early November Sir Henry was back in Downing Street, approving a draft of an Official Secrets Bill which made no progress by reason of press opposition. Then, on the 9th, four days before the beginning of his final illness, he spoke at the Lord Mayor's Banquet in the London Guildhall.

For a Presbyterian, a Communicant Member of the Church of Scotland and a lifelong advocate of disestablishment, Sir Henry took an untoward interest in the affairs of the Church of England, thus displaying an uncharacteristic inconsistency between his beliefs and practice. Even, given the Crown's exercise of patronage in the Church of England, there should have been some way of ensuring that a Prime Minister who was not an English Anglican was not involved, even nominally, with such matters.[367]

As for honours, Sir Henry recommended the creation of twenty-one peerages (say, an average of ten a year) as against an average of seven a year by Salisbury and six by Balfour. Asquith maintained the rate of ten a year without the justification of ten years in opposition and then matters got out of hand with Lloyd George. Although only forty-one peers (out of a voting total of 460) had voted for the Second Irish Home Rule Bill in 1893, there were about eighty-one Liberal peers in the House of Lords by December 1905 and some 102 (out of an overall total of 615) by April 1908.[368]

---

[366] Mackie (1914), p.130

[367] In connection with matters prelatic, Sir Henry was fortunate in not being a member of a Presbyterian denomination more inclined to discipline its members than was and is The Church of Scotland. In 1989, Lord Mackay of Clashfern (Conservative Lord Chancellor in 1987-1997) was excommunicated by the tiny Free Presbyterian Church, of which he was a member, for his involvement with another denomination to the extent of attending Roman Catholic funerals for judicial colleagues in 1986 and 1988. Lord Mackay then left the Free Presbyterian Church and thus was able to be Lord High Commissioner to the General Assembly of The Church of Scotland in 2005 and 2006. The Free Presbyterian Church, a breakaway in 1892 from the original Free Church of 1843-1900, is one of seven present-day very small Scottish-based Presbyterian Churches which stand apart from The Church of Scotland.

The Lords High Commissioner to the General Assembly during Sir Henry's tenure as Prime Minister were a Scottish Representative Peer, the 11th (Scottish) Earl of Leven, who was also 10th (Scottish) Earl of Melville, in 1906 and the 11th (Scottish) Lord Kinnaird, who was also 3rd (UK) Lord Kinnaird, in 1907. The Earl was also Lord High Commissioner in 1898-1905, that is during the tenures of Salisbury and Balfour as Prime Minister. He had been appointed for 1906 before the Conservative Government's resignation in December 1905. Lord Kinnaird, who was a Scottish Association Football Internationalist in 1873 and President of the (English) Football Association in 1890-1923, was also Lord High Commissioner in 1908 and 1909, that is, during Asquith's tenure as Prime Minister.

[368] Of course, if the 1911 Parliament Bill, curtailing the powers of the House of Lords, had not been approved in the Lords in August – by 131 votes to 114, with most Unionist peers abstaining and twenty-three Unionists and thirteen Bishops voting with the Liberals – the King

As for knighthoods, the award in 1907 to his Stirling Chairman, James B. Smith was challenged in the Commons. Sir James was also a director of a Government contractor, the Ayrshire Foundry Company which had supplied a defective rudder for a battleship with the defect concealed by cosmetic welding. The Speaker had to intervene to rule that the Prime Minister was not responsible to the Commons for advice to the King on honours. It was later held that none of the Company's directors were responsible for the fraud. W.S. Gilbert's knighthood, also in 1907, was much appreciated, being twenty-four years after Arthur Sullivan's in 1883.

Perhaps Sir Henry's most commendable recommendation was the award of the Order of Merit to Florence Nightingale, delayed because of the King's objection to women being given the Order – thus, when it went through in November 1907, she was beyond knowing what it was all about.[369] (The King's reluctance to give the Order to a woman contrasts with his grant of an honorary knighthood [KCVO] to the Abbot of the monastery which owned the mineral springs at Marienbad) Sir Henry's final acts as Prime Minister included recommending Lord Crewe – Rosebery's son-in-law – for the Order of the Garter, Lord Tweedmouth for the Order of the Thistle and Henry Higgs for a CB (Companion of the Order of the Bath).

(George V) had agreed to assent to the creation of (Liberal) peers sufficient in number to guard against any possible combination in opposition by which the Bill might be exposed a second time to defeat.

However, even if all the over two hundred potential Liberal peers listed by Asquith (Spender & Cyril Asquith [1932], Volume 1, pp.329-331) had been ennobled, the Liberal Party would not have secured a long-term majority in the House of Lords. The list, which included such *literati* as J.M. Barrie and Thomas Hardy, also included a number of men, such as Dr. Robert Farquharson, who were unmarried and/or childless and others, such as Lord Haddo (Courtesy Title) and Bertrand Russell, who were heirs to existing hereditary peerages. The list also included seventeen Liberal MPs with by-election implication in that number of Liberal-held constituencies.

[369] Florence Nightingale was a cousin of the father of the wife of Vaughan Nash, one of Sir Henry's Private Secretaries as Prime Minster. Vaughan Nash was also related by marriage to Sir Maurice Bonham Carter who, in due course, succeeded him as Asquith's Principal Private Secretary. Sir Maurice married Asquith's daughter Lady Violet and they were the parents of Mark Bonham Carter and Laura Grimond, Lady Bonham Carter of Yarnbury, a daughter of Mark Bonham Carter, has been a Liberal Democrat Life Peeress since 2004.

13 – 1905-1908 – Legislative and Executive Action and Frustration

South Africa

As already mentioned, the incoming Liberal Cabinet had decided, on 10 December 1905, to stop any further importation of indentured Chinese labour into the Transvaal and had set up a committee on South African matters generally.

However, given that a further 13,000 or more licences had been granted in early November by the outgoing Unionist Government, Sir Henry had to say, at Liverpool on 9 January 1906 and the next day at Chester that, on the advice of Asquith and the Cabinet's other legal experts, the licences could not be revoked. The matter was debated in the new House of Commons on 22 and 23 February 1906. This was in the context of consideration of the Government's motion effectively approving the King's Speech and a Unionist Opposition amendment to regret that the Government had 'brought the reputation of this country into contempt by describing the employment of Chinese indentured labour as slavery, whilst it is manifest [that the Government is] contemplating no official method of bringing it to an end'.

Although the debate concluded with the Government's unamended motion being carried by 416 votes to 91, there was no end in sight, much to the dismay of many of the Liberal back-benchers such as Hilaire Belloc who called for the deportation of all indentured Chinese labour from South Africa, with the whole cost falling on the mine owners. However, the end did come sixteen months later when Louis Botha, now Prime Minister of a self-governing Transvaal, announced, on 17 June 1907, that all the Chinese would be sent home immediately their contracts expired.[370]

There was never any doubt as to Sir Henry's commitment to grant, as soon as possible, self-government to the two new Crown Colonies in South Africa, which had also been promised, as soon as circumstances allowed, at Vereeniging in 1902.

In March 1905 the Unionist Government had published proposals to give the Transvaal a constitution (known as the Lyttelton Constitution) but with all executive authority to remain vested in officials appointed by the Crown and with the Governor to have a veto on legislation.[371] On the other hand, while favouring amendments to the Unionists' proposals, the more cautious elements in the new Liberal Cabinet favoured a transitional approach with all sorts of checks and safeguards, as indicated in a paper circulated by the Cabinet committee (set up on 10 December) on 30

---

[370] Spender (1923), Volume 2, pp.232-233

[371] The Lyttelton Constitution was named for Arthur Lyttelton who, as Unionist MP for Warwick and Leamington (1895-1906) had succeeded Joseph Chamberlain as Colonial Secretary in 1903. His first wife, Laura Tennant, who died in 1886, was a sister of Margot Asquith (née Tennant).

January 1906. Further, officials in the Colonial Office and UK officials in South Africa were in favour of continuity in policy, implying support for the Lyttelton Constitution. In the meantime, Louis Botha and Jan Christiaan Smuts had founded the Het Volk (Union of the People) Party with the objective of securing the immediate grant of <u>fully responsible</u> self-government to the two new Crown Colonies.

Accounts differ as to the details of what happened at the decisive Cabinet meeting on 8 February 1906, but for both the background and who was responsible for that day's decision, the most authentic accounts are perhaps such as were published in the *Glasgow High School Magazine* of June 1948 (pp.78-80 and 96).

<u>The Rt. Hon. Field Marshall Jan Christiaan Smuts, OM</u>

I am glad to place on record some of my recollections in connection with Sir Henry Campbell-Bannerman's share in the grant of self-government to the Transvaal and the Orange Free State in 1906 [and 1907]. His action will ever remain one of the highlights of British statesmanship, with far reaching effects on the future course of events. In these days of swiftly moving events and fading memories it is right that his great action should be remembered. And the pages of a magazine conducted by his old Scots school is a proper place in which to record once more the part he played.

After the conclusion of the South African War in 1902, Crown Colony rule of the standard type was imposed on the Boer republics. It was to be feared, in view of the length and obstinacy of the Boer resistance, that there might be a renewal of the trouble. But nothing happened. The behaviour of the Boer people, intent only on rebuilding their homes and restoring their destroyed country, was in every way exemplary. Nothing happened to disturb the peace or internal security.

[However] it soon became evident to the British authorities that in a country like Transvaal, with a Boer population traditionally wedded to law and order, and a British population always restive under the restraint of Crown Colony rule, the position was becoming untenable. And so in 1905 a plan was evolved by the then Conservative Government to grant what is called representative government to the Transvaal; that is to say, there would be popular representation in a legislative assembly, but the government would remain under the Crown. Among both the Boer and the British inhabitants there was considerable feeling against such a halfway solution, and it was clear to the Boer leaders that the scheme was likely to lead to differences between the British governing authority and the people, and so likely to disturb the good relationship that had existed since the peace.

Towards the end of 1905 a general election was pending in Britain, and it appeared likely that the Conservative Party might be beaten by the

Liberal Party led by Sir Henry Campbell-Bannerman. Personal exchanges between Lord Kitchener and myself at the Peace Conference in 1902 had raised hopes that the Boer people might look forward to a change of the Crown Colony regime when such a change of government should take place. My colleagues, therefore, asked me to go to London and explore the position with the new Liberal Government.

So I arrived in December, 1905, on my errand in London, where I had last been as a student ten years before. My presence was noted, and I remember an evening paper making a remark that a most dangerous man then walking the streets of London was a Boer emissary bent on upsetting the Boer War settlement. This looks a bad prophecy in the light of after events; but it still remains a question whether it might not have been a good shot if my mission had turned out a failure. Little more than ten years later I was once more walking the streets of London, but this time as a member of the British War Cabinet, helping in the conduct of the Great War. What an extraordinary turn of events, which completely upset the newspaper prophecy and amazed the world!

The man who wrought the miracle was Sir Henry Campbell-Bannerman, to all appearances an ordinary man, almost commonplace to a superficial view, but a real man, shrewd and worldly-wise, but rooted in a great faith which inspired a great action. I discussed my mission with many members of the Cabinet – perhaps the most brilliant Government Britain had had for a long time – and with men among them like Asquith, Edward Grey, Lloyd George, John Morley, and, last but not least, Winston Churchill. Campbell-Bannerman looked the least distinguished in that galaxy of talent. But what a wise man, what statesmanship in insight and faith, and what a sure grip on the future! My mission failed with the rest, as it was humanly speaking bound to fail. What an audacious, what an unprecedented request mine was practically for the restoration of the country to the Boers five years after they had been beaten to the ground in one of the hardest and most lengthy struggles in British warfare.

But with Campbell-Bannerman my mission did not fail. I put a simple case to him that night [7th February] in 10 Downing Street. It was in substance; *'Do you want friends or enemies? You can have the Boers for friends, and they have proved what their friendship may mean. I pledge the friendship of myself and my colleagues if you wish it. You can choose to make them enemies, and possibly have another Ireland on your hands. If you do believe in liberty, it is also their faith and their religion'*

I used no set arguments, but simply spoke to him as man to man, and appealed only to the human aspect, which I felt would weigh deeply with him. He was a cautious Scot, and said nothing to me, but I left the room that night a happy man. My intuition told me that the thing had been done. The rest of the story has been told by Mr. Lloyd George: how at a Cabinet meeting the next day the Prime Minister simply put to his colleagues the case for self-government to the Transvaal, and in ten minutes had created such an impression that not a word was said in opposition, and one of the Ministers had tears in his eyes.

A mission to work out the details was sent to the Transvaal, and next year the country had its free Constitution, in which Boer and Englishmen [sic] sat together, under a Prime Minister who had been Commander-in-Chief of the Boer armies in the field but Botha was a man of like stature to Campbell-Bannerman. Greatness of soul met equal greatness of soul, and a page was added to the story of human statesmanship, of unfading glory and inspiration to after ages. Seven years later Campbell-Bannerman had passed away, but Botha was once more a commander-in-chief in the field, this time, however, in common cause with Britain, and over forces in which Dutch and British were comrades.

The contagion of magnanimity has spread from the leaders to their peoples. Nor does the story end there. It was continued in the Second World War after Botha had also passed away. It has even been suggested that the action of South Africa saved our cause in the years that followed the Battle of Britain and when America [USA] had not entered the war. The story may never end. To great deeds wrought by the human soul there is no end. To-day we are living in distraught times, where in the confusion it is not easy to recognise the way.

But in this simple story I have told there is a light of statesmanship which shines like an inextinguishable beacon above the raging storm. We shall remember Campbell-Bannerman.

Last year [1947], when the Royal Family visited South Africa, the King [George VI] did my simple home (a relic from a British military camp of the Boer War) the honour of a visit. There, in my study, he saw a large portrait of Campbell-Bannerman hanging above my chair. Later he said to me: *I was so glad to see that portrait in your study. One seldom sees it in Britain to-day.* Alas! And so I say to you my young Scots friends, and my friends in all our Commonwealth, and to mankind everywhere where greatness of soul is honoured:

Don't forget Campbell-Bannerman.

James D.G. Davidson [1927-2017], Liberal MP for West Aberdeenshire in 1966-1970, served on HMS Vanguard which took the Royal Family to/from South Africa in 1947. As then the senior Sub-Lieutenant on HMS Vanguard he was awarded an

MVO. I first visited the Campbell-Bannerman grave in Meigle with James when we were en route to an event in Glasgow in September 1966.

An Extract from Lord Riddell's Diary 1913

(This was originally published in *Country Life*, London, 1934. Sir George Allardice Riddell [1865-1934] represented the British Press at the Paris Peace Conference as Chairman of George Newnes, Ltd. and *News of the World*. He was created Lord Riddell in 1920.)

> Lord Riddell: *The South Africa Constitution was the biggest thing established in our day. Who was responsible? Campbell-Bannerman or Asquith?*
>
> Lloyd George: *Oh, CB! He deserves all the credit. It was all done in a ten minutes' speech at the Cabinet – the most dramatic, the most important ten minutes speech ever delivered in our time. In ten minutes he brushed aside all the safeguards as devised by Asquith, Winston and Loreburn. At the outset only two of us were with him, John Burns and myself.*
>
> *But his speech convinced the whole Cabinet. It was the utterance of a plain, kindly, simple man. The speech moved at least one of the Cabinet to tears. It was the most impressive thing I ever saw. The result of CB's policy has been remarkable. It captured General Botha by its magnanimity, just as all great men are impressed when you display confidence in them. If we had a war to-morrow, Botha and fifty thousand Boers would march with us side by side. He would if necessary drive the Germans out.*

Thus the grant of fully responsible self-government to the Transvaal in December 1906 and to the Orange River Colony in June 1907, noting that the grants were in the form of Orders-in-Council to avoid the legislative involvement and obstruction of the House of Lords, much as the sale of army commissions had been abolished by Order-in-Council during the 1868-1874 Parliament.

I have heard it said – even in Liberal circles – that Sir Henry and his Government were responsible for the continuing disenfranchisement of the native people of South Africa and for the imposition of apartheid and separation development, particularly after the Afrikaner Nationalist victory at the South African General Election in 1948. In fact, the Liberal Government was bound by the terms of the Peace Treaty of Vereeniging, concluded on behalf of the then UK Unionist Government and the Boer leaders in May 1902. This prevented the Liberals giving any (further) political rights to the non-white people of South Africa before the grants of self-government to the Transvaal and the Orange River Colony.

The matter was debated in the House of Commons on 31 July 1906 in the context of consideration of a motion to approve the Government's Colonial Office Estimates.

Winston Churchill, as Colonial Under-Secretary, in opening the debate, referred to the undertaking, as from Vereeniging, which may be regretted, but adding that the Government was reserving to the Secretary of State the right to disallow any legislation which imposed disabilities on natives not imposed on Europeans. Further, Arthur Balfour, in winding-up the debate for the Opposition and speaking darkly about the 'native problem', said 'we have to face facts; it is not true, men are not born equal, the white and black races are not born with equal capacities... They will be eight to one' and concluded that the Government's policy was 'the most reckless experiment ever tried in the development of a great colonial policy'.

As it happened, Balfour's long repetitive speech left Sir Henry, 'rising just before 10 o'clock', only one minute to reply for the Government during which, he only managed to say, 'In the one minute left to me I will only say one thing, that never in the course of my Parliamentary career have I listened to a more unworthy, provocative and mischievous...' The Government's motion, and effectively its South Africa policy was then approved by a majority of 316 votes to 82. Margot Asquith, who thought her friend Balfour's speech 'quite wicked – a disgrace', 'wished that CB had had a little more time and could have crushed him with moderation instead of anger though every word he said was true'.[372] Significantly, one of the Unionists who did than vote against the policy, Austen Chamberlain wrote later (in 1921) that he wished he could have undone his vote if he could have seen further into the future.

Further, if the Boers had not been reconciled by Sir Henry Campbell-Bannerman's administration, there would, almost certainly, have been different alignments in South Africa in 1914, with the Boers actively supporting Germany, with thus the secured (rather than annexed) German colonies in South West and East Africa (now Namibia and the mainland part of Tanzania) providing facilities for German submarines in the south Atlantic and Pacific and the history of the First World War and the world might have been very different.

The following extracts were also published in the *Glasgow High School Magazine* of June 1948 –

Edited Extracts from Leader in *The Transvaal Leader* of 18 December 1906

> It is quite evident now that they [the leaders of Het Volk – Botha, Smuts, etc.] have engineered the Constitution under which this Colony will have to live. Mr. Smuts [has now confessed] that he himself suggested the appointment of an Imperial Commission to enquire into the terms of a Constitution that would best suit the Boers. Then Exeter Hall sprang up and, as representing the Nonconformist Conscience, imposed conditions which any decent Boer must regard with dislike and derision. Het Volk and the Liberals were acting on the good old

---

[372] As quoted in Wilson (1973), p.489

Liberal motto – let justice seek another clime as long as we keep our heavenly majority.

These observations must seem like a statement of platitude to anyone who knows of the parleys that have been maintained since <u>that draper man from Glasgow – one forgets his name – was gazetted as Prime Minister</u>. The Het Volk delegates [at their Party Congress] accepted terms that, where the natives are concerned, they have to be ruled by the mateless curates and disappointed spinsters who haunt the unholy purlieus of Exeter Hall.

[The Het Volk leaders] want to get power and the unprincipled rabble of clever young men which follows CB, wants to keep the power it has gained by methods so unscrupulous. In the meantime the Transvaal suffers…

Exeter Hall, a very large building in the Strand in London, was where meetings of the Anti-Slavery Society were held. Thus, 'Exeter Hall' became a synonym for the Anti-Slavery Lobby. The building was demolished in 1907 to provide a site for the Strand Palace Hotel

1907-1948

The Coalition Cabinet formed in the Transvaal in early 1907 included Botha as Prime Minister, Smuts as Minister of Education and effectively Deputy Prime Minister and two Ministers from the English-speaking National Party. On the formation of the Union of South Africa in 1910, Botha became Prime Minister, with James Hertzog, from the Orange River Colony, as Minister of Justice and Smuts as Minister of Defence and Minister of Mines. In 1913, as Minister of Mines, he (Smuts) had notable encounters with Mohandas Gandhi who from 1893 spent 21 years in South Africa opposing discrimination against Indians. Hertzog, having been ousted as Minister of Justice in 1912, founded the Afrikaner National Party in early 1914 and later in the year advocated neutrality during the First World War. Botha died in 1919 and Smuts succeeded as Leader of the South Africa Party and as Prime Minister and Minister for Native Affairs. In 1924 the South African General Election was won by the opposition parties, with Hertzog becoming Prime Minister in an Afrikaner National Coalition with the Labour Party. The world economic crisis forced the formation of a new Coalition in February 1933 with Smuts becoming Deputy Prime Minister and Minister of Justice. The Afrikaner National and South Africa Parties then amalgamated in 1934 to form the United Party with Herzog as Leader and Smuts as Deputy Leader. With the outbreak of the Second World War in September 1939, the United Party, the Cabinet and Parliament split over entry to the War with the neutralists (led by Hertzog) being defeated by one vote in the Cabinet and by thirteen votes in Parliament.

Hertzog resigned and Smuts became Prime Minister and Minister of Defence and Leader of a continuing United Party in coalition with the small Labour and Dominion Parties. The neutralist Afrikaners regrouped in a new Nationalist Party. Although leading in the popular vote, the United Party was defeated in the 1948 General Election by the (now pro-apartheid) Nationalist Party by reason of the electoral system and Smuts' support for the Fagan Commission Report which advocated the abandonment of all racial segregation in South Africa. Smuts had failed, while he had a parliamentary majority, to alter the electoral rules – as from the South African Constitution of 1910 – which greatly favoured rural constituencies and thus the Nationalists. For him adherence to the settlement of 1910 was a matter of good faith. On the basis of one vote, one value, he would have secured a comfortable majority. He died on 11 September 1950 on his farm near Pretoria.

India

With the governance of India remaining one of the most controversial other issues in colonial policy, some progress was made in increasing Indian representation in its government. In 1907 two Indians were appointed to the Secretary of State's (John Morley's) Council in London. (This was followed in 1909 by the appointment of one Indian to the Viceroy's Council in India and the Indian Councils Act which ensured that non-officials, many being elected, were in a majority in provincial councils). However, there remained only token Indian representation in Indian central government, with separate Muslim electorates for the provincial councils being an aspect of an implied divide-and-rule policy which would be a factor in bringing about partition some forty years later. An alternative approach, advocated by the Unionist-appointed Viceroy, the 4th Earl of Minto to involve the princely class in developing Indian institutions and thus to outflank middle class politicians and agitators was ruled out by John Morley.[373]

Ireland

In accordance with the agreed Liberal policy of home-rule-by-stages, Augustine Birrell, the new Chief Secretary, introduced the Irish Council Bill in the Commons on 7 May 1907. This provided for a Council of 82 elected and 24 nominated members with responsibility for Local Government, Agricultural and Technical Instruction, Congested Districts, Elementary and Intermediate Education, Reformatory and Industrial Schools and the Registrar-General's Office, with a £ 5 million annual grant from the UK Treasury to finance such responsibilities.

The Bill was initially accepted somewhat reluctantly by the Irish Parliamentary Party (Irish Nationalist MPs) at Westminster, including their Leader, John Redmond, although T.P. O'Connor was much more enthusiastic. However, the Bill made no progress as it was unanimously rejected by an Irish National Convention in Dublin during the Whitsun recess, given that it offered neither as much as Gladstone's Home Rule Bills nor the Dual Monarchy approach then favoured by the new Sinn Fein movement (founded in 1905 by Arthur Griffith) nor the aspirations of the semi-secret Irish Republican Brotherhood and also by reason of priestly

---

[373] The 4th Earl of Minto was a cousin of Bertrand Russell, 3rd Earl Russell, who was the father of Conrad Russell, 5th Earl who sat in the House of Lords as a Liberal/Liberal Democrat from 1987 until his death in 2004.

opposition to secular control of Irish Schools. Redmond himself moved the hostile resolution, saying that further scrutiny of the Bill's provisions had convinced him that it was not the way forward. His party was now in the position that any further appearance of compromising in relation to the fuller Irish demands would be fatal electorally as would be the case some eleven years later. (MPs elected in Ireland at the 1918 General Election were the now republican Sinn Fein 73, Unionist 26, Nationalist 6)

Next, an Irish Evicted Tenants Bill was introduced on 27 June, providing for compensation for some two thousand dispossessed tenants or their resettlement on good land purchased by compulsion if necessary. Although passed in the Commons, it was destroyed by amendments in the Lords resulting in a walk-out by the Irish Nationalists when the Bill returned to the Commons and was withdrawn by the Chief Secretary.

The last attempt to move forward towards Home Rule in Sir Henry's lifetime was in early 1908 when John Redmond and others drafted a motion which they hoped the Prime Minister himself would propose in the Commons. Given Sir Henry's illness, they had to communicate via Augustine Birrell, Chief Secretary for Ireland, with the reply on 27 January being that, before he and his colleagues could support such an approach, the motion must not give any indication of legislation in the present Parliament or of support for an <u>independent</u> Irish Parliament. The wording of a motion was then agreed with the intention being that, when the motion was debated in the Commons, Sir Henry would wind up the debate, speaking strongly in favour of the motion. However, he was unable to appear in the Commons or leave 10 Downing Street after 12 February, although that day he did speak to Redmond, with such being his last conversation on Ireland. Perhaps, the timing of the acceptance by the Irish Parliamentary leadership of the step-by-step approach was fatal in that it depended on one man who, when they accepted it in late 1905, had not much more than two years to live.

Thus, when the motion was eventually debated on 30 March, John Redmond, in proposing, said, 'At this moment when everybody, political friend and foe alike, are watching with strained anxiety by his [the Prime Minister's] bedside, it a sincere gratification to me to be able to say that it will never be forgotten by Ireland that no stress of circumstances induced him to lower the Home Rule flag...' The motion read –

> That the present system of government in Ireland is in opposition to the will of the Irish people, and gives them no voice in the management of their own affairs; that the system is consequently inefficient and extravagantly costly; that it does not enjoy the confidence of any section of the population; that it is productive of universal discontent and unrest, and is incapable of satisfactorily promoting the material and intellectual progress of the people; that the reform of Irish government is a matter vital to the interests of Ireland, and calculated greatly to promote the well-being of the people of Great Britain; and, in the opinion of this House, the solution of this problem can only be obtained

by giving to the Irish people the legislative and executive control of all purely Irish affairs.

The long debate – the last on Ireland in the Commons in Sir Henry's lifetime – concluded, after midnight, with two divisions. A Unionist amendment – effectively a direct negative – was defeated by 334 votes to 142. The main question, amended to add the words, 'subject to the supreme authority of the Imperial Parliament' – with that amendment having been moved by John Simon (Liberal) – was then agreed by 313 votes to 159.

1910-1948

So Sir Henry left the Irish problem unsolved. He did not live to see the events of 1910-1922. In 1910, the loss of the overall Liberal majority in the Commons and thus Asquith's dependence on Irish Nationalist votes. In 1912, the Lords' rejection of the third Irish Home Rule Bill which nevertheless, by reason of the 1911 Parliament Act, was enacted in 1914, although immediately suspended on the outbreak of the First World War. The agitation in Ulster, spurred on by the Unionists, Bonar Law and Edward Carson leading to the formation and arming of the Ulster Volunteers from 1912 followed, in the south, by the formation and arming of the Irish Volunteers from 1913. In 1916, the Easter Rising led by the Irish Republican Brotherhood, followed by the take-over of Sinn Fein by Republicans under the leadership of Eamon de Valera and the withdrawal of the Irish Parliamentary Party from Westminster in response to the possibility of the imposition of conscription in Ireland.

The virtual wipe-out of the Irish Parliamentary Party at Westminster by Sinn Fein at the 1918 General Election. The partition of Ireland in terms of the 1920 Government of Ireland Act, The bloodshed of 1919-1921, the Irish Free State Treaty of December 1921, the civil war of 1922-1923, the Irish Free State's declaration of independence in 1937, its neutrality during the Second World War and its adoption of a republican constitution and departure from the Commonwealth in 1948.

Scotland

As already mentioned (Chapter 11), Sir Henry was personally responsible, on 12 April 1907, for seeing through the new procedural rules in the Commons which, *inter alia,* resulted in the creation of the Scottish Grand Committee which had powers to take the Committee Stage of all exclusively Scottish Bills.

Otherwise, Scottish affairs in 1905-1908 benefited greatly from the close association of the Scottish Secretary, John (Jack) Sinclair with Sir Henry. However, Sinclair never got on too well with Asquith. So much so that he was translated to the Lords – which he thought was a branch of the Tory Party – as Lord Pentland in 1909 and the axe fell when he was appointed Governor of Madras in 1912, receiving the Freedom of the City and Royal Burgh of Edinburgh before his departure for India. (As considered in Chapter 2, as Sir Henry's literary executor, Sinclair edited and published a volume of the Prime Minister's early letters – with extracts from such being published in the *Glasgow High School Magazine* of June 1948)

Sinclair's tenure at the Scottish Office started with some non-contentious but enduring reforms. In 1906, the Education of Defective Children, the Fatal Accident and Sudden Death Inquiry, the Statute Law Revision and the National Galleries Acts. Thus, for example, School Boards were required to provide for handicapped children and the National Galleries in Edinburgh were provided with additional funding and a Board of Trustees, with a new School of Art being also built in the Capital. There were six Scottish Acts in 1907 – a Public Health Amendment Act, two Fisheries Acts, a Vaccination Act, a Sheriff Courts Act and the Qualification of Women (County and Borough Councils) Act, which gave widows and unmarried women ratepayers the right of election to such local authorities.

An Education (Scotland) Bill was introduced in 1907 and enacted in 1908. This provided for medical supervision and school meals, centralised educational finances, improved teacher training, remuneration, security of tenure and pensions, increased financial provision for the schools inspectorate, for the Scottish Universities, Technical, Agricultural and Art Colleges, with provision also for optional further education for school leavers up to the age of 17. In that timespan, Sinclair was also responsible for the 1908 Local Government (Scotland) Act which transferred greater housing powers to the Local Government Board for Scotland.

However, the Scottish Small Landholders Bill which Sinclair first introduced on 28 July 1906 (at the end of a Saturday afternoon session in the Commons) was much more contentious, very much depending for progress on Sir Henry's enthusiastic personal support, given that he had been committed to land reform since his 1868 campaigns in Stirling Burghs.

Further, in his first public speech as Prime Minister, in the Albert Hall in December 1905, he had said, 'We desire to give the farmer greater freedom and greater security, to secure a home and a career for the labourer. We desire to make the land less of a pleasure ground for the rich and more of a treasure home for the nation'.[374]

The Bill, which was drafted after deputations had been sent to examine small landholding tenure in Denmark, Canada and Australia, also reflected Sinclair's alarm at rural depopulation, believing that the exodus to the cities required radical action. The intention was to extend the provisions of the 1886 Crofters Act from the Highlands and Islands to the Lowlands, with the creation of a new Board of Agriculture to handle the creation of new holdings and a Land Court to deal with disputes and, if necessary, to take land by compulsory purchase The first (1906) attempt to legislate made no progress and Sinclair had to try again in March 1907.

The basic difficulty was that the provision for compulsory purchase had aroused the wrath of the landed gentry as well represented in the both the Commons and Lords,

---

[374] *The Times*, 22 December 1905

with even opposition in the Cabinet from Lords Elgin and Tweedmouth. However, the 1907 Bill, having spent 23 days in the Scottish Grand Committee and nine days on the floor of the House, was eventually passed by the Commons. Thereafter, given the extent of hostility in the Lords, including such from the increasingly reactionary Lord Rosebery who made a very personal attack on Sinclair, the Bill was withdrawn on 22 August (1907).

In the last speech of his life, in the Commons on 12 February 1908, Sir Henry outlined a new timetable for the Bill (and for the Land Values [Scotland] Bill which had also been blocked in the Lords), stating that it was an issue of who controlled Scottish affairs – Scotland's Liberal MPs or Peers and a small section of the Commons. The Bill was again passed in the Commons (with three Scottish Liberal MPs voting against) but rejected in the Lords (by 153 votes to 33) on 11 March (1908). Thus, with Sir Henry's resignation and death in the following month, the Bill went into limbo until after the passage of the 1911 Parliament Act.

Sinclair (now Lord Pentland) introduced the Bill for the fourth and last time in November 1911 and, after some minor concession, it was grudgingly passed by the Lords on 14 December, with Pentland being one of the peers who announced the Royal Assent to the Small Landholders (Scotland) Act two days later. The institution of the new Board of Agriculture for Scotland and the Scottish Land Court followed in 1912. Within three years, some 500 new holdings were created and nearly another 300 enlarged.

However, the Board of Agriculture for Scotland, as such, was abolished by the 1928 Reorganisation of Offices (Scotland) Act – thus ending, by reason of lack of funding and cumbersome administration, Sinclair's radical experiment in land reform in the Scottish lowlands. Nevertheless, the Scottish Land Court continues to do good work, with its Chairman now having the status of a Senator of the Scottish College of Justice.

Throughout the 1906-1908 period, Sinclair's land reforms were also opposed by Sir Reginald MacLeod, Permanent Under-Secretary at the Scottish Office, so much so that he resigned and eventually unsuccessfully contested the Inverness-shire county constituency as a Conservative at the December 1910 General Election. The Land Values (Scotland) Bill was dropped by Asquith in late 1908 but was incorporated in Lloyd George's 1909 Budget.

In late 1906, Sir Henry had to settle a dispute between two of his personal friends – Sinclair (as Scottish Secretary) and Thomas Shaw (as Lord Advocate) – as to who was responsible for submitting names for appointment as judges in Scotland. The Prime Minister's decision was that 'the Lord Advocate will recommend and the Secretary for Scotland will submit'.[375]

---

[375] Torrance (2006), p.65

(It is of interest to note that, as Secretary for Scotland, Sinclair was responsible for the exercise of the prerogative of mercy in Scotland, Thus, in mid-1909, he commuted the death sentence passed for murder on Oscar Slater to life imprisonment, following a petition organised by the trial judge. This was just as well as, in 1928 – that is, after the creation of the Scottish Court of Criminal Appeal in 1927 – the conviction was squashed and Slater [who died in 1948 aged 76] received compensation of £ 6,000 from which he had to pay all his considerable legal expenses. It was also just as well that in these former days the exercise of the prerogative of mercy was not subject to political or media or international challenges.)

The 1906 Trade Disputes and Workmen's Compensation Acts

It had been thought that the Liberal Trade Union and Criminal Law Amendment Acts of 1871 had given trade unions a legal status with protection of their funds and had also removed the threat of prosecution for unions engaged in peaceful picketing during industrial disputes. However, this presumption had been challenged by a series of court judgements, culminating in a 1901 decision of the House of Lords (acting judicially) in *Taff Vale Railway Company v Amalgamated Society of Railway Servants* which effectively ruled that unions could be sued for damages caused by the actions of their officials during industrial disputes. When the new Liberal Cabinet discussed the matter in early 1906, a minority, including Sir Henry and John Burns wanted a bill to be introduced stating that unions could not be sued for damages whereas the majority in the Cabinet, led by Asquith and the other lawyers, thought that such an approach would make the unions too powerful.

Accordingly, a Bill was introduced in the Commons on 28 March (1906) which, while relaxing the law of conspiracy and legalising peaceful picketing, did not go as far as to give union funds complete protection in the context of industrial disputes. The trade unionist reaction was that the Bill left a wide opening for litigation and so Walter Hudson (Labour MP for Newcastle-on-Tyne in 1906-1918 and President of the Amalgamated Society of Railway Servants in 1891-1899) introduced a Private Members' Bill along the lines for which the Prime Minister had argued in Cabinet. This alternative Bill was denounced by the Attorney-General but Sir Henry intervened later in the Second Reading debate to say that capital and labour should be placed in a position of equality so that any fight between them should be a fair one and that, accordingly, he would vote for Hudson's Bill.[376] So, at a stroke, he had thrown over the Bill introduced by his own Ministers. Asquith and his associates in the Cabinet continued to argue for their own Bill but, in August, the Cabinet accepted the alternative. Thus, given also the then apparent policy of the Unionists, not to antagonise organised Labour, a revised Government Bill proceeded to enactment and the trade unions received a privileged status which they were to retain for sixty-five years.

In the passage of the Workmen's Compensation Act, Sir Henry intervened in December (1906) in much the same way as he had done in the Trade Disputes debate. The Government's Bill was intended to extend and consolidate the provisions of the 1897 Act which only applied to workers in the railways, mining, quarrying, factories and laundries. The intention in 1906 was to extend the right to compensation on the mere occurrence of an accident or work-related illness to any person working by way of manual labour, clerical or otherwise under a contract of employment or apprenticeship, expressed or implied. However, the original Bill excluded domestic servants – then comprising a very significant percentage of the labour force – with

---

[376] *The Times,* 31 March 1906

the Ministers seeing through the legislation resisting their inclusion until the Report Stage debate on 5 December.

An amendment to include domestic servants had been tabled, with Labour leadership and Liberal and Unionist backbench support. Sir Henry then entered the Chamber, listened to four speeches in favour of the amendment and then stood up and, without consulting any colleague, accepted the amendment on behalf of the Government. Thus the amended Bill was enacted, again without significant Unionist opposition.

Sir Henry's habit of forming his own strong opinions and acting upon them, without hesitation, usually with the assured support of the Liberal back-benchers, stood him in good stead and, as in the above two cases, his Cabinet colleagues nearly always accepted his instincts were right even when expressed in such circumstances.

Social and Other Domestic Policy

Sir Henry's Government had early legislative success in 1906 with the enactment of a bill to allow local authorities in England and Wales to provide school meals for needy children, although not until 1914 were such made compulsory and, in the following year (1907), legislation was enacted providing for the medical supervision of school children. As already mentioned, there was similar legislation for Scotland.

Also in 1906 there were the Merchant Shipping Act, introduced by Lloyd George as President of the Board of Trade, which regulated standards of food and accommodation on UK registered ships and a Prevention of Corruption Act, providing penalties for inducements (bribery) in commercial transactions and the falsification of accounts, receipts and other documents.

In 1907 there were the Qualification of Women (County and Borough Councils) Act for England and Wales (in line with the already mentioned similar legislation for Scotland), and a Companies Act which updated company law and introduced the distinction between public and private companies.

Sir Henry's Government was also responsible for the Probation of Offenders Act which was passed on 21 August 1907 and which extended throughout the UK. Its principal innovation was to provide judges with the option of releasing an offender on probation as an alternative to a criminal conviction and associated punishments.

Further, a Deceased Wife's Sister's Marriage Bill was finally passed in 1907, with thus the success of the campaign which Henry had consistently supported in Parliament since 1871 (Chapter 4). Also as concerning family law, the Matrimonial Causes Act was passed in 1907, consolidating and enhancing earlier legislation relating to maintenance payments to separated and divorced women.

The 1908 Mines Eight Hours Act had its precursor in the eight hour working day which Sir Henry had introduced in the ordnance factory at Woolwich and in the Army Clothing Department when Secretary of State for War in 1892-1895.

Although the Old Age Pensions Act did not receive the royal assent until 1 August 1908, with implementation from 1 January 1909, this beginning of the UK's welfare state or society was initiated during Sir Henry's tenure as Prime Minister. [377] In December 1906 the Cabinet considered and approved a Treasury memorandum centred on a limited non-contributory means-tested pension scheme for the elderly poor, to be funded from general taxation, noting that none of the Government's other social initiatives involved significant central government funding although the school health and welfare initiatives did involve charges on ratepayers.

Accordingly, in preparing his 1907 Budget, Asquith, as Chancellor of the Exchequer, had to begin to provide for such Treasury funding, with that Budget anticipating pensions' legislation in 1908. Drafting of the actual details of the Pensions Bill was delegated to Reginald McKenna (President of the Board of Education), supported by Asquith and John Burns (President of the Local Government Board) with the Treasury placing a strict annual limit of £ 3 million on the cost of the scheme, as provided for in the 1908 Budget. Asquith, having prepared that Budget as Chancellor of the Exchequer, now, as Prime Minister, presented it in the Commons as Lloyd George (now Chancellor of the Exchequer) had not yet taken over full Treasury responsibilities.

However, it was Lloyd George who introduced the Pensions Bill in the Commons, rather hesitantly and apologetically, and ever after received personal credit for a scheme approved in outline by Sir Henry's Cabinet in December 1906 and with the financial implications and details worked-out by Asquith, McKenna and Burns. There was no real challenge to the Bill in the Commons, with the most interesting division being at the Third Reading stage. The official Unionist line was to abstain but twelve Unionists voted with the Government and eleven against, being joined by Harold Cox, a Liberal who objected to the Bill on extreme Free Trade or laissez faire grounds. He left the Liberal Party two years later when he was de-selected by his constituency association [Preston], by reason of his opposition to Liberal social policies, thus ending his parliamentary career. A number of amendments to the Bill were proposed in the Lords but rejected when the Bill returned to the Commons, with the Lords then letting the Bill pass without any further real trouble. In debate in the Lords, although he did not vote against, Rosebery described the Bill as 'Socialism pure and simple' and suggested that 'it is the beginning of a long progress which will culminate in the handing over of the hospitals to the state'.

(In the drafting and implementing of legislation the input of 'backroom boys' is often overlooked. Accordingly, mention should be made of Sir William Sutherland, who like Sir Henry had attended Glasgow High School and University. Later in Lloyd George's Coalition Cabinet as Chancellor of the Duchy of Lancaster for a few months in 1922, as a Civil Servant he had assisted in drafting and implementing the 1908 Old Age Pensions Act and the 1911 National Insurance Act. He also assisted

---

[377] Refer to Pat Thane on 'The Old Age Pensions Act 1908' in *Journal of Liberal History*, (Autumn 2008)

John Sinclair, Lord Pentland in drafting the 1911 Small Landholders [Scotland] Act.)

Foreign Affairs and Defence

> Now, consider France, the old hereditary enemy! Your hereditary enemy it may be, but not mine. I am too true a son of Caledonia to have anything but gratitude and affection for the ancient ally of my country.

(Sir Henry Campbell-Bannerman, Leeds, 19 March 1903)

Given such a commitment, it is of interest to note, with comments, what a French academic – Professor Henry Contamine of the University of Caen – wrote about Sir Henry, as published in the *Glasgow High School Magazine* of June 1948 (pp.90-92)

> Several British statesmen, who have been Prime Minister, hold hardly any place in the History of France, neither for good or ill – and it is better to regard one of them as an enemy, for example Pitt, than to have no regard for them at all, since it is through the long mingling of our pasts, once hostile, the United Kingdom and my country have become inseparable friends. And so it is that east of the Channel we speak of Peel and Disraeli only as foreigners or Europeans.
>
> Such is not the case with Sir Henry Campbell-Bannerman. And this is extraordinary, for if it is natural for a Scot to have been a friend of France, it is curious that a man, who was only the host in Downing Street for two years, and was already in his seventies, should be linked to our national history.
>
> It is the fact that he came to power at the right moment – or rather the bad moment, since posterity remembers the moments of anguish, which bring the nations together in a common bond, more than the peaceful periods which distance them in the daily course of small interests.
>
> So let's recall this drama in miniature, prelude to other dramas, bloody and boundless. In April 1904, London and Paris settled their old colonial differences [in the Entente Cordiale]. Since then, people talked generally of the 'Entente Cordiale', and Berlin became alarmed, which puts into practice the old saying: 'divide [and] rule'. In 1905, the Kaiser and his Chancellor, Bülow threatened France that its ally, Russia could not hold out any longer in an effective way, conquered as she [Russia] was in the Far East and shaken by revolution.

This refers to the defeat of Russia in its war with Japan from February 1904 to the Peace Treaty of August 1905 and to the internal disruptions in Russia from mid-1904 which led to the Tsar [Nicholas II] granting Russia its first constitution and the opening of the First Duma [Parliament] in April 1906.

> But London remained loyally behind Paris, and with even more energy than the French ministers wanted. By this attitude, British diplomacy avoided the forging of a great continental and anti-English [sic] coalition, which tradition is found from Napoleon to William II [the Kaiser] and again from William II to Adolf Hitler. For an isolated France would have fallen into the German trap, in 1905, thus delivering the continent and herself to the hegemony of a single [power].
>
> But in the course of this crisis, the pretext of which was Morocco, there was a Conservative Cabinet, that of Arthur Balfour [Prime Minister] and Lord Lansdowne [Foreign Secretary]. [Thereafter] worn out by [10] years in office and having lost the confidence of most of the electorate, [the Conservatives] resigned in December [1905] and the 1906 Election saw the triumph of the Liberal Party under the leadership of Sir Henry Campbell-Bannerman.

This refers to the situation in 1905-1906 when there was a dispute between France and Germany over their interests in Morocco and when France had to depend on the support of the UK. Although the French Foreign Minister Delcassé was forced to resign, the matter was temporarily settled, in favour of France, at an international conference at Algeceras [in southern Spain] by April 1906 when the new UK Liberal Government was in office.

> CB did not follow the advice of those who, knowing him to be of mediocre health, suggested a semi-retirement to the House of Lords, which would leave the main responsibility for affairs to Asquith. As a tenacious and courageous Scot, he knew that, in the 20th Century, the leader's place is in the [House of] Commons. There he was to become exhausted but he had given his friends the necessary impetus.
>
> In the matter of foreign policy, having understood France, its fundamental moderation and its democratic ideal, he greatly helped the Foreign Secretary, Sir Edward Grey, to continue the way towards friendly rapprochement started by the Conservatives under the high aegis of the King. His [influence] was not small, because there were in the victorious party men of influence who did not know France as well as he [Campbell-Bannerman] did, and who wrongly saw there a source of corruption and ambition, and others, such as Lord Rosebery, who retained numerous illusions about Germany.

When the Franco-British Agreement – The *Entente Cordiale* – had been concluded in 1904, Rosebery's was almost the only voice raised in opposition in the UK and he was generally accused of Germanophilism.

> So the Entente Cordiale survived the change in the majority at Westminster. Soon it even assumed a sort of ideological aspect, between the two democracies, one a monarchy which retains some

aristocratic traits, the other republican but comfortably fond of the 'Royals' forty years ago as it is today. Through it a European equilibrium has been saved, the essential value of which Great Britain has always been the herald.

At the cost of a great war, alas! But one may wonder whether in 1914 the strength and realism of Sir Henry Campbell-Bannerman, who died in 1908 were not lacking in the two nations who from being friends were to become allies. The goodwill of Premier Asquith and Sir Edward [Grey] was certainly as great as their loyalty. But were they sufficiently inspired by the example which CB had given them when in 1906, understanding that good diplomacy may also have possibilities of military action, he had [authorised] by his own high authority the first major [military staff] talks between Paris and London, held in absolute secrecy and contrary to a certain British formalism?

However that may be the history of France does not forget that if five magnificent divisions from the other side of the Channel contributed to saving our capital in 1914, it was greatly thanks to the first act of boldness of the great Scotsman of whom the High School of Glasgow is justly proud. The same spirit would have avoided many of the weaknesses between 1918 and 1939.

This refers to the Franco-British military staff talks in 1906, knowledge of which in the UK, beyond those directly involved (including the UK Military Attaché in Paris) was limited to the King, five members of the Cabinet (Prime Minister, Chancellor of the Exchequer, Foreign Secretary, Secretary for War and the Lord Privy Seal), the Parliamentary Under-Secretary at the War Office and a few senior civil servants such as the Permanent Under-Secretary at the War Office and the UK Ambassador in Paris. Accordingly, when Sir Henry saw M. Clemenceau, privately in Paris on 9 April 1907, the French Prime Minister said that, as from the staff talks, he assumed that the UK was now virtually committed to coming to the aid of France if and when she became involved in war with Germany. He then received a rude shock when Sir Henry replied that the UK was not in any way committed to taking part in a continental war on the side of France. Indeed, when the UK declared war in 1914, it was not by reason of any binding prior commitment to France but by reason of the German invasion of Belgium.

The Admiralty and War Office

Proposals to reduce the naval building programme were announced in the Commons on 27 July 1906, with the plans which the new Government had inherited to be reduced by one Dreadnought battleship, three destroyers and four submarines. It was also emphasised that the Board of Admiralty was satisfied that such savings of £ 1.5 million would not impair the UK's naval supremacy. Further, progress with one of the other three Dreadnoughts in the construction programme left by their Unionist predecessors was to be reviewed in the light of the outcome of the Second Hague Peace Conference called for mid-1907.

Inevitably, there were protests from the Unionists in support of the two-power standard which had operated since 1889, that the Royal Navy must always be larger than the fleets of the next two powers combined. Sir Henry responded by challenging the necessity for such a two-power UK naval standard by asking who were these powers? Were France and Germany, then the two other major naval powers, likely to be allied against the UK?

He also pointed out that, until 1909, when the UK would have four, no other country would have a single Dreadnought and that it was necessary for the UK to set an example with disarmament progress which, with its naval supremacy, it could do more easily than other powers.

At this time the UK was spending annually on the Royal Navy just over £ 30 million – that is, more than double the annual German naval budget, despite Germany building an average of just under three pre-Dreadnought battleships a year. In the March of the following year (1907), there was a further reduction of just under half-a-million pounds in the UK's Naval Estimates. In February 1908 there was a major row in the Cabinet, with a proposal for a significant increase in the Naval Estimates being opposed by Lloyd George, Morley, Burns and Louis Harcourt. So Sir Henry, who presided at his last eight Cabinet meetings between 21 January and 12 February, had to decide that the proposed increase in the Naval Estimates be reduced by almost half.

Haldane, at the War Office, continued the series of major Army reforms started by Caldwell with also Sir Henry's own contributions in 1871-1874, 1880-1882, 1886 and 1892-1895 and, as Haldane himself wrote to Sir Henry in early April 1908, 'None of your Cabinet has more real cause to be grateful to you. In a task of great magnitude and difficulty you trusted and helped through… Without your strong hand and guidance and complete sympathy my effort for you would have been a hopeless one.'(CB/BL)

Sir Henry was, of course, well aware that annual Army expenditure under the Unionists had increased from £ 18 million in 1895 to almost £ 37 million in 1904 and, while not for economy at any price, had appointed his friend Tom Buchanan as Financial Secretary to make sure that Haldane did not run wild' financially. However, by-and-large, Haldane's Army reforms were fully supported by the Prime Minister. One major doubt was the continuation of the Committee of Imperial Defence (as set up by Balfour in late 1902) which Sir Henry thought might challenge Cabinet and Ministerial responsibilities However, he accepted it as a *fait accompli* and chaired and worked with it, although there were not so many meetings as in 1903-1905.

After consulting the King, senior Army officers and Balfour (as Leader of the Unionist Opposition), Haldane circulated a draft Territorial and Reserve Forces Bill in late 1906, also ensuring that the Bill would be included in the Government's legislative programme for 1907. He then presented the definitive Bill in the Commons on 4 March, with it being debated from late March onwards. After attracting only un-coordinated opposition in the Commons and Lords, it received the Royal Assent in August, with full implementation from 1 April 1908.

Thus Sir Henry's support secured the creation of a striking force of some 160,000 regulars in six infantry divisions and a cavalry division – the basis of the Expeditionary Force of 1914 – with, in second line, fourteen territorial divisions. Balfour had personally opposed the creation of the striking force as ineffective against continental armies but this did not stop him writing to Haldane in 1914 demanding that the Expeditionary Force be mobilised and embarked, thus ditching the notion that the defence of the UK and the fulfilment of its international obligations were only safe in Conservative hands.

Since 1871 Sir Henry had been involved, off-and-on, in military affairs and Army reforms. 'Now, at the end of his life, he was leaving the War Office in good hands and the Army in a state of high efficiency. In less than seven years after his death it was to face, in 1914, its greatest and most terrible challenge'.[378]

The Second Hague Peace Conference of 1907

This International Conference was called for mid-1907, on the initiative of the US President, Theodore Roosevelt, in order to update and extend the Conventions agreed at the First Hague Conference in 1899, with particular reference to arbitration (as a peaceful way of settling disputes), the collection of debts, the rules of war (with a focus on naval and balloon warfare), the rights and obligations of neutrals and, hopefully, the limitation of armaments generally. The Conference, which met from 15 June to 18 October, was not a success in that while agreement was reached on many of the items on the agenda, the UK failed to secure agreement on armament limitation as Germany thought it was basically a UK attempt to stop the expansion of the German Navy. Germany also blocked proposals for compulsory rather than voluntary arbitration.

Sir Henry was very much concerned about European competition in armaments and had hoped that the Hague Conference would take a bold initiative for their reduction. Thus, after discussion with the Foreign Secretary, he took the initiative in writing an article headed 'The Hague Conference and The Limitation of Armaments – By the Prime Minister' for the first number of the new Liberal weekly, *The Nation* on 2 March (1907), of which some extracts follow –

> The disposition shown by certain powers, of whom [the UK] is one, to raise the question of the limitation of armaments at the approaching Hague Conference, has evoked some objections both at home and abroad, on the ground that such action will be ill-timed, inconvenient

---

[378] Wilson (1973), p.236

and mischievous. I wish to indicate... my reasons for holding these objections to be baseless.

We have already given earnest of our sincerity by the considerable reductions which have been effected in our naval and military expenditure, as well as the undertaking that we are prepared to go further if we find a similar disposition in other quarters. Our delegates, therefore, will not go into the conference empty-handed. It has, however, been suggested that our example will count for nothing as our preponderant naval position will still remain unimpaired. I do not believe it.

Our known adhesion to those two dominant principles – the independence of nationalities and the freedom of trade – entitles us of itself to claim that, if our fleets be invulnerable, they carry with them no menace across the waters of the world, but a message of the most cordial goodwill, based on a belief in a community of interests between the nations.[379]

However, within two months, the German Chancellor Prince Bülow announced in the Reichstag on 30 April that Germany would refuse to discuss disarmament at the Hague Conference. Accordingly, Sir Henry replied, on 10 May in a speech in Manchester, concluding –

We sought to carry out, we still seek to carry out, the policy advocated by Mr. Disraeli, after the Crimean War when he said, 'Let us terminate the disastrous system of rival expenditure, and mutually agree... to show by a reduction in armaments that peace is really our policy'. Prince Bülow and the German Government appear to believe that such a method is delusive, and so they recognise that they can have no share in it...[380]

With meaningful discussion of armament reduction having been removed from the Conference agenda, it was impossible for the UK Cabinet to discover any major role for its delegates. All they could manage to secure was the allocation of a day at the end of the Conference for an academic discussion on armament reduction when a meaningless resolution was passed, in the absence of the German delegates, declaring that such was desirable. A final decision provided that the next Peace Conference should take place in 1916 but that had to wait until 1919 (at Versailles). The Kaiser, in all his years of abdicated exile in the Netherlands, may have come to regret that Germany had declined the UK Prime Minister's initiatives on compulsory arbitration and armament reduction in 1907 and persisted in its preparations for war.

---

[379] The full text is given in Spender (1923), Volume 2, pp.328-330

[380] The full text is given in Spender (1923), Volume 2, pp.331-332

The UK delegation at the Conference was somewhat cosmopolitan. It was led by the 11th [Scottish] Lord Reay [1839-1921], Chief of Clan MacKay, who was a Dutch citizen until 1877 when he was naturalised as a UK citizen. He was created a UK Peer in 1881, and served as Governor of Bombay in 1885-1890 and Liberal Under-Secretary for India in 1894-1895. The other UK delegates included Sir Ernest Satow [1843-1929], a scholar, diplomat and Japanologist, whose German father had been naturalised as a UK citizen in 1846 and Sir Eyre Crowe [1864-192]), who served in the Foreign Office from 1885 until dying as Permanent Under-Secretary in 1925. His mother and wife were both German.

The House of Lords

More than anything else it was the opposition of vested interests and the associated disputes with the House of Lords which sapped the legislative vitality of Sir Henry's administration. Every Liberal Prime Minister had problems with the Lords and its inbuilt Conservative majority. However, particularly after the accession of Liberal Unionist peers, after the Liberal Irish Home Rule split in 1886, the vetoing of Gladstone's Second Irish Home Rule Bill in 1893 and again, after the Liberal General Election victory in early 1906, the Lords had come to take an unashamedly party stance in blocking most radical legislation, either by a direct veto or by wrecking amendments. Thus in 1906 they also killed the Education Bill for England and Wales and the (abolition of) Plural Voting Bill.

(The intention of this Bill was to introduce 'one man one vote', The University constituencies and business votes were not to be abolished. Instead, the Bill provided that electors entitled to more than one vote could only use one such vote)

As considered above, in 1907 and 1908 they caused the Government to withdraw Scottish land reform and land valuation legislation. After Sir Henry's resignation and death in April 1908, the Lords refused to give the Licensing Bill a second reading in November 1908, with all such obstruction culminating in the unprecedented rejection of a Budget (Lloyd George's) on 30 November 1909 and the resulting constitutional crisis.

As considered in earlier chapters – particularly, Chapter 8 about what he wrote and said in Dunfermline and Stirling and at Balmoral in 1894 – before becoming Prime Minister, Sir Henry had for long called for action to reduce the powers of the House of Lords.

However, as Prime Minister, he came face-to-face with the problem. Thus, when the Lords killed the Education Bill for England and Wales on 19 December 1906, he set up a Cabinet Committee, chaired by Lord Loreburn (Lord Chancellor). The Committee's report suggested that differences between the Lords and Commons be resolved at joint sittings of a delegation of 100 peers and all the MPs. The Prime Minister did not like this at all and, accordingly, circulated a long memorandum to all his colleagues on 31 May 1907. The Committee's plan was dismissed as too artificial and complicated, etc., etc. and, in any case, an assembly of 770 would be unmanageable with the plan also requiring any future Liberal Government to have a working majority of, say, 70 in the Commons. Instead, he suggested a version of a suspensory veto, concluding 'What is essential is that the power of overriding the Lords should be available as a last resort. If such a power existed the Lords would, except for dealing with a shaky Government or towards the close of a Parliament, nearly always give way at an earlier stage'.[381]

Another plan which had some support at this time was to submit Bills held up by the Lords to a referendum but this was rejected by the Cabinet as being contrary to the concept of parliamentary democracy and also in that if the Lords could thus force a referendum they would be given another weapon to use against a Liberal Government. Sir Edward Grey suggested an all-elected House of Lords but this was rejected in that such would challenge the Commons' democratic supremacy.

After a long debate, the Cabinet found common ground in supporting what Sir Henry had advocated in his memorandum. Thus, it was planned that the Prime Minister would propose a resolution in the Commons on Monday, 24 June in anticipation of legislation in the following year (1908). He had been due to be at Windsor that weekend but was released from that duty but nevertheless had to attend a Royal Garden Party for the King of Siam on the Saturday. Then, early on the Sunday he had a heart attack but quickly pulled himself together and determined to go ahead with his speech which he delivered on the Monday, with Arthur Ponsonby, with medication in a dispatch box, ready to defy all House rules if the attack was renewed.[382] All went well and there followed an animated and often stormy debate which lasted three days with the wording of the resolution, as carried by 432 votes to 147, being –

> In order to give effect to the will of the people, as expressed by their elected representatives, the power of the other House to alter or reject Bills, passed by this House must be restricted by law as to secure that within the limits of a single Parliament, the final decisions of the House of Commons shall prevail.

Sir Henry was fated not to take part in any further acts in the drama of Lords versus Commons but he had thus contributed decisively to the shaping of the 1911 Parliament Act. Indeed, the only major difference between what he had proposed in 1907 and what was enacted in 1911 was that he had not contemplated that, as in 1909, the Lords would interfere with a Budget/Money Bill.

---

[381] As quoted in Spender (1923), Volume 2, pp.351-355

[382] It was not so much that Ponsonby intended to administer medicine in the House but that, if Sir Henry had a heart attack while on the front bench, he (Ponsonby) intended to go directly to Sir Henry rather than follow protocol. Why Ponsonby didn't have a word with the Speaker beforehand and/or arrange for the close attention of a medically-qualified MP, was probably to avoid Sir Henry's heart attack becoming public knowledge.

14 – 1907-1908 – Final Illness, Resignation and Death

Beginning in late 1906, Sir Henry suffered a series of heart attacks which culminated in his death within 19 months. The first occurred at Belmont on 2 October, shortly after Charlotte's death. He recovered rapidly from this first one, as he did from the second on Sunday, 23 June 1907, after a Royal Garden Party for the King of Siam on the Saturday. He was back in the Commons on the Monday to move a successful motion on curbing the powers of the House of Lords.[383]

A fortnight later (7 July), he spoke at the National Liberal Club in London on a range of subjects including the Government's electoral mandate to keep intact the doctrine of Free Trade.[384] Then, after stays at Belmont and Balmoral in the late summer and early autumn, there were visits to Montrose, Peebles, Edinburgh (twice) and Dunfermline.

There followed a period of intense and exhausting activity in London and at Windsor in November. On the 12th, following a Cabinet meeting in London, he went to Windsor for a long audience with the King and a State Banquet and Reception for the Kaiser. On that occasion, he had to stand for more than two hours and was unable to retire to bed until nearly midnight. (Lord Ripon was so exhausted at the Reception that he lay on a table and got Mrs. Buxton, the wife of the Postmaster-General, to spread her skirt in front of him.)

However, next morning, Sir Henry was up and at breakfast by 7.30 a.m. and then attended to State business at the Castle before returning to London. He was kept busy at 10 Downing Street until it was time to go to the Guildhall to attend another Banquet for the Kaiser. There he had to remain standing for an hour before the Kaiser arrived. He was not able to leave the Guildhall until about 3.30 p.m. when he went back to 10 Downing Street to change and then left immediately for Paddington and a train to Bristol.

At Bristol, he spoke – as it transpired, his last public speech – at the annual Colson Banquet where he had to contend with interruptions from shrieking suffragettes. Although the memory of Edward Colston (1636-1721), a Bristol-born MP, merchant and philanthropist, was commemorated annually by Tories/Conservatives and Whigs/Liberals alike, this was essentially a party political speech on the eve of a Unionist gathering in Birmingham. Sir Henry referred to Arthur Balfour travelling to make his submission to Joseph Chamberlain and emerging 'as an honest protectionist – positive, settled, full-blooded and aggressive'. Then, after attacking the House of Lords, he concluded –

---

[383] *The Times,* 25 June 1907

[384] *The Times,* 8 July 1907

[This is] a country with the will and capacity to move quietly and steadily forward along the path of social reform towards a fairer and more enlightened common life free from the disgrace of the existence of unnecessary and unmerited misery and poverty.[385]

Returning exhausted to the home of his host, Sir William Howell Davies – Liberal MP for Bristol South – he nevertheless insisted on joining the company in the billiard-room. He socialised for a while, particularly with the young people present. He then went to bed and suffered another heart attack.

Fortunately, the son of his host was up late and heard noises – the ringing of a bell and/or groans – from the bedroom. Until a doctor arrived Sir Henry seemed to be hovering between life and death. However, he rallied during the night and by the morning was able to give instructions as to whom to break the news.

Unlike the earlier heart attacks this third one immediately became public knowledge. The newspapers were full of it. The King expressed his concern. 10 Downing Street was bombarded with inquiries. The Post Office had to send a specialist from London to ensure that the telephone system in Bristol could cope. The patient found himself the centre of a storm of solicitude.

However, after three days in bed, he was able to return to London, where he presided at Cabinet meetings on 18, 19, 25 and 26 November. He was, however, far from well and the medical advice was that he should go abroad immediately and take a rest for at least six weeks. He asked his London doctor, Robert Burnet – who was also a personal friend – how long he might expect to live. The reply was that if he lived restfully and gave up public duties, he might live for six or seven years; but if he remained in public life, he would live no more than two. Sir Henry concluded, "Then I'll remain where I am".[386]

On 27 November, Sir Henry left for Paris en route to Biarritz, accompanied by his Principal Private Secretary, Arthur Ponsonby. On arrival in Paris, he went out shopping for an hour or two and then dined at Foyot's. Then he had his fourth heart attack, in the Hotel Quai d'Orsay, in the early hours next morning. Ponsonby telegraphed Dr. Burnet and Mrs Alice Campbell – his niece by marriage and hostess since his wife's death – asking them to come out to Paris which they did. The medical verdict was that the Prime Minister had cardiac asthma, caused by overstrain and digestive derangement. This time the collapse did not become public knowledge, although a dinner with the French statesman, Léon Bourgeois had to be cancelled. Instead, M. Bourgeois was seen later when he called at the Hotel.

Léon Bourgeois [1851-1925] had led the French delegation at the previous year's Second Hague Peace Conference. In 1920 he was first President of the Council of the League of Nations and was awarded the Nobel Peace Prize.

---

[385] *The Times*, 14 November 1907

[386] *Stirling Observer*, 29 April 1908

However, on 2 December Sir Henry was able to leave with the others for Biarritz, where they were joined by Mrs Campbell's son, Hugh. Dr. Burnet returned to London on 6 December followed by Ponsonby on 20 December. Vaughan Nash arrived on 30 December to replace Ponsonby and, in the following month (January), succeeded him as Principal Private Secretary. Ponsonby had resigned by reason of his wife's ill-health, though he was politically active again within three months and she was to outlive him by some 17 years. Hubert Montgomery of the Foreign Office succeeded Nash as an Assistant Private Secretary.

The weather at Biarritz was not to Sir Henry's liking and, being out of season, he missed the cosmopolitan company he enjoyed at Marienbad. However, he enjoyed the company of Sir Gilbert Parker – Unionist MP for Gravesend – who was staying in the same hotel and with whom he had socialised at Marienbad. He also enjoyed visits from the local Church of England chaplain, Canon Fish – who went on to become the Archdeacon of Bath – with talk about Gladstone and discussions on Isaiah. There was even a good-going argument between the Canon and Hugh Campbell about the nationality of J.H. Taylor, then the temporary Biarritz golf professional. The question was believed to have been settled by a King's Messenger, who happened to be present, in favour of the Canon's assertion that Mr Taylor was a Yorkshireman.

In fact, John H. Taylor [1871-1963] was a native of Devon. He won the Open Championship five times between 1894 and 1913 and was non-playing captain of the winning UK Ryder Cup team in 1933.

On another occasion, speaking knowingly of how trying it was for those with weak hearts to stand at State functions, Sir Henry concluded, "You know that Lord Lansdowne says Providence has given royalties a special static muscle'.[387] There was also a brief excursion into Spain, travelling by motor car.

At Biarritz, where he usually stayed in bed until noon, he was attended by a Dr. Malpas who gave him carbolic baths. Although everything possible was done to relieve him of work and responsibilities, he continued to attend to telegrams and other correspondence, with King's Messengers arriving with letters and dispatches at least once a week. Nevertheless, he was now dictating letters to Nash instead of writing them himself. However, by mid-January, he seemed to have recovered much of his old buoyancy and energy, and no argument could persuade him not to return to London.

So on 16 January he went back to Paris, staying at the Metropolitan, a quiet hotel near the UK Embassy. While there, he had visits from the British Ambassador, various French statesmen, including Prime Minister Clemenceau, and John A Spender – one of Sir Henry's future biographers and then editor of the *Westminster Gazette* – and his wife.

---

[387] Spender (1923), Volume 2, pp.373-376

When the Spenders had lunch with him, they found him much distressed by the news of the death of Sir Lawson Walton, Liberal MP for South Leeds and Attorney-General since December 1905. He was also upset by the loss of the Ashburton (Devon) by-election, saying it would give encouragement to the House of Lords in its efforts to wreck the Government and how hopeless would be his task if the Liberal tide ebbed in the country.[388] (The By-Election result on 17 January 1908 was reversed at the January 1910 General Election.)

After four days in Paris, he returned to London, where he chaired eight meetings of the Cabinet over the following three weeks. Among the main topics of discussion were Ireland, the Transvaal, India, the Naval Estimates, a row between the Governor of Jamaica and a US Admiral and the progress of some Scottish Bills. At the start of these meetings he led the discussions briskly, but after an hour or so he showed signs of extreme fatigue. He attended his last dinner party on 22 January 1908, but was unable to travel to Windsor to see the King two days later and missed the opening of Parliament on 29 January. (There may have been a quick trip to Scotland at this time to see his brother, James Alexander who was ill – as it transpired, terminally ill – at Stracathro.)

However, he was back in the Commons on 4 February to move a vote of condolence on the assassination of the King and Crown Prince of Portugal, when he spoke strongly and clearly and had a very good reception. During the next week, when he did see the King, at Buckingham Palace (when the King advised him to take care of himself), he was present at Questions in the Commons and otherwise active with Cabinet and other business.

On 12 February, Sir Henry presided at his last Cabinet meeting and attended the House of Commons for the last time. There he spoke at length in moving a new procedural motion for the Small Landholders (Scotland) and Land Values (Scotland) Bills which the House of Lords had previously blocked. In his speech he also took the opportunity to refer to the resolution on reform of the relationship between the two Houses which he had successfully moved on 24 June 1907. (*The Times* noted afterwards that Gladstone's last speech in the Commons [in 1894] had also referred to the relationship between the Lords and Commons.)

> [This is an innovation in that] This is the first time, I believe, in the history of this House that Bills have been sent up a second time to the House of Lords within the lifetime of a single Parliament. But so was the Resolution passed by this House last year an innovation. Why should the House of Lords be able, when it chooses, to put this House to all the trouble and annoyance and sacrifice of useless, dilatory and superfluous debate on a matter so recently debated.

---

[388] Spender (1923), Volume 2, p.376

Then, after a conversation with the Irish Nationalist Leader, John Redmond, about an Irish Home Rule motion on which he intended to speak, he returned to Downing Street. That evening he was very unwell, with influenza being diagnosed, followed by another heart attack. He was thereafter confined to his bedroom in 10 Downing Street for the rest of his life.

During these last days he was attended by Mrs. Alice Campbell, Vaughan Nash, Dr. Robert Burnet and other doctors (including the King's physician, Sir Thomas Barlow), with two nurses also being in attendance. Otherwise, visits were restricted, although he was visited more than once by the Archbishop of Canterbury. Exceptions were also made for such colleagues and friends as Asquith, Lord Loreburn, John Morley, Lord Ripon, John Sinclair, Lewis Harcourt, Tom Buchanan, Arthur Ponsonby and Henry Higgs. He also received messages and flowers from Queen Alexandra.

His resignation as Prime Minister was delayed by the King's arrangements for a holiday at Biarritz. Before departing, when the King saw Sir Henry in Downing Street on 4 March, he discouraged a resignation before early May. This was followed by two messages from Biarritz also discouraging an early resignation. Nevertheless, the King had also seen Asquith on 4 March and had arranged that, if a change of Prime Minister did became necessary while he (the King) was away, Asquith would come out at once to see him at Biarritz.[389]

However, later in March, Sir Henry himself not only realised that there was absolutely no hope of a return to public life but was also under no delusion as to the approach of death. Indeed, Margot Asquith later recalled what his husband had told her after his last visit to see Sir Henry on 27 March.

> Henry [Asquith] came into my room at 7.30 p.m. and told me that Sir Henry Campbell-Bannerman had sent for him that day to tell him that he was dying... He was resigned and even cheerful, but after a while, with his strong immovability, he turned the subject deliberately on to material things, flimsy matters – such as patronage, titles and bishops, etc. Henry [Asquith] was deeply moved when he went on to tell me that Campbell-Bannerman had thanked him for being such a wonderful colleague. 'So loyal, so disinterested and so able'.[390]

Then, on 30 March, Sir Henry dictated a farewell letter to his constituents in Stirling Burghs – 'What do I not owe you all for loyalty, energy, courage and kindness. God bless you all'. (CB/BL) This was not sent by Vaughan Nash until after Sir Henry's death, to the Party officials in the Constituency and then published in the local newspapers. Two days later, on 1 April, Sir Henry dictated a letter to the King at Biarritz asking permission to resign without further delay.

---

[389] Spender and Asquith (1932), Volume 1, p.195

[390] Margot Asquith (1962), p.247

The King telegraphed on 3 April saying that under the circumstances he had no alternative but to accept Sir Henry's resignation. The King also wrote a personal letter to Sir Henry,

<u>Biarritz, April 3, 1908</u>

My dear Sir Henry – It is with sincere regret that I learn from your letter of 1st inst that it is your intention to place your resignation of the important and arduous post of Prime Minister in my hands. Though I reluctantly agree to your wishes, I fully understand that the present state of your health renders it absolutely necessary that you should avoid all strains of the great amount of work that your high office entails upon you.

I cannot conclude this letter without expressing my sincere regret that the intercourse we have had with one another ever since you became Prime Minister is at an end, as it has always been a great pleasure and satisfaction to me to do business with you at all times. Most sincerely do I hope that now you have ceased to bear the heavy responsibility of your office, your health may daily improve and that you may look forward to some years of quiet and comfort. –

Believe me, My dear Sir Henry, Yours very sincerely. EDWARD R [391]

Accordingly, Sir Henry dictated and signed a letter resigning as Prime Minister later on Friday, 3 April. The courier reaching the King at Biarritz on the Saturday evening – hence Sunday's Court Circular as reported from Biarritz by Reuters during the afternoon and announced from 10 Downing Street just after 8.00 p.m.

<u>Court Circular (Biarritz), 5 April 1908</u>

His Majesty The King has received a letter from the Rt. Hon. Sir Henry Campbell-Bannerman, MP in which, on the urgent recommendation of his medical advisers, he tenders to His Majesty his resignation as Prime Minister and First Lord of the Treasury. The King has received Sir Henry Campbell-Bannerman's communication with much regret, and has graciously accepted his resignation

The King had also written to Asquith on 4 April, calling on him to form a government and asking him to come out to Biarritz. Asquith spent the rest of the weekend interviewing colleagues and preparing a revised list of Ministers to be submitted to the King. To what extent Sir Henry was aware of the Cabinet and other ministerial changes is unknown, although it is known that he was pleased to hear that Asquith intended to keep on Vaughan Nash as a Private Secretary.

---

[391] Spender (1923), Volume 2, p.389

However, if he had known, the dying Sir Henry would certainly not have approved of the way in which Asquith dismissed the Earl of Elgin as Colonial Secretary and thus abruptly ended his long and distinguished public career As the Earl complained, 'Even a housemaid gets better warning'.[392]

Table 26 - Cabinet - Changes in April 1908	
Prime Minister First Lord of The Treasury and Leader of the House of Commons	Sir Henry Campbell-Bannerman replaced by Herbert Henry Asquith
Chancellor of the Exchequer	Herbert Henry Asquith replaced by David Lloyd George,
President of the Council	Robert Offley Ashley Crewe-Milnes, 1st Earl of Crewe replaced by Edward Marjoribanks, 2nd Lord Tweedmouth
Colonial Secretary	Victor Alexander Bruce, 9th (Scottish) Earl of Elgin, etc. replaced by Robert Offley Ashley Crewe-Milnes, 1st Earl of Crewe
First Lord of the Admiralty	Edward Marjoribanks, 2nd Lord Tweedmouth replaced by Reginald McKenna
President of the Board of Trade	David Lloyd George replaced by Winston Spencer Churchill
President, Board of Education	Reginald McKenna replaced by Walter Runciman

When the House of Commons reassembled on Monday, 6 April, brief tributes to Sir Henry were paid by Asquith for the Government and the Liberal Party, by Balfour for the Unionists and by Redmond for the Irish Nationalists. Also on 6 April, brief tributes to Sir Henry were paid in the House of Lords, by Lord Ripon for the Liberal Peers and Lord Lansdowne for the Unionist Peers. Asquith then departed for Biarritz to receive the King's commission as Prime Minister.

On returning to London on 10 April, Asquith and his wife, who had met him at Charing Cross Station, drove immediately to 10 Downing Street. Margot Asquith later recalled that late evening visit.

> I waited outside, while Henry went inside to enquire after Campbell-Bannerman. The street was empty, and but for the footfall of the few policemen there was not a sound to be heard. I looked at the dingy exterior of No. 10 and wondered how long we would live there. [They moved in on 5 May, two weeks after Sir Henry's death, and lived there until December 1916]... The door opened and the Archbishop came out [with] the doctor [Sir Thomas Barlow] going in... and as I reflected on the dying Prime Minister I could only hope that no sound had reached him of the crowd that had cheered his successor.[393]

---

[392] As quoted in Sheldon (2013), p.178

[393] Margot Asquith (1962), pp.248-249

The news of Sir Henry's resignation as Prime Minister was received with much regret but also with understanding in his constituency. As from the *Dunfermline Press* of 11 April, unaware that Sir Henry had been dissuaded by the King from resigning much earlier, 'It is understood that there has been no return of heart seizure or any nervous breakdown. His condition, though, is still grave. Any attempt to return to his old anxieties and fatigues would be attended by the most severe risk. Even if he should so far recover from his malady, as to be able to make the attempt, the Right Honourable gentleman definitely determined that the unsatisfactory situation of having a nominal chief who was ineffective for all practical purposes should not extend over the Easter holidays. That is why he has now yielded up the office he could no longer fill with satisfaction to himself'.

On returning from Biarritz, en route to Denmark, the King himself called but could not be admitted to the sick-room. By now Sir Henry was suffering from breathlessness, for which oxygen was prescribed, and having long periods of drowsiness and wandering.

After a period of unconsciousness, and another heart attack at 9.00.a.m on Wednesday, 22 April, Sir Henry died (aged 71) 15 minutes later. Mrs. Alice Campbell and Dr. Burnet were at his bedside. Vaughan Nash was then told and he immediately communicated the sad news to the King (who was in Copenhagen), the Prime Minister (Asquith) and other members of the Royal Family and Cabinet. An hour later the official public bulletin was issued by Dr. Burnet.
> Sir Henry Campbell-Bannerman passed away peacefully at 9.15 this morning. The cause of death was heart failure.
> (Signed) R. W. Burnet, MD

Later on the Wednesday, it was announced that there would be Memorial Services in Westminster Abbey and Glasgow Cathedral on Monday, 27 April followed, next day, by his burial, in accordance with his earnestly expressed wish, alongside his wife, beside Meigle Parish Church. [394]

Also that Wednesday afternoon Dr. Burnet gave an interview to a representative of the Press Association. During the interview it was confirmed that Sir Henry had never recovered from the death of his wife, and that 'he was a most plucky patient… always pleasant and never complained [and] bore up with the greatest fortitude'.[395]

The citizens of Dunfermline, Stirling, Culross, Inverkeithing and South Queensferry, on hearing of their MP's resignation as Prime Minister, hoped against hope that having been relieved of the burdens and anxieties of the Premiership he

---

[394] Much of this account of the events of 22 to 28 April 1908 is based on reports in *The Glasgow Herald, The Scotsman* and the Stirling and Dunfermline newspapers between 23 April and 1 May 1908.

[395] *The Glasgow Herald,* 23 April 1908

would be spared for a few years to continue as their Member. Thus the shock later on the Wednesday when, for example, Dunfermline Abbey's one set slow bell made known that the hope had been disappointed and that all were summoned to 'tread softly and speak low'. In Stirling the town bell was tolled, the Liberal Club closed and the Unionist Club's flag lowered to half-mast.

By 7.00 a.m. on the day of the Westminster Abbey Service, the short route from 10 Downing Street to the Abbey was thickly lined with people with the numbers growing until the coffin in an open hearse and carriages for the chief mourners, mainly family, left for the Abbey at about 11.30 a.m. All Government and Parliamentary buildings were flying their flags at half-mast as also many other buildings in the West End.

The Westminster Abbey Service, starting at 12 noon, including praise, prayer and scripture readings, was conducted by the Archbishop of Canterbury assisted by the Dean of Westminster. Prince George, (the future King George V) represented the King and M. Clemenceau, the French Prime Minister represented the Auld Alliance, the Entente Cordiale and the French President. Other members of our Royal Family, the Kaiser and the Kings of Denmark and Norway were also represented. Only two wreaths were brought in on the coffin, one from the Rt. Hon James Alexander Campbell, (Sir Henry's elder brother) and one from Mrs. Alice Campbell.

Prince George then came forward and placed the wreath from the King and Queen and his own wreath beside the coffin, followed by M. Clemenceau who placed the wreath from the French President and the German Ambassador who placed the Kaiser's wreath. The wreath from King Edward and Queen Alexandra was then placed between the two family wreaths on the coffin.

The pall-bearers were the Archbishop, Asquith (now Prime Minister), Lord Loreburn (Lord Chancellor), James Lowther, MP (The Speaker), the Duke of Fife (the King's son-in-law), the Earl of Aberdeen (Lord Lieutenant of Ireland), Lord Tweedmouth (now Lord President of the Council), John Morley, MP (Secretary for India), Herbert Gladstone, MP (Home Secretary), John Sinclair, MP (Secretary for Scotland), Walter Long, MP (for the Unionists) and Thomas Burt, MP (representing the Liberal back-benchers).

All the other members of the old and new Cabinets were present together with most of the junior ministers and other MPs, many members of the House of Lords and the Diplomatic Corps, representatives of the Dominions, clergy from all denominations, representative Liberals from all over the UK and members of the general public.

The next day Arthur Ponsonby wrote to his wife: 'I heard cackling and pushing behind us and there were the inevitable advertisers Winston Churchill and Lloyd George who had come late on purpose so as to attract attention. I told them to stand back.' [396]

---

[396] As quoted in Wilson (1973), p.631

After the Benediction the principal mourners and Prince George followed the coffin down the nave to the door and remained there until the coffin was placed in the waiting hearse. The procession, in which Prince George took part as far as Trafalgar Square, passed from the Abbey to Euston Station for the train north to take Sir Henry to Alyth Junction, Belmont and Meigle for the last time. The streets from the Abbey to the Station were lined with dense crowds, flags were at half-mast and, despite the heavy rain, the drivers of cabs and buses, stopped at the side of the streets, removed their caps as a sign of affection and respect.

At much the same time as the Westminster Abbey Service, another Memorial Service was held in Glasgow Cathedral with, in attendance, some eighteen of Sir Henry's Glasgow-based relatives. The Congregation also included the Lord Provost and other members of the Town Council and representatives of the Merchants' House, the Trades' House, the Clyde Navigation Trust, the Chamber of Commerce, the Glasgow and Govan School Boards, the University, the Consular Corps, the Liberal, Conservative and Liberal Unionist Parties, the Faculty of Physicians and Surgeons, the Faculty of Procurators, the Judiciary and the Army.

After the Westminster Abbey Service, the House of Commons met briefly to hear further tributes to Sir Henry by Asquith (as Prime Minister and Liberal Leader), by Akers-Douglas, the former Unionist Home Secretary (as Balfour was absent by reason of illness), by T.P. O'Connor for the Irish Nationalists (with John Redmond being absent), by Sir Alfred Thomas for the Welsh MPs and by Arthur Henderson for the Labour Party.

> Extracts – Mr. Asquith, Prime Minister and First Lord of the Treasury
> It is within a few months of forty years since Sir Henry Campbell-Bannerman took his seat in this Chamber. A new House, elected on an extended suffrage, had brought to Westminster new men, new ideas. Among the newcomers there were probably few who seemed less obviously destined than [the then] Mr. Campbell for ultimate leadership. There have been men who were universally judged to be fit for the highest place only until they attained and held it. Our late Prime Minister belonged to that rarer class whose fitness for such a place, until they attain and held it, is never adequately understood.
>
> But though he had too modest an estimate of himself to desire, and still less to seek, the first place in the State, it fell to him, after years of much storm and stress by a title which no one disputed; and he filled it with an ever-growing recognition in all quarters of his unique qualifications. In politics he may be may be fairly described as an idealist in aim, and an optimist by temperament. He was not ashamed to see visions and dream dreams. He has gone to his rest, and to-day in this House of which he was the senior and most honoured member, we may call a truce in the strife of parties while we remember our common loss and pay our united homage to a gracious and cherished memory.

Extracts – Mr. Akers-Douglas, Kent, St. Augustine's

We on this side of the House cannot but admire the determination and courage with which he [Sir Henry] stuck to his political convictions, never flinched from opinions because they might be unpopular, and never failed during the gloomiest period of his Party's fortunes. We often had occasion to admire his conduct, tact and resource, while we have appreciated to the full, although we have sometimes been disconcerted by, his wit and shrewdness.

By his removal a long and honourable career has been brought to an end; the public life of this country thereby is far poorer, while this House has suffered a loss from which it will not readily or quickly recover, a loss which has been felt by his political opponents as much as by his political friends.

Extracts – Mr. T.P. O'Connor, Liverpool, Scotland

Sir Henry Campbell-Bannerman boasted rightly that he was not only a Scot, but a Scot of Scots. We Irishmen feel that he had a love for our country and for our cause as though he was [also] one of us. We honoured and loved him and regret his death as one of the greatest and heaviest loses that our people and our country ever sustained.

Sir Alfred Thomas, Glamorgan, East

I beg on behalf of the Welsh Members to express the profound regret with which we heard of the passing away of the late Prime Minister. As one who keenly sympathised with small nationalities we are under a lasting debt of gratitude to his memory. His life was a noble example of a high-minded Christian gentleman. We can all say, as John Bright said of Cobden, 'I little knew how much I loved him until I found I had lost him'.

Extract – Mr. Arthur Henderson, Durham, Barnard Castle

We are the youngest Party in this House, and yet we have been here during the whole time the late Prime Minister presided over our Parliamentary destinies. His readiness sympathetically to consider the views of my colleagues and myself endeared him in an unmistakeable way to every member of the Labour Party. Nowhere is his loss more keenly felt than in the ranks of the Parliamentary Labour Party.

On same day, Arthur Balfour sent a most gracious letter to Asquith, of which some extracts follow –

> It is with the deepest concern that I find myself prevented by illness from taking any part in the tribute which the House of Commons will pay to the late Prime Minister... Greatly should I have valued the

opportunity of expressing on my own behalf, and on behalf of my friends, our high esteem for the departed statesman... It would, I think, be safe to say that he never served in any office without gaining and keeping the affections of his subordinates, that he never served in any Government but with an unswerving loyalty to the general interests, and that, after a long apprenticeship in office and in opposition, in sunshine and shade, he rose to the highest position under the Crown, all men felt that courage, consistency, high ideals, kindliness which never fell into weakness, shrewdness that never fell into malice, had received their fit reward.[397]

The special train (seven coaches) which took the coffin north, via Carlisle, Carstairs and Larbert, reached Alyth Junction at about 1.35 a.m. (Tuesday, 28 April). There were lights in many of the houses in the neighbourhood indicating that many of Sir Henry's neighbours had been waiting up to be at Alyth Junction or on the road to Belmont. (It was learned that at most of the stations on the way from London groups of people had gathered on the platforms to pay their last respects.)

Among those waiting at Alyth Junction was John Yeaman, Sir Henry's local factor who was also the local Agent for the Royal Bank of Scotland. Among the passengers on the train were Mrs. Alice Campbell and other Campbell relatives, some Government Ministers, Arthur Ponsonby and Vaughan Nash and Sir Henry's solicitors in London and Glasgow. Sir Henry's brother, James Alexander Campbell was terminally ill at Stracathro where he was being nursed by his unmarried daughter, Miss Elsie Louisa Campbell.

The coffin was removed from the train by some of Sir Henry's estate staff and the stationmaster and his staff and placed on the hearse which then proceeded to Belmont. There followed two large vans, with the wreaths which had been brought from London (Westminster Abbey and 10 Downing Street), and carriages with the passengers from the train. On arriving at Belmont the coffin and the London wreaths were placed in the Castle in the midst of some four hundred other wreaths which had already arrived at Belmont. Such included wreaths from the staff at Belmont, the people of Meigle, the teachers and pupils of Meigle School, other friends from all over Scotland, Princess Louise, Duchess of Argyll and other members of our Royal Family, the King and Queen of Norway, Canada and the Transvaal and Orange River Colonies.

There were also wreaths from members of the Government, other members of the Lords and Commons including the Unionist Whips, the Lord Provost and Corporation of Glasgow, the Scottish Liberal Association, the Scottish Woman's Liberal Federation, the Liberal Agents' Association, Glasgow Liberal Council, and Liberal Associations, Women's Liberal Associations and Young Scots Branches from all over Scotland, Cheltenham Liberal Association, the Scottish Liberal Club (Edinburgh) and the Glasgow and Dunfermline Liberal Clubs.

---

[397] *Stirling Journal (and Advertiser),* 1 May 1908

Later in the morning mourners were arriving from all over Scotland and beyond to join those in Meigle and district in paying their last respects to Sir Henry, with two special trains having been arranged. Then in the early afternoon a short service was held at Belmont mainly for Sir Henry's relatives and those public representatives who had been unable to attend a Memorial Service in London or Glasgow on the Monday. Between two and three hundred mourners crowded into the Castle with more than another seven hundred or so standing outside on the lawn.

The Service was conducted by the Rev. Hugh Climie (Parish Minister of Meigle, 1897-1948) and the Rev. Peter Maltman of Meigle United Free Church. Mr. Climie read Psalm 90 and some shorter scriptural passages, Mr. Maltman read 1 Corinthians 15:30-58, concluding with a short prayer/benediction by Mr. Climie.

During the service the coffin and some of the wreaths were moved by estate staff and others to a lorry, which had been partly reconstructed and painted and draped in black, drawn by two black horses. The other wreaths were moved to two carriages. After the service the cortege – with also a closed carriage for Mrs. Alice Campbell, her son, Hugh Campbell and two of Sir Henry's nieces, Mrs. Nora Jane Adamson of Careston and Mrs. Hilda Sophia Hunter of Dunmore – proceeded to the Parish Church. The thousand or so other mourners who had been at Belmont followed on foot – with some walking in front of, or beside the coffin – being joined en route by another thousand or so, with many others lining the route.

At the Church the coffin and wreaths were removed from the lorry and carriages and taken up to the Church by Belmont estate staff. The pall-bearers taking the coffin to the grave were the Lord Provosts of Edinburgh, Glasgow, Dundee and Perth, the Provosts of Stirling and Dunfermline, Sir John Kinloch of Kinloch and William Tasker, one of Sir Henry's tenants. Meanwhile the bells of the Parish Churches of Meigle, Alyth and Coupar-Angus were being tolled, all the blinds of the houses in the neighbourhood were drawn down and all local businesses and the School were closed for the afternoon.

The very short service at the graveside, conducted by the Rev. Hugh Climie, was centred on the reading of Collects (short prayers) for funeral services in the *Euchologion, A Book of Common Order*. By reason of the large number of people present (over 3,000), arrangements at the graveside were apparently other than what was originally planned

The *Euchologion* was originally published in 1867 by the Church Service Society as formed by a number of Ministers and Elders of the Church of Scotland in 1865. Mr. Climie must have been somewhat of a liturgical progressive as the General Assembly did not authorise a modern *Book of Common Order* until that published in 1940.

The pall-bearers at the grave were Hugh Campbell (Sir Henry's great-nephew), James Campbell-Bannerman (nephew), Shaw Adamson of Careston Castle (nephew-in-law), William Adamson (great-nephew), Matthew Pearce Campbell of

Glasgow (son of a cousin), Sir Henry Peto, Bt of Cheddington, Somerset (representing Sir Henry's sister-in-law's family), Lord Tweedmouth (now Lord President of the Council) and John Sinclair, MP for Forfarshire (Secretary for Scotland).

The mourners also included Parish and United Free Ministers from neighbouring Parishes (including Kettins), five very senior employees (each with over 50 years' service) of J. & W. Campbell (the family business in Glasgow), Liberal MPs for Midlothian, West Lothian, Leith Burghs, West Fife, Edinburgh Central, Kincardineshire, Paisley, Dumfries Burghs and West Perthshire. There were also other civic representatives from the Burghs of Alyth, Coupar-Angus, Hawick, Kirriemuir, Montrose and Tayport.

Organisations represented included the Scottish Liberal Association, and the Scottish Women's Liberal Federation, led by Lady Marjorie Sinclair, the wife of the Secretary for Scotland. Lady Marjorie Sinclair's father, the Earl of Aberdeen (Lord Lieutenant of Ireland) had to return to Ireland after the Memorial Service in London. He was represented in Meigle on 28 April by Lord Haddo, his heir, Lady Marjorie's brother.

The Countess of Aberdeen, a sister of Lord Tweedmouth, had been President of the London-based Women's Liberal Federation at the time of the 1906 General Election and, as by then Marchioness of Aberdeen and Tremair, was still active politically in North-East Scotland at the time of the 1929 General Election. The Earl of Elgin (no longer Colonial Secretary) and Thomas Shaw (Lord Advocate) were also unable to be present, being represented by the Earl's heir, Lord Bruce and John Lamb, Advocate.

The representatives of the Scottish Liberal Association (later Federation and then Party) of which Sir Henry had been President since 1900, included Dr. Robert Farquharson, as a former Chairman and William Webster, then Joint Secretary who, in retirement, some forty years later would write about Sir Henry in the *Glasgow High School Magazine* of June 1948.

Also represented were the Edinburgh United Liberal Committee, Glasgow Liberal Council, the Liberal Associations of Stirling, Dunfermline, South Queensferry, Alyth, Arbroath, Dundee, Edinburgh South and West (including Dr. J.E. Parrot, later a Liberal MP), Hawick and Wilton, Midlothian, Peebles, Perth, Perthshire East and West and Stirlingshire, the Scottish Liberal Club, Edinburgh (Thomas Gibson, Vice-Chairman), Glasgow Liberal Club, the Eighty Club, London (of which Sir Henry had been President),[398] the Guildry Incorporation of Stirling (of which Sir Henry had been an Honorary Member), the Town Councils of Culross, Inverkeithing and South Queensferry, Stirling Working Men's Association and the Scottish League for the Taxation of Land Values.

---

[398] Refer to Chapter 7

Another future MP present was (Sir) James Duncan Miller who was Liberal MP for St. Andrews Burghs briefly in 1910 and for North-East Lanarkshire in 1911-1918. He then represented East Fife as a Liberal in 1922-1924 and 1929-1931 and as a Liberal National in 1931-1932. His son, Major Ian A. Duncan Miller was Liberal Candidate for Kinross and West Perthshire at the 1950 General Election and at the 1963 By-Election.

On the day of the funeral, in many other Scottish towns and cities, flags were flown at half-mast on public buildings, political (Liberal and Unionist) and other clubs and some commercial premises, with the tolling of bells and the closing of many shops and offices at the time of the funeral. Memorial Services were also held in a number of other towns including Stirling, Dunfermline, Falkirk and Inverness, on the Tuesday. Flags on Government buildings in South Africa flew at half-mast for two days.

The following Sunday, Morning Worship in St. Columba's Scots Kirk in London was conducted by the Rev. Dr. Archibald Fleming, from whose sermon some extracts follow –

> The late Sir Henry Campbell-Bannerman was not a member of this congregation [He was a member of Meigle Parish Church] but he was deeply interested in its welfare. His elder brother, Mr. J.A. Campbell is one of the most venerated members of our Kirk Session, It is therefore appropriate that we should express our deepest sympathy with Mr, Campbell and with his family at this time of trial, especially as his own illness has been so severe and so prolonged…
>
> But, [of the late Prime Minister] I wish to tell you today of that which I have before me, and am permitted to use, his last letters and messages addressed to those nearest and dearest to him, at a time when he was under no delusions as to the near approach of death.
>
> And I am glad to tell you that his one solace and support in these testing hours was in the religious faith which was his heritage from his forefathers in the land of his birth. It was his 'only refuge' and he was 'perfectly resigned to whatever God had willed for him, and had faith in His [God's] tender mercy'… You will notice that there is nothing metaphysical or abstract about [these words]; they are simple and direct like the man himself, and they constitute a testimony to the sustaining value of an unsophisticated, but deep rooted, religious faith, which, in the view of those who knew and loved him, ought not to be withheld. In these 'merciful hands' – in the keeping of that 'tender mercy' – we leave him now.
>
> This only would I add – the Church of our fathers – the Church of Scotland, had a firm hold in his regard. One of his latest good deeds was to subscribe liberally to the rebuilding of our church at Crown Court [Covent Garden], and I have before me a letter, written last June [1907]

in which he wrote 'I am attached by very dear associations to the Church of Scotland'.

Just because these are the words of a man with whom it was a habit not to say more than he meant, we value this loyal tribute of regard from one of the eminent sons of our national Church,[399]

Life's race well run. Life's work well done. Life's victory won. Now cometh rest.

The House of Lords did not meet to pay tribute to Sir Henry until 5 May when the Earl of Crewe (now Colonial Secretary) spoke for the Liberal Peers and the Marquis of Lansdowne, a Liberal Unionist, for the Unionist Peers. Lansdowne took the opportunity to recall that, before he became a Liberal Unionist, he and Sir Henry had been close colleagues when both held junior office at the War Office in 1872-1874. Thirteen days later (on 18 May) the House of Lords agreed, *nemine dissentience,* to a motion by Lord Tweedmouth, that the following Address be presented to the King.

> That an humble Address be presented to His Majesty praying that His Majesty will give directions that a memorial be erected in the Collegiate Church of St, Peter, Westminster [Westminster Abbey], to the memory of Sir Henry Campbell-Bannerman, with an inscription expressive of the high sense entertained by this House of the eminent service rendered by him to the country in Parliament and in grist offices of State, and to assure His Majesty that this House will concur in giving effect to His Majesty's directions.

Such a memorial was' in due course, erected on 29 December 1911 and unveiled on 12 January 1912. (Refer to Appendix 5)

On 9 May 1908 – seventeen days after Sir Henry's death – his brother, the Rt. Hon. James Alexander Campbell died at Stracathro, leaving Stracathro to his grandson, Hugh Campbell. Obituaries for both brothers appeared in the *Glasgow High School Magazine* of June 1908.

> Extract from Obituary in the *Glasgow High School Magazine*, June 1908
>
> Among his [Sir Henry's] predecessors there have been none more beloved by his own party, or more esteemed by his opponents, or more kindly regarded throughout the country by men of all shades of political opinion. By all he was looked upon as a man of pure character and high motives.

---

[399] *Stirling Journal (and Advertiser),* 1 May 1908

The *Glasgow High School Magazine* of June 1948 recorded that with Sir Henry having no family, his niece, his brother's last surviving child, Miss Elsie L. Campbell was then living in Sussex. It is otherwise recorded that she had continued her father's interest in the surviving Church of Scotland Congregations in London. These were and are specifically, Crown Court (dating from 1711, with the present building dating from 1909), in Covent Garden and St. Columba's (dating from 1884, with the present building dating from 1955) in Pont Street, Belgravia.

At the time of his death Sir Henry had been nominated as Liberal Candidate for the Rectorship of Glasgow University 'Had he lived, [he] would probably have triumphed, in virtue of his local connections and personal popularity, over his Tory rival, Lord Curzon'[400] who was elected with Lloyd George having replacing Sir Henry as Liberal Candidate and with Keir Hardie as the Labour Candidate.[401]

Roy Hattersley (2006), p.132 was, of course, in error in stating that "Curzon was so angry [with Sir Henry for not recommending him for an Earldom] that he stood against Sir Henry for Rector of Glasgow University. Sir Henry won. It was his last victory."

As concerning the Liberal candidature for the Stirling Burghs vacancy, Sir Henry had wanted to be succeeded by a local man – specifically, Sir William Robertson of Dunfermline – but this was not to be [402]

The first person to be invited by the local Liberal Associations was Winston Churchill who, on 24 April had lost the Ministerial By-Election in Manchester North-West necessitated by his appointment to the new Liberal Cabinet as President of the Board of Trade.[403] However, he had instead accepted an invitation to contest the by-election in the two-member constituency of Dundee which he duly won on 9 May.

---

[400] Dr. Andrew Browning, Professor of History, University of Glasgow (*Glasgow High School Magazine,* June 1948, p.85).

[401] Torrance (2006), p.136. In the previous year (1907), Curzon had been elected as Chancellor of Oxford University, defeating Rosebery by 1,101 votes to 440 (Rhodes James [1985], p.463).

[402] During the 1910-1911 constitutional crisis. Sir William was on the list of Liberal Peers who would have been created if matters had not been otherwise resolved. In 1918, he was a supporter of the successful Lloyd George Coalition Liberal candidate in the new constituency of Dunfermline Burghs (also including Cowdenbeath, Inverkeithing and Lochgelly).who was opposed by a Labour candidate and by Arthur Ponsonby standing as an Independent. Following Asquith's by-election victory in Paisley in 1920 and the decision of what was now the Scottish Liberal Federation to endorse only Asquith's supporters as official Liberal candidates, Sir William resigned as the Federation's Chairman in opposition to the new policy. (Catriona M.M. Macdonsld [2000], p.242).

[403] *The Glasgow Herald,* 28 April 1908.

Eliot Crawshay-Williams, an unsuccessful Liberal candidate at the 1906 General Election and previously Assistant Private Secretary to Churchill at the Colonial Office, was suggested by the Master of Elibank, then the Government's Scottish Whip, but this was of no interest locally.[404]

However, the Scottish Liberal Association sponsored Arthur Ponsonby, formerly Sir Henry's Principal Private Secretary, and, given this close association with their former MP, this was accepted locally. The candidature was settled on the day of Sir Henry's funeral in Meigle and Ponsonby duly won the by-election on 22 May.

Forty years later, in the *Glasgow High School Magazine* of June 1948 (p.89), Lady Ponsonby wrote that her husband 'was elected by the biggest majority yet recorded. 'My husband did not attribute this to his own personality but regarded it as the highest compliment the constituency could pay to its late Member and the principles he stood for'. However, although Ponsonby's vote of 3,873 (against 2,512) was the largest Liberal vote so far in Stirling Burghs, his majority of 1,361 was less than Sir Henry's of 2,774 in 1880.

Sir Henry's Will was published in November (1908). Out of an assessment of £55,000 gross/£38.000 net, the ownership of Belmont was vested in trustees (for the benefit of Mrs, Alice Campbell, with reversion to her son, Hugh), his papers were left to John Sinclair, items worth £50 to Ponsonby, £1,000 to Vaughan Nash, 12 months wages to all his employees with over ten years' service and 6 months wages to his other employees.

Gravestone on the outside wall of Meigle Parish Church
SARAH CHARLOTTE CAMPBELL-BANNERMAN **Daughter of Major-General Sir Charles Bruce, KCB, and for forty-six years Wife and constant companion of Sir Henry Campbell-Bannerman, PC, GCB.MP** Died at Marienbad in Bohemia, on August 30 and was buried here on September 5, 1906 *"La cara moglie che di conforme cor mi ha data il cielo"* **Also by her side, the said** **RIGHT HONOURABLE SIR HENRY CAMPBELL-BANNERMAN, GCB** **Born September 7, 1836 + Died April 22, 1908** He represented the Stirling District of Burghs in Parliament from 1868 to 1908 and during that period held many Offices of State. He was twice Secretary of State for War and finally First Lord of the Treasury and Prime Minister up to

---

[404] Refer to Dr. J.G, Jones on 'Crawshay-Williams' in the *Journal of Liberal History* (Summer 2008). At both the 1910 General Elections in the then two-member constituency of Leicester, Crawshay-Williams was elected as a Liberal in tandem with Ramsay MacDonald (Labour). He was thereafter cited in a successful divorce action, resulting in his resignation as an MP in June 1913.

> within a few days of his death. He was at once Leader and Father of the House of Commons.
>
> *My trust is in the tender mercy of God for ever and ever*

The Italian is from *Gerusalemme Liberata* (Jerusalem Delivered) of 1575 by Torquato Tasso (1544-1595), with Sir Henry himself having substituted *cara* (dear) for Tasso's *antica* (aged). Thus, 'The <u>dear</u> wife who with her heart at one with his had made heaven for him'.

15 – An Appraisal

Rather than refer exclusively on my own views, much of this Chapter is based on what others have said and written about Sir Henry over the years.

Personal Characteristics

[Sir Henry Campbell-Bannerman] is absolutely unspoilt by high office. He wears it like an old well-fitting coat, in the most natural possible wavy – no trace of vanity or conceit, no symptom of affectation.... He is always the same – you can be quite sure of him. He will be certain to make the best of things, and will reject with a perfectly natural abhorrence all meanness and pettiness.

Arthur Ponsonby, Marienbad, August 1906
(Quoted by Lady Ponsonby in the *Glasgow High School Magazine,* June 1948, p.88)

I have never met a great public figure who so completely won the attachment and affection of the men who came in contact with him. He was not merely respected, he was loved by all. The masses of the people of this country, especially the more unfortunate of them, have lost the best friend they ever had in the high places of the land. He was truly a great man. A great head and a great heart. He was absolutely the bravest man I ever met in politics.

David Lloyd George, Manchester, 22 April 1808 (Quoted in *The Glasgow Herald,* 23 April 1908)

I should like to say, as one of the younger men of the Liberal Party, how generous and indulgent he always was. It was only at the end of his life that he emerged into the sunshine – the sunset it was – of popularity, of public affection, to the trust of the House of Commons, and to great political power.

Winston Churchill, Manchester, 22 April 1808 (Quoted in *The Glasgow Herald,* 23 April 1908)

On the day of Sir Henry's death, Lloyd George and Churchill were together in Manchester, where Churchill was contesting his Ministerial By-Election in Manchester North-West which he lost on 24 April.

There was in him a geniality of nature, unfeigned and unforced, a kindliness which permitted, indeed, hard blows to be struck, but was incompatible with rancour and malevolence. Many Prime Ministers have been more admired than Sir Henry Campbell-Bannerman, none has inspired more affection.

Extract from Obituary in *The Times,* 23 April 1908

Such then, was Campbell-Bannerman – a combination of remarkable political gifts with few of the ordinary and besetting weaknesses of the political life; with no disordered ambition, no irritable vanity, no lasting hatreds; brave in adversity, modest in triumph; the plain, honest, kindly man who added lustre to the even mighty position of Prime Minister by the simple virtues which brighten and adorn millions of British homes, and are the best and truest elements of the nation's honour, strength and fame

T.P. O'Connor [1908]. pp.166-167

[Sir Henry's] *courage was of a close-fitting quality that neither public anxiety nor private grief or ill-health could shake. It was sustained, as those who were nearest to him knew best, not only by his stubborn indomitable character and loyalty to his principles, but by a belief in the qualities of his countrymen, so intense and abiding as to enable him to possess his soul against the day when the dust and hubbub subsided and the 'decent, plain folk' were themselves again.*

Vaughan Nash as quoted in Spender [1923], p.410

If there is any man in the recent history of the country who, without claiming any of the heroic virtues, quietly and modestly lived up to them, it was Campbell-Bannerman.

John A. Spender (1923), Volume 2, p.411

He was by no means the simple personality that many people supposed. But of all the men with whom I have been associated in public life, I put him as high as any in both moral and intellectual courage.

Herbert Henry Asquith, *Sunday Times,* 4 November 1923

He was a most loveable man and one who could not but be impressed with the strength and simplicity of his manhood, the loyalty and constancy of his friendship, the sagacity and courage and inspiring power of his leadership. His loyalty to truth, as he saw it, exposed him to an obloquy of unparallel bitterness, but the loveable human being bore it all with bravery and tolerance, with gallantry and a dauntless good humour.

William Webster, *Glasgow High School Magazine,* June 1948, pp.75-74

William Webster, then (1948) retired and living in Corstorphine, Edinburgh, had been employed by the Scottish Liberal Association (later Federation and then Party) for over fifty years, including twenty-eight years as General Secretary. As Joint General Secretary, he attended Sir Henry's funeral at Meigle on 28 April 1908.

Sir Henry Campbell-Bannerman, to all appearances an ordinary man, almost commonplace to a superficial view, but a real man, shrewd and worldly-wise, but rooted in a great faith which inspired a great action. What a wise man, what statesmanship in insight and faith, and what a sure grip on the future, a light which shines like an inextinguishable beacon above the raging storm.

Jan Christiaan Smuts, *Glasgow High School Magazine,* June 1948, p.79

CB had the qualities of shrewd common sense and imperturbable good humour of the canny Scotsman; together with the steadfast grasp of moral principle which belongs to national character at its best. Vividly I remember that stout figure, rounded head, keen eye and kindly half-smiling mouth. He loved his fellow-men, and was happy in serving them.

Viscount Samuel, *Glasgow High School Magazine,* June 1948, p.81

And Sir Henry Campbell-Bannerman had one other quality which should commend him to history. His personal relationships – with his opponents, with his colleagues and, above all, with his wife – show him to have been a good man. That is not an attribute which, when judging politicians, history should overlook.

Roy Hattersley [2006], p.143

Indeed, above all, for forty-six years, Sir Henry's life was centred on his devotion to his wife and her devotion to him. She guarded his interests and her aspirations for his success compensated for his lack of ambition. Indeed, but for her interventions, he would not have accepted the office of Chief Secretary for Ireland in October 1884 and thus acquire, within seven to eight months, a reputation of being more than simply a competent junior minister in the War Office and Admiralty. In December 1905 he might have gone to the House of Lords and become merely a figurehead Prime Minister. Happily she lived long enough to know of, and share in his unparalleled triumph at the 1906 General Election.

It has been said that his unruffled calm was in evidence in good fortune and ill. Was it all his own, or was there a source beyond himself from which he drew an added strength and grace? There surely was. It was the harmony of his home life, the complete co-operation and support of his devoted wife, and it was [a] joy to him that she was spared to see him the most trusted man in the land.

Dr. Charles Duguid, Adelaide, South Australia
Glasgow High School Magazine, June 1948, p.92

Dr. Duguid, who also recalled 'the Khaki Election [1900] and its slanders', left The High School of Glasgow in 1902. After graduating in medicine in Glasgow, he emigrated to Australia where he became a successful campaigner for Aboriginal rights.

On the other hand, it is remarkable how Sir Henry coped, during his first nine months as Prime Minister, with Charlotte's illness and death and, thereafter, with his own failing health and strength. Also, in a family context, despite their different political allegiances, he maintained excellent personal relations with his father and brother.

He had remarkably good personal relations with both Queen Victoria and King Edward despite disagreements on such matters as the deployment of regiments and the like, House of Lords obstructionism and women's enfranchisement. Indeed he owed his first entry to the Cabinet in 1886 to royal intervention (the Queen and the Duke of Cambridge) with the Queen then describing him as 'a good honest Scotsman' and the Duke describing him as 'a very nice and pleasant man, well known to all here and who knows the War Office work, and with whom I have no doubt I shall be able to get on very smoothly and well'. (Wilson [1973], p.162) Even after he had dislodged the Duke as Commander-in-Chief in 1895, they continued to have good personal relations.

No doubt, his relations with the royal family generally were helped along by his and Charlotte's personal friendship with Princess Louise, his competence as Chief Secretary during the future King's visit, with Princess Alexandra, to Ireland in 1885, his services as Minister-in-Attendance (usually at the Queen's request) at Balmoral and elsewhere in 1886 and 1892-1894 and the Marienbad connection.

As a Constituency MP in 1868-1908

What more than anything else endeared Sir Henry to his constituents was his prompt attention to their interests no matter how small, and with the ease and freedom with which at all times he could be approached. Between him and the poorest citizen there was no barrier of pride.

Provost Scobie of Dunfermline, 31 October 1903 (Quoted in Mackie [1914], p.101)

Unquestionably Sir Henry Campbell-Bannerman was an ideal Parliamentary representative. There were in the Stirling District of Burghs many who differed from him politically, but they never had any fault to find with him so far as the performance of his duties as their Member was concerned. On the contrary, prominent Unionists have borne testimony to his unfailing courtesy and his readiness to render any service of which he was capable... It is impossible, too, to forget the regularity with which he fulfilled the task of visiting the constituency to give an account of his stewardship... Judged by whatever test one cares to apply, Sir Henry Campbell-Bannerman realised in an eminent degree all reasonable expectations that could be formed regarding a Parliamentary representative

Dunfermline Press, 25 April 1908

On his home ground CB was indestructible. He was entirely in tune with his constituents. One of them met him in the street and said to him, 'Sir Henry, I like you very much, but I would rather vote for the Devil'. CB promptly replied, 'As your friend is not a candidate, you might as well vote for me'.

Stirling Observer, 4 November 1913

For an enduring and happy connection between a Member of Parliament and his constituents a genuine political sympathy is essential. To agreement in political conviction must be added on the part of the Member devotion to the interests of his constituents, fidelity and efficiency in the discharge of his Parliamentary duties, a placable, reasonable temper that does not readily take or give offence, that smoothes away misunderstandings and prevents alienations. [Such] conditions of a happy political union were conspicuously present during the whole period of Sir Henry Campbell-Bannerman's connection with the Stirling Burghs.

John B. Mackie [1914], p.3

There can be no doubt that, not only by the standards of his time, Sir Henry was an exemplary constituency MP with systematic attention to such duties being rewarded with the provision of a secure electoral base on which his reputation throughout Scotland and at Westminster would be built. Thus, he did not have to experience the electoral vicissitudes of such other party leaders or future party leaders as Gladstone, Balfour, Bonar Law, Churchill, Asquith, Samuel and Sinclair. Indeed, it may be suggested that Rosebery would have been a much better party leader if he had ever had to face a constituency electorate or attend to constituency responsibilities.

Further, it is obvious that many of those who have criticised Sir Henry's record as a constituency MP were unaware that he was not only MP for Stirling but also for Dunfermline, Culross, Inverkeithing and South Queensferry,

In the House of Commons and on Public Platforms in 1868-1908

Mr, Campbell-Bannerman has himself to thank if he is not better known and better understood. There are very few abler men in the Government or in the House of Commons. But he makes no fuss and no show. He does not sufficiently sacrifice to the glorified spirit of self-advertisement which presides over the new era. But when he speaks people listen, attend and are convinced.

John Wilson (1973), pp.149-150, quoting a critic of 1895

Until he became Prime Minister, his speeches in the Commons were usually never more than adequate. He often stuck too closely to his texts, written in his own hand with points to be emphasised marked in red chalk and, as he was short-sighted, held his papers close to his eyes. For such reasons, and otherwise, he was for long consistently under-rated although his self-effacement may have been deliberately cultivated. But as Prime Minister in a new House of Commons he became a new man and, particularly after his clash with Balfour in March 1906, established a commanding position in the Commons which he held until his last appearance therein in February 1908.

Even before he became Prime Minister, he was often at his best in speeches in his own constituency and otherwise when he spoke off the cuff and allowed his natural wit and shrewdness to appear. As Prime Minister, some of his most memorable and significant interventions in debate were when he did speak off the cuff. He was always effective on public platforms where he drew encouragement from the large supportive audiences of his time and his major set-piece speeches invariably read well, as prepared with an eye to being read in the press as well as heard when delivered.

As a Junior Minister in 1871-1874 and 1880-1884

I am in despair at hearing that you are going to leave the Admiralty for Ireland. I suppose I ought to congratulate you. But it is a severe loss to us all. You may feel assured that you have made your mark at the Admiralty, and that you will be very much missed there.

> Earl Northbrook, First Lord of the Admiralty, 20 October 1884
> (Quoted in Spender [1923], Volume 1, p.57)

While Financial Secretary at the War Office and Parliamentary and Financial Secretary at the Admiralty, he had very good working relationships with his seniors in office, Caldwell, Childers and Northbrook (as also with Spencer in 1884-1885). At the War Office he was mainly confined to administrative duties – such as War Office finances and the Army Pay Department. However, with Northbrook in the Lords, he had to act as spokesman for the Admiralty in the Commons, being also prepared to take appropriate personal initiatives such as in connection with the Naval Estimates in 1884 and, with Charlotte, working conditions in Naval Dockyards.

As Chief Secretary for Ireland in 1884-1885

Lord Spencer formed a very high opinion of the qualifications and powers of Campbell-Bannerman while he held the post of Chief Secretary. I am not surprised; and it is quite conceivable that Campbell-Bannerman may take a great jump in the political world.

> Sir Edward Hamilton, November, 1885 (Quoted in Wilson [1973], p.161)

As I have said, it was from his seven to eight months of service in the most dangerous and disagreeable post in the public service that he gained a reputation of being something more than merely a competent junior minister in the War Office and Admiralty. Unlike his predecessors as Chief Secretary, he also gained the respect and trust of the Irish Nationalist MPs which was to stand him in good stead for the rest of his life.

As Secretary of State for War in 1886 and 1892-1895

Mr. Campbell-Bannerman [was] *certainly the most popular War Minister of this generation and had shown a real desire to improve the position of the officer and the soldier and had done much to speed up the rearming of the forces.*

Manchester Guardian, 24 June 1895

Will you allow me – as one of those who voted in the majority last night – to assure you that my vote was not given in any way as intended to cast blame upon yourself. It is no secret that the Army have generally looked upon you as the best War Minister of modern times, an opinion I cordially share. I could not endure the thought that you might consider me ungrateful for all you have done for the Army and the country.

Colonel Francis Bridgeman, Conservative MP, 24 June 1895
(Quoted in Wilson [1973]. p.207)

His five months at the War Office in 1886 were, of course, almost entirely overshadowed by the Irish Question and, apart from the passage of the Army Estimates in March and other routine business, there were only a few War Office or related reforms. His second term (three years) at the War Office was again somewhat overshadowed, at least until September 1893, by the Irish Question.

There were also a number of difficulties and successes with the royal family culminating in the dislodging of the Duke of Cambridge as Commander-in-Chief. Other successes including the creation of a Cabinet Defence Committee and the introduction of an eight-hour working day in the ordnance factory at Woolwich and then the Army Clothing Department. He also attempted to reconcile the differences in the Cabinet over the Naval Estimates which led to Gladstone's resignation in March 1894 and, in Rosebery's Cabinet which followed, it is said that he was the only member who was on speaking terms with all the others.

As Party Leader in 1899-1908

Campbell-Bannerman is the right man to hold a motley Government together. But a very motley Government it is: Home Rulers and anti-Home Rulers; Imperialists and anti-Imperialists; Capitalists and Labour men; Feminists and anti-Feminists; moderate Liberals and extreme Radicals, looking with anything but favour on each other.

Goldwin Smith, June 1906 (Quoted in Wilson [1973], p.509)

Lord Knowles [the King's Principal Private Secretary] *said he was told by Liberals that if anything happened to CB the Party would go burst in six months.*

Austen Chamberlain, Liberal Unionist MP, 4 December 1907 (Quoted in Wilson [1973], p.617)

He saved the ship of Liberalism from total shipwreck at a time when most of the crew and many of the pilots had lost all hope, all heart and all faith.

Extract from Obituary in *Public Opinion,* 24 April 1908

He was a strong party man, but it was for the success of the party, not for his own prestige as its leader, that he cared.

Sir Edward Grey, Viscount Grey of Fallodon (1925), Volume 1, p.66

Campbell-Bannerman was the best and most successful party leader that Liberals have ever had: a man who held his party together and held it to Liberalism, and who briefly went on to reap the rewards. How many times since has the party needed the twinkling wisdom, calm toughness and Liberal faith of a CB!

Tony, Lord Greaves in *Dictionary of Liberal Biography* (1998), p.71

As Party Leader in the Commons, Sir Henry had to cope with the antagonism of the Liberal Imperialists, led by Rosebery, during the Second Boer War and during their divisive activities in the Liberal League and, as he approached the Premiership, the plotting of Asquith, Grey and Haldane. However, in December 1905, he put all the divisive elements in their place and succeeded in forming an exceedingly electorally successful Administration, with a balanced allotment of posts. Further, in reuniting the Liberal Party, he put off the smash for another eleven years and thus provided a basis for another reforming ministry under Asquith.

As Prime Minister in 1905-1908

The Cabinet is the most harmonious that ever was, and the Prime Minister exercises in a singularly quiet and easy way an extraordinary ascendancy over both the Cabinet and the House of Commons... As head of the Cabinet CB was cool, acute, straight, attentive to affairs, considerate. He always knew his mind, and we were all aware that he knew it.

John Morley (Quoted in Wilson [1973], p.500)

From the moment his Cabinet was formed he made no distinction in personal relations, in intimacy and sympathy between those who had helped him and those who had made difficulties for him... For the two years of his Premiership the Cabinet was peculiarly free from personal differences and restlessness.

Sir Edward Grey, Viscount Grey of Fallodon (1925), Volume 1, pp.66-67

Premiers have to give so many important decisions and are pressed for so many concessions that they have to protect themselves by some sort of shield. Campbell-Bannerman's was a kindly manner which caused the applicant to go away feeling that his request would if possible be granted and that, if it was refused, the Premier would regret the refusal more than anyone else.

Winston Churchill, as from Lord Riddell's *Diaries 1908-1914*
(Quoted in the *Glasgow High School Magazine,* June 1948, p.108)

It is the peculiar misfortune of statesmen, especially of those whose period of power is short, that their greatest achievements are apt to be credited to their successors... Many achievements have been credited to Asquith [and Lloyd George] *which might with equal or greater justice have been attributed to Campbell-Bannerman – the restriction on the power of the House of Lords, the legislation of Home Rule in Ireland, the establishment of the Union of South Africa. All these ends had been indicated by Campbell-Bannerman as among the main objects of his policy. Had he survived a few years longer he would certainly have carried measures to secure them, and possibly in a more conciliatory manner than Asquith... But when all is said and done the reputation of Campbell-Bannerman must rest not on his achievements but on his personality... No premier has ever been more deservedly or more widely popular than he was.*

Professor Andrew Browning, Glasgow University
Glasgow High School Magazine, June 1948, pp.85-86

The Liberal victory of January 1906 [was] *above all... in its personal aspect a triumph for the Prime Minister... He dominated the new House of Commons, trusted not only by the serried ranks behind him but by the Irish Nationalists and the new Labour contingent... and, like the other young Members, I was won by his kindness and unaffected simplicity.*

G.P. Gooch (1958), p.105
(George P. Gooch, OM, CH was a Liberal MP for Bath in 1906-1910)

As Prime Minister CB achieved more than many who have been in No. 10 longer than him.

John Wilson in Herbert Van Thal (1975), p.191

[Sir Henry was] *the best Prime Minister that this Office has ever had to deal with.*

Sir Charles Hardinge, Lord Hardinge of Penshurst,
Permanent Under-Secretary, Foreign Office, 1906-1910 and 1916-1920, Viceroy of India, 1910-1916
(Quoted by John Wilson In Herbert Van Thal [1975], p.193)

He succeed in turning the Cabinet to his way of thinking on South Africa, on Trades Disputes and Workmen's Compensation legislation, on Scottish land reform and on relations between the Lords and Commons. Through no fault of his own, he failed to make progress with international disarmament or Irish Home Rule by stages.

Thus, I profoundly disagree with G.R. Searle's notion that 'with Campbell-Bannerman failing to give a firm lead, the first couple of years of Liberal rule [1906 and 1907] was a period of aimlessness and drift' – a notion Searle himself contradicted by going on to refer to important decisions in foreign affairs, the Trades Disputes and Workmen's Compensation legislation and other initiatives. (Searle [1992], p.80) As concerning Sir Henry if not others, I also profoundly disagree with both Lord Blake's suggestion that the personality of Prime Ministers between Gladstone and Churchill was not relevant to their effectiveness (Herbert Van Thal [1975], p.17) and with A.N. Wilson (2005, p.388) in his inclusion of Campbell-Bannerman in his (Wilson's) procession of dull twentieth-century prime ministers.

As a Scot of Scots

Every UK Whig, Peelite and Liberal Prime Minister from Melbourne to Asquith was a Scot by parentage (Aberdeen, Gladstone, Rosebery [although his mother was English] and Sir Henry) and/or had Scottish connections by education, marriage and/or constituency represented (Melbourne, Russell, Palmerston and Asquith). However, unlike all such other Prime Ministers, Sir Henry was very much a Scot of Scots, thus personifying Liberal hegemony in Scotland, the timespan of which, from 1832 until the First World War, was only ten years more than his own lifespan.

He was born and brought-up in Scotland and, apart from four years at Cambridge, had the benefit of a fairly full Scottish education. Apart from their commitment to Scotland's Auld Alliance with France, he and Charlotte were never happier when they were north of the Tweed, with their annual visits to the spa town of Marienbad in Bohemia being essentially for the benefit of Charlotte's health. Scotland was home. The south-east of England was for UK duties. Overseas was for holidays and Charlotte's recuperation

What Henry Thomas Buckle wrote about 'The Paradox of Scottish History' in his *History of Civilisation in England* (1857 and 1861) has relevance to those primarily educated in Scotland. Buckle noted that, in Scotland, the deductive method of reasoning – proceeding from first principles – was dominant. Whereas he noted that the inductive method – proceeding from experience or generalising from the particular – was dominant in England.

I have already considered the unfair criticism of Sir Henry for not ensuring the enfranchisement of the native peoples of South Africa. I have myself criticised him for his negative attitude to legislation facilitating Presbyterian reunion in Scotland. I have also criticised him for his inconsistent and untoward interest, as a Presbyterian Prime Minister, in the affairs of the Church of England. I would now consider some other of his (alleged) failures as Prime Minister.

Why was his and the House of Commons' commitment to reform its relations with the House of Lords not followed-up legislatively after he moved the successful resolution in the Commons in June 1907? The legislation was planned for 1908, by which time, by reason of his final illness, resignation and death, Sir Henry was in no position to do anything about it. Indeed, it was not until after a constitutional crisis and two General Elections that Asquith was able to secure the passage of the 1911 Parliament Act, on the basis of what Sir Henry had suggested in May 1907.

Why did he not attempt to introduce government legislation for women's enfranchisement at Parliamentary Elections, given his long-standing personal commitment to such? Not only was the Cabinet divided on the issue but, given the fate of the Private Member's Bill in March 1907 (which Sir Henry supported), there was probably not at that time a majority for the reform in the Commons.

However, there was some progress with women's enfranchisement in 1907, with the passage of the Qualification of Women [County and Town Councils] [Scotland] Act and the similar Act for England and Wales which gave widows and unmarried women ratepayers the right of election to all local authorities.

Within months of the passage of the 1907 Acts, Lavinia Malcolm, in Dollar, Clackmannanshire, became the first woman to be elected to a Burgh Council in Scotland. She was also the first woman to serve (1913-1919) as Provost of a Scottish Burgh.

It should also be appreciated that women ratepayers had already been enfranchised, mainly by Liberal legislation between 1869 and 1894, for elections to Urban and Rural District and Parish Councils, School Boards and Boards of Poor Law Guardians.

Incidentally, there was also considerable progress in women's enfranchisement in the Scottish Presbyterian Churches. Women could always act as patrons and had a say in the settlement of Ministers in the Secessionist Churches, in the original Free Church and, from 1844, in the Church of Scotland. Thus women were enfranchised in such Churches long before their full political enfranchisement in 1928. However, although women ministers were introduced in the post-1929 United Free Church from 1935, the women of the reunited Church of Scotland had to wait until 1966-1970 to be admitted as Ministers, Elders and Readers. (Refer to my PhD Thesis [2003], Chapter 4.01)

Why did he not attempt to progress his commitment to Scottish Home Rule? He was committed to Home All-Round (Federalism) and, accordingly, was opposed to asymmetrical devolution. Therefore, 'as Scottish Home Rule involves English Home Rule, Scottish Home Rule must wait until the sluggish mind of John Bull [the English collectively] is educated up to that point'. Irish Home Rule (including the by-stages approach) had to be dealt with separately, given the presence of 82 Irish Nationalist MPs at Westminster and because that was what the Irish electorate wanted.

Those who have suggested that Sir Henry was indolent merely confirm that they know next to nothing about him.

As from *The Times* of 27 April 1908, 'He got through his paper work quickly, showing a great gift for getting at the heart of a memorandum without wasting time; and his own notes and instructions were always short, adequate and to the point' As from Arthur Ponsonby, as quoted in Hirst (1947), p.261, 'Just as one imagined he was inattentive or indifferent, ready to take the line of least resistance, or do nothing, or yield suddenly, one came up against a rock, an obstinate determination, a perfectly clear and set conviction which in time upset everyone's calculations'.

He has also been criticised for spending too much time in Scotland and overseas. It should be appreciated, that in Sir Henry's time, Parliament did not usually meet after the summer adjournment until the New Year. (As already mentioned, during Sir Henry's thirty-nine autumns as an MP, the House of Commons only met in October and/or November in eight years.) Constituency correspondence was always forwarded to him and received his personal attention wherever he was and he developed and sustained very many valuable diplomatic contacts when abroad. Further, the presence of King Edward at Marienbad, particularly in 1905, was helpful in the development of good personal relations and, of course, Sir Henry was only once at Marienbad as Prime Minister, at the time of Charlotte's death in August 1906.

Indeed I would suggest that many of those who would denigrate Sir Henry are those who specialise in writing about matters about which they do not know enough to know how much they do not know.

All in all, I conclude, as I started, that Sir Henry should indeed be much better known and much better appreciated.

Had his [Sir Henry's] *great chance come earlier in life, he might have altered the course of political history; he might indeed have preserved the Liberal Party.*
                    Earl Winterton (1932), p.86

Indeed, if Sir Henry – who would also have been an excellent Foreign Secretary, Speaker of the House of Commons or Viceroy of India (all of which he came close to becoming) – had enjoyed better health and lived longer or had become Prime Minister earlier in life it would have enabled him to achieve all the reforms in which he believed (including perhaps the nationalisation of the Railways as he had anticipated in 1904), the First World War might have been averted, Ireland settled peacefully and the Liberal Party preserved as a party of government. Thus history would have been changed for the better.

Also, let Sir Henry, in speaking about Michelangelo as 'the perfect gentleman' and as from his 1900 Election Address, speak for himself –

A man and a citizen, pure, temperate and unblemished; proud and independent where duty called for the assertion of his position; generous, open and earnest; humble and lovely in his devotion to duty; true to his country; true and tender to his friends. Are not these the characteristics of a perfect gentleman?

As quoted in Mackie [1914], pp.46-47

it is not power, nor glory, nor wealth, that exalted a nation, but righteousness, justice and freedom

---

[Sir Henry] *was one of the nicest and most sensible men ever to be leader of a political party or prime minister. No prime minister was ever more loved by his followers. He was a modest man... but he had the wisdom and sagacity of a good family solicitor or of an old shepherd, and he was afraid of no one and nothing.*

John Wilson in Herbert Van Thal [1975], p.194

[Sir Henry] *was probably the most decent man ever to hold the office of Prime Minister*

Colin Clifford, (2002), p.134

Sir Henry Campbell-Bannerman, a man of great ability, courage and above all integrity

Professor Stewart J, Brown, Edinburgh, Letter of 6 May 2013

But the liberal deviseth liberal things; and by liberal things shall he stand.

Isaiah 32: 8 (King James Authorised Version)

Don't forget Campbell-Bannerman – *Duinecoir* – An Honest Man

Appendix 1 – Electoral History of Stirling Burghs 1708--1918

Much of the pre-1882 information in this Appendix is based on Joseph Forster's *Commissioners and) Members of Parliament, Scotland 1357-1882* as originally published in 1882. Until 1832 each of the five Burghs, effectively a delegate of their town councils, had one vote in contested elections. An asterisk indicates that there are entries for such MPs in the *Oxford Dictionary of National Biography* as also for Sir Henry Campbell-Bannerman and Arthur Ponsonby.

1708-1710 – The Hon. Colonel John Erskine (1662-1743) was a younger son of David Erskine, 2nd (Scottish) Lord Cardross of a junior branch of the Erskine Earls of Mar. His early career including service in the Netherlands in the army of William of Orange, with whom he landed in England at the start of the 'Glorious Revolution' in 1688. He was subsequently military Governor of Stirling and Dumbarton Castles and, from 1695, a Director of the Company of Scotland which was responsible for the ill-fated enterprise to establish a Scottish colony on the Darien isthmus in Central America. He represented the Royal Burgh of Stirling (as Provost) in the outgoing Scottish Parliament, being a member of the Court (Tory) Party and thus a supporter of the incorporating Parliamentary Union with England (and Wales). He was one of the 45 Scottish MPs appointed by the outgoing Scottish Parliament to serve in the UK House of Commons (all on a non-constituency basis) from May 1707 until being elected for Stirling Burghs at the first UK General Election in April/July 1708.

The sixteen Scottish Representative Peers for 1707-1708 were also appointed by the outgoing Scottish Parliament.

1710-1727 – Henry Cunningham (1697-1756), was the brother-in-law of his predecessor as MP for Stirling Burghs. He was MP for Stirlingshire in 1708–1710 before being elected for Stirling Burghs in 1710. He was elected for both Stirling Burghs and Stirlingshire in 1727 and chose to represent Stirlingshire, causing a gap in the Burghs' representation until Thomas Erskine was elected in 1728. Henry was thus again MP for Stirlingshire until being appointed Governor of Jamaica in 1734, in which post he died in 1736. Other appointments included being a Commissionary-General of Musters, a Commissioner of Forfeited Jacobite Estates and Provost of Inverkeithing.

1728-1734 – The Hon. Thomas Erskine (Died 1766) was the son of John Erskine, 22nd and 6th (Scottish) Earl of Mar who was attained in 1716 for his leadership of the Jacobite Rising of 1715. Thomas Erskine was later MP for Stirlingshire in 1747 and for Clackmannanshire in 1747-1754.

1734-1741 – Sir Peter Halkett, 2nd Baronet (1669-1755) was the son of Sir Peter Halkett, 1st Baronet who changed his surname from Wedderburn on marrying the sister of Sir James Halkett, who represented Dunfermline in the old Scottish

Parliament in 1705-1707 and served in the UK House of Commons (on a non-constituency basis) in 1707-1708.

1741-1747 – * The Hon. James Erskine (1679-1754) – known, after 1706, as **Lord Grange** – was a younger brother of the attained Earl of Mar (as above). As an advocate, James Erskine was appointed to the Court of Session in 1706 and to the High Court of Justiciary in 1707, taking the judicial title of Lord Grange and serving as Lord Justice Clerk in 1710-1714. Although a Jacobite intriguer, he took no part in the 1715 Rising and was, in due course, along with David Erskine, Lord Dun, allowed to buy back the family's forfeited estates in Clackmannanshire. In 1732 Lord Grange faked his deranged wife's death and funeral in Edinburgh whereas in reality he had her kidnapped and confined in the Highlands and Islands until she really died in 1745 in Skye. Having resigned his judicial offices, Lord Grange served as MP for Clackmannanshire in 1734-1741 until elected for Stirling Burghs.

1747-1758 – George Haldane (1722-1759) was of the Haldanes of Gleneagles and, therefore (as was his uncle and immediate successor, Robert Haldane as MP for Stirling Burghs) a distant relative of Sir Henry Campbell-Bannerman. He enlisted in the Army aged 17 and was on active service in 1743-1747 during the War of the Austrian Succession and the Jacobite Rising. After resigning from the Army as a Brigadier-General earlier in 1747, he served as MP for Stirling Burghs until, in 1758 he was appointed Governor of Jamaica where he died in 1759.

1758-1761 – Robert Haldane (1689-1768), elected at a by-election, uncle of the above, was the son of John Haldane who sat in the old Scottish Parliament for Perthshire in 1689-1693, for Dunbartonshire in 1700-1702 and for Perthshire again in 1702-1707. Robert's other brother, Kentigern was MP for Stirlingshire in 1715-1722 and for Perthshire in 1726-1727.

1761-1768 – * Sir Francis Holburne (1704-1771) entered the Royal Navy in 1720, eventually reaching the rank of Admiral. During his naval career he was commander-in-chief at the Leeward Islands in 1747-1748 and also had a command at Halifax, Nova Scotia in early 1757. Later, in 1757, while Port Admiral at Portsmouth, he was a member of the court-martial which tried and condemned Admiral Byng to death for the loss of Minorca during the Seven Year's War. The execution on HMS Monarch was satirised in Voltaire's *Candide*. In 1760, by intimidation and bribery, Admiral Holburne secured election as Provost of his native Inverkeithing and, a year later, was elected MP for Stirling Burghs which he represented until he was elected MP for Plymouth which he represented until his death. During the last six months of his life he was also Governor of Greenwich Hospital, a post to which he had been appointed by way of paid retirement from the Navy.

1768-1774 – James Masterton (Died 1778) served in the Army, reaching the rank of Colonel and is said to have been ADC to the Duke of Cumberland at Culloden in 1746. While MP for Stirling Burghs, he was Barrack-Master-General for Scotland in 1769.

1774-1780 and 1789-1791 – * Sir Archibald Campbell, KB (1739-1791) entered the Army (Royal Engineers) in 1758, eventually reaching the rank of General. While based in Calcutta, from 1768, as Chief Engineer of the British East India Company, he enriched himself through a partnership in a ship building and repairing business and as a silk trader and thus was able to buy a number of estates in his native Argyll and also houses in Inverkeithing and South Queensferry. On returning to Scotland, he was elected MP for Stirling Burghs in 1774 – after an unusually bitter contest with Colonel James Masterton, the former MP – and served, mainly *in absentia*, until the 1780 General Election. While commanding a Scottish infantry battalion, he was captured in Boston Harbour in 1776 during the American Revolutionary War and was not released, on the basis of a prisoner exchange, until 1778. He then had further commands during the War before returning to the UK in 1779 and then served as Governor of Jamaica in 1782-1784 and of Madras in 1786-1789. On returned to the UK prematurely in 1789 (by reason of ill-health) he succeeded his elder brother, as from a by-election, as again MP for Stirling Burghs. He died on 31 March 1791 and was buried in Westminster Abbey.

1780-1789 – Sir James Campbell (1737-1805), the elder brother of General Sir Archibald Campbell, had kept his brother's parliamentary interests 'warm' both in 1776-1780 when Sir Archibald was only nominally MP for Stirling Burghs and from the 1780 General Election until 1789 when Sir James was himself MP for the Constituency.

1791-1797 – * The Hon. Andrew James Cochrane (1767-1833) – known, after his first marriage in 1793, as **Cochrane-Johnstone** – was a younger son of the 8th Earl of Dundonald and an uncle of (Admiral) Thomas Cochrane, naval hero, Member of Parliament and, from 1831, 10th (Scottish) Earl of Dundonald. Andrew Cochrane served in the Army from 1783 until 1805 when, after being acquitted by a court-martial on such charges as corruption and wrongful arrest during his controversial Governorship of Dominica, he resigned his commission. He was first elected MP for Stirling Burghs at a by-election in May 1791 but resigned as an MP on his appointment as Governor of Dominica in 1797. He was later elected as MP for Grampound – then a corrupt, two-member 'rotten borough' – in Cornwall at the 1807 General Election but was disqualified within ten months for failing to possess the necessary property qualifications. He then returned to the West Indies where he acted as a civilian agent for the Royal Navy until legal proceedings against him for corruption drove him back to UK by 1809. He then went to Spain where he was involved in currency transactions for the UK Treasury and in various dubious and disastrous commercial ventures until, again returning to the UK, he was re-elected for Grampound at the 1812 General Election, having presumably now acquired the necessary property qualifications. However, he was now in deep financial trouble and in 1814, along with other defendants including his nephew, Thomas Cochrane, he was found guilty of Stock Exchange fraud. Cochrane-Johnstone did not attend the trial, having fled abroad never to return to the UK.

(In later years. Thomas Cochrane's heirs received substantial compensation for his wrongful conviction)

Refer also to Stewart Allen, 'Admiral Cochrane, The Real Master and Commander' in *History Scotland* (January/February 2012).

1797-1800 – William Tait (Died 1800), elected at a by-election, was the second son of Alexander Tait, Clerk of the Sasines at Edinburgh. William was admitted to the English Bar (Lincoln's Inn) in 1777. He died within three years of his election as MP for Stirling Burghs.

1800-1806 – * The Hon. Sir Alexander Cochrane, GCB (1758-1832) was another younger son of the 8th (Scottish) Earl of Dundonald and, therefore, an elder brother of Andrew Cochrane Johnstone and also an uncle of Thomas Cochrane Alexander Cochrane joined the Royal Navy at an early age and served in the West Indian station from 1778 until the American Revolutionary War ended in 1783. After a period as a Captain on half-pay, he resumed active service in 1790 during which time his nephew, Thomas Cochrane started his colourful career under his uncle as a midshipman in 1793. During the early war with Revolutionary France, Alexander Cochrane had commands in the North Sea, with the Channel Fleet and in the Mediterranean. He was elected MP for Stirling Burghs in 1800 but, with the breakdown of the 1802 Peace of Amiens in 1803, he was recalled to active service without relinquishing his seat which he continued to represent *in absentia* until defeated at the 1806 General Election. He was appointed naval commander in the Leeward Islands in 1805, served again in the North Sea from 1806, returned to the West Indian station in 1809 and, during the war of 1812-1814/1815 with the USA, was Vice-Admiral commanding the North American station. As already mentioned, he was responsible for the bombardment of Baltimore on 13-14 September 1814 when the use of rockets and bombs prompted the poem which became *The Star-Spangled Banner*. He was also responsible for the ineffective naval operations in support of the attack on New Orleans in January 1815 with the land battle being fought and lost on 8 January 1815 – that is after the Peace Treaty of Ghent had been agreed and signed on 24 December 1814 although not ratified by the US Senate until 16 February 1815. Later in 1815 Alexander Cochrane sought to return to Parliament but his interest in candidature in a Westminster By-Election received no support. Promoted to Admiral in 1819, his last appointment was as Commander-in-Chief Plymouth in 1821-1824.

1806-1807 – Sir John Henderson, Bt (1752-1817) was previously MP for Dysart Burghs (also including Kirkcaldy, Burntisland and Kinghorn) in 1780-1784 and for Seaford (Sussex) in 1785-1786. He also served for a term as Provost of Inverkeithing from 1802.

1807-1818 – Alexander Campbell (Died 1832) was previously MP for Anstruther Burghs (including also Kilrenny, Crail and Pittenweem) in 1779-1806. He also served simultaneously in the Army, reaching the rank of General, with overseas commands in North America and the West Indies.

1818-1819 – John Campbell was elected for Stirling Burghs on 15 July 1818 and served until the election was declared void, by reason of electoral bribery, on 29 March 1819,

1819-1820 – Francis Ward Primrose (1785-1860), elected at a by-election, was a younger son of Sir Neil Primrose, KT, 3rd (Scottish) Earl of Rosebery, who was the grandfather of Archibald Primrose, MP for Stirling Burghs in 1832-1841 and great-grandfather of the 5th Earl, Liberal Prime Minister in 1895-1895.

1820-1830 – Robert Downie (Died 1841) had prospered as a Merchant in India. On return to Scotland in 1813, he bought property in and near Dunfermline and land in Appin in Argyllshire.

1830-1832 – James Johnstone (1802-1841), a Tory, of Straiton in Midlothian was defeated at the first General Election after the 1832 Reform Acts.

1832 General Election - Electorate 956

Archibald Primrose	Whig	492
James Johnston	Tory	366

05/05/1835 Ministerial By-Election

Archibald Primrose	Whig	Unopposed

1835 General Election - Electorate 1,060

Archibald Primrose	Whig	418
J. Cruwford	Radical	345

1837 General Election - Electorate 1,241

Archibald Primrose	Whig	459
T.P. Thompson		4

1841 General Election - Electorate c,1,141

Archibald Primrose	Whig	438
J. Aytoun	Radical	420

1832-1847 – The Hon. Archibald Primrose (1809-1851) – known as **Lord Dalmeny** from 1814 until his death – was the eldest son and heir of Sir Archibald Primrose, KT, 4th (Scottish) Earl of Rosebery and 1st (UK) Lord Rosebery. Dalmeny served as Civil Lord of the Admiralty in Viscount Melbourne's Second Whig Government in 1835-1841. After defeating James Johnston the former MP for the Constituency in 1832, he representing Stirling Burghs for fifteen years. As already mentioned, his premature death in 1851 resulted in his only son, Archibald Primrose (Liberal Prime Minister in 1894-1895) succeeding, aged 21, as 5th Earl on the death of the 4th Earl in 1868.

1847 General Election – Electorate 1,125

John B. Smith	Radical	435
A.C.R.G. Maitland	Whig	312
A. Alison		156

1847-1852 – * John Benjamin Smith (1796-1879), a Manchester merchant, unsuccessfully contested Blackburn in 1837 and Walsall and Dundee in 1841. After representing Stirling Burghs for five years, he was elected for Stockport at the 1852 General Election and continued to serve as its Whig and then Liberal MP until he retired in 1874. In earlier years he was President of Manchester Chamber of Commerce and first Chairman of the Anti-Corn Law League. His brothers-in-law –

William and James Lawrence – both served as Liberal MPs and Lord Mayors of London.

1852 General Election - Electorate 1,097			1857 General Election - Electorate 1,149		
<u>Sir James Anderson</u>	Radical	431	<u>Sir James Anderson</u>	Radical	Unopposed
O.J. Miller	Whig	411			

1852-1859 – Sir James Anderson (1800-1864), a Glasgow manufacturer, was elected Lord Provost of the City in November 1848 and knighted on Queen Victoria's visit to the City in August 1849. He also unsuccessfully contested Falkirk Burghs at the 1852 General Election but was then elected for Stirling Burghs and served until retiring at the 1859 General Election.

1859 General Election – Electorate 1,224

<u>(Sir) James Caird</u>   Liberal   Unopposed

1859-1865 – * The Rt. Hon. Sir James Caird, KCB, FRS (1816-1892), an Edinburgh-educated agricultural administrator and writer, was an unsuccessful candidate for Wigtown Burghs in 1852 and Whig MP for Dartmouth in 1857-1859. After representing Stirling Burghs for six years, he was appointed as Senior Commissioner for Enclosures in 1865 and an Indian Famine Commissioner in 1878. He was President of the Royal Statistical Society in 1880-1882 and Land Director of the Board of Agriculture in 1889-1891. Having been invested as a Knight Commander of the Order of the Bath (KCB) in 1882, he was appointed to the Privy Council in 1889.

1865 General Election – Electorate 1,262

<u>Laurence Oliphant</u>   Liberal   Unopposed

1865-1868 – * Laurence Oliphant (1829-1888), son of a former Chief Justice of Ceylon, was called to the Scottish Bar in 1854 and to the English Bar (Lincoln's Inn) in 1855. Otherwise, from 1853 onwards, he was an overseas civil servant in the USA, Canada, China and Japan. In 1861, while First Secretary to the UK Legation in Japan, he was severely wounded during a xenophobic attack on the Legation. He resigned from the service on returning to the UK and, after representing Stirling Burghs for three years, resigned (in order to join a United States-based spiritualist community), thus causing a By-Election. He remained connected to the community for about thirteen years, but during this time also worked as a correspondent for *The Times* during the Franco-Prussian War and travelled extensively in the Ottoman Empire, including the Holy Land within which he had an active commitment to Jewish settlement. After severing his connection with the community, he and his first wife lived for a few years in the Holy Land, with his wife dying therein in 1886. His second wife (married in 1888, the year of his death, in Twickenham) was a granddaughter of Robert Owen, the philanthropist, social theorist and manager of New Lanark in Scotland. Oliphant also wrote a number of (mainly travel) books, a satirical novel, *Piccadilly* in 1870 and another novel, *Masollam* in 1885.

1868 - John Ramsay (1814-1892), Liberal

1868-1908 - Henry Campbell ⇒ (Sir) Henry Campbell-Bannerman (1836-1908), Liberal

22/05/1908 By-Election - Electorate 7.556			Jan 1910 General Election - Electorate 8,147		
Arthur Ponsonby	Liberal	3,873	Arthur Ponsonby	Liberal	4,471
W. Whitelaw	Conservative	2,518	N.J.K. Cochran-Patrick	Conservative	2,419

Dec 1910 General Election - Electorate 8,147		
Arthur Ponsonby	Liberal	Unopposed

In 1918 the Constituency was split four ways. Stirling was included in the new constituency of Stirling and Falkirk Burghs (also including Grangemouth) with Liberal MPs in 1918-1922 and 1923-1924, a Conservative MP in 1931-1935 and otherwise Labour MPs. Dunfermline and Inverkeithing were included in the new constituency of Dunfermline Burghs (also including Cowdenbeath and Lochgelly) which had a Coalition Liberal MP in 1918-1922, a Liberal National MP in 1931-1935 and otherwise Labour MPs. Culross was included in the county constituency of West Fife which had a Conservative MP in 1931-1935, a Communist MP in 1935-1950 and otherwise Labour MPs. South Queensferry was included in the county constituency of West Lothian which had Conservative MPs in 1918-1922, 1924-1928, and 1931-1935 and otherwise Labour MPs.

Stirling is currently in the county constituency of Stirling (as created in 2005) which includes such rural areas as The Trossachs and was represented by a Labour MP (first elected for the old Stirling constituency in 1997), until 2015, by an SNP MP from 2015-2017 and by a Conservative MP from 2017. Dunfermline, Inverkeithing and Culross are in the county constituency of Dunfermline and West Fife (as created in 2005) as represented by a Labour MP in 2005-2006, by a Liberal Democrat MP in 2006-2010, by a Labour MP from 2010 to 2015, and since 2015 by an SNP MP. South Queensferry is now included in the constituency of Edinburgh West as represented by Liberal Democrat MPs from 1997 to 2015 and again from 2017.

Appendix 2 – Liberal Hegemony in Scotland 1832 to 1918

Table 27 - General Elections - Scotland - 1832 to 1918

Excluding Scottish University Constituencies as created in 1868

Candidates (Unopposed), Percentages and MPs Elected

	1832				1835				1837			
Whigs & Radicals	70	(12)	79.0	43	52	(15)	62.8	38	49	(15)	54.0	33
Conservatives	29	(4)	21.0	10	33	(8)	37.2	15	35	(7)	46.0	20

	1841				1847				1852			
Whigs & Radicals	40	(13)	60.8	31	48	(21)	61.7	33	43	(15)	72.6	33
Conservatives	35	(18)	38.3	22	35	(16)	38.3	20	31	(18)	27.4	20
Chartist	1	(0)	0.9	-								

Conservatives in 1847, 1852, 1857 and 1859 include Peelites (Free Traders)

	1857				1859				1865			
Whigs & Radicals	49	(25)	84.6	39	44	(34)	66.4	40				
Liberals									51	(30)	85.4	42
Conservatives	19	(13)	15.2	14	17	(11)	33.6	13	17	(7)		14.6
	11											

Whigs, Radicals and Peelites united after the June 1859 General Election to form the Liberal Party.

	1868				1874				1880			
Liberals	70	(23)	82.5	51	61	(16)	68.4	40	60	(12)	70.1	52
Conservatives	20	(3)	17.5	7	36	(6)	31.6	18	43	(0)	29.9	6

	1885				1886				1892			
Liberals	70	(5)	53.3	51	68	(7)	53.6	43	70	(0)	53.9	50
Conservatives	55	(0)	34.3	8								
Unionists					63	(2)	46.4	27	68	(0)	44.4	20
Others	32	(0)	12.4	11					11	(0)	1.7	-

Unionists from 1886 = Conservatives and Liberal Unionists

The 11 Others elected in 1885 were Independent Liberals
including four Crofter MPs and one elected with Conservative support.

	1895				1900				1906			
Liberals	66	(1)	56.8	39	66	(0)	50.2	34	70	(1)	56.4	58
Unionists	68	(4)	47.1	31	70	(3)	49.0	36	69	(0)	38.2	10
ILP	7	(0)	0.8	-								
Labour									4	(0)	2.3	2
Others	1	(0)	0.1	-	3	(0)	0.8	-	8	(0)	3.1	-

ILP = Independent Labour Party as founded in 1893

As from by-elections after 1900, there were, by March 1905, 38 Liberal and 32 Unionist MPs.

The Labour MPs elected in 1906 were nominees of the Labour Representation Committee
, with the Labour Party, as such, being formed when Parliament assembled.

	1910 (January)				1910 (December)				1918 (December)			
Liberals	68	(0)	54.2	58	67	(11)	53.6	58	33	(0)	15.0	8
Coalition Liberals									28	(7)	19.1	25
Unionists	70	(0)	39.6	9	57	(1)	42.6	9	37	(1)	32.8	30
Coalition Labour, etc.									4	(0)	2.8	1
Labour	10	(0)	5.1	2	5	(0)	3.6	3	42	(0)	24.7	6
Others	4	(0)	1.1	1	3	(0)	0.2	-	21	(0)	3.6	1

The Other MP elected in January 1910 was an Independent Liberal, formerly a Liberal Unionist, who rejoined the Liberal Party during 1910 and was re-elected as a Liberal in Decembers 1910.

The Other MP elected in 1918 was an Independent Labour Candidate
who joined the Labour Party immediately after the Election

The January 1910 General Election

Net Gains/Losses in MPs Elected compared to the 1906 General Election

	England	Wales	Scotland	Ireland	Universities	UK
Liberals	minus 118	minus 5	No Change	minus 2	-	minus 125
Unionists	plus 111	plus 2	minus 1	plus 4	No Change	plus 116
Labour	plus 7	plus 4	No Change	-	-	plus 11
Irish Nationalists	No Change	-	-	No Change	-	No Change
Others	No Change	minus 1	plus 1	minus 2	-	minus 2

Accordingly, unlike the Liberals in England and Wales, the Liberals in Scotland held their position (as also at the December 1910 General Election) with the Labour advance being due primarily to former Liberal/Labour MPs in England and Wales moving over to the Labour Party.

In terms of votes and MPs elected, the Labour Party became the lead party in Scotland at the 1923 General Election - a position it has held ever since, at UK General Elections, except in 1924, 1931, 1935 and 1951,

The fact of Liberal hegemony in Scotland from 1832 to 1918 was of considerable political significance in the United Kingdom generally. Like Labour's Scottish strength in the second half of the 20th century, it gave a solid base to the Party's strength across the UK, providing many of the Prime Ministers and other ministerial personnel and contributed substantially to both the philosophical base of the Party and its programme and political priorities.

The approach and motivation of many of those who adhered to the Party in Scotland in this period was well – indeed inspiringly – expressed by Alexander Taylor Innes, who served as an Advocate Depute during the time of Liberal Administrations in 1880-1885 and 1892-1894-1895.

Alexander Taylor Innes on *Why I am a Liberal* (1885)

> I am a Liberal because I am a Scotsman. As a matter of personal constitution, the claim of the past, the authority of the present, the sacred continuity of both, so press on my imagination as almost to make me a Conservative. But in the history of my own country, I find something deeper than the thin stream of its Conservative tradition. I find there in every age a passion for the ideal, and a sense of the obligation of the men who deal with public affairs to build upon nothing less than the principles of right. And as time goes on, Scotland has fallen back more and more on such principles – principles of individual freedom no doubt, but of individual freedom to unite in construction and reconstruction, and so to join with the new principle of toleration, the old passion for truth and right. And in proportion as it has done for our Liberalism, without becoming less Scottish than it was in the days of George Buchanan [1506-1682]. Scotland has become more cosmopolitan. I know, therefore, that Scotland, in thus adhering to Liberalism, has chosen the better part in politics. For it has chosen that which need not be taken away from it in the future, by any accident however strange, by any development however slow.

Alexander Taylor Innes in Andrew Reid [Editor], *Why I am a Liberal* [1885] pp.64-65. A.T. Innes (1833-1913) was a lawyer, biographer and church historian. He was a brother-in-law of Alexander Dingwall Fordyce who is mentioned in Chapter 6 as a guest of the Campbell-Bannermans at Belmont in December 1897. Some of the contributors to Reid's book in 1885 – such as Joseph Chamberlain, Sir John Lubbock and John Webster (as follows) – became Liberal Unionists in the following year. In 1996 Duncan Brack, Editor of the *Journal of Liberal History*, published *Why I am a Liberal Democrat*, including some extracts from Andrew Reid's 1885 book.

Otherwise, it is suggested that there were three underlying historical factors sustaining Liberal electoral hegemony in Scotland for most of the 19th century.

Firstly, the Scottish commitment to a proto-democratic constitutional monarchy, aligned with the Community of the Realm, as from the Declaration of Arbroath of 1320.

Secondly, as from the late 15th century and the 16th century, the development of traditions of protest, radicalism and reform – that is, as from 'the days of George Buchanan'.

Indeed, it has recently been suggested by Roger A, Mason (Professor of Scottish History in the University of St. Andrews) that George Buchanan 'lay at the heart of Scottish self-fashioning at the time of [the approach of] the Union of the Crowns' in 1603. Even apart from his radical politics, Buchanan is significant in that while a source of reassurance that Scotland's unique status would not be assimilated into a greater English *imperium,* he also emphasised as fundamental law, in his *De iure regni apud Scotos* (1579), the right to hold errant rulers to account. ('George Buchanan and Scottish Self-Fashioning', [*The Scottish Historical Review,* April 2013])

George Buchanan was Principal of St. Leonard's College, St. Andrews from 1566, Moderator of the 1567 General Assembly and a tutor of the young King James VI in 1570-1578. The claim that, before he [Buchanan] left Scotland, aged 14, to study Latin at the University of Paris, he attended what became the High School of Glasgow is unsupported, although he was an associate of the Rev. Thomas Jack, the Grammar School's Rector in 1567-1574.

Also as from the late 16th century the development of the Presbyterian form of Church Government contributed to later adherence to Liberalism in Scotland. As John Webster (Liberal MP for Aberdeen in 1880-1885) also wrote in *Why I am a Liberal* [1885].pp.105-106 –

> Why then, is Scotland so decidedly, sternly on the side of Liberalism? Mainly by the influence of her Democratic – it may even be called her Republican – form of Church government. Some eighty or eighty-five per cent of her people are attached to one section or another of the Presbyterian church, and from the popular spirit and character inherent in Presbytery *when not hampered by state connection,* has ever flowed the love of civil freedom in the body of the nation.

Significantly, the name Whig – from *whiggamore,* meaning 'one who drives cattle' – originated as a description for the more militant Scottish Covenanters in the 17th century. The name was then adopted in England by those who also supported a constitutional monarchy and, accordingly, were also opposed to the succession of Charles II's brother, the Roman Catholic James, in 1685. (The word Tory is derived from the Irish *toraidhe,* meaning 'a highwayman [or] outlaw')

Thirdly, the input of the wide-ranging Scottish Enlightenment in the 18th century, given also, by then, the relatively high incidence of literacy in Scotland – 75 % by 1750 – as from the educational policies in the *First Book of Discipline* of the Church of Scotland (as endorsed by the Scottish Privy Council in 1561) and the old Scottish Parliament's Education Acts in the 17th century. In this context, as Robert Falkner wrote (p.372) in the 2007 *Dictionary of Liberal Thought* (Duncan Brack and Ed

Randall, Editors), 'the rich body of political liberalism' which can be found in the writings of Adam Smith (1723-1790) contrasts with his popular image as a laissez-faire doctrinaire'.

Incidentally, it is not generally appreciated that Immanuel Kant – who was born in what was then Königsberg in East Prussia in 1724 and is described in the *Dictionary of Liberal Thought* (p.194) as 'one of the most influential thinkers in Europe' – was of Scottish parentage. His paternal grandfather had migrated from Scotland and his father continued to use the surname Cant. One of the family – Andrew Cant (1584-1663), Moderator of the 1650 General Assembly – is said to have been 'the most actively bigoted supporter of the Covenant in the North of Scotland'. Andrew Cant's son, Alexander, Parish Minister of Banchory-Ternan from 1646, was deposed by the Scottish Privy Council in 1662 for seditious activities. (Refer to my 2003 PhD Thesis – *A History of the Parish of Banchory=Ternan to 1929,* Chapter 2.01)

The Scottish traditions of protest, radicalism and reform continued into the late 18th century and then the 19th century. For example, mention has already been made of firstly, the Glasgow-based Reform Association and the sentencing of its Thomas Muir to transportation in 1794 (Chapter 1), secondly, of the Radical Laird, of the Kinloch family with which Sir Henry Campbell-Bannerman was later well acquainted, who was declared an outlaw in Edinburgh in 1819 (Chapter 6), and thirdly, of the Scottish Chartists of the 1840s of whom two – Daniel Lawson of Glasgow and Thomas Morrison of Dunfermline – would later interact with Sir Henry Campbell-Bannerman. (Chapter 2, etc.)

However, such factors did not have much in the way of electoral implications until the Scottish Reform Act of 1832. This not only increased the Scottish electorate from about 4,500 to 64,447, but also ensured that the newly enfranchised electors were not likely to support the Scottish Tories who had, almost without exception, opposed their enfranchisement. (The Scottish Burgh Reform Act of 1833 was also significant in that elected town councils replaced self-perpetuating councils, thus also increasing popular representation among the Elder Commissioners appointed by the Royal Burghs to the General Assembly of the Church of Scotland.) Indeed, such was the virulent and passionate hostility to which the Tories were subjected that, for many years, in many constituencies, there was not enough local support to nominate, never mind elect, a Tory candidate. Thus, until about 1886, contests between Whigs and Radicals or, after 1859, between different kinds of Liberals were almost as frequent as contests between Whigs/Radicals/Liberals and Conservatives.

Further, and particularly after the Disruption of the Church of Scotland in 1843 (for which the Tories were rightly blamed) the divisions in Scottish Presbyterianism tended to entrench political alignments. As from Chapter 4, Table 10, Presbyterian dissenters tended to vote Liberal whereas Presbyterians who adhered to the Church of Scotland tended to vote Conservative. This was in the context of members and adherents of the Church of Scotland being in a Presbyterian minority for about a generation after the Disruption. The number of Scottish Presbyterians adhering to the Church of Scotland was 40 % in 1851 and 56 % by the end of the century. There were, of course, always a significant number of Liberals, including Sir Henry

Campbell-Bannerman, who continued to adhere to the Church of Scotland, with those opposed to the disestablishment of the Church of Scotland – in, for example, in the Church Defence Association – known as Church Liberals.

However, at the time of the Irish Home Rule Liberal split in 1886, many Scottish Presbyterian dissenters became Unionists (Liberal Unionists or Conservatives). Indeed, as indicated in Chapter 5, even before 1886, there was an alignment between the Orange Order and the Conservative Party in Scotland, with the Glasgow Lodges having a representative on the City's Conservative Executive, On the other hand, the increase in the then mainly Liberal-voting (except in 1885 and 1900) Roman Catholic electorate (mainly of Irish origin) tended to off-set losses to the Unionists.

Roman Catholics, as a proportion of all Scottish church members and adherents, increased from 5 % in 1851 to 27 % by the end of the century. (The reason for [Irish] Roman Catholics voting Conservative in Scotland, in 1885 was considered in Chapter 5 and the reason for their voting Unionist in 1900 was considered in Chapter 9)

Further, as Professor Richard Finlay of Strathclyde University has suggested, other reasons for the Liberal hegemony in Scotland were the Scottish commitment to individualism, the use of the Tories as bogeymen, the 'broad church' to which the Liberal Party appealed and the ability to portray itself as very much the Scottish Party. (Refer to Robert Brown's report in the *Journal of Liberal History* [Winter 2009-2010] on the Liberal Democrat History Group meeting, at which Professor Finlay spoke, in Perth on 13 March 2010. Professor Finlay has, with Claire Wood, subsequently written 'A House Divided? – The Impact of the First World War on Scottish Liberals and Labour' (*History Scotland,* May/June 2013)

Moreover, as already mentioned, every UK Whig, Peelite and Liberal Prime Minister and Leader from Melbourne to Asquith was a Scot by parentage and/or had Scottish connections by education, marriage and/or constituency represented. Such a consideration may be added to the other reasons for Whig/Radical/Liberal electoral supremacy in Scotland, except in 1900, from 1832 until the First World War.

Since 1926, when Asquith demitted the Liberal Leadership, of the eleven Liberal/Liberal Democrat Leaders, five have been Scots (Sinclair, Grimond, Steel, Kennedy and Campbell), two have been Welsh (Lloyd George and Davies), with five being essentially English (Samuel, Thorpe, Ashdown, Clegg and Cable). Mention should also be made of two other Scots – Sir Donald Maclean who led the Liberal MPs in the Commons after the 1918 General Election until the return of Asquith to Parliament as from the Paisley by-election in February 1920 and Robert Maclennan who was, with David Steel, briefly Joint Liberal Democrat Leader in 1988. Further, Roy Jenkins, Leader of the SDP in 1981-1983, represented a Scottish constituency (Glasgow Hillhead) in 1982-1987.

Further, also since 1926, no fewer than seven Scots have been or are Liberal/Liberal Democrat Chief Whips – Sir Robert Hutchison (1926-1930), Sir Archibald Sinclair (1930-1931), Jo Grimond (1950-1956), David Steel (1970-1976), Jim Wallace

(1987-1992), Archy Kirkwood (1992-1997) and Alastair Carmichael (2010-2013) – with Jo Grimond, Jim Wallace and Alastair Carmichael being MPs for Orkney and Shetland. Moreover, of the five Liberal Democrats in the UK Coalition Cabinet (2010-2015), two were Scots (Danny Alexander and Alastair Carmichael) and Vince Cable was, for some years, based in Glasgow where he was a Labour Councillor, the unsuccessful Labour candidate for Glasgow Hillhead in 1970 and received his PhD from the University in 1973

It is also of interest to note that, apart from the combined Liberal/SDP Alliance votes in 1983 and 1987, the 528,076 Liberal Democrat vote at the 2005 General Election was the largest ever 'Liberal' vote in Scotland. However, with the Scottish electorate having increased from 728,725 in 1906 to 3,839,900 in 2005, the 2005 vote represented only 22.6 % of total votes (on a 60.8 % Turnout) compared to 56.4 % (on a 80.9 % Turnout) at the 1906 General Election.

Appendix 3 – Biographical Notes

* Scottish connection by parentage, education, marriage and/or constituency represented

Other Liberal Cabinet Ministers 1905-1908

* ASQUITH. The Rt. Hon. Sir Herbert Henry, KC, KG, FRS (1852-1928), 1st Earl of Oxford and Asquith from 1925. Born in Morley, Yorkshire on 12 September 1852, being the second son of J. Dixon Asquith and Emily Willams. Educated at Huddersfield College (1860-1861), Fulneck Moravian School near Leeds (1861-1863), City of London School (1863-1870) and Balliol College, Oxford (First Class Degree in *Literae Humaniores*) in 1870-1874, President of the Oxford Union in 1874, Fellow of Balliol College in 1875-1882 and Honorary Fellow from 1908. Called to the English Bar (Lincoln's Inn) in 1876. Married (1) Helen Melland (Died 1891) on 23 August 1877. Liberal MP for East Fife (excluding St. Andrews Burghs), 1886-1918. Home Secretary (6th and 7th Liberal Cabinets), 1892-1895. Married (2) Margaret/Margot Tennant (Died 1945) on 10 May 1894. Rector of the University of Glasgow, 1905-1908. **Chancellor of the Exchequer (8th Liberal Cabinet), 1905-1908.** Prime Minister and Liberal Leader (9th Liberal Cabinet), 1908-1915, Rector of the University of Aberdeen, 1908-1914. Secretary of State for War (9th Liberal Cabinet). 1914. Prime Minister and Liberal Leader (Asquith Coalition Cabinet), 1915-1916, Liberal Leader (in Opposition from May 1918), 1916-1926. Liberal MP for Paisley, 1920-1924. Died in Berkshire on 17 February 1928.

* BIRRELL, The Rt. Hon. Augustine, KC (1850-1933). Born at Wavertree, Cheshire on 19th January 1850, being the son of the Rev. C.M. Birrell and Harriet Jane Grey of Edinburgh. Educated at Amersham Hall School, Cavershaw and Trinity Hall, Cambridge. Called to the English Bar (Inner Temple) in 1875. Married (1) Margaret Mirrielees (Died 1879) in 1878. Married (2) Mrs. Eleanor Tennyson, née Locker-Lampson (Died 1915) in 1888. Liberal MP for West Fife, 1889-1900, Professor of Law, University College, London, 1896-1899. President of the National Liberal Federation and Liberal Publication Department, 1902-1906. President of the Sir Walter Scott Club of Edinburgh, 1903. **President of the Board of Education (8th Liberal Cabinet), 1905-1907.** Liberal MP for Bristol North, 1906-1918. **Chief Secretary for Ireland (8th and 9th Liberal Cabinets), 1907-1915,** Rector of the University of Glasgow, 1911-1914, Chief Secretary for Ireland (Asquith Coalition Cabinet), 1915-1916. Died in London on 20 November 1933

* BRYCE, The Rt. Hon. Sir James, OM, GCVO, FRS (1838-1922), 1st Viscount Bryce of Dechmont from 1914 Born in Belfast on 10th May, 1838, being the first son of Dr. James Bryce, (Mathematics and Geography Master at the High School of Glasgow, 1846-1874) and Margaret Young.[405] Educated at **The High School of**

---

[405] Dr. Bryce's father, James Bryce the Elder was a Scottish Secessionist Minister who settled in Ulster in 1805. The Bryce family were originally landowning farmers at Dechmont, south-east of

Glasgow (Two years behind Sir Henry Campbell-Bannerman) in 1847-1852, Belfast Academy, 1852-1853, University of Glasgow, 1854-1857 and Trinity College, Oxford in 1857-1862 (Double First) and Heidelberg University in 1863, after being elected a Fellow of Oriel College, Oxford in 1862. President of the Oxford Union in 1862. Called to the English Bar (Lincoln's Inn) in 1867. Regius Professor of Civil Law, University of Oxford, 1870-1893. He was also, in 1870-1875, Professor of Jurisprudence at Owen's College, Manchester. He ascended Mount Ararat in 1876, being a notable mountain climber and President of the Alpine Club in 1899-1901. Liberal MP for Tower Hamlets, London, 1880-1885 and for South Aberdeen, 1885-1907. Parliamentary Under-Secretary at the Foreign Office (5th Liberal Administration), 1886. Married Elizabeth Marion Ashton in 1889, Chairman of the Royal Commission on Secondary Education, 1894-1896, Chancellor of the Duchy of Lancaster (6th Liberal Cabinet), 1892-1894. President of the Board of Trade (7th Liberal Cabinet), 1894-1895. **Chief Secretary for Ireland (8th Liberal Cabinet), 1905-1907).** UK Ambassador to the USA, 1907-1913. President of the British Academy (which he had helped to found in 1902) in 1913-1917. Participated in the Hague Tribunal in 1913 and investigated and reported on German atrocities in Belgium in 1914-1915. He was also, in July 1915, the first person to speak about Armenian massacres in the Ottoman Empire. He died on 22 January 1922 in Sidmouth, Devon. At the time of his death he was due to be granted the Freedom of the City and Royal Burgh of Glasgow. In 1965 the James Bryce Chair of Government (Politics from 1970) in Glasgow University was endowed in his honour. On the initiative of the Ulster History Circle and the Ulster-Scots Agency, a blue plaque in Viscount Bryce's honour was unveiled in Belfast on 10 May 2013. (Refer also to Appendix 6)

James Bryce had degrees, including honorary degrees, from thirty-one universities, with his twelve major publications including *The Holy Roman Empire* (1864) and *The American Commonwealth* (1888). Described in the *Glasgow High School Magazine* of June 1948 as 'this polymath of ours', the *Magazine* also quoted H.H. Asquith as saying –

> If I were asked who among the people directly or indirectly involved in politics in our time was the best educated, I should be disposed to single out James Bryce. No man in these days can take all knowledge for his province, but Bryce was near to being a universal specialist as any of his contemporaries.

* **BURNS, The Rt. Hon. John Elliott (1858-1943).** Born, of Scottish parentage, in Lambeth, London on 20 October 1856. Educated at St. Mary's National School,

---

Glasgow in Lanarkshire – hence 'Viscount Bryce of Dechmont'. However, as Covenanters, the family lost most of its property during the 17th century. (Viscount once said in the House of Lords, 'I have the broadsword of my ancestor who fought at Bothwell Brig', a battle fought in Lanarkshire in 1679 when government troops. led by the Duke of Monmouth and Graham of Claverhouse, defeated some 6,000 Covenanters) From c.1900 onwards. Dechmont has been best known for its Rifle Ranges which were at one time used by the Glasgow High School and other Army Cadets. However, with changes in the law after the Dunblane massacre in 1996, the Ranges are now only used by civilians for field target shooting with air rifles.

Battersea, London. Member of the Social Democratic Federation, 1881-1889. Married Martha Gale in 1882. Independent Labour and then Liberal/Labour MP for Battersea, 1892-1918. Attended the inaugural conference of the Labour Representation Committee in 1900 but refused to join. **President of the Local Government Board (8th and 9th Liberal Cabinets), 1905-1914.** President of the Board of Trade (9th Liberal Cabinet), 1914 (Resigned in opposition to Declaration of War). Died in London on 24th January 1943.

BUXTON, The Rt. Hon. Sir Sydney Charles, GCMG (1853-1934), 1st Lord Buxton from 1914, 1st Earl Buxton from 1920, Born in London on 25 October 1853, being the son of Charles Buxton (a Liberal MP in 1857-1871). Educated at Clifton College and Trinity College, Cambridge. Married (1) Constance Lubbock (Died 1892) in 1882. (She was the second daughter of Sir John Lubbock, 1st Lord Avebury) Liberal MP for Peterborough, 1883-1885. Liberal MP for Tower Hamlets, Poplar, London, 1886-1914, Under-Secretary for the Colonies (6th and 7th Liberal Administrations), 1892-1895, Married (2) Mildred Smith in 1896. **Postmaster General (8th and 9th Liberal Cabinets), 1905-1910,** President of the Board of Trade (9th Liberal Cabinet), 1910-1914, Governor General of South Africa, 1914-1920. Died at Newtimber, Sussex on 15 October 1934

CARRINGTON, The Rt. Hon. Sir Charles Robert Wynn-, KG, GCMG (1843-1928), 3rd (Irish) Lord Carrington and 3rd (UK) Lord Carrington from 1868, 1st Earl of Carrington from 1895, 1st Marquis of Lincolnshire from 1912. Born on 16 May 1843. Educated at Eton and Trinity College, Cambridge. Liberal MP for Wycombe, 1865-1868. Lord in Waiting/ Whip (4th Liberal Administration), 1881-1885. Governor of New South Wales, 1886-1890. Lord Chamberlain (6th and 7th Liberal Administrations), 1892-1895. Ambassador-at-Large to announce accession of King Edward in 1901. **President of the Board of Agriculture (8th and 9th Liberal Cabinets), 1905-1911.** Hereditary Lord Great Chamberlain as from accession of George V in 1910. (Title rotates between different descendants of the 4th Duke of Ancaster). Lord Privy Seal (9th Liberal Cabinet), 1911-1912. Died on 13 June 1928.

* **CREWE, The Rt. Hon. Sir Robert Offley Ashley Crewe-Milnes, KG (1858-1945), 2nd Lord Houghton from 1885, 1st Earl of Crewe from 1895, 1st Marquis of Crewe from 1911.** Born, as Robert O.A. Milnes, in London on 12 January 1858, Educated at Harrow and Trinity College, Cambridge. Married (1) Sibyl Maria Graham (Died 1887) in 1880. (They were the maternal grandparents of Sir John Colville, Joint Principal Private Secretary to Sir Winston Churchill in 1951-1955 and Terence O'Neil, Prime Minister of Northern Ireland in 1963-1969). Lord in Waiting /Whip (5th Liberal Administration), 1886. Lord Lieutenant of Ireland (6th and 7th Liberal Administrations), 1892-1895 Married (2) Lady Peggy Primrose, Daughter of the 5th Earl of Rosebery, in 1899, **Lord President of the Council (8th Liberal Cabinet), 1905-1908.** Colonial Secretary (9th Liberal Cabinet), 1908-1910. Lord Privy Seal (9th Liberal Cabinet), 1908-1911. Liberal Leader in House of Lords, 1908-1922. Secretary of State for India (9th Liberal Cabinet), 1910-1915. Lord Privy Seal (9th Liberal Cabinet), 1912-1915. Lord President of the Council (Asquith Coalition Cabinet), 1915-1916. President of the Board of Education (Asquith Coalition Cabinet), 1916. UK Ambassador to France, 1922-1928. Secretary of State for War (National Government), 1931. Liberal Leader in House of Lords, 1936-1944. Died in Surrey on 20 June 1945.

* **ELGIN, The Rt. Hon. Sir Victor Alexander Bruce, KG (1849-1917), 9th (Scottish) Earl of Elgin. 13th (Scottish) Earl of Kincardine and 2nd (UK) Lord Elgin from 1863.** Born in Government House near Montreal, Canada on 16 May 1849 when his father was Governor-General of Canada. Educated at Glenalmond, Eton and Balliol College, Oxford (Third Class Degree in *Literae Humaniores*, 1873). Married (1) Lady Constance Carnegie (1853-1909) in 1876, Treasurer of the Household (5th Liberal Administration) and First Commissioner of Works (5th Liberal Administration), 1886, Viceroy of India, 1894-1899, Chairman of Royal Commission on Salmon River Pollution, 1900. Chairman of Royal Commission on Military Preparations for the Boer War, 1903. Chairman of Royal Commission on the Scottish Churches Case, 1905. **Colonial Secretary (8th Liberal Cabinet), 1905-1908.** Married (2) Mrs. Gertrude Lillian Ogilvy, née Sherbrooke (Died 1971) in 1913. Died at Broomhall, Fife on 18th January 1917.

* **FOWLER, The Rt. Hon. Sir Henry Hartley, GCSI (1830-1911), 1st Viscount Wolverhampton from 1908.** Born in Sunderland on 16th May, 1830, being the son of the Rev. Joseph Fowler and Elizabeth Laing of Glasgow. Educated at Woodgrove School, Rawdon near Leeds and St. Saviour's School, Southwark, London. Married Ellen Thorneycroft (1830-1911) of Wolverhampton on 6 October 1857. Liberal MP for Wolverhampton, 1880-1885 Under-Secretary at the Home Office (4th Liberal Administration), 1884-1885 Liberal MP for Wolverhampton East, 1885-1908. Financial Secretary to the Treasury (5th Liberal Administration), 1886. President of the Local Government Board (6th Liberal Cabinet), 1892-1894. Secretary of State for India (7th Liberal Cabinet), 1894-1895. **Chancellor of the Duchy of Lancaster (8th and 9th Liberal Cabinets), 1905-1908.** Lord President of the Council (9th Liberal) Cabinet), 1908-1910. Died in Wolverhampton on 25 February 1911.

* **GLADSTONE, The Rt. Hon Sir Herbert John, GCB, GCMG, GBE (1854-1930), 1st Viscount Gladstone from 1910.** Born in 11 Downing Street, London on 7th January 1854, being the fourth and youngest son of William Ewart Gladstone.[406]. Educated at Eton and University College, Oxford. Liberal MP for Leeds, 1880-1885. Junior Lord of the Treasury/Whip (4th Liberal Administration) 1881-1885. Liberal MP for West Leeds, 1885-1910. Financial Secretary at the War Office (5th Liberal Administration), 1886. Under-Secretary at the Home Office (6th Liberal Administration), 1892-1894, First Commissioner of Works (7th Liberal Administration), 1894-1895. Liberal Chief Whip, 1899-1905. Married Dorothy Paget in 1901. **Home Secretary (8th and 9th Liberal Cabinets), 1905-1910.** First Governor General of South Africa, 1910-1914. Died in Hertfordshire on 6 March 1930.

---

[406] 11 Downing Street was William Gladstone's residence as Chancellor of the Exchequer in 1852-1855.

GREY, The Rt. Hon Sir Edward, Bt, KG (1862-1933), 1st Viscount Grey of Falloden from 1916. Born in London on 25 April 1862. Educated at Winchester and Balliol College, Oxford. Liberal MP for Berwick-upon-Tweed, 1885-1916. Married (1) Miss Dorothy Widdrington (Died 1906) in 1885. Under-Secretary at the Foreign Office (6th and 7th Liberal Administrations), 1892-1895. **Foreign Secretary (8th and 9th Liberal Cabinets), 1905-1915.** Foreign Secretary (Asquith Coalition Cabinet), 1915-1916. Temporary Ambassador to the USA in 1919. Married (2) Pamela Wyndham (Died 1929) – widow of Edward Tennant, 1st Lord Glenconner (Asquith's brother-in-law) – in 1922. Liberal Leader in the House of Lords, 1923-1924, Died at Falloden, Northumberland on 7 September 1933.

* HALDANE, The Rt. Hon. Sir Richard Burton, KC, KT, OM (1856-1928), 1st Viscount Haldane from 1911. Born in Edinburgh on 30 July1856. Educated at Edinburgh Academy and Universities of Edinburgh and Göttingen, Called to the English Bar (Lincoln's Inn) in 1879. Liberal MP for Haddingtonshire (East Lothian), 1885-1911. Rector of the University of Edinburgh, 1905-1908. **Secretary of State for War (8th and 9th Liberal Cabinets), 1905-1912.** Lord Chancellor (9th Liberal Cabinet), 1912-1915. Lord Chancellor (First Labour Cabinet), 1924. Labour Leader in the House of Lords, 1924-1928, Died at Cloanden, Perthshire on 19 August 1928.

HARCOURT, The Rt. Hon. Lewis (Loulou) Vernon (1863-1922), 1st Viscount Harcourt from 1917. Born in London on 31 January 1883, being the elder son of Sir William Harcourt, a Liberal Cabinet Minister in 1880-1885, 1886 and 1902-1905. Educated at Eton. Married Mary Ethel Burns in 1899. Liberal MP for Rossendale, Lancashire, 1904-1917. First Commissioner of Works (8th Liberal Administration), 1905-1907. **First Commissioner of Works (8th and 9th Liberal Cabinets), 1907-1910.** Colonial Secretary (9th Liberal Cabinet), 1910-1915. First Commissioner of Works (Asquith Coalition Cabinet), 1915-1916, Died in London on 24 February 1922.

LLOYD GEORGE, The Rt. Hon. David, OM (1863-1945), 1st Earl Lloyd George from 1945. Born, of Welsh parentage, in Manchester on 17 January 1863. Educated at Llanystumdwy School. Qualified as a Solicitor, 1884. Married (1) Miss Margaret Owen (Dame Margaret Lloyd George, Died 1941) in 1888. Liberal MP for Caernarfon Burghs, 1890-1918. **President of the Board of Trade (8th Liberal Cabinet), 1905-1908.** Chancellor of the Exchequer (9th Liberal Cabinet), 1908-1915. Minister of Munitions (Asquith Coalition Cabinet), 1915-1916, Secretary of State for War (Asquith Coalition Cabinet), 1916. Prime Minister (Lloyd George War Cabinet), 1916-1919. Coalition/National Liberal MP for Caernarfon Burghs, 1918-1923. Prime Minister (Lloyd George Coalition Cabinet), 1919-1922. Rector of the University of Edinburgh, 1920-1923 Liberal MP for Caernarfon Burghs, 1923-1931, Acting Liberal Leader in House of Commons, 1924-1926. Liberal Leader, 1926-1931. 'Father' of the House of Commons, 1929-1945. Independent Liberal MP for Caernarfon Burghs, 1931-1935. Liberal MP for Caernarfon Burghs, 1935-1945. Married (2) Frances Stevenson (Died 1972) in 1943. Died on 26 March 1945.

* **LOREBURN, The Rt. Hon. Sir Robert (Bob) Threshie Reid, KC, GCMG (1846-1923), 1st Lord Loreburn from 1906, 1st Earl Loreburn from 1911.** Born in Corfu on 3 April, 1846 when his father. Sir James John Reid (a native of Dumfries-shire in Scotland) was Chief Justice of the Ionian Islands. Educated at Cheltenham College and Balliol College, Oxford. Married Emily Fleming (Died 1904) in 1871. Called to the English Bar (Inner Temple) in 1871. Liberal MP for Hereford, 1880-1885. Liberal MP for Dumfries Burghs, 1886-1906. Solicitor General for England and Wales (7th Liberal Administration), 1894. Attorney General (7th Liberal Administration), 1894-1895. **Lord Chancellor (8th and 9th Liberal Cabinets), 1905-1912.** Died on 30 November 1923.

McKENNA, The Rt. Hon. Reginald (1863-1943), Born in London on 6 July 1863. Educated at King's College School, London and Trinity Hall, Cambridge. Called to the English Bar (Inner Temple) in 1887. Liberal MP for Monmouthshire North, 1895-1918, Financial Secretary to the Treasury (8th Liberal Administration), 1905-1907, **President of the Board of Education (8th Liberal Cabinet), 1907-1908.** Married Pamela Jekyll (Died 1943) in 1908, First Lord of the Admiralty (9th Liberal Cabinet), 1908-1911. Home Secretary (9th Liberal Cabinet), 1911-1915. Chancellor of the Exchequer (Asquith Coalition Cabinet), 1915-1916. Chairman of the Midland Bank, 1919-1943. Died in London on 6 September 1943.

* **MORLEY, The Rt. Hon. John, OM (1838-1923), 1st Viscount Morley of Blackburn from 1908.** Born in Blackburn on 24 December 1838. Educated at University College School, London, Cheltenham College and Lincoln College, Oxford. Married Rose Ayling in 1870. Liberal MP for Newcastle-upon-Tyne, 1883-1895. Chief Secretary for Ireland (5th Liberal Cabinet), 1886. Chief Secretary for Ireland (6th and 7th Liberal Cabinets), 1892-1895. Liberal MP for Montrose Burghs, 1896-1908 **Secretary of State for India (8th and 9th Liberal Cabinets), 1905-1910.** Chancellor of Manchester University, 1908-1923, Lord President of the Council (9th Liberal Cabinet), 1910-1914, (Resigned in opposition to Declaration of War). Died in Wimbledon on 23 September 1923.

RIPON, The Rt. Hon. Sir George Robinson, KG (1827-1909), 3rd Earl de Grey and 2nd Earl of Ripon from 1859, 1st Marquis of Ripon from 1871. Born in 10 Downing Street, London on 24 October, 1827, being the son of Viscount Goderich, then Prime Minister. Married Miss Henrietta Vyner, his cousin (Died 1907) in 1851. Educated privately and did not attend school or university. Radical MP for Hull, 1852-1853. Radical MP for Huddersfield, 1853-1857. Radical MP for West Riding of Yorkshire, 1857-1859. Under-Secretary of State for War (1st Liberal Administration), 1859-1861. Under-Secretary of State for India (1st Liberal Administration), 1861, Under-Secretary of State for War (1st Liberal Administration), 1861-1963. Secretary of State for War (1st and 2nd Liberal Cabinets), 1863-1866. Secretary of State for India (2nd Liberal Cabinet), 1866. Lord President of the Council (3rd Liberal Cabinet), 1868-1873. A high-ranking Freemason from 1861 until his conversion to Roman Catholicism in 1874. President of the Co-operative Congress, 1878. Viceroy of India (4th Liberal Administration), 1880-1884. First Lord of the Admiralty (5th Liberal Cabinet), 1886. Colonial Secretary (6th and 7th Liberal Cabinets), 1892-1895. Chancellor of the University of Leeds, 1904-1909. Liberal Leader in House of Lords, 1905-1908. **Lord Privy Seal (8th and 9th Liberal Cabinets), 1905-1908.** Died on 9 July 1909.

* **SINCLAIR, The Rt. Hon. Sir John (Jack), GCSI, GCIE (1860-1925), 1st Lord Pentland of Lyth from 1909.** Born in Edinburgh on 7 July 1860, being the first child of Captain George Sinclair (youngest son of Sir John Sinclair, 6th Baronet of Dunbeath in Caithness) [407] Educated at Edinburgh Academy, Wellington College and Sandhurst. Military Service, 1879-1887. Captain in the 5th Royal Irish Lancers, 1881-1886, being on escort duty in Dublin when Henry Campbell-Bannerman was Chief Secretary for Ireland (1884-1885). Aide-de-Camp and Official Secretary to Sir John Hamilton-Gordon, 7th (Scottish) Earl of Aberdeen as Lord Lieutenant of Ireland, 1886. Toynbee Hall studying law and economics, 1887-1889, Liberal MP for Dunbartonshire, 1892-1895. Parliamentary Private Secretary to Henry Campbell-Bannerman as Secretary of State for War (6th and 7th Liberal Administrations), 1892-1895. Secretary to Sir John Hamilton-Gordon, 7th (Scottish) Earl of Aberdeen as Governor-General of Canada, 1895-1897. Liberal MP for Forfarshire, 1897-1909. Sir Henry Campbell Bannerman's Chief Political Assistant, 1897-1905. Honorary Secretary of Gladstone National Memorial Fund Committee, 1898. Scottish Liberal Whip in the House of Commons, 1900-1905. Married (12 July 1904) Lady Marjorie Hamilton-Gordon (1880-1970), daughter of Sir John Hamilton-Gordon and Dame Isobel Hamilton-Gordon (née Majoribanks), 7th (Scottish) Earl and Countess of Aberdeen. **Secretary for Scotland (8th and 9th Liberal Cabinets), 1905-1912.** Sir Henry Campbell Bannerman's Literary Executor and a Trustee from 1908. Honorary President of the Campbell-Bannerman Memorial Committee, 1908-1913, Freedom of the City of Edinburgh, 1912. Governor of Madras, 1912-1919. Died on 11 January 1925

* **TWEEDMOUTH, The Rt. Hon. Sir Edward Marjoribanks, Bt, KT (1849-1909), 2nd Lord Tweedmouth from 1894.** Born on 8 July 1849. Educated at Harrow and Christ Church, Oxford. Married Lady Fanny Spencer-Churchill (1853-1904) on 9 June 1872. (Daughter of the 7th Duke of Marlborough and Aunt of Winston Churchill). Called to the English Bar (Inner Temple), 1874 Liberal MP for Berwickshire, 1880-1894. Comptroller of the Household/Whip (5th Liberal Administration), 1886. Parliamentary Secretary to the Treasury/Chief Whip (6th Liberal Administration), 1892-1894. Lord Privy Seal and Chancellor of the Duchy of Lancaster (7th Liberal Cabinet), 1894-1895. **First Lord of the Admiralty (8th Liberal Cabinet), 1905-1908.** Lord President of the Council (9th Liberal Cabinet), 1908. Died in Dublin on 15 September 1909.

The Prime Minister's Private Secretaries 1905-1908

* **PONSONBY, The Rt. Hon Arthur Augustus William Henry (1871-1946), 1st Lord Ponsonby of Shulbrede from 1930.** Born on 16 February 1871 in Windsor Castle, being the youngest son of Sir Henry Ponsonby, one of Queen Victoria's Principal Private Secretaries and a younger brother of Frederick Ponsonby (Lord

---

[407] The Sinclairs of Dunbeath and the Sinclairs of Ulbster (Sir Archibald Sinclair, Viscount Thurso, etc,) are both descended from an early Sinclair Earl of Caithness.

Sysonby), Assistant Private Secretary to Queen Victoria and then to King Edward. Royal Page, 1882-1887. Educated at Eton, 1885-1890 and Balliol College, Oxford, 1890-1892. Overseas learning French and German, 1892-1894. Foreign Office and Diplomatic Service (Constantinople and Copenhagen), 1894-1902. Married Dorothea (1876-1963), daughter of Sir Charles Parry, the composer, in 1898. Secretary of the Liberal Central Association, 1902--1905. Unsuccessful Liberal Candidate for Taunton at the January 1906 General Election. **Principal Private Secretary to Sir Henry Campbell-Bannerman as Prime Minister, 1906-1908**, resigning in January 1908 by reason of his wife's ill-health. (He was politically active again within three months and she outlived him by some 17 years) Liberal MP for Stirling Burghs (in succession to Sir Henry Campbell-Bannerman), 1908-1918. A Leader of the anti-war Union of Democratic Control, 1914-1918. Unsuccessful Independent Candidate for the new constituency of Dunfermline Burghs at the 1918 General Election, Labour MP for Sheffield Brightside, 1922-1930, Under Secretary at the Foreign Office, January-December 1924 (First Labour Administration), Under Secretary at the Dominions Office, June-December 1929 and Parliamentary Secretary, Ministry of Transport, 1929-1931 (Second Labour Administration). Chancellor of the Duchy of Lancaster, March-August 1931 (Second Labour Cabinet). Labour Leader in the House of Lords, 1931-1935, resigning, as a founder of the Peace Pledge Union, when (Major) Clement Attlee replaced George Lansbury, a pacifist, as Labour Leader. Resigned from the Labour Party in 1940 when it agreed to join Churchill's Coalition Government. Died in Surrey on 23 March 1946.

NASH, Vaughan Robinson, CB, CVO (1861-1932). Born on 5 October 1861 in Bristol. Privately educated Resident in Toynbee Hall, the University Settlement in the East End of London, 1887-1889. Freelance Writer and Journalist, 1889-1893. Married Rosalind Smith (1862-1952) in 1892. Her father was a cousin of Florence Nightingale. *Daily Chronicle,* 1893-1899, being dismissed for being pro-Boer during the South African War. *Manchester Guardian,* 1900. *Daily News,* 1901-1905. In 1903, as a member of the New Reform Club, he was involved in encouraging the electoral pact between Herbert Gladstone (Liberal Chief Whip) and Ramsay MacDonald (Labour). **Assistant Private Secretary to Sir Henry Campbell-Bannerman as Prime Minister, from December 1905 to January 1908. Principal Private Secretary to Sir Henry Campbell-Bannerman as Prime Minister, from January until Sir Henry's resignation on 3 April.** Assistant Private Secretary to Asquith as Prime Minister from 5 April but continuing to act as Private Secretary to Sir Henry Campbell-Bannerman until his death on 22 April. Principal Private Secretary to Asquith as Prime Minister from December 1908 until 1912 when he was succeeded by his wife's second cousin, (Sir) Maurice Bonham-Carter, who had been an Assistant Private Secretary since 1910. (Bonham-Carter married Violet Asquith and they were the parents of Mark Bonham-Carter and Laura Grimond.) Commissioner and then Principal of the Development Commission charged with recommending Treasury grants for rural industries, countryside services, harbours, fisheries and forestry, 1912-1915. Extra Private Secretary to Asquith as Prime Minister from August 1915. Appointed, in December 1916, to Secretariat of the Cabinet's Reconstruction Committee which, from July 1917, formed the nucleus of the staff of the new Ministry of Reconstruction. Re-appointed to the Development

Commission as from January 1919 and served until 1929. Died on 16 December 1932 in Hampshire.

HIGGS, Henry, CB (1864-1940). Born on 4 March 1864 in Cornwall. Civil Service Clerk, 1881-1884. Secretary's Office, GPO when not involved educationally, 1884-1899. University College, London, University of Berlin and, from 1887, Lecturer in Economics at Toynbee Hall, 1884-1890. Called to the English Bar (Middle Temple) in 1890. Treasury (Serving as Private Secretary to a succession of Ministers and as Assistant Private Secretary to Salisbury and Balfour before December 1905), 1899-1921 Secondment as Special Commissioner in Natal, 1902-1903. Secondment as **Assistant Private Secretary to Sir Henry Campbell-Bannerman as Prime Minister from December 1905 to April 1908.** Married Winifred Sarah South (1877-1939) on 16 July 1908. Secondment as Inspector-General of Finance in Egypt, 1912-1915. Retired from Treasury as Principal Clerk in 1921. Unsuccessful Liberal Candidate for Putney at the 1922 General Election. Lecturer in Economics, University of Wales, Bangor, 1925-1929. Died on 21 May 1940.in Brighton. He was a prolific writer on UK public finance, being also founding Secretary of what is now the Royal Economic Society and joint editor of its *Economic Journal* in 1892-1905.

MONTGOMERY, Sir (Charles) Hubert, CB, KCMG, KCVO (1874-1942). Born on 24 August 1874 in Co. Tyrone, being the fifth son of Hugh Montgomery, Conservative MP for Leitrim in 1852-1858. Educated at Charterhouse School. Foreign Office (Serving, in 1904-1918, as Private Secretary to a succession of Ministers), 1900-1933. **Seconded to** act as an **Assistant Private Secretary to Sir Henry Campbell-Bannerman as Prime Minister, from January to April 1908.** Seconded to act as a Secretary to the Earl Marshall's Office for the Coronation of King George V in 1911. Seconded to UK Embassy in Washington, 1918. Chief Clerk and Assistant Secretary, Foreign Office, 1919-1922   Assistant and then Deputy Permanent Under-Secretary of State for Foreign Affairs, 1922--1933. UK Ambassador to the Netherlands, 1933-1938. Died on 3 December 1942.

Four Other Glasgow High School Parliamentarians

* CAMPBELL, The Rt. Hon. James Alexander Campbell (1825-1908). Born in George Square, Glasgow on 20 April 1825, being the elder son of Sir James Campbell (1790-1876), Lord Provost of Glasgow in 1840-1843 and elder brother of Sir Henry-Campbell-Bannerman. Educated at the High School of Glasgow (1834-1838 and 1840-1841) and the University of Glasgow (Honours in Arts and Classics). Engaged in the family business, becoming a partner in 1860 and thereafter senior managing partner, 1851-1876. Married Ann Peto (died 1887) on 25 April 1854. Convener of the Lord Advocate's Glasgow University Committee charged with raising funds for the building and maintenance of the new buildings at Gilmorehill, 1865-1894.[408] Served on four Royal Commissions, 1868-1889. Honorary Doctor of

---

[408] The leading architect for the new University buildings at Gilmorehill was Sir George Gilbert Scott who, in his early career, had been employed by James Alexander's father-in-law, Sir Morton Peto.

Laws (LLD), Glasgow, 1868. Member of the Glasgow University Court as Assessor to two Rectors and two Chancellors, 1869-1884. First Deputy Chairman of the Glasgow School Board and, Convener of its Property and High School Committees, 1873-1876. Succeeded to his father's estate of Stracathro in Forfarshire (Angus) in 1876, Conservative MP for the Universities of Glasgow and Aberdeen, 1880-1906. Honorary Doctor of Laws (LLD), St. Andrews, 1885. Died on 9 May 1908 at Stracathro

As an Elder of the Church of Scotland, James Alexander served on a number of occasions as a General Assembly Commissioner, being also for many years Convener of the Endowments Committee. He was also first Secretary of the Glasgow Sabbath School Union. Prior to his appointment to the Privy Council in 1897, he was offered a baronetcy which he refused. He was also a considerable benefactor of the Church of Scotland Congregations in London. After his election as an MP in 1880, he had become an Elder in Crown Court in Covent Garden and then St. Columba's in Pont Street, Belgravia. In 1884 he was Convener of the Committee, with Lord Balfour of Burleigh (Conservative Secretary for Scotland in 1895-1903) as a co-opted member, whose report led to St. Columba's and Crown Court being disjoined in 1885 (Dr. George G. Cameron's *The Scots Kirk in London*, Becket Publications, Oxford, 1979)

* BUCHANAN, The Rt. Hon. Thomas (Tom) Ryburn Buchanan (1846-1911). Born on 2 April 1848 in Partick (then in Lanarkshire, now in Glasgow), being the third son of John Buchanan and Jane Buchanan (née Young). Educated at the High School of Glasgow (1855-1860), Shelbourne School and Balliol College Oxford (BA 1870, MA 1872) Fellow of All Souls College, Oxford, 1871-1888. Called to the English Bar (Inner Temple), 1873. Liberal MP for Edinburgh (Two-Member Constituency) from By-Election in 1881 until 1885. Liberal MP for Edinburgh West, 1885-1886 Liberal Unionist MP for Edinburgh West from 1886, resigning on re-joining the Liberal Party in 1888. Liberal MP for Edinburgh West as from a By-Election in February 1888 until 1892. Married Emily Bolitho of Trengwainton, Cornwall in 1888. Liberal MP for Aberdeenshire East from By-Election in December 1892 until 1900. Liberal MP for Perthshire East from By-Election in February 1903 until 1910, thus being the Campbell-Bannermans local MP for three to five years. Financial Secretary at the War Office (8th Liberal Government), 1905-1908 Under-Secretary at the India Office (9th Liberal Government), 1908-1909, representing the India Office in the House of Commons as the Secretary of State, Viscount Morley was in the House of Lords. Died on 7 April 1911 in Bournemouth.

* LAW, The Rt. Hon. Andrew Bonar Law (1858-1923). Born on 16 September 1858 in Rexton (formerly Kingston), New Brunswick, Canada. His father, the Rev. James Law (1822-1882), an Ulster Scot, was born in Portrush, Northern Ireland, became a Minister of the Free Church of Scotland and served as Minister of St. Andrew's Presbyterian Church in Rexton (now St. Andrew's United Church) from 1845 to 1877. His mother, Mrs. Elizabeth Law (nèe Kidston) was from Helensburgh in Scotland. After his mother died in childbirth in 1860 he was looked after by his mother's sister, Janet, who had come over from Helensburgh. When his father remarried in 1870, his aunt returned to Scotland taking Andrew with her to live in Helensburgh with her three male Kidston cousins who were merchant bankers in Glasgow. As the Kidston brothers were all unmarried or childless, they saw him as a substitute son and heir and indeed it was a substantial legacy on the death of one of the Kidstons which enabled him to undertake a political career as from 1900. The family home in Helensburgh was the now demolished Ferniegar. (In later life Bonar Law's Canadian connections were maintained through his friendship with William Aitken Lord Beaverbrook). He attended Gilbertfield School, Hamilton (presumably as a boarder) in 1870-1873 and The High School of Glasgow (presumably commuting from Helensburgh) in 1873-1875. For the next ten years he was employed in the Kidston's merchant bank. During this period he also attended evening classes at the University and was also, until 1900, an active member (North Staffordshire) of the Glasgow Parliamentary Debating Association. (GPDA). Following the take-over of the Kidston's bank by the Clydesdale Bank in 1885, he entered into partnership in William Jacks and Company of Glasgow. Mr. Jacks was a neighbour in Helensburgh. The partnership traded speculatively in pig iron and gold futures. During this time he also served on the first committee of Helensburgh Golf Club and was also a founding member of Helensburgh Lawn Tennis Club.' In 1891 he married Anne (Annie) Robley (Born 1867), daughter of Harrington Robley, a Dumbarton ship broker. They were married in Helensburgh West Free Church and set up home locally in Seabank (beside the former Clyde Centre) a house originally owned by Janet Kidston. When Annie's father died they moved to his house, Kintillo in Suffolk Street, Helensburgh. This house was sold in 1909 when the family moved to London. Conservative MP for Glasgow Blackfriars in 1900-1906, being Parliamentary Secretary, Board of Trade and President of the Glasgow High School Club (Former Pupils) in 1902-1905. Having been defeated at the 1906 General Election, he was Conservative MP for Dulwich, London (Elected at a By-Election in May 1906) until the December 1910 General Election. Mrs. Law died in London after a gall bladder operation in 1910. Having been defeated in North West Manchester at the December 1910 General Election, he was Conservative MP for Bootle, Lancashire (Elected at a By-Election in March 1911) until the 1918 General Election. Leader of the Conservative Party, 1911-1921. Colonial Secretary (Asquith Coalition Cabinet), 1915-1916,[409] Chancellor of the Exchequer (Lloyd George War Cabinet), 1916-1918 and Leader of the House of Commons in 1916-1921. Conservative MP for Glasgow Central in 1918-1923. Rector of Glasgow University (1919-1922) of which he was also an honorary graduate. Lord Privy Seal (Lloyd George Coalition Cabinet), 1919-1921. Resigned from the Cabinet and as Conservative Leader in 1921 by reason of ill health. Attended the Carlton Club meeting on 19 October 1922 at which, on his advice, the Conservatives decided to withdraw from the Lloyd George Coalition. Leader of the Conservative Party and

---

[409] Bonar Law was personally in a very weak position at the time of the formation of Asquith's Coalition on 19 May 1915 which is probably why he accepted the then relatively minor position of Colonial Secretary. Although he was no longer a partner in Jacks and Company, he was still financially committed and his brother, Jack was a partner. Thus the embarrassment when earlier in the month the Company was charged with trading with the enemy in that just after the Declaration of War in August 1914, the Company had delivered a cargo of iron ore from Nova Scotia to Krupps, the German iron and armaments manufacture. His brother narrowly escaped prosecution but two other partners, both friends of Bonar Law, were imprisoned.

Prime Minister from 23 October 1922 to 22 May 1923 when he resigned by reason of returning ill health. Died in London on 30 October 1923. He wanted to be buried in the family plot beside the north wall of Helensburgh Cemetery beside his wife and sons who had been killed in 1917 while serving in the KOSB and RFC but the family agreed that, as a Prime Minister, his ashes should be buried in the Nave of Westminster Abbey.

* **SUTHERLAND, The Rt. Hon. Sir William Sutherland, KCB (1880-1949).** Born in Glasgow on 4 March 1880, being the son of Alan Sutherland of Glasgow. His uncle, Angus Sutherland (1848-1922) was Liberal MP for Sutherland from 1886 until appointed Chairman of the Scottish Fisheries Board in 1894. After education at The High School of Glasgow and the University of Glasgow (MA), he joined the Civil Service and was initially appointed to the Board of Trade of which Lloyd George was President in 1905-1908 and Winston Churchill in 1908-1911. In 1907 he published *Old Age Pensions, in Theory and Practice, with some Foreign Examples.* Assisted in drafting and implementing the 1908 Old Age Pensions Act. In 1909-1913 he published (1) *The Call of the Land,* (2) *The Land Question* and (3) *Rural Regeneration.* Assisted in drafting and implementing the 1911 National Insurance Act and also assisted the Liberal Secretary for Scotland (John Sinclair, Lord Pentland) in drafting the 1911 Small Landowners (Scotland) Act Secretary, Cabinet Committee on the Supply of Munitions, 1915. Private (and Press) Secretary to Lloyd George as Minister of Munitions, Secretary of State for War and Prime Minister, 1915-1918. (During his association with Lloyd George when Prime Minister, he was much involved in the honours scandal.) Coalition Liberal MP for Argyll, 1918-1922. Parliamentary Private Secretary to Lloyd George as Prime Minister in 1919-1920. Junior Lord of the Treasury/Whip, 1920-1922, Married Anne Christine Fountain, CBE (Died 1949) of Yorkshire on 27 August 1921. Chancellor of the Duchy of Lancaster (Lloyd George Coalition Cabinet), April to October, 1922. National Liberal MP for Argyll, 1922-1923, defeating the official Liberal Candidate, Harry Watt (also a Glasgow High School Former Pupil). Liberal MP for Argyll from 1923 until defeated by a Conservative in 1924. Owner of a group of collieries in Yorkshire and Director and Managing Director of other colliery companies in 1924-1949. Unsuccessful Liberal Candidate for Barnsley in 1929. Died at Sheffield on 19 September 1949.

Appendix 4

Table 28 – Other Members of the Liberal Administration 1905-1908

* Royal Household

From 11 December 1905

Lord Lieutenant of Ireland	Sir John Hamilton-Gordon 7th (Scottish) Earl of Aberdeen & 4th (UK) Viscount Gordon

From 12 December 1905

Parliamentary Secretary, Treasury	George Whiteley, MP for Pudsey (Chief Whip)
Financial Secretary, Treasury (to 29 January 1907)	Reginald McKenna, MP for Monmouth
Under-Secretary, Home Office	Herbert Samuel. MP for Cleveland
Under-Secretary, Colonial Office	Winston S. Churchill, MP for North-West Manchester
Under-Secretary, War Office	Newton Wallop, 6th Earl of Portsmouth
Under-Secretary, India (to 29 January 1907)	John E. Ellis, MP for Rushcliffe
Parliamentary and Financial Secretary, Admiralty	Edmund Robertson, MP for Dundee
Attorney-General (to 28 January 1908)	Sir John Lawson Walton, KC, MP for Leeds South
Solicitor-General (to 28 January 1908)	Sir William S. Robson, KC, MP for South Shields
Lord Advocate (Scotland)	Thomas Shaw, KC, MP for Hawick Burghs
Lord Chancellor of Ireland	Sir Samuel Walker (Chief Justice)

From 14 December 1905

Financial Secretary, War Office	Thomas R. Buchanan, MP for East Perthshire

From 18 December 1905

Junior Lords of the Treasury (Assistant Whips)	John Herbert Lewis, MP for Flintshire Joseph A. Pease, MP for Saffron Walden
Civil Lord, Admiralty	George Lambert, MP for North Devon
Under-Secretary, Foreign Office	Edmond George Petty-Fitzmaurice, 1st Lord Fitzmaurice
Parliamentary Secretary, Education	Thomas Lough, MP for West Islington
Parliamentary Secretary, Board of Trade	Hudson E. Kearley, MP for Devonport)
Parliamentary Secretary, Local Government Board (to 29 January 1907)	Walter Runciman, MP for Dewsbury
Solicitor-General (Scotland)	Alexander Ure, KC, MP for Linlithgowshire = West Lothian
Paymaster-General	Richard K. Causton, MP for West Southwark
Government Chief Whip, House of Lords (to 29 May 1907)	Thomas Lister, 4th Lord Ribblesdale

* Lord Steward (to 31 July 1907)	Cecil G.S. Foljambe, 1st Earl of Liverpool
* Lord Chamberlain	Charles Robert Spencer, 1st Viscount Althorp
* Vice-Chamberlain (to 27 February 1907)	Wentworth Beaumont, MP for Hexham
* Master of the Horse (to 6 September 1907)	Osbert Cecil Molyneux, 6th Earl of Sefton
* Treasurer	Sir Edward Strachey, MP for South Somerset
* Comptroller of the Household (Scottish Whip)	Alexander W.C.O. Murray, MP for Peebles and Selkirk, The Master of Elibank
* Captain of Gentlemen at Arms (to 31 July 1907)	William Lygon, 7th Earl Beauchamp
* Captain of the Yeoman of the Guard (to 29 April 1907)	William Montagu, 9th Duke of Manchester
* Lords in Waiting (Whips)	Richard Forbes, 8th (Irish) Earl of Granard (to 31 July 1907) (and Assistant Postmaster-General) Thomas Denman, 3rd Lord Denman (to 31 July 1907) Richard Lyon-Dalberg-Acton, 2nd Lord Acton Granville Leveson-Gower, 3rd Earl Granville Gavin Hamilton, 2nd Lord Hamilton of Dalzell

From 20 December 1905

Attorney-General (Ireland)	Richard R. Cherry, KC, MP for Liverpool Exchange
Solicitor-General (Ireland)	Redmond Barry, KC, MP for Tyrone North from March 1907

From 21 December 1905

Junior Lord of the Treasury (Assistant Whip)	Cecil Norton, MP for West Newington

From 2 February 1906

Junior Lord of the Treasury (Assistant Whip)	John Fuller, MP for Westbury, Wiltshire

From 21 February 1906

* Lord in Waiting (Whip)	Edward Colebrooke, 1st Lord Colebrooke

From 29 January 1907

Financial Secretary, Treasury	Walter Runciman, MP for Dewsbury
Under-Secretary, India	Charles Hobhouse, MP for East Bristol
Parliamentary Secretary, Local Government Board	Dr. Thomas J. Macnamara, MP for Camberwell North

From 27 February 1907

Junior Lord of the Treasury (Assistant Whip)	John Henry Whitley, MP for Halifax
* Vice-Chamberlain	John Fuller, MP for Westbury

From 29 May 1907

Government Chief Whip, House of Lords

	Thomas Denman, 3rd Lord Denman (as above)
From 31 July 1907	
* Lord Steward	William Lygon, 7th Earl Beauchamp
* Captain of Gentlemen at Arms	Thomas Denman, 3rd Lord Denman (as above)
* Lord in Waiting (Whip)	Richard Herschell, 2nd Lord Herschell
From 6 September 1907	
* Master of the Horse	Richard Forbes, 8th (Irish) Earl of Granard
From 1 November 1907	
* Lord in Waiting (Whip)	Maurice Towneley-O'Hagan, 3rd Lord O'Hagan
From 28 January 1908	
Attorney-General	Sir William S. Robson, KC, MP (as above)
Solicitor-General	Sir Samuel T. Evans, KC, MP for Mid Glamorgan

Appendix 5 – Commemorations

Monument to Sir Henry in Westminster Abbey

The Monument, by Paul Raphael Montford (Sculptor) and Maurice Webb (Architect), is situated in the north nave aisle of the Abbey. It was erected on 29 December 1911 and unveiled on 12 January 1912. The monument shows an over life-size bust in bronze in in the robes of a Knight Grand Cross of the Order of the Bath. The background is of black marble with bronze Ionic pillars framing a round-headed niche with enamelled heraldic shield above. The inscription on the red marble base reads: 'Erected by Parliament to the Right Honourable Sir Henry Campbell-Bannerman, GCB, Prime Minister' and, within a bronze wreath, 'Born 1836, Died 1908'. The date of birth was originally given as 1839, due to the last figure being turned upside down but this was corrected soon after the unveiling.

The heraldic shield shows Bannerman quartered with Campbell of Stracathro. Sir Henry's coat of arms was as granted and recorded by Lord Lyon King of Arms in Edinburgh in 1872, the year in which he assumed the surname Campbell-Bannerman. The coat of arms of his father, Sir James Campbell, as Campbell of Stracathro, was similarly granted and recorded in 1859, twelve years after he bought the Stracathro Estate in Forfarshire (Angus) from the Cruickshank family.

The crests and mottos associated with Sir Henry's coat of arms having been considered in the Personal Prologue, the quarterings in the shield were stated in Harvey Johnston's *The Heraldry of the Campbells* (1921, pp.46-47) as – 1 and 4 [Bannerman] – *Parted per pale red and black a banner displayed bend ways silver, thereon a canton blue charged with a silver saltire.* 2 and 3 [Campbell] – *Gyronny of eight, gold and black, on an engrailed silver chief a galley, oars in action, between two hunting horns stringed, all of them black,*

Paul Raphael Montford

Paul Raphael Montford (1868-1938), who went to Australia in 1923, was also the sculptor for Sir Henry's statue in Stirling (as follows) and for a marble bust of Sir Henry in the Stirling Smith Art Gallery and Museum. Montford also designed the four sculpture groups on Glasgow's Kelvin Way Bridge (over the River Kelvin) in Kelvingrove Park and thus downstream from the site of Kelvinside House where Sir Henry was born in 1836. The Bridge was designed in 1912 by Alexander Beith McDonald, the City Engineer, and erected in 1914. Montford's sculpture groups design was selected in a competition in 1914 but the groups were not erected until 1926. The groups were badly damaged by enemy action in March 1941 and were, in 1951, repaired by Benno Schotz (as follows).

Unveiling of Sir Henry's Statue in Stirling
by H.H. Asquith as Prime Minister on Saturday, 1 November 1913

This part of Appendix 5 is based on reports in the *Stirling Observer* of 4 November 1913, and the *Stirling Journal (and Advertiser)* of 6 November 1913

The Honorary President of the Memorial Committee, John Sinclair, Lord Pentland, who had been, *inter alia,* Sir Henry's Secretary for Scotland, was not present as he was serving as Governor of Madras. The first Chairman of the Committee, Sir James B. Smith, for long Sir Henry's Chairman in Stirling, had died. Accordingly, the Committee's second Chairman, Sir John Graham, Bt of Larbert in Stirlingshire presided during the proceedings, both in the open air and afterwards in the Albert Hall.

Sir John Graham (1837-1926) had been at Glasgow University with Sir Henry some sixty years earlier and, like Sir Henry, had served as an officer (Captain) in the First Lanarkshire Rifle Volunteers.

To the great disappointment of the very large number of spectators, the ceremony at the statue was very brief, lasting for only about ten minutes. Sir John, speaking from a temporary platform, said it was his privilege to preside that day and also to have the privilege of asking the Prime Minister to complete the work begun by their late friend, Sir James B. Smith, and carried out on their behalf by Mr. Paul Raphael Montford, the sculptor. He then asked Mr. Asquith to unveil the statue, and to hand it over to the care of the Provost and Magistracy of the Royal Burgh of Stirling, (Applause).

Mr. Asquith then stepped forward and pulled the cord which released the covering of the statue, revealing to view the figure of Sir Henry, with the unveiling being greeted with much cheering. The Prime Minister then said, 'I have the honour to unveil this statue, and to hand it over to the care of the Provost and Magistrates of this ancient and Royal Burgh, to perpetuate the memory of a man who, through their confidence, was for the best part of forty years a distinguished member of the Imperial Parliament, and who rendered in his time the most solid and signal service to his country and to the Empire'. (Cheers)

The open air proceedings concluded with the Rt. Hon. Eugene Wason (Liberal MP for Clackmannan and Kinross) proposing a vote of thanks to the Prime Minister for being present on such a memorable occasion. (Loud Cheers). The platform party then moved to the Albert Hall to join the 1,350 privileged ticket-holders who were waiting to listen to Asquith's eulogy of the late Prime Minister and other speeches.

> The site on which the statue has been erected… will commend itself more and more as the improvements in the locality, especially the erection of the new municipal buildings, are carried out… The statue is of bronze, the figure standing 9½ feet high, and represents Sir Henry in his robes as a [Knight Grand Cross of the Order of the Bath]. The likeness is an excellent one, the features bearing a smiling characteristic expression. The pedestal is of bronze-tinted granite. In front there is a bronze female figure of "Peace" standing out in relief, and over and behind in Egyptian symbolics the words "South Africa". Surmounting the panel there is inscribed in raised letters, "Campbell-Bannerman, 1836-1908". Other panels record the fact[s] that Sir Henry represented the Stirling Burghs from 1868 to 1908 and was Prime Minister from 1905 to 1908…
>
> (*Stirling Observer,* 4 November 1913)
> …

In opening the indoor proceedings, Sir John Graham again referred with gratitude to the late Sir James B. Smith, his predecessor as Chairman of the Memorial Committee and also to the late Robert Taylor, for long Sir Henry's Agent in Stirling and the Committee's first Secretary and Treasurer. Sir John also said that the list of subscribers to the memorial, comprising as it did prominent public men, high officials, humble citizens of all shades of opinion from all walks of life and from all parts, was a testimony to the fact that Sir Henry's moral courage and perseverance, his unflinching rectitude and his sincerity were appreciated throughout the length and breadth of the land.

Mr. Asquith started his speech by saying that 'we are met to do honour to a great citizen and a great Scotsman (applause) who used the trust so long and so constantly confided in him by the Stirling Burghs in the unselfish service of his generation and his country'. (Applause) The Prime Minister then went on to recall the main stages in Sir Henry's public life and his many other interests including his real love of books and pictures.

> But he was also – although I believe he did not take a very high degree at Cambridge – a well-read classical scholar. I remember an incident in Mr. Gladstone's Cabinet of 1892. That Cabinet contained, in addition to its illustrious chief, quite a number of distinguished classical scholars One day a discussion arose – for even Cabinets do not always keep to the point (laughter) – as to the true reading of a line in the Latin poet Juvenal. Most of our big classical guns were in favour of one meaning, while Campbell-Bannerman was almost alone in favour of another. The text was sent for, and it was proved that they were wrong and he was right. (Laughter and applause)
>
> I remember being somewhat nettled myself, because I was on the side of the majority. [So] I pointed out to him that the line with which he had

shown such an uncanny familiarity was in one of the satires of Juvenal which are not ordinarily allowed to be read in schools (Laughter)

The Prime Minister concluded by referring to the tenacity of Sir Henry's convictions, his shrewdness and humour, his courage as a political fighter, concluding that 'we had in him what a country most needs in its statesmen – a man true as steel, simple in heart and life, a devoted and unselfish servant of the State. (Cheers) May his memory here in Stirling and throughout the Empire never fade', (Loud cheers)

The other speakers were the Rt. Hon. John Burns (President of the Local Government Board), Dr. William Chapple (Liberal MP for Stirlingshire), T.P. O'Connor (Irish Nationalist MP for Liverpool Scotland and a personal friend of Sir Henry), and Arthur Ponsonby (Sir Henry's successor as Liberal MP for Stirling Burghs). Two messages received by cable from overseas were also read out –

> [From Louis Botha, Prime Minister of the Union of South Africa] – *South Africans will always retain a grateful memory of the Statesman who had the courage to carry into effect self-government for the Transvaal and the Orange Free State, which paved the way for the establishment of the Union of South Africa. I deem it a great privilege to be associated with the movement in connection with the memorial to Sir Henry Campbell-Bannerman.* (Cheers)

> [From the Rt. Hon. John Sinclair, Lord Pentland, Governor of Madras] – *Heartily rejoice with Scottish Liberals all the world over in honour done to your Sir Henry to-day.* (Cheers)

Earlier in the day Asquith had received the Freedom of the Royal Burgh of Stirling and was admitted as an honorary member of the Guildry Incorporation of Stirling, honours which Sir Henry himself had received some 21 years earlier on 15 December 1892.

However, although in Stirling the day passed off without any untoward incident, the Prime Minister and his daughter, Violet (the future Lady Bonham Carter, Jo Grimond's mother-in-law) were the victims of a suffragette attack while on their way to Stirling., They had been staying with Sir John and Lady Graham in Larbert and were travelling to Stirling with them in a chauffeur-driven, open-topped car which was forced to stop, near Bannockburn, by four militant suffragettes who were lying down on the road. One of the women then threw some pepper into the car, whilst another attempted to strike the Prime Minister with a dog whip. A Scotland Yard officer from London, who had been sitting beside the chauffeur, immediately jumped out and drove the women off. Four local constables who had been patrolling the road on bicycles then arrived on the scene, the women were taken to Bannockburn Police Station and then to the County Police Office in Stirling where they were detained.

Asquith took the incident quite calmly but Violet appeared to be somewhat alarmed and upset. Much indignation was expressed in Bannockburn and in Stirling when news of the attack became known but by then the women were safely under lock and key. They had given false names but were later identified by detectives from Edinburgh and Glasgow. They were brought before Sherriff Mitchell in Stirling on the Monday morning, granted bail of £ 10 each and left Stirling in the afternoon.

As areas mentioned, The Stirling Smith Art Gallery and Museum has a Marble Bust of Sir Henry, also by Paul Raphael Montfort. This was presumably a by-product of the sculptor's work on the above statue, although the marble bust shows Sir Henry in 'civilian' clothes whereas the statue shows him in the robes of a Knight Grand Cross of the Order of the Bath.

Centenary Commemorations in Scotland 2008

Given that I attended four of the five events, this part of Appendix 5 is based on my reports in the *Journal of Liberal History* (Summer 2008 and Summer 2009), noting that Dr. Ewen A. Cameron was appointed as Sir William Fraser Professor of Scottish History and Palaeography in the University of Edinburgh in February 2012;

The five Scottish events were in commemoration of the Centenary of Sir Henry's death. Refer also to the *High School of Glasgow Magazine* for 2008-2009.

The Meigle and District History Society held a Campbell-Bannerman Evening in the Kinloch Memorial Hall, Meigle, Perthshire on Tuesday, 22 April.

With some 80 people in attendance, the speaker was Dr. Ewen A. Cameron, then a Senior Lecturer in Scottish History at Edinburgh University (now Sir William Fraser, Professor of Scottish History and Palaeography at Edinburgh Univeristy) and a contributor to the *Journal of Liberal History*. His talk followed much the same approach as in his article about Sir Henry in the *Journal* (Spring 2007). However, Dr. Cameron also referred to a number of other aspects of Sir Henry's career during the talk and in discussion. There was, for example, reference to Sir Henry's unsuccessful candidature at the Stirling Burghs By-Election in April 1868 and his success, seven months later on an extended franchise at the General Election after which he remained MP for Stirling Burghs for the rest of his life.

The talk was supported by an excellent handout including a biographical chronology, details of Sir Henry's constituency election results, summarised Scottish and UK General Election results from 1868 to 1906, a selection of quotations (on all of which Dr. Cameron commented) and a bibliography from T.P. O'Connor's 1908 memoir to Dr. Cameron's own 2007 article. (Dr. Cameron's critical comments on the 2006 biography of Sir Henry by Roy Hattersley were much appreciated).

Other topics discussed included Sir Henry's emergence from a Tory background (described as suspicious by the *Stirling Journal [and Advertiser]* in March 1868), his (perhaps deliberately cultivated) image of self-effacement, Irish and Scottish Home Rule and 'home rule all round' (or federalism), the 'disestablishment' of the Church of Scotland, the South African War of 1899-1902, imperialism, free trade versus tariff reform, extension of the franchise (including votes for women), land reform, and restricting the powers of the House of Lords.

Also discussed was what would or would not have happened if Sir Henry had lived longer with reference to the careers of Asquith, Lloyd George and Churchill, the Irish dimension, the First World War, interaction with Bonar Law (Conservative Leader from 1911 and, as was Sir Henry, a Former Pupil of The High School of Glasgow), Liberal-Labour relations and Liberal election prospects.

A Campbell-Bannerman Centenary Commemoration, endorsed by the Liberal Democrat History Group, took place in Meigle on Sunday, 27 April.

The day's programme started with Morning Worship in the Parish Church where, as already mentioned (Chapter 6), there is a plaque near the East Gallery where the Campbell-Bannermans worshipped when living at the nearby Belmont Castle, their Scottish home from 1887,

The Service was led the Rev. John (Ian) W. Knox, a retired Minister, who managed to mention Sir Henry in his Introductory Remarks/Welcomes, Children's Address, Intercessory Prayer and Sermon. At one point Mr. Knox suggested that Sir Henry was a precursor of Sir William Beveridge's social initiatives.

We then visited Belmont Castle which, as a listed building, is much as reconstructed and refurbished for the Campbell-Bannermans in 1885-1886. They acquired the Castle after much of it had been destroyed by fire in 1884. It was leased from Dundee Corporation by the Church of Scotland as a Home for Senior Citizens from 1930, being formally opened as such in 1931. We were welcomed by Dr. Sue Marshall, then Deputy Unit Manager, who pointed-out various features and memorabilia associated with the Campbell-Bannermans including portraits. We were then allowed to move freely between the main lounge and the other public rooms and into the stair hall (originally a covered-in courtyard) and up its grand staircase.[*]

By reason of fire safety precautions, there is no longer direct access between the main lounge (or living hall) and the stair hall. Thus we were unable to have an overall view of the space (entrance, living and stair halls) which accommodated between two and three hundred relatives and public representatives (and some four hundred wreaths) on the day of Sir Henry's funeral. (The Church of Scotland's decision in April 2013 to give up its lease of Belmont Castle was considered in Chapter 6.)

Lunch followed in the Kinloch Arms Hotel (in the centre of Meigle) starting with Grace by the Rev. Dr. Malcolm H. MacRae, Meigle's Interim Moderator (Acting Parish Minister) and concluding, as did refreshments on the Tuesday evening, with buttered gingerbread with which Sir Henry liked to end his meals.

Dr. MacRae was then basically Parish Minister of Kirkmichael, Straloch and Glenshee linked with Rattray. He retired to Stirling (where he had been a Parish

---

[*] The castle closed as a care home in 2013

Minister previously) in 2010 and coincidentally was succeeded in Kirkmichael, etc. by the Rev. (Mrs) Linda Stewart who had previously been Parish Minister of Meigle, etc. and then Port of Menteith, etc. (Refer to Chapter 1)

We then proceeded to the Campbell-Bannerman grave beside the Parish Church. After an Introduction by Dr. MacRae, and a Biographical Eulogy by Dr. Sandy Waugh, a Former Pupil of the High School of Glasgow and a Member of the Liberal Democrat History Group, Dr. MacRae read *'Let Us Now Praise Famous Men'* from *Ecclesiasticus*. A wreath – featuring the old Scottish Liberal colours of red and yellow – was then laid by Liberal Democrat Councillor Willie Wilson as then Provost Depute of Perth and Kinross. (Councillor Willie Wilson, with other Liberals, had also taken part in a similar wreath-laying at the time of the 75th anniversary of Sir Henry's death.)

The programme concluded with the singing of Scottish Metrical Psalm 23, *The Lord's my Shepherd* to the tune *Stracathro* (named for the house and estate in Forfarshire [Angus] which Sir Henry's father, Sir James Campbell acquired in 1847), followed with Prayer and Benediction by Dr. MacRae and an expression of thanks to all concerned by the Provost Depute, who had also undertaken similar courtesies at Belmont Castle and at Lunch.

By way of appreciation and thanks, those present and some others, who were unable to be present, contributed not only to the cost of the wreath but also to donations sent afterwards to Meigle Parish Church and to Friends of Belmont Castle.

The Stirling Liberal Democrats organised a Centenary Commemoration at Sir Henry's statue in Stirling on the afternoon of Monday, 28 April.

Wreaths were laid by Nicol Stephen (Lord Stephen 2011), then an MSP and Scottish Liberal Democrat Leader, and Councillor Fergus Wood (SNP) as Provost of Stirling.

(It was noted at this time that the marble bust of Sir Henry by Paul Raphael Montford in the Stirling Smith Art Gallery and Museum was arrayed with a wreath of daffodils to mark the centenary.

As already mentioned, the Gallery and Museum also has a sea-scape which Sir Henry bought and presented in 1897 (Chapter 3) and, as above, a portrait sketch of Sir Henry by Sir James Guthrie, probably painted in the autumn of 1907, and gifted by J.J. Monroe in 1944.

The High School of Glasgow – which Sir Henry attended in 1845-1850 – had its own Centenary Commemoration on the morning of Tuesday, 16 September 2008

The audience in the Assembly Hall included members and former members of staff, all the sixth formers, history scholars from the fifth form and from two other Glasgow schools, past and present School Governors and Trustees and Office-

Bearers of the School Club (Former Pupils) including the then President, the Rt. Hon. Lord Philip and other invited guests.

After introductory welcomes by Colin Mair (then Rector), Leona Duff, then Girls' Captain of Bannerman House (named for Sir Henry) outlined Sir Henry's career at the High School. The programme then centred on a lecture by Dr. Ewen A. Cameron, by then Reader in Scottish History in Edinburgh University. who offered answers to the question "Why study Campbell-Bannerman?", following much the same approach as in his article on Sir Henry in the *Journal of Liberal History* (Spring 2007) and his talk on Sir Henry at Meigle on 22 April 2008 (as above) After a presentation on Bannerman House's then current charitable fund-raising project in Sir Henry's memory, Thomas Nicholl, then Boys' House Captain concluded the proceedings in the Assembly Hall by expressing the thanks of all present to Dr. Cameron.

During the morning the guests also had the opportunity to see the bronze plaque commemorating Sir Henry (by Benno Schotz, RSA) and a picture of John M. Bannerman, Lord Bannerman of Kildonan (1901-1969), another Former Pupil, who played Rugby for Scotland on thirty-seven occasions and who, when Chairman of the Scottish Liberal Party (1955-1965), came within 966 votes of winning Inverness in 1955 and within 1,658 votes of winning Paisley in 1961.

In the same row as the bronze plaque for Sir Henry, there is a plaque (also by Benno Schotz) commemorating Bonar Law, the School's other Prime Minister. Benno Schotz [1891-1984] was an Estonian who settled in Glasgow in 1912. He was appointed the Queen's Sculptor-in-Ordinary in Scotland in 1963 and received the Freedom of Glasgow in 1969. His other works include Lord Boyd Orr, Hugh McDiarmid, David Ben Gurion and Golda Meir in bronze, James Bridie in terracotta and Stanley Baxter in plaster.

The above-mentioned fund-raising by Bannerman House in Sir Henry's memory raised £5,900 in 2007-2008 in support of Mary's Meals (formerly Scottish International Relief) which provides a daily school meal for over three quarters of a million children in some of the world's poorest communities where poverty and hunger would otherwise prevent children from gaining an education. The funds were used to finance the construction of a Kitchen at Cobbe Barracks Primary School, Zomba, Malawi where a plaque, in Sir Henry's name, is now situated.

The final Scottish Centenary event was the unveiling of a bronze plaque at 129 Bath Street, Glasgow (Sir Henry's family home in 1836-1860) by the Rt. Hon. Lord Steel of Aikwood (Liberal Leader in 1976-1988) on the afternoon of Friday, 5 December 2008, the 103rd anniversary of Sir Henry's appointment as Prime Minister on 5 December 1905. In 2008 the building was The ABode Glasgow Hotel, as renamed The Arthouse Glasgow in 2014.

Those present also included the late Rt. Hon. Charles Kennedy, MP (Liberal Democrat Leader in 1999-2006), representatives of the Lord Provost and the High

School, a number of Liberal Democrat MSPs and Councillors and other Liberal Democrats from many parts of Scotland and one from England.

After a reception, hosted by the Hotel's General Manager, there were welcomes and introductory remarks by the leading promoters of the project – Nigel Lindsay (formerly a Liberal Councillor in Aberdeen) and Robert Brown (then an MSP and now a Liberal Democrat Councillor in South Lanarkshire.) We were then piped outside by Thomas Nicholl of the High School (as above). In unveiling the plaque, Lord Steel praised Sir Henry as an "overlooked radical" whose 1906 General Election landslide victory had paved the way for a succession of reforming governments. "He had led the way for the longest period of successful radical government ever [and] gets overlooked because Asquith and Lloyd George were Prime Ministers for longer."

**SIR HENRY
CAMPBELL-BANNERMAN
1836 – 1908
LIBERAL PRIME MINISTER
BORN IN GLASGOW AND LIVED
HERE UNTIL 1860
A RADICAL. A PEACEMAKER
A GOOD MAN**

Events in London in 2009 and 2010

This part of Appendix 5 is based on items in the *Journal of Liberal History* (Autumn 2009 and Winter 2009-2010), in the *High School of Glasgow Magazine* for 2009-2010 and in the Online *Three Former Prime Ministers – UK Parliament* and on correspondence with James Gray, MP.

Portrait Busts of Sir Henry and Andrew Bonar Law, now in the Members' Lobby adjacent to the Debating Chamber of the House of Commons, were unveiled in Portcullis House, Westminster on 15 July 2009.

As from a letter (30 April 2013) from James Gray, MP, who attended the High School in 1966-1971 –

> When I arrived in Parliament [as Conservative MP for Wiltshire North] in 1997, and having been told that the busts around the Members' Lobby were of all the Prime Ministers since 1900, I quickly set off to seek out my two fellow Glasgow High School MPs [Sir Henry and Bonar Law]. I was very surprised to discover that neither of them was commemorated in… the Palace of Westminster. I then approached Mr. Speaker's Advisory Committee on Works of Art to point out this omission and after some to-ing and fro-ing the busts were commissioned…

Wiltshire North includes the former Parliamentary Borough of Malmesbury, whose MP in 1818-1820 was Kirkman Finlay (1773-1842) who was also a pupil at Glasgow High School (when known as the Grammar School). Kirkman Finlay, a Free Trade Tory, had previously been Lord Provost of Glasgow and MP for the Glasgow District of Burghs. His son, Alexander, educated at Harrow, was Liberal MP for Argyll in 1857-1868.

The remit of the Speaker's Advisory Committee includes ensuring that leading and notable parliamentarians are represented in either portraits or sculptures in the Permanent Collection of the House of Commons.

The portrait bust of Sir Henry was commissioned from Martin Jenkins with that of Bonar Law being copied from an original by John E. Hyatt in Ashridge Business College in Hertfordshire. The College was formerly a centre for training Conservative agents and organisers, purchased from funds made available by Bonar Law.

Accordingly, the event in 2009 when also unveiled then and there were a portrait bust of Neville Chamberlain by Kathleen, Lady Kennett – the widow (from her first marriage) of Captain Robert Scott of the Antarctic – on loan from Birmingham, and a portrait bust of Jeremy Thorpe (Liberal Leader in 1967-1976) cast by Pangolin Editions from an original by Avril Vellacott.

Coincidentally, before his ill-fated Antarctic Expedition (1910-1913), Captain Scott raised funds during a lecture tour and, encouraged by the then Rector, the boys of The High School of Glasgow raised funds to finance a pony sledge which was named Glasgow. (Lockhart [2010], p.367) There is another High School connection with Antarctica in that Sir William Beardmore, Bt (1st Lord Invernairn 1921), a Former Pupil, heavily funded Ernest Shackleton's expedition of 1907-1909 – hence the naming by Shackleton of the Beardmore Glacier, the largest in the world. (Lockhart [2010], p.108)

Those present at the event in 2009, in addition to the Speaker, included Hugo Swire (Conservative MP for East Devon and Chairman of the Advisory Committee), James Gray, MP, Jeremy and Marion Thorpe, Martin Jenkins and Avril Vellacott, Colin Mair (Rector of The High School of Glasgow). Hugh A. Campbell Adamson (a descendant of Sir Henry's elder brother, James Alexander Campbell, MP), Graham Lippiatt (Secretary of the Liberal Democrat History Group and of the Lloyd George Society) and Sir Nick Clegg, Liberal Democrat Leader from 2007 to 2015.

It is of interest to note what Martin Jenkins said about his commission. After referring to the incident in 1913 when, on his way to unveil the Stirling statue of Sir Henry, Asquith was set upon by suffragettes, he concluded –

> It is not clear to what extent their [the suffragettes'] ire concerned the unveiling of the statue but looking at photographs of Campbell-Bannerman, it is hard to imagine how such anger could have been aroused by so kindly a face. He seems shrewd admittedly but hardly careworn in the manners of today's leaders. In making the portside I was interested in bringing out the story these photos told – of an open-faced, smiling, avuncular figure from an age in which, for better or worse, politicians were not constantly under the microscope. Like him they could even sometimes look contented, fulfilled and happy with their lot.

A Reception, hosted by James Gray, MP, took place in the Palace of Westminster on 26 May 2010

This provided, *inter alia,* an opportunity for those present to view the above-mentioned portrait busts of Sir Henry and Bonar Law as placed next to each other in the Members' Lobby of the House of Commons. Those present also included Colin Mair (as above), Gordon Wishart, then President of the High School Club, David Eales, then President of the School's London Club and other representatives of the School and School Clubs and friends of the School.

James Gray's father, the Very Rev. Dr. John Gray [1913-1984] also attended the High School in 1927-1930. He was Moderator of the 1977 General Assembly before which, when a Parish Minister in Glasgow, he was the High School's Chaplain. When Moderator he dedicated the new High School at Old Anniesland when it was formally opened by Lord Home of the Hirsel on 28 September 1977.

Dr. Gray's other sons also attended the High School. James Gray's elder brother, Charles Gray, CMG, LVO (Born 1953) was Marshall of the Diplomatic Corps in 2008-2014. As such he was a member of the Royal Household, being the Queen's link with the diplomatic community – headed by Ambassadors and Commonwealth High Commissioners – in London

Dame Anne Fyfe Pringle, DCMG (Born 1955), a Former Pupil of the Girls' High School in Glasgow, was UK Ambassador to the Czech Republic in 2001-2004 and to the Russian Federation in 2009-2011.

Appendix 6 – Glasgow High School Parliamentarians

Sir Henry had the company of six other Glasgow High School Former Pupils (FPs) in the 1900-1906 Parliament and, until his death in April 1908, between nine and ten in the 1906-1910 Parliament, with another returning to the Commons as from a by-election in March 1909.

Table 29 - Glasgow High School Former Pupils as MPs in 1900-1910

Name	Party	Constituency	Years
Sir Henry Campbell-Bannerman *	Liberal	Stirling Burghs	1868-1908
Sir James Bryce * (Viscount Bryce 1914)	Liberal	Tower Hamlets, London Aberdeen South	1880-1985 1985-1907
James Alexander Campbell ^ (Sir Henry's brother)	Conservative	Glasgow and Aberdeen Universities	1880-1906
Thomas (Tom) Ryburn Buchanan *	Liberal Liberal Unionist Liberal	Edinburgh)Two Members) Edinburgh West Aberdeenshire East Perthshire East	1881-1885 1885-1886 1886-1888 1888-1892 1892-1900 1903-1910
John Archibald Murray Macdonald *	Liberal	Bow and Bromley, London Falkirk Burghs Stirling and Falkirk Burghs	1892-1895 1906-1918 1916-1922
Andrew Bonar Law *	Conservative	Glasgow Blackfriars Dulwich Bootle Glasgow Central	1900-1906 1906-1910 1911-1918 1918-1923
Hugh Crawford Smith	Liberal Unionist	Tyneside, Northumberland	1900-1906
Charles Scott Dickson* (Lord Dickson [Judicial Title] 1915)	Conservative	Glasgow Bridgeton Glasgow Central	1900-1906 1909-1915
James Cleland	Liberal	Glasgow Bridgeton	1906-1910
John Annan Bryce (Brother of James, Viscount Bryce)	Liberal	Inverness Burghs	1906-1918
Henry (Harry) Watt	Liberal	Glasgow College	1906-1918
Sir Walter Menzies	Liberal	Lanarkshire South	1906-1913
Sir Henry Craik, Bt *	Conservative	Glasgow and Aberdeen Universities Scottish Universities (Three Members)	1906-1918 1918-1927
Robert Duncan	Conservative	Lanarkshire Govan	1906-1910

* Privy Councillors

In addition to Sir Henry, James Bryce and Bonar Law, one other Glasgow High School Former Pupil has been a member of a UK Cabinet. Sir William Sutherland (1880-1949), while a Coalition Liberal MP for Argyll in 1918-1922, was briefly Chancellor of the Duchy of Lancaster from April to October 1922. (Refer also to Chapter 13 and Appendix 3).

Such peaks of Glasgow High School representation in the Commons have never again been achieved, with the most significant debilitating factor, as from the First World War, being the massive reduction in the number of Former Pupils available for any career, given 478 fatalities in 1914-1918.

Currently (2013) there are only five Glasgow High School Parliamentarians – a Conservative Life Peer, a Conservative MP in England (Refer to Appendix 5), a Labour MP in England, a SNP MSP and the Speaker of the House of Keys in the Isle of Man.

Steve Rodan (Born 1954) has been a member of the House of Keys since 1995, Minister of Education in 1999-2004, of Health and Social Security in 2004-2006 and Speaker since 2006. He was previously Chairman of the Heriot-Watt University Liberal Club and of the Scottish Young Liberals, a member of the National Executive of the Scottish Liberal Party and the unsuccessful Liberal Candidate for Moray and Nairn at the 1979 General Election.

All in all, since 1707, twelve Former Pupils of the Grammar/High School of Glasgow have served or serve in the House of Lords, thirty-eight in the House of Commons, one in the new Scottish Parliament (as above), one in the European Parliament (as follows), one in the House of Keys (as above) and eight in legislatures in Australia, Burma, Canada, and South Africa. James, Viscount Bryce is the only Former Pupil to have served in both Houses of the UK Parliament and his younger brother, John Annan Bryce is the only Former Pupil to have served in both a colonial legislature and the House of Commons. (Refer to Appendix 3 for Biographical Notes for James Bryce, James Alexander Campbell, Tom Buchanan, Bonar Law and Sir William Sutherland).

The Rt. Hon. Sir Joseph Paton Maclay, Bt. (1857-1951), educated at The High School of Glasgow, was Minister of Shipping in Lloyd George's Administrations in 1916-1921 without then being a member of either House of Parliament. He was created 1st Lord Maclay in 1922. During the 1923 General Election campaign, Lord Maclay hosted Lloyd George's Liberal Reunion visit to Paisley in support of Asquith's re-election as Liberal MP for Paisley.

The Rt. Hon. Sir William Weir, GCB (1877-1959), also educated at The High School of Glasgow, was briefly President of the Air Council in Lloyd George's Administration in 1918, being created 1st Lord Weir that summer and 1st Viscount Weir in 1938. On his father's side, Lord Weir was the great-grandson of Elizabeth Paton, an illegitimate daughter of Robert Burns.

Iain MacDonald MacCormick (Born 1939), who attended the High School in 1944-1957 and was SNP MP for Argyll in 1974-1979 joined the Social Democrat Party (SDP) in the year of its foundation (1981). His brother. Professor Sir Neil MacCormick (1941-2009) who attended the High School in 1946-1959 (being both School Captain and Dux in 1958-1959) was a SNP Member of the European Parliament (MEP) in 1999-2004

Given the association of the Old Girls' Club of Glasgow High School for Girls with the re-constitution of The High School as a co-educational school in 1976, mention should also be made of two pupils of the Girls' School who became MPs. Mrs. Mary Agnes Hamilton, née Adamson (1882-1966) was a Labour MP for Blackburn in 1929-1931. She was a BBC Governor in 1933-1937, being awarded a CBE in 1947. Mrs. Anna McCurley, née Gemmell (Born 1943) was Conservative MP for Renfrew West and Inverclyde in 1983-1987. She joined the Liberal Democrats in 1988. Further, William M.R. Pringle (1874-1928), who attended the co-educational Garnethill School before it became the Girls' High in 1894, was Liberal MP for North-West Lanarkshire in 1910-1918 and for Penistone, Yorkshire in 1922-1924.

As mentioned in Appendix 3, on the initiative of the Ulster History Circle and the Ulster-Scots Agency, a blue plaque commemorating James, Viscount Bryce (a member of Sir Henry's Cabinet in 1905-1907 and a fellow Glasgow High School Former Pupil) was unveiled in Belfast on 10 May 2013. The occasion marked the 175th Anniversary of his birth on 10 May 1838 in 40 Upper Arthur Street, Belfast, with the plaque being located at 13 Chichester Street which is part of Upper Arthur Street. The plaque was unveiled by Ian Crozier, Chief Executive Officer of the Ulster-Scots Agency, with those present also including Berkley Farr (formerly Chairman of the Ulster Liberal Party) representing the Liberal Democrat History Group.

VISCOUNT BRYCE OM
1838-1922
Jurist, Historian and Diplomat
Born in a house in this street

BIBLIOGRAPHY

The five previous biographies of Sir Henry and two selected autobiographies are included, with biographical notes, in a separate section as are sources for general political data.

ALEXANDER S. WAUGH – UNIVERSITY OF ABERDEEN
A History of the Parish of Banchory-Ternan to 1929
A Study in National and Local Ecclesiastical Interaction
There are copies of this 2003 PhD Thesis in the University and Christ's College Libraries, Aberdeen, in New College Library, Edinburgh and in the Banchory and Oldmeldrum Public Libraries

ALEXANDER S. WAUGH – PRIVATELY PUBLISHED PAPERS
A Scottish Liberal Perspective 1836-2008 –
A Centenary Commemoration for Sir Henry Campbell-Bannerman 1836-1908
(2008/2009)
Sir Henry Campbell-Bannerman (Presentation in Glasgow, June 2009)
The Scottish Reformation (Presentation in Banchory, March 2011)
The Disruption of the Church of Scotland in May 1843 (Presentation in Banchory, September 2011)
Comparing Aspects of Scottish and Welsh Liberalism
(Presentation in Llandrindod Wells, February 2012)

ROSIE CAMPBELL ADAMSON – UNIVERSITY OF DURHAM
CB – The Thwarted Prime Minister (Dissertation, 2009)

DUNFERMLINE CARNEGIE LIBRARY
Campbell or Ramsay – Which?, 1868
The Campbells are Coming, 1868
(Sir) Henry Campbell-Bannerman's Election Addresses of 1886 (February), 1892, 1895, 1900 and 1906
Dunfermline Liberal Polling Cards of 1892 and 1895
Sir H. Campbell-Bannerman and The Bloemfontein Letters, 1900
(Reprinted from the *Stirling Sentinel* of 2 October 1900)
Menu Card for Dinner in the Royal Hotel, Dunfermline on 29 December 1905

MISCELLANEOUS

Bradshaw's Handbook of Great Britain and Ireland (1863)
(Special Collector's Edition, Old House Books & Maps, Oxford, 2012)
Guide to The House of Commons for 1880 (Ward Lock, London, 1880)
Transactions of the Aberdeen Ecclesiological Society for 1895 (W. Jolly and Sons, Aberdeen, 1897)
This included the text of the Court Circular (Balmoral Castle) of 19 June 1895
The Times – Speeches by the Rt. Hon. Sir Henry Campbell-Bannerman, 1899-1908

The House of Commons in 1906 (*Pall Mall Gazette Extra*, London, 1906)
The Harmsworth Encyclopaedia, Ten Volumes
(Amalgamated Press and Thomas Nelson, London, 1906)
The High School of Glasgow Prospectus for 1906-1907
High Parish Church, Inverness – Tuesday, 28 April 1908
Front Page of Order of Service for Memorial Service for Sir Henry Campbell-Bannerman
Bradshaw's Continental Railway Guide and General Handbook (Henry Blacklock, London, 1913)
(Facsimile Edition, Old House Books & Maps, Oxford, 2012)
Meigle SWRI, *Our Meigle Book* (William Kidd & Sons, Dundee, 1932)
Church Hymnary, Fourth Edition (Canterbury Press, Norwich, 2005)
Belmont Times, 75th Anniversary Edition (2006)
(Crossreach, The Church of Scotland Social Care Council)
CAMERON, Dr. Ewen A. – CB Centenary Commemoration – Meigle Handout, 22 April 2008
CB Centenary Commemoration – Meigle Parish Church Intimations, 27 April 2008
WAUGH, Alexander S. – CB Centenary Commemoration – Meigle Papers, 27 April 2008
Port of Menteith Parish Church, *Restoration 2011-2012*
Port of Menteith Parish Church Leaflet, as at 12 February 2013
Perth and Kinross Heritage Trust, *Meigle Historic Churchyard,* as at 18 February 2013

ONLINE ACCESS

Ancestry of British Prime Ministers, Archontology
(USA) Civil War Newspaper Clippings (New York Military Museum)
Clan Campbell Society of North America (Septs of Clan Campbell), Clan Gregor History – Lanrick Commercial Overprint Society of Great Britain, The Earldom of Menteith
Gazetteer for Scotland, Hansard, 1803-2005, Historic Scotland
Leigh Rayment's *Peerage* and *Baronetage Measuring Worth*
Memorials and Portraits of One Hundred Glasgow Men (1885), Glasgow Digital Library
AOC Archaeology Group Oxford Dictionary of National Biography (ODNB), Perth and Kinross Council Archives Scottish Railways Scottish Towns Sue Young Histories
Three Former Prime Ministers – UK Parliament/ Visitors Ulster History Circle
Who's Who in Glasgow in 1909, Glasgow Digital Library

NEWSPAPERS

Daily Chronicle (London), *Daily News* (London), *Dunfermline Journal,*

Dunfermline Press, The (Manchester) Guardian, The (Glasgow) Herald,

Pall Mall Gazette, The Scotsman (Edinburgh), *Stirling Journal (and Advertiser), Stirling Observer, Stirling Sentinel, The Times* (London), *Westminster Gazette*

The *Stirling Journal* and the *Stirling Advertiser* merged in 1833 The *Stirling Sentinel* was published from 1888 to 1906. The *Pall Mall Gazette* was absorbed by the

(London) *Evening Standard* in 1923. In 1928 the *Westminster Gazette* merged with the *Daily News* which merged with the *Daily Chronicle* in 1930 to form the *News Chronicle* which survived until 1960, The *Dunfermline Journal* continued, as The *Dunfermline and West Fife Journal,* until 1951. *The Manchester Guardian* became *The Guardian* in 1959. *The Glasgow Herald* became *The Herald* in 1992, The *Stirling Observer* took over the *Stirling Journal* in 1970.

ARTICLES

Current Archaeology
'Pict-and-Mix, Meigle, Perthshire' (December 2012)
History Scotland
ALLEN, Stewart, 'Admiral Cochrane, The Real Master and Commander' (January/February 2012)
EMSLEY, Clive, 'Why Crucify Tommy' (November/December 2012)
FINLAY, Professor Richard and WOOD, Claire,
'A House Divided? – The Impact of the First World War on Scottish Liberals and Labour'
(May/June 2013)
GROUNDWATER, Dr. Anna, 'Ben Johnson in Scotland' (May/June, 2013)
INGLIS, Bill, 'Sir Henry Campbell-Bannerman and the Boer War' (July/August 2008)
JENKINS, Terry, 'The Orsini Affair and the Crisis of 1858' (January/February 2008)
McNIVEN, Peter, 'Place-Names and the Medieval Church in Menteith' (November/December, 2012)
TALBOTT, Dr. Siobhan, 'The Auld Alliance' (January/February 2013)
History Today
EMSLEY, Clive, 'Why Crucify Tommy' (November 2012)
Journal of British Studies (Chicago Journals)
BERNSTEIN, George L., 'Sir Henry Campbell-Bannerman and the Liberal Imperialists' (Autumn 1983)
Journal of Liberal History
BRACK, Duncan (Editor), 'Nick Clegg unveils History Group plaque' (Spring 2013)
BROWN, Robert, 'The Struggle for Radical Supremacy in Scotland, 1885-1929' (Winter 2009-2010) CAMERON, Dr. E.A., 'Maistly Scotch – Campbell-Bannerman & Liberal Leadership' (Spring 2007)
DUTTON, David and PUGH, Martin, 'Liberals in 1906 – Flourishing or Doomed?' (Spring 2007)
ELDER, R. Ian, 'The Young Scots Society' (Autumn 2002)

FARGHER, James, 'The South Africa War and its Effect on the Liberal [-Irish Nationalist] Alliance'
(Summer 2013)
GOLDMAN, Lawrence, 'Campbell-Bannerman and Asquith' (Winter 2008-2009)
ILES, Lawrence, 'Organiser Par Excellence – Herbert Gladstone, 1854-1930 (Summer 2006)
JONES, Dr. J. G., 'Eliot Crawshaw-Williams – Biography of the Leicester Liberal MP' (Summer 2008)
MEADOWCROFT, Michael, 'Leeds and the Liberal Pantheon' (Winter 2010-2011)
MORGAN, Kenneth O. '1906: Blissful Dawn? – A Hundred Years On'
(Summer 2006)

NEWMAN, Anne, 'Dundee's Grand Old Man – Edmund Robertson, MP' (Spring 2005)
THANE, Pat, 'The Old Age Pensions Act 1908' (Autumn 2008)
WAUGH, Dr. A.S., 'Campbell-Bannerman Centenary Commemorations 2008 – 1' (Summer 2008)
WAUGH, Dr. A.S., 'Campbell-Bannerman Centenary Commemorations 2008 – 2' (Summer 2009)
WAUGH, Dr. A.S., 'Discovering Kincardineshire's Liberal History' (Spring 2012)
Unfortunately, the photograph of the so-called 'Kincardine Castle' – which was published with this Spring 2012 article – was a photograph of Kincardine (O'Neil) House (in Aberdeenshire), some 20 miles north of the site of the now ruined Kincardine Castle in Kincardineshire.

Life and Work – The Magazine of The Church of Scotland
MACADAM, Jackie, 'Songs of History' (April 2013)
This was the article about the wee Chartist hymnbook of 1845 to which reference was made in an Endnote in Chapter 1.

The Scots Magazine
FRASER, Garry, 'Focus on Stirling' (July 2013)

The Scottish Historical Review
BROWN, Professor Stewart J.,
'Echoes of Midlothian – Scottish Liberalism and the South African War, 1899-1902' (October 1992)
MANSON, Professor Roger A, 'George Buchanan and Scottish Self-Fashioning' (April 2013)

OTHER PERIODICALS

The Church of Scotland Year Books, Glasgow High School Magazines,
Liberal Democrat News Whitakers Almanacks
Times Guides to the House of Commons,

The weekly *Liberal Democrat News* was replaced by the monthly AD LIB in December 2012

PREVIOUS BIOGRAPHIES OF SIR HENRY

HATTERSLEY, Roy, *Campbell-Bannerman* (Haus Publishing, London, 2006)

The Rt. Hon. Roy Hattersley (Born 28 December 1932) was educated at Sheffield Grammar School and Hull University (Economics). His mother, Enid was Lord Mayor of Sheffield in 1981. He was Labour MP for Birmingham Sparbrook from 1964 until 1997, Minister of State at the Foreign and Commonwealth Office in 1974-1976 and Secretary of State for Prices and Consumer Protection in 1976-1979. He was subsequently Deputy Leader of the Labour Party and Shadow Home Secretary and Chancellor of the Exchequer. He was created Lord Hattersley (Life Peerage) on 24

November 1997. Hattersley's short biography of 2006 was published in the '20 British Prime Ministers of the 20th century' series from Salisbury to Blair.

MACKIE, John B., *The Model Member – Sir Henry Campbell-Bannerman* (Dunfermline Journal, 1914)

John Beveridge Mackie (1848-1919), a native of Dunfermline, was Editor and Proprietor of the *Dunfermline Journal* (founded in 1840) from 1903 to 1918 and a Fellow of the Institute of Journalists. As at 1914, the *Dunfermline Journal* was published on Saturdays and cost One Penny. He also published three other local weeklies. He was related to Sir William, Lord Beveridge whose father, Henry (an Indian Civil Servant) was born in Dunfermline in 1837. His elder son, John Duncan Mackie was Professor of Scottish History and Literature (1930-1957) in the University of Glasgow and later Historiographer Royal in Scotland. J.B. Mackie also wrote biographies of Andrew Carnegie and Duncan McLaren (an Edinburgh Liberal MP in 1865-1881 and, through his third wife, a brother-in-law of John Bright, with whom he became a Liberal Unionist in 1886).

O'CONNOR, T.P., *Sir Henry Campbell-Bannerman* (Hodder & Stoughton, London, 1908)

The Rt. Hon. Thomas Power O'Connor (1848-1929), journalist and author, was Irish Nationalist MP for Galway, 1880-1885 and for Liverpool Scotland from 1885 until his death on 18 November 1929, being re-elected unopposed at the 1923, 1924 and 1929 General Elections. He was a personal friend of Sir Henry Campbell-Bannerman and, like a number of other Irish Nationalist MPs, was a member of the National Liberal Club in London. In 1917 he became the first President of the British Board of Film Censors with his name becoming very familiar as from his signature on projected certificates. He was 'Father' of the House of Commons from 1918 and a Privy Councillor from 1924. O'Connor himself described this biography of 1908, published shortly after Sir Henry's death, as 'a memoir'.

SPENDER, J.A., *Life of the Rt. Hon. Sir Henry Campbell-Bannerman, GCB,* Two Volumes
(Hodder & Stoughton, London, 1923)

John Alfred Spender, CH (1862-1942) – Editor, *Eastern Morning News,* Hull (1886-1891), Assistant Editor (1892), *Pall Mall Gazette,* Assistant Editor and Editor, *Westminster Gazette* (1893-1896-1922), contracted to the *Westminster Gazette* (1922-1928), the *Daily News* incorporating the *Gazette* (1928-1930) and the *News Chronicle* incorporating the *Daily News* and the *Daily Chronicle* (1930-1935). He was thereafter a contributor to *The Times,* etc. and a BBC broadcaster. His first published book (1892) advocated the state provision of old-age pensions and his other biographies included *Asquith* (1932) with the authorship shared with Cyril Asquith (as follows). He was President of the National Liberal Federation in 1926, was appointed a Companion of Honour (CH) in 1937 and served as (Honorary) President of the Chartered Institute of Journalists from 1940 until his death in 1942. Spender was commissioned to write the *Life* in 1923 by John Sinclair, Lord Pentland, Sir Henry's literary executor. A sum was provided by Sir Henry's family towards the cost of publication but this was refunded when the book came out.

WILSON, John, *A Life of Sir Henry Campbell-Bannerman*
(Constable and Purnell Book Services, London, 1973)

The Rt. Hon. Sir Richard John McMoran Moran Wilson, KCMG known as John Wilson (Born 22 September 1924, Died 14 February 2014) was the son of the 1st Lord Moran (Winston Churchill's physician). John Wilson was educated at Eton and King's College, Cambridge (BA). After serving (1943-1945) in the Royal Naval Reserve he entered the Diplomatic Service in 1945 and held various subordinate posts in Turkey, Israel, Brazil, the USA and South Africa until being appointed Head of the West Africa Department in London in 1970 and being concurrently non-resident UK Ambassador to Chad. He was then UK Ambassador to Hungary (1973-1976), to Portugal (1976-1981) and UK High Commissioner in Canada from 1981 until he retired from the Diplomatic Service. Having succeeded as 2nd Lord Moran in 1977, he had, since 1999, sat in the House of Lords as an elected cross-bench hereditary peer. He wrote his biography of CB – for which he received a Whitbread Award – while based in London in 1970-1973. He had extensive organisational and literary interests as a naturalist.

SELECTED AUTOBIOGRAPHIES

FARQUHARSON, Robert, *In and Out of Parliament*
(Williams and Norgate, London, 1911)
(Reprint, Lightening Source, Milton Keynes, 2012)

The Rt. Hon. Dr. Robert Farquharson (1837-1918), physician and author, was educated at Edinburgh Academy and University, served as a medical officer in the Coldstream Guards and at Rugby School and thereafter was on the staff of St. Mary's Hospital, London. He was Liberal MP for West Aberdeenshire in 1880-1906. He inherited the Finzean Estate on Deeside (as 11th Laird) in 1887 and, with Finzean being fairly near to Balmoral, was created a Privy Councillor in 1906 as he could easily attend Council meetings when the King was in residence on Deeside. During the 1910-1911 constitutional crisis Dr. Farquharson was third on the list of Liberal Peers who would have been created if matters had not been otherwise resolved. He was succeeded as 12th Laird of Finzean by his younger brother, Joseph Farquharson, RA, the distinguished pastoral and landscape artist. The present-day Farquharsons of Finzean are descended from the 17th century 2nd Laird,

SHAW, Thomas, *Letters to Isabel* (George H. Doran, New York, 1921)

The Rt. Hon. Thomas Shaw, QC/KC (1850-1937), educated at Dunfermline High School and Edinburgh University and called to the Scottish Bar in 1875. He was Liberal MP for Hawick Burghs (also including Galashiels and Selkirk) n 1892-1909, being Solicitor-General for Scotland in 1894-1895 and Lord Advocate in 1905-1909. He served as a Lord of Appeal (House of Lords) in 1909-1929 with the Judicial Title of Lord Shaw and, on retiring in 1929, was created Lord Craigmyle. His son and heir, The Hon. Alexander Shaw was elected as Liberal MP for Kilmarnock Burghs (also including Dumbarton, Port Glasgow, Renfrew and Rutherglen) in 1915, after William Glynne Charles Gladstone was killed in action. Alexander Shaw was thereafter Coalition and National Liberal MP for the Kilmarnock Division of Ayrshire from December 1918 until he resigned just before the 1923 General Election.

Dr. Farquharson and Thomas Shaw were personal friends of Sir Henry and provide personal and domestic information not available from other sources.

GENERAL POLITICAL DATA

CRAIG, F.W.S., *Scottish Parliamentary Election Manual (1918-1963)*,
(John McQueen & Son, Galashiels, 1964)
CRAIG, F.W.S., *British General Election Manifestos* (Macmillan, London, etc., 1975)
CRAIG, F.W.S., *British Parliamentary Election Results 1832-1885* and *1885-1918*
(Parliamentary Research Services, Aldershot, 1989).
FOSTER, Joseph, *(Commissioners and) Members of Parliament, Scotland 1357-1882*
(Hazell, Watson and Viney, London and Aylesbury, 1882)
(Reprint, Lightening Source, Milton Keynes, 2012)
JOYCE, Peter, *Politico's Guide to UK General Elections* (Politico's Publishing, London, 2004)
KINNEAR, Michael, *The British Voter – An Atlas and Survey since 1885*
(Batsford, London, 1968 and 1981)
RALLINGS, Colin and THRASHER, Michael, *British Electoral Facts 1832-2005*
(Ashgate, Aldershot, 2006 & Biteback, London, 2009)
STENTON, Michael, *Who's Who of British Members of Parliament, 1832-1885*
(Harvester Press, Sussex and Humanities Press, New Jersey, 1976)
STENTON, Michael and LEES, Stephen, *Who's Who of British Members of Parliament, 1886-1918*
(Harvester Press, Sussex and Humanities Press, New Jersey, 1978)
STENTON, Michael and LEES, Stephen, *Who's Who of British Members of Parliament, 1919-1945*
(Harvester Press, Sussex and Humanities Press, New Jersey, 1979)
STENTON, Michael and LEES, Stephen, *Who's Who of British Members of Parliament, 1945-1979*
(Harvester Press, Sussex and Humanities Press, New Jersey, 1981)
VINCENT, J. and STENTON, M., *McCalmont's Parliamentary Poll Book 1832-1918*
– Eighth Edition
(Harvester Press, Sussex, 1971)
WALKER, R.M. (Editor), *Parliamentary Election Results in Ireland 1801-1922*
(Royal Irish Academy, Dublin, 1978)

OTHER PUBLICATIONS

ASHMALL, Harry A., *The High School of Glasgow*
(Scottish Academic Press for the Glasgow High School Club, 1976)
Harry Ashmall taught History in the High School from 1961, being Principal Teacher from 1965 until 1971 when he was appointed Rector of Forfar Academy.

ASPINALL, Arthur, *Lord Brougham and the Whig Party,* Modern Edition (Nonsuch, Stroud, 2005)
ASQUITH, The Earl of Oxford and Asquith, *Memories and Reflections,* Two Volumes
(Cassell, London, etc., 1928).

ASQUITH, Margot, *The Autobiography of Margot Asquith*
One Volume Edition edited by Mark Bonham Carter (Eyre & Spottiswoode, London, 1962)
BALFOUR, Lady Frances, *A Memoir of Alexander Hugh Bruce, 6th Lord Balfour of Burleigh*
(Hodder and Stoughton, London, 1924)

BALFOUR, Lady Frances, *Ne Obliviscaris, Dinna Forget*, Two Volumes
[(Hodder and Stoughton, London, 1929-1930].
BARR, James, *Lang Syne – Memoirs* (William McLellan, Glasgow, 1948)
BASTABLE, Jonathan, *Prime Ministers – Amazing and Extraordinary Facts*
(David & Charles. Newton Abbot, 2011)
BEBBINGTON, David and SWIFT, Roger (Editors), *Gladstone Centenary Essays*
(Liverpool University Press, 2000)
BELL P.M.H., *Disestablishment in Ireland and Wales* (SPCK, London, 1969)
BELL, Peter (Editor), *Ministers of the Church of Scotland, 1560-1929*
An Index to *Fasti Ecclesiae Scoticanae* (Portsburgh Press, Edinburgh, 2004)
BENTLEY, Michael, *The Climax of Liberal Politics, 1868-1918* (Edward Arnold, London, 1997)
BERTIE, David M, *Scottish Episcopal Clergy* (T&T Clark, Edinburgh, 2000)
BINGHAM, Robert and BRACK, Duncan (Editors),
Peace, Reform and Liberation – A History of Liberal Politics in Britain 1679-2011
(Biteback, London, 2011)
BLACK, C. Stewart, *Glasgow's Story* (J. & J. Cook, Paisley, c.1952)
BLAIR, J. and CHAPEL, David, *A Handbook of Parliamentary Elections in Scotland*
(William Hodge, Edinburgh & Glasgow, 1909)
BOOTHROYD, David, *Politico's Guide to the History of British Political Parties*
(Politico's Publishing, London, 2001)
BRACK, Duncan (Editor), *Why I am a Liberal Democrat*
(Liberal Democrat Publications, Dorchester, 1996)
BRACK, Duncan (Editor), *A Dictionary of Liberal Biography* (Politico's Publishing, London, 1998)
BRACK, Duncan and LITTLE, Tony (Editors), *Great Liberal Speeches*
(Politico's Publishing, London, 2001)
BRACK, Duncan and RANDALL, Ed (Editors), *Dictionary of Liberal Thought*
(Politico's Publishing, London, 2007)
BRACK, Duncan (Editor), *Mothers of Liberty – Women who built British Liberalism*
(Liberal Democrat History Group, London, 2012)
BRADLEY, Ian, *God Save the Queen* (Darton, Longman and Todd, London, 2002)
BROWN, Robert and LINDSAY, Nigel (Editors),
The Little Yellow Book – Reclaiming the Liberal Democrats for the People
(Fastprint Publishing, Peterborough, 2012)
BROWN, Stewart J. and NEWLANDS, George (Editors), *Scottish Christianity in the Modern World*
(T&T Clark, Edinburgh, 2000)
BURLEIGH, J.H.S., *A Church History of Scotland* (Oxford UP, 1960)
CAMERON, Ewen A., *Impaled upon a Thistle – Scotland since 1880* (Edinburgh UP, 2010)
CAMERON, George G. *The Scots Kirk in London* (Becket Publications, Oxford, 1979)

CAMERON, Nigel M. de S. (Organising Editor), *Dictionary of Scottish Church History & Theology*
(T & T Clark, Edinburgh, 1993)
CAMPBELL, Margaret Olympia, *A Memorial History of the Campbells of Melfort, Argyllshire*
(Simmons Botten, London, 1882 – Reprint Lightening Source, Milton Keynes, 2012)
CAMPBELL, Sir Menzies, *My Autobiography* (Hodder & Stoughton, London, 2008)
CAWOOD, Ian, *The Liberal Unionist Party – A History* (Tauris, London, 2012)
CECIL, David, *Melbourne* (Reprint Society, London, 1955)
CLIFFORD, Colin, *The Asquiths* (John Murray, London, 2002)
COLE, Sue, *Discovering Meigle* (Sue Cole, Meigle, 2000)
CONACHER, J.B., *The Peelites and the Party System 1846-1852*
(David & Charles, Newton Abbot, 1972)
COOK, Chris, *A Short History of the Liberal Party 1900-1997,* Fourth Edition
(Macmillan, Basingstoke & London, 1998)
COWAN, Dr. Robert. M.W., *The Newspaper in Scotland* (George Outram, Glasgow, 1946)
Dr. Cowan had joined the English Department of The High School of Glasgow in 1926 anf his 1946 book was based on his 1944 DLitt Thesis.
DANGERFIELD, George, *The Strange Death of Liberal England*
(Harrison, New York, 1935 and Grenada Publishing, London, 1983)
DE BANZIE, Louis (Editor), *The High School of Glasgow Scrapbook* (1995)
DUFF, David (Editor), *Queen Victoria's Highland Journals* (Webb & Bower, Exeter, 1983)
DUTTON, David, *A History of the Liberal Party* (Palgrave Macmillan, Basingstoke & New York, 2004)
DOUGLAS, Roy, *Liberals – A History of the Liberal and Liberal Democrat Parties*
(Hambledon and London, London & New York, 2005)
EKWALL, Filert, *The Concise Oxford Dictionary of English Place-Names,* Fourth Edition
(Oxford UP, 1960
ELLIS, Roger, *Who's Who in British History – Victorian Britain 1851-1901*
(Shepheard-Walwyn, London, 1987 and Stackpole Books, Pennsylvania, 2001)
FAIRBAIRN's *Book of Crests,* 4th Edition, Two Volumes (London, 1905) – One Volume Edition
(*Heraldry Today,* Ramsbury, Wiltshire, 1984 and 1996)
FARQUHARSON-LANG, W.M., *The Manse and the Mansion* (Pentland Press, East Lothian, 1987)
FAWCETT, Richard, *Scottish Abbeys and Priories*
(Historic Scotland/Batsford, London, 1994/2000)
FERGUSON, Norman, *The Glasgow Book of Days* (The History Press, Stroud, 2013)
FLEET, Christopher et al, *Scotland – Mapping the Nation*
(Birlinn in association with the National Library of Scotland, Edinburgh, 2011)
FOREMAN, Amanda, *The World on Fire* (Allen Lane/Penguin, London, 2010/2011)|
FOREMAN, Carol, *Glasgow Street Names,* New Edition (Birlinn, Edinburgh, 2007)
FRASER, Antonia, *Perilous Question – The Drama of the Great Reform Bill 1832*
(Weidenfeld & Nicolson, London, 2013)
FRY, Michael, *Patronage and Principle – A Political History of Modern Scotland*
(Aberdeen University Press, 1991)
GARDINER, A.G., *Prophets, Priests and Kings* (Alston Rivers, London, 1908)

(Classical Reprint Series, Forgotten Books, London, 2012)
GIFFORD, John, *The Buildings of Scotland – Perth and Kinross*
(Yale University Press, New Haven, USA and London, 2007)
GIFFORD, John, *The Buildings of Scotland – Dundee and Angus*
(Yale University Press, New Haven, USA and London, 2012)
GILLIES, Patrick H., *Netherlorn, Argyllshire and its Neighbourhood* (Virtue & Co, London, 1909)
(Reprint, BiblioLife, Charleston, South Carolina, 2012)
GOOCH, G.P., *Under Six Reigns* (Longmans, London, 1958)
GORING, Rosemary, *Chambers Scottish Biographical Dictionary*
(Chambers, Edinburgh and New York, 1992)
GRAHAM, Patrick, *Sketches of Perthshire* (London, 1812)
(Reprint, Lightening Source, Milton Keynes, 2013)
GREY, Sir Edward (Viscount Grey), *Twenty-Five Years,* Two Volumes
(Hodder & Stoughton. London, 1925)
HAMER, D.A., *Liberal Politics in the Age of Gladstone and Rosebery* (Oxford UP, 1972)
HAMMERTON, Sir John A., *Outline of Great Books* (Amalgamated Press, London, 1906)
HANKS, Patrick et al (Editors), *The Oxford Names Companion* (Oxford UP, 2002)
HARVIE Christopher, *The Lights of Liberalism* (Allan Lane, London, 1976)
HAY, J.R., *The Origins of the Liberal Welfare Reforms 1906-1914* (Palgrave, Basingstoke, 1983)
HIRST, Francis W., *In The Golden Days* (Frederick Muller, London, 1947)
HITCHENS, Mark, *Prime Ministers' Wives – and One Husband* (Peter Owen, London, 2004)
HOUSE, Jack, *Square Mile of Murder* – Four Murders in Glasgow's fashionable Victorian West End
(Richard Drew, Glasgow, 1988)
HOUSE, Jack, *The Heart of Glasgow* (Neil Wilson, Glasgow, 2005)
HUTCHINSON, I.G.C., *A Political History of Scotland 1832-1924* (John Donald, Edinburgh, 1986)
HUTCHISON, Andrew Fleming, *The Lake of Menteith – Its Islands and Vicinity*
(Eneas Mackay, Stirling, 1899 – Reprint, Lightening Source, Milton Keynes, 2010)
JACKSON, Patrick, *Harcourt and Son* (Fairleigh Dickinson UP, Madison, New Jersey, 2004)
JACKSON, Patrick, *Morley of Blackburn* (Fairleigh Dickinson UP, Madison, New Jersey, 2012)
JENKINS, Roy, *Asquith* (Collins, Glasgow & London, 1964 & 1986)
JENKINS, Roy, *Gladstone* (Macmillan, London, 1995)
JENKINS, Roy, *The Chancellors* [of the Exchequer] (Macmillan, London, 1998)
JENKINS, Roy, *Churchill* (Macmillan, London, 2001)
JENKINS, Roy, *Dilke – A Victorian Tragedy* (Papermac, Collins, London, 1965)
JOHNSTON, Harvey, *Heraldry of the Campbells,* Volume 2 (W. & A.K. Johnston, Edinburgh, 1921)
KEAY, John and Julia (Editors), *Collins Encyclopaedia of Scotland* (HarperCollins, London, 1974)
KELLY, The Rev. Tom Davidson, *Living Stones: The Daughter Churches of Govan Parish 1730-1919*
(Friends of Govan Old, Glasgow, 2007)

KOSS, Stephen, *Asquith* (Allen Lane, London, 1976)
LOCKHART, Brian R.W., *Jinglin' Geordie's Legacy – A History of George Heriot's Hospital and School*
(John Donald/Birlinn, Edinburgh, 2003)
LOCKHART, Brian R.W., *The Town School – A History of The High School of Glasgow*
(John Donald/Birlinn, Edinburgh, 2010)
Brian Lockhart was on the staff of George Heriot's School. Edinburgh from 1968, becoming Principal Teacher of History in 1972. He was Deputy Rector of The High School of Glasgow in 1982-1996 and Headmaster of Robert Gordon's College, Aberdeen from 1996 until he retired in 2004. He has also written histories of Robert Gordon's College and Aberdeen Grammar School.
LYALL, Francis, *Of Presbyters* and *Kings – Church and State in the Law of Scotland*
(Aberdeen UP, 1980)
MACBAIN, Dr. Alexander, *An Etymological Dictionary of the Gaelic Language* (1896 and 1911)
(Reprint, Gairm Publications, Glasgow, 1982)
MACDONALD, Dr. Catriona M.M.,
The Radical Thread – Political Change in Scotland – Paisley Politics 1885-1924
(Tuckwell Press, East Linton, East Lothian, 2000)
MACFARLANE, Leslie J., *William Elphinstone and the Kingdom of Scotland,*
Quincentenary Edition
(Aberdeen University Press, 1995)
MACDONALD, Finlay A.J. (Editor), *Fasti Ecclesiæ Scoticanæ,* Volume XI
(T&T Clark, Edinburgh, 2000)
MACKAY, George, *Scottish Place Names* (Lomond Books, New Lanark, 2000)
McLAREN, Moray (Editor), *The Shell Guide to Scotland*
(Shell-Mex and BP Ltd., London, 1965)
McLAREN, Moray and MACNIE, Donald Lamont (Editors), *The New Shell Guide to Scotland*
(Shell UK Ltd., London, 1977)
MALLISON, Allan, *The Making of the British Army* (Bantam Press, London, 2009)
MATTHEW, H.G.C., *The Liberal Imperialists* (Oxford UP, 1973)
MEREDITH, Martin, *Diamonds, Gold and War* (Public Affairs, New York, 2007)
MOREY, Desmond, *Hunton, A Kentish Village* (St. Mary's Church, Hunton, 2000)
MORGAN, Kenneth O, *Wales in British Politics* (University of Wales Press, Cardiff, 1991)
MORLEY, John, *The Life of William Ewart Gladstone,* New Edition, Two Volumes
(Macmillan, London, 1905)
MUNRO, Alasdair and SIM, Duncan, *The Merseyside Scots* (Liver Press, Birkenhead, 2001)
OAKLEY, C.A., *The Second City* (Blackie, London & Glasgow, 1946)
PACKER, Ian, *Liberal Government and Politics, 1905-1915* (Palgrave Macmillan, Basingstoke, 2006)
PANKHURST, Sylvia, *The History of the Militant Women's Suffrage Movement*
(Gay and Hancock, London, 1911)
PEACOCKE, Marguerite D., *Buckingham Palace* (Odhams Press, London, 1951)
PENTLAND, Lady, *The Rt. Hon. John Sinclair, Lord Pentland – A Memoir* (Methuen, London, 1928)

PENTLAND, Lord (Editor), *Early Letters of Sir Henry Campbell-Bannerman, 1850-1851*
(T. Fisher Unwin, London, 1925)
PICKARD, Willis, *The Member for Scotland – A Life of Duncan McLaren*
(John Donald/Birlinn, Edinburgh, 2011)
POWELL, David, *The Edwardian Crisis – Britain 1901-1914* (Palgrave, Basingstoke, 1996)
REID, Andrew (Editor), *Why I am a Liberal* (Cassell, London, 1885)
RHODES JAMES, Robert, *Rosebery*
(Weidenfeld & Nicolson, London, 1963 and Phoenix, London, 1995)
RISK, James C., *The History of the Order of the Bath* (Spink & Son, London, 1972)
ROBBINS. Dr. Keith, *Sir Edward Grey* (Cassell, London, 1971)
ROOT, Margaret E, *Stirling Castle* (HMSO, Edinburgh, 1948)
RUSSELL, A.K., *Liberal Landslide – The General Election of 1906*
(David & Charles, Newton Abbot, 1973)
RUSSELL, George W.E., *Prime Ministers and Some Others* (Palmerston to Campbell-Bannerman)
(Reprint – Echo Library, Teddington, Middlesex, 2007)
SEARLE, G.R., *The Liberal Party – Triumph & Disintegration, 1886-1929*
(Macmillan, London, 1992)
SHANNON, Richard, *Gladstone – Peel's Inheritor, 1809-1865* (Hamish Hamilton, London, 1982)
SHANNON, Richard, *Gladstone – Heroic Minister, 1865-1898* (Allan Lane, London, 1999)
SHELEDEN, Michael, *Young Titan – The Making of Winston Churchill*
(Simon & Schuster, London, 2013)
SINCLAIR, Sir John (Editor), *(First) Statistical Account of Scotland 1791-1799*
Volume XI – South & East Perthshire, etc. (Edited Reprint, EP Publishing, Wakefield, 1976)
Culross (1793) by the Rev. Robert Rolland (1728-1815), Joint Parish Minister, 1754-1815
and the Rev. Walter McAlpine (1741-1823, Joint Parish Minister, 1770-1823
Meigle (1791) by the Rev. Dr. James Playfair (1736-1819), Parish Minister, 1777-1800.
Volume XII – North & West Perthshire, (Edited Reprint, EP Publishing, Wakefield, 1977)
Blackford including Tullibardine (1792) by the Rev. John Stevenson (1730-1815), Parish Minister, 1777-1815
Port of Menteith (1791-1793) by the Rev. William Macgregor Stirling (1771-1833), Parish Minister, 1791-1823
SMART, Aileen, *Villages of Glasgow South of the Clyde* (John Donald, Edinburgh, 1996)
SMART, Aileen, *Villages of Glasgow North of the Clyde* (John Donald, Edinburgh, 2002)
SMYTH, Alfred F. et al, *A Biographical Dictionary of Dark Age Britain* (B.E. Seaby, London, 1991)
SNELL, K D.M. & ELL: Paul S., *Rival Jerusalems – The Geography of Victorian Religion*
(Cambridge UP, 2000)
SPENDER, J.A. and ASQUITH, Cyril, *Life of Lord Oxford and Asquith*. Two Volumes

(Hutchinson, London, 1932)
TAYLOR, Andrew, *Bonar Law* (Haus Publishing, London, 2006)
THOMSON, B., *The Parliament of Scotland 1690-1702* (St. Andrews University Press, 1929)
THOMSON, Claude, *Scottish Councils at Work*
(National Council for the Training of Journalists, Epping, 1981)
This includes a chapter on 'Interpreting Election Results' by Alexander S. Waugh
TENNANT, Charles, *The Radical Laird – George Kinloch of Kinloch, 1775-1833*
(Roundwood Press, Kineton, Warwickshire, 1970)
TORRANCE, David, *The Scottish Secretaries* (Birlinn, Edinburgh, 2006)
URQUHART, Gordon R., *Along Great Western Road* (Stenlake, Ochiltree, Ayrshire, 2000)
URQUHART, R.M., *Scottish Burgh and County Heraldry* (*Heraldry Today,* London, 1973)
VANE, Henry, *Affair of State – A Biography of the 8th Duke and Duchess of Devonshire*
(Peter Owen, London, 2004)
VAN THAL, Herbert (Editor), *The Prime Ministers,* Volume Two (Lord John Russell to Edward Heath)
(George Allen & Unwin. London, 1975)
WATERHOUSE, Michael, *Edwardian Requiem – A Life of Sir Edward Grey*
(Biteback, London, 2013)
WEINTRUB, Stanley, *The Importance of being Edward – King in Waiting, 1841-1901*
(John Murray, London, 2000)
WEIR, Alison, *Britain's Royal Families – The Complete Genealogy* (Vintage, London, 2008)
WILLIAMSON, G. et al, *The Welsh Church from Reformation to Disestablishment 1603-1920*
(University of Wales, Cardiff, 2007)
WILSON, A.N., *After the Victorians* (Arrow Books, London, 2005)
WINTERTON, Earl, *Pre-War* (Macmillan, London, 1932)
WISHART, A.W., *Why a United Free Church Continues*
(Glasgow & District United Free Church Office-Bearers Union, 1953)

A

Aberdeen University 101
Aberdeen, 4th (Scottish) Earl of 40, 58, 60
Aberdeen, 4th Scottish Earl of 40
Aberdeen, King's College 48
Acland, Francis Dyke 245
Adam, William Patrick 102
Adamson, Nora Jane, nee Campbell (niece) 58
Adamson, William 243
Adamsons, of Careston and Stracathro (descendants of niece) 43
Admiralty 107, 281–82, 281–82
Alexander, (Sir) Danny 331
Alexandra, Queen 249, 291, 295
All Souls Church, Langham Place, London 63
Anderson, Sir James 75, 324
Annandale, 1st (Scottish) Marquis of, 49
Anti-semitism 199
Argyll, 8th (Scottish) Duke of 17, 40, 91
Army Estimates 93, 119, 157, 162
Army Pay Department 93, 311
Army reforms 93–94, 163, 282–83, 282
Ashdown, Paddy (Lord Ashdown of Norton-sub-Hamdon) 330
Asquith, Helen, nee Melland 58
Asquith, Herbert Henry (Earl) 209
　1907 budget 278
　absence from House of Commons debate on the Sudan 175
　agreement to become Chancellor of the Exchequer 206
　biographical note 332
　candidature in East Fife constituency 1886 143
　coalition of 1915-16 61
　Committee on South African matters 215
　defence of Cunninghame-Graham 30
　Eighty Club 143–44
　encounter with suffragettes in Stirling, 1913 248, 350–51, 357
　friendship with Sir Arthur Milner 176

Imperial Liberal Council 179
indentured Chinese labour in the Transvaal 263
invitation to form government 1908 292
Liberal Imperialist League 184
Marriage 64
Meeting with Grey and Haldane at Relugas, 1905 205
moves no confidence motion 1892 153
pallbearer at Sir Henry's funeral 295
Sir Henry's final illness 291
speech at unveiling of statue of Sir Henry, 1913 59
strategic and tactical deficiencies 208
support for Sir Henry after Charlotte's death 248–51
support for Sir Henry becoming Liberal Party leader 172
tributes to Sir Henry 296, 307, 296
unveiling of Sir Henry's statue, 1913 348–51
victory in Paisley by-election, 1920 303
Workers' Compensation Act 1906 276
Asquith, Margot, nee Tennant (Countess) 64, 176, 268, 291, 293
Auld Alliance, of Scotland and France 139, 201

B

Balfour, Arthur James (Earl) 191, 208, 255
　Boer War 186
　Church of Scotland 40
　Colonial Office Estimates debate, 1906 267–68
　defeat in 1906 General Election 237
　Irish Home Rule 117
　resignation as Prime Minister 208
　return to House of Commons, 1906 245–46
　Scottish Home Rule 148

Territorial and Reserve Forces Bill, 1906	282–83
tribute to Sir Henry	297
Ballioll, John	43
Bannerman, David (cousin)	53
Bannerman, Henry (uncle)	20, 91
Bannerman, James Alexander (cousin and brother-in-law)	53, 59, 92
Bannerman, Janet, nee Motherwell	32
Bannerman, Louisa, nee Campbell (sister, and wife of James Alexander Bannerman)	24, 53, 59
Bannerman, Mary, nee Wyld (wife of Henry Bannerman)	32, 192
Bannerman, William (grandfather)	32
Baring, Evelyn (Lord Cromer)	210
Baring, Thomas George (Lord/Earl Northbrook)	93, 107, 118, 311
Barr, Rev. James	233, 254
Barrie, James M	221
Belfast	110
Belloc, Hilaire	221
Belmont Castle	
history	126–29, 130
later years	140–42
purchase by CB	64
Purchase by CB	130
purchase by Sir Henry	124
restoration	130–31
Biarritz	288
Birrell, The Rt. Hon. Augustine	332
Blackburn constituency	241
Blue plaques, London	100
Boer War (Second)	163, 177–79, 178, 179, 185–88
concentration camps	185, 187
Jamieson raid 1895	169
origins	168–70, 176
Peace treaty	190–91
Royal Commission on conduct of	187
Botha, Louis	255, 263, 264, 268, 269, 350
Bourgeois, Léon	288
Brewster, Rev Patrick	38
Bridgeman, Colonel Francis	312
Bristol	287
British League of Young Liberals	222
Brougham, Henry (Lord)	62
Brown, Robert	24, 330, 355
Browning, Professor Andrew	314
Bruce, Colonel Herbert (brother-in-law)	41
Bruce, Victor Alexander (9th) Earl of Elgin	293
Bryce family	332
Bryce, James (Viscount)	52, 57, 122, 198, 211, 252, 332, 361
Buchan, John	188
Buchanan, George	328
Buchanan, Thomas	198, 341
Burghs of Barony	27
Burns, John Elliott	333
Burt, Thomas	97, 242
Buxton, (Sir) Sydney Charles	334
By-elections	21, 67, 75, 76, 82, 84, 96, 105, 106, 109, 112, 119, 137, 144, 146, 147, 150, 154, 166, 168, 170, 178, 179, 183, 188, 198, 221, 224, 237, 238, 243, 245, 255, 256, 290, 301, 303, 304, 320, 321, 322, 323, 324, 330, 341, 342, 351, 359

C

Cabinet reshuffle 1907	252
Caird, Rt Hon (Sir) James	324
Caird, Sir James	140
Cambusketh Abbey	70
Campbell (Sir) Archibald	321
Campbell family business	31–32, 38, 42, 44, 45–47, 99
origins	32, 31–32
Campbell, (Sir) James	321
Campbell, (Sir) James (father)	35, 42, 43, 52
apprenticeship	31
censure as Lord Provost	36–37
death	99
marriage	32, 33
political career	36
Campbell, Alexander	322
Campbell, Alice Morton	251
Campbell, Elsie Louisa (neice)	303

Campbell, Hugh (grandson of brother) 43
Campbell, James (cousin) 168
Campbell, James Alexander (brother) 42, 45, 52, 58, 99, 100, 106, 145, 250, 302, 340
Campbell, Janet, (Lady), nee Bannerman (mother) 52, 99
   marriage 32, 33
Campbell, Jessie, nee Black (wife of James Campbell) 168
Campbell, John 322
Campbell, Margaret, nee Roxburgh (wife of William Campbell)
   marriage 32
Campbell, Menzies (Lord Campbell of Pittenweem) 28, 101, 330
Campbell, William (uncle) 35, 38, 40, 41, 42
   marriage 32
Campbell-Bannerman, Charlotte, (Lady), nee Bruce 58, 63–64, 100, 207, 226, 234, 244, 308
   death 248–51
   illness 191
Campbell-Bannerman, Sir Henry
   Admiralty 107, 281–82
   appointment of first cabinet 211
   Auld Alliance of Scotland and France) 139
   becomes Liberal Leader 173
   Belmont Castle 130
   birth (as Henry Campbell) 34
   Boer War (Second) 180, 189
   Boer War speech "When is a war not a war?" 186
   Cambridge University 41, 58
   Campbell family business 61, 62
   centenary commemorations 2008 351
   Chief Secretary for Ireland 108, 109–11
   Chinese labourers in South Africa 200
   church disestablishment 157
   Church of England 261
   Church of Scotland 40, 170
   Church Patronage (Scotland) Bill 1874 98
   Churches (Scotland) Act 1905 193
   commemoration events, London, 2009-10 356
   constituency election address 1906 227–31
   constituency work 83, 84, 96, 260
   Cordite vote 1895 162–63
   death 294
   decision not to go to the House of Lords 211
   Douma is dead-long live the Douma\ speech 248
   election as MP, 1868 80
   enough of this foolery speech to Arthur Balfour 246
   enrolment at the High School of Glasgow (as Henry Campbell) 50
   Entente Cordiale 1904 201
   entry into active Liberal politics 67
   family life 260
   farewell letter to consitituents 291
   Father of House of Commons 256
   final illness 291
   financial affairs 42, 92
   First Lanarkshire Rifle Volunteers 61
   France, views on 279, 281
   free trade 194, 195, 229–31, 255, 256
   freedom of City and Royal Burgh of Glasgow 253
   freedom of Royal Burgh of Dunfermline 197
   freedom of Royal Burgh of Montrose 258
   freedom of Royal Burgh of Stirling 154–55
   funeral, Meigle 298–301
   general election 1868 81, 78–81
   general election 1874 96
   general election 1880 103
   general election 1885 113
   general election 1886 123
   general election 1892 151
   general election 1895 165
   general election 1900 179, 183

general election 1906 225–35
Glasgow Cathedral memorial service 296
Glasgow University 57
Glasgow University rectorship candidacy 303
Hague Peace Conference (Second) 1907 283–84, 284
health 148, 185, 261, 286, 287, 288, 291–94
Home Rule all round (Federalism) 316
Honorary degrees 256
House of Commons tributes on death 296–97
House of Commons tributes on resignation 293
House of Lords 108, 160, 258, 285–86, 315
House of Lords, tributes on death 302
Immigration bill 1905 199
Imperial Conference (1907) 255
imperialism 189
infant mortalilty 254
influences on entry into Liberal politics 41
Inter-Parliamentary Conference (14th) 248
Irish Home Rule 114, 121, 190, 205, 206
knighthood 164
knighthoods awarded by 262
Lady Campbell-Bannerman, death of 248–51
last appearance in House of Commons 290
last public speech 287
Liberal Imperialists 201
Liberal Party splits 187
London homes 87, 94, 100, 202
maiden speech 89
Marienbad, Bohemia 95–96
marriage to Charlotte 63
meets Charlotte Bruce (future wife) 58
ministerial by-election 1884 109

ministerial by-election 1886 119
ministerial by-election 1892 137
motto and coat of arms 17
MPs, payment of salaries to 245
naval estimates 312
old age pensions 175
overseas travel 57, 59–60, 64–66, 94, 206, 256, 288
peerages created 261
personal life and routine 137–39
political influences 41
press tributes on death 306, 309–10, 312
Prime Minister, appointment as 209
public finances 228
resignation as Prime Minister 292
resignation from Government 1895 163
Royal Burgh of Edinburgh, freedom of 258
Royal Burgh of Peebles, Sir Henry 258
Royal Navy 282
Royal Titles Act 1876 101
Russia 248
Scottish Home Rule 149
Scottish local government 149
Scottish roots 315
Secretary of State for War 118, 154
Smuts, Jan Christiaan, meeting 1907 265
South Africa 228, 263
South Africa, Chinese labour in 263
South African self-government, speech to cabinet on 267
Stirling Burghs by-election 1868 76–78
Stirling Burghs constituency 123
Stirling statue 348–51
surname change (to Campbell-Bannerman) 92
Union of Scotland with England and Wales 259
United Free Church of Scotland 192
War Office 94, 98, 106, 119, 147, 154, 156–57, 162, 282, 282–83, 312

Westminster Abbey memorial service 295–96
Westminster Abbey Monument 347
will 304
women's suffrage 90, 316, 247
Workmen's Compensation Act 1871 276

Canals, Royal Commission on 215
Cant, Alexander 329
Cant, Andrew 329
Carmichael, Alastair 331
Carnegie, Andrew 198
Carrington, (Sir) Charles Robert Wynn 334
Cavendish, Lord Frederick 58, 108
Cavendish, Spencer 98
Chamberlain, Austen 312
Chamberlain, Joseph 100, 111, 145, 146, 167, 195, 196, 245
Channel Tunnel (proposal 1907) 253
Chartists 37
Church Defence Association 330
church disestablishment 158, 170
Church of England 261
Church of England in Ireland 79
Church of Scotland 39, 126, 170, 192–94, 261, 329
 General Assembly of 49, 71
Churchill, (Sir) Winston 147, 196, 216, 245, 252, 295, 303, 306, 314
Churchill, Lord Randolph 112, 146
Clark, Dr Gavin 148
Clegg, (Sir) Nick 330
Clemenceau, Georges 289
Cochrane, The Hon (Sir) Alexander 322
Cochrane, The Hon Andrew James 321
Colebrooke family 250
Conan Doyle, Arthur 221
Contamine, Professor Henry 279
Cordite vote 1895 162–63
Corn duty 194
Cox, Harold 278
Craik, Sir Henry 45, 57
Crewe-Milnes, (Sir) Robert 334
Crimean War 49
Crofter MPs 119
Crowe, Sir Eyre 285

Culross 73
Cunningham, Henry 319
Curzon, George, 1st (Irish) Lord of Kedleston 256

D

Davidson, James D G 266
Davies, Clement 330
Davis, Jefferson (Confederate President) 30
Declaration of Arbroath 1320 327
Derby, 14th (English) Earl of 58
Derby, 4th (English) Earl of 60
Dickinson, Willoughby 245
Disraeli, Benjamin (Earl of Beaconsfield) 76, 78, 86, 97, 101, 103, 105, 107
Disruption, of Church of Scotland, 1843 38, 39, 62, 71, 99, 126, 329
Downie, Robert 323
Duguid, Charles (Dr) 308
Dundee 140
Dundee constituency 242
Dunfermline 71–72, 197, 260

E

Earldoms of Mar (Scottish) 69
East & North of Scotland Liberal Assocation 102
Easter rising 1916 272
Edward VII, King 205, 247, 249, 288, 291, 292, 309
Elgin, (Sir) Victor 335
Elphinstone, William 48
Entente Cordiale 1904 201, 279, 280
Erskine, The Hon Colonel John 319
Erskine, The Hon James (Lord Erskine) 320
Erskine, the Hon Thomas 319

F

Fasque 43
Fawcett, Millicent Garrett 88
Federalism 148
Fenwick, Charles 242
First Lanarkshire Rifle Volunteers 61
Fleming, Dr Archibald 301

Fletcher, Andrew of Saltoun 27
Fonda, Henry 30
Fonda, USA 30
Fowler, (Sir) Henry 335
France 279–81
Free Church of Scotland 40
Free trade 43, 194–97, 229–31, 255

G

Gawthorpe, Mary 247
General election 1906
   Gladstone-MacDonald pact 219, 242
   Irish Defence League 223
   Jewish vote 223
   Labour candidates 241
   Labour Party 219
   Liberal organisation and strategy 218–22
   Liberal Party allies 223
   Liberal Party ancillaries 222–23
   National Free Church Council 223
   press 223
   Prime Minister's campaign 225–35
   results 236–42
   Welsh Liberals 220
General elections
   1837 36
   1841 37
   1847 43
   1852 58
   1857 60
   1859 60
   1865 66, 67
   1868 86–87, 96
   1874 97
   1880 105, 166
   1885 116, 144
   1886 122
   1892 151, 152
   1895 165
   1900 179, 182
   1906 218–42
George V, King 256, 261
George VI, King 266
Germany 283, 284
Gladstone, (Sir) John 43
Gladstone, Herbert (Viscount) 119, 176, 218, 219, 335
Gladstone, Sir John 41
Gladstone, William 39, 40, 41, 79, 86, 88, 90, 96, 97, 98, 101, 102, 105, 106, 113, 117, 120, 144, 148, 153, 156, 157, 270
   Midlothian campaign 102–3
Glasgow 35, 254
   Botanic Gardens 35
   population and expansion 35
Glasgow Academy 42
Glasgow Liberal Club 45
Gooch, G.P. 314
Goschen, George (Viscount) 146
Graham, Sir James 39
Graham, Sir John 348
Grahams, of Gartmore 29
Greaves, Tony (Lord) 313
Grey, (Sir) Edward 204, 210, 286, 313, 336
Grey, Albert 117
Grimond, Jo (Baron Grimond) 238, 330
Guthrie, Sir James 258

H

Hague Peace Conference (Second) 1907 282, 283–85, 288
Haldane, George 320
Haldane, Richard (Viscount) 26, 210, 282, 336
Haldane, Robert 320
Haldanes, of Gleneagles 74
Halkett, (Sir) Peter (2nd Baronet) 319
Hamilton, (Sir) Edward 311
Hamilton, 4th (Scottish) Duke of 49
Harcourt, Lewis (Viscount) 336
Harcourt, Sir William 98, 146, 150, 157, 159, 169, 170, 171, 200
Hardie, Keir 152, 167, 243, 303
Hartington, Marquis of, (8th (English) Duke of Devonshire) 100, 117
Hattersley, Roy 308
Henderson, (Sir) John 322
Henderson, Arthur 297
Herschell, Lord 146
Hertzog, James 269

Higgs, Henry 340
High School of Glasgow 42, 48–50, 62, 353, 359
Hobhouse, Emily 186
Holburne, (Sir) Francis 320
Home Rule all round (Federalism) 190, 316
House of Commons
   Standing Committees 256
House of Lords 160–61, 258, 261, 285–86
Hunton, Kent 91–93
Hutchison, (Sir) Robert 330

I

Immigration 199
Imperial Conference (1907) 255
Imperial Liberal Council 179, 184
Inchmaholme Island, Augustinian Priory 28
Independent Labour MP 242
India 270
Innes, Alexander Taylor 327
Inter-Parliamentary Conference (14th) 248
Inverkeithing 72
Irish Defence League 223
Irish Home Rule 89, 112, 113, 117, 120–23, 145, 155, 205, 261, 270, 271–72
Irish Home Rule Party 89
Irish Nationalists 167

J

Jenkins, Roy 238
Johnson, Ben 73
Johnstone, James 323

K

Kant, Immanuel 329
Kennedy, Charles 101, 330
Kenney, Annie 247
Kinloch, George (the Radical Laird) 134
Kirkwood, Archy (Baron Kirkwood of Kirkhope) 331

L

Labour MPs 198, 242
Labour Party 242–43, 327
Labour Representation Committee 219
Labour Representation League 87
Laing, Very Rev Marshall 40
Lake of Menteith 28, 27–28
Lanrick Castle 26
Law, Andrew Bonar 35, 40, 50, 52, 239, 255, 341
Lee, General Robert E 100
Legislation
   Aliens Act 1905 199
   Ballot Act 1872 20, 96, 97
   Burgh Police (Scotland) Act 1892 27
   Church of Scotland (Property and Endowments Act 1925 194
   Church of Scotland Act 1921 194
   Church Patronage (Scotland) Act 1874 98
   Churches (Scotland) Act 1905 193
   Coal Mines Regulation Act 1908 277
   Companies (Consolidation) Act 1908 277
   Constituency Redistribution Bill 1905 200
   Corn Laws 43
   Criminal Law Amendment Act 1871 96, 276
   Crofters Holdings Act 1886 120
   Deceased Wife's Sister's Marriage Act 1907 277
   Deceased wife's Sister's marriage Bill 1871 90
   Education (Provision of Meals) Act 1906 277
   Education (Scotland) Act 1872 42, 90
   Education (Scotland) Act 1908 273
   Education Act 1902 198
   Education Bill 1906 285
   Elementary Education in Ireland Bill 1887 111
   Endowed Hospitals (Scotland) Bill 1869 89
   Fatal Accident and Sudden Deaths Inquiry (Scotland) Act 1906 273
   Fisheries Acts 1907 273

Irish Church Act 1869 88
Irish Council Bill 190
Irish Council Bill 1907 270
Irish Crimes Act 1887 145
Irish Evicted Tenants Bill 1907 271
Irish Home Rule Bill 1885 120
Irish Home Rule Bill 1886 113
Irish Home Rule Bill 1893 155, 261
Irish Home Rule Bill 1912 (enacted 1914) 272
Irish Land Act 1871 88
Irish Land Act 1887 146
Irish Local Government Act 1898 171
Irish Local Government Bill 1892 151
Irish Universities Act 1908 88
Irish Universities Bill 1873 88
Judicature Act 1873 96
Land Values (Scotland) Bill 1906 290
Licensing Act 1904 199
Licensing Bill 1908 285
Local Government (Scotland) Act 1889 149
Local Government (Scotland) Act 1908 273
Marriage Act 1835 90
Matrimonial Causes Act 1907 277
Merchant Shipping Act 1906 277
Militia Acts 1792 126
Ministers Act 1693 (Act of Scottish Parliament) 193
National Galleries of Scotland Act 1906 273
Official Secrets Bill 1907 261
Old-Age Pensions Act 1908 278
Parliament Act 1911 261, 286
Plural Voting Bill 1906 285
Prevention of Corruption Act 1906 277
Private water company unification (London) Bill 1880 103
Probation of Offenders Act 1908 277
Public Health (Scotland) Amendment Act 1907 273
Qualification of Women (County and Borough Councils) Act 1907 273, 277
Redistribution Act 1885 112
Reform Act 1867 (England and Wales) 76
Reform Acts 1832 62, 129, 183
Reform Acts 1868 (Scotland and Ireland) 76
Representation of the People Act 1884 112
Representation of the People Act 1948 147
Roads and Bridges Act 1875 82
Royal Titles Act 1876 101
Scottish Burgh Reform Act 1833 71, 329
Scottish Home Rule bills 149
Scottish Marriage Act 1567 90
Scottish Parochial Schools (Scotland) Bill 1869 90
Scottish Reform Act 1832 329
Scottish Small Landholders Bill 1906 273, 274, 273
Scottish Temperance Bill 1877 100
Sheriff Courts (Scotland) Act 1907 273
Small Landholders (Scotland) Act 1911 274
Small Landholders (Scotland) Bill 1908 290
Suspensory Act 1914 158
Titles of Religious Congregations Act 1850 41
Trade Union Act 1871 96, 276
Universities Tests Act 1871 89
Welsh Church Act 1914 157
Welsh Disestablishment Bill 1909 157
Welsh Disestablishment Bills 1894 and 1895 157
Women's Enfranchisement Bill 1907 247
Women's suffrage Bill 1870 90
Workmen's Compensation Act 1906 276–77
Liberal Cabinet (8th) 1905 212, 213, 215
Liberal Central Association 87, 121, 218
Liberal hegemony in Scotland 327–31
Liberal Imperialist League 184

Liberal Imperialists 185, 188, 189, 201, 204
Liberal League 189, 202, 219, 221
Liberal Party
   formation of 61
   splits 187, 330
   splits over Second Boer War 178, 179
Liberal Reform Club 88
Liberal Registration Association 87
Liberal re-unification 146
Liberal Unionists 122, 123, 144, 146, 167, 183, 239
Liberal/Labour MPs 97, 105, 144, 167, 182, 237, 242–43
Liberal/Liberal Democrat Chief Whips 330
Liberal/SDP Alliance 331
Lindsay, Nigel 23, 24, 355
Lloyd George, David (Earl) 40, 150, 199, 246, 267, 295, 306, 330, 336
   Boer war 185
Lloyd George, Gwilym 245
London Liberal and Radical Union 218
London Liberal Federation 218
Lord High Commissioner 158
Loreburn, Robert (Earl) 285, 337
Louise, Princess (Duchess of Argyll from 1900) 91, 160, 212
Lyttleton, Arthur 263

M

MacCormick, Iain MacDonald 360
MacDonald, Ramsay 219
Mackay, James (Lord Mackay of Clashfern) 261
Mackie, John B 310
Maclay, (Sir) Joseph Paton 360
Maclean, (Sir) Donald 330
Maclenna, Robert (Baron Maclennan of Rogart) 330
Maitland, (Sir) James Gibson 104
Marienbad, Bohemia 94, 95–96, 191, 205, 248
Mason, Professor Roger A 328
Masterton, James 320

Maule, Fox (2nd Lord Panmure, 11th [Scottish] Earl of Dalhousie) 39
McGill, James 48
McKenna, Reginald 337
McOran family military service 47
McOran, James (paternal grandfather) 29
McOran-Campbells
   ancestry 25–26
   in later years 29–30
Meigle 89, 124–26
Menzies, Robert 133
Merthyr Tydvil constituency 241
Midlothian Campaign (Gladstone's) 102
Mill, John Stuart 88, 91
Ministerial by-elections 21, 75, 84, 109, 119, 137, 154, 303
Montford, Paul Raphael 347
Montgomery, (Sir) Charles 340
Montgomery, Hubert 289
Morley, John (Viscount) 133, 146, 168, 175, 270, 313, 337
Morrison, Thomas 67
MPs, payment of salaries to 245

N

Napier Commission on crofters and cottars 1883 119
Nash, Vaughan 262, 289, 307, 339
National Free Church Council 223
National Liberal Club 88, 107, 287
National Liberal Federation 100, 106, 120, 157, 171, 175, 181, 185, 189, 218
National Liberal Federation of Scotland 121
National University of Ireland 88
Naval Estimates 312
Nightingale, Florence 262
North and South Wales Liberal Federations 121

O

O'Connor, T.P. 110, 116, 206, 270, 297, 307, 350
Old age pensions 175

Oliphant, Laurence 67, 75, 324
Order of the Garter 164
Order of the Thistle 164
O'Shea, William 150
Otto, Dr Ernst 212, 249

P

Palmerston, 3rd (Irish) Viscount 57, 60
Parliamentary Labour Party, formation of 242
Parnell, Charles 106, 112, 150
Peel, Sir Robert 39, 43
Peerages 21–22
Peto, Sir Morton (father-in-law of brother) 58
Playfair, Dr. Lyon, (Lord) 89
Playfair, Rev Dr James 89, 126
Plural voting 147
Ponsonby, Arthur (Lord Ponsonby of Shulbrede) 138, 218, 244, 251, 286, 289, 304, 306, 317, 338
Port of Menteith 27, 30, 99
Primrose, Archibald (Lord Dalmeny) 39, 75, 323
Primrose, Francis Ward 323
Primrose, Harry 244
Primroses, of Culross 73

Q

Queen's College, Belfast 88
Queen's University, Belfast 88

R

Ramsay, John 67, 68, 76, 78, 82
Reay, Lord 285
Redmond, John 150, 270, 271, 291
Reform Club 88
Relugas Compact (to stop Sir Henry becoming Prime Minister) 204
Ripon, George (Marquis) 337
Robertson, Sir William 303
Rodan, Steve 360
Roosevelt, Theodore 283
Rosebery, 4th (Scottish) Earl of 323
Rosebery, 5th (Scottish) Earl of 40, 98, 101, 159, 160, 167, 170, 187, 188, 189, 202, 204, 207, 244, 252, 274, 278, 280
Rosyth, naval base and dockyard 197
Russell, Bertrand, 3rd (Earl) Russell 256, 270
Russell, Lord John (Earl) 43, 57, 79, 159
Russell, Rt. Hon. Sir Thomas Wallace 237
Russia 248, 257, 279

S

Salisbury, 3rd Marquis of 107, 144, 146, 151, 153, 164, 165, 167
Samuel, Herbert (Viscount) 308, 330
Satow, Sir Ernest 285
Scobie, Andrew, Provost of Dunfermline 309
Scotland 272–75
Scott, Captain 357
Scottish Enlightenment 328
Scottish Grand Committee 272
Scottish Home Rule 148–49
Scottish Home Rule Association 148
Scottish Land Court 274
Scottish Liberal Association 107, 121, 157, 178, 202, 221, 300
Scottish Liberal Club 88
Scottish Liberal Federation 121, 185
Scottish Liberal Party 121
Scottish National Party 29
Scottish Presbyterian churches 316, 328
Scottish Women's Liberal Federation 222, 300
Searle, G.R. 315
Secretary for Scotland, office of 112
Secretary of State for Scotland 275
Shaw, Thomas 67, 274
Sinclair, (Sir) Archibald 330
Sinclair, John (Lord Pentland) 53, 111, 144, 147, 154, 156, 164, 167, 170, 183, 188, 202, 220, 224, 272, 273, 274, 338, 350
Sinn Fein movement 270
Slater, Oscar 275
Smith, Adam 329
Smith, Goldwin 312

Smith, John Benjamin 323
Smuts, Jan Christiaan 176, 185, 264–66, 268, 269, 308
South Africa 200, 257, 263–70
   Transvaal (Lyttelton) constitution 263
South Queensferry 74
Spencer, John, 5th Earl 108, 191
Spender, John A 307
Spottiswoode, John 48
St Andrews 125
St Bernard's Football Club 62
Steel, David (Lord Steel of Aikwood) 33, 78, 330
Stirling 69–71
Stirling Burghs constituency 67, 69, 85, 214, 234, 250, 294, 303, 319–25, 339
   1868 by-election 76
   by-election 1868 76–78
   by-election 1884 109
   general election 1868 80
Stirling Burghs Liberal Association 84
Stirling Castle 70
Stracathro Estate 43
Strauss, Johann the Younger 56
Sudetenland 94
Suffragettes 225, 247, 287, 350
Sutherland, (Sir) William 278, 343

T

Tait, William 322
Tariff Reform League 223
Taylor, J.H. 289
Third Lanark Football Club 62
Thomas, Sir Alfred 297
Thorpe, Jeremy 330
Tory, origin of name 328

Trevelyan, (Sir) George Otto 88, 107, 108, 144, 146, 153, 158
Tullibardine, Perthshire 32
Tweedmouth, Edward (Lord Tweedmouth) 338

U

Union of the Crowns 1603 328
United Edinburgh Liberal Council 202
United Free Church of Scotland 194
University constituencies 86, 87
US Civil War 30, 41

V

Victoria, Queen 36, 61, 91, 156, 158, 160, 163, 184, 309

W

Wallace, Jim (Baron Wallace of Tankerness) 330
Walton, Sir Lawson 290
War Office 98, 106, 119, 282–83
Webster, John 328
Webster, William 307
Wee Frees 192
Weir, (Sir) William 360
Wells, H.G. 51
West & South of Scotland Liberal Association 102
Whig, origin of name 328
William, Prince (Duke of Cambridge) 108
Wilson, John 310, 314
Women's suffrage 90, 247–48, 316

Y

Young Liberals 222
Young Scots Society 222